THE OXFORD ENCYCLOPEDIA OF
AMERICAN BUSINESS, LABOR, AND ECONOMIC HISTORY

THE OXFORD ENCYCLOPEDIA OF
AMERICAN BUSINESS, LABOR, AND ECONOMIC HISTORY

Melvyn Dubofsky

EDITOR IN CHIEF

VOLUME 1
ABRA–MUTU

OXFORD
UNIVERSITY PRESS

Oxford University Press is a department of the University of Oxford.
It furthers the University's objective of excellence in research,
scholarship, and education by publishing worldwide.

Oxford   New York
Auckland   Cape Town   Dar es Salaam   Hong Kong   Karachi
Kuala Lumpur   Madrid   Melbourne   Mexico City   Nairobi
New Delhi   Shanghai   Taipei   Toronto

With offices in
Argentina   Austria   Brazil   Chile   Czech Republic   France   Greece
Guatemala   Hungary   Italy   Japan   Poland   Portugal   Singapore
South Korea   Switzerland   Thailand   Turkey   Ukraine   Vietnam

Oxford is a registered trademark of Oxford University Press
in the UK and certain other countries.

Published by Oxford University Press, Inc.
198 Madison Avenue, New York, NY 10016
www.oup.com

The Library of Congress Cataloging-in-Publication Data

The Oxford encyclopedia of American business, labor, and economic history /
Melvyn Dubofsky, editor in chief.
p. cm.
Includes bibliographical references and index.
ISBN 978-0-19-999304-8 ((volume 1; hardcover) : alk. paper)
ISBN 978-0-19-999305-5 ((volume 2; hardcover) : alk. paper)
ISBN 978-0-19-973881-6 ((set; hardcover) : alk. paper)

1. United States—Commerce—History—Encyclopedias.   2. Industries—United States—History—Encyclopedias.
3. Business—History—Encyclopedias.   4. United States—Economic policy—Encyclopedias.
5. United States—Economic conditions—Encyclopedias.   6. Labor—United States—History—Encyclopedias.
7. Industrial relations—United States—History—Encyclopedias.   I. Dubofsky, Melvyn, 1934-
II. Title: Encyclopedia of American business, labor, and economic history.
HF3021.O94 2013
330.973003—dc23
2012039475

3 5 7 9 8 6 4 2

Printed in the United States of America
on acid-free paper

EDITORIAL AND PRODUCTION STAFF

CONTENTS

LIST OF ENTRIES

INTRODUCTION

The Oxford Encyclopedia of American History carries on a tradition of scholarly publishing by Oxford University Press that began in 1478, fourteen years before Christopher Columbus set out from Palos de la Frontera in Spain and sailed westward across the Atlantic. As for American history, Oxford's first contribution was John Smith's annotated *Map of Virginia*, published in 1612, five years after 104 English men and boys had founded the Jamestown settlement.

This tradition has continued over the centuries, including *The Oxford Companion to United States History* (2001), affectionately called "OCUSH," which I had the pleasure and privilege of editing along with a distinguished group of associates. To this long and noteworthy record, Oxford now proudly adds this new work. Building on the one-volume *Companion*,

this twelve-volume set of six encyclopedias offers a far more capacious format, making it possible to include a greater number of entries and to provide more detailed, in-depth coverage than was possible in the briefer compass of the *Companion*.

The rationale for such a work is obvious. Awareness of, and interest in, our collective past is part of what makes us human, and the recording of history has characterized every great civilization. The case for this specific set of encyclopedias is equally compelling. From the time when the first human beings made their way from present-day Siberia across a now-vanished land bridge to what we call North America, the history of the peoples of this great geographic region has been rich in its diversity and interest. From the late sixteenth century onward, the various settlements in what Europeans called first the New World and then, after 1776, the United States have loomed large on the world stage—first in the realm of the imagination and then, increasingly, as unavoidable reality. The nation's political, social, economic, and cultural lives have always roused interest, sometimes as the target of criticism and ridicule, sometimes as an ideal to be envied and emulated. As Johann Wolfgang von Goethe wrote in an 1827 poem (in Daniel Platt's translation):

> America, you've got it better
> Than our old continent. Exult!
> You have no decaying castles
> And no basalt.
> Your heart is not troubled,
> In lively pursuits,
> By useless old remembrance
> And empty disputes.

The actual America of 1827, distracted by controversy over the tariff and by angry feuds within John Quincy Adams's unpopular and dysfunctional presidential administration, was, of course, irrelevant to Goethe. As others have done before and since, he was conjuring up a finer America of his dreams, a fresh, new society uncorrupted by the all-too-human flaws of tired, old Europe. (That strange reference to "basalt," some scholars believe, may be a metaphorical allusion to volcanoes as symbols of social unrest and revolutionary turmoil.) Of more substantive, less abstract interest has been America's global military, diplomatic, economic, and strategic role, which has grown steadily more significant and inescapable over the years. In short, for a variety of reasons, the case for a comprehensive reference work covering all of American history is clear.

But is such a work really needed in the twenty-first century, given the tsunami of "information" endlessly churning through the media, accessible at a keystroke? The answer is a decisive "Yes." This set of encyclopedias arose from a core assumption shared by the editors at Oxford University Press, by the gifted scholars constituting the editorial teams, and certainly by me. In an era in which the production and dissemination of knowledge have become wholly diffuse, often anonymous and un-sourced, and frequently idiosyncratic and unreliable, we are convinced that there is still a place—indeed, a vital necessity—for a historical reference work that is authoritative, carefully planned, analytically sophisticated, written by scholars familiar with the latest findings, and carefully edited for accuracy, clarity, and readability.

Grounded in these basic principles, *The Oxford Encyclopedia of American History* is chronologically comprehensive, from the earliest human settlements to the twenty-first century, from the Stone Age to the Computer Age. The work is topically comprehensive as well. This is a daunting task, particularly because the field of American history has expanded dramatically in recent decades: the field has come to include much more extensive coverage of social, cultural, scientific, medical, and demographic topics than was true in the past. Recent scholarship has vastly broadened our knowledge of the historical experience of all Americans of the past, not just the elite figures who once dominated the story. This set of encyclopedias fully reflects this broader understanding of the American past.

HISTORY: AN ANCIENT DISCIPLINE, YET EVER NEW

History is among the oldest of the scholarly disciplines, tracing its origins to West African griots, ancient Chinese chroniclers, and Mesopotamians who combined the skills of historian, elocutionist, scribe, and stonemason, celebrating the exploits of their rulers in viva voce orations and on steles and tablets for future generations to transcribe and wonder at. The

Greek historian Herodotus, who lived in the fifth century BCE, wrote an account of successive rulers of Persia, with whom Greece fought several wars. Filling his narrative with stories about the peoples and places he had heard about, he was an early practitioner of what is now called social and cultural history. Herodotus's younger contemporary Thucydides devoted his great talents to a history of the Peloponnesian war, the long conflict between Athens and Sparta. Focusing on battles and diplomacy and avoiding Herodotus's charming penchant for digression, Thucydides nevertheless recognized the importance of personality traits and social factors, such as the terrible plague that struck Athens in the midst of the war. In an authorial decision that would place him at odds with some participants in modern America's culture wars, Thucydides strictly excluded divine intervention from his causal forces, and he avoided suggesting that the gods favored one side or another in the conflict he was describing.

But history writing, this ancient pursuit, is also ever new, which helps account for its appeal to so many bright young scholars. It continually reinvents itself, not only because more things keep happening, but also because historians' understanding of their field, and of what merits their attention, is continually shifting and enlarging. In former times, the historian typically focused his attention (and it almost invariably was a "he") on politics, war, law, and diplomacy. Together with industrialization, finance, and other economic matters, these were considered history's driving forces and thus the historian's proper subject matter.

But gradually a broader understanding emerged. George Bancroft, the prolific nineteenth-century historian, famously included a chapter on social history in his monumental ten-volume history of the United States (1834–1874). Henry Adams began his multivolume *History of the United States during the Administrations of Thomas Jefferson and James Madison* (1889–1891) with a chapter each on the "popular characteristics" of the American people, on "American ideals," and on the intellectual life of New England, the mid-Atlantic states, and the South. By offering new approaches to the history of ideas, Vernon L. Parrington's *Main Currents in American Thought* (1927) and Merle Curti's *The Growth of American Thought* (1943) helped create a new field, combining history and literature, that came to be known as American studies.

Later scholars have vastly expanded these initiatives. The twenty-first century's historians recognize that the history of social groups, class conflict, sexuality, popular culture, ideas and ideology, religious belief, literature, music, and the arts, as well as developments in science, medicine, technology, and the economy, all lie within their purview and merit careful attention and study. The traditional areas of politics, the law, military history, and foreign relations remain central, of course, but these fields, too, have been enriched by attention to the broader sociocultural context within which elections, legislative battles, legal decisions, wars, and diplomatic maneuverings unfold.

Indeed, all these subfields are interconnected. One cannot understand the social and military history of colonial America, for example, without understanding the devastating effects of the bacteria and viruses that the European newcomers unwittingly brought with them: lacking the immunity to these bacteria and viruses that comes with long exposure, native peoples were decimated by disease. The history of slavery remains incomplete without attention to the changing technology of cotton production. One cannot grasp the full impact on America of World War I without also grasping the impact of the virulent influenza virus (the precise point of origin remains uncertain) that spread across the battlefields of Europe and home-front military bases, causing a global pandemic that took at least 50 million lives. The nation's military and political history is enriched by attention to the ways in which perceptions of wars, battles, elections, and political careers are shaped by the popular culture, from ballads and broadsides to cartoons, films, and television programs. Our picture of working-class America is enriched if we examine workers' families, leisure activities, religious lives, and consumption patterns, as well as their voting habits and participation in labor unions—important as voting patterns and unions obviously are. On and on the list could go, illustrating that American history, like all history, is really a seamless web; however, we divide it into subfields for analytic and pedagogical purposes.

Along with the subject matter of history, the demographic profile of the profession of American history itself has changed. Once the domain of white males of British or northern European ancestry, in the twenty-first century the profession is far more diverse in terms of gender, race, and ethnicity. This has made for a livelier and more stimulating intellectual environment, as well as for a greater sensitivity to the diverse historical experience of the many subgroups within American society.

Historians' understanding of America's place in the world has evolved as well. In the past, U.S. historians tended to stress the uniqueness of the American experience. Underlying this view was the notion that America was not only different from, but superior to, other nations, and that it was somehow immune to the historical processes that could be seen in the rise and decline of other once-powerful civilizations and nation-states, from Babylon, Greece, and Rome to Spain, Portugal, Sweden, the Netherlands, and Great Britain. Sometimes, as in the writings of the New England Puritans, this view of America's uniqueness took on explicitly religious overtones. Even George Bancroft, a liberal Unitarian with a European

education including a Ph.D. from Germany's University of Göttingen, saw America as enjoying God's special favor. Such explicitly supernaturalist understandings of American history gradually faded, but notions of American exceptionalism survived, shaping historians' approach to their subject. This, too, has changed since the later twentieth century. U.S. historians now recognize that the forces shaping American history are hardly unique to the United States, but replicate processes also observable in other societies. This broader comparative dimension has both enriched American historical scholarship and added a chastening note of humility.

The heightened transnational awareness has not been only at the abstract level. American historians have vastly benefited from the work of foreign scholars, including the British historian E. P. Thompson, whose book on the making of the English working class was pathbreaking, and the French historians Lucien Febvre, Marc Bloch, Fernand Braudel, and Emmanuel Le Roy Ladurie, who did pioneering work in social history and founded the so-called *Annales* school, with its shift from providing a narrative of passing events to focusing on the *longue durée*, or long-term, processes that shape human societies over centuries.

Influential, too, has been the Italian historian Carlo Ginzburg, with his attention to the illuminating insights to be gained from "microhistory," the close analysis of specific events or small communities. Ginzburg's *Il formaggio e i vermi: Il cosmo di un mugnaio del Cinquecento* (1976; English trans., *The Cheese and the Worms: The Cosmos of a Sixteenth-Century Miller*, 1980), based on detailed Inquisition records that Ginzburg discovered in long-neglected archives of the Catholic Church, told of an obscure miller, Domenico Scandella, better known as Menocchio, burned at the stake in 1600 in the northeastern Italian town of Montereale for beliefs that he summed up this way:

I have said that in my opinion, all was chaos…and out of that bulk a mass formed—just as cheese is made out of milk—and worms appeared in it, and these were the angels. There was also God, he too having been created out of that mass at the same time.

Such heresy shocked church authorities, and Menocchio went to his fiery death. In writing about this forgotten event in an obscure town, Ginzburg offered a wealth of fresh insights into the procedures and processes of the Inquisition, late medieval folk belief and oral culture, and the ramifications of the Counter-Reformation in Italy. Such scholarship proved appealing to American historians, who explored microhistories of their own to see what they would reveal. Laurel Thatcher Ulrich's Pulitzer Prize–winning *A Midwife's Tale* (1991) offered a biography of Martha Ballard, an obscure Maine midwife of the turn of the nineteenth century, based on Ballard's diary recording the unremarkable routines of her life. In the diary's "exhaustive, repetitive dailiness," Ulrich argued, lay its value as a historical document.

As this suggests, American historians' methodologies and sources have expanded as well. While retaining a strong sense of the value of their traditional text-based approaches, historians have learned from sociologists and political scientists the value of quantification in illuminating the past. Census records, voting data, tax lists, and many other forms of quantified information have yielded rich results. Such pathbreaking books using quantified data as Lee Benson's *The Concept of Jacksonian Democracy: New York as a Test Case* (1961) and Stephan Thernstrom's *Poverty and Progress: Social Mobility in a Nineteenth Century City* (1964) provided a means of testing cherished American myths about the "era of the common man," "rags to riches," and the United States as a "land of opportunity"—myths reinforced by Horatio

Alger stories and the oft-told biographies of exceptional figures like Andrew Carnegie. (That Thernstrom's book was pathbreaking is indicated by its being relegated by the *American Historical Review* to a brief notice in a section called "Other Recent Publications" and by its being overlooked entirely by the *Journal of American History*, whose editor assumed that it was a work of sociology.)

Fully aware that statistically based findings must be interpreted for and presented in prose accessible to people who are not mathematicians, historians are in little danger of becoming computing automatons, spewing out numbers, statistics, and formulas. And the profession has learned that statistical data, like any other form of evidence, can be fudged and misrepresented and thus must be approached with due skepticism. Nevertheless, American historians have grown more conscious of the rich resources buried in the nation's vast repositories of quantified data. So, too, have they discovered the research value of material-culture products, visual materials, industrial designs, fashion shows, television commercials, and mundane everyday objects from toys, comic books, tombstones, and toilets to domestic structures. Approached with insight and imagination, such materials are invaluable historical sources.

To be sure, all this ferment and change within the profession of American history has raised troublesome questions. If historians focus too exclusively on subgroups within society, how can they formulate a larger conception of *American* history? Put another way, what meaning does the familiar phrase "one nation indivisible" from the original Pledge of Allegiance to the flag ("under God" was inserted later) retain in the twenty-first century, apart from the banal point that a second secession movement like that of 1861 would be unlikely to succeed? Or, again, if historians adopt a snapshot approach, documenting the experience of specific groups during one brief period of their history, how can they explain change over time? Other questions have been raised as well. As historians, from wholly laudable motives, turned their attention to the poor, disenfranchised, and disinherited—doing "history from the bottom up," as it was called—did they risk losing sight of the important role of powerful elites and interest groups in society? In abandoning the notion of American exceptionalism as self-serving and parochial, did they risk missing what might, in fact, be distinctive and unique about the American experience? At the practical level, could historians successfully integrate quantified statistical data and other new forms of evidence with the written sources upon which they have traditionally relied? Such questions have for decades energized the profession of American history, and echoes of these questions will be found in the pages of this set of encyclopedias.

THE OXFORD ENCYCLOPEDIA OF AMERICAN HISTORY: A REFERENCE WORK FOR THE TWENTY-FIRST CENTURY

All these trends—the greater diversity of the profession of American history, historians' broader understanding of the discipline's scope and available range of sources and methodologies, the greater openness to multicultural and transnational perspectives—have informed the planning and execution of *The Oxford Encyclopedia of American History*. This becomes immediately evident as one looks at the basic structure of the work. The effort to bring organizational and intellectual coherence to such a vast and unwieldy topic has been formidable indeed. We have been reminded more than once of Immanuel Kant's much-quoted observation: "Out of the crooked timber of humanity, no straight thing was ever made." Yet we have given it a try—with, we hope, some success. To make this set of encyclopedias of maximum benefit to its users, we have divided the sprawling, almost boundless field of American history into six topical subcategories, each comprising two volumes and each with its own editor or editors in chief. Here are these six subcategories, with the name of the editor or editors in chief and his or her academic affiliation:

The Oxford Encyclopedia of American Business, Labor, and Economic History
Editor in Chief
Melvyn Dubofsky
Binghamton University, State University of New York

The Oxford Encyclopedia of American Cultural and Intellectual History
Editors in Chief
Joan Shelley Rubin
University of Rochester

Scott E. Casper
University of Nevada, Reno

The Oxford Encyclopedia of American Military and Diplomatic History
Editor in Chief
Timothy J. Lynch
University of Melbourne

The Oxford Encyclopedia of American Political and Legal History
Editors in Chief
Donald T. Critchlow
Arizona State University

Philip R. VanderMeer
Arizona State University

The Oxford Encyclopedia of the History of American Science, Medicine, and Technology
Editor in Chief
Hugh Richard Slotten
University of Otago

The Oxford Encyclopedia of American Social History

Editor in Chief
Lynn Dumenil
Occidental College

These editors, distinguished scholars all, have been assisted by teams of associate editors, ranging from prominent senior scholars to gifted younger scholars. Through extended discussions, these teams carefully formulated their entry lists to ensure comprehensive coverage of the core topics in their field, supplemented by mid-length and shorter entries on topics of interest. The editors then solicited entries from historians who had relevant expertise. This great project would be impossible without the participation of hundreds of scholars who welcomed the opportunity to offer an account of their work to a broader public, beyond the circle of colleagues who routinely review their books, evaluate their research proposals, and share panels at scholarly meetings. The specialization and compartmentalization of the profession of history can be rewarding, as one exchanges ideas with others who share one's specific interests, but it can also seem confining and a bit claustrophobic. Participation in a large-scale collaborative project like *The Oxford Encyclopedia of American History* provides an opportunity to move beyond one's professional comfort zone and to share one's research with an interested worldwide readership.

Incorporating the most recent research and interpretive approaches, the entries are designed to be of value to scholars, advanced students, and all those seeking high-level analytic treatment of key topics in American history. The entries include essential facts, of course—names, dates, and so on—but they go further, contextualizing the topic, conveying its human dimensions, suggesting its larger historical significance, and addressing matters of controversy or interpretive disagreement.

Along with matters of content, methodology, and scope, we have given high priority to the entries' organization and style. Historians have long hovered ambivalently between the social sciences and the humanities, unwilling to abandon the social sciences' commitment to methodological rigor, but also determined to retain the humanities' concern for clarity and persuasiveness of presentation. For all the changes since the days of Herodotus and Thucydides—and Edward Gibbon, Voltaire, Francis Parkman, George Bancroft, Henry Adams, and scores of other historians admired for their writing style—historians still take pride in writing lucid, accessible, even elegant prose. They pay attention not only to the information being conveyed, but also to the manner in which it is conveyed.

In choosing our contributors, describing their assignments, and editing their entries, therefore, we have emphasized style as well as content. Lewis Mumford once rather cattily observed that reading John Dewey was like riding on the Boston subway: one eventually got to one's destination, but considerably the worse for wear. We have made every effort to ensure that such a criticism will not be leveled against the contributors to this set of encyclopedias. Acquiring historical knowledge should not be the intellectual equivalent of a visit to the dentist.

USING THE ENCYCLOPEDIA

Taken together, the twelve volumes of *The Oxford Encyclopedia of American History* include more than 3,500 entries, arranged in alphabetical order within each two-volume topical set, for ease of research. Composite entries gather together discussions of similar or related topics under one entry title. For example, under the entry "Internal Migration" in *The Oxford Encyclopedia of American Social History*, the reader will find four subentries:

"Colonial Era," "Nineteenth-Century West-ward," "Twentieth Century and Beyond," and "African Americans." A headnote listing the various subentries introduces each composite entry.

A selective bibliography at the end of each entry directs the reader who wishes to pursue a topic in greater detail to the most important recent scholarly work. Most entries include references at the end that guide interested readers to related entries. Blind entries direct the user from an alternate form of an entry title to the entry itself. For example, in *The Oxford Encyclopedia of American Social History*, the blind entry "Mormon Rebellion" tells the reader to look under "Utah War of 1857."

Throughout the planning and execution of this work we have been guided by a single goal: to make the full panorama of American history accessible and understandable to the maximum number of users. We hope that we have succeeded in this purpose.

Finally, the editors would like to extend sincere thanks to the professionals at Oxford University Press who aided immeasurably in the preparation of this work: Grace Labatt, who patiently and cheerfully oversaw the process of selecting the editors in chief; Stephen Wagley, executive editor, who shared his wisdom and experience and saw the project successfully launched; Damon Zucca, editorial director, and Alixandra Gould, senior editor, who aided us in thinking about the emerging world of online reference; and Eric Stannard and Andrew Jung, the developmental editors, who with unfailing good humor moderated early discussions among the editors over where specific entries should go, dealt with problems as they arose, and gently prodded us to maintain the pace. Our thanks to one and all.

Paul S. Boyer
Merle Curti Professor of History Emeritus,
University of Wisconsin–Madison
July 2011

PREFACE

Not quite twenty years ago, my good friend Paul Boyer asked me to serve as an associate editor for the *Oxford Companion to United States History* (2001), a one-volume encyclopedic history of the United States and its antecedents. My responsibility was to solicit and to edit the contributions that covered the nation's economic, social, and labor history, categories that at the time included nearly all that was neglected in the more conventional fields of history. The *Oxford Companion* consisted of various short entries such as brief biographies of notable individuals, decisive events, and significant movements and organizations. More importantly, it featured substantial entries that covered history from the pre–Colonial Era in North America to the present. These entries covered such subjects as economic develop- ment, immigration, business organization, industrialization, slavery, the varieties of capitalism, government promotion and regulation of the economy, and labor movements. Nearly all the entries were written by mid-1997 at the latest and most even earlier. Eleven years have now passed since the publication of the *Companion* and more than fifteen since most of its entries were written.

Much has changed over the intervening years in how scholars, students, and concerned citizens go about studying subjects and researching historical issues. Printed literature has become less used and perhaps less essential than the broader range of information—historical and contemporary—now available through computer search engines that guide the curious to online sites offering a plethora of original sources for historical research as well as references to the best literature available on myriad subjects. Ask Google a question on nearly any historical subject and its search engine will guide the inquisitor to an impressive, nearly endless array of potential sources. Turn to Wikipedia, the online free-for-all (that's a pun) encyclopedia, and the user will surely find an entry on whatever she is seeking, including impressively lengthy ones on even minor historical topics. Nevertheless, Oxford University Press decided to expand its *Companion to United States History* into six two-volume sets devoted to each of the following subject areas: social history; cultural and intellectual history; political and legal history; scientific, technological, and medical history; military and diplomatic history; and, finally, my area of responsibility, business, labor, and economic history.

GENERAL PRINCIPLES GOVERNING THE ENCYCLOPEDIA

What can a contemporary twelve-volume print encyclopedia offer that Google or Wikipedia lack? A good question. Let me try to answer it briefly. Google and Wikipedia have their uses, as do other computerized and Internet-related utilities, but the sites to which they lead their users are not always reliable nor do they necessarily represent the best or latest scholarly consensus. Wikipedia and similar sites may offer easily accessible and digestible information about historical subjects but they are not necessarily accurate or reliable, especially on subjects that have generated heated scholarly controversy. For the Oxford Press's twelve volumes, including the two that I have edited, we have obtained entries from outstanding senior scholars, emerging younger scholars, talented doctoral students, and even international economists and historians, all of whom are exceptionally knowledgeable about the subjects on which they write and present the best

and most recent scholarly literature on their subjects. Their entries are then read and evaluated by the volume editors for accuracy, reliability, and interpretive perspective before being approved for publication; a subsequent stage coordinated by the press's editorial staff fact checks further and ensures accuracy. This careful attention to accuracy and reliability aims to ensure that established scholars and their graduate student apprentices will find in these volumes a ready and reliable guide to the finest current knowledge and scholarly literature on subjects that pique their interest; it also ensures that undergraduate and secondary school students as well as general readers will find accurate information in their search for information on historical subjects.

Although the volumes are organized alphabetically from A to Z, we chose the entries to capture the most salient long-term trends in business, labor, and economic history. We drew nearly a third of our entries from the *Oxford Companion*, selecting those that represented the best scholarship and that were written most fluently. They included many extended entries on central aspects of U.S. history, somewhat shorter ones on important events, organizations/movements, and individuals, and brief concise entries on similar subjects often neglected but nevertheless important. Nearly all the entries drawn from the *Companion* were revised and updated in light of new scholarship, shifting interpretations, and developments that have occurred since they were written initially. Most of the entries in these volumes, however, are completely new and original and cover aspects of the past that could not be fitted into the spatial confines of the *Companion*.

In planning the volumes, we realized that not only the distinctions among business, labor, and economic history were artificial but also those between these two volumes and the other ten in the larger series. No hard and fast line separates business, labor, and economic history from social history, political and legal history, or even scientific and technological history. Hence these volumes cover some of the same subjects treated in the other encyclopedias and even draw on the contributions of the same scholars. After all, how does one distinguish labor movements from social movements that consist largely of working people? Class and class consciousness are as much a part of business, labor, and economic history as of social history. Immigration is as central to economic and labor history as it is to social history. The history of government promotion and regulation of the economy and business belongs as much to economic and business history as to political history. The same can be said concerning how the law impinges on economic, business, and labor history. And, to be sure, science and technology are fully imbricated in economic and business history. Thus the two volumes include entries that deal with political, legal, social, scientific, and technological aspects of U.S. history.

THE LOGIC OF BUSINESS, LABOR, AND ECONOMIC HISTORY

It is equally true that no clear, bright lines separate business, labor, and economic history from each other. Historians have studied and written about economic and business history for more than a century and both fields have published scholarly journals of record for many decades. Labor history as a serious field of study for historians as distinguished from labor economists is of more recent origin. It was rarely included in the collegiate history curriculum before the 1960s. The first scholarly American journal devoted to the field did not appear until 1959; its then managing editor was neither a historian nor an academic and the majority of its editorial board consisted of labor economists and industrial relations scholars. Only in the 1960s with the arrival of the so-called "new labor his-

tory" and its practitioners, most notably David Brody, Herbert Gutman, and David Montgomery, did the field become an accepted and respected aspect of the study and teaching of U.S. history. Simultaneously economic history seemed to disappear from the history department curriculum at most colleges and universities as "econometrics," the application of mathematical techniques and formulae to the study of the past, came to dominate the field. Economists skilled at quantification, comfortable with calculus, and lodged mostly in economics departments dominated the field by the end of the twentieth century, treating economic history as a field of applied neoclassical economics. Such skilled economic historians as Robert Fogel and Stanley Engerman taught within history as well as economics departments and trained doctoral students in history into the last decades of the twentieth century, but they remained the rare exceptions. Business historians, like economic historians, found a welcome home outside of history departments, most especially in graduate schools of business or management. The field's leading journal, *Business History Review*, had its editorial offices at the Harvard Business School and was published with the school's imprimatur.

By the end of the twentieth century the best scholarship integrated economic, business, and labor history. Sandy Jacoby's excellent books examining how American business enterprises obtained employees and managed them, *Employing Bureaucracy: Managers, Unions, and the Transformation of Work in the Twentieth Century* (2004) and *Modern Manors: Welfare Capitalism since the New Deal* (1997), used the tools of economic, business, and labor history to describe expertly the evolution of corporate personnel policies from the era of World War I to the end of the twentieth century. Philip Scranton did much the same in his pathbreaking books on the rise and decline of the textile industry in Philadelphia over the course of two centuries: *Proprietary Capitalism: The Textile Manufacture at Philadelphia, 1899–1885* (1983); *The Philadelphia System of Textile Manufacturing, 1884–1984* (1984); and *Figured Tapestry: Production, Markets, and Power in Philadelphia, 1885–1941* (1989). Richard White's revisionist history—*Railroaded: The Transcontinentals and the Making of Modern America* (2011)—of the transcontinental railroads went a step further as he added detailed accounts of political and legal history to his narrative of the railroads' economic, business, and labor history. Tom Sugrue accomplished a similar scholarly feat in his history of the deindustrialization of Detroit in the decades immediately after World War II, *The Origins of the Urban Crisis: Race and Inequality in Postwar Detroit* (1996). And the dean of American business historians, Alfred D. Chandler Jr., in two masterful books, *The Visible Hand: The Managerial Revolution in American Business* (1977) and *Scale and Scope: The Dynamics of Industrial Capitalism* (1990), joined business to economic history in explaining the evolution of the modern American corporation from the late nineteenth to the late twentieth century in the former and in the latter adding an international dimension by including Great Britain, Germany, and Japan, among other nations, in his history of the evolution of modern business organization and practice.

MAIN TRENDS IN BUSINESS, LABOR, AND ECONOMIC HISTORY

The nearly five hundred entries in the two volumes aim to demonstrate the links among the separate fields of business, labor, and economic history. Although many of the entries, especially those that describe notable individuals, individual business enterprises, key labor organizations, more technical aspects of economic history, and specific events, focus on discrete aspects of the past, taken together, as they should be, these entries illustrate the interrelationships among the three separate fields. The long entries treat what French historians have called the "longue duree," stasis and change over centuries, or truly significant subjects that require integration of several related factors.

The central, extended entries describe and analyze how the American economy, its business institutions and practices, its entrepreneurs, middle managers, and workers have evolved from the Colonial Era to the early twenty-first century. Readers will learn how overseas European colonies founded at the dawn of the age of capitalism grew and evolved into a new nation whose history by the twenty-first century had encapsulated the evolution from the early capitalism of merchants and petty producers through the heyday of a domestically based corporate capitalism to a system dominated by financial institutions and megaretailers that operated on a global scale previously unimaginable. They will discover how an economy based initially on the production and export of staple agricultural crops, most especially tobacco and cotton in the seventeenth, eighteenth, and first half of the nineteenth centuries, evolved into an industrial economy built on steam, steel, oil, internal combustion, and mass production and then shifted into one in which financial services, retail activities, and personal services grew.

Entries describe how an economy built largely on the labor of unfree workers—indentured servants and slaves—changed steadily if slowly into one in which workers became free legally but too often dependent economically, with only their labor power to barter in return for subsistence wages. These entries devote particular attention to the structural and demographic aspects of the labor market. Several explore how three waves of mass immigration, first during the 1840s and 1850s, later from 1881 to 1921, and finally since 1965, altered the ethnic and racial characteristics of the labor force. Others describe the gendered characteristics of the work force, noting the contributions that women made in the domestic sphere, where they were responsible for the reproduction of the labor force, and, then, how over time women steadily shifted from their role as unwaged domestic caregivers to low-waged domestic servants, textile workers, factory operatives, and later clerical and personal-service providers, until by the early twenty-first century women formed as large a proportion of the paid labor force as men. In the first half of the nineteenth century the southern cotton states became the wealthiest region of the nation on the labor coerced from enslaved blacks, all too many of whom after emancipation continued to provide essential labor in the former slave states as quasi-free workers tied to the land through sharecropping arrangements, victims of unfair employment relationships, or, worst of all, uncompensated convict laborers. By the end of the nineteenth century and into the early twentieth, the labor force grew ever more racially diverse as western railroad entrepreneurs recruited Chinese laborers as construction workers, by Japanese immigrants who labored in Far Western fields and homes, and then Filipinos who succeeded the Chinese denied entry by exclusion laws and the Japanese laborers excluded by informal presidential agreements. Until the Great Depression of the 1930s, Mexicans steadily drifted north across the border, where they joined a substantial population of U.S. citizens of Mexican origin who had become Americans as a consequence of the territories seized by the United States in the aftermath of the Mexican–American War of 1846–1848. Finally, after Congress reformed immigration law in 1965, eliminating quotas based on race and national origin, a new wave of mass immigration commenced, with the vast majority of newcomers emigrating from East and South Asia, Central America, and Africa. Recent estimates suggest that by the middle of the twenty-first century at the latest, a majority of the population and an even larger proportion of the labor force will be nonwhite.

Additional entries examine how working people sought to better their circumstances and to rise economically either through individual effort or by collective action. Extended entries examine the evolution of national worker movements from the late 1860s to the early twenty-first century, as well as how workers used strikes and other forms of direct action to achieve higher wages and improve working conditions. Shorter entries focus on key individual labor unions, decisive industrial conflicts, and some of the most influential labor leaders, including women too often neglected when writing the history of organized labor. While workers sought through collective action to better their lives, their employers implemented policies and actions aimed at dissuading employees from joining unions or broke unions formed by their workers.

The growth of the American economy and the history of its working people cannot be written and understood without an appreciation of the role played by government and the law. Thus many entries describe how government policies and actions evolved historically, from those implemented in the early republic to secure public finance and tie regions together through internal improvements to the subsidization of transcontinental railroads and, later, interstate highways that promoted economic growth. Just as government promoted economic development to enrich citizens, it has also from the beginning regulated private economic activity to protect citizens from exploitation, inequities, and the effects of the actions of others, including pollution. Many of the entries also show how at different times government promoted and protected the interests of working people individually and collectively, but all too often left workers economically adrift and their organizations suspect. The law, as interpreted and implemented by federal and state judges, at times reinforced the policy preferences of legislators and executors but sometimes subverted them. Judges occasionally protected workers and defended collective action but more often left workers defenseless against their employers and deemed collective action illegal. All this and more is treated in multiple entries.

USING THIS VOLUME

We have sought to make the two volumes as user-friendly as possible. The essay-length entries open with a headnote that lists the subentries to follow. Every entry includes at its end a selective bibliography on the subject as well as cross-references to related entries. Blind entries guide readers to full entries that cover the same subject under a different headword or title. Readers interested in finding all the articles on a particular subject can consult the systematic topical outline that shows how articles relate to one another. The encyclopedia's back pages include a directory of contributors, which provides a complete alphabetical list of all the contributors with their current academic or professional affiliations. A comprehensive index lists all the topics covered in the encyclopedia, including those that are not headwords themselves. The topical outline, the directory of contributors, and the index are all located at the end of Volume 2.

These volumes could not have been completed without the advice and guidance of the late Paul Boyer, an outstanding historian and a good friend for more than four decades, with whom I worked on the progenitor of this encyclopedia beginning two decades ago and without whom the *Oxford Encyclopedia of American Business, Labor, and Economic History* might never have become reality. It is truly a shame that his untimely death denied Paul the plea-sure of seeing his introduction to the encyclopedia in print.

I owe an equal debt to my two associate editors on the project, Gerald Friedman and Joseph McCartin. They helped me select the subjects and specific entries that we included, plan the overall design, seek and obtain many of the contributors, and edit numerous entries. Jerry, who is an economist and economic historian by academic training and disciplinary location, proved especially helpful in choosing economic history subjects for inclusion and finding scholars to write the more technical and specialized economic history entries. Joe, who is one of my former doctoral students, proved more knowledgeable and adept than I in knowing younger scholars whom he convinced to write entries in labor history and about how government and law impinged on labor and economic history. Jerry and Joe also volunteered to write several essential entries for which we had great difficulty obtaining contributors. Without their assistance these two volumes would not have been nearly as good.

Last but not least, I must thank the various editors at Oxford University Press who guided this project from its inception through to completion. Stephen Wagley worked with me on the earliest stages and then turned the responsibility over to Eric Stannard, with whom I consulted during the bulk of the preparation, and finally to Andrew Jung, who assisted me in its final stages. Without their wise counsel and consistent support, this would have been a far more laborious and less satisfying experience. The same might well be said about the mostly anonymous Oxford University Press staff who diligently fact-checked the entries, edited them expertly, and ushered them into print.

Melvyn Dubofsky

COMMON ABBREVIATIONS USED IN THIS WORK

AD	*anno Domini,* in the year of the Lord	l.	line (pl., ll.)
AH	*anno Hegirae,* in the year of the Hajj	n.	note
		n.d.	no date
b.	Born	no.	number
BCE	before the common era (= BC)	n.p.	no place
		n.s.	new series
c.	*circa,* about, approximately	p.	page (pl., pp.)
CE	common era (= AD)	pt.	part
cf.	*confer,* compare	rev.	revised
d.	died	ser.	series
diss.	dissertation	supp.	supplement
ed.	editor (pl., eds.), edition	USSR	Union of Soviet Socialist Republics
f.	and following (pl., ff.)	vol.	volume (pl., vols.)
fl.	*floruit,* flourished		

THE OXFORD ENCYCLOPEDIA OF
AMERICAN BUSINESS, LABOR, AND ECONOMIC HISTORY

A

ABRAHAM LINCOLN BRIGADE

"Abraham Lincoln Brigade" is the name popularly given the American contingent of the Communist-dominated International Brigades that fought for the Spanish Republic against its enemies in mid-1936. About three thousand Americans, volunteers from U.S. Communist and leftist organizations, served in Spain; organized formally in early 1937, the so-called brigade in fact never reached brigade strength. Many union members volunteered, especially those from left-wing unions of the Congress of Industrial Organizations—most notably, merchant seamen.

As the forces of the Spanish Republic, the Loyalists, fought to save the republic from the Nationalists, forces headed by General Francisco Franco and strongly aided by Fascist Italy and Nazi Germany, the Lincolns participated in defeats, victories, and some inconclusive battles. The Americans, although poorly officered, inadequately armed, and ineptly trained, demonstrated fierce bravery in combat, suffering significant casualties; of those who served, about a third were killed before Spain—seeking favor with the Non-Intervention Committee, an international group that sought to localize the conflict—agreed in autumn 1938 to withdraw the International Brigades.

After withdrawal from Spain and repatriation to the United States the Lincoln Brigade veterans did not fare well. They had broken federal law by fighting in Spain and thus became political and social outcasts. In 1939 the Veterans of the Abraham Lincoln Brigade (VALB) was founded to aid its members, "assist refugees of the Spanish struggle," and protest U.S. ties to the Franco regime. Those who remained Communists suffered during the McCarthy era and beyond.

In 1979 the VALB formed the Abraham Lincoln Brigade Archive (ALBA), which came to be housed at New York University's Tamiment Library. ALBA, a "comprehensive archive dedicated to the preservation and dissemination of the history of the North American role" in the Spanish Civil War, has done much to enhance the reputation of the Lincoln Brigade.

[*See also* **Labor and Anti-Communism.**]

BIBLIOGRAPHY

Beevor, Antony. *The Battle for Spain: The Spanish Civil War, 1936–1939*. New York: Penguin Books, 2006. Originally published in 1982.

Carroll, Peter N. *The Odyssey of the Abraham Lincoln Brigade: Americans in the Spanish Civil War*. Stanford, Calif.: Stanford University Press, 1994.

Eby, Cecil D. *Comrades and Commissars: The Lincoln Battalion in the Spanish Civil War*. University Park: Pennsylvania State University Press, 2007.

Daniel J. Leab

ACCUMULATION, SOCIAL STRUCTURES OF

A social structure of accumulation (SSA) is a coherent, mutually reinforcing, and long-lasting set of institutions that promotes capital accumulation in a capitalist economy. The institutions making up an SSA encompass the economic, political, and ideological aspects of society. For example, the post–World War II SSA in the United States featured the economic institution of regular collective bargaining between management and labor to determine wages and working conditions, the political institution of government provision of substan-tial social programs such as unemployment compensation and Social Security, and a mixed-economy ideology that held active government intervention in the economy to be essential to achieve acceptable economic performance.

Concept and Theory. First proposed in the United States by David M. Gordon in 1980, the concept of a social structure of accumulation forms the basis of a theory of how capitalist economies develop and change over time. A few years earlier, French historians and economists had pioneered a somewhat similar theory of the stages of capitalist development called "regulation theory," which characterized the post–World War II structure of political economy as "Fordism." The SSA theory holds that a lengthy period of vigorous and relatively stable capital accumulation can begin only if an SSA is in place. An SSA promotes capital accumulation by creating relative stability and predictability, as well as by ensuring a high rate of profit for business. Left to its own devices, capitalism leads to disruptive conflicts, both between capital and labor and among capitalists, that discourage productive investment. An SSA stabilizes the relations in capitalism that create conflict, although it cannot entirely eliminate such conflict. Every SSA regulates relations between capital and labor and competition among capitalists, as well as establishing a particular role for the state in the economy and a dominant set of ideas related to the economy.

The central claim of the SSA theory is that, although an SSA can effectively promote accumulation for a long period of some twenty to thirty years, it cannot do so indefinitely. Every historically existing SSA eventually has turned from a facilitator of accumulation into an obstacle to it. There follows a period of economic crisis marked by some combination of slow or no economic growth, high unemployment, and high inflation. The period of crisis gives way to a new period of relatively stable capital accumulation only if a new SSA is constructed.

Since capitalist society changes over time, each new SSA arises in new historical conditions, and hence each new SSA differs from earlier ones. Thus the SSA theory posits a theory of stages of capitalism.

Successive SSAs in the United States.
In the 1890s an SSA arose in the United States that included a concentrated industrial structure characterized by banker dominance of much of industry, control of the new semi-skilled assembly-line workers through machine pacing, the first significant state regulation of the economy, and a new ideology stressing corporate responsibility. This SSA entered its crisis phase, rather dramatically, after the great stock market crash of 1929.

The construction of the next SSA began in the midst of the Great Depression of the 1930s and was completed around 1948. This SSA included peaceful collective bargaining, control of labor through bureaucratic organization, a welfare state, state regulation of the macroeconomy through Keynesian techniques as well as regulation of key industries, active state promotion of economic growth, and a dominant ideology that combined a favorable view of government intervention in the economy with Cold War fear of Communism. This SSA also included important international dimensions, such as the Bretton Woods monetary system of fixed exchange rates based on a gold-backed U.S. dollar and U.S. dominance in the capitalist world.

Beginning in the late 1960s this SSA began to show signs of crisis. The crisis, which intensified through the end of the 1970s, was marked by slower economic growth, a more severe business cycle, rising unemployment and inflation, and international monetary instability. Starting in the late 1970s, a new

institutional structure emerged that was based on the weakening of trade unions, deregulation of markets both domestically and internationally, cutbacks in the welfare state, privatization of public services, growing global economic integration, and an antigovernment, pro-free-market ideology. At first many SSA theorists questioned whether these developments constituted a new SSA or were instead a continuation of the crisis of the previous SSA. Eventually almost all analysts concluded that a new SSA had indeed emerged, since the developments proved to constitute a coherent, mutually reinforcing set of institutions that promoted capital accumulation for several decades. Initially referred to as "free-market" or "conservative" economics, this SSA eventually came to be called the "neoliberal" SSA, based on the traditional European meaning of "liberal" as a call for limited state intervention in the economy. It appears that this latest SSA entered its period of crisis with the financial crisis and sharp recession that began in 2008.

The SSA theory was initially developed in reference to the economic history of the United States, but it has come to be applied to many other countries and to the global economy. The SSA theory provides a new way of understanding capitalism and the ways in which it changes over time. According to this approach, capitalism takes an institutional form that is relatively stable for several decades. During such periods, a shift in governance from one political party to another does not bring significant economic change. Although the post–World War II SSA was constructed under presidents from the Democratic Party, Republican presidents in the 1950s and 1960s did not attempt to significantly change the main economic institutions. Similarly, the neoliberal SSA had its beginnings under a president from the Democratic Party, Jimmy Carter; was deepened under a president from the Republican Party, Ronald Reagan;

and was maintained during the Democratic Party presidency of Bill Clinton.

Significant economic change takes place when an SSA goes into crisis. At that point, institutions that had seemed invulnerable to opposition now can be reformed or replaced. According to the SSA theory, there is no economic law governing the outcome of such a period of institutional restructuring. Rather, the result is the outcome of complex struggles among various groups and classes, with a significant role played by the interpretation of what caused the crisis of the previous institutional structure. Not surprisingly, in such periods a sharp battle always occurs over the explanation of why the previous institutional structure gave rise to an economic crisis.

[*See also* **Capitalism; Depressions, Economic; Economic Theories and Thought; Ford, Henry, and Fordism; Long Swings and Cycles in Economic Growth;** *and* **Neoliberalism.**]

BIBLIOGRAPHY

Gordon, David M. "Stages of Accumulation and Long Economic Cycles." In *Processes of the World-System*, edited by Terence K. Hopkins and Immanuel Wallerstein, pp. 9–45. Beverly Hills, Calif.: Sage, 1980.

Gordon, David M., Richard Edwards, and Michael Reich. *Segmented Work, Divided Workers: The Historical Transformation of Labor in the United States.* Cambridge, U.K.: Cambridge University Press, 1982.

Kotz, David M., Terrence McDonough, and Michael Reich, eds. *Social Structures of Accumulation: The Political Economy of Growth and Crisis.* Cambridge, U.K.: Cambridge University Press, 1994.

McDonough, Terrence, Michael Reich, and David M. Kotz, eds. *Contemporary Capitalism and Its Crises: Social Structure of Accumulation Theory for the 21st Century.* Cambridge, U.K.: Cambridge University Press, 2010.

David M. Kotz

ADAMSON ACT

Enacted on 3 September 1916 at the insistence of President Woodrow Wilson, the Adamson (Eight-Hour) Act narrowly averted the threatened general strike of 400,000 running-trades workers employed by more than fifty different railway companies—a strike that might have disrupted the nation's railways just when the United States was on the verge of war with Mexico and was becoming more involved in World War I. The law's roots can be traced both to earlier federal legislation regulating the hours worked by government employees and also to President Wilson's need to build trade union support for his reelection in 1916. More important, the Adamson Act represents the first time that the federal government mandated the eight-hour workday for employees in the private sector.

President Wilson asserted that "the eight-hour day now, undoubtedly, has the sanction of the judgment of society in its favor." Although the Adamson Act affected only 20 percent of the nation's railway employees—and only when their work crossed state lines—union leaders proclaimed it a great victory for American workers.

The immediate cause of this legislation was a demand from leaders of the four major railway brotherhoods for the eight-hour day or a maximum of one hundred miles traveled—whichever was less—with no reduction in pay from the standard ten-hour day. The railway executives rejected the unions' demands and instead offered to submit the matter to the U.S. Mediation Board. Both the workers and the railway executives began preparing for a nationwide strike that threatened President Wilson's war-preparedness program and his reelection. To prevent the shutdown of the railways, Wilson hosted a White House conference between brotherhood officials and the railway owners.

His mediation efforts failed. Wilson then asked Congress to pass the Adamson Act. The railway companies immediately challenged the constitutionality of the act and refused to implement it when it became operative on 1 January 1917. On 18 March 1917, Wilson finally pressured the railway owners to accept the eight-hour day. A day later the Supreme Court, rendering its verdict on the constitutional challenge (*Wilson v. New*), ruled in favor of the government.

[*See also* **Eight-Hour Day; Railroad Brotherhoods;** *and* **Railroads.**]

BIBLIOGRAPHY

Kerr, K. Austin. *American Railroad Politics, 1914–1920: Rates, Wages, and Efficiency.* Pittsburgh, Pa.: University of Pittsburgh Press, 1968.

Link, Arthur S. *Woodrow Wilson and the Progressive Era, 1910–1917.* New York: Harper, 1954.

Montgomery, David. *The Fall of the House of Labor: The Workplace, the State, and American Labor Activism, 1865–1925.* Cambridge, U.K.: Cambridge University Press, 1987.

James Mochoruk

ADKINS v. CHILDREN'S HOSPITAL

During the early twentieth century, Progressives sought to ameliorate the consequences of industrialization by enacting minimum-wage laws. Conservatives and business groups challenged these laws in the courts. In *Adkins v. Children's Hospital* (1923), the U.S. Supreme Court, by a vote of 5 to 3, struck down a 1918 congressional statute setting a minimum wage for women in the District of Columbia. The 1918 law, the Court held, violated the liberty of contract protected by the due process clause of the Fifth Amendment. Writing for the majority, Justice George Sutherland emphasized that under the Constitution, freedom of contract was the general rule and restraint the exception. Minimum-wage laws, he argued, foisted on employers a welfare function that properly belonged to society as a whole. Moreover, Sutherland insisted, in light of the Nineteenth Amendment, women could not be more restricted in the exercise of contractual freedom than men were.

Chief Justice William Howard Taft and Justice Oliver Wendell Holmes Jr. each wrote a dissenting opinion. Taft maintained that legislators could, under the government's police powers, regulate the hours of work or minimum wages of women. Holmes expressed doubt about the constitutional basis for the liberty-of-contract doctrine.

The *Adkins* decision stands as a classic expression of the Court's commitment to contractual freedom. It made clear the Court's determination to keep wages and prices free of regulatory interference. During the New Deal era of the 1930s, however, the Supreme Court moderated its long-standing commitment to economic liberty and freedom of contract. *Adkins* was overruled in *West Coast Hotel v. Parrish* (1937), in which the justices, by a vote of 5 to 4, sustained a Washington State minimum-wage law.

[*See also* **Employment-at-Will; Factory and Hours Laws; Freedom of Contract;** *and West Coast Hotel v. Parrish.*]

BIBLIOGRAPHY

Arkes, Hadley. *The Return of George Sutherland: Restoring a Jurisprudence of Natural Rights.* Princeton, N.J.: Princeton University Press, 1994.

Ely, James W., Jr. *The Guardian of Every Other Right: A Constitutional History of Property Rights.* 3d ed. Oxford: Oxford University Press, 2008.

Mayer, David N. *Liberty of Contract: Rediscovering a Lost Constitutional Right.* Washington, D.C.: Cato Institute, 2011.

James W. Ely Jr.

ADVERTISING

From its origins in colonial handbills, sign-boards, and newspaper announcements, American advertising by the twenty-first century had grown into a multibillion-dollar industry, one with broad significance for the nation's culture as well as its economy. Its transformations reflect both the course of American business and the shifting patterns of American culture. For most of its history, observers have seen advertising as a central feature of the American social landscape and have considered the United States the "promised land" of advertising. For example, the historian David Potter (*People of Plenty*, 1954) treated advertising as emblematic of American abundance and a pervasive means of democratic social control.

Before Mass Retail.   In the Colonial Era, when production for market was constrained, currency was in short supply, and goods were rarely identified with their producers, advertising remained small in scale and intermittent. Yet by the eighteenth century a network of shopkeepers and colonists sought customers among the growing number of colonists who could afford manufactured amenities and luxuries such as pottery, books, furniture, and musical instruments. Sellers trumpeted the wide range of choices available and portrayed their goods as appropriate for refined and fashionable men and women. Benjamin Franklin's *Pennsylvania Gazette* introduced innovations such as headlines, illustrations, and advertising notices placed next to news items. At times, more than half of his newspaper was devoted to advertising. Though it may be an exaggeration to speak of an eighteenth-century Anglo-American "consumer revolution," the spread of advertising impressed observers on both sides of the Atlantic. Indeed, T. H. Breen has argued forcefully that consumer consciousness sparked the American Revolution. The "baubles of Britain" both appealed to colonists and provoked anxieties about dependency and the corruptions of luxury. Advertisements intensified this ambivalence and drew pre-Revolutionary Americans into a web of consumption.

Down to the Civil War, newspaper advertising developed slowly. Steam-powered presses and cheap newsprint allowed the emergence of the penny press in the 1830s, but most of these innovations limited attractive displays and confined advertisements within column rules. Display advertising became common only in the 1870s. Magazines generally segregated advertisements in the back pages and barred eye-catching display. "Announcement" remained a near-synonym for "advertisement." Nevertheless, the so-called market revolution of Jacksonian America opened up opportunities for persuasive commercial communications.

There were several individuals who made exceptional use of advertising in the mid-nineteenth century. P. T. Barnum's promotions usually involved finding free publicity rather than paying for space in media, but he wrote accurately in his autobiography, "I thoroughly understood the art of advertising." Jay Cooke's marketing of Union bonds across the North during the Civil War borrowed commercial advertising's techniques and merged them with nationalistic appeals. The pioneers of persuasive advertising copy, however, were usually medicine makers. Employing a range of media, these "toadstool millionaires" (the title of a 1961 book by James Harvey Young) won customers for their nostrums with emotional appeals to fear and faith. By the early twentieth century, however, the dishonest and hyperbolic claims of the medicine makers clashed with the needs of new corporate marketers and advertising agents eager to professionalize and legitimate advertising. Muckraking exposés and legislation sought to draw a line between advertising as a tool of a modernizing business society and the dishonest blandishments of the makers of pills and potions.

The Rise of Agencies.

The appearance of mass retailers, in particular downtown department stores, and the rise of mass-produced brand-name consumer goods after 1880 gave advertising much of its modern form. Volney Palmer, generally considered the nation's first advertising agent, and his successors had solicited advertisers to fill space in the newspapers and magazines they represented. By the 1890s, however, advertising agencies were taking over the preparation of advertising copy and design, and they were being compensated through a discount for the space that they purchased from publishers. Freelance copywriters gave way to a new generation of agency employees. In the early 1900s, agencies increasingly boasted of their broad competence as sales and marketing professionals. The 1911 introduction of Procter & Gamble's shortening, Crisco, involved a multifaceted marketing campaign. To reach broad middle-class audiences, new general-interest magazines like the *Saturday Evening Post* became leading advertising media. By World War I, the advertising business's institutional triad of advertisers, agencies, and media had assumed roles that largely endured throughout the twentieth century. Advertising self-regulation sought to win popular respect and assert claims to professionalism. The leading trade journal, *Printer's Ink*, and the Associated Advertising Clubs of America launched an energetic, if self-serving, "truth in advertising" movement to upgrade ethical standards. It pushed a model statute through state legislatures that aimed to ban false advertising; in most cases, the statute proved hard to apply, because it required prosecutors to prove that ads were intended to deceive.

The historian Pamela Walker Laird has shown how a motif of progress came to prevail in advertising discourse in the Gilded Age and Progressive Era. Ironically, this theme initially may have detracted from the persuasiveness of national advertising. Rather than aiming to persuade consumers of the benefits of their products, late nineteenth-century advertisers often featured their factories, their machinery, or even stock images of American power and might as measures of industrial progress. The language of these ads, vague and bombastic, drew sharp criticism by the early twentieth century. Advertising descriptions were too often "a mass of dead verbiage that would apply to one commodity as well, or as poorly, as to any other," lamented Daniel Starch, one of the first psychologists to study advertising. When advertisers began to employ advertising agencies to prepare their messages, however, the focus shifted from manufacturer to consumer. Progress came to be equated with the satisfactions of consumption.

Two seemingly conflicting doctrines about how to appeal to consumers emerged in the early twentieth century. In a revelatory moment in 1904, the freelance copywriter John E. Kennedy vouchsafed his secret to the young advertising prodigy Albert Lasker of the Lord & Thomas advertising agency. Advertising, Kennedy insisted, must be "salesmanship in print." It had to give readers a "reason why" they should buy the seller's product. At the same time, however, others were emphasizing the nonrational side of persuasion. "Human-interest" copy could attract customers through appeals to emotion and "instinct" and through recognizing the power of habit in human action. In practice, however, the two approaches were complementary. By the 1920s, advertising copywriters reached a consensus that consumers were generally ignorant and unreasonable. Advertising was persuasion designed to pull Americans toward accommodation with the modern world that business was molding; to do so, advertisements were to "aim low." Decades later, David Ogilvy, one of the stars of the industry in the late twentieth century, took a different approach, declaring, "The consumer is not an idiot. She is your wife." Growing levels of income and education had lessened the perceived gap between advertising practitioners and those they hoped to persuade, but it had hardly eliminated it.

Challenges to Consumption during the Depression and War.

Although President Calvin Coolidge in 1926 proclaimed advertising "part of the greater work of the regeneration and redemption of mankind," advertising experts customarily thought of themselves in less exalted terms. They hoped to lead ill-informed and manipulable consumers toward adjustment to modern, corporate-dominated society. The accoutrements of a consumer society, from personal-hygiene products (such as Listerine mouthwash and Kotex sanitary napkins) to large-scale consumer durables (automobiles, radio consoles, refrigerators), became markers of advertisers' success in promoting this new way of life. Advertisements stressed popularity and social acceptance as the rewards for appropriate consumer behavior. Ostracism and shame awaited those who failed to meet the new norms of consumption. Despite Herbert Hoover's warning against letting radio be "drowned in advertising chatter," broadcasting soon became a major medium, alongside the older print media.

In the 1930s Depression, advertising turned shrill, playing upon Americans' economic worries and matching the industry's combative response to the New Deal's consumer-protection proposals. The regulatory impact of the New Deal's efforts was limited, but many in the advertising industry equated government controls with threats to capitalism. J. B. Matthews, a former left-winger and consumer advocate, contended that "communists believe that to sabotage and destroy advertising is … a revolutionary tactic." On the other hand, such firms as General Electric and General Motors used the tools of advertising in corporate image campaigns to portray businesses as human and humane, endowed with what Roland Marchand called a "corporate soul."

World War II posed both challenges and opportunities for the advertising industry. Wartime shortages of consumer goods forced advertising experts to devise ways to promote products that consumers could not immediately purchase. At the same time, however, businesses invested money in advertising that would otherwise have been taxed at high corporate-profit tax rates. Moreover, the confrontations between Depression-Era consumer activists and advertisers faded with the coming of war. As they had back in 1917–1918, advertising leaders in World War II sought legitimation through contributions to the war effort. The War Advertising Council, founded in 1942, lived on after 1945 as the Advertising Council, usually promoting uncontroversial causes such as forest-fire prevention. The subtexts consistently touted advertising's social benefits and the industry's service to the nation.

Postwar Culture of Consumption.

Advertising in the postwar era grew alongside economic prosperity and undergirded a culture of consumption. Expenditures grew from under $3 billion in 1945 to over $200 billion in 1998. Television advertising accounted for approximately one quarter of this. TV's combination of visual appeals, motion, and sound gave advertisements new dimensions and greater power. Although postwar advertising continued to promote conformity through consumption of standardized products, by the 1960s segmentation was becoming a dominant marketing strategy. Product distinctions proliferated, mass media gave way to specialized ones, and advertisements "positioned" products for targeted "niche markets." Voted the outstanding advertising campaign of its era, Volkswagen advertising appealed to consumers to "think small," telling the cars' buyers that they were part of a special and presumably superior group. Other campaigns sought to attract members of particular sociological or psychological categories to goods and services tailored for them. Advertising, as observers such as Daniel Boorstin (in *The Americans: The Democratic Experience*, 1973) noted, could even create "consumption communities," groups identifying themselves by loyalty to a particular brand or product. For Boorstin, consumption communities were democratic and flexible; anyone could join or leave through his or her buying choices. For others, segmentation both reflected and portended a fragmentation of American culture.

Advertising agencies diversified as well. Until the second half of the twentieth century, the advertising business was a white-shoe industry. In the 1960s and beyond, a younger generation of men and women, often from ethnic minorities, undertook what they liked to call a "creative revolution": elements of fantasy, humor, irony, and even self-mockery assumed a larger place in the repertoire of persuasion. However, advertising remained a business; agencies knew that clients' sales constituted the bottom line. Geographic expansion also characterized the advertising industry in the late twentieth century. Though New York's Madison Avenue still symbolized the industry, large firms were increasingly multinational, and agencies from Richmond, Virginia, to Portland, Oregon, gained industry acclaim. Indeed, by late in the twentieth century the United States had lost its unquestioned supremacy in advertising. By the 1970s the Japanese agency Dentsu had become the largest advertising agency in the world. Increasingly, ad agencies became linked in global networks. Advertising grew globally as government-controlled and tax or license-fee financing of broadcasting gave way to commercial broadcasting. American advertising specialists often turned to foreign campaigns for inspiration and ideas.

Politics, Branding, and the Internet.
Advertisements had become tools of election campaigns early in the twentieth century. Albert Lasker, one of the titans of advertising in that era, had served as an adviser to Warren Harding in the 1920 presidential race. After World War II, advertising became a central element in political contests. The 1952 presidential race saw the first television commercials. Dwight Eisenhower gave brief answers to scripted questions about policy from seemingly ordinary Americans; these film clips were shown with the title "Eisenhower Answers America." These spots, crude by later standards, prefigured more sophisticated advertising such as Ronald Reagan's 1984 "Morning in America" campaign. "Morning in America" was feel-good advertising, bathing iconic American images of family, faith, and flag in a gauzy glow, but often political ads turned negative, attacking and sometimes distorting opponents' personal records and policy stands. The 2010 U.S. Supreme Court decision in *Citizens United v. Federal Election Commission* removed restrictions on corporate financing of political campaigns and threatened to increase further the influence of paid publicity in election battles.

Complementing the rise of segmentation strategies in mid-twentieth-century American advertising was the growing attention to branding. Advertisers had long known that a distinctive brand identity was a valuable asset. Those in the advertising business had long maintained that advertising could create corporate goodwill—not just favorable sentiments, but also monetary value above and beyond a firm's tangible and financial assets. Now, however, advocates of branding strategies focused on building that distinctiveness. Not only were businesses to demonstrate that they had a "corporate soul," but they were exhorted to build a corporate personality. In 1955, David Ogilvy introduced the notion of a "brand personality." Eventually, advocates extended the concept of branding beyond commercial persuasion. They advised political candidates, philanthropic organizations, even individuals to create their own brand image. Branding became a strategy for identity formation and individuation in daily life.

At the end of the twentieth century, the growth of the Internet opened new pathways for commercial publicity. Scholars need to avoid the temptation to exaggerate the role of the Internet in advertising. Online advertising volume in 2009 was estimated at $22.7 billion, only a little more than 10 percent of total advertising outlays. Older media, beleaguered in various ways, remain mainstays of the advertising business. Yet the Internet has wrought radical changes in the industry. It has allowed a previously impossible degree of targeting and personalization of advertising messages. Ads that track a user's browsing and choose a message based on his or her paths around the World Wide Web raise disturbing questions about privacy and manipulation.

Scholarly and critical attention is not new: from the early twentieth century, as it became more ubiquitous, advertising attracted such attention. Though some scholars pointed out the uncertainties and limits of its sway, a host of cultural critiques—from James Rorty's Veblenesque indictment in *Our Master's Voice: Advertising* (1934) through Vance Packard's *The Hidden Persuaders* (1957) to the "culture-jamming" efforts of the Canadian magazine *Adbusters* in the twenty-first century—warned of its persuasive powers and of the materialism and consumerism that it was said to promote. Yet despite the attacks, advertising has remained central to the nation's economy and culture. With its ever-changing forms and styles, its omnipresence seemed assured.

[*See also* **Consumer Culture; Mass Marketing; Radio;** *and* **Television.**]

BIBLIOGRAPHY

Blaszczyk, Regina Lee. *American Consumer Society, 1865–2005: From Hearth to HDTV.* Wheeling, Ill.: Harlan Davidson, 2009.

Breen, T. H. *The Marketplace of Revolution: How Consumer Politics Shaped American Independence.* New York: Oxford University Press, 2004.

Laird, Pamela Walker. *Advertising Progress: American Business and the Rise of Consumer Marketing.* Baltimore: Johns Hopkins University Press, 1998.

Lears, Jackson. *Fables of Abundance: A Cultural History of Advertising in America.* New York: Basic Books, 1994.

Marchand, Roland. *Advertising the American Dream: Making Way for Modernity, 1920–1940.* Berkeley: University of California Press, 1985.

McDonough, John, Karen Egolf, and the Museum of Broadcast Communications, eds. *The Advertising Age Encyclopedia of Advertising.* 3 vols. New York: Fitzroy Dearborn, 2003.

McGovern, Charles F. *Sold American: Consumption and Citizenship, 1890–1945.* Chapel Hill: University of North Carolina Press, 2006.

Pope, Daniel. *The Making of Modern Advertising.* New York: Basic Books, 1983.

Presbrey, Frank. *The History and Development of Advertising.* Garden City, N.Y.: Doubleday, Doran, 1929.

Tedlow, Richard S. *New and Improved: The Story of Mass Marketing in America.* New York: Basic Books, 1990.

Daniel Pope

AFL-CIO

See **American Federation of Labor; American Federation of Labor and Congress of Industrial Organizations;** *and* **Congress of Industrial Organizations.**

AFRICAN AMERICAN LABOR ORGANIZATIONS

Ever since the era of Reconstruction, African American workers in the United States have formed numerous racially distinct organizations to advance the needs of their members in the labor market and in the union movement. Prior to the passage of the 1964 Civil Rights Act—and in some regions even after its passage—widespread employment discrimination kept black workers out of key sectors of the economy or segregated them into unskilled, poorly paid positions. In some cases, trade unions excluded blacks from membership—and at times, union membership was a condition of employment—or relegated them to inferior auxiliary locals. From the late nineteenth through the mid-twentieth century, associations of black workers directed their energies toward breaking down barriers to employment and opening up union membership, goals that they largely if not entirely accomplished in the final decades of the twentieth century.

First Organizations. The first major all-black labor body, the Colored National Labor Union (CNLU), emerged after the Civil War. With virtually all trade unions of skilled workers closed to blacks—including the new federation the National Labor Union—the Baltimore activist Isaac Myers organized black workers in the upper South and founded the CNLU in 1869, bringing together black trade unionists, community leaders, and Republican Party officials. Insisting on the harmony of interest between capital and labor, the CNLU made "no discrimination as to nationality, sex, or color," for a "labor movement based upon such discrimination, and embracing a small part of the great working masses of the country," would be of "very little value" and "suicidal." Promoting as a matter of American citizenship rights the organization of black mechanics to procure employment without discrimination, the organization faded into obscurity by the early 1870s as the battle over Reconstruction intensified and an economic depression sent unemployment rising.

Although a large majority of black workers remained aloof from organized labor, from the 1880s through the early to mid-twentieth century a significant minority in the South did organize to promote their economic and racial advancement. Virtually all who did so joined racially distinct unions in the trades where blacks predominated; where whites also labored, racial segregation proved the rule. Boasting that it knew no color line, the Knights of Labor welcomed black members in all-black locals in the 1880s. Although the American Federation of Labor (AFL) was less welcoming—many of its constituent internationals barred black members—individual unions in trades that had significant numbers of black workers, such as longshoring and coal mining, experimented with biracial unionism. Among dockworkers, all-black locals coexisted with all-white locals in a number of ports, negotiating identical contracts and observing identical work rules, to black workers' advantage. In other cases, stronger white locals dominated weaker black ones. And in still other cases, white unions consigned black workers to racially distinct auxiliary unions with fewer rights and benefits.

Beginning in the World War I era, organizations of black workers proliferated in a number of crafts. The Railway Men's International Benevolent Industrial Association, as much a fraternal organization as a union federation, did not outlive the immediate postwar years, but the Colored Trainmen of America, based in Texas and Louisiana, and the Colored Association of Railroad Employees, based in Memphis, Tennessee, did; the International Association of Railway Employees, established 1934, operated until the 1960s. Excluded from the all-white railroad brotherhoods and other craft unions, black railroaders joined independent all-black associations that interceded on their members' behalf before management, fought to preserve black workers' jobs, and relied upon petitions, court suits, and testimony before federal agencies. Relatively small and weak, these organizations battled against the odds to maintain their institutional independence and serve their members' needs.

The BSCP's Broad Influence. The Brotherhood of Sleeping Car Porters (BSCP), inaugurated in 1925 and composed of Pullman porters and maids, transformed the debate in black communities toward unionization. A long-standing antiunionism prevailed among many black community leaders, a response to white union practices and a segregated job market that was popularized by Booker T. Washington and other conservative editors, clergymen, and politicians. The socialist activist A. Philip Randolph, hired by the porters to direct the new union, preached the gospel of trade unionism to black workers and black elites alike, arguing that the "next emancipation" required an economic independence and dignity that only self-organization in unions could provide. Under the provisions of the Railway Labor Act, the BSCP won a union representation election in 1935; its first contract, signed with the Pullman Company two years later, was a cause for celebration in the black press.

The porters' victory, Randolph predicted, would reverberate far beyond the ranks of Pullman employees and "serve as one great stimulant to the organization of Race workers in all industries throughout the country." Randolph's high profile and the BSCP's success did, in fact, inspire numerous groups of black workers to organize. In the mid- and late 1930s, railroad red caps established the International Brotherhood of Red Caps (later the United Transport Service Employees of America), which affiliated with the new Congress of Industrial Organizations (CIO), and the Joint Council of Dining Car Employees, which, like the BSCP, remained in the AFL, expanded in size. Unlike the World War I era, when many black workers were cool to white unions that had unimpressive track records on race, the late 1930s and 1940s witnessed an unprecedented wave of black unionization, much of which came in integrated CIO unions. By 1943, some 400,000 African American workers had joined the labor movement; by 1955 that number had grown to one and a half million.

Targeting Discrimination. Black trade unionists were key participants in several pioneering organizations targeting discrimination in the 1930s and 1940s. In cities as diverse as New York, Chicago, Minneapolis, Washington, D.C., and Seattle, local groups promoted "don't buy where you can't work" campaigns and pressed utilities to open up municipal transit and telephone jobs. The National Negro Congress, formed in 1936, initially attracted a diverse membership to promote black unionization and civil rights; in 1939, however, Communist domination drove out most non-Communists. The March on Washington Movement, spearheaded by A. Philip Randolph in 1941 and drawing upon the energies of the BSCP and many others, forced President Franklin D. Roosevelt to issue Executive Order 8802, which barred racial discrimination in national defense industries. Weak enforcement of the order and persistent discrimination kept the movement active with protests, pickets, and lobbying for the duration of World War II. To combat inferior auxiliary unions in the booming wartime shipyards on the West Coast, black workers joined the San Francisco Committee against Segregation and Discrimination and the East Bay Shipyard Workers against

Discrimination to advocate on behalf of complete union integration.

The persistence of discrimination within the unified AFL-CIO and its tolerance of exclusionary white unions prompted black activists to intensify their attack on the federation's racial policies and practices in the late 1950s and early 1960s. The labor movement "cannot say it is democratic unless it cleans its house and says that, regardless of race, color and creed, any worker can join any A F of L union," A. Philip Randolph charged in 1942. In 1960, Randolph formed the Negro American Labor Council (NALC) to press the AFL-CIO toward greater action on civil rights. With as many as ten thousand members, the NALC also highlighted the economic problems afflicting black America and sponsored the 1963 March on Washington for Jobs and Freedom; in 1972 the newly formed Coalition of Black Trade Unionists absorbed the NALC. In the late 1960s, locals of all-black sanitation workers and multiracial hospital workers won the support of the larger labor movement and achieved modest successes.

Although the AFL-CIO eventually embraced many of the civil rights movement's demands, in the late 1960s and early 1970s some activists on the left adopted more militant rhetoric and a Marxist perspective, forming groups such as the League of Revolutionary Black Workers and the Dodge Revolutionary Union Movement. From the 1970s onward, deindustrialization, fiscal crises, and contracting employment in various economic sectors at times generated conflict between white workers and more recently employed black workers. Relying upon a variety of smaller associations, the NAACP Legal Defense Fund, and their own attorneys in affirmative action challenges, black workers continued to seek to preserve or extend black employment. Since the 1970s, caucuses of black workers within union internationals—for instance, the Teamsters National Black Caucus, established in 1971—have continued to challenge discrimination, promote the interests of their members, and encourage greater union activism among blacks.

[*See also* **Brotherhood of Sleeping Car Porters; Dockworkers' Unions, Multiracial; Dodge Revolutionary Union Movement; Memphis Sanitation Strike (1968); Racism; Randolph, A. Philip;** *and* **Webster, Milton.**]

BIBLIOGRAPHY

Arnesen, Eric. *Waterfront Workers of New Orleans: Race, Class, and Politics, 1863–1923*. New York: Oxford University Press, 1991.

Bates, Beth Tompkins. *Pullman Porters and the Rise of Protest Politics in Black America, 1925–1945*. Chapel Hill: University of North Carolina Press, 2001.

Jones, William P. *The Tribe of Black Ulysses: African American Lumber Workers in the Jim Crow South*. Urbana: University of Illinois Press, 2005.

Letwin, Daniel. *The Challenge of Interracial Unionism: Alabama Coal Miners, 1878–1921*. Chapel Hill: University of North Carolina Press, 1998.

Stein, Judith. *Running Steel, Running America: Race, Economic Policy, and the Decline of Liberalism*. Chapel Hill: University of North Carolina Press, 1998.

Zieger, Robert H. *For Jobs and Freedom: Race and Labor in America since 1865*. Lexington: University Press of Kentucky, 2007.

Eric Arnesen

AGRICULTURAL ADJUSTMENT ADMINISTRATION

In 1933, American agriculture neared collapse as farm bankruptcies and foreclosures multiplied and agricultural prices fell below the cost of production. President Franklin Delano Roosevelt instructed his agricultural experts to draft legislation. The result was the Agricultural

Adjustment Act (AAA) of May 1933. The law's fundamental goal was "parity": raising basic farm prices until they were in balance with the general economy. One way was to eliminate existing commodity surpluses by taking farm acreage out of production and inducing farmers to produce only what was needed for domestic consumption. The government paid benefits to farmers who contracted to reduce acreage and also offered "parity" payments on the crops actually grown. To finance these payments, the secretary of agriculture taxed the domestic processors of basic commodities—wheat, cotton, tobacco, corn hogs, and milk products. Since pork and milk production could not be controlled effectively by reducing acreage, the government negotiated agreements among the meatpackers and dairy companies to regulate markets and fix prices.

The law created the Agricultural Adjustment Administration to administer the new system. The first administrator was George N. Peek, a businessman and agricultural reformer. Because Peek assumed power in 1933 after crops had been planted and sows were bearing litters of pigs, his agency contracted with farmers to plow under nearly half of their crops and to slaughter baby pigs. Although calculated to increase prices and raise farm income, the destruction of crops and livestock stirred widespread dismay.

By late 1935 the AAA had enabled agriculture to approach a parity position. AAA payments especially benefited larger commercial farmers and southern planters. Acreage reduction, however, hurt tenant farmers and sharecroppers, many thousands of whom were evicted or received pitifully small payments.

The AAA saved agriculture from collapse, but as the crisis eased, constitutional questions arose. In 1936 the U.S. Supreme Court struck down the act for exceeding the government's interstate commerce powers. To keep the AAA operating, Congress passed a new law that preserved AAA programs under the pretext of soil conservation. In 1938, Congress passed a second AAA that emphasized price supports and subsidies. Congress ended the AAA during World War II when agricultural prices rose sharply and demand exceeded supply; the Department of Agriculture assumed many of the AAA's programs and implemented them as the core of post–World War II agricultural policy.

[*See also* **Agriculture,** *subentry on* **Since 1920; Dust Bowl Era and Farm Crisis; New Deal and Institutional Economics; Sharecropping and Tenancy;** *and* **Subsidies, Agricultural.**]

BIBLIOGRAPHY

Conrad, David E. *The Forgotten Farmers: The Story of Sharecroppers in the New Deal.* Urbana: University of Illinois Press, 1965.

Nourse, Edwin G., Joseph S. Davis, and John D. Black. *Three Years of the Agricultural Adjustment Administration.* Washington, D.C.: Brookings Institution, 1937.

David E. Conrad

AGRICULTURAL EXTENSION AND EDUCATION

The system of agricultural education and extension consists of the land-grant colleges with their associated agricultural experiment stations and cooperative extension services, as well as secondary schools that offer vocational instruction in agriculture. The sixty-nine land-grant colleges that existed by the end of the twentieth century were established under the provisions of the Morrill Land Grant Act of 1862, which required that they offer residential instruction in agriculture.

The Hatch Act of 1887 appropriated federal funds for the establishment in each state of one or more experiment stations to undertake systematic study of agricultural problems and to formulate scientific knowledge that could be presented in college classrooms. The stations were usually located at the land-grant colleges and commonly shared faculty with them.

The experiment stations were required to disseminate their findings among farmers, but the printed word proved to be an ineffective form of communication, as also were farmers' institutes. In 1903, Seaman A. Knapp introduced in Texas the demonstration method, by which farmers learned improved agricultural practices under the direction of a skilled adviser, later to be known as a county agent. Success with this teaching innovation led to boys' and girls' corn and tomato clubs, which developed into the 4-H club movement for farm youth, and to home-demonstration work with rural women. The Smith–Lever Act of 1914 provided additional federal support for a nationwide educational program for all members of the farm family.

Vocational instruction in agriculture began around 1897 with nature study in the public schools of New York State and elsewhere. In the first decade of the twentieth century, some states authorized the establishment of agricultural high schools. These institutions disappeared when public high schools began to employ graduates of the land-grant colleges to offer courses in vocational agriculture and home economics. The Smith–Hughes Act of 1917 funded such educational programs. This system of agricultural education contributed greatly to the development of the United States in the twentieth century. By increasing dramatically agricultural productivity, it permitted a sharp reduction in farm population while providing abundant and low-cost food and fiber.

[*See also* **Agriculture,** *subentry on* **Since 1920; Family Farm; Farm Machinery; Household Technology and Domestic Labor;** *and* **Technology.**]

BIBLIOGRAPHY

Eddy, Edward D. *Colleges for Our Land and Time: The Land-Grant Idea in American Education.* New York: Harper, 1957.

Marcus, Alan I. *Agricultural Science and the Quest for Legitimacy: Farmers, Agricultural Colleges, and Experiment Stations, 1870–1890.* Ames: Iowa State University Press, 1985.

Roy V. Scott

AGRICULTURAL WORKERS

Agricultural workers pick, pack, harvest, irrigate, prune, plant, weed, spray, and tend crops both on small, family-run farms and on large-scale industrial operations, usually as temporary wage employees. On small, diversified farms in the American colonies during the 1600s and early 1700s, families handled most work, supplemented when necessary by neighbors and hired hands. On the Spanish missions of the American Southwest between the late 1700s and the early 1800s, natives labored for padres on what amounted to self-sufficient agricultural plantations. As labor shortages developed in the American South in the early 1700s, tobacco farmers in Virginia and Maryland increasingly turned to indentured workers. By 1750 indentured workers constituted more than half of the immigrants south of New England. Agricultural slavery emerged slowly at this time between Maryland and Georgia. By 1810 a million slaves worked on rice, cotton, corn, tobacco, and indigo farms in the South; by 1860 that number had quadrupled.

Change and Continuity. Family farming and hired hands progressively gave way after the Civil War. The total amount of farm land remained static, while the sizes of farms increased. In the 1870s and 1880s, African American sharecroppers in the South cultivated twenty- to fifty-acre plots of cotton by paying landlords one third to one half of the crop, or more than this when the landlord furnished a mule, seed, fertilizers, and implements, or less when the sharecropper provided some or all of those items. The arrangement kept African Americans perpetually in debt and frequently resulted in debt peonage.

Three broad patterns of seasonal labor migration developed between the 1880s and 1900. African Americans from the South joined Italian Americans from Philadelphia, Poles from Baltimore, and Bahamians from Florida and migrated between truck farms and orchards up and down the Atlantic coast. A succession of dispossessed peoples and immigrant groups from Asia, Mexico, and India circulated between farms along the Pacific coast. A midcontinent stream, originating in Texas, branched north into Michigan and Wisconsin. Between 1890 and 1927, as many as 200,000 workers harvested and threshed wheat crops from Oklahoma to Canada.

During the Great Depression, agricultural workers were excluded from New Deal legislation and programs such as the National Labor Relations Act, workman's compensation insurance, Social Security, and many key minimum-wage and maximum-hour protections in the Fair Labor Standards Act. Under the guise of a World War II labor shortage, growers gained access to a continuous supply of cheap labor through a series of laws and diplomatic arrangements that created the bracero labor program. Between 1942 and 1964, 4.5 million Mexican men traveled north to work as braceros on farms from California to Florida and as far north as Michigan. The bracero program depressed wages, undermined agricultural unions, and drove away local workers, while braceros' remittances helped stabilize Mexico. Millions of Mexican Americans trace their roots in the United States to the arrival of a father or grandfather as a bracero. Similar to the bracero program, the H-2 program allows employers to petition for skilled labor, mainly with advanced degrees, to meet temporary or seasonal needs when U.S. workers are unavailable, with an annual cap of sixty-six thousand workers. The H2-A program provides work visas for workers from Mexico, the West Indies, and other Latin American countries to perform low-wage, temporary labor harvesting crops. More than ten thousand H-2A Mexican farmworkers arrive annually to work in the North Carolina tobacco fields. In 2012 there were about thirty thousand temporary H-2A agricultural workers. There is no annual cap on visas for H-2A workers. Both the bracero and the H-2A programs created a class of foreign workers differentiated from other American workers by their limited access to the labor market, temporary residence, nonimmigrant status, and circumscribed human rights.

Combines eliminated hand labor in the wheat harvest in the 1920s. The mechanical cotton picker eliminated hundreds of thousands of jobs in the 1940s and 1950s, and thirty-two thousand farmworkers lost their jobs to the mechanical tomato picker in the 1970s. On the other hand, large-scale technological displacement of agricultural workers has been offset by massive labor requirements on irrigated fruit and vegetable farms.

Strikes and Organizing. Two of the largest labor strikes by agricultural workers occurred in 1887, when ten thousand African Americans walked out of the sugarcane fields of Louisiana under the banner of the Knights of Labor, and in 1933, when fifteen thousand Mexicans and Okies walked out of the cotton fields in California's San Joaquin valley. During the 1930s the Southern Tenant Farmers' Union (STFU), which grew to thirty thousand members by 1937, fought evictions and terror in the southern states. In 1946 the STFU became the National Farm Labor Union (NFLU) and affiliated with the American Federation of Labor (AFL). After losing a protracted a strike against the Di Giorgio fruit corporation in California's San Joaquin valley, the NFLU shifted tactics and concentrated on exposing the abuses of the bracero program. After the NFLU's demise, the organization of migrant farmworkers was carried on by the Agricultural Workers Organizing Committee (AWOC), an AFL union that led more than 150 strikes. In the 1960s and 1970s the United Farm Workers of America (UFW), led by Cesar Chavez, struck the California table-grape industry, developed an international boycott of table grapes, and ultimately won many contracts. In 1975, California enacted the first state legislation to protect union organizing among farmworkers. Other states did not follow, and subsequently the California law was gutted. The Farm Labor Organizing Committee (FLOC), active mainly in the Midwest, and the Coalition of Immokalee Workers (CIW), active mainly in the Florida tomato industry, carry on the struggle in the twenty-first century. CIW boycotts of large businesses such as Taco Bell and McDonald's, as well as alliances with consumer and environmental groups, have achieved marginal improvements in working conditions and curbed pesticide exposure. Growers fight the organization of farmworkers, believing that the perishable nature of their crops makes every harvest a crisis solved only by a surplus of labor.

The 2010 U.S. Census classified 1.5 million people as agricultural workers. Some nongovernmental sources have identified up to 3 million agricultural workers. Of these workers, 77 percent were born in Mexico, 80 percent were male, 66 percent were younger than thirty-five years old, 20 percent were in their first year of agricultural work, 22 percent were U.S citizens, 24 percent were legal permanent residents, 52 percent were undocumented immigrants, and 80 percent worked less than nine months every year. Their average age was thirty-one. In 2005 the average annual income for individual farmworkers was $10,000 to $12,499 (for comparison, in 2007 the federal poverty level for individuals was $10,210) and the average annual income for farm families was $15,000 to $17,499 (for comparison, in 2007 the federal poverty level for families was $20,650). Agricultural labor remains the second-most-dangerous occupation in the United States. Common pejorative terms for agricultural workers include "fruit tramps," "sugar tramps," "harvest gypsies," "apple knockers," *betabeleros* (sugar-beet harvesters), "stoop laborers," and "bindlestiffs."

[*See also* **Agricultural Extension and Education; Agriculture; Braceros; Chavez, Cesar; Dust Bowl Era and Farm Crisis; Factory Farming; Family Farm; Farm Machinery; Granger Movement and Laws; Indentured Labor; Labor Movements; Migratory Labor and Migrant Workers; National Farmers Union; Sharecropping and Tenancy; Slavery; Southern Tenant Farmers' Union;** *and* **United Farm Workers of America.**]

BIBLIOGRAPHY

Cohen, Deborah. *Braceros: Migrant Citizens and Transnational Subjects in the Postwar United States and Mexico.* Chapel Hill: University of North Carolina Press, 2011.

Hahamovitch, Cindy. *The Fruits of their Labor: Atlantic Coast Farmworkers and the Making of Migrant Poverty, 1870–1945.* Chapel Hill: University of North Carolina Press, 1997.

Mapes, Kathleen. *Sweet Tyranny: Migrant Labor, Industrial Agriculture, and Imperial Politics.* Urbana: University of Illinois Press, 2009.

Street, Richard Steven. *Beasts of the Field: A Narrative History of California Farmworkers, 1769–1913*. Stanford, Calif.: Stanford University Press, 2004.

Valdés, Dennis Nodín. *Al Norte: Agricultural Workers in the Great Lakes Region, 1917–1970*. Austin: University of Texas Press, 1991.

Wyman, Mark. *Hoboes: Bindlestiffs, Fruit Tramps, and the Harvesting of the West*. New York: Hill and Wang, 2010.

Richard S. Street

AGRICULTURE

This entry contains four subentries: Colonial Era; 1770 to 1890; The Golden Age (1890 to 1920); *and* Since 1920.

COLONIAL ERA

Agriculture dominated the colonial economy, and the great majority of the population lived in the countryside. The agricultural practices of colonial farmers often earned the scorn of European contemporary observers, and their reputation fared little better at the hands of later historians. They were portrayed as wasteful and slovenly farmers who abused the land, neglected their livestock, accepted small yields and low incomes, used primitive tools, and resisted useful innovations, preferring customary practices and constrained by the dead hand of tradition. Recently historians have challenged that view for two reasons. First, the denigration of colonial agriculture often arose from an inappropriate comparison with European farmers, who faced a much different situation. In America, where land was relatively cheap and labor costly, following the best European practices seldom made sense. Farm practices that appeared wasteful to Old World observers often reflected efforts to save labor in an economy of high wages. Second, the critics of colonial farm-

ers often underestimated their impressive accomplishments, most evident in the creation of what might be called a "mestizo" agriculture. At its best, colonial agriculture combined crops and farming techniques from America, Africa, and Europe to produce a unique system of husbandry that was more productive than any of its individual sources. American agriculture was mestizo in another, more sinister sense. It combined labor stolen from Africa with land stolen from Native Americans to produce commodities, and sometimes luxuries, for European consumers.

Diversity. Colonial agriculture was strikingly diverse. The plantation districts of the coastal South, where slaves, often working on large units with one hundred or more laborers, produced rice, indigo, and tobacco for export to Europe, differed radically from the southern backcountry and the northern colonies, where small family farms produced a diverse range of products for their own subsistence and small surpluses for export or sale in local markets. Agriculturally, the colonies represent a spectrum ranging from north to south, from farm region to plantation district. Though agriculture in the farming regions of the backcountry and northern colonies appears relatively homogeneous, one should distinguish between New England, where thin soils and a short growing season limited the size of surpluses available for export, and the mid-Atlantic colonies, where a warmer climate and richer soils yielded much larger crops for export.

By the end of the eighteenth century, wheat cultivation was well established in the mid-Atlantic colonies, where it had expanded into the Hudson, Mohawk, Delaware, and Susquehanna river valleys. Plows drawn by oxen or, increasingly, by horses were in common use. Corn, barley (used in beer making), and oats for feed were raised as well. Sheep were common in New England, and cattle were raised for export in Delaware, New Jersey, and Massachusetts. Livestock grazed on English grasses imported and planted for the purpose. Farmers in New England and New York raised flax as a commercial crop.

The plantation South, too, was far from homogeneous, as differing principal crops with differing labor and capital requirements led to sharply differing agricultural practices and social systems and cultures. In the lower South—the coastal portions of Georgia and South Carolina—the major export crops were rice and indigo, plantations were large, planters were wealthy, and a majority of the population was enslaved. In the upper South colonies of Maryland and Virginia around the Chesapeake Bay, where tobacco was the main crop, plantations were smaller—indeed, much tobacco was grown on family farms—planters were less rich, and the slave presence, though still substantial, was less overwhelming.

Another source of diversity—and another much-debated topic among historians—was the degree to which farmers produced surpluses for market, a distinction that tended to reinforce and deepen the dichotomy between plantation and farm. Plantations, especially the largest ones, were highly commercialized, often engaged in single-crop production, and imported from abroad much of what they needed for consumption. Yet even the largest, most commercialized operations grew some of the food that their workers consumed, and even the smallest, most self-sufficient farms sold some surplus on the market and purchased some consumer goods.

Despite its diversity, all colonial agriculture did share common characteristics. The first was its relatively high productivity, along with the high incomes that it generated for farm residents—especially in the eighteenth century, when farm prices rose steadily as trade patterns shifted in favor of agriculture. This high productivity had several sources, including colonial

farmers' creativity, evident in the mestizo system they created; the abundance and fertility of land; and the hard work of farm families, including farm wives, who often helped in the fields, did dairying, and kept a garden, in addition to performing the household work traditionally associated with women. The high productivity and incomes generated by colonial agriculture meant that the free population in rural areas lived quite well by early modern standards, as is evident in their diet and material culture. The quality of the colonial diet is revealed in the height of the population: by the time of the Revolutionary War, American-born men of European ancestry were, on average, just over five feet eight inches tall, about three and a half inches taller than their English counterparts and about the same height as American males who served in the military during World War II.

Further evidence of the vitality of agriculture in the colonial North comes from late twentieth-century research challenging the conventional wisdom that industrialization in America began in the cities and was imported from England. This research points to the domestic origins of America's Industrial Revolution and argues that agriculture provided the labor force, capital, and much of the expertise that made industrialization possible.

The Plantation Workforce. Before about 1680, most unfree workers on colonial plantations were indentured servants recruited to the colonies from Britain. In the eighteenth century, most unfree workers were slaves of African ancestry. Initially, high mortality and a shortage of women kept the slave population from reproducing itself, so planters had to rely on continual imports to maintain their workforce. American-born slaves experienced lower death rates and had a balanced sex ratio, so as the native-born share of the population rose, the rate of natural population growth rose as well.

By the 1720s in the Chesapeake colonies, though much later in the lower South, the colonial slave population was growing by reproduction. When most slaves were African born, slaves were largely confined to work in the fields; with the rise of an American-born slave population, however, the occupations available to slaves diversified, and they took over much of the skilled work on plantations.

The plantations that produced staple crops—tobacco, rice, and indigo, for export—shipped their surplus and purchased the bulk of their consumer goods through the services of British merchants, or factors, who controlled the flow of foreign commerce. Prices for these agricultural staples, moreover, were set in European markets, most notably those in England but also in Amsterdam and Paris. By the eve of the American Revolution, many of the colonial plantation masters were deeply in debt to the British factors who marketed their surpluses and managed the purchase of the expensive consumer goods that plantation owners displayed as a mark of their rank and status.

Northern agriculturists who produced surpluses for market rarely dealt with foreign merchants and factors. More typically, smaller farmers in New England and the middle colonies bartered their surplus with local merchants who provided them with store credit for the agricultural implements and consumer goods that they could not themselves manufacture on the farm. The larger farmers in the mid-Atlantic region produced a greater surplus, especially of grains, that found a ready market in the expanding seaport cities and the Caribbean sugar islands. Their surplus that was sold to Caribbean plantations was carried largely in colonial bottoms, thus enriching colonial merchants, covering the cost of the sugar, molasses, and rum that colonials imported, and building capital for the more industrious and productive farmers.

[*See also* **Cotton Trade, Antebellum Era; Family Farm; Indentured Labor; Native Americans, Economic Aspects of U.S. Relations with; Slavery;** *and* **Tobacco Trade.**]

BIBLIOGRAPHY

Carr, Lois Green, Russell R. Menard, and Lorena S. Walsh. *Robert Cole's World: Agriculture and Society in Early Maryland.* Chapel Hill: University of North Carolina Press for the Institute of Early American History and Culture, Williamsburg, Va., 1991.

Chaplin, Joyce E. *An Anxious Pursuit: Agricultural Innovation and Modernity in the Lower South, 1730–1815.* Chapel Hill: University of North Carolina Press for the Institute of Early American History and Culture, Williamsburg, Va., 1993.

Clemens, Paul G. E. *The Atlantic Economy and Colonial Maryland's Eastern Shore: From Tobacco to Grain.* Ithaca, N.Y.: Cornell University Press, 1980.

Engerman, Stanley L., and Robert E. Gallman, eds. *The Cambridge Economic History of the United States.* Vol. 1: *The Colonial Era.* Cambridge, U.K.: Cambridge University Press, 1996.

Kulikoff, Allan. *The Agrarian Origins of American Capitalism.* Charlottesville: University Press of Virginia, 1992.

Lemon, James T. *The Best Poor Man's Country: A Geographical Study of Early Southeastern Pennsylvania.* Baltimore: Johns Hopkins University Press, 1972.

McCusker, John J., and Russell R. Menard. *The Economy of British America, 1607–1789.* Chapel Hill: University of North Carolina Press for the Institute of Early American History and Culture, Williamsburg, Va., 1985.

Rothenberg, Winifred Barr. *From Market-places to a Market Economy: The Transformation of Rural Massachusetts, 1750–1850.* Chicago: University of Chicago Press, 1992.

Vickers, Daniel. *Farmers and Fishermen: Two Centuries of Work in Essex County, Massachusetts, 1630–1850.* Chapel Hill: University of North Carolina

Press for the Institute of Early American History and Culture, Williamsburg, Va., 1994.

Russell R. Menard

1770 TO 1890

Following the Revolutionary War, the new nation built its economy largely on the marketing of agricultural products. New crops, innovative technologies, and aggressive territorial expansion fostered agricultural expansion in the nineteenth century. The cotton kingdom, founded on slavery, developed in the southern United States, producing the era's most important cash crop and principal U.S. export. In the North, the agricultural economy flourished by marketing its grain crops and livestock. The new lands acquired through the Louisiana Purchase and the Mexican War spread the market economy of agriculture to the Pacific coast, and rivers, canals, and railroads linked farmers, distributors, and consumers. The largest contributor to economic expansion in the first half of the nineteenth century, antebellum American agriculture was marked by regional distinctions. Cotton characterized the South, and wheat, corn, beef, and pork characterized the Midwest and, soon, the Great Plains. Farmers of the Northeast, with its large urban concentrations, supplied the cities with perishable commodities such as fruit, vegetables, and dairy products.

In the aftermath of the Revolution, it took time to reestablish domestic commodity markets and open new international ones. The federal government, initially under the Articles of Confederation, promoted an economy built on small family farms. The Land Ordinance of 1785, followed by the Northwest Ordinance of 1787, established a system of land distribution and rapid territorial transition to statehood. Vermont, Kentucky, Tennessee, and Ohio became states as settlers sought out new farmland—a process that continued throughout the nineteenth century.

Several economic problems beset small farmers in the early republic, including tight credit, the lack of hard currency, and an inability to pay taxes. In 1786, under the leadership of Daniel Shays, debt-ridden farmers in western Massachusetts organized militias and closed courts to forestall being penalized for failing to pay bills and taxes. Only military repression ended Shays's Rebellion. Federal taxation spurred a comparable rural rebellion in 1791. Opposed to excise taxes on whiskey—a primary money-making product because it proved easier to ship alcohol than grain to market over poorly maintained roadways (whiskey also enjoyed a far greater value per unit than grain)—farmers in the mid-Atlantic and upper South regions fueled the Whiskey Rebellion. President George Washington sent federal troops to end the uprising.

Other events in the 1790s, especially the cotton-gin patent secured by Eli Whitney in 1793, had a more lasting impact. Whitney's relatively simple machine spread the cultivation of short-staple cotton across the South. By 1860 the region produced as much as 6 million bales of cotton, accounting for two thirds of the nation's exports. Although the southern states continued to grow tobacco, rice, and sugarcane, as well as to raise livestock, the cotton gin accelerated the spread of the cotton economy and, with it, slavery and the plantation system. This, in turn, gave rise to a two-tier southern agricultural system consisting of a small minority of wealthy plantation owners and a vast majority of slaves and poor, white subsistence farmers.

Impact of the Transportation Revolution. In the North, early nineteenth-century agriculture was characterized by the production of livestock (sheep, hogs, and cattle) and such grains as wheat and corn. Roads and trails, rivers and canals, and eventually railroads connected farmers to their markets. For the most part, transportation improvements were funded by state, local, or private monies. Except for the National Road, Congress did not fund such improvements in the antebellum era. In 1825 the Erie Canal, built by New York State, connected eastern markets with the newer western states and territories. Initially, the canal benefited farmers in upstate New York, who could now ship their surplus more quickly and economically to the New York City market, whose merchants could sell it domestically and abroad. The success of the Erie Canal led New York to finance the building of feeder canals and led other states to subsidize the construction of their own canal systems. Because the Erie Canal's western terminus connected with Lake Erie, the canal linked much of the Midwest to the New York City market, thus opening the plentiful and fertile land of the region to rapid development. Seeking more ample and fertile land, agriculturists from New England, the middle states, and the upper South flocked west. Water transport boomed as canals in Ohio, Michigan, and Illinois connected farmland to the Great Lakes and then to the Erie Canal. Buffalo became the second-largest city in New York State and one of the ten largest in the United States by serving as a milling, slaughtering, and transshipment center for midwestern grains and livestock.

If canals linked midwestern agriculture to New York City and thence to Europe, the Ohio and Mississippi rivers linked the more southern portions of the Midwest to the South and, via New Orleans, to foreign markets. Cincinnati, Ohio, gained a reputation as "Porkopolis," and Saint Louis, Missouri, became the "Queen City." Just as northern agriculturists flocked to the more fertile western lands, southern cotton planters did the same, carrying slaves with them and in the 1820s and 1830s creating flush times in Alabama and Mississippi. In the 1840s and 1850s, slave owners crossed the Mississippi and carried cotton culture to Louisiana, Arkansas, and eastern Texas. The rapid expansion of the cotton and slave belt, by

earning the bulk of American foreign-trade returns and offering a market for the surplus produced by midwestern farmers, built the capital that stimulated national economic development and fostered industrialization.

By the 1840s and 1850s, railroads developed and spread to offer an alternative transport system, one that was less susceptible to seasonal suspensions and was quicker, if more expensive, than water transport. The railroads tied the West more tightly to the East (the South entered the railroad age relatively late) as the new mode of transport linked the ports of Baltimore, Philadelphia, Boston, and, most impressively, New York City to western markets. What historians later characterized as the "transportation revolution" promoted the movement of Americans relentlessly westward toward the Pacific coast. The transportation revolution also made possible what has been called the "farmers' age," the years from roughly 1815 to 1860. The rapid geographic expansion of agriculture stimulated new farm technology. Farmers quickly discovered that implements that worked in the thinner soils of the East failed on heavier midwestern and western soils. Hence the invention of new agricultural implements—including Hiram and John Pitts's threshing machines, John Deere's cast-iron plows, and Cyrus McCormick's reapers—became essential in the early to mid-nineteenth century. Hiram Moore pioneered in the development of the combine, which could perform both harvesting and threshing operations, and in 1886 George S. Berry patented a steam-powered and self-propelled combine that could cut as much as fifty acres of wheat per day. The introduction of steam- and gasoline-powered farm equipment significantly increased per capita productivity and laid the groundwork for the later emergence of large-scale agribusinesses.

Expansion before and after the Civil War. Agriculture experienced neither steady expansion nor unbroken prosperity prior to the Civil War. At times, hopes outran realities, as western farmers and plantation masters took on excessive debt to increase their landholdings and their production of grains and cotton. Inflated land costs and contracting markets that reduced the price for agricultural products made it difficult for many agriculturists to finance their debts—pushing them into bankruptcy—during the economic contractions or depressions of 1816–1819, 1837–1843, and 1857–1859. Overall, however, the period was one of prosperity for northern farmers and southern cotton growers as demand for foodstuffs rose in domestic and foreign markets and New England and British cotton mills sought ever-more raw cotton. On the eve of the Civil War, land values in the North and the West had risen, and prime field and house hands fetched $1,600 in southern slave markets, representing billions of dollars of capital for slaveholders.

Following the Civil War, agriculture continued its expansion. The Homestead Act, the Morrill Land Grant Act, the Pacific Railway Act, and the creation in 1862 of the U.S. Department of Agriculture (USDA) all promoted agricultural expansion. Although cotton remained king in the South, a new system of labor replaced slavery: sharecropping. Combining sharecropping and other forms of farm tenancy with a crop-lien system, southern planters kept their impoverished labor force tied to the land. In the North, agricultural specialization advanced apace. Dairy and truck farming (raising fruits and vegetables for urban markets) became ever-more specialized and standardized. Midwestern farms continued to flourish on a base of corn, hogs, and beef, while Wisconsin emerged as a leader in dairy products.

The greatest changes occurred on the Great Plains and beyond, where cattle and wheat produced on bonanza farms and ranches financed by eastern and foreign investment became the key commodities. With the arrival of railroads

and the establishment of the first cattle town in Kansas by Joseph McCoy in 1867, the Great Plains and Rocky Mountain regions soon dominated cattle ranching. Large herds, large ranches, and large-scale investments characterized the livestock industry's expansion in the 1870s and 1880s. Absentee investors who purchased ranches in hopes of making a quick profit soon transformed centuries-old Spanish, Mexican, and Native American modes of livestock culture into a modern, market-driven industry based on the labor of cowboys, who eventually became the stuff of myth and legend. But drought and harsh winters bled the profits out of the livestock industry in the late 1880s, dashing the hopes of the speculative investors. Wheat cultivation followed a similar pattern, as climatic and market changes brought failure to those who had gambled on bonanza farms. By 1900 the production of both these commodities had been reorganized and reestablished on a smaller scale.

Agriculture's Testing Time. If most of the nineteenth century was the farmers' age, the century's last twenty-five years proved agriculture's testing time. In economic history this period is known as the "long depression," an unbroken era of price deflation. In the United States, deep depressions sparked by financial panics occurred in 1873–1877 and 1893–1897, with a milder downturn in 1883–1885. Unfavorable terms of trade—that is, the ratio of farm products to effective demand—caused falling prices. The cause was simple: globally, agricultural productivity increased far more rapidly than population in farmers' primary markets. Cotton cultivation expanded overseas, and as cotton cultivation in the South recovered from war and the abolition of slavery, supply far outran demand, causing cotton prices to collapse. As their income fell, farmers found it increasingly difficult to pay their mortgages, taxes, and other debts. Bankruptcies increased, farm tenancy increased, and share-cropping spread among both white and black farmers as cultivation expanded into Texas and Oklahoma. Economic ills tended to be concentrated primarily among agriculturists who had gone deeply into debt to finance both the acquisition of more land and also the expensive machinery needed to work extensive holdings that produced crops whose price was set in the world market. Economic misery was concentrated in the cotton South, the wheat belt of the Great Plains, and among cattle ranchers in the arid West.

Thus the late nineteenth century was characterized by agricultural discontent that manifested itself in farmer organization and action. The Patrons of Husbandry, or the Grange, organized by Oliver Hudson Kelley in the late 1860s, soon gave rise to more politically active movements in rural America. Southern farmers' alliances under the leadership of Charles McCune, organized in the late 1870s and 1880s, allied with farm groups in the North and the Midwest, led by Milton George, to form a national confederation. Never cohesive, in the early 1890s the alliances put aside their economic and ideological differences to form the Populist Party. Although the Populist insurgency faded after William Jennings Bryan's unsuccessful presidential bid in 1896, many of the political reforms sought by farmers later became law. More important, after 1897 the terms of trade shifted back in favor of agriculture, bringing a new prosperity to farmers.

[See also Canals and Waterways; Cotton Trade, Antebellum Era; Cowboys; Family Farm; Farm Machinery; Grains; Granger Movement and Laws; Greenback Labor Party; Homestead Act; Livestock Industry; Native Americans, Economic Aspects of U.S. Relations with; Public Land Policy; Railroads; Sharecropping and Tenancy; Slavery; Transportation Revolution; Turnpikes and Early Roads; and Whitney, Eli.]

BIBLIOGRAPHY

Blassingame, John W. The Slave Community: Plantation Life in the Antebellum South. New York: Oxford University Press, 1972.

Bogue, Allan G. From Prairie to Corn Belt: Farming on the Illinois and Iowa Prairies in the Nineteenth Century. Chicago: University of Chicago Press, 1963.

Cronon, William. Nature's Metropolis: Chicago and the Great West. New York: W. W. Norton and Company, 1991.

Fite, Gilbert C. The Farmers' Frontier, 1865–1900. New York: Holt, Rinehart and Winston, 1966.

Hurt, R. Douglas. American Agriculture: A Brief History. Ames: Iowa State University Press, 1994.

Hurt, R. Douglas. American Farm Tools: From Hand-Power to Steam-Power. Manhattan, Kan.: Sunflower University Press, 1982.

Jordan, Terry G. North American Cattle-Ranching Frontiers: Origins, Diffusion, and Differentiation. Albuquerque: University of New Mexico Press, 1993.

Russell, Howard S. A Long, Deep Furrow: Three Centuries of Farming in New England. Hanover, N.H.: University Press of New England, 1976.

Slaughter, Thomas P. The Whiskey Rebellion: Frontier Epilogue to the American Revolution. New York: Oxford University Press, 1986.

Szatmary, David P. Shays' Rebellion: The Making of Agrarian Insurrection. Amherst: University of Massachusetts Press, 1980.

Stephanie A. Carpenter

THE GOLDEN AGE (1890 TO 1920)

A brief era of rare prosperity and hopes fulfilled, the so-called golden age of American agriculture was a time when most everything went right for the nation's farmers. Historians generally situate this period between the Spanish–American War (1898) and World War I, or, more precisely, from 1909 to 1914, when strong agricultural prices translated into parity, a boost in purchasing power for farm men and women that matched or surpassed that of other economic sectors. A period characterized by optimism and modernization, it was summed up by one contemporary as an era of "corn, cattle, and contentment." Of lasting consequence, notes R. Douglas Hurt in *American Agriculture: A Brief History* (1994), is the concept of parity prices and income—the notion that this was a time when the cost of agricultural production and the prices received for farm products had come into proper balance—which soon became the basis of American agricultural policy.

What set this "golden age" apart from other periods in American agricultural history was the absence of the hard times and agrarian discontent characteristic of several earlier eras. After the Civil War, many farmers suffered from mortgage indebtedness, high railroad rates, price deflation, and surplus production. To increase their productivity, farm men and women invested more capital in implements and machinery, such as improved plows, reapers, and combines. Moreover, the movement to settle and cultivate western lands, which doubled the number of farms in the United States between 1870 and 1890, contributed significantly to the surplus crop production. As agricultural expansion outpaced consumer demand, foreign and domestic farm prices fell.

The worsening plight of farmers was lost on a larger American society in the midst of shifting from a predominantly rural agricultural basis to an urban industrial one. To resist social, economic, and political marginalization, agriculturists from the late 1860s through the 1890s formed organizations such as the Grange, the Farmers' Alliance, and the People's, or Populist, Party. Through these, the farm sector voiced its discontent and sought economic improvement and, ultimately, political change, all of which typified this period of agrarian revolt.

New Prosperity. As conditions improved for the farm sector by the early twentieth century,

the angry voices partially faded away. A favorable combination of factors related to crop yields, farm prices, land values, and an expanded domestic market precipitated the dawn of agriculture's golden age. Agricultural expansion slowed around 1890, as most of the new land being brought under cultivation was marginal, in need of irrigation, and less conducive to surplus crop and livestock production. As production stabilized by the late 1890s, the output of farm goods, unlike in previous decades, better matched consumer demand, bringing farmers higher prices. In both the United States and Europe, the urban population grew more rapidly than the rural population did, as superfluous European rural dwellers immigrated to the United States or migrated to European cities, in the process increasing demand for foodstuffs.

Land values rose, in some cases dramatically, as rising farm prices increased the demand for good land. One estimate puts the average price increase of farmland from 1900 to 1910 at between 200 and 300 percent. Industrialization and the rapid urbanization that accompanied it expanded the domestic market and consumer demand for farm goods. Chicago and Cleveland, Ohio, grew by 55 percent and 46 percent, respectively, between 1890 and 1900, and Los Angeles and Atlanta swelled by 211 percent and 72 percent, respectively, between 1900 and 1910. Such phenomenal urban growth, even more than rising demand in foreign markets, stimulated and sustained the era of agricultural prosperity.

For farm men and women, the new prosperity manifested itself in several significant ways. A mood of optimism, propagated by the press, popular magazines, and public discourse, enlarged the sense that all was well with farmers, especially in the Midwest. References to the "new agriculture" implied that more modern methods and equipment had replaced the outmoded practices of pioneer days. Prosperity was especially apparent in the improved credit position of many farmers, who now enjoyed exceptional borrowing and purchasing power.

This enhanced purchasing power reflected the advantageous price relationship between farm goods and nonfarm goods. With nonfarm prices increasing far more slowly than farm prices, argues Gilbert C. Fite in *American Farmers* (1981), farmers received substantially higher prices for the goods that they sold than they paid for the goods that they purchased. The U.S. Department of Agriculture (USDA), later determining that the period 1909–1914 represented a time of price parity for farmers—an economic relationship in which farm goods could be exchanged for a fair amount of nonfarm goods—designated this period as the baseline for formulating future policy regarding agricultural prices.

The Country-Life Movement. However, the prosperity associated with the golden age of agriculture was neither ubiquitous nor synonymous with satisfaction or respect. While the Midwest seemed to bask in good times, the South experienced little of the period's well-being. Most of that region's sharecroppers and tenant farm families lived amid abject poverty and long continued to do so, largely because of landowners' reluctance to abandon cotton as the primary cash crop and adopt diversified agriculture. Further, despite the farm sector's overall prosperity, rural life still presented hardship and had few amenities: as city dwellers came to enjoy central heating, electricity, natural gas, flush toilets, telephones, trolley lines, elevated railways, subways, and well-paved, clean streets, farm families rarely enjoyed those amenities. They heated their homes with wood- or coal-burning stoves and fireplaces, used candles and kerosene lamps for illumination, cooked on wood or coal stoves, continued to use outhouses, and suffered from rough roads that were often impassable both in winter

weather and during spring thaws when dirt and gravel turned to mud. As a consequence, many young people left the family farm for the city.

This trend alarmed a group of mainly urban professionals and social reformers affiliated with the Progressive Party. Their concern with the quality of rural life and the promotion of efficient farming practices formed the core of the country-life movement. To these urban reformers, David B. Danbom contends in *Born in the Country: A History of Rural America* (1995), farm men and women seemed out of step with an industrialized society and thus represented a problem to be studied. Once seen as the backbone of American society, rural America and its institutions now appeared more like a backwater. In 1908, President Theodore Roosevelt appointed the Country Life Commission to propose ways to improve rural life and keep young people from leaving the farm. The commission's 1909 report identified substandard schools, poor roads, inadequate communication, and social isolation as significant problems in life and community leadership in farming regions.

Although a number of the country lifers' objectives were achieved, neither the larger American society nor rural and agricultural people in general participated in the movement. Instead, rural and farm people determined their own response to the prosperity of the age. Enjoying enhanced purchasing power, they became uncharacteristically oriented toward consumption. Many reinvested their profits in farm operations; others, however, purchased items that made their homes more comfortable, modern, and pleasant, such as carpets, drapes, wallpaper, and kitchen conveniences. Farm men and women also invested in the era's new technologies and amenities, installing not only hand pumps but also plumbing, electricity, and telephones when they became available, primarily in less-isolated rural areas. They also bought automobiles, which substantially altered patterns of rural life. Their communities benefited from the prosperity as well, as farmers paid taxes to improve rural roads and schools, financed churches, and sought rural free delivery of mail.

The prosperity and increased consumer spending during agriculture's golden age hastened numerous changes in rural life. In 1920 the average farm family produced only 40 percent of what it consumed, as opposed to 60 percent twenty years earlier. Store-bought items increasingly supplanted traditional patterns of home production. Modernization of farms and the purchase of machine technology led, some historians argue, to shifts in gender, family, and community relations. Inasmuch as the family farm was part of a complex web of community ties, modernization disrupted traditional practices of interdependence often found in rural areas.

World War I and the End of the Golden Age.

America's entrance into World War I in 1917 marked the beginning of the end of America's golden age of agriculture. The stabilized production levels that had contributed to farmers' prosperity now seemed a problem to be overcome as the administration of Woodrow Wilson realized that successful prosecution of the war depended on America's ability to feed not only its own citizens but also those of its British and French allies. Acting under the 1917 Food Production Act and Food Control Act, Wilson named Herbert Hoover as food administrator. Government propaganda encouraged farmers to increase production by putting more land into cultivation or intensifying production on existing acreage. Government also subsidized the cost of seed, fertilizer, machinery, and even capital to induce farmers to produce more food.

The end of the war, however, shattered the structure of agriculture that had been built during hostilities. In May 1920 the government ended its wartime subsidies. Agricul-

tural exports fell as European nations recovered from the war and soon were growing enough to feed themselves. The falling farm prices that followed spelled trouble for the nation's farm sector: too many farmers had heeded the patriotic call to produce more by borrowing money to expand production. As the agricultural depression of the 1920s descended upon America's farm men and women and agrarian discontent erupted once again, the golden age of agriculture collapsed with a thud.

[*See also* **Consumer Culture; Family Farm; Farm Machinery; Granger Movement and Laws; Household Technology and Domestic Labor; National Farmers Union; Poverty; Subsidies, Agricultural; Technology;** *and* **Wartime Economic Regulation.**]

BIBLIOGRAPHY

Danbom, David B. *The Resisted Revolution: Urban America and the Industrialization of Agriculture, 1900–1930*. Ames: Iowa State University Press, 1979.

Fite, Gilbert C. *Cotton Fields No More: Southern Agriculture, 1865–1980*. Lexington: Universiy Press of Kentucky, 1984.

Hurt, R. Douglas. *Agricultural Technology in the Twentieth Century*. Manhattan, Kan.: Sunflower University Press, 1991.

Neth, Mary. *Preserving the Family Farm: Women, Community, and the Foundations of Agribusiness in the Midwest, 1900–1940*. Baltimore: Johns Hopkins University Press, 1995.

Ross, Earle D. *Iowa Agriculture: An Historical Survey*. Iowa City: State Historical Society of Iowa, 1951.

Schwieder, Dorothy. *Iowa: The Middle Land*. Ames: Iowa State University Press, 1996.

Tweton, D. Jerome. "The Golden Age of Agriculture: 1897–1917." *North Dakota History* 37 (1970): 41–55.

Ginette Aley

SINCE 1920

In the 1920s American agriculture entered hard times economically and politically, and for the first time in the nation's history, the number of farmers and farms declined. Yet thanks to mechanization, new plant strains, better grades of livestock, more scientific cultivation practices, more potent insecticides, and increased use of fertilizer, production increased dramatically. These innovations raised the costs of farming, encouraged the development of large commercial farms, and reduced the number of small, subsistence farms.

In the upper Midwest, tractor-drawn equipment, combines, and farm trucks facilitated large wheat-farming operations. Cotton remained prominent in the South, but it continued to be grown and harvested largely by tenant farmers and sharecroppers. Tobacco, a labor-intensive crop produced mostly in the upper South, was cultivated on smallholdings, mostly by tenant farmers. Corn, the most universal crop, benefited from improved practices, but its harvesting was not yet fully mechanized. Increasingly, midwestern corn growers developed hog production in large-scale operations. Irrigated citrus farming and truck farming in Florida, California, and Texas's Rio Grande valley developed rapidly in the 1920s.

Commodity values plunged over the course of the 1920s, however, creating a crisis that Herbert Hoover and the Federal Farm Board were unable to alleviate. The Farm Board, created by the Agricultural Marketing Act of 1929, was intended to help farmers eliminate inefficiencies by encouraging the formation of cooperative marketing organizations for each principal commodity. With its budget quickly exhausted by attempts to stabilize wheat and cotton prices, the board became overwhelmed by the scale of the developing depression that was now affecting the wider economy, and it ceased to be a significant agency by the time of the 1932 election.

The AAA. The Great Depression of the 1930s worsened the agricultural crisis, as consumers had less and less money to buy food and clothing. When Franklin Delano Roosevelt entered the White House in 1933, farm foreclosures were at their highest since the 1890s. Roosevelt's advisers urgently drafted an emergency farm bill, which became the Agricultural Adjustment Act of 1933. This sweeping measure created broad new government powers and agricultural programs. Its basic idea was to give farmers a "fair exchange value" for their products in relation to the general economy. In practice, this became known as "parity."

This landmark law embodied several new concepts. One was domestic allotment, an attempt to limit the production of basic agricultural commodities to the quantity needed for domestic use. This approach was predicated on the belief that if commodity production fell substantially, prices would rise, benefiting farmers and the entire economy.

A new government agency, the Agricultural Adjustment Administration (AAA), received extraordinary powers to administer the act. The domestic-allotment plan mandated acreage-reduction programs. The government offered farmers contracts whereby they received payments for reducing their planted acreage by as much as 40 percent. For perishable commodities, New Deal administrators negotiated marketing agreements among processors to raise prices to parity levels.

By 1935 the AAA had raised agricultural prices to near parity levels and saved many large and midsize farmers from ruin. In the cotton South, the New Deal's acreage-reduction program made it more profitable for landowners to evict thousands of tenant farmers and sharecroppers and to receive checks for taking their plots out of commission. Criticism of the program poured in from across the political spectrum. Some conservatives bridled at the expansion of government powers and foresaw the AAA as a step toward a command economy. Many on the left found it unthinkable that the government should pay farmers to leave food to rot in the fields of a hungry nation. The Supreme Court in 1935 held the Agricultural Adjustment Act unconstitutional, but Congress quickly passed legislation that reinstated many AAA programs, and a changed Court upheld it. In 1938 another Agricultural Adjustment Act revived many of the early programs, including price supports. Overall, by the end of the New Deal era, American agriculture had regained a near-parity position. In the process, farmers had become a protected class, insulated by the government from free-market forces.

Surpluses and a Shift in Policy.

World War II brought global food shortages. American farmers were exhorted to produce as much as possible, and the risks of overproduction were quickly forgotten. As farmers met the challenge by growing bumper crops, farm income tripled between 1939 and 1945, far outpacing the increases in industrial wages and corporate profits. American agriculture played a vital role in the Allied victory and thereby prospered.

As farmers continued to produce at high levels after the war, the problem of surpluses predictably returned. Despite government price supports, farm income declined. The so-called farm problem became a burning political question, forcing Congress to act. Agricultural legislation in 1948 and 1949 made feeble efforts to address the problem with "flexible" (lowered) price supports, but these measures had little effect. By late 1963, parity stood at 76 percent, the lowest since 1934.

With the nation plagued by agricultural surpluses, Congress in 1956 enacted a "soil bank" program that took entire farms out of produc-

tion. Still later, in 1985, the Conservation Reserve Program eliminated 37 million acres of erodible land from cultivation. These measures spoke to the increased concern about preserving the quality of land that began in the Dust Bowl years of the 1930s.

Through to the 1970s there remained a clear conflict in interest between consumers who wanted cheap food prices and farmers who wanted a high return on their commodities. Facing public pressure from increased prices during Richard Nixon's second term, Secretary of Agriculture Earl Butz engineered the most significant shift in government farm policy since the New Deal. Instead of seeking to create scarcity to bolster commodity values, he instructed farmers to plant more land and create ever-greater yields. Rather than supporting a system of loans and idle land, the USDA would provide direct payments to farmers and subsidize what they could produce, ensuring that a target price was reached for each crop. The unleashed forces of agribusiness harvested yields that had once been unimaginable, and food prices shifted downward in the coming decades. Genetically modified seeds devised by companies such as Monsanto came to be regarded as intellectual property and were widely sought after for their robust capacity to endure adverse climatic conditions that in the past could have wiped out a crop. As the most significant source of scientific agricultural technology and the world's leading surplus producer of arable crops, America increasingly influenced the developing world through farm policy, a process that had begun with the so-called green revolution in the 1940s.

In the 1980s, declining world markets produced great surpluses, forcing the government to lower loan and price-support levels. Several laws, including the Farm Act of 1990, continued the trend toward world-market orientation, and renewed exports after 1987 gave farmers record incomes.

Post-1920 American agriculture has also seen great demographic changes. Government programs, market forces, and the dynamics of modern life gave rise to large agribusinesses and a new farmer elite, while worsening the prospects for smallholder farmers and stimulating a dramatic rural-to-urban movement. From 1920 to 1995, the U.S. farm population fell from 31.5 million to 5 million. In 1990, only one in ten sons and daughters of farmers could hope to become farmers themselves.

Public-Health Hazards. The bounty of inexpensive food brought consequences that became increasingly obvious and troubling as the twentieth century came to a close. The prevalence of diets that were high in carbohydrates and sugars had far-reaching repercussions upon public health. Diabetes and heart disease, as well as obesity, became far more common. Between 1980 and 2010 the number of obese adults doubled, to 34 percent, and the number of obese children tripled, to 17 percent. Such developments came at great expense: the rise of conditions derived from poor eating habits increased the costs of private medical insurance and contributed to the increasing costliness of government entitlement programs such as Medicare and Medicaid.

Responses to the hazards of the American diet were impassioned and creative, but they failed to make a great impact beyond members of the more affluent classes. Concern about the conditions faced by workers involved in food production, as well as about the quality of heavily processed foods, gave rise to a boom in the popularity of farmers' markets and organic retailers, most notably Whole Foods. By the 1990s the production of organic food, for a long time a small niche within the market, became a multimillion-dollar industry as companies scaled up organic production for an ever-greater market. This caused debates between "purists" and agribusiness over what could plausibly be defined as an "organic" product. Entering the twenty-first century, debates about food production came to take on an ever-greater importance in the academic and public spheres as the challenges of environmental sustainability and public health appeared to be increasingly interconnected, yet the struggle to find an alternative to agribusiness that could work on a grand scale continued to be elusive.

[*See also* **Agricultural Adjustment Administration; Agricultural Extension and Education; Brannan Plan; Corn, Hybrid; Corporate Agriculture; Dust Bowl Era and Farm Crisis; Factory Farming; Family Farm; Farm Bureau Federation; Farm Machinery; Food and Diet; Globalization; Marketing Cooperatives; Mass Marketing; McNary–Haugen Bill; Southern Tenant Farmers' Union; Subsidies, Agricultural; Trade Policy, Federal; United Farm Workers of America;** *and* **Water and Irrigation.**]

BIBLIOGRAPHY

Drache, Hiram M. *History of U.S. Agriculture and Its Relevance to Today.* Danville, Ill.: Interstate, 1996.

Fite, Gilbert C. *American Farmers: The New Minority.* Bloomington: Indiana University Press, 1981.

Genung, Albert Benjamin. *Farm Aid Programs: A Brief Survey of 35 Years of Government Aid to Agriculture Beginning in 1920.* Ithaca, N.Y.: Northeast Farm Foundation, 1955.

Higbee, Edward. *Farms and Farmers in an Urban Age.* New York: Twentieth Century Fund, 1963.

Krause, Kenneth R., and Leonard R. Kyle. *Midwestern Corn Farms: Economic Status and the Potential for Large and Family-Sized Units.* Washington, D.C.: Economic Research Services, U.S. Department of Agriculture, 1971.

David E. Conrad;
revised by Patrick M. Dixon

AIRPLANES AND AIR TRANSPORT

The centuries-old dream of powered, heavier-than-air, controllable flight became reality on 17 December 1903 when Orville Wright lifted his fragile biplane off the sands of Kill Devil Hill, North Carolina, and traveled 120 feet in twelve seconds. Orville, his brother Wilbur, and other pioneer aviators quickly recognized and exploited the military and commercial potential of the new means of transport. The first air express delivery in the United States took place in November 1910 when a department store in Columbus, Ohio, flew a bolt of silk to Dayton, Ohio. The following year, on 25 September, Earle Ovington flew the first U.S. Post Office–sanctioned airmail as part of an aerial meet at Garden City, New York. The first sustained effort to carry passengers came in 1914. Operating from January to March, the Saint Petersburg–Tampa Airboat Line safely carried some twelve hundred people between the Florida cities in a two-seat (pilot and one passenger) Benoist flying boat.

Single-passenger airline operations were not, obviously, economically viable. With their limited lifting capacity and unreliable engines, airplanes could best be employed in carrying lightweight, high-value cargo. The U.S. Post Office early recognized the advantages and limitations of air transport. In 1918, farsighted postal officials established the U.S. Air Mail Service. Over the next nine years, this government-operated adjunct of the Post Office established a transcontinental air route from New York to San Francisco, inaugurated systematic night flying, and experimented with radio and instrument navigation. Between 1918 and 1927, postal airmen flew more than 13.7 million miles and carried more than 300 million letters, setting a standard of excellence for bad-weather and night flying unmatched in the world and laying the foundations for U.S. commercial aviation.

The outstanding performance of the Air Mail Service drew the attention of private investors. Congress facilitated their entry into aviation by passing the Air Mail Act of 1925 and the Air Commerce Act of 1926, measures that ensured profit and established the essential regulatory structure for the early development of commercial aviation. Encouraged by Charles Lindbergh's dramatic transatlantic solo flight in May 1927, an event that brought enormous public attention to aviation, the private sector began to make substantial investments in air-transport enterprises.

Subsidies and the Development of Passenger Travel.

By the early 1930s the four major domestic airlines that would dominate the industry for the next forty years had emerged. All were headed by dynamic individuals: William A. Patterson of United Air Lines, Edward V. Rickenbacker of Eastern Air Lines, C. R. Smith of American Airlines, and Jack Frye of Trans World Airlines (TWA). One airline, meanwhile, came to monopolize international travel. Pan American Airways, the government's chosen instrument for international service, established long-distance operations throughout Latin America and across two oceans. Under the adroit leadership of Juan Trippe, this superbly run company also flew a series of impressive flying boats, culminating in the four-engine Boeing 314. The federal government underwrote the development expenses for Pan American's international routes by providing generous postal subsidies. Between 1929 and 1940, Pan American received $47.2 million in mail payments, compared to the $59.8 million received by all domestic airlines. This funding enabled Pan American not only to expand worldwide but also to turn a modest profit.

In an effort to lessen their dependency on federal subsidies, the domestic airlines emphasized passenger travel in the 1930s. Their transition from mail contracts to passenger operations was facilitated by a series of technological developments that produced a new generation of airlines. Important advances in airframe design led to the adoption of stressed-skin metal wings and fuselages in place of the previous fabric-covered, wood-framed construction. At the same time, improved cylinder heads and pistons, plus better fuel, resulted in engines that were more efficient, more reliable, and more powerful.

The first modern passenger transport, the twin-engine Boeing 247, went into service with United Air Lines in 1933. A streamlined, all-metal stressed-skin plane powered by two 550-horsepower Pratt & Whitney engines mounted into nacelles on the wing, the 247 could carry ten passengers at a cruising speed of approximately 160 miles per hour. The Douglas DC-3 appeared in 1936. The twenty-one-passenger DC-3, which within three years was carrying 80 percent of all U.S. air travelers, gave airlines the first real opportunity to make a profit from flying passengers.

The federal government promoted airline-industry growth before World War II not only by providing subsidies but also by licensing airmen and aircraft and by constructing and operating the ground facilities that made safe point-to-point navigation possible. In addition to its existing responsibility for radio aids to navigation, Washington expanded its regulatory activities in 1936 by taking over three air-traffic-control centers that had been set up by the airlines six months earlier to deal with expanding air traffic. In 1938 the Air Commerce Act established the framework for government policy toward aviation that would last for the next forty years, creating a regulatory structure that encompassed strict economic control, safety oversight, and federal operation of the nation's airways and air-traffic-control facilities.

America's entry into World War II temporarily ended the rapid growth of the airline industry, which carried 3.4 million passengers—primarily business travelers—in 1941. By June 1942 the army had requisitioned 200 airplanes out of the industry's total of 360. The war years saw a dramatic increase in aircraft utilization as the airlines struggled to meet the demands for priority air travel. Despite the sharp reduction in equipment, the airlines, by filling most seats, carried nearly as many passengers in 1942 and 1943 as they had in 1941.

Golden Years. The U.S. air-transport industry underwent rapid expansion during the 1950s, one reflection of the nation's vibrant economic growth. The decade witnessed two watershed events. Flying larger, pressurized four-engine Douglas DC-6s and Lockheed Constellations that could carry more than fifty passengers from San Francisco to New York in ten hours, domestic airlines boarded 38 million passengers in 1955—marking the first year that airlines hauled more people than railroads did. Three years later, international airlines took more travelers to Europe than steamship companies did.

The explosive growth of the air-transport industry during the 1950s imposed an intolerable strain on an air-traffic-control system designed for DC-3s. Following a series of midair collisions, Congress passed the Federal Aviation Act in 1958. The new law created the Federal Aviation Agency, which united all the government's principal safety-related functions in a single, powerful organization that reported directly to the president.

The new regulatory structure was in place in time for the jet revolution of the 1960s, which saw piston-engine and turboprop airplanes give way to faster, more efficient jet transports. At the same time, changes in airline fare structures lured leisure travelers away from trains and buses. By the mid-1960s, some 50 percent of airline passengers were traveling for pleasure rather than for business, a pattern that remained constant for the rest of the century.

The 1960s were golden years for the air-transport industry. The major trunk carriers grew larger, regional airlines prospered, and scheduled air-taxi lines brought air service to small communities. By the end of the decade, few people were outside the aerial network that was coming to dominate intercity transportation. The number of passengers carried by scheduled airlines rose from 56.3 million in 1960 to 158.5 million in 1969. At the same time, the net operating income of domestic airlines averaged $255.4 million a year, while international airlines averaged $139.4 million.

Struggles, Deregulation, and More Struggles. The good times ended in the early 1970s. The appearance of the wide-bodied "jumbo jets"—the Boeing 747, Douglas DC-10, and Lockheed L-1011 Tristar—added capacity at a time when demand was leveling off. The oil crisis of 1973–1974 quadrupled airline fuel prices. Finally, in 1974 the nation entered a period of inflation and economic stagnation that the press labeled "stagflation."

As the airlines struggled, the federal government abandoned the regulatory structure that had been in place since 1938. In October 1978, President Jimmy Carter signed the landmark Airline Deregulation Act, by which Washington gave up the control over routes and fares that it had exercised since 1938. Airlines now were free to add or drop routes as market conditions dictated and to charge whatever fares they pleased.

Deregulation could not have come at a worse time. Another round of cost increases occurred in 1979 and 1980, together with a deep recession that lasted into 1982. In the midst of these economic woes, the Professional Air Traffic Controllers Organization began an illegal strike, crippling the nation's air-traffic system. President Ronald Reagan fired eleven thousand strikers, breaking both the strike and the union. Several years passed before the air-traffic-control system fully recovered.

New airlines proliferated in the unregulated environment, increasing from thirty-six in 1978 to ninety-six in 1983 (although only two survived the decade). Of the new airlines that entered the industry in response to deregulation, only one, Southwest, proved an economic success, becoming the most profitable and efficient among all airlines in the 1990s and 2000s. Overall, however, between 1979 and 1983, the domestic airline industry suffered a staggering net loss of $1.2 billion. The later 1980s witnessed a wave of mergers and bankruptcies as the air-transport industry struggled to adjust to deregulation. Not until the mid-1990s did a measure of stability and profitability return to an industry once again dominated by a handful of giant carriers. That period of temporary stability gave way to further crisis during the economic contraction of 2008–2010 when traffic fell and then fuel prices rose rapidly. Economic contraction pushed major airlines toward bankruptcy—most notably, American Airlines, once the industry leader—and spurred additional mergers. Delta and Northwest and United and Continental merged with each other in 2010 and 2011; even Southwest took over a competing low-cost carrier, AirTran, in 2011. By 2012 the passenger airline industry was more concentrated than ever, and two companies, Federal Express and United Parcel Service, dominated air cargo.

Over the years, air travel had changed from an individual adventure to a routine feature of the national scene. By the twenty-first century, with U.S. airlines carrying some 750 million passengers a year, plus a significant portion of high-value-cargo traffic, the industry clearly had become a vital component of the nation's transportation infrastructure. For both business and leisure travel, Americans had come to rely on air transport no less than earlier generations had relied on railroads, buses, and steamships. Air travel, however, brought a speed that had not been possible previously, contributing to the accelerated pace of life that characterized the early twenty-first century in the United States.

[*See also* **Air Traffic Controllers' Strike (1981); Economic Deregulation and the Carter Administration; Federal Regulatory Agencies; Postal Services;** *and* **Transportation Revolution.**]

BIBLIOGRAPHY

Bender, Marylin, and Selig Altschul. *The Chosen Instrument: Pan Am, Juan Trippe—The Rise and Fall of an American Entrepreneur.* New York: Simon and Schuster, 1982.

Bilstein, Roger E. *The American Aerospace Industry: From Workshop to Global Enterprise.* New York: Twayne, 1996.

Bilstein, Roger B. *Flight in America, 1900–1983: From the Wrights to the Astronauts.* Baltimore: Johns Hopkins University Press, 1984.

Davies, R. E. G. *Airlines of the United States since 1914.* London: Putnam, 1972.

Komons, Nick A. *Bonfires to Beacons: Federal Civil Aviation Policy under the Air Commerce Act, 1926–1938.* Washington, D.C.: U.S. Department of Transportation, Federal Aviation Administration, 1978.

Leary, William M. *Aerial Pioneers: The U.S. Air Mail Service, 1918–1927.* Washington, D.C.: Smithsonian Institution Press, 1985.

Lewis, W. David, and Wesley P. Newton. *Delta: The History of an Airline.* Athens, Ga.: University of Georgia Press, 1979.

Miller, Ronald, and David Sawers. *The Technical Development of Modern Aviation.* New York: Praeger, 1968.

Smith, Henry Ladd. *Airways: The History of Commercial Aviation in the United States.* New York: Alfred A. Knopf, 1942.

William M. Leary

AIR TRAFFIC CONTROLLERS' STRIKE (1981)

The walkout by more than twelve thousand members of the Professional Air Traffic Controllers Organization (PATCO) on 3 August 1981 proved to be one of the most significant strikes of the twentieth century. Under federal law, the air traffic controllers, employed by the Federal Aviation Administration, had no right to strike. Within hours of their walkout, President Ronald Reagan, who had been in office for less than seven months, went on national television and issued a dramatic ultimatum to PATCO. He warned that if strikers did not return to work within forty-eight hours, they would be terminated and permanently replaced. When roughly 11,500 strikers refused to heed Reagan's warning—most believing that the air-traffic-control system could not operate without them—Reagan carried out his threat. They lost their jobs, and PATCO was decertified.

No strike at that time received such extraordinary public attention, and no instance of strikebreaking was more widely reported and commented upon. The event was thus broadly influential. It helped Reagan cement his image as a tough-minded president, and it highlighted unions' growing inability to win strikes. Although the PATCO strike took place in the public sector, it influenced behavior in the private sector. Courts had long held that private employers could replace striking workers, but employers' reluctance to trigger divisive conflicts had restrained strikebreaking. The public support that Reagan received in confronting PATCO, however, encouraged many private-sector employers to believe that they, too, could break strikes. A string of prominent broken strikes soon followed during the 1980s. By the end of the century, strikes no longer played a significant role in U.S. labor relations.

[*See also* **Aviation Industry; Labor Movement, Decline of the;** *and* **Strikes.**]

BIBLIOGRAPHY

McCartin, Joseph A. *Collision Course: Ronald Reagan, the Air Traffic Controllers, and the Strike That Changed America.* New York: Oxford University Press, 2011.

Shostak, Arthur B., and David Skocik. *The Air Controllers' Controversy: Lessons from the PATCO Strike.* New York: Human Sciences Press, 1986.

Joseph A. McCartin

ALIEN CONTRACT LABOR LAW

The 1885 Alien Contract Labor Law—popularly known as the Foran Act, for its chief sponsor, Representative Martin Foran, a Democrat from Ohio—was a signature piece of congressional legislation that for the first time in American history prohibited employers from recruiting immigrant workers from abroad or paying such workers' passage to the United States. It pointedly reversed the earlier Contract Labor Act of 1864, which had been passed in response to the labor shortages caused by the American Civil War. The 1864 act encouraged employers to import workers to the United States, deducting travel expenses from their future wages, in a form of indentured servitude. Although the 1864 act was popular among industrialists, it generated opposition from the rising American labor movement because employers sometimes imported workers to break strikes and to keep wages down, as well as to swell the labor pool, making immigrant contract laborers easy scapegoats for late nineteenth-century unemployment.

By the mid-1880s, multiple economic downturns contributed to rising anti-immigrant sentiment and increased calls for immigration restriction, calls often initiated by American trade unionists, who blamed new immigrants for undermining the wages of laborers and weakening their position in American society. One of the most vocal proponents of immigration restriction was the Knights of Labor, which favored the 1882 Chinese Exclusion Act, part of the increasingly exclusionary American policies toward immigrant workers. As the 1880s progressed, unions and civic groups generated numerous petitions that focused on banning contract workers from abroad.

The Alien Contract Labor Act that passed Congress on 26 February 1885 prohibited American companies from recruiting or contracting workers from abroad prior to their emigration, and it also prohibited them from transporting or paying the passage of workers from abroad to the United States. Although the law both levied fines against employers and transportation companies who violated it and also provided for the deportation of workers caught arriving under contract, it proved difficult to enforce. The government lacked full authority to deport workers before 1890, and the 1885 law included numerous exceptions to its ban on the importation of contract employees. Further, the Foran Act failed to address the issue of cross-border worker recruitment in North America or its effects on Canada and Mexico. In practice, the law did relatively little to stem the larger tide of immigrants seeking work, of whom few actually entered into contracts prior to emigration. Nonetheless, the Foran Act played its own small part in moving American immigration policy in the direction of "closing the gates" and incorporating organized labor as a partner in the formulation of immigration policy.

[*See also* **Immigration; Immigration-Restriction Laws; Indentured Labor; Racism;** *and* **Sandlot Riots and Anti-Chinese Movement.**]

BIBLIOGRAPHY

LeMay, Michael C. *From Open Door to Dutch Door: An Analysis of U.S. Immigration Policy since 1820.* New York: Praeger, 1987.

Peck, Gunther. *Reinventing Free Labor: Padrones and Immigrant Workers in the North American West, 1880–1930.* Cambridge, U.K.: Cambridge University Press, 2000.

Susan Roth Breitzer

ALLIANCE FOR LABOR ACTION

The Alliance for Labor Action (ALA), a trade union federation established by the United Auto Workers (UAW) and the International Brotherhood of Teamsters in July 1968, was formed in opposition to the American Federation of Labor and Congress of Industrial Organizations (AFL-CIO), the dominant U.S. trade union federation. The impetus behind the establishment of the labor combination was to organize the millions of nonunion workers throughout the country and to advocate for the social issues that the two founding unions perceived were being disregarded by the AFL-CIO.

The ALA emerged out of the strained relationship during the mid-1960s between the AFL-CIO and its largest affiliate, the UAW, headed by Walter Reuther. Reuther, who also directed the AFL-CIO's Industrial Union Department (IUD), accused George Meany, then the AFL-CIO's president, of devoting too little time and resources to the progressive goals that had been adopted by the two federations prior to the merger in 1955 and that were included in the AFL-CIO's constitution. As a sign of his frustration with the AFL-CIO's direction, on 3 February 1967, Reuther tendered his resignations from both the organization's vice presidency and its executive council.

In April 1967, at a special UAW convention, the delegates sought to rejuvenate the U.S. labor movement. When the AFL-CIO rejected the UAW's request for a special convention in December 1968 to consider its reform proposals, the AFL-CIO subsequently suspended the UAW for nonpayment of per capita dues and removed Reuther from the IUD presidency, effective 15 May 1968. On 1 July the UAW wrote to Meany officially to separate from the AFL-CIO.

On 23 July 1968, Reuther and the Teamsters president Frank Fitzsimmons announced the establishment of the ALA. Their announcement claimed that the ALA would aggressively attempt to unionize the unorganized and would collaborate with other organizations in the creation of "community unions" to help poor and unemployed people throughout the United States. The ALA also promised to lobby for progressive legislation at the federal and state levels that would establish a guaranteed income, national health insurance, and free education to all U.S. citizens.

The partnership between the progressive UAW and the corruption-ridden Teamsters proved a strange one. From the first the UAW and the Teamsters had an acrimonious relationship. It was a partnership of convenience through which the Teamsters sought instant respectability, while the UAW hoped to gain greater strength in its conflict with the AFL-CIO.

Reuther's hopes to attract other unions unhappy with AFL-CIO policies to the new federation were dashed when only two small unions affiliated with the ALA; at its zenith the ALA claimed 3.6 million members and four affiliates, or about 30 percent of the 12-million-member AFL-CIO.

The ALA's major activity during its brief existence was a citywide organizational campaign in Atlanta from 1969 to 1971 that overall proved a disappointment. Although it won nearly 60 percent of its certification elections in Atlanta, the ALA obtained collective-bargaining rights for only 9,360 workers at a cost of nearly $4 million for its first year.

Walter Reuther's death in May 1970 harmed the ALA's operations but was not the decisive factor in its collapse. More important was a two-month UAW strike against General Motors that depleted the union's treasury and forced it to borrow funds from other unions. Financial stringency compelled the UAW to rationalize its operations and terminate more than two hundred staff personnel. Concurrently, it reduced its monetary contributions to the ALA by 50 percent; soon after, it ended all funding for the organization. By the spring of 1972, the ALA's fifty-person staff had been reduced to one employee, and the ALA died not with a bang, but with a whimper.

[*See also* American Federation of Labor and Congress of Industrial Organizations; International Brotherhood of Teamsters; Reuther, Walter; Union Reform Movements; *and* United Auto Workers.]

BIBLIOGRAPHY

Devinatz, Victor G. " 'To Find Answers to the Urgent Problems of Our Society': The Alliance for Labor Action's Atlanta Union Organizing Offensive, 1969–1971." *Labor Studies Journal* 31, no. 2 (June 2006): 69–91.

Treckel, Karl F. *The Rise and Fall of the Alliance for Labor Action (1968–1972)*. Kent, Ohio: Center for Business and Economic Research, Graduate School of Business Administration, Kent State University, 1975.

Victor G. Devinatz

ALTGELD, JOHN P.

(1847–1902), Democratic Party leader and reformer who championed labor and working-class rights. Altgeld served one term as Illinois governor and is best remembered for pardoning three of the Haymarket defendants and for opposing the use of federal troops during the Pullman lockout of 1894.

Born in western Germany on 30 December 1847, John Peter Altgeld grew up in Ohio after his family immigrated there. In 1875 he moved to Chicago. Real estate investments made him a millionaire by 1890 and enabled his election as Illinois governor in 1892. As governor, Altgeld studied the cases of the surviving three defendants who had been arrested and convicted after the 4 May 1886 bombing at Haymarket Square in Chicago. Altgeld pardoned all three: because none had been suspected of throwing the bomb, he decided that they had been convicted not for their actions, but for their anarchist political ideology.

In 1894, Altgeld asserted that President Grover Cleveland's dispatch of federal troops to break the American Railway Union's strike at the Pullman Palace Car Company was unnecessary, unconstitutional, and potentially dangerous. When the federal troops arrived, violence erupted, proving that Altgeld's understanding of the strike was not totally mistaken.

Although Altgeld is remembered mainly for his actions regarding the Haymarket defendants and the Pullman lockout, his championing of the rights of immigrants, women, and the working class mark him as one of the creators of a new, more progressive platform for the Democratic Party at the turn of the twentieth century. Altgeld died of a cerebral hemorrhage after speaking publicly against imperialism on 12 March 1902.

[*See also* Haymarket Affair *and* Pullman Strike.]

BIBLIOGRAPHY

Barnard, Harry. *"Eagle Forgotten": The Life of John Peter Altgeld*. New York: Duell, Sloan and Pearce, 1938.

Ginger, Ray. *Altgeld's America: The Lincoln Ideal versus Changing Realities*. New York: Funk & Wagnalls, 1958.

Mimi Cowan

AMALGAMATED ASSOCIATION OF IRON, STEEL, AND TIN WORKERS

Founded in 1876, the Amalgamated Association of Iron, Steel, and Tin Workers (AAISTW, or simply AA) was one of the earliest national unions created by skilled workers in the metal trades, most especially puddlers, whose skill was essential to the rapidly expanding iron industry. As workers whose labor was indispensable, puddlers built strong unions, wrested agreements from their employers, and maintained considerable power and autonomy at work. A charter affiliate of the American Federation of Labor (AFL), the AA was one of the federation's largest and most successful affiliates in its early years.

By the 1890s, however, steel had superseded iron as the more dynamic and dominant core of the metal trades, and it had less need for the puddlers' skill. Steel employed a larger and more diverse labor force than the iron industry did. As a craft union, the AA included only workers with the requisite skills as defined by the union, and its members were nearly all U.S.-born citizens or immigrants of northern European stock. By the 1890s unskilled workers of eastern and southern European origin dominated the labor force in the steel industry. Employers, moreover, determined to limit the power of the AA, because—in the words of Andrew Carnegie—the union effectively had placed a tax on production and reduced profit margins. When the AA's contract at Carnegie's Homestead steel mill, near Pittsburgh, Pennsylvania, terminated in 1892, the company refused to sign a new one and locked out the workers.

In an ensuing violent struggle, the union succeeded temporarily in uniting skilled and unskilled workers, old-stock Americans and new immigrants. Yet with the assistance of Pennsylvania state militia, the company won its lockout, eliminated the union, and began the AA's decline.

When Carnegie sold his company to J. P. Morgan in 1901—who then created its successor, U.S. Steel—the AA struck to achieve recognition. The result was a decisive victory for the company. By 1909, U.S. Steel had succeeded in eliminating the AA from all its mills, and a union that had once had 35,000 members claimed slightly more than 6,000 on the eve of World War I, mostly puddlers still employed in the iron industry. The war offered the AA a new opportunity to organize the steel industry, and assisted by the AFL and several other metal-trades unions, the campaign to organize the industry made great progress in 1918. The steel companies, however, refused to recognize unions, resulting in a nationwide steel strike in 1919 that involved more than 300,000 workers. The steel companies won a decisive victory from which the AA never recovered.

By the time of the New Deal, the AA had only about two thousand members and little appeal to steelworkers of new-immigrant origin; its most valuable remaining asset was the charter that it held from the AFL for exclusive jurisdiction in the iron and steel industries. In 1935 when John L. Lewis formed the Committee for Industrial Organization (CIO) and targeted the steel industry for unionization, he wooed the leaders of the AA because of the charter. Lewis's seduction succeeded: Michael Tighe, the president of the AA, succumbed and led his tattered followers into the CIO's Steel Workers Organizing Committee, where their independence and autonomy vanished.

[*See also* **American Federation of Labor; Congress of Industrial Organizations; Home-**

stead Strike (1892); Iron and Steel Industry; Labor Movements; Steel Strike of 1919; *and* Strikes.]

BIBLIOGRAPHY

Brody, David. *Steelworkers in America: The Nonunion Era.* Cambridge, Mass.: Harvard University Press, 1960.

Montgomery, David. *Workers' Control in America: Studies in the History of Work, Technology, and Labor Struggles.* Cambridge, U.K.: Cambridge University Press, 1979.

Rose, James D. *Duquesne and the Rise of Steel Unionism.* Urbana: University of Illinois Press, 2001.

Melvyn Dubofsky

AMERICAN ANTI-BOYCOTT ASSOCIATION

The American Anti-Boycott Association (AABA) was an anti-trade-union organization formed in 1902 by Dietrich Loewe and Charles Merritt, hat manufacturers in Danbury, Connecticut. The AABA's impact was greatest in courtrooms, where its attorneys defended employers against union-organized boycotts of businesses and denounced closed-shop unionism. With a membership of one thousand in 1915, the organization sought, in its words, to "promote good citizenship, individual liberty, [and] the open shop."

Two cases decided by the Supreme Court, *Loewe v. Lawlor* (1908) and *Gompers v. Buck's Stove and Range Company* (1911), illustrate the AABA's importance. Responding to the boycott of D. E. Loewe & Company, a hat-making factory, led by the American Federation of Labor (AFL), Loewe, with assistance from the AABA attorney Daniel Davenport, sought damages against union members, arguing that boycotters, including the business agent Martin Lawlor, had violated the 1890 Sherman Anti-

trust Act. The Supreme Court heard this case, and all nine judges ruled that unions could be held responsible for restraining trade.

Gompers v. Buck's Stove followed a similar pattern. In 1906, striking metal polishers demanded a nine-hour workday at the Saint Louis–based Buck's Stove and Range Company, whose president, James Van Cleave, was also the president of the National Association of Manufacturers. At the same time, the AFL added the company to its so-called unfair list. In response, the AABA helped Van Cleave obtain an injunction against the boycott; the AFL's continued publication of its unfair list violated the injunction, and its leaders were convicted of contempt. This case also reached the Supreme Court, which ruled unanimously in the company's favor.

In addition to offering legal representation to employers embroiled in labor conflicts, the AABA distributed pamphlets to employers about effective ways to confront the labor movement. In 1919 the AABA changed its name to the League for Industrial Rights and began publishing a journal, *Law and Labor.*

[*See also* **Antiunion Law Firms; Citizens' Committees and Alliances; Danbury Hatters' Case; Open-Shop Movement; Repression of Unions;** *and* **Right-to-Work Committees and Organizations, National.**]

BIBLIOGRAPHY

Bensman, David. *The Practice of Solidarity: American Hat Finishers in the Nineteenth Century.* Urbana: University of Illinois Press, 1985.

Bonnett, Clarence E. *Employers' Associations in the United States: A Study of Typical Associations.* New York: Macmillan, 1922.

Ernst, Daniel R. *Lawyers against Labor: From Individual Rights to Corporate Liberalism.* Urbana: University of Illinois Press, 1995.

Helfand, Barry F. "Labor and the Courts: The Common-Law Doctrine of Criminal Conspiracy and

Its Application in the Buck's Stove Case." *Labor History* 18 (Winter 1977): 91–114.

Chad Pearson

AMERICAN BANKERS ASSOCIATION

Organized at a meeting of bankers in Saratoga Springs, New York, in 1875, the American Bankers Association (ABA) is one of the oldest national trade associations, engaged in lobbying, public relations, and educational programs. Historically the association has attempted to present a unified voice for a diverse financial industry comprising national banks, state banks, savings banks, private banks, and trust companies. The ABA coordinates the activities of fifty state banking associations. By the 1950s about 98 percent of American banks belonged to the ABA.

In its early days the association lobbied for resumption of specie payment on U.S. currency and repeal of Civil War taxes on bank deposits and checks. The early ABA also worked to develop uniform and efficient local banking practices. After the financial panics of 1893 and 1907, the ABA joined in the call for a more flexible money supply controlled by a central bank and based on commercial borrowing. Although the Federal Reserve Act of 1913 differed somewhat from these proposals, the ABA found much to praise in the new system.

During the Great Depression and World War II, the ABA approved of a larger role for the federal government in the creation of financial credit for industry and agriculture. After initial opposition, it also supported the federal guarantee of bank deposits provided for by the 1933 act that created the Federal Deposit Insurance Corporation. After the emergency was over, however, the ABA demanded a reduction in government spending and a less active federal role in credit expansion. The association criticized government regulations that favored its rivals, the savings and loan institutions and credit unions. When in the 1970s brokerage firms and credit-card companies offered checking and savings accounts to the public, the ABA lobbied for deregulation that would allow banks to compete in a full range of financial services. In 1996 the association contributed about $1.6 million to election campaigns to ensure that its position on issues affecting banking would be heard.

[*See also* **Deregulation, Financial; Financial and Banking Promotion and Regulation;** *and* **New Deal Banking Regulation.**]

BIBLIOGRAPHY

Klebaner, Benjamin Joseph. *American Commercial Banking: A History*. Boston: Twayne, 1990.

Schneider, Wilbert M. *The American Bankers Association: Its Past and Present*. Washington, D.C.: Public Affairs Press, 1956.

Norman Nordhauser

AMERICAN ECONOMIC ASSOCIATION AND THE NEW ECONOMICS

Organized in 1885, the American Economic Association (AEA) is the principal professional association for economists working in the United States. Explicitly nonpartisan, the organization promotes the discipline through research publications—chiefly the *American Economic Review*—professional meetings, and the defense of academic freedom. The organization's initial membership was overwhelmingly academic, but by the twenty-first century the roughly eighteen-thousand-member association was approximately half academic, with the remaining members in business, government, and the non-profit sector. The AEA played a decisive role in the professionalization of economics. Throughout its history, the association has struggled to balance the need to appeal to an ideologically and politically diverse membership with the reality that the discipline's central questions are inherently social and political.

The AEA began with an 1885 meeting at Saratoga Springs, New York, in which economists trained in Germany under the German historical school banded together to professionalize the discipline and promote what they believed was their new, scientific approach to economics. The organization was the brainchild of Richard T. Ely, a professor at Johns Hopkins University, the first major U.S. school to import the German academic model of PhD programs and an emphasis on research. Ely and his colleagues were skeptical of mainstream economics approaches that emphasized Ricardian orthodoxy and advocated laissez-faire policies. Inspired by their training in Germany, they argued that institutions and country-specific historical development were integral to understanding the workings of economies, and they emphasized these factors over the search for universal economic laws. This institutional approach came to be known as the new economics. In creating the AEA, the founders hoped that a new professional organization would secure economics' place as a science and contrasted their attitudes and findings with the economic principles accepted by the public and the business community.

In 1892 the AEA embraced a more moderate, nonpartisan approach, welcoming economists from all backgrounds, including those skeptical of the new economics. Though this move triggered Ely's temporary resignation and alienated the more radical economists working at non-eastern land-grant universities, this explicitly nonpartisan approach legitimized the AEA by appealing to conservative economists

at elite schools like Yale and Princeton. With its members' increasing focus in the 1890s on such theoretical questions as marginal productivity analysis, the AEA promoted the discipline's scientific prestige, while avoiding the divisive political issues that had made conservative economists skeptical of the early AEA.

In the next few decades, the AEA's emphasis on economics as science collided with the inherently political nature of the discipline's subject matter, testing the AEA's commitment to nonpartisanship. Several key cases related to academic freedom targeted economists—including an 1894 case against Ely for allegedly promoting socialist views while at the University of Wisconsin—and the AEA's reaction to these cases forged economists' collective identity. Though the AEA did not play a direct role in these cases, its informal participation, through discussion of such subjects as academic freedom, solidified economists' commitment to their collective interest. Nevertheless, the AEA's reluctance to take a formal position reflected its concerns about appearing partisan.

During the twentieth century the association solidified its place at the heart of the economics profession. The creation of the *American Economic Review* in 1911 helped the AEA assert the discipline's intellectual independence from elite universities. The *Review*'s first editor, Davis R. Dewey, balanced scholarly research with the need to cater to the AEA's sizable nonacademic membership. Though the association struggled during the Depression, World War II brought renewed strength as the ranks of nonacademic economists grew rapidly. When postwar university enrollment boomed, the AEA saw its ranks grow, and members standardized college economics curricula. The association also worked to classify economists' specialties, formalizing the discipline's subfields, many of which came to have their own journals and subassociations.

From the late 1960s onward, the AEA faced criticism from intellectual and social minorities.

Radical economists claimed that the AEA was uncritically capitalist and committed to an implicitly conservative notion of nonpartisanship, while women and economists from minority backgrounds criticized race and gender bias in the discipline. Though the association addressed such concerns in a limited way, its leadership struggled to remain nonpartisan by emphasizing its commitment to promoting theoretical research.

In the twenty-first century the AEA remains the preeminent professional group for economists working in the United States. Nonpartisanship serves as its bedrock principle and has helped legitimate both the profession and the association in the face of academic and ideological conflict.

[*See also* **Economic Theories and Thought** *and* **Institutional and Historical Economics.**]

BIBLIOGRAPHY

Bernstein, Michael. "A Brief History of the American Economic Association." *American Journal of Economics and Sociology* 67, no. 5 (November 2008): 1007–1023.

Coats, A. W. "The American Economic Association and the Economics Profession." *Journal of Economic Literature* 23, no. 4 (December 1985): 1697–1727.

Margo, Robert A. "The Economic History of the *American Economic Review:* A Century's Explosion of Economics Research." *American Economic Review* 101, no. 1 (February 2011): 9–35.

Joshua Specht

AMERICAN FEDERATION OF LABOR

Formed in 1886 as an umbrella organization to represent craft unions, the American Federation of Labor (AFL) emphasized practical, bread-and-butter unionism, promoted the integrity of its affiliates, and upheld the sanctity of union contracts. Apart from one two-year interval (1893–1895), Samuel Gompers served as president from 1886 to 1924. Early on, the AFL's leaders mediated jurisdictional conflicts among affiliates and promoted legislation considered beneficial to organized labor, including immigration restriction. Indeed, much of its early history consisted of mediating disputes in the construction industry. The AFL achieved a form of equilibrium when it created departments to oversee industry-wide amalgamations, such as the Railway Employees' Department, the Metal Trades Department, and the Maritime Trades Department.

Gompers insisted that the AFL steer away from partisan politics. That is, affiliated unions should support not one political party or the other, but instead the politician who best served the interests of workers and their unions. Thus the affiliates adopted a policy of rewarding their friends and punishing their enemies. Such a clear distinction was not always followed in practice. Affiliated unions like the International Association of Machinists (IAM) and the Brewery Workers endorsed the Socialist Party of America (SPA). Nonetheless the AFL's preferred policy was to remain cool to third parties, whether socialist or labor parties. Nevertheless the AFL lobbied vigorously for legislation that benefited its affiliates and their members. It supported the Clayton Antitrust Act (1914) as a way to counter employers' efforts to criminalize union behavior and to enjoin such labor actions as picketing and strikes. The AFL also fought hard for immigration restriction. Though it had to tread carefully because so many of its members were European immigrants, it nonetheless targeted Asian immigrants for exclusion. Mirroring the efforts of West Coast affiliates, such as those in the building trades, the AFL vigorously supported passage of the 1882 Chinese Exclusion

Act and its subsequent extensions. It also endorsed nearly all the immigration restriction acts from 1900 to 1918 and the restriction acts of 1921 and 1924. Echoing the racist ideology of the day, the AFL was convinced that Asian immigrants could not possibly assimilate into American society.

The AFL by the early twentieth century also practiced racial exclusion and segregation. African Americans were confined to separate locals, such as those on the docks in New York City and New Orleans. It never challenged the racially exclusive policies of such affiliates as boilermakers, carpenters, and railroad workers. These trades' unions explicitly banned African Americans from joining. The AFL regarded women workers with deep suspicion. Although it included such affiliates as the International Ladies' Garment Workers' Union and the nearly all-female Bookbinders' Union, the AFL rarely offered women workers a warm welcome. When the AFL did organize women, it often did so partly to protect men's wages and working conditions. Indeed, the AFL too often left the organization of women workers to such cross-class organizations as the Women's Trade Union League.

The AFL's emphasis on practical, basic economic gains ensured that it would not challenge the capitalist system. Instead, the AFL's leaders associated with leading businesspeople in such cross-class organizations as the National Civic Federation. Gompers was intent on creating an alliance with responsible and moderate capitalists. He strove to garner respectability and a place at the table of power.

The AFL also sought to establish powerful city and state federations. Several city and state federations became extremely powerful and could, and did, create an effective base for local political action. The burgeoning strength of its member unions in the early twentieth century created a vibrant AFL and solidified trade union power. The presidential administration of Wil-

liam Howard Taft bestowed critical recognition on the AFL and the labor movement as a whole by establishing a separate cabinet-level department, the Department of Labor, on Taft's last day in office in 1913. An alliance between labor and the Democratic Party took shape before and especially during World War I when Woodrow Wilson's administration created the National War Labor Board, which helped in disputes between employers and workers and encouraged employers' recognition of trade unions. A grateful Gompers worked tirelessly for Wilson's war programs, promoting the American Alliance for Labor and Democracy and attacking more radical labor organizations. Stimulated by the AFL's alliance with the administration, trade union membership expanded from 1,562,000 in 1910 to 4,125,000 in 1919. The war's end brought an employer backlash. Employers unleashed an open-shop assault under the rubric of what became known as the American Plan, decimating union membership. The 1922 railroad shopmen's strike proved symptomatic of this employer offensive. In a titanic struggle pitting railroad corporations against 400,000 AFL members, the shopmen were eventually defeated with the active support of the administration of Warren G. Harding. The 1920s witnessed a series of unsympathetic Republican administrations that weakened the AFL still more.

The Great Depression of the 1930s brought further strains as the industrial unions within the AFL's ranks, most notably John L. Lewis's United Mine Workers of America, challenged it to organize mass-production workers. Refusing to devote scarce resources to a risky endeavor, the more cautious members of the AFL's executive board balked. This strategy backfired in 1938 when eleven industrial unions created the rival Congress of Industrial Organizations (CIO).

Although the AFL had initially lagged at organizing the millions of nonunion workers seeking representation rights, it competed aggressively for new members throughout World War II and the postwar years, growing more rapidly than the CIO did. Diluting their craft principles, AFL affiliates accepted masses of new members regardless of skill or job title. By the mid-1950s the AFL had 50 percent more members than the CIO, 9 million to 6 million. In 1952 the incumbent presidents of the two rival labor organizations died, clearing the way for a merger. The merged AFL-CIO held its first convention in December 1955.

[*See also* **American Federation of Labor and Congress of Industrial Organizations; Gompers, Samuel; Industrialization and Deindustrialization; Labor Movements; Racism;** *and* **Strikes.**]

BIBLIOGRAPHY

Arnesen, Eric. *Waterfront Workers of New Orleans: Race, Class, and Politics, 1863–1923*. New York: Oxford University Press, 1991.

Cobble, Dorothy Sue. *Dishing It Out: Waitresses and Their Unions in the Twentieth Century*. Urbana: University of Illinois Press, 1991.

Davis, Colin J. *Power at Odds: The 1922 National Railroad Shopmen's Strike*. Urbana: University of Illinois Press, 1997.

Greene, Julie. *Pure and Simple Politics: The American Federation of Labor and Political Activism, 1881–1917*. Cambridge, U.K.: Cambridge University Press, 1998.

Kaufman, Stuart B., ed. *The Samuel Gompers Papers*. 12 vols. Urbana: University of Illinois Press, 1986–2010.

Kessler-Harris, Alice. " 'Where Are the Organized Women Workers?' " *Feminist Studies* 3 (Autumn 1975): 92–110.

McCartin, Joseph A. *Labor's Great War: The Struggle for Industrial Democracy and the Origins of Modern American Labor Relations, 1912–1921*. Chapel Hill: University of North Carolina Press, 1997.

Taft, Philip. *The A. F. of L. from the Death of Gompers to the Merger*. New York: Harper, 1959.

Taft, Philip. *The A. F. of L. in the Time of Gompers*. New York: Harper, 1957.

Robert H. Zieger

AMERICAN FEDERATION OF LABOR AND CONGRESS OF INDUSTRIAL ORGANIZATIONS

The American Federation of Labor and Congress of Industrial Organizations, or AFL-CIO, came into being at a convention in New York City in December 1955 when the two hitherto-separate labor federations merged. The delegates elected the AFL president George Meany to lead the AFL-CIO. Six vice presidents, three from each federation, along with the president and secretary-treasurer, formed an executive committee. President Meany emerged as the dominant force in the organization. The negotiators agreed to finance the AFL-CIO through a monthly assessment, set at four cents per member in each affiliated union. By the AFL-CIO's twenty-sixth convention in 2009, this monthly per capita assessment had grown to sixty-five cents: yielding about $72 million a year, the money thus raised constituting the bulk of the AFL-CIO's annual budget.

A Unified Voice. The AFL-CIO intended to provide a unified voice for the labor movement in public arenas, particularly in political and legislative matters. In the period immediately after the merger, the United Auto Workers (UAW) president Walter Reuther sought unsuccessfully to commit the AFL-CIO to an ambitious organizing agenda. Meany, however, believed that centralized efforts to expand union membership would be unproductive. In 1968, Reuther's frustration with the Meany-led federation's lethargy, along with differences over organized labor's role in U.S. foreign affairs, led

Reuther to march the 1.4-million-member UAW out of the AFL-CIO.

Under Meany (1955–1979) and his successor, Lane Kirkland (1979–1995), the AFL-CIO focused on political and legislative activity. In the 1950s and 1960s its Committee on Political Education (COPE) pioneered in efforts at voter education and mobilization, and the labor federation played a key role within the Democratic Party. Both the combative Meany and the more subdued Kirkland demanded federal programs to promote economic growth, expansion of military spending, and enactment of liberal tax, social-welfare, and civil rights legislation. Both men cooperated with both Republican and Democratic presidents and government officials in the formulation and implementation of Cold War anti-Communist foreign and military policies.

The AFL-CIO reached the peak of its influence in the mid-1960s. Fresh from helping to reelect Lyndon B. Johnson and to elect the most liberal Congress since the New Deal, Meany told the 1965 convention that "To a greater degree than ever before . . . the stated goals of the administration and of Congress . . . and of the labor movement . . . are practically identical." AFL-CIO leaders, along with the leaders of most affiliated unions, were enthusiastic supporters of Johnson's Great Society programs.

The Vietnam War and the social conflicts of the later 1960s, however, diminished the AFL-CIO's role in the post–New Deal liberal coalition. Many liberals were alienated by Meany's strident support of the efforts by the administrations of John F. Kennedy, Johnson, and Richard M. Nixon to maintain South Vietnam's anti-Communist government. In 1972—for the first and only time—the AFL-CIO refused to endorse the Democratic presidential nominee, antiwar candidate George McGovern. At the same time, organized labor began to experience what became a long-term decline in union membership. At the time of the merger, unions represented one third of the nonagricultural labor force, but by 1980 they represented less than 24 percent. Despite major gains in recruiting public employees, membership in affiliated unions continued to decline, standing in 2010 at about 12 percent—and among workers in private employment, a mere 7 percent.

As early as the mid-1970s, the AFL-CIO's influence in legislative and governmental affairs weakened. Through the 1980s and into the 1990s the AFL-CIO suffered successive defeats with respect to collective bargaining, organizing, and political and legislative influence. In 1981, for example, the administration of Ronald Reagan crushed a strike by AFL-CIO-affiliated federal air-traffic controllers, an action that encouraged employers throughout the economy to intensify their resistance to unionism. In 1992 the election of the Democrat Bill Clinton brought a welcome change, but in 1993, at Clinton's urging, the Democrat-controlled Congress passed the North American Free Trade Agreement (NAFTA), which was fiercely opposed by the AFL-CIO. Then in 1994 the Republicans swept to victory in the congressional elections, gaining strong majorities in both houses of Congress for the first time since 1953. Republican success called into question the efficacy of the AFL-CIO's once-vaunted political operations.

Under Kirkland's leadership, the AFL-CIO did enjoy some successes. Its support of the Solidarity labor movement in Communist Poland in the early 1980s reinforced its reputation as a champion of human rights. In the 1980s and 1990s the AFL-CIO drew closer to women's rights, environmental, and civil rights movements. Reaffiliation in 1981 of the UAW and in 1987 of the Teamsters—expelled in December 1957 because of corrupt and undemocratic practices—brought two of the country's more dynamic unions back into the so-called House of Labor.

Even so, critics, especially among the expanding unions of public workers and employees in the service sector, called for Kirkland to retire. At the AFL-CIO's 1995 convention, the Service Employees International Union (SEIU) president John Sweeney, heading a ticket called the New Voice, defeated Kirkland's handpicked successor, and he assumed the federation's presidency. By then, unions such as the SEIU and the American Federation of State, County, and Municipal Employees were among the largest in the labor movement.

Under Sweeney's leadership, which lasted until 2009, the AFL-CIO reached out to progressive-minded groups. An initiative known as Union Cities sought to revitalize the federation's hitherto-neglected local organizations. Labor operatives helped conduct state and local living-wage campaigns in an effort to improve compensation for lower-income workers. The federation also coordinated organizing campaigns in selected cities, notably Houston and Los Angeles.

The AFL-CIO also intensified its political operations, stressing grassroots approaches to political mobilization. It contributed heavily to the effort to reelect Clinton in 1996 and to defeat antiunion House and Senate candidates. These political efforts enjoyed some successes: in 1997 the new Congress defeated an effort by the Clinton administration to expand NAFTA, and in 1998 the AFL-CIO mobilized voters to defeat a referendum in California that was intended to cripple organized labor's political activities. But the AFL-CIO and many of its affiliates poured resources into the 2000 presidential election only to see their preferred candidate, Vice President Al Gore, deprived of victory, despite winning the popular vote.

Continuing Tribulations. Meanwhile, membership continued to decline. In 2005, dissatisfied with Sweeney's leadership, a group of unions, led by his successor as SEIU chief, Andy Stern, withdrew from the AFL-CIO. They established the Change to Win alliance (CTW), which included unions holding about 40 percent

of the AFL-CIO's membership. In 2009, Sweeney stepped down as AFL-CIO president, and the convention chose Secretary-Treasurer Richard Trumka to succeed him. The convention's election of Elizabeth Shuler as secretary-treasurer and of Arlene Holt Baker, an African American, as executive vice president reflected the growing importance of women and workers of color in the AFL-CIO's dwindling ranks.

In 2008, the election of Barack Obama, along with substantial Democratic majorities in both houses of Congress, initially buoyed hopes for positive action on the AFL-CIO's legislative priorities, health care and labor-law reform. But the health reforms that were enacted disappointed union officials, and efforts to secure union-friendly changes in labor law became a dead letter after the election of a massive Republican majority in the House in 2010. Even worse from the AFL-CIO perspective were the actions of newly elected Republican governors and legislative majorities in several states. In Wisconsin, Ohio, Indiana, Florida, and elsewhere, attacks on public employees and their unions—by 2011 constituting a majority of the AFL-CIO's membership—mounted, culminating in the undermining of public workers' right to collective bargaining in several states. Trumka and other AFL-CIO spokespeople hailed the massive protest demonstrations that erupted in response and hoped to translate such activism into the basis for a renewal of a beleaguered and divided labor movement.

[*See also* **Alliance for Labor Action; Change to Win; Labor Movements; Meany, George;** *and* **Sweeney, John.**]

BIBLIOGRAPHY

AFL-CIO. http://www.aflcio.org.

Dark, Taylor E., III. *The Unions and the Democrats: An Enduring Alliance.* Ithaca, N.Y.: ILR Press, 1999.

Early, Steve. *The Civil Wars in U.S. Labor: Birth of a New Workers' Movement or Death Throes of the Old?* Chicago: Haymarket Books, 2011.

Goldberg, Arthur J. *AFL-CIO: Labor United.* New York: McGraw–Hill, 1956.

Goulden, Joseph C. *Meany.* New York: Atheneum, 1972.

Wehrle, Edmund F. *Between a River and a Mountain: The AFL-CIO and the Vietnam War.* Ann Arbor: University of Michigan Press, 2005.

Zieger, Robert H., and Gilbert J. Gall. *American Workers, American Unions: The Twentieth Century.* 3d ed. Baltimore: Johns Hopkins University Press, 2002.

Colin J. Davis

AMERICAN FEDERATION OF STATE, COUNTY, AND MUNICIPAL EMPLOYEES

By the early twenty-first century the American Federation of State, County, and Municipal Employees (AFSCME) was the largest public-sector union in the United States and the largest affiliate of the American Federation of Labor and Congress of Industrial Organizations (AFL-CIO). In 2009 the union had more than 1.6 million members.

Chartered by the AFL as Federal Labor Union 18213 in May 1932, the AFSCME was first called the Wisconsin State Administrative Employees Association (WSAEA). Initially the organization served primarily as a vehicle to defend the state's civil-service system against the resurgence of patronage politics, and its membership was limited to white-collar clerical and technical workers employed at the state capitol. In October 1934 the AFL's executive council awarded jurisdiction over state and municipal government workers to the American Federation of Government Employees (AFGE), folding the WSAEA and similar organizations into the more established federal workers'

union. When the original leaders of the WSAEA threatened to affiliate with the CIO, the AFL reversed course. In October 1936 the AFSCME was officially granted a charter by the AFL, with jurisdiction over all state and local government employees in the United States not already covered by an existing union.

Early Years. During its first two decades the AFSCME focused most of its energy on preserving and extending state civil-service systems. Arnold Zander, the union's first president, personified the organization in its early years: holding a PhD in public administration from the University of Wisconsin, Zander genuinely believed that government service was sacrosanct and that the civil-service merit system was the union's sacred protection.

With this relatively narrow focus, the union grew modestly but steadily, from less than ten thousand members when it was chartered in 1936 to twenty-nine thousand in 1940. But this pace slowed during the next decade, in part because of the chilling effect of the wartime climate and in part because of the inability of the union to gain footholds in the large urban centers of the Eastern Seaboard. Whereas the union had nearly tripled its membership in its first four years, it barely doubled over the next decade.

The union's orientation began to change during the early 1950s. Around 1952, the compensation of government employees fell behind that of unionized industrial workers. Pressure mounted within the rank and file for formal contracts. Consequently, the 1954 AFSCME convention passed a resolution calling for "increasing the number of written agreements between the city and state . . . governments and AFSCME locals."

The union doubled in size between 1954 and 1961, reaching more than 200,000 members. This growth was thanks in part to the influx of members from the United Public Workers after the AFL-CIO merger in 1955, but it also reflected the continued expansion of the public sector as a whole. The growth of the union mostly stemmed from its new strength in the job-rich cities of the industrial Northeast. A new generation of union leaders, epitomized by Jerry Wurf in New York City, joined the union in the late 1940s. They employed more militant tactics than the AFSCME's founders had, expressed less faith in civil service, and strove for the enactment of formal, signed agreements. The union benefited from the legalization of public employees' collective bargaining at the state and local levels—first in New York City (1954), then in Wisconsin (1959)—and finally at the federal level, with John F. Kennedy's Executive Order 10988 (1962).

By the early 1960s the union had strong footholds in Philadelphia and New York City. Buoyed by these gains in membership and legal standing, a coalition of local and regional leaders began to coalesce around demands for a greater institutional commitment by the AFSCME to collective bargaining. The most active and influential members of the reform movement shared similar career paths: all had been brought into the union as international organizers, only to find security and power in regional councils. Though their particular grievances varied, they shared a common opposition to the dominance of the rural, Midwest faction.

Drawing on his successful leadership of New York City's District Council 37, Jerry Wurf became the dominant figure in the reform caucus. At the 1960 convention, District Council 37 represented one seventh of the AFSCME's total membership. Wurf unsuccessfully challenged Zander at the union's 1962 convention in Milwaukee, Wisconsin, but defeated him two years later by the narrow margin of 1,450 to 1,429.

Growth and Backlash. The AFSCME grew tremendously through the 1960s and 1970s. In 1964 the union had 234,000 members nationwide; by 1970 it had more than half a million, two thirds of whom worked in occupations classified as blue collar. The union's growth was particularly strong among minority and female workers. Many important segments of the public-sector labor market, particularly the low-paid, semiskilled service departments, were dominated by minorities and women, and the union lent strong support to both the civil rights and the feminist movements during the 1960s. The AFSCME's leadership positions were unusually open to minority and female members; Bill Lucy became the union's highest-ranking African American when he was elected secretary-treasurer in 1972. The union became one of the leading forces behind the enactment and expansion of so-called comparable worth legislation designed to equalize gendered pay disparities.

The union's tremendous growth and visibility drew increasing criticism from conservative activists during the late 1970s. This was first evident in the inability of the AFSCME and other public-sector unions to win a national collective-bargaining law—a law like the National Labor Relations (Wagner) Act, but for public employees—during the mid-1970s. The urban fiscal crises of the decade and related anti-tax movements both drew from and fueled the expansion of a backlash against the gains that public-sector unions had won.

On the state and local levels, AFSCME affiliates teamed with community groups and welfare advocacy organizations to defend social services against conservative calls for cutbacks and privatization. But the antigovernment message of Ronald Reagan's Republican Party dramatically altered the political terrain on which the AFSCME operated. Its membership gains slowed dramatically in the 1980s and 1990s, though it weathered the antiunion storm far better than its private-sector counterparts did.

In the 1980s the AFSCME began organizing health-care workers employed by the state, culminating in the 1989 affiliation of the National Union of Hospital and Health Care Employees. During the 1990s the union continued to expand its jurisdictional boundaries, organizing private-sector service workers, university employees, and health-care professionals.

In 1995 the AFSCME was one of the eleven members of the Committee for Change that orchestrated John Sweeney's defeat of Thomas Donahue for the presidency of the AFL-CIO. Unlike some other members of the New Voice slate, however, the AFSCME did not join in Change to Win's breakaway movement in 2005, preferring instead to remain in the AFL-CIO.

[*See also* **American Federation of Labor and Congress of Industrial Organizations; Labor Movements; Memphis Sanitation Strike (1968); Service Employees International Union;** *and* **Wurf, Jerry.**]

BIBLIOGRAPHY

Bellush, Jewel, and Bernard Bellush. *Union Power and New York: Victor Gotbaum and District Council 37.* New York: Praeger, 1984.

Billings, Richard N., and John Greenya. *Power to the Public Worker.* Washington, D.C.: R. B. Luce, 1974.

Goulden, Joseph C. *Jerry Wurf: Labor's Last Angry Man.* New York: Atheneum, 1982.

Kramer, Leo. *Labor's Paradox: The American Federation of State, County, and Municipal Employees, AFL-CIO.* New York: Wiley, 1962.

Joseph E. Hower

AMERICAN FEDERATION OF TEACHERS

Forged in the same reform hothouse of Progressive Era Chicago that sparked the settlement-house movement and industrial unionism, the American Federation of Teachers (AFT) united rank-and-file educators in pursuit of better pay, secure pensions, and greater autonomy. Founded in 1916 in response to a Chicago Board of Education rule forbidding teachers from joining unions, the AFT soon attracted membership from such cities as New York, Atlanta, and San Francisco. Unlike its rival, the National Education Association (NEA), formed earlier as a professional organization dominated by school administrators who rejected the idea of teacher unionization until decades later, the AFT was conceived as part of the labor movement, a craft union dedicated to the rights of "brain workers," as the American Federation of Labor president Samuel Gompers called teachers.

In the absence of legal recognition by state governments, the AFT for its first forty years acted primarily as a pressure group on local school boards, pushing for bread-and-butter issues such as wages and professional concerns such as academic freedom. In contrast to the much larger NEA, the AFT remained a small, largely urban phenomenon, counting fewer than forty-one thousand members in 1950. By 1960, although the AFT had secured tenure, due process protections, and married women's job rights for many teachers, wages still lagged; according to the AFT, the average teacher earned $400 less per year than a typical factory worker did.

Inspired by the success of the industrial union movement, in the late 1950s AFT leaders began an aggressive push for states to grant teachers collective-bargaining rights. Wisconsin was the only state to do so by 1960, but by 1980, twenty-eight other states had joined the list. State legislation fostered the AFT's explosive growth in the 1960s and 1970s, but just as crucial was the union's increasing use of strikes, often in defiance of the law. Such was the case in New York City in 1962 when the organizers

David Selden and Albert Shanker led the city's teachers on an illegal walkout that won a significant wage increase and no reprisals. Victory in the nation's largest school district emboldened teachers all across the country to organize and strike, often in the face of mass firings and arrests, and the results were spectacular: in 1960, fewer than a dozen school districts had collective-bargaining agreements; by 1980, 72 percent of all teachers were represented by contracts that stipulated pay rates, job protections, and workplace rules. By 1980 the AFT had more than half a million members, making it one of the largest labor unions in the United States.

By the turn of the twenty-first century, although the AFT remained one of the nation's biggest unions, its members faced new challenges: financially strapped boards of education pushed for givebacks during contract negotiations, and prominent education reformers argued that collective bargaining inherently undermined student achievement and the public interest. Even though teaching remained a low-salary vocation relative to other fields requiring an equivalent level of training, teachers faced challenges to their rights, status, and pay reminiscent of those that caused Chicago educators to organize nearly a century before.

[See also Labor Movements; National Education Association; New York Teachers' Strike (1968); Shanker, Albert; and Strikes.]

BIBLIOGRAPHY

Kahlenberg, Richard D. *Tough Liberal: Albert Shanker and the Battle over Schools, Unions, Race, and Democracy.* New York: Columbia University Press, 2007.
Murphy, Marjorie. *Blackboard Unions: The AFT and the NEA, 1900–1980.* Ithaca, N.Y.: Cornell University Press, 1990.

Daniel A. Graff

AMERICAN NEWSPAPER GUILD

The American Newspaper Guild (ANG) began during the summer of 1933 as a spontaneous response by editorial workers to management's attempt to influence a New Deal agency's oversight of wages and working conditions in the newspaper industry. Aroused journalists, dissatisfied with their working conditions and lack of respect, decided to band together. Some had already done so when Heywood Broun, a prominent columnist, announced in August 1933 that he would help organize them.

When the journalists met in December 1933, Broun became president; he led the ANG with panache until his death in 1939. Although members agreed on the need to improve working conditions, they differed about whether to become a union, and as a result the organization was called a "guild." Under Broun's guidance the ANG joined the American Federation of Labor in 1936 and left in 1937 for the Congress of Industrial Organizations. The ANG opened its ranks to noneditorial workers, and its membership more than doubled, to about nine thousand. Journalists more interested in a professional organization dropped out.

Communists played a significant role in the transformation of the guild into a union. The ANG's largest unit numerically, and its most important financially, was located in New York City. The Communists acted as a disciplined and effective caucus within what was called "the New York crowd," which controlled the organization. During the Popular Front of the 1930s, that caucus held undisputed sway; after 1939 the anti-Communist caucus, aided by the Association of Catholic Trade Unionists, rose in power, winning control of the national organization in 1941 and of the New York affiliate in 1947.

The fledgling organization negotiated a variety of contracts during the 1930s, but it also engaged in bitter conflicts with chain opera-tions, especially the Hearst newspapers, and with several independent publishers.

During World War II and afterward the ANG's jurisdiction expanded in a flourishing industry, labor relations progressed smoothly, and membership rose to more than forty thou-sand. But beginning in the 1950s, competition for the reader dollar—first from television and then from newer media—publisher misman-agement, and a changing advertising environ-ment as Americans moved from the center city to the suburbs all combined to begin a decline in the U.S. newspaper industry that has acceler-ated ever since.

Charles Perlik Jr., who rose from union rep-resentative to president, led the union in its final successful era, from 1969 to 1987. He oversaw its change of name in 1971 to the Newspaper Guild—in recognition of its Cana-dian affiliates—and set in motion a merger with the larger, more powerful Communications Workers of America in 1995. During his tenure the guild supported minorities and women in the industry, endorsed presidential candidates, confronted automation, and endeavored to broaden its membership base.

Since the later 1990s the guild has taken a less activist role politically and socially as its leadership deals with the many problems that threaten not only its own existence but also that of the traditional newspaper industry. Be-cause of continuing change in the delivery of news, as well as continuing technological in-novations, the guild has found itself on the de-fensive as its members face pay freezes and layoffs. More than ever before, in the twenty-first century the guild—like the industry and the employees it represents—faces an uncer-tain future.

[See also **Communications Workers of Amer-ica** and **Printing and Publishing.**]

BIBLIOGRAPHY

Emery, Michael C., Edwin Emery, and Nancy L. Roberts. *The Press and America: An Interpretive History of the Mass Media.* Boston: Allyn & Bacon, 2000.
Leab, Daniel J. *A Union of Individuals: The Formation of the American Newspaper Guild, 1933–1936.* New York: Columbia University Press, 1970.

Daniel J. Leab

AMERICAN SYSTEM OF MANUFACTURING AND INTERCHANGEABLE PARTS

By the time that Henry Ford mass-produced the Model T, U.S. firms were acknowledged leaders in manufacturing mechanisms with in-terchangeable parts. The U.S. advantage dated to firearms production in the early nineteenth century and was recognized when Americans displayed firearms made of interchangeable parts at London's Crystal Palace Exposition in 1851. The American system of manufacturing, as U.S. methods came to be called, had two fun-damental components. First, parts were pro-duced to a uniform standard and hence could replace one another, which facilitated firearm repair on the battlefield. Such production en-tailed jigs and fixtures to hold parts in the proper position and gauges to test for accuracy. Second, specialized machinery made the parts, which reduced labor time and, if technologi-cally advanced, improved accuracy and reduced the need for skilled labor. Both features were integral to the success of firms in many indus-tries. But neither developed easily, the govern-ment played a vital role, and skilled labor was essential.

Origins and Development. Interchange-able parts and specialized machinery were not distinctly American. French armorers attempted to produce interchangeable-parts firearms using craft methods. British engineers devised specialized machinery to mass-produce ship blocks for the navy. But the U.S. federal government led a process that brought American methods to world leadership. It issued large contracts and advanced capital to private armories. The first important contractor, Eli Whitney, promised interchangeability but did little to deliver it. Simeon North, however, advanced interchangeability by developing a uniformity system and inventing the milling machine, a key mass-production machine tool. Federal armories in Springfield, Massachusetts, and Harpers Ferry, Virginia (later West Virginia), advanced techniques of precision measurement, gunstocking, milling, and drop forging. Springfield became the center of a well-organized network through which knowledge was shared among public and private armories. Using machines, gauges, and hand finishing, federal and private armories achieved a modicum of interchangeability by 1830.

Interchangeability advanced even as the system of government contractings declined after 1840. The Springfield Armory deepened machinery investments, cut labor time, improved precision through mechanization and augmented skills, and spread knowledge of its methods. Developments in the private sector also contributed. Firms such as Colt and Remington sold firearms largely to civilians. Two firms that displayed at the Crystal Palace—Robbins & Lawrence and Colt—attracted a British parliamentary commission to study American methods. Both firms learned from the Springfield Armory, enjoyed government contracts, and advanced mechanization, including improved turret lathes and drop forges. Worker mobility spread methods widely within New England but less so elsewhere. The spread of the industrial lathe and the metal planer enabled firms to make machines that were more accurate. From the 1850s, machine tool firms

sold mass-production machinery to firearms firms. The two most important—Brown & Sharpe and Pratt & Whitney—both learned from firearms manufacturers. Brown & Sharpe's vernier and micrometer calipers improved measurement capabilities. Over the rest of the nineteenth century, machine-based interchangeability reduced but never eliminated hand filing.

Widening. In principle, the American system could apply wherever mechanisms were made in large quantities, but it took a century to spread this system widely. The potential was inherent in the technological convergence, in Nathan Rosenberg's term, of production methods among industries with very different products. Though interchangeability had multiple origins, including Connecticut clock production, firearms proved central to its diffusion. New England sewing machine firms were early beneficiaries. Wheeler & Wilson used knowledge from several firearms-trained machinists to build its leading interchangeable-parts factory in 1863. Brown & Sharpe applied its knowledge and tools to mass-produce the Willcox & Gibbs machine. To make better machines, Joseph Brown invented two important machine tools, the universal milling machine and the universal grinding machine. Firearms and sewing machine firms were Brown & Sharpe's biggest customers through 1880. Interchangeable methods spread unevenly; Singer, the market leader, did not introduce them until the 1880s.

After 1880, many industries adopted American-system methods. The automobile industry was the most important, and the bicycle linked it to earlier interchangeable-parts production. The leading bicycle maker, Albert Pope, employed a sewing machine producer based in Hartford, Connecticut, and trained at Robbins & Lawrence and at Colt to manufacture bicycles with machine-made, interchangeable parts. Other firms applied metal stamping techniques. Innovations such as grinding ball bearings improved accuracy and durability. Technological convergences contributed to the quick introduction of interchangeable-parts methods to make the Oldsmobile, the Cadillac, and the Model T. Worker movement was a principal mode of diffusion. Henry Leland worked at the Springfield Armory, Colt, and Brown & Sharpe before organizing production at Olds and then Cadillac. Ford made similar use of methods that Walter Flanders learned at Singer and at machine tool companies. Machine tool firms supplied automobile companies and developed heavier mass-production metalworking machines such as Charles Norton's grinder. Automobile firms designed and built special-purpose machines and organized the flow of work, most importantly through Ford's assembly line. Ford's methods spread quickly to General Motors and Chrysler.

Effects. The transition from small-scale, nonmechanized craft production to large-scale, mechanized, interchangeable-parts production reshaped labor, businesses, and the economy. Machine operatives and assemblers replaced craft laborers. Until products were assembled without fitting, workers retained significant skills. Even after that, production entailed a variety of skill levels; alongside the Ford assembly-line worker, factories and their suppliers employed highly skilled machinists and engineers to design, build, and maintain machines, tools, and gauges.

American-system factories often had significant economies of scale, and their firms frequently were industry leaders. But the relationship among interchangeable-parts methods, costs, and industry leadership was complex. Special-purpose machinery reduced costs, but other factors did as well, including high-speed steel cutting tools and the use of electric motors to power individual machines. Higher productivity need not reduce prices: Singer and Pope sold at the high end of their markets, but Ford led in using mechanization to drive down prices. Scale hardly ensured success: Ford's concentration on the Model T caused its market share to plummet, while General Motors, with shorter runs of more diverse products, flourished. Further, the growth of large firms rested on more than production economies. The largest firms making sewing machines, business machines, automobiles, and other complex, mass-production machinery invested in distribution systems. Singer's lead in sewing machines rested not on production economies but on its extensive system of company agencies.

Interchangeable-parts manufacturing helped propel the growth of industries in the United States and abroad. Of course, mass production was much broader, including textiles, iron and steel, and much else. Moreover, small-batch and custom work persisted even at such giants as General Electric and Westinghouse. But the number and importance of interchangeable-parts industries expanded over time. Firearms, clocks, and locks used these methods in 1860. Sewing machines, bicycles, typewriters, watches, and locomotives joined them by 1900. By 1930, automobiles, tractors, small electrical motors, and many consumer durables expanded the list. The American system that the government pioneered early in the nineteenth century initiated methods in which private U.S. firms led the world in the twentieth.

[*See also* **Automotive Industry; Business Growth and Decline; Deskilling; Factory System; Ford, Henry, and Fordism; Industrialization and Deindustrialization; Industrial Policy, Theory and Practice of; Mass Production; Technology; Technology and Labor;** *and* **Vertical Integration, Economies of Scale, and Firm Size.**]

BIBLIOGRAPHY

Gordon, Robert B. "Who Turned the Mechanical Ideal into Mechanical Reality?" *Technology and Culture* 29 (October 1988): 744–778.

Hounshell, David A. *From the American System to Mass Production, 1800–1932: The Development of Manufacturing Technology in the United States.* Baltimore: Johns Hopkins University Press, 1984.

Mayr, Otto, and Robert C. Post, eds. *Yankee Enterprise: The Rise of the American System of Manufactures.* Washington, D.C.: Smithsonian Institution, 1981.

Rosenberg, Nathan. *Perspectives on Technology.* Cambridge, U.K.: Cambridge University Press, 1976.

Rosenberg, Nathan, ed. *The American System of Manufactures: The Report of the Committee on the Machinery of the United States 1855, and the Special Reports of George Wallis and Joseph Whitworth 1854.* Edinburgh, U.K.: Edinburgh University Press, 1969.

Smith, Merritt Roe. *Harpers Ferry Armory and the New Technology: The Challenge of Change.* Ithaca, N.Y.: Cornell University Press, 1977.

Thomson, Ross. *Structures of Change in the Mechanical Age: Technological Innovation in the United States, 1790–1865.* Baltimore: Johns Hopkins University Press, 2009.

Thomson, Ross. "Understanding Machine Tool Development in the United States: Uniting Economic and Business History." *Business and Economic History On-line* 8 (2010): 1–32. Available at http://www.thebhc.org/publications/BEHonline/2010/thomson.pdf.

Ross Thomson

ANARCHISM AND LABOR

Anarchists played key roles in the American labor movement, from the native-born labor reformers who came together in the middle of the nineteenth century to launch the New England Labor Reform League and kindred organizations to the immigrant workers who became a majority among wageworkers.

Several anarchists were active in the New England Labor Reform League, an organization founded in 1869 that united a wide array of labor-reform efforts. These labor reformers were primarily dedicated to addressing what they saw as systemic causes of labor exploitation, such as excessive working hours, monopoly, usury, and chattel and wage slavery.

Often labeled "individualists," anarchists such as Joseph A. Labadie played a key role in reform associations, as well as in the Knights of Labor. Labadie, a printer by trade, involved himself in many social-reform movements, including organizing the Knights of Labor's Detroit Local Assembly 901 in 1878 and serving as president of the Detroit Trades Council, the eight-hour-day movement, and Haymarket defense efforts. In 1888 he helped launch the Michigan Federation of Labor as an alternative to the Knights.

Perhaps best known are the activities of the Chicago anarchists, who organized primarily among the city's immigrant workers. The anarchists led several local unions, grouped in the Central Labor Union (a rival to the local affiliate of the American Federation of Labor, or AFL), played a leading role in the 1886 eight-hour-day movement, and published a German-language daily newspaper, the *Chicagoer Arbeiter-Zeitung*.

But anarchists were active in many unions, from the marble cutters of Barre, Vermont, to the largely Spanish-speaking East Coast marine firemen who in 1913 left the AFL-affiliated Seamen's Union to join the Industrial Workers of the World's Marine Transport Workers Industrial Union—which maintained IWW halls into the 1950s. Anarchists were influential enough in the garment trades that the International Ladies' Garment Workers' Union regularly purchased advertisements in the Yiddish anarchist weekly, *Di Fraye Arbeter Shtime* (Free Voice of Labor).

Anarchists and other radicals were central to the launching not only of the Industrial Workers of the World, but also of the men's clothing and textile workers' unions launched in response to the conservatism of the AFL-affiliated garment unions. The scores of mostly foreign-language weeklies and other newspapers published by the anarchist movement devoted as much attention to contemporary labor struggles as to anarchist doctrine, and unions regularly called on anarchist agitators such as Philadelphia's Chaim Weinberg when they needed someone to speak to immigrant workers or to motivate a crowd.

Anarchists also played important roles in the mainstream labor movement, largely as rank-and-file activists but sometimes rising to positions of leadership. Anton Johannsen, for example, was prominent in both Chicago and California as an organizer and business agent of the United Brotherhood of Carpenters and Joiners, and late in life he served as vice president of the Chicago Federation of Labor. Rose Pesotta served as an organizer and vice president of the International Ladies' Garment Workers' Union. Early in the twenty-first century many anarchists continued to hold local office and staff positions.

[*See also* Eight-Hour Day; Garment Industry; Goldman, Emma; Great Upheaval of 1886; Haymarket Affair; Industrial Workers of the World; Labor Movements; Parsons, Albert; Radicalism and Workers; *and* Sacco and Vanzetti Case.]

BIBLIOGRAPHY

Anderson, Carlotta R. *All-American Anarchist: Joseph A. Labadie and the Labor Movement*. Detroit, Mich.: Wayne State University Press, 1998.
Avrich, Paul. *The Haymarket Tragedy*. Princeton, N.J.: Princeton University Press, 1984.
Leeder, Elaine. *The Gentle General: Rose Pesotta, Anarchist, and Labor Organizer*. Albany, N.Y.: State University of New York Press, 1993.
Topp, Michael Miller. *Those without a Country: The Political Culture of Italian American Syndicalists*. Minneapolis: University of Minnesota Press, 2001.
Weinberg, Chaim Leib. *Forty Years in the Struggle: The Memoirs of a Jewish Anarchist*. Translated by Naomi Cohen; edited and annotated by Robert P. Helms. Duluth, Minn.: Litwin Books, 2008.

Jon Bekken

ANTILABOR MOBILIZATION AFTER 1945

The three decades following the end of World War II are generally seen as the high point of labor-union power in twentieth-century America. Unions represented about one third of the workforce, with much higher rates of union membership in manufacturing industries and in the Northeast and Midwest. Yet the evident power of labor in postwar America did not prevent businesses from seeking to limit the gains that unions had made. Almost as soon as World War II ended—some would say even before the war ended—the business community began seeking ways to restrict the power of unions.

Containment of Unions' Gains. Although the modern American labor movement began in the 1930s with the passage of the National Labor Relations (Wagner) Act and the birth of the Congress of Industrial Organizations (CIO), only during World War II did unions gain the institutional strength that came to define their postwar history. At the end of the 1930s it was unclear whether labor unions would be able to consolidate the gains they had made with the passage of the Wagner Act and the birth of the CIO to win a lasting place in the American economy. But by the end of the war, almost 70 percent of manufacturing workers worked under contracts negotiated by unions, and in some industries, more than 80 percent of workers were unionized. The federal government's interest in limiting strikes during wartime led to the National War Labor Board's encouragement of the adoption of so-called maintenance-of-membership clauses that granted union security. As a result, union membership grew dramatically during the war, and the landscape that American business confronted at the end of World War II was very different from that of the late 1930s. This caused no small amount of anxiety in corporate circles about the right way to confront the new power of organized labor after the war, a time when business also feared both the return of economic depression and also the possibility that the federal government would continue the active involvement in the economy that had defined wartime policy. Though few employers believed that it would be possible to reverse labor's gains and substantially eliminate unions after the war—as had been done in the wave of repression that followed World War I—there were still major questions about the scope of union power and collective bargaining in the postwar years.

But management was quickly able to regain the upper hand in the immediate postwar period, effectively containing unions to the industries and regions that had been organized in the 1930s. The massive strike wave of 1945–1946—in which about 5 million workers participated in more than forty-six hundred strikes—made it clear that unions would not be substantially rolled back after the war. Still, the labor movement was not able to win some of its more radical demands, such as Walter Reuther's insistence that General Motors "open the books" to provide evidence about the wages that it could afford to pay its workers. In 1947 the passage of the Taft–Hartley Act indicated the waning momentum of the labor movement. The new law, reflecting many of the ambitions of groups such as the National Association of

Manufacturers, granted states the right to pass right-to-work laws, limited the ability of unions to engage in secondary strikes and boycotts, codified the rights of employers to campaign during union elections, and revised the preamble of the Wagner Act so that the labor-relations policy of the United States was no longer so directly committed to union rights. The difficulties encountered by Operation Dixie—the CIO's campaign to organize in southern states—also indicated that although labor might remain strong in the industries and regions that it had already organized, it would not be able to expand its power.

Truce. The result was that the postwar period was defined less by labor-management peace than by a sort of armed truce. In the 1950s and 1960s, although many companies felt compelled to bargain with their unions, they also sought in a variety of ways to limit union power and to prevent it from expanding. Nonunion companies fought organizing drives, developing a wide range of strategies that took advantage of the "free speech" provisions granted employers in Taft–Hartley to lobby against union representation and sometimes hiring antiunion consultants such as Nathan Shefferman, a former employee of Sears, Roebuck, to advise them on the best ways to fight unions. Some unionized companies, most notably General Electric, whose influential strategy was designed by its vice president Lemuel Boulware, developed and sought to popularize highly politicized contract negotiation and public relations strategies that were intended to undermine the power of the union by promoting free-market ideas. The National Association of Manufacturers engaged in extensive public relations campaigns intended to sway public opinion about labor unions. Corporations helped to fund think tanks, such as the Foundation for Economic Education and the American Enterprise Institute, that were devoted to opposing liberalism more broadly. The National Right to Work Committee, founded in 1955, helped to coordinate state-level right-to-work campaigns.

After the election of President Dwight D. Eisenhower, employers campaigned hard to ensure that new appointees to the National Labor Relations Board would be sympathetic to business interests, and the board under Eisenhower was much less friendly toward unions. In the late 1950s the Senate's Committee on Improper Activities in Labor-Management Relations provided a steady stream of images of union corruption, images that conservative politicians such as the Arizona senator Barry Goldwater were able to play upon in their bids for electoral office. Sometimes companies relocated factories in order to evade unions.

When the economic boom of the postwar years came to an end in the 1970s, many more employers began to be willing to attack labor unions openly, hiring professional antiunion consultants to fight organizing drives and employing strikebreakers. The increasingly aggressive opposition to labor unions in the 1970s and 1980s, however, built upon many of the institutions, ideas, and practices that had developed during the heart of the postwar boom.

[*See also* **Antiunion Law Firms; Employee Free Choice Act; National Association of Manufacturers; National Labor Relations Board; Open-Shop Movement; Repression of Unions; Right-to-Work Committees and Organizations, National; Right-to-Work Committees and Organizations, State Laws Related to; Taft–Hartley Act; Treaty of Detroit and Postwar Labor Accord;** *and* **Union Corruption.**]

BIBLIOGRAPHY

Fones-Wolf, Elizabeth A. *Selling Free Enterprise: The Business Assault on Labor and Liberalism, 1945–60.* Urbana and Champaign: University of Illinois Press, 1994.

Gross, James. *Broken Promise: The Subversion of U.S. Labor Relations Policy, 1947–1994.* Philadelphia: Temple University Press, 1995.

Harris, Howell John. *The Right to Manage: Industrial Relations Policies of American Business in the 1940s.* Madison: University of Wisconsin Press, 1982.

Phillips-Fein, Kim. *Invisible Hands: The Making of the Conservative Movement from the New Deal to Reagan.* New York: W. W. Norton and Company, 2009.

Kim Phillips-Fein

ANTITRUST LEGISLATION

Opposition to concentrated corporate power occupies a noteworthy if ambiguous place in American history. Ever since Congress passed the Sherman Antitrust Act of 1890, public consensus supported antitrust values in principle, even as repeated disputes arose over their application in particular cases. Such inconsistency paralleled the nation's unfolding experience with big government and managerial capitalism; the shifting significance of small business and organized labor; the growing importance of economic experts; and the central policy-making role of lawyers and courts, particularly the U.S. Supreme Court. A popular faith in competition governed antitrust development. What "competition" meant, however, and who benefited, was subject to change.

Gilded Age Beginnings. The antitrust movement originated as managerial capitalism burgeoned near the end of the nineteenth century. Following the Civil War, technological innovation and mass marketing fostered the development of large-scale corporate combinations, leading to a separation between owners and managers. In this new form of corporate enterprise, managers increasingly acted as the principal decision makers. The rise of big business spawned corporate mergers, as well as loose cartel arrangements and other trade restraints. (A cartel is a secret agreement among supposedly competing businesses to establish a monopoly by price fixing or other means.) Although some states successfully limited both forms of combination, New Jersey enacted a law in 1889 that permitted the formation of holding companies and facilitated the formation of corporate combinations controlled by managers. Because the New Jersey law conflicted with other states' laws, its critics demanded federal action.

The Sherman Act was a product of countervailing market and political pressures. Small business and farm groups, eager to limit the growth of large corporate combinations, supported federal action in principle. Big-business interests and their lawyers, by contrast, were divided over the possible results of a more uniform national antitrust policy. Fearing that federal power might be used against it, organized labor opposed federal antitrust legislation. Popular opinion, at the time and ever since, reflected these divergent sentiments. Americans profoundly distrusted giant concentrations of corporate wealth and power, while at the same time they yearned for the consumer benefits that bigness often seemed to facilitate; people were also anxious about the apparent lack of legal accountability of huge, "soulless" corporations. Congress responded to those conflicting desires and interests with a law that embodied several general provisions: Section 1 of the Sherman Act banned "[e]very contract, combination, or conspiracy" that restrained interstate or foreign trade of commerce; Section 2 prohibited individual firms from monopolization and attempted monopolization. The act's enforcement relied upon the state and federal courts. Federal or state prosecutors, as well as private litigants, could win treble damages by proving violations of the law.

The Sherman Act's general provisions invited diverse interpretation. During the first decade of the law's operation, the Supreme Court encouraged corporations to adopt the holding-company approach. (A holding company is a corporation that owns a controlling share of the stock of one or more other firms.) In 1895 the Court held that the E. C. Knight Company, a holding company that monopolized sugar production in the United States, did not violate the antitrust law. The Supreme Court and state courts also decided, however, that loose cartel practices were illegal under both the Sherman Act and state laws. The Court's simultaneous enforcement of rules against cartel practices and toleration of holding companies facilitated a great turn-of-the-century merger wave. By 1903 most of the nation's largest firms were holding companies in which decisions were generally left to managers. Meanwhile, the Supreme Court and lower federal judges increasingly applied the Sherman Act against organized labor, enabling employers to defeat strikes and boycotts.

The Progressive Era. After 1900, demands for stricter antitrust enforcement increased. In the Northern Securities Case (1904), Theodore Roosevelt's administration became the first to prosecute successfully a holding company. This victory brought an end to the first merger wave. Federal officials, corporate leaders, economists, Wall Street lawyers, and Supreme Court justices soon concluded that a more flexible "rule of reason" should govern merger cases. Adopting a rule of reason as the basic doctrine governing merger cases, the Supreme Court in 1911 struck down predatory pricing practices that Standard Oil and American Tobacco were using to crush smaller firms.

Louis Brandeis, a prominent lawyer who championed small business and opposed big corporations, favored employing the rule of reason to allow for loose collusion among small enterprises, while urging the breakup of giant corporations. In taking this position, Brandeis adopted an Americanized version of European cartel policy. But in 1911 the Supreme Court frustrated Brandeis's hopes, outlawing loose cartel arrangements even among smaller companies.

Woodrow Wilson's victory in the 1912 presidential election brought the enactment of two new antitrust laws. The Federal Trade Commission Act of 1914 created an administrative agency with broad powers to prevent "unfair methods of competition." The terms "unfair" and "competition" remained sufficiently general, however, that judicial interpretation was inevitable. Similarly, the 1914 Clayton Act included provisions condemning the anticompetitive implications of price discrimination, exclusive arrangements, interlocking directorates, and stock-purchase mergers, particularly holding companies. The Clayton Act also contained language that seemed to prohibit injunctions against labor. However, the Supreme Court construed both laws so narrowly that the advocates of more vigorous antitrust enforcement grew frustrated. The Justice Department prosecuted single-firm monopolies, but oligopolistic competition among a few managerially centralized big corporations characterized most leading industries. Still, the federal government's persistent prosecution of price-fixing violations did enhance competitive opportunities for small businesses. Farmer cooperatives and exporters also benefited from antitrust legislation.

The New Deal Era and Beyond. As the twentieth century progressed, antitrust legislation achieved mixed results. The Norris–LaGuardia Anti-injunction Act of 1932 decisively exempted labor organizations from the antitrust laws. Yet following the early New Deal's unsuccessful experiment with federally authorized cartelization under the National Recovery Administration, antitrust enforcement became more vigorous. Small business benefited from various fair-trade laws. In antitrust cases heard by the Supreme Court under Chief Justice Earl Warren, from 1953 to 1969, the Court favored smaller business as it curtailed many horizontal and vertical mergers. Simultaneously, however, corporate managers created conglomerates of competitively unrelated firms joined together primarily for investment purposes. The Hart–Scott–Rodino Act of 1976 added antitrust provisions that authorized the Justice Department's Antitrust Division to pursue a more proactive policy against mergers that had antitrust implications. The Supreme Court's and the Antitrust Division's embrace of free-market theories during Ronald Reagan's administration in the 1980s, however, turned the Hart–Scott–Rodino Act to the benefit of new forms of financially driven vertical mergers. The Court, moreover, expanded the application of the rule of reason to permit what previously had been treated as clear-cut violations of the antitrust laws. By the 1990s a reaction against the more extreme free-market enthusiasm of the 1980s arose, creating new possibilities for the future of antitrust enforcement.

Bringing antitrust law into the computer age, the Justice Department won a landmark case against the software giant Microsoft in 2000. Microsoft appealed, however, and the final outcome remained uncertain.

[*See also* **American Anti-Boycott Association; Clayton Antitrust Act; Danbury Hatters' Case; Federal Trade Commission; Industrial Policy, Theory and Practice of; Merger Movement; Norris–LaGuardia Act; Northern Securities Case;** *United States v. E. C. Knight*; *and* **Vertical Integration, Economies of Scale, and Firm Size.**]

BIBLIOGRAPHY

Fligstein, Neil. *The Transformation of Corporate Control.* Cambridge, Mass.: Harvard University Press, 1990.

Freyer, Tony. *Regulating Big Business: Antitrust in Great Britain and America, 1880–1990.* Cambridge, U.K.: Cambridge University Press, 1992.

May, James. "Antitrust in the Formative Era: Political and Economic Theory in Constitutional and Antitrust Analysis, 1880–1918." *Ohio State Law Journal* 50 (1989): 257–395.

McCraw, Thomas K. *Prophets of Regulation: Charles Francis Adams, Louis D. Brandeis, James M. Landis, and Alfred E. Kahn.* Cambridge, Mass.: Belknap Press of Harvard University Press, 1984.

Peritz, Rudolph J. R. *Competition Policy in America: History, Rhetoric, Law.* Rev. ed. New York: Oxford University Press, 2000.

Sklar, Martin J. *The Corporate Reconstruction of American Capitalism, 1890–1916: The Market, the Law, and Politics.* Cambridge, U.K.: Cambridge University Press, 1988.

Tony A. Freyer

ANTIUNION LAW FIRMS

Lawyers have long played an important role in the fight against unions. In the nineteenth century they learned how to procure judicial injunctions to break strikes; in the early twentieth century they worked with organizations such as the American Anti-Boycott Association to fight secondary boycotts and the closed shop. But it was not until the post–World War II years that law firms that specialized in resisting unionization arose. Their lawyers learned to exploit aspects of the 1947 Taft–Hartley Act to discourage unionization, decertify unions, and defeat strikes.

An early influence on such firms was the Chicago-based management consulting firm run by Nathan Shefferman: Labor Relations Associates (LRA). With twenty full-time consultants by the 1950s and branch offices in New York City, Detroit, and Chicago, the LRA pioneered the techniques of union resistance and became a training ground for lawyers who went on to found their own antiunion law firms. Among these were Louis Jackson and Robert Lewis, who together founded what became the leading antiunion law firm, Jackson Lewis, in New York City in 1958. By the 1970s a large cohort of such firms had emerged, including Seyfarth Shaw of Chicago, Fisher & Phillips of Atlanta, Littler Mendelson of San Francisco, and Kullman & Lang of New Orleans. Among them, Jackson Lewis was the largest. By 2012 the firm employed more than seven hundred lawyers working in forty-nine branch offices.

Such firms developed the tactics of so-called union avoidance. They contested the scope and content of bargaining units, filed charges of unfair labor practices against unions, developed techniques for enlisting workers in antiunion activism in workplaces that were being organized, and spoke on behalf of employers to their workers. These techniques, combined with changes in the economy after 1973 that hit unionized industries hard, proved effective in helping employers defeat union elections or deny labor contracts in workplaces that had been organized. Rulings by the National Labor Relations Board (NLRB) during the administration of Ronald Reagan made the work of these firms easier. By the end of the twentieth century, they had largely neutralized the NLRB as an effective protector of workers' rights to organize, contributing to the erosion of the private-sector union-membership rate.

[*See also* **American Anti-Boycott Association; Antilabor Mobilization after 1945; Labor Movement, Decline of the; National Labor Relations Board; Repression of Unions;** *and* **Taft–Hartley Act.**]

BIBLIOGRAPHY

Ernst, Daniel R. *Lawyers against Labor: From Individual Rights to Corporate Liberalism.* Urbana: University of Illinois Press, 1995.

Logan, John. "The Union Avoidance Industry in the United States." *British Journal of Industrial Relations* 44, no. 4 (December 2006): 651–675.

Smith, Robert Michael. *From Blackjacks to Briefcases: A History of Commercialized Strikebreaking and Unionbusting in the United States.* Athens, Ohio: Ohio University Press, 2003.

Joseph A. McCartin

APPRENTICED LABOR

Apprenticed labor is work done by young people under contract to an older supervisor, the master, typically for several years. Two types of apprenticeships developed in the United States, each descending from a different English law. The more prominent, craft apprenticeship, descended from the Statute of Artificers of 1563, which set the duration of the contract at seven years and limited entry into various trades. Boys in the colonial period entered craft apprenticeships in order to become relatively low-status tailors or shoemakers, middling-status blacksmiths or carpenters, or highly paid silver- or goldsmiths. Fathers placed boys with master craftsmen whom they knew through family or neighborhood connections. For the first few years, when the boy was young, inexperienced, and physically not as strong as he would become, he performed necessary drudge work. For this he received room and board while living with the master's family. Gradually he was introduced to the "art and mystery" of his master's trade, as many contracts described it. By the end of the "indenture," as contracts were known, he had learned enough to find work as a journeyman. To encourage the young man to remain on the job even after he developed enough skill to work on his own, masters often promised their apprentices a cash payment or set of tools to be awarded at the end of his time.

The other type of apprenticed labor was pauper or orphan apprenticeship. These workers, too, were young people, many of them girls, who labored under a master. But whereas craft apprenticeships primarily aimed to train a young person in a trade, pauper apprenticeships were more of a social-welfare program. Descending from the English Poor Law of 1601, pauper apprenticeships bound poor young people so that they could earn their keep and thus stay off poor relief. Some pauper apprentices were bound to masters by a surviving parent or family member, and others were bound by local overseers of the poor. Pauper apprentices were less likely than craft apprentices to learn a specific trade; pauper boys were more likely to be bound as general farm laborers, and pauper girls were more likely to learn housewifery.

An obvious abuse of the practice of apprenticeship emerged during Reconstruction. In the chaos of the Civil War's aftermath, white landowners attempted to restore black slavery indirectly, by binding children to them as laborers with formal apprenticeship indentures. The goal was less to teach a trade or provide poor relief than to re-create a legally bound labor force. The Freedmen's Bureau thwarted these efforts by applying laws that governed (white) apprenticeship to the newly freed young people.

Both craft apprenticeships and pauper apprenticeships declined in use after the early part of the nineteenth century. The causes of decline are not well documented, but they seem related to the growing feasibility of absconding (especially to the West), the rise of common schools, and the increasing financial ability of even poor families to keep children at home. Later in the nineteenth century, management of industrial craft apprenticeships shifted from employers to unions. There it remains in the twenty-first century, particularly among the building trades.

[*See also* **Apprenticeship Systems; Child Labor; Indentured Labor; Master and Servant Law;** *and* **Worker Training.**]

BIBLIOGRAPHY

Herndon, Ruth Wallis, and John E. Murray, eds. *Children Bound to Labor: The Pauper Apprentice System in Early America.* Ithaca, N.Y.: Cornell University Press, 2009.

Jacoby, Daniel. "The Transformation of Industrial Apprenticeship in the United States." *Journal of Economic History* 51, no. 4 (1991): 887–910.

Rorabaugh, W. J. *The Craft Apprentice: From Franklin to the Machine Age in America.* New York: Oxford University Press, 1986.

John E. Murray

APPRENTICESHIP SYSTEMS

The training of craft workers involves an investment with distinct risks to all involved. Although low-cost trainees may be highly profitable to master craftsmen, unregulated supply can lead to lower wages and the subdivision of work into less-skilled, more-specialized components. Thus the control of apprenticeship systems has been an important point of contention between organized labor and employers.

Apprenticeship was transplanted from Europe to America during the Colonial Era. Europe's guilds stabilized competition by restricting the number of apprentices that masters were allowed to employ and also by enforcing long periods of service under indenture contracts. In the United States, apprenticeship proved difficult to regulate, not only because the nation lacked Europe's guild system, but also because the introduction of new production technologies rapidly restructured the nation's industrial crafts.

In the eighteenth and nineteenth centuries, factory and mass production reduced prospects for learners' stable progression from apprentices to skilled journeymen and then on to independent masters who owned their own enterprises. Increasing capital requirements made it less likely that a journeyman would work his way up to become a factory owner who hired other workers. Mass production also increased demand for factory work that was more specialized and required less training. The length of indentures declined steadily over the nineteenth century, and eventually, formal indentures nearly disappeared.

In the United States, trade unions attempted to monitor and enforce apprenticeship. Though a few unions, especially those in the building trades, succeeded in raising wages and training, the apprenticeship system more generally gave way to on-the-job training for less-skilled jobs and to school-based vocational or professional education. Ultimately, unions' inability to control training institutions affected the shape of America's labor movement: it became more concerned with organizing semiskilled workers along industrial rather than craft lines.

[*See also* **Apprenticed Labor; Artisanal Labor; Deskilling; Indentured Labor; Industrialization and Deindustrialization; Master and Servant Law;** *and* **Worker Training.**]

BIBLIOGRAPHY

Hamilton, Gillian. "The Decline of Apprenticeship in North America: Evidence from Montreal." *Journal of Economic History* 60, no. 3 (2000): 627–664.

Jacoby, Daniel. "The Transformation of Industrial Apprenticeship in the United States." *Journal of Economic History* 51, no. 4 (1991): 887–910.

Rorabaugh, W. J. *The Craft Apprentice: From Franklin to the Machine Age in America.* New York: Oxford University Press, 1986.

Daniel Jacoby

ARNOLD, THURMAN

(1891–1969), important and iconoclastic twentieth-century lawyer who is best known for being a key member of the administration of Franklin D. Roosevelt and later a prominent attorney in Washington, D.C. His father, C. P. Arnold, was a prominent lawyer in Laramie, Wyoming, during its early statehood years. Thurman attended the Princeton University and then Harvard Law School. After a brief time in private practice in Chicago, Arnold returned home to practice law with his father and soon entered politics. He served as mayor of Laramie and as the sole Democratic member of the Wyoming legislature.

Arnold left Wyoming to accept a position as dean of the law school of West Virginia University. Shortly thereafter he joined the faculty of Yale Law School. At Yale he achieved national prominence as a member of the legal realist movement, which emphasized how the law operated to favor powerful interests in society. Arnold wrote numerous books and articles during his academic career. His book about the myths and symbols used by businesspeople and jurists to defend the established U.S. economy, the *Folklore of Capitalism* (1937), became a surprise best seller and brought him national prominence.

In 1938, President Roosevelt appointed Arnold assistant attorney general in charge of the Antitrust Division of the Justice Department, a position in which Arnold received credit for revitalizing antitrust law and restoring the nation's legal commitment to free-market competition. Arnold served for five years, fighting cartels and monopolies in national and international commerce. His controversial cases against both major corporations and labor unions eventually led the president in 1943 to remove him from the Justice Department and to install him instead on the U.S. Court of Appeals for the District of Columbia.

Dissatisfied with his life as a judge, Arnold left the court to found the firm that became known as Arnold & Porter. His original partners were Abe Fortas—who later served as a justice of the Supreme Court—and Paul Porter, each of whom also had served in key positions in the Roosevelt administration. In private practice, Arnold served both the powerful and the oppressed. Arnold and the firm devoted countless hours to representing government workers accused of being Communists during the McCarthy era, as well as major corporations in all areas of the law. Arnold served affluent clients in antitrust, civil liberties, and other litigation matters. The firm steadily grew into one of the major law firms in Washington, D.C.

Late in life, Arnold suffered a series of heart attacks, but he remained active at the firm until his death. He is remembered as a staunch liberal and one of the few lawyers of the twentieth century to make major contributions as a politician, academic, government lawyer, judge, and private practitioner.

[*See also* **Antitrust Legislation.**]

BIBLIOGRAPHY

Arnold, Thurman W. *The Folklore of Capitalism*. New Haven, Conn.: Yale University Press, 1937.

Waller, Spencer Weber. *Thurman Arnold: A Biography*. New York: New York University Press, 2005.

Spencer Weber Waller

ARROW, KENNETH

(1921–), economist and joint winner of the 1972 Nobel Prize in Economics. Every society faces a fundamental problem of allocating scarce resources to productive uses and distributing the resulting product among its members in a way that achieves some degree of consent or legitimacy. This involves two related questions. One is a question of ends: What should be the preferred mix of product and allocation? And the other is a question of means: How should the chosen solution be implemented?

Born in New York City and educated at City College and Columbia University, Kenneth Joseph Arrow achieved preeminence among economists for making fundamental contributions to both questions. Together with Gerard Debreu, he formulated what became the canonical model of a general equilibrium. In the Arrow–Debreu formulation, decentralized competitive processes—those in which no buyer or seller has any influence on the price at which exchanges take place—can attain equilibrium with prices at which demand equals supply in all markets. Every such equilibrium, moreover, satisfies the normative criterion of being a Pareto optimum, at which there is no alternative allocation such that at least one individual is better off and no other individual is worse off.

The Arrow–Debreu model has been taken to be the modern expression of Adam Smith's postulate of the "invisible hand." This, however, involves some misinterpretation of their work. Finding an equilibrium that is Pareto-optimal captures something of Smith's postulate that every market participant is "led by an invisible hand to promote an end which was no part of his intention," that end being society's. But Smith meant something more, not only that the unfettered operation of free commodity markets will promote society's end—meaning that a Pareto-optimal general-equilibrium set of prices exists—but also that society can be led by the market: that is, that a stable solution exists and markets will return to a general-equilibrium set of prices if disturbed. Although proof of the existence of equilibrium has been mostly unproblematic, there exists no general proof of the stability of market equilibrium.

As momentous as Arrow's reconstruction of the theory of the market has been, his even greater claim to fame rests on his impossibility theorem: the proposition that, given a reasonable meaning of "democratic legitimacy," society will fail to reach agreement on the choice question. It is self-evident that the impossibility theorem must take precedence over the Arrow–Debreu model, because the Arrow–Debreu model presupposes a given distribution of individual endowments the legitimacy of which, according to the impossibility theorem, cannot be proved. If it is impossible for a democratic society to agree on a distribution, then it is impossible to state that the society would agree on the allocation coming from the Arrow–Debreu general-equilibrium system.

[*See also* **Economic Theories and Thought.**]

BIBLIOGRAPHY

http://www.nobelprize.org/nobel_prizes/economics/laureates/1972/arrow-autobio.html.

J. Mohan Rao

ARTISANAL LABOR

Artisans were skilled workmen—women rarely performed such work—who turned out everything from clothing and furniture to buildings and jewelry. In Europe, artisans formed a hierarchy of master craftsmen (employers), journeymen (wageworkers), and apprentices (journeymen in training), and the conditions of their crafts were strictly regulated by guilds; in America, guilds never took root, which meant that access to skilled work was democratic and that training was far less formal, typically amounting to learning on the job. The vast panoply of trades broke down into two broad groupings: the "lesser" trades of shoemaking, tailoring, and so on, and the "better trades" of carpentry, printing, and so on, which were harder to learn and paid much better, if barely enough to support a family in comfort.

Two great forces—the division of labor and machines—inexorably cheapened craft skills in the course of the nineteenth century. Entrepreneurial masters, sometimes in partnership with merchant capitalists, exploited the developing mass market for consumer goods by breaking down skills into smaller and smaller specialized tasks. Thus employers divided shoemaking, for example, into cutting leather, sewing the uppers, and attaching the uppers to soles. When the McKay stitching machine was invented in the early 1860s to attach the uppers to the soles, the pace of production quickened, and more and more tasks were divided and subdivided. By the end of the Civil War a journeyman shoemaker, when asked what he did for a living, responded that he was "one sixty-fourth" of a shoemaker. Machines did not uniformly eliminate all skills. Some tradesmen assigned to specialized tasks continued to practice skilled work; printers, for example, yielded running presses to pressmen but continued to perform the skilled job of setting type. In the main, however, the advent of the division of labor and machine-paced production reduced craft workers to semiskilled hands performing repetitive jobs that were easily learned and paid much less.

Craftsmen enjoyed a long tradition of political activism and self-organization. They led the opposition to British rule during the American Revolution, and then, believing that the new government would usher in economic prosperity, they embraced the Constitution. Soon after, individual trades unionized sporadically, and in the 1820s the first citywide trade unions and labor parties appeared. Citywide unions emerged again and again throughout the century, galvanized by the powerful idea that workers were entitled to the "full product of their labor."

Craft unions were fragile. They were brought down by depressions, by disruptive waves of immigrants, and, starting in the 1870s, by stiffer opposition from employers—opposition bolstered by militias and troops that were mobilized to quell chronic labor unrest. In addition, though opportunities for self-advancement contracted, it was still possible for ambitious workers to set up on their own. As a result, labor organization remained fitful and weak until the formation in 1886 of the American Federation of Labor, a loosely organized confederation of skilled craftsmen that hewed to a conservative form of trade unionism.

[*See also* **American Federation of Labor; Apprenticeship Systems; Deskilling; Labor Movements; Labor Organizations, Pre–Civil War;** *and* **Mass Production.**]

BIBLIOGRAPHY

Laurie, Bruce. *Artisans into Workers: Labor in Nineteenth-Century America.* New York: Hill and Wang, 1989.

Wilentz, Sean. *Chants Democratic: New York and the Rise of the American Working Class, 1788–1850.* New York: Oxford University Press, 1984.

Bruce Laurie

ASTOR, JOHN JACOB

(1763–1848), fur trader, real estate developer, and financier. Born in Germany, Astor immigrated to the United States in 1783. A chance shipboard conversation with a fellow passenger familiar with the Pacific Northwest led to his decision to enter the fur trade. Organizing fur-trading expeditions with the Indians of the Northwest, Astor founded several trading posts, including Astoria, Oregon, at the mouth of the Columbia River, the first American settlement west of the Rocky Mountains. In 1808 he established the American Fur Company. The fur trade proved immensely profitable, encompassing China, the United States, and Europe. Known for exchanging liquor for furs, Astor gained an unsavory reputation in some quarters. He invested much of his large fortune in real estate in and around New York City. He also became a financier, joining with Stephen Girard, a Philadelphia banker, during the War of 1812 to raise $16 million for the U.S. Treasury—at a substantial profit to themselves. This episode was later cited by politicians as an example of the business elite's taking advantage of the Treasury in times of crisis.

In contrast to his earlier reputation for sharp dealings and cutthroat trade with the Indians, Astor in his later years became a well-known philanthropist. He contributed $350,000 to found the Astor Library, forerunner of the New York Public Library. At his death he was the richest man in America, with a fortune estimated at $20 million. His wealth founded a family dynasty that would remain prominent through the nineteenth and early twentieth centuries.

[*See also* **Fur Trade.**]

BIBLIOGRAPHY

Haeger, John Denis. *John Jacob Astor: Business and Finance in the Early Republic.* Detroit, Mich.: Wayne State University Press, 1991.

Irving, Washington. *Astoria, or Anecdotes of an Enterprise beyond the Rocky Mountains* (1836). Edited by Richard Dilworth. Boston: Twayne, 1976.

Charles Geisst

AUTOMOTIVE INDUSTRY

Dynamism and uncertainty characterized the early American automotive industry. Its scores of tinkerers and entrepreneurs typically assembled rather than manufactured their products, subcontracting for parts from carriage builders, bicycle manufacturers, and machinists. Most companies catered to wealthy consumers until 1908, when Henry Ford's Model T permanently changed the industry.

Sturdy, powerful, and inexpensive, the Model T combined innovative engineering with revolutionary manufacturing methods to become the first mass-produced car. Ford and his employees introduced economies of scale, creating the world's first assembly line by 1914. That same year, to address the absenteeism and turnover problems of the assembly line, Ford doubled his already competitive wages to $5 a day. As other manufacturers struggled to keep pace, a wave of mergers swept the industry. Before World War I interrupted production, the industry had expanded its operations, boosted production, cut prices, and made important technological advances.

Americans' Growing Automotive Habit. Automobiles pervaded American life in the 1920s, embodying both the tensions and the flash of the era's developing consumer culture. The decade's volatile market caused 60 percent of all auto manufacturers to fail and caused the remainder—based mainly in Detroit, Michigan—to struggle. While Henry Ford solidified his personal control over the Ford Motor Company, Alfred P. Sloan brought professional management, market forecasting, and basic technical research to General Motors (GM). As cheap used cars challenged the Model T in the low-price market, sales of new cars flattened after 1923 at roughly 3.6 million per year. Ford responded by further cutting prices for the Model T, while Sloan introduced the annual model change—an innovation that Ford adopted in 1927 with his Model A.

Though automobile sales slipped even before Wall Street crashed in 1929, the

Depression of the 1930s failed to break America's automotive habit. Cars outnumbered telephones and bathtubs throughout the decade, and if stagnant sales forced GM, Chrysler, and Ford temporarily to halt production in 1932, all three companies—the "Big Three"—again earned profits in 1933, solidifying their dominance as waves of independents went bankrupt. The "Little Five"—Nash, Hudson, Packard, Willys–Overland, and Studebaker—battled insolvency, watching their market share erode over the decade from 25 to 10 percent.

Hefty paychecks had always helped Detroit sustain an open (nonunion) shop, but the Depression divided management and labor. Speedups, slashed wages, and layoffs generated unrest, unionization, strikes, and violence. The National Labor Relations (Wagner) Act of 1935 guaranteed unions the right to organize, precipitating an often brutal struggle between Detroit manufacturers and the United Auto Workers (UAW) of the Congress of Industrial Organizations (CIO). The UAW's forty-four-day sit-down strike against GM in Flint, Michigan, forced the industry to recognize the union in February 1937. Only Ford resisted, though after a strike in which the National Labor Relations Board (NLRB) intervened in 1941, Ford signed the most generous union contract in the industry.

After the United States entered World War II, Detroit became the nation's primary armaments producer. Americans temporarily suppressed their desire for new cars, but the war's end unleashed a flood of pent-up demand. In the five years after 1945, Americans purchased 21.4 million vehicles, nearly doubling the number of cars in the country. While the UAW became better organized under Walter Reuther, Americans transformed their landscape to accommodate their automobiles, constructing a forty-one-thousand-mile interstate highway system and thronging to new suburban devel-

opments. GM, Chrysler, and Ford prospered, but of the Little Five, only Nash survived. Even well-financed and innovative newcomers such as Preston Tucker and Kaiser–Frazer failed to crack the market, going bankrupt by the mid-1950s.

Effects of Fuel Efficiency. New problems plagued the industry in the 1960s. While Ralph Nader publicized what he called the "designed-in dangers" of American cars, new labor tensions emerged, foreign competition grew, and Congress instituted the first national emissions controls. GM's problems were emblematic: averaging under twelve miles per gallon, its line provoked consumer dissatisfaction when the 1973 oil embargo by the Organization of Petroleum Exporting Countries raised gasoline prices by 30 percent. Big-car sales plummeted as small foreign imports penetrated the market (imports had an 18.3 percent market share by 1975), prompting the industry to pledge—and the government to require—improved fuel efficiency.

After clamoring for smaller, fuel-efficient cars in the 1970s, Americans again embraced large cars in the 1980s and 1990s as fuel prices dropped. Foreign manufacturers that had broken into the American market in the 1970s joined Detroit in supplying less-fuel-efficient minivans, pickups, and sport-utility vehicles to eager buyers. State governments competed with one another to attract plants where Toyotas, Nissans, Hondas, and later Hyundais were assembled.

By the early twenty-first century there were once again incentives toward moving away from fossil fuels toward sustainable alternatives. Hybrid vehicles retained an internal combustion engine, while converting kinetic energy into electricity and charging a battery that reduced overall fuel consumption. The hybrid that led the way was the Toyota Prius, which was introduced in the U.S. market in 2000 and of which more than a million were sold in its first eleven years.

In the wake of near bankruptcy in 2008, American manufacturers sought to produce models similar to the Prius. As auto sales plummeted and credit lines closed during the financial crisis, the Big Three sought government assistance to stave off insolvency and the prospect of being forced to lay off perhaps hundreds of thousands of workers. In early 2009 the U.S. Treasury used the Troubled Asset Relief Program to lend $25 billion to Chrysler, GM, and the customer financier the General Motors Acceptance Corporation. A presidential taskforce was formed that restructured the recipients of government funds and implemented a series of recommendations. These included ending production of unprofitable lines such as Pontiac, Saturn, and Hummer and demanding a renewed emphasis upon devising fuel-efficient vehicles. The global automotive industry of the 2000s barely resembled its early predecessor, though throughout its first century the industry had been instrumental in establishing patterns of life, economy, and mobility.

[*See also* **American System of Manufacturing and Interchangeable Parts; Battle of the Overpass (1937); Congress of Industrial Organizations; Consumer Culture; Dodge Revolutionary Union Movement; Energy Crises, Late Twentieth Century; Five-Dollar Day; Flint General Motors Strike; Ford, Henry, and Fordism; General Motors Strike (1945); Highways and Interstates; Industrialization and Deindustrialization; Mass Production; Reuther, Walter; Scientific Management; Sloan, Alfred P.; Toledo Auto-Lite Strike; Treaty of Detroit and Postwar Labor Accord; United Auto Workers;** *and* **Welfare Capitalism.**]

BIBLIOGRAPHY

Flink, James J. *The Automobile Age.* Cambridge, Mass.: MIT Press, 1988.

Flink, James J. *The Car Culture.* Cambridge, Mass.: MIT Press, 1975.

Hounshell, David A. *From the American System to Mass Production, 1800–1932: The Development of Manufacturing Technology in the United States.* Baltimore: Johns Hopkins University Press, 1984.

Ingrassia, Paul J., and Joseph B. White. *Comeback: The Fall and Rise of the American Automobile Industry.* New York: Simon & Schuster, 1994.

Meyer, Stephen, III. *The Five Dollar Day: Labor, Management, and Social Control in the Ford Motor Company, 1908–1921.* Albany: State University of New York Press, 1981.

Nevins, Allan, and Frank Ernest Hill. *Ford.* 3 vols. New York: Charles Scribner's Sons, 1954–1963.

Christopher W. Wells; revised and updated by Patrick M. Dixon

AVIATION INDUSTRY

At the time of the first flight by Wilbur and Orville Wright in 1903, aircraft builders in the United States constituted a disparate group of amateurs. During 1908 and 1909, Orville Wright completed a series of highly publicized flights in America for the U.S. Army; overseas, his brother Wilbur dazzled European royalty and enthusiastic crowds. Against this backdrop of public acclaim and investor interest, the Wrights formed a manufacturing company in 1909; dozens of other entrepreneurs soon did the same. Military contracts represented the core market, and the outbreak of World War I in 1914 brought additional orders from Europe. When the United States declared war in 1917, Congress authorized massive aircraft contracts for domestic production. Although subsequent investigations revealed widespread fraud, the wartime effort provided valuable experience in high-volume production and the manufacture of myriad basic components such as engines, propellers, magnetos, and instrumentation.

During the 1920s and 1930s, manufacturers successfully incorporated numerous technological innovations developed by the National Advisory Committee for Aeronautics. The military services also carried on practical research, and new curricula in aeroengineering at major universities contributed to an expanding population of trained engineers. Trade associations and professional societies appeared. Government regulatory agencies, such as the Civil Aeronautics Authority (1938) and the later Federal Aviation Administration (1958), helped stabilize the industry, thereby encouraging airlines and private pilots alike to order new aircraft. Douglas Aircraft Company launched the historic DC-3 airliner in 1935, and builders of light planes for private pilots delivered classic designs like the two-seat Piper Cub and Beechcraft's twin-engine models for executive travel.

The success of the American aviation industry during the interwar years rested on a mix of corporate innovation, federal research and development, and the contribution of émigrés from Europe such as Igor Sikorsky (flying boats and helicopters), Theodore von Kármán (theorist and educator), and others in both the private and public sectors. A late 1930s wave of orders from European air forces, accelerated after 1941 by the Lend–Lease program, had a significant impact on the aviation industry's record production during World War II, during which 300,000 aircraft were produced. Development of planes like the complex Boeing B-29 bomber rested on sophisticated management and production procedures, including the coordination of thousands of suppliers. At the same time, the introduction of jet-propulsion engines and aircraft by Britain and Germany proved crucial

in subsequent American progress, as did other German developments.

After 1945, Cold War antagonisms intensified the wartime concentration of aviation industries in the Northeast and along the Pacific coast—including the Seattle-based Boeing Company—although diversification in the South and Middle West occurred as well. Electronics became a major component of both civil and military aircraft, increasing their costs. Postwar prosperity and business expansion created a strong demand for airliners, and vast production resources gave U.S. manufacturers the lead in global sales. During the 1960s, American jet transports dominated the world market. The light-plane industry also increased dramatically, turning out 18,000 planes in the record year 1978, compared to 240 civil transports and 1,000 military aircraft. During the 1990s, despite financial difficulties and the end of the Cold War, manufacturers continued to produce annually 900 light planes, 500 transports, and 700 military planes. Exports remained crucial to the industry, and multinational agreements proliferated. Although American manufacturers led the world, corporate mergers reduced the number of domestic firms.

Meanwhile, sales of airliners made in the United States dominated the world market, much to the chagrin of European manufacturers. Eventually the Europeans formed a special consortium, called Airbus Industrie, in order to compete with U.S. giants like Boeing and Douglas Aircraft. The first Airbus transport, a widebody twin jet called the A300, entered service in 1974. A complete family of Airbus models followed, competing head-to-head with McDonnell Douglas and Boeing. Aggressive sales and marketing accelerated deliveries of Airbus transports. Douglas, which had been the world's number-two sales leader (Boeing dominated as number one), fell behind Airbus in 1983. By 2005, Airbus sales had also outstripped those of Boeing, leading to a tumultuous rivalry for global domination. In time, Airbus became a division of a larger conglomerate, the European Aeronautic Defence and Space company (EADS), which continued to develop Europe's independence from American manufacturers.

[*See also* **Airplanes and Air Transport; Technology;** *and* **Transportation Revolution.**]

BIBLIOGRAPHY

Bilstein, Roger E. *The American Aerospace Industry: From Workshop to Global Enterprise.* New York: Twayne, 1996.

Newhouse, John. *The Sporty Game.* New York: Alfred A. Knopf, 1982.

Vander Meulen, Jacob A. *The Politics of Aircraft: Building an American Military Industry.* Lawrence: University Press of Kansas, 1992.

Roger E. Bilstein

B

BANK OF AMERICA

The Bank of America was opened in San Francisco. A. P. Giannini, the son of Italian peasants who immigrated to San Jose, California, to benefit from the gold rush, founded the first branch of the Bank of Italy, later rebranded the Bank of America, in 1904. A self-made man, Giannini built a financial empire with a populist bent. Bank of America pioneered mass advertising at a time when other banks barely deigned to loan money to the masses. Giannini's vision of a national bank, with branches in every town, ran him afoul of regulators, not to mention anti-Catholics and Wall Street bankers. Though he did not hold a controlling interest in the bank, Giannini's magnetic personality allowed him to lead stockholder campaigns against any opposition to his leadership. He plied the same skills in politics, where he became an important ally of James Phelan, a mayor of San Francisco and later a U.S. senator, and Franklin D. Roosevelt, though he had an acrimonious split with Roosevelt over regulatory policy. In 1945, Giannini resigned from his position as chairman of the board; that same year the Bank of America became the world's largest privately owned bank.

The Bank of America's early years were pivotal in economic history because of its liberal lending policies and its role in promoting the growth of California. Eager to improve its public image during the Great Depression, Bank of America financed construction of the Golden Gate Bridge. It lent generously to agriculture and the movie industry; Giannini personally gave Walt Disney start-up money. Most important, it pioneered installment plans for consumer goods, laying the foundation for modern consumer credit.

[*See also* **Consumer Credit and Credit Cards.**]

BIBLIOGRAPHY

Bonadio, Felice A. *A. P. Giannini: Banker of America.* Berkeley: University of California Press, 1994.

Nash, Gerald D. *A. P. Giannini and the Bank of America.* Norman: University of Oklahoma Press, 1992.

Christopher England

BANK OF THE UNITED STATES, FIRST AND SECOND

Between 1791 and 1811 and again from 1816 to 1836, the U.S. government created and operated a national bank that by most historical assessments met the nation's financial needs effectively. But the banks' size and scope led to political controversy.

The First Bank of the United States (BUS) served the economic policies of Alexander Hamilton, the nation's first secretary of the treasury. In his "Report on a National Bank" (1790), Hamilton argued that the nation needed a federally chartered bank to establish the public credit, attract foreign investment, serve as an administrative arm of the federal treasury, and draw the support of wealthier citizens to the new government. Despite the opposition of Thomas Jefferson, President George Washington signed the bill authorizing a national bank after it passed both houses of Congress by solid majorities. The U.S. government held one fifth of the $10 million of stock offered; individuals purchased the remaining four fifths. The BUS served as the fiscal agent for the U.S. Trea-

sury: it held federal funds, transferred them throughout the United States, and disbursed these funds to pay interest and principal on the national debt. Its banknotes, which functioned much like today's paper currency, acted as legal tender in payment of U.S. debts. This gave the BUS unusual power, for it enjoyed access to government receipts, and it could and did establish branches throughout the country.

Although the First Bank of the United States fulfilled Hamilton's intentions, a bill to recharter the BUS was tabled in 1811 by a one-vote margin in both houses of Congress. This reaction arose largely because the Federalist Party had established the BUS and Federalists served as directors and officers of the bank and its branches. For many Jeffersonian Republicans, however, the question transcended politics; they were wary of the bank's inordinate power over state and local economic development.

The Second Bank of the United States was created by Congress in 1816 on much the same terms that had governed the first, although the law authorizing its establishment raised its capitalization to $35 million and required the BUS to pay a bonus of $1.5 million to the federal government. After a rocky start, the Second BUS met the needs of the government and its stockholders while promoting the nation's economic development. Nicholas Biddle (1786–1844), a Philadelphia financier who assumed the bank presidency in 1823, deserved credit for much of this success.

But again the BUS became entangled in national politics. In 1829, President Andrew Jackson declared his opposition to the BUS. Noting that it was by far the largest bank in the nation, he accused the BUS of using monopoly power and exclusive privileges to deny common citizens access to credit and economic opportunity. Angered by Jackson's veto of the bill to recharter the bank in 1832, Biddle used the bank's power to seek support in Congress and the press. Jackson retaliated by removing federal deposits from the BUS, which he had begun to call "the Monster." With compromise no longer possible, the federal charter of the BUS lapsed in 1836.

[*See also* **Federal Reserve System; Financial and Banking Promotion and Regulation; Hamilton, Alexander, and Economic Development;** *and* **Monetary Policy, Federal.**]

BIBLIOGRAPHY

Hammond, Bray. *Banks and Politics in America from the Revolution to the Civil War.* Princeton, N.J.: Princeton University Press, 1957.

Holdsworth, John Thom, and Davis R. Dewey. *The First and Second Banks of the United States.* 61st Cong., 2d sess., U.S. Senate, Doc. 571. Washington, D.C.: Government Printing Office, 1910.

Diane Lindstrom

BARBED WIRE

In 1873, Joseph Glidden, a farmer from De Kalb, Illinois, designed a form of "armored fencing" that was highly effective and could be inexpensively produced: ultimately his design launched a transformation of the rural landscape. The Great Plains farmers of the nineteenth century had long been wrangling with the challenge of fencing the West. They had neither the Northeast's abundance of stone that could be used to create walls nor the South's readily available timber. Hedgerows were a possibility, but they could take up to three years to grow, and they attracted vermin.

The early users of barbed wire were agriculturalists who sought to protect their crops from the roaming cattle of the open range. Many cattle herders objected, considering the wire cruel and unnatural, and were concerned about the wounds it inflicted upon animals. In 1874 a hundred pounds of barbed wire sold for $20. In 1897 the same length cost as little as $1.80. As the open range disappeared in the 1880s and 1890s and the West became more crowded, barbed wire made possible the mass enclosure of public lands. By this point it was used as often by cattlemen seeking to protect land for grazing as by agriculturalists.

In the twentieth century the uses of barbed wire diversified considerably: vicious heavy-duty forms were developed for warfare, and later forms were developed to keep people either in or out of facilities such as penitentiaries and power stations.

[*See also* **Agriculture** *and* **Public Land Policy.**]

BIBLIOGRAPHY

McCallum, Henry D., and Frances T. McCallum. *The Wire That Fenced the West.* Norman: University of Oklahoma Press, 1965.

Webb, Walter Prescott. *The Great Plains.* New York: Grosset & Dunlap, 1931.

Patrick M. Dixon

BATTLE OF THE OVERPASS (1937)

The Battle of the Overpass was a violent clash between Ford Motor Company servicemen and United Auto Workers (UAW) organizers at Ford's River Rouge factory in Dearborn, Michigan. On 26 May 1937, as part of an early public effort to unionize Ford, UAW organizers gathered at the Rouge to distribute leaflets at the factory's entrances. At the Miller Road overpass leading to the Rouge's main entrance, members of Ford's notorious service department confronted organizers. After demanding their immediate dispersal, the servicemen set upon the UAW leaders Walter Reuther and Richard Frankensteen, beating the two brutally and methodically. Others suffered a similar fate; in all, eighteen sustained injuries, nearly half of them members of the UAW Women's Auxiliary.

Photographers and news reporters witnessed the attacks, and though servicemen attempted to destroy cameras and film, news of what was dubbed the "Battle of the Overpass" spread quickly. The *Detroit News* photographer James E. Kilpatrick captured the clash in a series of photographs that served as a visual representation of Ford's brutality and that were so influential that they inspired the creation of the Pulitzer Prize for Photography, first awarded in 1942. News of the Battle of the Overpass transformed public perceptions of Ford and led to widespread condemnation.

Though the Battle of the Overpass initially restrained the UAW's effort to unionize Ford, the conflict exposed Ford's viciousness and strengthened the union's resolve. During a revitalized effort to unionize Ford in 1940, the Battle of the Overpass became a rallying call, and in 1941 the UAW succeeded in gaining union recognition from Ford—an accomplishment that was unthinkable at the time of the Battle of the Overpass.

[*See also* **Automotive Industry; Ford, Henry, and Fordism;** *and* **United Auto Workers.**]

BIBLIOGRAPHY

Lichtenstein, Nelson. *The Most Dangerous Man in Detroit: Walter Reuther and the Fate of American Labor.* New York: Basic Books, 1995.
Norwood, Stephen H. *Strikebreaking and Intimidation: Mercenaries and Masculinity in Twentieth-Century America.* Chapel Hill: University of North Carolina Press, 2002.

Zach Sell

BEHAVIORAL ECONOMICS

Behavioral economists question the assumptions regarding the basis and process of human decision making and behavior that underpin neoclassical economic models. In reaction to the interpretive and predictive shortcomings of models based on the assumption of hyper-rational individuals, behavioral economists use findings from other disciplines, including psychology and sociology, to show how economic actors use rules of thumb and intuition rather than optimal prediction. Using laboratory experiments and surveys, they have shown the behavioral importance of salience and framing, as well as of such concepts as loss aversion, anchoring, over- and underconfidence in the face of uncertainty, inertia, time inconsistency, and fairness.

The rise of behavioral economics since the late twentieth century represents in part a re-emergence of concepts that were central to early Keynesian analysis—for example, money illusion, animal spirits, and "useful mental habits." Behavioral economics is a direct reaction to the shortcomings of the standard models in explaining important phenomena: in labor markets, such phenomena as strikes; in financial markets, such phenomena as booms, bubbles, and crises; and in macroeconomics, such phenomena as unemployment.

Behavioral economics has been controversial in economics because of its assault on the dominant microeconomic model. The field has been attacked because of its implication that people do not always act in their own interest, as well as because the flexibility of responses and preferences means that unique or stable outcomes cannot be predicted, thus limiting generalized application. Orthodox critics charge that the field is little more than a collection of anomalies and critiques rather than a coherent alternative theory of behavior. Heterodox critics observe that it remains rooted in the methodological individualist tradition. Its unit of interpretation remains the individual; coordination and conflict beyond the predictions of the traditional model may emerge, but only from individual behavior rather than aggregate formations.

Behavioral economics has logged impressive successes in demonstrating the flaws in the dominant optimization-based economic theory. Its future significance depends on its ability to supplant existing theory with an alternative that offers parsimonious explanations, accurate predictions, and guidance for research and policy.

[*See also* **Economic Theories and Thought** *and* **Rational-Choice Theory.**]

BIBLIOGRAPHY

Akerlof, George A., and Robert J. Shiller. *Animal Spirits: How Human Psychology Drives the Economy, and Why It Matters for Global Capitalism.* Princeton, N.J.: Princeton University Press, 2009.

Ariely, Dan. *Predictably Irrational: The Hidden Forces That Shape Our Decisions.* New York: Harper, 2008.

Pech, Wesley, and Marcelo Milan. "Behavioral Economics and the Economics of Keynes." *Journal of Socio-Economics* 38, no. 6 (2009): 891–902.

Michael Ash

BERLE, ADOLF, AND GARDINER MEANS AND THE MODERN CORPORATION

By the time that Adolf Augustus Berle Jr., a lawyer, and Gardiner C. Means, an economist, published their landmark book, *The Modern Corporation and Private Property* (*TMCPP*), in 1932, two of the three central regulatory issues of the large corporation had been largely resolved. The "giant corporation" became a threatening presence on the American economic and political landscape during the latter part of the nineteenth century; by the turn of the twentieth century, following massive consolidation of industrial enterprises during the great merger wave of 1897–1904, it was a central fixture.

Commentators and policy makers at the time worried about three issues related to the giant corporation's advent: first, its size and potential for monopolizing markets and entire industries; second, its faceless personality and potential for corrupting democratic political processes and institutions; and third, its separation of ownership from control and potential for enabling managerial agents to misappropriate a large share of the nation's economic resources. From 1890 onward, Congress, state legislatures, and the courts had addressed the first of these issues through a combination of antitrust legislation and utility regulations. Congress and the states had addressed the second of these issues through legislation that precluded corporations from participating in electoral processes—in particular, forbidding campaign spending by corporations. (This legislation has more recently been overturned in effect.) The third issue, however, was still without regulatory solution when the Great Depression hit. And it was in that context that Berle and Means's timely analysis became a centerpiece of American political economic theory and policy.

TMCPP's **Premises and Arguments.** The central premise of *TMCPP* is that capitalism had traditionally depended on the control of property owners over their wealth: owners would allocate their wealth and oversee it to ensure that their expectations were being met. This "unity of property ownership" is destroyed when ownership is separated from control, as it is in large, publicly traded firms "whereby the wealth of innumerable individuals has been concentrated into huge aggregates and whereby control over this wealth has been surrendered to a unified direction" (Berle, 1932, p. 2). The "new relationships between the owners on the one hand and control on the other" (Berle, 1932, p. 7) must be examined; such an examination, then, shapes the book.

The book has three parts. The first is a study of the two hundred largest, publicly traded industrial and commercial firms. Berle and Means analyzed the role and place of the large corporation in the U.S. economy: they found that these corporations already owned roughly half of the corporate industrial and commercial wealth in the United States and that the trend was toward ever-growing concentration. They projected that without intervention, concentration levels might reach 70 percent by the 1950s. This concentration of industrial power seemed dangerous if the managers were not accountable to the traditional expectations of property ownership.

Accordingly, Berle and Means consider accountability. To do so, they analyzed share ownership among these two hundred firms. As firms grew, the numbers of shareholders tended to grow as well: the ownership of American Telephone and Telegraph (AT&T), for instance, concentrated in the hands of 10,000 shareholders in 1900, had by 1931 been dispersed among more than 642,000 shareholders, almost all of whom were passive in the management of AT&T's affairs. Large numbers of widely dispersed shareowners have no cheap and quick means for acting collectively. By default, then, boards of directors, elected by the shareholders, and managers, whom the directors have chosen to run the firm day to day, are in control. Boards of directors of the two hundred largest firms, which nominally exercised control, tended to represent either the interests of unusually powerful shareholders (often,

"minority control") or, more often, the interests of managers on whom the directors relied for information, strategic insight, proper execution of plans, and so on. The result was an estrangement of control from ownership, which in turn threatened lower returns on investor capital than might have been expected under unified share ownership and strategic direction. This risk was particularly strong when top managers and inside directors used their powers to "perpetuate" their control—for instance, by securing the election of friendly directors—and then adopted policies that in effect misallocated or misappropriated corporate resources.

In the absence of norms, economic incentives, and regulative rules to reinforce shareholders' interests, shareholder dispersion, along with the growing concentration of wealth, in these firms posed a serious potential threat to the economy. The second part of *TMCPP*, then, is an analysis of the legal checks and balances on control: the extent to which courts limit "control" from asserting its will over the interests of the shareholders. The third part of the book is an analysis of the securities markets and the extent to which markets allow investors to exercise oversight of publicly traded firms through the buying and selling of their shares.

Critiques of *TMCPP*. Since its publication, *TMCPP* has been subjected to considerable critique. Praised for contributions that it did not make—for instance, it is wrongly said to have been the first to recognize the separation of ownership from control in large, publicly traded firms—it has also been criticized for moral and policy positions that it did not take. Indeed, many critics, in particular from the political right, have relied as much on the folklore surrounding Berle, the guiding force behind *TMCPP*, as on what he actually wrote in the book. Berle, for his part, was an iconoclast, ranging along the political spectrum from left to right. Economists have mainly focused their critique on the statistical study of the two hundred largest publicly traded firms. Some economists fault Berle and Means for not addressing what has come to be termed the "[financial] agency" problem: namely, the difficulty of getting managers to carry out the articulated policies of the board of directors. The agency problem, however, is secondary to the estrangement problem that *TMCPP* addresses: that is, the point of *TMCPP*'s study was to suggest the extent and economic implications of shareholding dispersion in the context of industrial concentration. Herbert Simon began elaborating on the problems of managerial agency in the 1940s, and a series of financial economists addressed it beginning in the 1960s.

In any case, those critics have lost sight of the implications of the book's second and third parts, in which Berle sketched out two alternative models for corporate regulation: a law-centered model that followed "trust" principles, and an economic-centered model that followed "market" principles. Under the trust model, shareholders would be treated as dependents (that is, trust beneficiaries), and the corporate control agents (directors, managers) would be treated as their trustees or guardians, obligated to hold the shareholders' interests paramount under the law. Notwithstanding ambiguous statutory language that seemed to give "control" absolute powers, the courts, Berle argued, were empowered to preserve the equitable interests of the dependent beneficiaries in trusts and so could intervene against control to protect shareholder rights.

Under the market model, in contrast, shareholders were regarded as independent, self-reliant actors, and the central concern was to render the stock markets reliable so that investors could act rationally. In the book's analysis, regulations must ensure that investors have adequate information for rational decisions, and they must correct market imperfections such as liquidity constraints, information asymmetries such as insider trading, and market and accounting manipulations that lead to short-term windfalls (that is, before the manipulation can be discovered). In short, according to Berle, the third part of *TMCPP* "became the foundation" (Berle, 1967, p. 253) for congressional enactment of the Securities Exchange Act of 1934 and other legislation.

Since the New Deal, U.S. corporate regulation in general—that is, not only with regard to financial investors, but also with regard to workers, consumers, and other corporate interests—has followed the twofold path that *TMCPP* outlines, alternating between trust (legal) and contract (market) models.

[*See also* **Antitrust Legislation; Capitalism; Economic Theories and Thought; Merger Movement; New Deal Corporate Regulation;** *and* **Securities and Exchange Commission.**]

BIBLIOGRAPHY

Berle, Adolf A., Jr. "The Equitable Distribution of Ownership." In *Business Management as a Human Enterprise*. New York: Bureau of Personnel Administration, 1930.

Berle, Adolf A., Jr., and Gardiner C. Means. *The Modern Corporation and Private Property*. New York: Macmillan, 1932.

Berle, Adolf A., Jr., and Gardiner C. Means. *The Modern Corporation and Private Property*. Rev. ed. New York: Harcourt, Brace and World, 1967.

Kaufman, Allen, and Lawrence S. Zacharias. "From Trust to Contract: The Legal Language of Managerial Ideology, 1920–1980." *Business History Review* 66 (1992): 523–572.

Kirkendall, Richard S., and Adolf A. Berle, Jr. "Student of the Corporation 1917–1932." *Business History Review* 35 (1961): 43–58.

Schwarz, Jordan A. *Liberal: Adolf A. Berle and the Vision of an American Era*. New York: Free Press, 1987.

Stigler, George J., and Claire Friedland. "The Literature of Economics: The Case of Berle and Means." *Journal of Law and Economics* 26 (1983): 237–268.

Lawrence S. Zacharias

BIEMILLER, ANDREW

(1906–1982), labor leader and lobbyist. Born in Sandusky, Ohio, on 23 July 1906, Andrew John Biemiller was the first legislative director of the American Federation of Labor and Congress of Industrial Organizations (AFL-CIO), a position he held from 1956 until 1978. Working closely with the AFL-CIO's president, George Meany, on behalf of what he termed "the people's lobby," Biemiller was a resourceful insider on Capitol Hill who worked for labor and social legislation. He is especially identified with civil rights.

By the time he was a lobbyist, Biemiller was a veteran of union and electoral politics. In 1932 he and his wife, Hannah Perot Morris, moved from Philadelphia to Milwaukee, Wisconsin; a Socialist, he became a Socialist-Progressive, then a Democrat. He served on the executive board of the Milwaukee Federated Trades Council and the Wisconsin State Federation of Labor, and in 1936 he was elected to the Wisconsin state assembly. In 1941 he was appointed to the War Production Board, but he left in 1944 when he was elected to the U.S. House of Representatives; he lost office in 1946, was reelected in 1948, then lost in 1950 and 1952. After a stint at the U.S. Department of the Interior (1951–1952), he became a lobbyist for the AFL in 1952.

Biemiller considered feminism a middle-class movement, not one for working women; thus he supported protective labor legislation and for a long period opposed the Equal Rights Amendment. In contrast, he believed strongly in civil rights, which he considered more germane to union and worker interests, and he wrote a breakthrough civil rights plank introduced by Hubert Humphrey at the 1948 Democratic National Convention. In the 1960s as a member of the Leadership Conference on Civil Rights, he pushed hard for new laws and successfully added an equal-employment provision to the Civil Rights Act of 1964.

[*See also* **American Federation of Labor and Congress of Industrial Organizations; Labor's Role in Politics;** *and* **Title VII.**]

BIBLIOGRAPHY

Dark, Taylor E. *The Unions and the Democrats: An Enduring Alliance.* Updated ed. Ithaca, N.Y.: ILR Press, 2001.
Deslippe, Dennis A. *Rights, Not Roses: Unions and the Rise of Working-Class Feminism, 1945–80.* Urbana: University of Illinois Press, 2000.
Norman, Michael. "Andrew J. Biemiller Dies at 75; Was A.F.L.-C.I.O.'s Top Lobbyist." *New York Times,* 4 April 1982, p. 36.

Jacquelyn Southern

BIOTECHNOLOGY INDUSTRY

Robert Swanson and Herbert Boyer founded the Genentech Corporation in South San Francisco, California, in April 1976, giving birth to the biotechnology industry. In a broad sense, biotechnology has a long history. People have modified plants and animals for millennia by selective breeding to generate better agricultural plants and more productive livestock. Makers of wine, beer, and cheese have long relied on fermentation with microorganisms. However, the term "biotechnology" in the late twentieth century came to denote procedures involving genetic engineering and the tools of molecular biology. Genetic engineering became possible in 1973 when Stanley Cohen at Stanford University and Herbert Boyer at the University of California, San Francisco, accomplished the first recombinant DNA experiment. Joining together two independent pieces of DNA, they introduced that hybrid DNA molecule into an *E. coli* bacterium, where the DNA was inherited as part of the bacterium's genetic material. Genes, discrete pieces of DNA that commonly code for specific proteins, could now be manipulated. The next important discovery showed that it was possible to put a human gene in bacteria and then to express the protein that the gene encoded. This feat was accomplished when Genentech expressed human somatostatin protein in bacteria in 1977. Genentech then cloned the gene for human insulin into bacteria and, in 1982, marketed human insulin purified from the genetically engineered bacteria as the first drug based on recombinant DNA technology.

By the early 1980s, numerous biotechnology companies, including Biogen, Cetus, Genex, and Amgen, had appeared. Biotechnology gave rise to an independent industry, while at the same time contributing to other, more established industries—pharmaceutical, agricultural, and medical—and to the manufacture of various industrial and consumer goods, such as oil-eating bacteria and enzymes that are high-grade detergents. The major pharmaceutical companies all purchased biotechnology companies in the 1980s and 1990s and established multibillion-dollar research-and-development divisions using the tools of biotechnology. The resulting pharmaceutical products included human growth hormone (somatropin), erythropoietin (EPO), tissue plasminogen activator (tPA), interferon-alpha (IFN-α), GM-CSF (granulocyte–macrophage colony-stimulating factor), the hepatitis B vaccine, and Herceptin (trastuzumab), as well as human insulin.

Major agribusiness companies used biotechnology to engineer better crops. The first genetically modified crop was a virus-resistant tobacco plant, produced in 1983. The first genetically modified whole food marketed to consumers was the rot-resistant Flavr-Savr tomato, introduced in 1994. Many other genetically modified plants—cotton, soybeans, and corn, among others—were made in the 1980s and 1990s. Most were resistant to viruses, insects, or herbicides. Genetically modified foods sometimes led to controversy, particularly in Europe, where some people feared that the genetic modification might be hazardous to human beings, plants, or animals. However, most short-term field trials of such foods showed them safe for both human beings and the environment.

Biotechnology, particularly in the pharmaceutical industry, could be very expensive. To bring a product to market sometimes cost upward of $100 million and ten years of effort. Approximately nine out of ten biotechnology products failed commercially because of patent, production, efficacy, or side-effect problems.

The future of the industry at the beginning of the twenty-first century looked promising, but advances came slowly. Three major scientific developments—the cloning of Dolly the lamb in Scotland (1996), the first successful gene-therapy trials (2000), and the complete mapping of the human genome (2003)—generated particular excitement. The cloning of a lamb by Ian Wilmut and colleagues was important less because of the cloning per se than because the technology paved the way for more rapid and extensive transgenic livestock development. Gene therapy—the process of introducing a gene into a human being to remedy a genetic disease—offered hope to people suffering from such diseases as hemophilia, cystic fibrosis, and diabetes. The mapping of the full human-genome sequence, the molecular blueprint for human life, was simultaneously completed by the National Institutes of Health Human Genome Project and the biotechnology company Celera Genomics. Although the mapping of the human genome seemed unlikely to lead to immediate medical breakthroughs, it promised substantially to influence biotechnology and medicine for many years to come.

As the twenty-first century has progressed, both new commercial opportunities for profitable use of advances in biotechnology and political resistance to aspects of such advances have remained much in evidence. Resistance has been especially strong to research using human embryonic stem cells to develop treatments for degenerative diseases. Opposition to such research by the Roman Catholic Church and many evangelical Protestants has resulted in a series of executive and legislative restrictions on government subsidization of such research. Resistance to the cultivation of genetically modified crops has remained potent, perhaps less so in the United States than in Europe, but it has achieved far less political purchase than resistance to stem-cell research has. Private, for-profit enterprises have sought to use the findings of the Human Genome Project to sell their services to prospective consumers willing to pay high fees in order to learn more about their ancestry or to determine whether they have inherited genes that favor specific debilitating or fatal diseases. Despite resistance to aspects of biotechnological development and the dubious practices of several for-profit genetic-testing companies, research and advances in the field are likely to continue.

[*See also* **Agriculture,** *subentry on* **Since 1920; Pharmaceutical Industry;** *and* **Technology.**]

BIBLIOGRAPHY

Bud, Robert. *The Uses of Life: A History of Biotechnology.* Cambridge, U.K.: Cambridge University Press, 1993.

Crotty, Shane. *Ahead of the Curve: David Baltimore's Life in Science.* Berkeley: University of California Press, 2001.

Robbins-Roth, Cynthia. *From Alchemy to IPO: The Business of Biotechnology.* Cambridge, Mass.: Perseus, 2000.

Watson, James D., Richard M. Myers, Amy A. Caudy, and Jan A. Witkowski. *Recombinant DNA: Genes and Genomes—A Short Course.* 3d ed. New York: W. H. Freeman, 2007.

Shane Crotty

BISBEE STRIKE AND DEPORTATION

By 1917, Bisbee, Arizona, situated in southern Arizona close to the Mexican border, had been transformed from a smoke-filled copper-mining camp of shacks and adobe huts into a site for modern industry. The town's largest copper company, Phelps Dodge, had underwritten modernization by installing electricity, gas, water, and telephone service as Bisbee's growing middle class financed the construction of schools, churches, libraries, and hospitals. Its leading citizens also vigorously defended white racial dominance and privileges, as did many white miners, who belonged to the American Federation of Labor (AFL).

By late 1916, growing numbers of immigrant and Mexican workers began to demand recognition from the AFL and Bisbee's copper companies. Neither the employers nor the AFL offered concessions to immigrant and Mexican miners, however, and when the radical Industrial Workers of the World (IWW, or Wobblies) came to town in 1917, it quickly gained the allegiance of a large majority of the miners. In late June the IWW-affiliated Metal Mine Workers Industrial Union No. 800 held its first formal meeting, and within days the miners walked off the job. By early July more than twenty-five thousand miners across the region had quit work and demanded wage increases, shorter hours, union recognition, an end to employer discrimination against union members and Mexicans, and the abolition of the dual-wage system that exploited Mexican miners, ensuring their subordination not only to employers but also to white workers.

On the morning of 12 July 1917, Bisbee's newspapers carried a notice that vagrants, strangers, and disturbers of the peace would be arrested by a sheriff's posse of twelve hundred men; the notice was also posted on fences and railings throughout the town. Early that day approximately twenty-two hundred vigilantes—organized and led by Bisbee's sheriff, Harry Wheeler, and armed with guns, clubs, and lists of the names of strikers and their leaders—fanned out across Bisbee. The posse rounded up nearly two thousand men and marched them to the local baseball field. At midday, Wheeler's men forced at gunpoint more than twelve hundred of the detainees onto railroad boxcars that carried them some two hundred miles east to Columbus, New Mexico, where they were abandoned in the desert. Sheriff Wheeler justified the deportation by insisting that the deportees were Mexican revolutionaries who had cached weapons in nearby mountains. His justification shifted when it emerged that only a small minority of the deportees were of Mexican ancestry. Instead local enemies of the IWW alleged German and Austrian influence among the miners—many of whom had emigrated from the Austro-Hungarian Empire—intimating that foreign-born miners planned to weaken the United States in the ongoing war against Germany and Austria. Indeed, months after the deportation, the Phelps Dodge chief Walter Douglas confidently concluded that the strike had been the work of Austrians.

Civil libertarians, however, condemned the action in Bisbee as a violation of fundamental constitutional rights, and the administration of Woodrow Wilson, noting that many of the deportees were U.S. citizens by birth or naturalization, announced its refusal to tolerate vigilantism. A presidential committee created to investigate the Bisbee deportation recommended that its organizers be indicted and tried for illegally detaining and deporting U.S. citizens. Local juries, however, declined to convict respected citizens who took action against unpatriotic and un-American strikers who intended to disrupt essential copper production during wartime.

[*See also* **Industrial Workers of the World; Mining Industry;** *and* **Racism.**]

BIBLIOGRAPHY

Benton-Cohen, Katherine. *Borderline Americans: Racial Division and Labor War in the Arizona Borderlands.* Cambridge, Mass.: Harvard University Press, 2009.

Byrkit, James W. *Forging the Copper Collar: Arizona's Labor-Management War of 1901–1921.* Tucson: University of Arizona Press, 1982.

Dubofsky, Melvyn. *We Shall Be All: A History of the Industrial Workers of the World.* 2d ed. Urbana: University of Illinois Press, 1988.

Gerald Ronning

BRACEROS

Braceros, whose name comes from the Spanish word *brazo*, or "arm," were single Mexican males who were recruited and brought north to the United States as temporary workers under a government-sponsored labor-importation arrangement. The laws and bilateral diplomatic agreements governing their employment were popularly known as the "bracero program." Most braceros were between the ages of eighteen and fifty. Four of ten were illiterate. They came from small, rural villages and communities in northern Mexico. The number of braceros rose from 4,203 in 1942 to 49,454 in 1945, 192,095 in 1951, and 445,197 in 1956, the peak year of their employment. Eventually more than 4 million braceros were housed in isolated barracks, sent from field to field, and deported if they spoke up. Remittances formed a key element sustaining the Mexican economy.

The bracero program emerged from the labor shortages of World War II. Once institutionalized, the program insulated growers from competing for labor in the domestic labor market. Government agencies failed to ensure minimal working standards. President Harry S. Truman's Commission on Migratory Labor reported massive abuses, lax enforcement, and deplorable living and working conditions. Trade unions and liberal organizations condemned the bracero program as a national scandal. On 31 December 1964, Congress failed to renew the bracero program, thereby removing the single most important impediment to farm labor organizing. Cesar Chavez and the United Farm Workers seized the opportunity to launch a grape strike and boycott that in the summer of 1970 won contracts with the entire California table-grape industry.

[*See also* **Agricultural Workers; Immigration; Labor Markets;** *and* **Migratory Labor and Migrant Workers.**]

BIBLIOGRAPHY

Cohn, Deborah. *Braceros: Migrant Citizens and Transnational Subjects in the Postwar United States and Mexico.* Chapel Hill: University of North Carolina Press, 2011.

García y Griego, Manuel. "The Importation of Mexican Contract Laborers to the United States, 1942–1964." In *Between Two Worlds: Mexican Immigrants in the United States,* edited by David G. Gutiérrez, pp. 45–85. Wilmington, Del.: Scholarly Resources, 1996.

Gonzalez, Gilbert G. *Guest Workers or Colonized Labor? Mexican Labor Migration to the United States.* Boulder, Colo.: Paradigm, 2006.

Richard S. Street

BRANNAN PLAN

Charles F. Brannan, the secretary of agriculture from 1948 to 1953, introduced a plan in 1949 that was intended to be the most sweeping transformation of U.S. farm policies since the New Deal. A core component of President Harry S. Truman's Fair Deal, the so-called Brannan Plan aimed to solidify the electoral base of the Democratic Party. In the years immediately following World War II, small farmers criticized New Deal farm policies for directing price supports and acreage-reduction payments primarily to large commercial farmers. Consumers and industrial workers complained that farm policies drove up food prices. Brannan responded to such criticisms with the eponymous plan he unveiled in April 1949.

Brannan proposed to guarantee farm incomes rather than commodity prices. Large farmers would receive proportionately less government assistance than smaller farmers. The plan included incentives for farmers both to raise more livestock and to reduce production of surplus commodity crops like cotton or tobacco. Subsidized prices for beef and milk would help consumers buy more of these high-value products, boosting farm incomes and enriching consumer's diets.

Republicans and southern Democrats in Congress, along with farm lobbyists from the American Farm Bureau Federation, denounced Brannan's plan as a step toward state socialism. The House Agriculture Committee tabled the plan in July 1949. In 1950, after America's entry into the Korean War led to rising farm incomes, the plan was permanently rejected.

Eventually, in August 1973, President Richard M. Nixon signed a farm bill that instituted direct payments to farmers, thus guaranteeing certain farmers' incomes rather than crop prices.

[*See also* **Agriculture,** *subentry on* **Since 1920; Farm Bureau Federation;** *and* **Subsidies, Agricultural.**]

BIBLIOGRAPHY

Dean, Virgil W. *An Opportunity Lost: The Truman Administration and the Farm Policy Debate.* Columbia: University of Missouri Press, 2006.

Hansen, John Mark. *Gaining Access: Congress and the Farm Lobby, 1919–1981.* Chicago: University of Chicago Press, 1991.

Matusow, Allen J. *Farm Policies and Politics in the Truman Years.* Cambridge, Mass.: Harvard University Press, 1967.

Shane Hamilton

BRETTON WOODS CONFERENCE

The breakdown of the world economic system during the 1930s Great Depression convinced American and British planners of the need for a new international economic framework as part of the postwar settlement. Anglo-American discussions led by U.S. Assistant Secretary of the Treasury Harry Dexter White and the British Treasury representative John Maynard Keynes began in 1942. These talks, as well as intragovernmental planning in both countries, led to an international conference held in Bretton Woods, New Hampshire, in July 1944. Attended by representatives of forty-five nations, the conclave produced the blueprints for two new institutions, the International Monetary Fund (IMF) and the International Bank for Reconstruction and Development, better known as the World Bank, as well as discussions of a third, the International Trade Organization.

The underlying principles of the Bretton Woods agreements followed American, not British, preferences: this is hardly surprising considering that at the end of World War II the United States owned half the world's supply of monetary gold and produced half the world's gross national product. Embracing the capitalist ethos of the United States, the Bretton Woods system assumed that prosperity brought peace and that the best guarantee of prosperity was an international economic system based on the freest possible flow of money and goods.

American planners had hoped that the wartime participation of the Soviet Union in the Grand Alliance with the United States and Great Britain would convince the Soviet government to join the new international economic order. Soviet attendance at the Bretton Woods conference seemed to augur well, but the following year the Soviet dictator Joseph Stalin vetoed Soviet participation in the Bretton Woods organizations. Although operational arrangements of the Bretton Woods institutions evolved in the decades after 1944, the agreements nonetheless provided the basic framework for the capitalist economic system during the Cold War and after.

[*See also* **Capitalism; Foreign Trade; GATT and WTO; International Monetary Fund; Trade Policy, Federal;** *and* **World Bank.**]

BIBLIOGRAPHY

Gardner, Richard N. *Sterling-Dollar Diplomacy: The Origins and the Prospects of Our International Economic Order.* New ed. New York: McGraw–Hill, 1969.

Woods, Randall Bennett. *A Changing of the Guard: Anglo-American Relations 1941–1946.* Chapel Hill: University of North Carolina Press, 1990.

Diane B. Kunz

BREWING AND DISTILLING

Adrian Block and Hans Christensen established the first brewery in British North America in 1612 in New Amsterdam (now New York City). Others soon followed, although many taverns brewed their own beer, making it difficult for commercial breweries to succeed. In 1793, Philadelphia was the brewing center of the colonies. By 1810, 132 U.S. breweries produced 185,000 barrels, or 31 gallons each, of beer.

Rum, distilled from molasses produced by slaves on West Indian sugar plantations, figured prominently in the economy of England's mainland colonies. In the early nineteenth century, settlers moving into Kentucky and Tennessee began making whiskey, which became beer's major competitor. Whiskey, distilled from wheat, rye, and corn, soon became a lucrative alternative to selling grain. Noted early distillers included Dr. James C. Crow, Jasper Newton, "Jack" Daniel, and James Beam. Bourbon, acorn-based whiskey, was first distilled in Bourbon County, Kentucky.

The brewing industry, meanwhile, moving west with the settlers, responded to the influx of European immigrants, especially Germans. Jacob Best, a German immigrant, established the Best Brewery in Milwaukee in 1844, four years before Wisconsin became a state. Renamed the Pabst Brewery, it was the country's leading brewery by 1874. A second Milwaukee brewery, started by John Braun in 1846, became the Blatz Brewery when Valentine Blatz, a former employee, married Braun's widow shortly after his death. August Krug started a brewery in Milwaukee in 1849, which later became the Schlitz Brewery. A brewery launched in Saint Louis, Missouri, by George Schneider in 1850 became the Anheuser–Busch Brewery when Eberhard Anheuser bought the company and four years later was joined by Adolphus Busch. In 1855 the German-born

Frederick E. Miller of Milwaukee purchased a local brewery and renamed it the Miller Brewing Company. By 1860 the nation's 1,269 breweries produced more than a million barrels of beer, 85 percent of it still brewed in New York and Pennsylvania. In 1873, 4,131 U.S. breweries—an all-time high—produced 9 million barrels of beer. The years from 1880 to 1910 saw a decline in brewery numbers as improvements in production and distribution enabled fewer plants to produce more beer. The number of breweries fell to 1,500 by 1910.

Americans' taste in distilled spirits, meanwhile, had expanded to include mixed drinks, or "cocktails" (an American slang coinage), that used imported Scotch and Irish whiskey; gin, a grain-based, juniper-flavored liquor invented by the Dutch; and vodka, a flavorless but potent drink made from rye and barley malt, or sometimes from potatoes, that originated in Russia, Scandinavia, and eastern Europe. The bourbon-based mint julep enjoyed particular popularity in the South.

The Eighteenth Amendment, ratified in 1919, forced all breweries and distilleries to stop making beer and spirits. Some breweries continued by producing candy, soft drinks, and near-beer (no more than 0.5 percent alcohol). Prohibition ended in 1933, but by 1934 only 756 breweries were back in operation. The number of U.S. breweries reached a low of 80 in 1983, but with interest in microbreweries and pub breweries (on-site breweries) the total increased thereafter. By 1996, more than 1,500 breweries, many of them small, local enterprises, were operating in the United States. The leading national breweries at century's end were Anheuser–Busch, Miller, Coors, and Stroh. In the early twenty-first century, the mass-market brewing industry became more concentrated and globalized than ever. Even Anheuser–Busch, the most successful of the mass-market domestic brewers, was acquired by a Brazilian brewer that had already become the world's largest brewing enterprise in Latin American and European markets. Simultaneously, smaller domestic specialty brewers and microbreweries continued to grow in popularity, and some—such as the Boston Beer Company, the maker of the Samuel Adams brand—developed a relatively large market for their products.

Consumption of distilled drinks declined in the late twentieth century owing to health and fitness concerns and the growing popularity of specialty beers and domestic and imported wines. From 1980 to 1995, U.S. production of distilled spirits fell from 236 to 104 million gallons, including a 20 percent drop in whiskey production. Mixed drinks remained important in American drinking patterns, however, as evidenced by the more than $2 billion in distilled spirits imported in 1996. The early twenty-first century, moreover, saw a sudden explosion in the consumption of martinis: the distillers of gin and vodka produced flavored spirits, and so-called mixologists (bartenders) created from these an array of exotically flavored martinis. Cocktails based on tequila and rum experienced a similar popularity, and even rye-based drinks such as manhattans shared in the cocktail revival. Overall, however, a domestic focus on health and fitness tempered the growth of alcohol consumption in the United States, and Americans' per capita consumption of beers and distilled spirits lagged behind that of many European, Latin American, and Asian nations.

[*See also* **Food and Diet** *and* **United Brewery Workers.**]

BIBLIOGRAPHY

Apps, Jerry. *Breweries of Wisconsin.* 2d ed. Madison: University of Wisconsin Press, 2005.

Baron, Stanley Wade. *Brewed in America: A History of Beer and Ale in the United States.* Boston: Little, Brown, 1962.

Downard, William L. *Dictionary of the History of the American Brewing and Distilling Industries.* Westport, Conn.: Greenwood Press, 1980.

Jerold "Jerry" W. Apps

BRIDGES, HARRY

(1901–1990), prominent labor leader. Harry Renton Bridges was born on 28 July 1901 near Melbourne, Australia. Christened Alfred Renton Bridges, he later took the name Harry, emulating a favorite uncle who advocated for the Australian Labor Party. Bridges went to sea in 1917, arrived in the United States in 1920, participated in a seamen's strike in 1921, and briefly joined the Industrial Workers of the World.

Bridges began working on the San Francisco docks in 1922. In 1934 the Pacific Coast District (California, Oregon, and Washington) of the International Longshoremen's Association went on strike, and seafaring unions soon went on strike, too. Chairman of his local's strike committee, Bridges displayed an uncompromising militancy that made him the strike's real leader. After nearly three months and a general strike in San Francisco, longshoremen secured nearly all their demands through arbitration.

Bridges became president first of his local and then of the Pacific Coast District. In 1937 the Pacific Coast District joined the Congress of Industrial Organizations as the International Longshoremen's and Warehousemen's Union (ILWU), with Bridges as president. In California, Oregon, Washington, British Columbia, Alaska, and Hawai'i, the ILWU forged a strong union among longshoremen and warehouse workers, as well as among agricultural and hotel workers in Hawai'i. The ILWU also institutionalized extensive rank-and-file participation in bargaining, and it usually made major decisions through membership referendums.

From 1934 onward, rumors spread that Bridges was a Communist Party (CP) member and hence subject to deportation. He openly supported the CP but insisted that he never joined. (Comintern files, however, indicate that Bridges was elected secretly to the CP's Central Committee in 1936: see Klehr and Haynes, 1992.) In 1939 a hearing by the Immigration and Naturalization Service (INS) acquitted Bridges. A second INS hearing, in 1941, found against Bridges, but ultimately the Supreme Court reversed that decision. In 1949, federal authorities charged Bridges with lying about his CP membership when he applied for naturalization. Convicted in 1950, he appealed, and in 1953 the Supreme Court overturned his conviction on procedural grounds. In 1955, federal attorneys initiated yet another trial, but the judge dismissed the charges. Five years earlier the CIO had expelled the ILWU on the grounds that it was led by Communists. Unlike most expelled CIO unions, the ILWU maintained nearly all its jurisdictions and members.

After a three-month strike in 1948, Bridges and the ILWU built a stable relationship with the Pacific Maritime Association. In the late 1950s, Bridges proposed that the ILWU should not fight technology but benefit from it, and the 1960 contract accepted full mechanization in return for generous retirement arrangements and pay guarantees for working longshoremen.

By the 1950s Bridges had become a living legend: the militant, democratic leftist who repeatedly triumphed against federal persecution. Not many ILWU members shared his admiration for the Soviet Union, but most nonetheless pledged him their respect, loyalty, and affection. After 1960, Bridges was also praised for his contributions to the maritime industry. Joseph Alioto, mayor of San Francisco, appointed Bridges to the Citizens Charter Revision Committee in 1968 and to the Port Commission in 1970. Bridges retired as ILWU president in 1977 and died on 30 March 1990.

[*See also* Labor and Anti-Communism; Labor Leaders; Longshoremen and Longshoremen's Unions; *and* San Francisco General Strike (1934).]

BIBLIOGRAPHY

Cherny, Robert W. "Constructing a Radical Identity: History, Memory, and the Seafaring Stories of Harry Bridges." *Pacific Historical Review* 70 (2001): 571–600.

Klehr, Harvey, and John Haynes. "The Comintern's Open Secrets." *American Spectator* (December 1992): 34–43. Summarizes evidence from the Comintern archives regarding the election of Bridges to the CP Central Committee.

Kutler, Stanley I. *The American Inquisition: Justice and Injustice in the Cold War*. New York: Hill and Wang, 1982.

Larrowe, Charles P. *Harry Bridges: The Rise and Fall of Radical Labor in the United States*. New York: Lawrence Hill, 1972.

Robert W. Cherny

BROOKWOOD LABOR COLLEGE

Brookwood Labor College was a school for union activists located on a fifty-three-acre campus near Katonah, New York, from 1921 to 1937. Founded by union leaders and radicals who had opposed World War I, the school was first led by A. J. Muste, a well-known minister who had led the 1919 textile strike in Lawrence, Massachusetts. With the avowed aim of teaching "workers to work in the workers' movement," Brookwood had a two-year residential program (changed to one year in 1929) that included classes in the social sciences, history, English and journalism, and labor relations. Students came from a broad range of unions and trades, including miners, machinists, garment and textile workers, and building-trades workers. Approximately 40 percent of

Brookwood's 450 graduates were women, most of whom had previously attended one of several residential "summer schools for working women in industry."

When Muste and others associated with Brookwood promoted industrial unionism and criticized the American Federation of Labor (AFL) for its lethargy, AFL leaders abruptly censured the school in 1928 and called on its affiliates to cease supporting it. Although this freed Brookwood to champion militancy more openly, the Depression ultimately drove the school into bankruptcy. After Muste departed in 1933, Brookwood operated within the orbit of the Socialist Party, and the Reuther brothers and other future leaders of the United Auto Workers came to Brookwood as students or faculty. Brookwood closed in 1937, but its educational model influenced labor education and labor studies programs in later years.

[*See also* **Muste, A. J.,** *and* **Worker Colleges and Education.**]

BIBLIOGRAPHY

Bloom, Jonathan D. "Brookwood Labor College." In *The Re-education of the American Working Class,* edited by Steven H. London, Elvira R. Tarr, and Joseph F. Wilson. Westport, Conn.: Greenwood Press, 1990.

Bloom, Jonathan D. "Brookwood Labor College: The Final Years, 1933–1937." *Labor's Heritage* 2 (April 1990): 24–43.

Jonathan D. Bloom

BROPHY, JOHN

(1883–1963), leader of the United Mine Workers of America. Born in Lancashire, England, John Brophy migrated to the United States with his family as a child. He started working in bituminous coal mines at age eleven. Brophy moved to Nanty-Glo, Pennsylvania, in 1906, where he was elected to local and district offices of the United Mine Workers of America (UMWA); he was president of the UMWA's District 2 (Central Pennsylvania) from 1916 to 1926. Brophy championed what his supporters called the Miners' Program that promoted labor education and called for nationalization of the coal industry. Under his direction, District 2 established a permanent Workers' Education Department and sent miners to the Brookwood Labor College.

Brophy was a leader of the Save the Union committee that challenged John L. Lewis for control of the UMWA, and he lost a highly disputed election campaign for union president in 1926. In 1928, with the defeat of the union's left wing and a sharp decline in its membership, Lewis revoked Brophy's union membership. In 1933, however, Lewis invited Brophy to participate in the organizing drive that helped to rebuild the union. Brophy's willingness to work for Lewis, his connections to others on the labor and political left, and his success in the organizing campaign led Lewis to appoint him as the first national director of the Congress of Industrial Organizations (CIO), a position that he held from 1935 to 1938. Lewis and Brophy split when Lewis opposed Franklin D. Roosevelt during the election of 1940 and, in the aftermath of Roosevelt's reelection, left the CIO. In 1941, Brophy became the CIO's Director of Industrial Union Councils. After World War II, Brophy, a devout Catholic, became an anti-Communist who played a major role in driving Communist organizers out of the union movement. He served as a CIO representative to international labor organizations and as a labor representative to a number of government agencies. Brophy deserves much of the credit usually assigned to John L. Lewis for the labor upsurge of the 1930s. His autobiography remains a classic account of twentieth-century American labor history.

[*See also* Congress of Industrial Organizations; Labor and Anti-Communism; Labor Leaders; Labor Movements; Lewis, John L.; United Mine Workers; *and* Worker Colleges and Education.]

BIBLIOGRAPHY

Brophy, John. *A Miner's Life*. Edited and supplemented by John O. P. Hall. Madison: University of Wisconsin Press, 1964.

Laslett, John H. M., ed. *The United Mine Workers of America: A Model of Industrial Solidarity?* University Park: Pennsylvania State University Press, 1996.

Singer, Alan. "John Brophy's 'Miners' Program': Workers' Education in UMWA District 2 during the 1920s." *Labor Studies Journal* 13, no. 4 (Winter 1988): 50–64.

Alan Singer

BROTHERHOOD OF SLEEPING CAR PORTERS

The saga of the Brotherhood of Sleeping Car Porters and Maids (BSCP) is interwoven into the fabric of American society from the Progressive Era through World War II. It reveals how a group of African American workers, despite being confined to the lower ranges of the market, carved out an arena in the labor movement in which their voices made a difference. The BSCP's participation—the participation of both individual members and the organization as a whole—in the modern civil rights movement also altered America's racial discourse.

George Pullman, the creator of the sleeping car, initially selected African Americans as porters because they were perceived as natural servants and economically exploitable. The Pullman Company continued this race-based hiring practice well into the twentieth century. Pullman's racialized hiring practices inadvertently contributed to the emergence of an African American trade union.

Ashley Totten, William H. Des Verney, Roy Lancaster, and others, veteran porters in New York City, formed the Brotherhood of Sleeping Car Porters and Maids in 1925. Totten, Des Verney, and Lancaster convinced the Harlem radical and activist A. Philip Randolph to serve as the BSCP's public face. Within a year the leaders established branches throughout the country. Like other labor organizations of the time, the new union sought to secure adequate wages for its members, better working conditions, and union recognition from the Pullman Company. Unlike its counterparts, however, it also fought to eradicate racial discrimination within organized labor. A critical moment in the relationship between Pullman and the BSCP occurred three years after the union's founding. Since 1925 the BSCP had struggled with Pullman over its right to represent the porters, and in 1928 the porters voted to strike. Just hours before the strike was to begin, however, Randolph called it off, some say at the request of William Green, the president of the American Federation of Labor (AFL). The AFL persistently sought to limit the BSCP's autonomy. Randolph's public relations skills and the organizational work of Milton P. Webster, C. L. Dellums, and other leaders kept the BSCP alive.

Finally, in 1935 the Pullman Company acknowledged the BSCP as the sole representative of the porters, and the company grudgingly agreed to negotiate a contract. Although the BSCP signed a contract with the Pullman Company, two more years passed before the AFL issued the BSCP an independent international charter—making it the first predominately African American union affiliated with the AFL.

The union's leadership and general membership became symbols of strength for African American working people. Many members also belonged to local civil rights organizations, and Randolph and BSCP members were critical to organizing both the threatened 1941 March on Washington that prompted President Franklin D. Roosevelt to create the Fair Employment Practices Committee and also the more famous 1963 March on Washington that led to the Civil Rights Act of 1964 and the Voting Rights Act of 1965.

[*See also* **African American Labor Organizations; American Federation of Labor; Labor Movements; Racism; Railroad Brotherhoods; Randolph, A. Philip;** *and* **Webster, Milton.**]

BIBLIOGRAPHY

Anderson, Jervis. *A. Philip Randolph: A Biographical Portrait.* New York: Harcourt Brace Jovanovich, 1973.

Chateauvert, Melinda. *Marching Together: Women of the Brotherhood of Sleeping Car Porters.* Urbana: University of Illinois Press, 1998.

Harris, William H. *Keeping the Faith: A. Philip Randolph, Milton P. Webster, and the Brotherhood of Sleeping Car Porters, 1925–37.* Urbana: University of Illinois Press, 1977.

Kersten, Andrew E. *A. Philip Randolph: A Life in the Vanguard.* Lanham, Md.: Rowman & Littlefield, 2007.

Tye, Larry. *Rising from the Rails: Pullman Porters and the Making of the Black Middle Class.* New York: Henry Holt, 2004.

Paul C. Young

BROWN BROTHERS HARRIMAN & COMPANY

Brown Brothers Harriman & Company (BBH) is a prestigious New York City investment bank, founded in 1818. George and John Brown established Brown Brothers and Company in Philadelphia in 1818 as a financer of the Atlantic trade of American export goods such as tobacco, wheat, and cotton. By the twentieth century Brown Brothers had moved away from the import and export industry in favor of a focus upon banking operations. Left exposed and overextended with devalued corporate and government securities during the Great Depression, Brown Brothers merged in 1931 with the more recently founded Harriman Brothers & Company, named after the sons of the railroad magnate E. H. Harriman. This transaction was eased by the connections that a great many board members of the merged firm had formed as graduates of Yale University.

The presence of numerous Yale alums was significant in shaping BBH's reputation as a conservative institution and a protector of so-called old money. Among the more renowned partners were the diplomat and governor of New York, W. Averell Harriman, and the U.S. senator from Connecticut, Prescott Bush. Yet BBH's caution was also the result of the bank's decision not to be insured by the Federal Deposit Insurance Corporation, a decision that meant that the partners shared unlimited liability. By the end of the twentieth century, BBH acted to rejuvenate its image through offering innovation in its services and reaching out to attract newly wealthy clientele. In the late 1990s the bank's boardroom finally achieved a greater measure of diversity when, for the first time, two women were named partners.

BIBLIOGRAPHY

Abramson, Rudy. *Spanning the Century: The Life of W. Averell Harriman, 1891–1986.* New York: William Morrow, 1992.

Kouwenhoven, John A. *Partners in Banking: An Historical Portrait of a Great Private Bank, Brown Brothers Harriman & Co., 1818–1968.* Garden City, N.Y.: Doubleday, 1968.

Patrick M. Dixon

BUREAU OF LABOR STATISTICS

The Bureau of Labor Statistics (BLS), estab-lished in its modern form in July 1913 within the U.S. Department of Labor, is the principal fact-finding agency for the federal government in the broad field of labor economics and statis-tics. The BLS produces regular reports on un-employment and employment, inflation, and other areas of labor economics.

From its Progressive Era origins to the twenty-first century, the BLS has striven to maintain a veneer of nonpartisan objectivity, even during periods of severe budget cutbacks and interdepartmental conflict. After World War II the public perception of the BLS as an objective, nonpartisan agency gained wide ac-ceptance, and union and business negotiators began to accept BLS data, such as the con-sumer price index (CPI), as objective precepts on which to base wage negotiations. The ac-ceptance of BLS data as objective is perhaps emblematic of a postwar liberal-corporate consensus: a system characterized by business and labor working, with government encour-agement, toward an economic stability that includes the negotiation of compensation through nondisruptive collective bargaining. Until the early 1980s, most union collective-bargaining contracts were linked with the BLS's price indexes.

As the American economy evolved from being based on manufacturing to being based on service and, at the same time, union power declined, the corporate consensus cracked. BLS statistics thus suffered increased criticism from the 1980s onward. The best known of these criticisms, the 1996 Boskin Commission Report commissioned by the Senate Finance Committee, accused the BLS of overestimating inflation rates with the CPI. Others have criti-cized the CPI for underestimating inflation. As the structure of the American economy evolves, the BLS faces new political challenges to its construction of so-called objective measure-ments of unemployment and employment rates, real price changes, and levels of union membership.

[*See also* **Collective Bargaining; Inflation and Deflation; Labor Markets;** *and* **Unemploy-ment.**]

BIBLIOGRAPHY

Abraham, Katherine G. "What We Don't Know Could Hurt Us: Some Reflections on the Measurement of Economic Activity." *Journal of Economic Perspec-tives* 19, no. 3 (Summer 2005): 3–18.

Clague, Ewan. *The Bureau of Labor Statistics*. New York: Praeger, 1968.

Goldberg, Joseph P., and William T. Moye. *The First Hundred Years of the Bureau of Labor Statistics*. Washington, D.C.: Bureau of Labor Statistics, 1985. Available online at http://www.bls.gov /opub/blsfirsthundredyears.

Greenless, John S., and Robert McClelland. "Recent Controversies over CPI Methodology." *Business Economics* 45, no. 1 (January 2010): 28–37.

Stapleford, Thomas A. "Shaping Knowledge about American Labor: External Advising at the U.S. Bureau of Labor Statistics in the Twentieth Cen-tury." *Science in Context* 23, no. 2 (June 2010): 187–220.

James G. Cassedy

BUSINESS CYCLES

As far back as reliable statistics for the Ameri-can economy exist, periods of expanding output and employment have alternated with periods in which output and employment have con-tracted. This pattern has also characterized the economies of other industrialized nations. Al-though such fluctuating "cycles" have been ir-regular in amplitude and duration, the word "cycle" does emphasize their recurring nature.

Systematic research into the U.S. business cycle dates to the early and mid-twentieth-century work of Wesley C. Mitchell, Arthur Burns, and others associated with the National Bureau of Economic Research (NBER), a private organization whose widely used dating of business-cycle peaks and troughs has been accepted the U.S. Department of Commerce. The NBER considers a recession to have occurred when output, income, and employment have declined for at least several months. A particularly severe recession has been termed a "depression," although no formal definition of "depression" exists.

Chronology. Because of the paucity of data for earlier periods, the NBER begins its business-cycle chronology with the recession that followed the cyclical peak of December 1854. Significant economic downturns clearly occurred before the mid-1850s, however. Major recessions, perhaps severe enough to be considered depressions, took place in 1819 and 1837. The close linkages between the U.S. and foreign economies were evident in these early contractions. The 1819 downturn followed a downturn in U.S. exports, particularly cotton. The protracted downturn that began in 1837 was set off when the Bank of England tightened credit. Because statistics for prices for these years are more readily available than are statistics on production and employment, some economic historians have argued that pre–Civil War business cycles mainly affected prices and wages and not production and employment. Contemporary accounts, however, establish that noticeable increases in unemployment occurred in urban areas during contractions; soup kitchens for the jobless, for example, appeared as early as 1819.

In the Gilded Age, major recessions occurred during the 1870s, 1880s, and 1890s. The downturn that began with the cyclical peak of January 1893 was particularly severe, probably meriting being labeled a depression, and caused high unemployment through the remainder of the decade. The pace of industrialization exposed more workers to unemployment during these downturns. During the depression of the 1890s, unemployment probably peaked at well above 10 percent of the labor force and might have reached 15 percent. As the fraction of the labor force experiencing business-cycle contractions increased, so did agitation for government intervention. The most visible manifestation of the pressure for action by the federal government during these years was the march of the unemployed on Washington, D.C., in 1894, led by Jacob Coxey of Ohio and popularly known as Coxey's Army. Local governments and private agencies, however, provided the bulk of assistance to the unemployed during the nineteenth century, chiefly by expanding existing programs of poor relief or by occasionally creating public works programs.

Most recessions in the post–Civil War period were accompanied by financial panics during which banks, unable to satisfy their depositors' demands, suspended withdrawals, thereby exacerbating the crisis. For this reason, after a particularly severe panic and recession in 1907, support grew for reform of the banking system. The 1913 Federal Reserve Act was designed to moderate recessions by providing a lender of last resort to banks experiencing liquidity problems. Although a brief but severe recession occurred in 1920–1921, economists attributed it to adjustment problems following the end of World War I. Most observers were thus surprised by the length and severity of the downturn that began in 1929.

According to the NBER, the Great Depression of the 1930s began with the cyclical peak of August 1929 and reached its trough in March 1933, at which point the unemployment rate exceeded 20 percent. Unemployment remained high until 1941 when the reinstatement of the military draft and increased military spending stimulated the economy and expanded civilian job opportunities. Economists continue to debate the causes of the Great Depression, some blaming the 1929 stock market crash, others the series of bank panics that began in the fall of 1930, and still others a series of government policies, including passage of the Smoot–Hawley Tariff in June 1930. President Franklin Delano Roosevelt's New Deal—which in some respects built on initiatives dating to the administration of Herbert Hoover—represented the first significant attempt by the federal government to ameliorate the effects of the business cycle.

Although many economists and policy makers feared that depression would return after World War II, the postwar business cycle proved relatively mild. The long expansion during the 1960s led many to declare the business cycle "dead," but severe recessions in 1974–1975 and 1981–1982 revived concern about macroeconomic stability. The twenty-five-year period following the end of the 1982 recession saw low rates of inflation and only two mild recessions, in 1990–1991 and in 2001. This strong macroeconomic performance led some economists to label the period the "Great Moderation." The Great Moderation came to a dramatic end with the recession that began in December 2007 and lasted to June 2009. The 2007–2009 recession was the longest and most severe since the Great Depression and was accompanied by a financial crisis that also was the worst since the Depression. The slow recovery from the recession brought issues of macroeconomic policy to the forefront of public debate and political campaigns.

Explanations. Economists have advanced many explanations for the business cycle. In earlier agricultural economies, some observers—notably the nineteenth-century British economist Stanley Jevons—linked business cycles to sunspots, which have a fairly regular periodicity. In the mid-nineteenth century, Karl Marx proposed that cycles resulted from the tendency for capital accumulation to cause an overproduction of goods relative to the purchasing power of the working class. The twentieth-century British economist John Maynard Keynes provided a particularly influential explanation for business cycles. In *The General Theory of Employment, Interest, and Money* (1936), Keynes attributed business cycles to fluctuations in total spending, or aggregate demand. Controversy long raged between supporters of Keynes's theory and supporters of its main rival—monetarism, or the neo-quantity theory of money. The monetarist school, led by Milton Friedman of the University of Chicago, attributed business cycles to fluctuations in the stock of money. Toward the end of the twentieth century, many economists embraced a theory that sees the business cycle as a result of the rational responses of workers and firms to the economic effects of underlying changes in technology, broadly defined.

[*See also* **Capitalism; Depressions, Economic; Economic Development; Economic Growth and Income Patterns; Federal Reserve System; Financial Crises, 1980s–2010; Friedman, Milton, and the Chicago School of Economics; Great Depression (1929–1939); Great Recession of 2008 and After; Industrialization and Deindustrialization; Keynesian Economics; Long Swings and Cycles in Economic Growth; Monetarism; Monetary Policy, Federal; National Bureau of Economic Research;** *and* **Unemployment.**]

BIBLIOGRAPHY

Bordo, Michael D., Claudia Goldin, and Eugene N. White, eds. *The Defining Moment: The Great Depression and the American Economy in the Twentieth Century.* Chicago: University of Chicago Press, 1998.

Burns, Arthur F., and Wesley C. Mitchell. *Measuring Business Cycles*. National Bureau of Economic Research, Studies in Business Cycles, no. 2. New York: National Bureau of Economic Research, 1946.

Friedman, Milton, and Anna Jacobson Schwartz. *A Monetary History of the United States, 1867–1960*. Princeton, N.J.: Princeton University Press, 1963.

Glasner, David, ed. *Business Cycles and Depressions: An Encyclopedia*. New York: Garland, 1997.

Anthony Patrick O'Brien

BUSINESS GROWTH AND DECLINE

Modern capitalist economic progress began during the seventeenth and eighteenth centuries, just when the thirteen colonies that would form the United States were being settled. Such corporate enterprises as the Massachusetts Bay Company, the Virginia Company of London, and the Royal African Company even brought immigrants to the New World. The Royal African Company's commerce in human beings constituted only a small fraction of the transatlantic slave trade, but it symbolized the extent to which businesspeople on both sides of the Atlantic were willing to go to make a profit. Most white immigrants to America during the eighteenth and early nineteenth centuries came as indentured servants. In this business transaction, the would-be immigrant exchanged three to seven years of service for passage to a land of enhanced opportunity. Mostly self-selected risk takers, indentured servants embraced an entrepreneurial culture once their terms of servitude ended.

Statistical Gauges of Business Success.
The modern capitalist era marked a profound historical discontinuity. For the eight thousand years of recorded human experience up to around 1700, most people lived on the edge of survival. Their incomes grew slowly, if at all. But beginning with the First Industrial Revolution in about 1760, business growth accelerated. Between 1820 and 2000, per capita incomes in the United States doubled every forty-two years—a phenomenal business achievement and apparent miracle of economic growth.

Only a few major countries attained such growth, and all were organized around capitalist economies. Of the twenty-five countries classified as "high-income" by the early twenty-first century, the United States had long occupied a special position. Its economy was the world's largest—double that of the runner-up, Japan. The per capita purchasing power of Americans ranked first among major countries. The volume of U.S. industrial production also ranked first, as it had since the 1880s. So, too, during much of this period, had its productivity (value of output per hour of work) in manufacturing, distribution, services, construction, mining, and most other business activities.

The Ongoing Role of Immigrants.
People of many nationalities and ethnic groups made fundamental contributions to American business throughout the nation's history. The early treasury secretaries Alexander Hamilton (from the West Indies) and Albert Gallatin (Switzerland) played vital roles in shaping a national economy hospitable to entrepreneurship. Immigrant businessmen formed companies that became internationally leading firms. In 1837, for example, William Procter, a candlemaker from England, and James Gamble, a soap boiler from Ireland, founded Procter and Gamble, which became the world's largest consumer-products company. John Jacob Astor, a poor immigrant from Germany, amassed a vast fortune in the fur trade, transoceanic commerce, and New York City real estate. Daniel McCallum (Scotland), general superintendent of the New York & Erie Railroad, published in

1855 the earliest-known treatise on business administration. In the 1870s, while working for the Louisville & Nashville Railroad, Albert Fink (Germany) devised such an ingenious method of separating fixed costs from variable costs—a distinction vital in accounting and business planning—that he later became known as the father of railway economics. Andrew Carnegie, who emigrated from Scotland, became the world's greatest steel magnate.

Twentieth-century immigrants continued to make vital contributions to American business. David Sarnoff, born in a Russian shtetl, immigrated to the United States as a boy. Without formal education beyond the eighth grade, he became the architect and chief executive officer (CEO) of the Radio Corporation of America (RCA), a leader both in radio network broadcasting (RCA launched the National Broadcasting Company, or NBC, in 1926) and also in television research and development. Other Jewish immigrants from eastern Europe, such as Samuel Goldwyn (Poland) and Louis B. Mayer (Russia), built movie studios that made Hollywood the world's entertainment capital.

During the 1970s, An Wang (China) innovated in producing minicomputers and office workstations. In the 1980s, Roberto Gouizeta (Cuba) became CEO of the Coca-Cola Company and led it to unprecedented growth. In the 1990s, Alex Trotman (Scotland) served as CEO of the Ford Motor Company and presided over its globalization.

Just as the "American" business achievement drew freely on the abilities of diverse immigrants, so did business-related American science and technology. In the 1790s, during the First Industrial Revolution, Samuel Slater (England) brought the power loom to the budding American textile industry. The du Pont family (France) founded a small gunpowder firm in 1802 that eventually became the world's leading chemical company. In the early twentieth century, Charles Steinmetz (Germany), the resident inventive genius at General Electric, led that company's move into high-tech products.

In the 1930s and 1940s a cadre of brilliant physicists, chemists, and mathematicians fleeing Nazi Europe, including Albert Einstein (Germany), Enrico Fermi (Italy), Niels Bohr (Denmark), Hans Bethe (Germany), and John von Neumann (Hungary), advanced the frontiers of American science. Augmenting this distinguished group were immigrant German rocket scientists who had worked for the Nazi regime, the best known of whom was Wernher von Braun. Much of late twentieth-century American leadership electronics, nuclear, and aerospace technology derived from the scientific and entrepreneurial talents of immigrants. Andrew Grove (Hungary), a key figure in the rise of the Intel Corporation, played such a key role in the development of microprocessors that *Time* magazine named him its "Person of the Year" for 1997. Intel and hundreds of other information-technology firms, including Hewlett–Packard, Apple Computer, Sun Microsystems, Oracle, and Cisco Systems, set up their headquarters in California's Silicon Valley, southeast of San Francisco. Collectively these companies spearheaded American economic growth at the turn of the twenty-first century—and became a powerful magnet for still another flood of immigrant talent, notably from East Asia and South Asia.

Attitudes and Ideologies. From the start, many American businesspeople were unabashedly ambitious about increasing their fortunes. Benjamin Franklin wrote in his autobiography that as a young Philadelphia printer he had taken care "not only to be in reality industrious and frugal but to avoid all appearances to the contrary." In *The Protestant Ethic and the Spirit of Capitalism* (1904–1905; English trans., 1930), the German sociologist

Max Weber declared that Franklin's sentiments expressed "above all the idea of a duty of the individual toward the increase of his capital, which is assumed as an end in itself." In earlier times, Weber added, this new way of thinking, which "called forth the applause of a whole [American] people, would have been proscribed as the lowest sort of avarice and as an attitude entirely lacking in self-respect."

Yet even in the colonial and early national eras, a large proportion of Americans fervently embraced the opportunities afforded by the North American continent's rich resources. They also benefited from a pro-business legal system inherited from the British, particularly rules protecting property rights. Taking the sanctity of contracts almost for granted, they started thousands of proprietorships and partnerships in cities along the Eastern Seaboard: Boston, Newport, New York, Philadelphia, Baltimore, and Charleston. Moving westward, they not only established farms, but also opened innumerable small businesses.

Early nineteenth-century Americans enacted laws to promote this business growth, such as general incorporation laws, very low tax rates, and liberal bankruptcy proceedings. Relying on this last advantage, which shifted part of the risk of doing business from entrepreneurs to creditors, Americans showed themselves singularly willing to traffic in personal and business credit. This trait, fully evident by the mid-nineteenth century, has remained a hallmark of the nation's business and consumer culture. By 2000, business and consumer debt stood at several trillion dollars each, and Americans possessed well over a billion credit cards.

Throughout the nation's history, most of the American electorate endorsed the business system. Americans took political action to restrain it less frequently than did voters in other democratic capitalist countries, not to mention socialist ones. They tolerated the gyrations of the business cycle more willingly, including dozens of recessions and several deep economic depressions. The worst of all business downturns, the worldwide Great Depression of the 1930s, hit the United States harder than almost any other nation, but resulted in less political turmoil than occurred in Germany, Japan, Britain, France, Italy, and many other countries.

The individualistic laissez-faire ideology embraced by most Americans promoted a high degree of entrepreneurial effort and released an immense amount of business energy. But the social and environmental cost of business success sometimes proved woefully high. Up until the New Deal era of the 1930s, and in many ways beyond that, business exploited children, women, minorities, and laborers of all types. The United States consistently had a lower percentage of unionized workers than did comparable countries. Even in the early twenty-first century, in contrast to the situation in Great Britain, France, Germany, and Japan, American business and its political allies did a relatively ineffectual job of protecting those who found it hard to compete within the system. By 2000 the gap between rich and poor had become greater in the United States than in any other developed country, reversing both a national commitment to equality and a sixty-year statistical trend. Some CEOs of large American firms were receiving four hundred times the earnings of the lowest-paid members of their own companies. This multiple far exceeded the averages in Europe or Japan, and it was ten times the rate in the United States itself as recently as 1975.

African Americans and Women. The extraordinary mixture of cultures and nationalities resulting from mass immigration became the defining trait of the American business system. The 1900 U.S. Census revealed that a majority of the nation's 76 million people were nonwhite, immigrants, or second-generation Americans. Despite the record of economic exploitation, one of the signal triumphs of

American society and its business system was to absorb the best contributions of a myriad of cultures without disintegrating under the stress of racial and ethnic strife. The great exception, of course, was the Civil War. But although that conflict ended slavery and gave millions of African Americans a chance to participate in the business opportunities available to their fellow citizens, progress proved slow for a century after emancipation. Open racism prevailed in business up until the post–World War II civil rights movement and the landmark voting rights and public-accommodation laws enacted during the 1960s. Equality in employment opportunity was the last barrier to fall, and in mainstream American business it did not begin to come down until about the 1970s. Despite significant progress, latent racism continued to plague American business into the twenty-first century.

Discrimination also hampered most American women who attempted business careers. In 1900, females constituted only 4.5 percent of all U.S. managers, proprietors, and other business officials, and by 1940 this had risen to only 11 percent. But women's business opportunities grew markedly after 1970, epitomized by the careers of Estée Lauder, Mary Kay Ash, Oprah Winfrey, Margaret Whitman, and other entrepreneurs. By 2000, about 40 percent of all new firms were being started by women, and women had made extraordinary gains in business-related professions such as law and accounting. In big business, however, the glass ceiling remained formidable. In 2000, only three of America's five hundred largest firms had female chief executive officers, and only two were headed by African Americans.

Even so, throughout the country's history, entrepreneurial activity by African American, Asian, and Hispanic businesspeople—both men and women—has been far greater than is commonly recognized. Devoting their energies to enterprises often overlooked by historians, who have tended to focus on large firms, members of these groups operated service businesses such as insurance companies, small stores, dressmaking and millinery boutiques, barbershops and beauty salons, and shoe-repair shops, catering primarily to members of their own ethnic or gender groups.

The First Industrial Revolution. Scholars disagree over whether the term "Industrial Revolution" is applicable to business. Critics point out that economic growth seldom occurs in tumultuous spurts analogous to violent political upheavals. Instead, business typically evolves through the steady accretion and dissemination of small- and medium-size gains in technology and organizational design.

Yet breakthroughs such as the telegraph, railroad, electric motor, internal combustion engine, computer, polymerization of chemicals, and the mapping of the human genome do tend to accelerate business growth. And even in normal times, business never stands still. Entrepreneurial energies and competitive pressures promote what the economist Joseph Schumpeter aptly termed a "perennial gale of creative destruction." New products, new firms, and new forms of business organizations are forever sweeping away old ones. So the idea of industrial revolutions, though flawed, does offer a useful framework for understanding the evolution of American business.

During the First Industrial Revolution, from about 1760 to 1840, the new roads and canals markedly improved American business productivity. In a few industries, factories first appeared, steam power began to replace water and animal power, and work was regulated by the clock rather than by the sun and seasons. Machine-based mass production was adopted for some products, most notably cotton textiles, and the prices of these products dropped precipitously.

Most businesses remained small in these years, employing at most a few hundred workers and never more than a thousand. An artisanal and mercantile economy predominated, as opposed to a full-fledged industrial one. Thousands of modest proprietorships and partnerships—grocers, blacksmiths, fabric merchants, printers, tailors, dressmakers, milliners—sold specialized goods. Most remained local, and almost no products were branded. Because they helped to enforce commercial commitments through noneconomic sanctions, kinship and religious affiliations figured significantly in financing and maintaining business relationships. The same had been true in colonial times for New England's Puritan merchants and for southern planters marketing their products.

The largest companies of the First Industrial Revolution, measured by their market value, were in banking, insurance, and canals. Some of these firms survived into the twenty-first century as big businesses, such as Citigroup, Fleet Financial Group, and Cigna Corporation. Through special acts passed by state legislatures, a few hundred such firms operated as corporations. To put this early nineteenth-century figure in perspective, tens of thousands of corporations were doing business by 1900, and 4.5 million were doing business by 2000. Still, most American enterprises have always been small proprietorships or partnerships, of which there were more than 15 million in 2000.

The Second Industrial Revolution.
The corporate form accelerated the progress of business during the Second Industrial Revolution, the crucial era from roughly 1850 to 1950. Practically all states stopped requiring special acts of incorporation and instead passed general laws permitting groups to incorporate for any legitimate business purpose. Some states vied with each other in offering generous terms. This so-called charter mongering led to the incorporation of many prominent firms' headquarters in New Jersey and Delaware, each of which offered low fees for incorporation and

permitted holding companies to own subsidiary corporations.

The advantages of corporations over proprietorships and partnerships included limited liability, easier financing, and institutional permanence. Most important, corporations afforded far more efficient means of governance, through stockholder oversight and hierarchical management structures based on merit rather than on family connection or social standing.

The 1880s proved an especially portentous decade for the development of American business. As the commercialization of electricity, the telephone, and the internal combustion engine began in earnest, entrepreneurs founded scores of important new companies. Among the firms started in this decade (some with different names originally) one finds Scott Paper, the Times Mirror Company, Kroger, Dresser Industries, Consolidated Edison, Eastman Kodak, Chiquita Brands, Honeywell, Johnson & Johnson, Tyco International, Avon Products, Coca-Cola, Sears, Roebuck, Sun Oil, Union Carbide, Unisys, Upjohn, US West, Hershey Foods, Westinghouse, Merck, Alcoa, Abbott Laboratories, Amoco, Pennzoil, and Berkshire Hathaway.

During the Second Industrial Revolution, the telegraph and then the telephone made instantaneous communication possible on a broad scale. Between 1840 and 1890, railroad firms laid down more than 200,000 miles of new tracks. Around 1900, the automobile, truck, and airplane all materialized in a remarkably brief time. Both the Ford Motor Company and General Motors were founded during the first decade of the new century; Boeing was founded in 1916; and Chrysler, Lockheed, Douglas Aircraft, Yellow Freight, Delta Airlines, and United Airlines were founded during the 1920s.

Meanwhile, alongside mass production, most of the modern institutions of mass marketing—department stores, franchised outlets, catalog stores, and chain retailers—also appeared during this era. Numerous companies, including many of those listed above, integrated vertically—that is, they both produced and marketed goods. In some cases they also procured raw materials and conducted research and development in-house.

This multifunctional approach gave rise to what is known as the multidivisional structure in the governance of firms, as several large corporations began to organize their divisions according to products rather than functions, giving bottom-line responsibility to division heads who oversaw both the production and the marketing of particular products. The older, functional system, under which sets of executives handled production, sales, and purchasing of all items across the company, made it difficult to pinpoint responsibility when problems arose. The new multidivisional system, by contrast, carved giant companies into smaller segments categorized by individual products, and it gave aspiring managers a clear path up the corporate ladder. Created in the early 1920s almost simultaneously by Alfred P. Sloan Jr. at General Motors and by several DuPont executives, the multidivisional structure proved to be the most influential organizational innovation of the twentieth century. Companies in the United States and worldwide emulated it, particularly after World War II, when many firms began offering different lines of products.

Although the vast majority of Second Industrial Revolution businesses remained small or medium in size, a few became giants. The Pennsylvania Railroad employed more than 100,000 people by the 1890s, General Motors employed several hundred thousand by the 1940s, and the American Telephone and Telegraph Company (AT&T) employed about 1 million before its breakup under antitrust pressures during the 1980s. Some companies, such as Singer Sewing Machines, H. J. Heinz, and Ford Motor

Company, grew large through internal expansion. Others, such as United States Steel, International Harvester, and General Electric, resulted from major mergers. Prominent financiers such as the investment banker J. P. Morgan organized several large combinations. But in the United States during the Second Industrial Revolution, finance proved less important as a source of business innovation than it was in other major economies, notably those of Germany and Japan.

Most companies that became big businesses shared certain common characteristics, all of which differed from those common during the First Industrial Revolution. Big businesses tended to be capital-intensive and vertically integrated and to serve national (and sometimes international) mass markets with standardized, machine-manufactured products. They typically generated enormous cash flows and financed their operations more through retained earnings than by issuing stocks and bonds. These Second Industrial Revolution firms employed large staffs of professional managers who were organized in formal hierarchies.

The Third Industrial Revolution, 1950s and Beyond. In this fertile business era, the percentage of jobs in the service sector came to exceed the total in manufacturing, mining, construction, and agriculture combined. Beginning in the 1980s, many corporations downsized their staffs, flattened their hierarchies, and outsourced their noncore functions. These steps derived from intensified competition both domestically and from overseas challengers such as Japanese automobile and consumer-electronics companies. Another trend in business growth, and in the long run the most important, was the driving force of science and technology. This was not an altogether new phenomenon, of course. The steam engine had symbolized the First Industrial Revolution and the electric motor and internal combustion engine the

Second. But the Third Industrial Revolution brought unparalleled levels of scientific knowledge readily applicable to business: jet engines, rocket power, nuclear power, satellite communications, lasers, computer hardware and software, robotics, and a dazzling array of new chemicals based on polymer science and of pharmaceuticals based on genetic research and development.

A simple listing of representative new companies and their founding dates illustrates the nature of the Third Industrial Revolution. Note the preponderance of service firms, high-tech companies, and marketers of international scope in the 1940s, Wal-Mart, Mattel, Toys "R" Us, McDonald's, and Circuit City; in the 1950s, Eckerd Drugs, Caldor, and Service Merchandise; in the 1960s, MCI Communications, Turner Broadcasting, Nike, Intel, The Gap, The Limited, and Columbia HCA Healthcare; in the 1970s, Federal Express, Microsoft, Apple Computer, and Home Depot; in the 1980s, Compaq, Sun Microsystems, Dell Computer, and Gateway; in the 1990s, an explosion of Internet-based firms such as eBay and Amazon.com.

The "information age" component of the Third Industrial Revolution seemed to peak at the turn of the twenty-first century, with its multitudinous start-ups of dot-com and bio-technology businesses. The term "IPO"—the initial public offering of a company's common stock—entered the vernacular. As a means of measuring the value and prospects of firms and the health of the national economy, the NASDAQ Composite Index, consisting mostly of high-tech stocks, began to rival the venerable Dow Jones Industrial Average, which originated in 1884 for railroads and in 1897 for industrial corporations. In several high-tech industries, venture capitalism displaced traditional investment banking as the quickest route to personal fortunes for both founding entrepreneurs and their financial backers.

As firms that grew out of the Second and Third Industrial Revolutions internationalized their operations and moved much of their manufacturing to offshore sources of inexpensive labor, the number of well-paying jobs in American manufacturing declined. Simultaneously, franchised service operations such as McDonald's, Kinko's copy centers, and 7-Eleven convenience stores proliferated. These companies typically paid low initial wages, but they offered masses of immigrants first-time jobs and numerous students entry into the workforce as part-time employees. They also provided entrepreneurial opportunities for owner-operator franchisees, of which there were nearly 1 million by the early twenty-first century.

The economic inequality that accompanied the Third Industrial Revolution accelerated in the early twenty-first century as the financial sector garnered an ever-rising share of total business income and profits. Beneficiaries of legislation that removed New Deal regulations on banking and finance, large banks, investment firms, venture capitalists, and hedge-fund operators began to make risky investments that initially returned large profits. The clear lines of demarcation that the New Deal had drawn between conventional commercial banking and riskier investment or speculative financing all but disappeared. The enormous profits generated by the financial sector prior to 2008 resulted in levels of remuneration for executives in that sector unseen elsewhere in the advanced world or ever before in U.S. history. The top 1 percent of income earners received nearly 90 percent of the total gain in national income between 2000 and 2008, and the top one tenth of the 1 percent were the greatest winners.

Among the most speculative and profitable of the investments made early in the new century were those in real estate, where mortgage brokers and bankers granted mortgages with small down payments and loose credit standards. Bankers then converted individual mortages into mortgage-backed bonds that promised their holders attractive interest rates and that credit-rating agencies gave their highest ratings. The whole system was based on ever-rising prices in residential real estate, a vastly inflated bubble that was sure to burst—as so many similar economic bubbles had burst, beginning with the seventeenth-century Dutch tulip craze and continuing with the late 1990s Internet stock bubble. When the real estate bubble burst in 2008, it threatened to collapse the entire global financial sector, the United States' included. The bubble burst had all the makings of another great crash and great depression on the order of that of the 1930s. In the United States, only prompt and financially generous intervention by the federal government and the Federal Reserve Board rescued major banks, insurance companies, and investment banks from disaster. Federal loans also saved General Motors and Chrysler from bankruptcy. The financial sector and the American automobile industry were saved with billions of dollars of public funds, but for most citizens, wages and earnings had stagnated; for millions of people unable to pay mortgages that represented sums greater than the value of their homes, eviction threatened; and for even more millions, unemployment became an inescapable reality. A truly Schumpeterian gale of destruction had ravaged the American economy.

By 2012, how the economic crisis of 2008–2010 would ultimately turn out remained to be seen. But throughout its history, the American business system had exhibited a remarkable resilience and adaptability. So it seemed likely that Schumpeter's "perennial gale of creative destruction" would remain a fitting metaphor for its future course.

[*See also* **American System of Manufacturing and Interchangeable Parts; Business Cycles; Capitalism and Immigration; Communications Revolution; Consumer Culture; Depressions, Economic; Deskilling; Economic Development; Economic Growth and Income Patterns; Financial Crises, 1980s–2010; Globalization; Hamilton, Alexander, and Economic Development; Immigration; Industrial Policy, Theory and Practice of; Labor Productivity Growth; Laissez-Faire and Classical Economics; Long Swings and Cycles in Economic Growth; Mass Marketing; Mass Production; Productivity; Profits, Changes in Rates of; Scientific Management; Technology; Technology and Labor;** *and* **Vertical Integration, Economies of Scale, and Firm Size.**]

BIBLIOGRAPHY

Bailyn, Bernard. *The New England Merchants in the Seventeenth Century.* Cambridge, Mass.: Harvard University Press, 1955.

Blackford, Mansel G. *A History of Small Business in America.* New York: Twayne, 1991.

Bruchey, Stuart. *Enterprise: The Dynamic Economy of a Free People.* Cambridge, Mass.: Harvard University Press, 1990.

Chandler, Alfred D., Jr. *The Visible Hand: The Managerial Revolution in American Business.* Cambridge, Mass.: Belknap Press of Harvard University Press, 1977.

Hounshell, David A. *From the American System to Mass Production, 1800–1932: The Development of Manufacturing Technology in the United States.* Baltimore: Johns Hopkins University Press, 1984.

Hughes, Jonathan R. T. *The Vital Few: American Economic Progress and Its Protagonists.* Boston: Houghton Mifflin, 1965.

Kwolek-Folland, Angel. *Incorporating Women: A History of Women and Business in the United States.* New York: Twayne, 1998.

Lamoreaux, Naomi R. *Insider Lending: Banks, Personal Connections, and Economic Development in Industrial New England.* Cambridge, U.K.: Cambridge University Press, 1994.

McCraw, Thomas K. *American Business, 1920–2000: How It Worked.* Wheeling, Ill.: Harlan Davidson, 2000.

Scranton, Philip. *Endless Novelty: Specialty Production and American Industrialization, 1865–1925.* Princeton, N.J.: Princeton University Press, 1997.

Tedlow, Richard S. *New and Improved: The Story of Mass Marketing in America.* New York: Basic Books, 1990.

Walker, Juliet E. K. *The History of Black Business in America: Capitalism, Race, Entrepreneurship.* New York: Macmillan Library Reference USA, 1998.

Thomas K. McCraw

BUSINESS ROUNDTABLE

The Business Roundtable, an elite lobbying and advisory organization of chief executive officers (CEOs) from two hundred of the nation's largest business enterprises, was established in 1972 in response to a surge of regulatory legislation that began in the mid-1960s. New laws that protected the environment, affected consumer goods, regulated energy use, secured worker safety and health, and guaranteed equal employment opportunity all combined to increase production costs and diminish business profits. Big business reacted aggressively to defend its interests.

During the 1975–1985 decade of relatively slow economic growth, income polarization, intense foreign competition, divisive social issues, and rising conservatism, the roundtable's influence grew steadily. Its initial victories, however, were defensive. The roundtable defeated efforts by the American Federation of Labor and Congress of Industrial Organizations to reform federal labor law, as well as Ralph Nader's campaign to create a consumer protection agency. Subsequently, roundtable committees learned to influence the national political agenda and to achieve legislative and administrative victories that climaxed in multibillion-dollar corporate tax reductions and selective business deregulation during and after the presidency of Ronald Reagan. By the 1980s and 1990s, roundtable representatives regularly participated in broad coalitions of corporate and noncorporate groups to affect legislation in such diverse areas as civil rights, reform of liability law, and reduction of health-care costs. The roundtable proved especially effective at lobbying legislators who represented congressional districts and states where its corporate members had large investments and employee payrolls.

Accommodating itself to the party in power, the roundtable rarely resorted to open confrontation. More often than not, it succeeded in convincing the government to promote the interests of big business in an increasingly global economy in which high-technology development and subsidized trade increased corporate profits. Tax incentives, export-promotion programs, federally insured overseas investment, and the privatization of formerly public services all improved corporate balance sheets. Hence, most big-business executives saw federal power as a permanent presence in the economic marketplace and utilized the roundtable to defend their interests in Washington.

[*See also* **Chambers of Commerce; Deregulation, Financial; National Association of Manufacturers;** *and* **Trade Policy, Federal.**]

BIBLIOGRAPHY

Levitan, Sar A., and Martha R. Cooper. *Business Lobbies: The Public Good and the Bottom Line.* Baltimore: Johns Hopkins University Press, 1984.

McQuaid, Kim. *Uneasy Partners: Big Business in American Politics, 1945–1990.* 1994. See in particular pp. 125–185. Baltimore: Johns Hopkins University Press, 1994.

Kim McQuaid

C

CAMPBELL SOUP

The Campbell Soup Company is the leading maker of soups in the world and has often been at the forefront of developments in the convenience-foods industry, marketing, and labor relations. Founded in 1869 in Camden, New Jersey, as a collaboration between the produce wholesaler Joseph Campbell and the tinsmith Abraham Anderson, it was one of many canneries in southern New Jersey in the late nineteenth century that was created to take advantage of the area's agricultural bounty, especially tomatoes. In 1899 the Campbell chemist John T. Dorrance developed a method for condensing soup that substantially reduced shipping and warehousing costs. This innovation, combined with an aggressive and imaginative marketing campaign, catapulted the company beyond its competitors and into the front ranks of the emerging prepared-foods industry. Dorrance became president of the company in 1914 and sole owner the following year. Focusing on the production of condensed soup, the firm built a second plant in Camden and another in Chicago in 1929. Although it expanded to Canada and Britain in the early 1930s, its international penetration was limited largely to sales and marketing until it began serious global growth in the 1950s.

Throughout its history, Campbell has been notable for a number of innovations in sourcing, production, and marketing. Dorrance set the tone through his early efforts in breeding new varieties of tomatoes, constantly revolutionizing production methods, and pioneering new media for advertising. In all these areas, he and his successors strove to gain tight control over every aspect of the company's operations, yet they often faced opposition, especially in the production plants. Employees formed militant unions in the 1930s and 1940s, and Campbell was forced to concede to demands from well-organized unions in Camden and Chicago in 1946. The company built new plants, this time in dispersed, rural locations where representation by less aggressive unions enabled it to impose its conditions on a divided workforce. A spectacular nationwide strike and consumer boycott in 1968, however, threatened to shift the power balance back to the unions; this was averted when the most committed union, the United Packinghouse Workers, disbanded owing to unrelated membership declines in its primary industry.

The company was privately held by the Dorrance family until 1954, and the family continued to hold a substantial stake in the company as it expanded its acquisitions of other food-related firms in the United States and internationally, including the frozen-foods maker C. A. Swanson & Sons and the baked-goods producer Pepperidge Farms. With the development in the 1960s of the mechanical tomato harvester, core production facilities could be relocated away from sources of raw materials. By 1990, Campbell had closed its original plants in Camden and Chicago as newer facilities took over production of soups and other products. The final years of the twentieth century were marked by disagreements among Dorrance heirs, product recalls, and struggles to retain market share. Nonetheless, the company's reputation as the maker of the quintessential comfort food, immortalized in Andy Warhol's soup-can paintings of the 1960s, appeared to be validated on 29 September 2008. On that day, the day of the largest point drop in the history of Standard & Poor's S&P 500 index, Campbell's stock was the only one of the companies on that index to rise.

[*See also* **Food and Diet** *and* **Mass Marketing.**]

BIBLIOGRAPHY

Collins, Douglas. *America's Favorite Food: The Story of Campbell Soup Company.* New York: H. N. Abrams, 1994.

Sidorick, Daniel. *Condensed Capitalism: Campbell Soup and the Pursuit of Cheap Production in the Twentieth Century.* Ithaca, N.Y.: ILR Press, 2009.

Daniel Sidorick

CANALS AND WATERWAYS

The first waterway engineers in the Americas were the prehistoric builders who constructed fish weirs and ditches. The ancient Pueblo Indians of Mesa Verde reclaimed the high desert with a sophisticated system of storage reservoirs. European navigators encountered snags, sandbars, and rapids. In 1785, George Washington organized a company that cleared rocks from the Potomac. Canal builders also developed the Santee, James, Delaware, Susquehanna, Schuylkill, and Merrimack rivers.

Canals in the antebellum era were typically semipublic stock corporations supported by state and municipal bonds. In 1808, Secretary of the Treasury Albert Gallatin asked Congress to supplement local investment with $20 million for roads and canals. John C. Calhoun's Bonus Bill, an elaborate attempt to implement Gallatin's concept, was vetoed by President James Madison in 1817. New Yorkers, twice denied federal assistance, raised $7 million in state revenues and bonds for the 364-mile Erie Canal, completed in 1825.

The Erie Canal inspired a boom in state and federal waterway projects. Encouraged by the U.S. Supreme Court's outspoken nationalism in *Gibbons v. Ogden* (1824), Congress purchased $300,000 in canal stock to finance a cut through the Delmarva Peninsula. Virginians chartered a larger enterprise, the Chesapeake and Ohio Canal. By 1830, New Jersey, Ohio, Indiana, and Illinois had launched ambitious projects, and Pennsylvania spanned the Alleghenies with the Main Line canal from Philadelphia to Pittsburgh, opened in 1834.

Antebellum canal engineers were mostly millwrights, surveyors, mechanics, or masons, some field-trained on the Erie Canal and others formally schooled at the U.S. Military Academy at West Point. Construction fell to dollar-a-day laborers, increasingly Irish Americans. The Panic of 1837 hurt canal investors, pushing Maryland, Ohio, Michigan, Indiana, and Illinois to the brink of bankruptcy. In 1838, as the nation's attention shifted to railroads and steamboats, Congress suspended federal aid to canal corporations. From 1815 to 1861 the total U.S. expenditure on canal construction was about $195 million—two thirds of it public money.

After the Civil War, the federal investment in waterways focused on levees, jetties, locks, and dams. One popular project was the deepwater shipping channel that opened the Mississippi River below New Orleans. Serious flooding in Louisiana, meanwhile, led to the 1879 establishment of a levee-oversight bureau called the Mississippi River Commission. In 1902, Congress extended federal financing through the U.S. Reclamation Service, later renamed the Bureau of Reclamation. Senator George W. Norris of Nebraska, a crusader for public hydropower, sponsored the 1933 law that created the Tennessee Valley Authority (TVA).

Federal responsibility for flood control increased dramatically after the great Mississippi flood of 1927. The Mississippi River Commission oversaw a vast network of tall levees, storage reservoirs, navigation cutoffs that straightened rivers, and floodways that spread high water through swamps. On the Mississippi above Saint Louis, meanwhile, the U.S. Army Corps of Engineers constructed a lock-and-dam slack-water project for barge navigation.

Rural demand for electricity helped justify massive construction. One engineering triumph was Boulder Dam on the Colorado River, finished in 1935 and renamed Hoover Dam in 1947. The 1936 Flood Control Act greatly expanded the Army Corps of Engineers' jurisdiction, granting $310 million for some 250 projects. Flood control became a primary justification for the corps' basinwide dam and canal projects such as the Saint Lawrence Seaway, the Pick–Sloan project on the Missouri River, and the Tennessee–Tombigbee Waterway. In all, about seventy-five thousand large dams have been built in the nation's rivers.

A major twentieth-century waterway project was the Saint Lawrence Seaway. This joint Canadian–U.S. engineering project was authorized by Canada in 1951 and by the U.S. Congress in 1954. The seaway opened in 1959. By a system of canals, dams, and locks extending over twenty-three hundred miles westward from Montreal, the Saint Lawrence Seaway links the Great Lakes to the Saint Lawrence River and the Atlantic Ocean by a channel twenty-seven feet deep that can accommodate freighters with a capacity of nearly thirty thousand tons. The seaway proved an economic boon to such ports as Buffalo, New York; Cleveland, Ohio; Detroit, Michigan; Chicago; Milwaukee, Wisconsin; and Duluth, Minnesota, enabling the agricultural and industrial products of the upper Middle West to reach world markets and bringing imported goods and raw materials to the American heartland.

Once widely praised as monuments to American know-how, dams, environmentalists now maintain, have degraded water quality and killed migrating fish. In 1997 the Federal Energy Regulatory Commission (FERC) responded to environmental protest by calling for the removal of Edwards Dam in Maine. In the Pacific

Northwest, meanwhile, a study by the Army Corps of Engineers concluded that the most effective way to restore seagoing salmon and steelhead was to breach Snake River dams.

Levees and canals can also degrade the natural process of flooding and silting that replenishes marshes and swamps. In 2005, in the sinking marsh below New Orleans, a deepwater shipping canal magnified the damage of Hurricane Katrina. In 2007, Congress closed the canal.

[*See also* Fisheries; Gallatin, Albert, and Economic Development; *Gibbons v. Ogden*; Hydroelectric Power; Maritime Transport; Public Works Administration; Railroads; Tennessee Valley Authority; Transportation Revolution; *and* Turnpikes and Early Roads.]

BIBLIOGRAPHY

Armstrong, Ellis L., ed. *History of Public Works in the United States, 1776–1976.* Chicago: American Public Works Association, 1976.
Bartlett, Richard A., ed. *Rolling Rivers: An Encyclopedia of America's Rivers.* New York: McGraw–Hill, 1984.

Todd A. Shallat

CAPITALISM

The term "capitalism" has frequently been used to describe the American economy. The general usage of the term, however, dates to the late nineteenth century and was largely drawn from Karl Marx's multivolume work *Das Kapital.* Initially used mainly by Marxist critics of capitalism, the term came to mean an economic system with private ownership of land and capital, an individual's right to his or her own labor, and the existence of competitive markets that determine prices and quantities for goods and services and for factors of production (land, raw materials, labor, capital). Often it has been defined as "free enterprise" or "laissez-faire," an economy in which government plays a limited role. "Capitalism" is, however, a term more frequently used and debated than clearly defined; its precise meaning has seldom been widely agreed upon.

Characteristics. Capitalism has often been contrasted with other basic types of economic systems that preceded or coexisted with it. In the Marxist scheme, all societies followed, or will follow, a predictable set of economic stages. First comes the transition from feudalism to capitalism, leading to freer markets and freer labor, thus permitting rapid economic growth. Marx predicted that capitalism, in turn, would lead to Communism, as a result of labor revolt. In the Cold War era, social scientists and government leaders drew a sharp political contrast between the capitalist world (the United States and, in some cases, western Europe) and the Communist bloc (the Soviet Union, its eastern European allies, and the People's Republic of China), a comparison based on the two blocs' relative economic development and differences in political freedoms. Capitalism's supporters credited it with generating more rapid growth and greater political freedoms than Communism.

Some scholars assert that capitalism itself passes through successive stages, reflecting changing economic structures. In the early stages of merchant, or commercial, capitalism in western Europe, from the sixteenth to eighteenth centuries, expanding commerce, especially overseas trade with colonial empires, drove the economic system. Industrial capitalism, based on a manufacturing sector and factory production using free labor, followed as the next stage. The final stage, finance capitalism, characterized by V. I. Lenin and others as the highest stage of capitalism, was marked by excess production and savings that needed foreign outlets. Hence, according to this interpretive scheme, imperialism arose in the late nineteenth century to preserve domestic capitalist economies from collapse. Such divisions into stages have been applied more easily to England and to western Europe than to the United States, where, by contrast, capitalism's different stages have generally revolved around changes in the relation of government to business.

American capitalism began with English colonial policy, which established basically free markets internally, combined with mercantilistic regulations to control international trade. Mercantilism, however, under which governments sought to promote home industry and maximize exports, existed alongside most elements of capitalism, such as individual freedoms and the role of markets in internal and external trade. That mercantilism as conventionally defined was not inconsistent with capitalism is apparent from the fact that the newly independent United States adopted a form of mercantilism, using state power to promote economic growth. In the late nineteenth century, the government began to regulate businesses through antitrust legislation and related measures, but throughout the century governments had played an important, positive role in the economy through expenditures to build transportation, tariffs to protect industries, banking controls to police the financial system, and public education to improve human capital. The late nineteenth-century rise of government economic regulation, however, represented a shift away from earlier governmental stress on the promotion of business and economic growth. Even with the growth of regulation, considerable room for competitive markets and freedom of individual choice existed within the economic sphere.

Connotations and Prospects.

The term "capitalism" has carried both positive and negative connotations. The positive connotation, as suggested by the title of Carl Snyder's 1940 book, *Capitalism: The Creator*, celebrates the alleged link between capitalism and political freedom. The negative connotations are clearly conveyed in such terms as "capitalist exploiter," "capitalist imperialist," or simply "filthy capitalist." Praise of capitalists and capitalism has been a central theme among those who desire to limit public restrictions on business behavior, while many reformers and reform movements in U.S. history have emphasized the social costs of "unfettered" or "unbridled" capitalism. Capitalism's critics have focused on how it unevenly distributes income and wealth, on the problems created by large fluctuations, and also on how the market system trivializes culture.

Capitalism's long-term survival prospects have been much discussed. Seemingly whenever a financial crisis occurs, some argue that capitalism as we know it is doomed. During the Great Depression of the 1930s, commentators frequently proclaimed capitalism's decline or demise, often in contrast to the ability of the Communist economies to avoid such severe economic collapse. By contrast, the economic revival of the capitalist economies in the post–World War II era—particularly through the 1970s, a period of unusually rapid growth by any historical standard—elicited praise. Social scientists extolled the post–World War II economies alternatively as a return to capitalist principles or as the development of a new economic system with an enlarged governmental role and the introduction of elements of socialism—a hybrid economic system with only some capitalistic elements surviving. Some labeled this system "managed capitalism," reflecting an enhanced government commitment to influence macroeconomic policy (monetary and fiscal policies), as well as to regulate microeconomic behavior of markets. Whether this system will come to be regarded as a new stage of economic and political development or as another example of capitalism's basic adaptability and flexibility remains to be seen.

[*See also* **Capitalism and Immigration; Economic Theories and Thought; Financial and Banking Promotion and Regulation; Laissez-Faire and Classical Economics; Marxian Economics; Mercantilism; Neoclassical Economics; Neoliberalism; Slavery and Capitalism;** *and* **Welfare Capitalism.**]

BIBLIOGRAPHY

Appleby, Joyce. *The Relentless Revolution: A History of Capitalism*. New York: W. W. Norton and Company, 2010.

Friedman, Milton. *Capitalism and Freedom*. Chicago: University of Chicago Press, 1962.

Hughes, Jonathan R.T. *The Governmental Habit Redux: Economic Controls from Colonial Times to the Present*. Princeton, N.J.: Princeton University Press, 1991.

Neal, Larry. *The Rise of Financial Capitalism: International Capital Markets in the Age of Reason*. Cambridge, U.K.: Cambridge University Press, 1990.

Schumpeter, Joseph A. *Capitalism, Socialism, and Democracy*. New York: Harper & Brothers, 1942.

Sombart, Werner. "Capitalism." In *Encyclopedia of the Social Sciences*, edited by Edwin R. A. Seligman and Alvin Johnson, vol. 3, pp. 195–208. New York: Macmillan, 1930.

Stanley L. Engerman

CAPITALISM AND IMMIGRATION

Capitalism creates migrants, and the globalization of capitalism produces immigrants. Capitalist development inevitably entails a radical transformation of institutions, ideas, and relationships. The shift from a peasant or command economy to a market economy is highly disruptive, displacing people from existing occupations and ways of life. Within countries, the substitution of capital for labor and the creation of markets for land brought about massive displacements from the countryside, leading to rural–urban migration and the urbanization of society. Although some countries underwent capitalist development without sending many migrants abroad, most nations historically have experienced mass emigration as well.

The world has experienced two eras of capitalist globalization. The first lasted from 1800 to 1914 and involved the integration of European markets with each other and with their overseas colonies and offshoots. The core of the system was a transatlantic economy in which European nations exported capital and people to the Americas and received back commodities and raw materials first and later on manufactured goods. During this period, global markets for goods, capital, commodities, and labor were increasingly integrated, and with few restrictions on immigration, more than 50 million people emigrated from Europe, mostly to the United States but also to other countries such as Canada, Argentina, Brazil, and Australia.

The first era of globalization came to an abrupt end with the outbreak of World War I, which halted transatlantic trade, investment, and immigration and led to rising nationalism, protectionism, and immigration restrictions in the 1920s. What was left of the global economy collapsed in 1929, and international migration fell to a trickle.

In the aftermath of a global depression and World War II, a series of multilateral institutions were created to preserve peace, encourage trade, and promote economic development. Supported by institutions run by the United Nations, the World Bank, the International Monetary Fund, and the General Agreement on Tariffs and Trade, the global market economy began to revive, first among the United States, western Europe, and Japan, then incorporating the so-called Asian Tigers of South Korea, Taiwan, and Singapore and southern European countries such as Greece, Spain, and Portugal. The collapse of the Soviet Union and China's abandonment of a command economy in the late 1980s brought the second wave of capitalist globalization to full fruition.

Accompanying the global renewal of trade and investment was a global revival of immigration from the developing to the developed world. As newer capitalist economies matured and joined the global trading regime as developed nations, they progressively shifted from the export to the import of labor. By the early twenty-first century, roughly 3 percent of all people lived outside the country of their birth. Unlike the first era of globalization, however, the early twenty-first century has been characterized by closed global labor markets. Although all developed nations receive immigrants, they attempt to restrict their numbers, leading to the phenomenon of undocumented migration as a hallmark of the era. In the United States, for example, roughly one third of all immigrants are present without authorization.

[*See also* Globalization; Immigration-Restriction Laws; Indentured Labor; Labor Markets; Migratory Labor and Migrant Workers; *and* Trade Policy, Federal.]

BIBLIOGRAPHY

Massey, Douglas S. 1988. "International Migration and Economic Development in Comparative Perspective." *Population and Development Review* 14 (1988): 383–414.

Massey, Douglas S. "The Political Economy of Migration in an Era of Globalization." In *International Migration and Human Rights: The Global Repercussions of US Policy,* edited by Samuel Martinez, pp. 25–43. Berkeley: University of California Press, 2009.

Massey, Douglas S., Jorge Durand, and Nolan J. Malone. 2002. *Beyond Smoke and Mirrors: Mexican Immigration in an Age of Economic Integration.* New York: Russell Sage Foundation, 2002.

Douglas S. Massey

CAPITALISM AND INDUSTRIAL DEMOCRACY

See **Industrial Democracy.**

CARNEGIE, ANDREW

(1835–1919), industrial entrepreneur and philanthropist whose life embodied the rags-to-riches myth of the self-made man. Born to a working-class family in Dunfermline, Scotland, Carnegie immigrated to America in 1848 and settled near Pittsburgh, Pennsylvania. Soon after his arrival, he began work in a textile mill for $1.20 per week. Five decades later, he stood at the pinnacle of the U.S. steel industry, the richest man in the world.

Carnegie rose rapidly, by 1853 becoming the personal assistant to Thomas A. Scott, the future head of the Pennsylvania Railroad. In 1856, Carnegie invested his savings in a sleeping-car company that netted him $5,000 in annual dividends. That same year he assisted Scott in suppressing union organizers, winning for himself the superintendency of the Pennsylvania Railroad's western division.

Carnegie's investments grew throughout the 1860s. Aided by a loan from Scott, Carnegie founded the Keystone Bridge Company in 1867 and within a year controlled assets in excess of $400,000. By then, his earnings were so large that he pledged to retire from business and pursue scholarship and philanthropy because, he feared, the quest for wealth would inevitably lead to personal degradation.

But Carnegie did not keep his promise. He continued to invest heavily in the iron business that he had purchased in the 1860s and by 1872 was planning the world's most advanced steel mill. Over the course of the next three decades, Carnegie competed ruthlessly against his rivals in the steel industry, while also resisting the initiatives of organized labor. He became a trailblazer in reducing production costs and extending managerial control over workers. In 1875, Carnegie's new steel mill, the Edgar Thomson Works near Pittsburgh, ushered in a revolution in industrial production and organization. He rid the mill of union workers and produced rails at a lower cost and earned more money than any other U.S. metal maker. The Bessemer process of steelmaking—which Carnegie was the first to use—produced vast quantities of hard, durable metal at low cost. In combining the essential stages of metal production (smelting, refining, and rolling), Carnegie achieved a new level of automation and technological integration.

Carnegie's profits, investments, and fame continued to expand during the 1880s, a time when he found new sources of personal fulfillment as well. He married Louise Whitfield, with whom he later had one child, Margaret; he began to dispense his wealth by donating money for thousands of Carnegie libraries; and he summed up his social thought in *Triumphant Democracy* (1886). In several influential essays, notably "Wealth" (*North American Review*, 1889), he defended the theoretical right of workers to join unions and proclaimed the responsibility of the wealthy to redistribute their money for the good of the community. In 1892, however, Carnegie and his close business associate Henry Clay Frick chose to maximize profits rather than respect their workers' right to a union. The result was the violence-ridden Homestead steel strike that thwarted unionism in the steel industry until the 1930s.

Carnegie paid dearly for his victory at Homestead in the arena of public opinion, but he remained active publicly. In the late 1890s he campaigned against the Spanish–American War and opposed the annexation of the Philippines. In 1901 he sold the Carnegie Steel Company to J. P. Morgan for $480 million, freeing himself to pursue such philanthropic ventures as the Carnegie Foundation for the Advancement of Teaching, the Carnegie Hero Fund, and the Carnegie Endowment for International Peace. His total benefactions—including more than twenty-eight hundred Carnegie libraries—amounted to $350 million.

In his declining years, Carnegie served as a kind of ambassador at large for world peace. From the late 1880s on, he spent much of each year at his estate in Scotland. World War I seemed to crush his otherwise undaunted spirit, and he died in 1919 at Shadowbrook, his estate in the Berkshire hills of Massachusetts.

[*See also* **Homestead Strike (1892)** *and* **Iron and Steel Industry.**]

BIBLIOGRAPHY

Hendrick, Burton J. *The Life of Andrew Carnegie.* Garden City, N.Y.: Doubleday, Doran, 1932.
Wall, Joseph Frazier. *Andrew Carnegie.* New York: Oxford University Press, 1970.

Paul Krause

CATTLEMEN'S ASSOCIATIONS

The term "cattlemen's association" encompasses a range of organizations. The first were informal gatherings of cattle owners who were concerned about rustling. Unfortunately, some became a law unto themselves, and numerous supposed rustlers, whether guilty or not, found themselves hanged from the nearest tree. Soon the cattlemen's associations became more disciplined and organized.

The Texas and Southwestern Cattle Raisers Association, for example, began when forty cattlemen met on 15–16 February 1877 in Graham, Texas, to deal with rustling. The association served only northern Texas, but by 1921 smaller organizations throughout the state, as well as in Oklahoma and New Mexico, merged with it. By the twenty-first century, even cattle raisers from Mexico and Haiti made up its fifteen thousand members. Special rangers are official police officers who arrest lawbreakers, and additional market inspectors enter descriptions of cattle and brands into a database. As part of its mission of "protecting the stewards of land and livestock in the Southwest," the association provides members such services as insurance, workers' compensation, and discounts. Similar cattlemen's associations exist in other states.

Assisting the various state associations is a national association that began in Denver, Colorado, in 1898 as the National Live Stock Growers Association. Though over time it went through mergers, splits, and name changes, the surviving National Cattlemen's Beef Association (NCBA), the name since 1996, serves twenty-first-century cattlemen.

Economics dominated the thinking of cattlemen from the beginning. Rustling, government policies, innovative marketing measures, and feeding programs affected profits. Joint efforts, whether at the state, regional, or national level, benefit all cattlemen.

[*See also* **Barbed Wire; Cowboys; Livestock Industry; Marketing Cooperatives;** *and* **Public Land Policy.**]

BIBLIOGRAPHY

"A Brief History of Texas and Southwestern Cattle Raisers Association." Texas and Southwestern Cattle Raisers Association. http://www.texascattleraisers.org/about-tscra/mission-history.html.

"National Cattlemen's Association." National Cattlemen's Beef Association. http://www.beefusa.org/nationalcattlemensassociation.aspx.

Pate, J'Nell L. *America's Historic Stockyards Livestock Hotels.* Fort Worth, Tex.: Texas Christian University Press, 2005.

J'Nell L. Pate

CHAMBERS OF COMMERCE

Often led by bankers, realtors, and representatives of other service industries, chambers of commerce are a type of organization that represent a broad range of business interests in a given city or state. Such organizations were formed as early as the 1780s, but their numbers and their political role blossomed in the Gilded Age in response to the challenges of rapid economic growth, labor unrest, and urban political reform. Unlike more narrowly focused employers' or trade associations, local and regional chambers focused on such issues as property taxes, zoning and regulation, and business promotion.

In 1912, a group of leading municipal chambers and trade associations formed the United States Chamber of Commerce (USCC) to unite business interests on public-policy issues. Through the middle years of the twentieth century, the USCC was less confrontational than organizations like the National Association of Manufacturers and was more likely to encourage its members to accommodate to changing patterns of labor relations and political regulation. The USCC cooperated closely with the federal government in mobilizing the economy for World War I and with Herbert Hoover's Commerce Department during the 1920s. The USCC initially attempted to work with the New Deal, but like the larger business community that it represented, it grew increasingly disenchanted with many of President Franklin Delano Roosevelt's policies. Though the USCC participated in the postwar business backlash against the New Deal, it also acted as a leading business advocate for a limited welfare state built on public spending and the "politics of growth." After the 1930s, the USCC was led by a loose coalition of internationalists, shippers, exporters, bankers, and natural-resource interests. Through political lobbying, informational services to members, and its magazine, *Nation's Business*, the USCC proved a moderate and politically pragmatic vehicle for business opinion and influence.

[*See also* **National Association of Manufacturers.**]

BIBLIOGRAPHY

Collins, Robert M. *The Business Response to Keynes, 1929–1964*. New York: Columbia University Press, 1981.

Werking, Richard Hume. "Bureaucrats, Businessmen, and Foreign Trade: The Origins of the United States Chamber of Commerce." *Business History Review* 52, no. 3 (1978): 321–341.

Colin Gordon

CHANGE TO WIN

The roots of the Change to Win (CTW) federation date to the summer of 2003 when five national union presidents, four of whose unions were affiliates of the American Federation of Labor and Congress of Industrial Organizations (AFL-CIO), met over the Fourth of July holiday to discuss the decades-long fall in union density. After subsequent meetings, these union officers advanced a strategy for both increasing union membership and revitalizing the U.S. trade union movement. Calling their alliance the New Unity Partnership (NUP), the Service Employees International Union (SEIU), the

Union of Needle Trades, Industrial, and Textile Employees (UNITE), the Hotel Employees and Restaurant Employees (HERE), the Laborers' International Union of North America (LIUNA), and the United Brotherhood of Carpenters (UBC) decided to pool their funds in joint organizing drives, while advocating that the AFL-CIO's fifty-seven unions combine into fifteen or twenty mega-unions.

Although the NUP formally dissolved in January 2005, during that winter and early spring the dissident unions searched for support among federation affiliates for reorganizing the AFL-CIO along their proposed lines. Upon realizing that it would be impossible to implement their reforms, on 14 June 2005 the SEIU, UNITE HERE (UNITE and HERE merged in 2004), the LIUNA, the Teamsters, and the United Food and Commercial Workers (UFCW) established the Change to Win Coalition. On 27 September 2005 these five unions, along with the UBC and the United Farm Workers, created the CTW, with 5.4 million members, and announced that the new federation would dedicate itself to unionizing hundreds of thousands of the nation's unorganized workers.

In contrast to the AFL-CIO's per capita dues of sixty-five cents, the CTW's rate was only twenty-five cents in 2006, with 75 percent devoted to organizing. The CTW's unionization efforts targeted service workers in industries protected from outsourcing—industries such as health care, hospitality, retail building services, transportation, and construction. Additionally, the CTW's strategy favored militancy in union organizing as the best means of obtaining cooperation and partnership with business. In September 2011, for instance, CTW unions were conducting major organizing drives among Wal-Mart employees and ports' truck drivers and warehouse workers in southern California.

In January 2009, five CTW unions conferred with seven large AFL-CIO affiliates to explore reunification, but they failed to reach agreement. Later in the year, internal problems disrupted the CTW. By mid-September 2009 the UBC had left the federation. After a bitter internal fight that resulted in the departure of one-third of UNITE HERE's members for the SEIU, UNITE HERE's rump rejoined the AFL-CIO. In August 2010 the LIUNA announced that it would abandon the CTW; that October the union formally reaffiliated with the AFL-CIO.

In spite of increased funding, the CTW's organizing successes have been limited. The Teamsters unionized several thousand school-bus drivers, and UNITE HERE, when still a CTW affiliate from 2005 to 2007, organized an additional 6,700 hotel workers in those years and obtained employer neutrality agreements for organizing new hotels in six large cities. Moreover, by a vote of 2,041 to 1,879, the UFCW won a certification election victory at North Carolina's Smithfield Foods in December 2008.

In the final analysis, the CTW's formation appears to have been a mistake. The federation ultimately offered no new ideas for revitalizing the U.S. trade union movement, and its organizing successes have been far from stellar. The CTW unions could have pursued similar strategies as AFL-CIO affiliates.

[*See also* **American Federation of Labor and Congress of Industrial Organizations; Labor Movement, Decline of the; Service Employees International Union; Union Reform Movements; United Brotherhood of Carpenters and Joiners;** *and* **United Farm Workers of America.**]

BIBLIOGRAPHY

Chaison, Gary. "The AFL-CIO Split: Does It Really Matter?" *Journal of Labor Research* 28, no. 2 (2007): 301–311.

Masters, Marick F., Ray Gibney, and Tom Zagenczyk. "The AFL-CIO v. CTW: The Competing Visions, Strategies, and Structures." *Journal of Labor Research* 27, no. 4 (2006): 473–504.

Victor G. Devinatz

CHARLES RIVER BRIDGE v. WARREN BRIDGE

Charles River Bridge v. Warren Bridge was an 1837 Supreme Court ruling relating to corporate development. In 1650 the Massachusetts legislature gave Harvard College an exclusive right to operate a ferry from Boston across the Charles River to Charlestown. Under acts of 1785 and 1792, Massachusetts transferred all rights of Harvard's monopoly to the Charles River Bridge Company and gave that company a seventy-year charter to operate a toll bridge between Charlestown and Boston. In 1828 the legislature chartered the Warren Bridge Company to build a new bridge that would revert to the state within six years after its completion. The stock owners of the Charles River Bridge complained that the charter for the new Warren Bridge violated its contract with the state. The Charles River Bridge Company argued that its original monopoly to operate the ferry included the bridge and that, in effect, the state had granted the company an exclusive right to operate a bridge between the two cities. The Charles River Bridge Company sued, citing the contracts clause of the U.S. Constitution (Article 1, Section 9), which bars states from "impairing the Obligations of Contracts."

By a vote of 4 to 3, the U.S. Supreme Court in 1837 upheld Massachusetts's right to charter the Warren Bridge. Writing for the Court, Chief Justice Roger B. Taney ruled that the charter granted to the Charles River Company should be read strictly; it did not include the promise of a monopoly, and therefore the state had the power to charter a new company.

This ruling allowed new industries to develop alongside—and even to supplant—existing technologies and companies. It gave states flexibility in developing public policy toward industries and utilities. It encouraged more competitive enterprise yet allowed states to grant monopolies to enterprises that served the public interest. Adhering to the logic of *Charles River Bridge*, however, states often included contract clauses enabling them to revoke all or some of the charter rights.

[*See also* **Contract, Sanctity of.**]

BIBLIOGRAPHY

Kutler, Stanley I. *Privilege and Creative Destruction: The Charles River Bridge Case.* Philadelphia: Lippincott, 1971.
Monroe, Elizabeth B. "Abridging Vested Interest: The Battle of the Massachusetts Bridge." In *Historic U.S. Court Cases: 1690–1990*, edited by John W. Johnson, pp. 174–181. New York: Garland, 1992.

Paul Finkelman

CHASE MANHATTAN BANK

In 1877 the banker and financial publisher John Thompson established a nationally chartered bank in New York City. He named it "Chase National Bank" in honor of his late friend Salmon P. Chase, who had served as President Abraham Lincoln's secretary of the Treasury. The new institution quickly became a bankers' bank: by 1914 two thirds of its assets were deposits made by other banks. The establishment of the Federal Reserve at the end of 1913 forced Chase National to pursue other opportunities, something it did by distributing Liberty bonds and acquiring new commercial and industrial customers. During the 1920s the bank grew rapidly through a series of mergers and acquisitions, and in 1930 it became the nation's largest commercial bank. It retained that status until the mid-1940s.

Chase National's focus on big business threatened to leave it behind during a postwar economic boom fueled largely by consumers, so in 1955 chairman John J. McCloy facilitated a merger with the consumer-oriented Bank of the Manhattan Company. That institution traced its roots back to 1799, when the state of New York chartered a water company but also permitted it to operate as a lending institution. The new bank, named "Chase Manhattan," had branches throughout New York City and grew rapidly following the merger. Chase Manhattan expanded into global markets, became a major player in the credit-card industry, and was an early provider of electronic home banking. It also lobbied heavily for repeal of the Glass–Steagall Act. In 1996, Chemical Bank acquired Chase Manhattan, adopting the latter's more recognizable name. On the last day of 2000, Chase Manhattan finalized a merger with the investment bank J. P. Morgan, and the "Chase Manhattan" name officially passed into history.

[*See also* **Consumer Credit and Credit Cards** *and* **Glass–Steagall, Repeal of.**]

BIBLIOGRAPHY

JPMorgan Chase & Co. *The History of JPMorgan Chase & Co.: 200 Years of Leadership in Banking.* 2008. Available at http://www.jpmorganchase.com/corporate/About-JPMC/document/short history.pdf.
Wilson, John Donald. *The Chase: The Chase Manhattan Bank, N.A., 1945–1985.* Boston: Harvard Business School Press, 1986.

Timothy S. Wolters

CHAVEZ, CESAR

(1927–1993), labor activist and founder and president of the United Farm Workers of

America. Cesar Chavez was born to the farmers and store owners Librado and Juana Chavez in Arizona in 1927. During the Great Depression, his parents lost both their farm and their business interests and turned to migrant farm work to survive. Barely seventeen, Chavez joined the navy in 1944; he served in the Mariana Islands and in Guam. After the war, he returned to California and married Helen Fabela. They eventually settled in San Jose, where he met Fred Ross of the Community Service Organization (CSO). Chavez so impressed Ross that by 1953 he had recruited Chavez to work for the CSO. Chavez became the CSO's general director in 1960. Through his work with the CSO, Chavez began to appreciate the growing concerns of Mexican Americans about the overabundance of braceros in the fields. In 1962, Chavez resigned from the CSO when he found that its leadership would not support programs for a farmworkers' union. Chavez then moved his family to the farm town of Delano and began a door-to-door campaign to build the National Farm Workers Association (NFWA). When the bracero program ended in 1964, Chavez had a chance for success. In March 1965, union workers in a rose field in McFarland, about twelve miles from Delano, struck for higher wages. They did not gain union recognition, but the workers were pleased with the promised pay raise.

In September, Larry Itliong, the leader of the Agricultural Workers Organizing Committee (AWOC), asked the NFWA to join the AWOC's strike against the grape growers who were refusing to pay the same wages that workers had received earlier in the year in other parts of the state. Chavez called NFWA members together for a successful strike vote on 16 September, Mexico's independence day. The resulting grape strike targeted grape growers mostly in the San Joaquin valley. When the workers found that immigrant workers from Mexico still easily replaced them, Chavez began a boycott of non-union grapes. During this strike and boycott, the mostly Hispanic NFWA and the mostly Filipino AWOC decided to merge rather than risk losing elections to the Teamsters. The result was the 1966 formation of the United Farm Workers Organizing Committee. The strike and boycott concluded in 1970, at which point Chavez had under union contract 85 percent of California table-grape growers. Chavez had succeeded in organizing the first truly successful farm labor movement in California.

Other strikes and boycotts were not so effective. Increasingly Chavez found his union at odds with the Teamsters, and in 1973 when the 1970 union contracts expired, many growers signed with the Teamsters. Although he tried leading similar strikes and boycotts for other types of produce such as lettuce, none was as successful as the original grape strike.

Chavez's greatest significance is his legacy as a nonviolent labor leader. He managed to use the tactics of the contemporary civil rights era and the philosophies of Mohandas Gandhi to promote nonviolent strategies within labor movements. As such, he is widely remembered as both a labor leader and a civil rights leader, although his work was mostly in labor struggles.

[*See also* **Agricultural Workers; Braceros; Labor Leaders;** *and* **United Farm Workers of America.**]

BIBLIOGRAPHY

Ganz, Marshall. *Why David Sometimes Wins: Leadership, Organization, and Strategy in the California Farm Worker Movement.* New York: Oxford University Press, 2009.

Griswold del Castillo, Richard, and Richard A. Garcia. *César Chávez: A Triumph of Spirit.* Norman: University of Oklahoma Press, 1995.

Andrea Johnson

CHEMICAL INDUSTRY

The largest industry in America, the chemical industry supplies roughly a quarter of the world's chemicals, more than any other nation. In the Colonial Era, chemical manufacturing was confined to such rudimentary products as indigo dyes, naval stores, leather, glass, soap, and candles. In the early 1800s, producers relied heavily on imports of alkalies—especially soda ash, caustic soda, and bleach—from Great Britain. The typical nineteenth-century American chemical manufactory was owner managed, employed eight to twelve workers, and served local markets. Philadelphia, an industry center, hosted the first professional organization (Chemical Society of Philadelphia, 1792) and publication (*American Journal of Pharmacy*, 1825). The DuPont Corporation, a giant in the chemical industry, had its origins in 1802 when E. I. du Pont started a gunpowder company near Wilmington, Delaware.

In the late nineteenth century, American producers excelled at prospecting, mining, smelting, and refining iron ore, coal, copper, lead, zinc, tungsten, and other inorganic minerals into fertilizers, explosives, nitric acid, and sulfuric acid. Progress with dyestuffs, coal–tar compounds, and other organics accelerated after the adoption of the Solvay process, a commercial technology for the manufacture of sodium carbonate, in the 1880s. Some American firms, exploiting abundant hydroelectric power, became large producers of electrochemicals. In 1914, inorganic chemicals accounted for roughly half of U.S. production, organics for about one quarter, and acids and electrochemicals for one quarter.

American producers made significant progress in advanced technologies—pharmaceuticals, dyestuffs, and fine chemicals—in the early twentieth century. Vital to the World War I military effort, the industry was supported by tariffs and the government's confiscation and licensing of key German technologies, especially dyestuffs and the Haber–Bosch process for nitrogen fixation. Between 1900 and 1930, the U.S. chemical industry's growth far outstripped that of Germany or Great Britain. Rapid expansion of the automotive industry in the 1920s spurred demand for thermoplastics, protective coatings, and petroleum products. A merger wave in that decade created Allied Chemical and Dye and Union Carbide and Carbon, which joined DuPont and American Cyanamid as the nation's largest producers. Robust sales of rayon, cellophane, pesticides, fertilizers, and other key products in the 1930s earned the industry a reputation as "depression proof." Leading firms invested heavily in research and development, opening some 430 new laboratories between 1918 and 1945.

World War II brought heavy government involvement through an enormously successful synthetic-rubber program; aggressive investment in government-owned, company-operated plants; and a new round of confiscation of German technology. The postwar decades brought both a petrochemicals revolution and new challenges. Exploiting abundant sources of oil and natural gas, American chemical and petroleum companies mass-produced so-called miracle plastics such as polyester, polyethylene, polypropylene, and polyvinyl chloride. Foreign competition and the energy crisis of the 1970s led to overcapacity and falling profits. Meanwhile, the industry confronted new regulatory controls in the early 1970s, following public outcry over the health and environmental risks of agricultural chemicals and water- and airborne wastes. In 1984, methyl isocyanate gas escaping from a Union Carbide plant in Bhopal, India, killed more than three thousand people and injured thousands more. Despite its problems, however, the American chemical industry was one of the few key sectors of the American economy to retain its global dominance.

[*See also* Environmental Regulations; Petroleum Industry; Pharmaceutical Industry; Plastics and Synthetics; *and* Technology.]

BIBLIOGRAPHY

Arora, Ashish, Ralph Landau, and Nathan Rosenberg. *Chemicals and Long-Term Economic Growth: Insights from the Chemical Industry.* New York: Wiley, 1998.

Haynes, Williams. *American Chemical Industry.* 6 vols. New York: Van Nostrand, 1945–1954.

David B. Sicilia

CHICAGO SCHOOL

See Friedman, Milton, and the Chicago School of Economics.

CHILD LABOR

Child labor, long a feature of American rural life, grew enormously and changed character with the industrialization of the late nineteenth century. On farms and in coal mines, on city streets and in tenements, in mills and canneries, almost 2 million children, some as young as five and six years old, worked long hours for a pittance, often under harsh conditions.

In response, some people began to fight the evil of child labor. In 1901, Edgar Gardner Murphy, a clergyman, organized the Alabama Child Labor Committee, the first organization of its kind in the United States. A year later, Florence Kelley, Lillian Wald, and Robert Hunter created the New York Child Labor Committee. In the early twentieth century, twenty-eight states restricted child labor by law, but most of the laws were vaguely worded, full of exemptions, and laxly enforced. To achieve better enforcement of these laws on a national basis, reformers in 1904 created the National Child Labor Committee (NCLC). The NCLC, under the leadership of such reformers as Felix Adler, Samuel McCune Lindsay, Alexander McKelway, and Owen R. Lovejoy, led the fight against child labor.

By 1909, despite further success in securing state regulation of child labor, the NCLC sought federal legislation. Despite vigorous opposition from various groups, Congress in 1916 passed, and President Woodrow Wilson signed into law, the Keating–Owen Child Labor Act, the first federal law addressing the issue. Two years later, however, in *Hammer v. Dagenhart*, the U.S. Supreme Court ruled the measure unconstitutional as an unwarranted exercise of the power to regulate interstate commerce granted to the federal government in the Constitution. When Congress quickly passed a second federal child-labor statute, this time using its taxing power, the Supreme Court invalidated that measure as well.

For the reformers, the only remaining course appeared to be a constitutional amendment. Winning broad public support, the proposed amendment sailed through both houses of Congress in 1924 by large majorities. Opponents, however, organized an aggressive counterattack, led by big business—especially the National Association of Manufacturers—in alliance with conservative organizations and publications. Some leaders of the Catholic Church, moreover, opposed the amendment as a threat to parental rights and parochial education. Falling eight states short of ratification, the proposed amendment died.

In June 1938, however, Congress passed, and President Franklin Delano Roosevelt signed into law, the Fair Labor Standards Act, which effectively prohibited child labor. The Supreme Court unanimously upheld the act in February 1941. Even before the 1938 law, however, the use of machines on farms and in factories had diminished the need for unskilled manual labor. As a result, by the 1950s child labor had been largely eliminated in America.

Around the turn of the twenty-first century, however, the practice reappeared. An influx of immigrants from Asia and Latin America, including undocumented immigrants, gave new life to tenement sweatshops, and the fast-food industry employed masses of young workers. Simultaneously, a rise in both school-dropout rates and juvenile delinquency prompted many people to promote paid employment for youngsters as a positive good. Thus despite legislative and judicial victories, the issue of child labor remained troubling and unresolved.

[*See also* **Factory and Hours Laws; Fair Labor Standards Act; Keating–Owen Act; Kelley, Florence;** *and* **Undocumented Workers.**]

BIBLIOGRAPHY

Trattner, Walter I. *Crusade for the Children: A History of the National Child Labor Committee and Child Labor Reform in America.* Chicago: Quadrangle, 1970.

Walter I. Trattner

CITIZENS' COMMITTEES AND ALLIANCES

From the early twentieth century to the 1930s the citizens' committee—a variation of "Citizens' Alliance," the name used by a number of groups throughout the United States—was the most innovative grassroots institution fashioned by American business to champion the open shop and to oppose the spread of organized labor. In towns and cities across America the citizens' committee enabled the business community to enter the public sphere as a dis-

interested third party. Through the agency of the citizens' committee, the business community could assemble resources to oppose organized labor in the public sphere, to fight strikes through court-ordered injunctions, to recruit strikebreakers, guards, and labor spies, and to create and sustain blacklists to be employed against labor activists.

J. West Goodwin created the first Citizens' Alliance, in Sedalia, Missouri, on 19 August 1901; by 1904, Goodwin had helped to establish the organization in twenty-eight cities. Others were formed without his direct involvement, and by 1904, Citizens' Alliances existed in cities across America. An early chronicler of the movement, Ray Stannard Baker, observed that the Citizens' Alliance had "sprung into existence with the explosive enthusiasm of a vigilance committee" (p. 283).

Ostensibly, the Citizens' Alliance was a civic organization concerned with shaping opinion and public policy through access to the public sphere. The inclusion of the term "Citizens'" in the organization's title gestured toward the organization's concern with the public interest. Thus the "Citizens'" Alliance asserted a moral authority that was denied to Employers' Associations, which made no claim to being other than an instrument of business. However, the secret membership of the Citizens' Alliance allowed a broader antilabor agenda and invited dissimulation and abuse. When the authorities and a Citizens' Alliance disagreed about how to control industrial conflict, vigilantism sponsored by the Citizens' Alliance often resulted.

The Citizens' Alliance movement gained national leadership in 1903 when David M. Parry, president of the National Association of Manufacturers (NAM), called for a "crusade against unionism." The NAM sponsored the creation of the Citizens' Industrial Alliance (CIA). Its creators described the CIA as a "federation of employers' associations organized to promote peace and harmony between employers and employees" ("Movement to Spread the Open Shop Plan," *New York Times*, 27 November 1904). "Peace and harmony" sat uncomfortably with Parry's claims in 1903 that "organized labor knows but one law, and that is the law of physical force—the law of the Huns and Vandals, the law of the savage" (*Proceedings of the Eighth Annual Convention of the National Association of Manufacturers of the United States of America*, 1903 in Richard W. Gable, "Birth of an Employers' Association," *The Business History Review*, 33:4 (Winter, 1959), 541–542).

The Minneapolis Citizens' Alliance, established in 1903, was one of the more active such organizations. It used secret surveillance, blacklists, and legal action to combat what it considered the spirit of lawlessness and intimidation that it alleged governed the activities of all unions. In the mid-1930s it and other Citizens' Alliances came under increased scrutiny, including by the 1938 La Follette Senate committee hearings into antilabor practices. These hearings disclosed how the Citizens' Alliance and kindred organizations manipulated public opinion and turned civic and state authorities against organized labor in the interest of private capital.

[*See also* **American Anti-Boycott Association; Labor Spies and Pinkertons; Open-Shop Movement;** *and* **Repression of Unions.**]

BIBLIOGRAPHY

Baker, Ray Stannard. "Organized Capital Challenges Organized Labor: The New Employers' Association Movement." *McClure's Magazine* 23 (July 1904): 279–292.
Millikan, William. *A Union against Unions: The Minneapolis Citizens Alliance and Its Fight against Organized Labor, 1903–1947*. Saint Paul: Minnesota Historical Society Press, 2001.
Silverberg, Louis G. "Citizens' Committees: Their Role in Industrial Conflict." *Public Opinion Quarterly* 5 (March 1941): 17–37.

Tom Mitchell

CIVILIAN CONSERVATION CORPS

In late March 1933, during his first hundred days in office, President Franklin D. Roosevelt implored Congress to create the Civilian Conservation Corps (CCC) to help alleviate the 25 percent unemployment rate then plaguing the nation. Two weeks later, on 5 April 1933, he signed an executive order that created the CCC. Though best known for planting 2 billion trees, slowing soil erosion on 40 million acres of farmland, and developing eight hundred new state parks, the CCC also had a dramatic impact on the country's economic and labor history.

Each of the more than 3 million young men between the ages of eighteen and twenty-five who enrolled in the CCC between 1933 and 1942 received $1 a day for their labor, along with room and board in CCC camps scattered across the country. The federal government mailed $25 of each enrollee's $30 monthly paycheck back home to the enrollee's family, which had to be listed on state relief registers. Vocational classes offered at night in CCC camps also helped prepare these young men for jobs after their stint in the CCC. Thus the CCC economically benefited not only the more than 3 million young men who served in it, but also their families.

The CCC also proved economically beneficial to those Americans who lived in local communities situated near the approximately fifteen hundred camps operating at any given moment during the Great Depression years. On average, each CCC camp pumped $5,000 per month back into the local economy through the purchase of materials and services. Approximately $2,000 per month in spending money from each camp also found its way from enrollees' pockets into local movie theaters, pool halls, bars, restaurants, and shops as the young men flocked to nearby towns for recreation on their days off. A single CCC camp therefore injected

$7,000 per month into the nearby economy, or more than $80,000 a year. "Hundreds of communities have discovered since the CCC was organized two years ago," reported *Business Week* in May 1935, "that the neighboring camp is the bright spot on their business map." As it conserved the nation's natural resources, the Civilian Conservation Corps simultaneously stimulated the country's economy.

[*See also* **Great Depression (1929–1939)** *and* **New Deal and Institutional Economics.**]

BIBLIOGRAPHY

Cole, Olen, Jr. *The African-American Experience in the Civilian Conservation Corps.* Gainesville: University Press of Florida, 1999.

Maher, Neil M. *Nature's New Deal: The Civilian Conservation Corps and the Roots of the American Environmental Movement.* Oxford: Oxford University Press, 2008.

Salmond, John A. *The Civilian Conservation Corps, 1933–1942: A New Deal Case Study.* Durham, N.C.: Duke University Press, 1967.

Neil M. Maher

CLARK, JOHN BATES

(1847–1938), neoclassical economist. The first American economist to gain an international reputation, John Bates Clark was born in Providence, Rhode Island. After graduating from Amherst College, he studied at the Universities of Heidelberg and Zurich. On his return to the United States he began an academic career that ended at Columbia University. He was one of the founders of the American Economic Association in 1885.

Clark's reputation rested on his development of the marginal-product theory of wages and profits, making him one of the founders of neoclassical economics. He formulated his theory in the late nineteenth century when the United States experienced a wave of strikes. Clark attributed the strike wave to an imbalance of bargaining power between labor and business and proposed government arbitration to avert industrial conflict. To help develop a standard for government arbitration boards to use in determining wages and profits, Clark investigated how the marginal-product theory could determine wages and profits and then analyzed how that theory operated in a world of large businesses and unions.

Clark's formulation of the marginal-product theory was based on a static economy—which assumed a timeless, changeless world—and relied on abstract concepts to ascertain how competition established wages and profits as equal to the marginal product of labor and capital, that is, the amount of output each added to total production. Clark, it is usually maintained, developed the marginal-product theory to argue that competition resulted in a fair distribution of income. Clark himself, however, insisted that his theory was only a competitive model of the world. In his later work, he offered a real-world analysis of wages that focused on technical change as a primary factor: he contended that wages fell below the marginal product of labor when changes in production methods caused unemployment and downward pressure on wages.

In the real world, Clark called for collective bargaining in which all workers who were willing to take a job in an industry were allowed to join a union. In return for dues, the union would bargain for their wage. He differentiated collective bargaining from union monopolies that benefited their members by fighting employers who paid low wages: such union monopolies were detrimental to society because they kept wages above the marginal product of workers. Clark concluded that the theory of marginal product was most effective when competing employers negotiated with local unions and that the wage agreed upon in such private bargains was the best standard for government arbitration boards to use in similar situations. Clark thus agreed with other intellectuals and social reformers of the time that unions could be a positive force in society, so long as they behaved responsibly.

[*See also* Collective Bargaining; Neoclassical Economics; *and* Strikes.]

BIBLIOGRAPHY

Clark, John Bates. *The Distribution of Wealth: A Theory of Wages, Interest, and Profits.* New York: Macmillan, 1899.

Clark, John Bates. *Essentials of Economic Theory, as Applied to Modern Problems of Industry and Public Policy.* New York: Macmillan, 1907.

Henry, John F. *John Bates Clark: The Making of a Neoclassical Economist.* New York: St. Martin's Press, 1995.

Stabile, Donald R. "Unions and the Natural Standard of Wages: Another Look at the 'J.B. Clark Problem.'" *History of Political Economy* 32 (Fall 2000): 585–606.

Donald R. Stabile

CLARK, JOHN MAURICE

(1884–1963), economist. Born in Northampton, Massachusetts, John Maurice Clark earned his undergraduate degree at Amherst College. He completed a doctorate at Columbia University and spent most of his academic career there. He had an eclectic approach to economics, combining the concept of marginalism from his father, John Bates Clark, with the institutional economics associated with Thorstein Veblen.

Clark's foremost work analyzed how overhead costs, costs that continue when production ceases, affected the market economy. Clark used overhead costs to develop the theory of the accelerator. When expenditures for the capital equipment that constituted overhead costs were concentrated into short time periods, small changes in consumer demand led to larger changes in investment demand. This accelerator process gave booms and recessions reinforcing effects that amplified their impact. Clark also considered social overhead costs that had an indirect effect on society, especially concerning labor. When workers were responsible for their own sustenance and either their wages were not adequate to sustain them or they became unemployed, their health and productivity deteriorated. When businesses coped with recessions through layoffs and wage reductions, they left it to society to sustain the workforce. Clark did not see a market solution to this problem, because wage bargains were the result of the weak bargaining strength of workers compared to that of employers. To control the business cycle he proposed national economic planning through the cooperation of business, labor, and government.

When the United States experienced the Great Depression of the 1930s, Clark argued that national economic planning was necessary for a balanced economy, one in which the productive potential of industry balanced social needs. He was optimistic that the National Industrial Recovery Act (NIRA) of the New Deal would promote such national planning. When the Supreme Court voided the NIRA in 1935, President Franklin D. Roosevelt created the Committee of Industrial Analysis—to which he appointed Clark—to evaluate the economic impact of the NIRA. The committee concluded that the NIRA's attempt to secure voluntary cooperation of business and labor to foster planning had failed.

After this experience, Clark abandoned national economic planning, believing that labor was incapable of effective participation. Businesses had the technical skills for planning, but businessmen captured the NIRA and used it to form cartels. Clark felt that business would control any system of planning to serve its own purposes and not those of society. The rise of the Congress of Industrial Organizations in the late 1930s did not add to labor's ability to participate in planning, Clark argued, because union leaders would prove as loath as businesspeople to act in the interest of society. In his subsequent writings Clark criticized unions for gaining power without using that power for social good.

[*See also* **Business Cycles; National Industrial Recovery Act and National Recovery Administration;** *and* **New Deal and Institutional Economics.**]

BIBLIOGRAPHY

Clark, John Maurice. *Strategic Factors in Business Cycles*. New York: National Bureau of Economic Research, 1934.

Clark, John Maurice. *Studies in the Economics of Overhead Costs*. Chicago: University of Chicago Press, 1923.

Shute, Lawrence. *John Maurice Clark: A Social Economics for the Twenty-First Century*. London: Macmillan, 1997.

Stabile, D.R. "Pigou, Clark and modern economics: the quality of the workforce." *Cambridge Journal of Economics* 20 (May 1996): 277–288.

Donald R. Stabile

CLASS CONSCIOUSNESS

Class consciousness is one of the most elusive and contested concepts in American social and political history. On its most fundamental level, class consciousness can be understood as a measure of political awareness stemming from the "rational" understanding and pursuit of one's economic position and interests, as well as the understanding of how those interests conflict with those of other classes. Karl Marx theorized that working-class class consciousness could lead to a wider solidarity, that is, a shared sense of interests and destiny, among members of the working class. This shared consciousness would lead workers to challenge and reject the dominant or bourgeois ideology of class, moving from what Marx called a "class in itself," that is, a class externally defined by economic circumstances, to a "class for itself," one that could take collective action and mobilize in pursuit of its own political and economic interests.

Because almost nowhere, especially in the United States, did the great mass of workers ever fully develop a Marxian sense of class consciousness, later disciples of Marx developed the concept of "false consciousness": the substitution of illusory ideas for a "true" recognition by a class of its position in an oppressive system. Among the factors that undermined belief in the material struggle of class against class were faith in upward mobility, religion, race, a narrow focus on increased wages (economism), and other that ideas that systematically obscure or mask the true or "objective" nature of class relations. By recognizing the complexity of any social identity, subsequent theorists have also recognized the limits of the idea of false consciousness.

Class Consciousness in the United States. Class consciousness has historically been weak and fragmented in the United States, and the types of objectivity and coherence suggested by the term "class consciousness" have often been the product of other forces. Even though Friedrich Engels predicted that the "more favored soil of America, where no medieval ruins bar the way," would deliver the new nation to a more immediate and radical form of class consciousness, the objective realization of class interests, and certainly of revolutionary potential, has been, at best, elusive. Issues of class and inequality have been important motivations for protest, politics, and industrial relations in American history, but they have almost universally been a product of divided or ambiguous forms of consciousness.

Arguments about the weakness of orthodox understandings of class consciousness abound. Selig Perlman, for instance, argued that American workers were uniquely "job conscious," that is, largely nonideological and focused only on issues that affected their jobs directly—separated by an enormous gulf from the forms of solidarity theorized by radical intellectuals. Others, such as Barrington Moore, suggested that oppositional culture emerges, not from a forward-looking revolutionary ideology, but from the "precipitates of past historical experience." Craig Calhoun went a step further to suggest that working-class activism, which might otherwise appear as widespread class-conscious protest, should be seen as the work of "reactionary radicals" who were not fighting systematic labor exploitation, but rather were leading a backward-looking fight against the intrusion of industry upon their cherished traditions of skill, pride, community, and autonomy. Perhaps the most notable aspect of the power of tradition in class consciousness is the ongoing populist appeal for a return to the core precepts of the American Revolution as one of the wellsprings of working-class ideology. The so-called new labor historians after the 1960s tended to see community as one of the most powerful resources that workers had in their contest with the new industrial order, but they did not often probe its limits as a resource in the struggle of class against class.

Other scholars have examined the influence in the United States of what the Italian theorist Antonio Gramsci called the process of "cultural hegemony." Between accommodation and resistance to capitalism lies an ideological compromise of sorts, argued Gramsci, in which the dominant bourgeois ideology is imposed, in a porous and flexible way, upon the hearts and minds of the working class. Hegemony is less a form of cultural domination, as the term seems to imply, than it is a mass culture in which the working class gives its consent to a system that must legitimate itself to their satisfaction ideologically.

Another important set of arguments about class consciousness in the United States examines the fractious roles that race, gender, skill, and immigration have played. "The working class" implies a term neutral of other forms of identity—an inclusive, multicultural movement of economic interests—but the term has often passed for something much narrower. From the mill girls of Lowell, Massachusetts, to the emancipated slaves to the waves of immigrants from southern and eastern Europe, the American working class has been a thing of extraordinary diversity. Often, however, the interests of the skilled, white, native-born, male workers became synonymous with the term "working class." Even more confounding, as such historians as David Roediger, taking his cues from W. E. B. Du Bois, have argued, free wage laborers often chose their race, their "whiteness," over their class. American class consciousness, Roediger argued, developed in tandem with racial identity, making racial identity inseparable from how class consciousness works in the U.S. context.

During the 1930s and 1940s, it appeared that the working class had achieved a massive breakthrough in both consciousness and representation as the Congress of Industrial Organizations managed to knit workers together despite divisions of race, skill, gender, and ethnicity. Yet as the dust settled on the postwar era, this upheaval ended up being part of what became known as "industrial pluralism" or "interest-group liberalism," an incorporation of workers and their unions into the political and economic system, rather than the type of pure oppositional class consciousness that might overthrow the system. Even that success proved historically limited as trade union presence, even the core idea of the working class, faded after the 1970s.

Twenty-First-Century Critiques. The twenty-first-century postmodern critiques of class consciousness cut in multiple directions. One view suggests that the United States, and indeed the developed world, has entered a phase of "post-materialism" in which issues of class consciousness are essentially rendered anachronistic, as other forms of identity and issues such as environmentalism and quality of life have become far more important. ("The class war is over," declared the British Labour Party's Tony Blair in 1999.) Others look to the social construction of issues of class and class consciousness, rejecting both the "death of class" and the pure and objective Marxian version for a more performative and mutually constitutive understanding of class consciousness linked to other forms of identity. Class may shape people's understandings of the world, these thinkers argue, but it is neither determinative nor even primary in developing people's consciousness.

[*See also* **International Unionism and International Solidarity; Labor Movements;** *and* **Poverty.**]

Jefferson Cowie

CLAYTON ANTITRUST ACT

Enacted in October 1914, the Clayton Antitrust Act was essentially a detailed expansion of the vaguely worded Sherman Antitrust Act of 1890. In conjunction with the Federal Trade Commission Act, the Clayton Antitrust Act was designed to fulfill the final part of President Woodrow Wilson's New Freedom platform from the election of 1912. The original draft of the act promised to limit the power of trusts and monopolies by prohibiting price discrimination, contracts that required exclusive dealing, "tying" (forcing a customer to purchase other, linked goods from a firm rather than from a competitor), and mergers of firms that would result in a de facto monopoly within a particular industry or otherwise put the merged firm in a position to limit competition. But the proposed legislation said nothing about exempting unions or farm organizations from being viewed as "illegal combinations or conspiracies in restraint of trade," a definition that had allowed federal judges to use the Sherman Act to charge farmers' organizations and especially trade unions with illegally restraining trade. The organized-labor movement believed that it had been promised an exemption from judicial injunctions during Wilson's 1912 campaign, and as such it saw the original draft of the Clayton Act as a betrayal. After much wrangling, leaders of the American Federation of Labor, the railway brotherhoods, farm organizations, and their friends in the House and Senate wrested a compromise from the Wilson administration; though falling short of giving labor complete immunity from prosecution, the compromise offered labor some protection. In Section 6 the Clayton Act declared that "The labor of a human being is not a commodity or article of commerce. Nothing contained in the antitrust laws shall be construed to forbid the existence and operation of labor, agricultural, or horticultural organizations . . . nor shall such organizations, or the members thereof, be held or construed to be illegal combinations or conspiracies in restraint of trade, under the antitrust laws." Such language led Samuel Gompers to describe the Clayton Antitrust Act as "labor's Magna Carta," although many contemporary commentators believed that this was hyperbole—and subsequent legal decisions and the verdict of most historians bear this out.

[*See also* **Antitrust Legislation** *and* **Norris–LaGuardia Act.**]

BIBLIOGRAPHY

Dubofsky, Melvyn. *The State and Labor in Modern America*. Chapel Hill: University of North Carolina Press, 1994.

Kutler, Stanley I. "Labor, the Clayton Act, and the Supreme Court." *Labor History* 3, no. 1 (December 1962): 19–38.

Sklar, Martin J. *The Corporate Reconstruction of American Capitalism, 1890–1916: The Market, the Law, and Politics*. Cambridge, U.K.: Cambridge University Press, 1988.

James Mochoruk

CLERICAL WORKERS

Known colloquially as "paper pushers," clerical workers encompass all those white-collar employees of businesses whose work involves the production, manipulation, and tracking of business records. Historically this has included everyone from typists, stenographers, and secretaries to bookkeepers and accountants. As a category of employment, clerical work expanded dramatically from the late nineteenth through the early twentieth centuries, growing faster than even basic industrial sectors. This growth of the clerical workforce accompanied the appearance of modern corporations; as businesses became increasingly elaborate, they required new layers of white-collar clerical workers to keep track of both products and profits. Concurrent technological innovations such as the typewriter and the adding machine both simplified this process of tracking and helped extend it further.

At exactly the same time, clerical work also became more and more feminized. In 1870, less than 3 percent of all the nation's office workers were women; by 1929 more than half were. A variety of factors contributed to the entrance of women into clerical work. Around the turn of the century, women tended to graduate from high school at a higher rate than did men, giving them the basic literacy tools necessary in an office setting. At the same time, few other occupations attracted this supply of educated young women, thereby lowering the wages at which they would work. In this setting, new technologies such as the typewriter quickly became sex-typed as "female" in the nation's offices. These factors combined with prevalent social expectations to ensure that businesses viewed women as suited for the type of routinized and dead-end employment that low-level office work had become.

[*See also* **9to5 and Women Office Workers;** *and* **Women Workers.**]

BIBLIOGRAPHY

Bjelopera, Jerome P. *City of Clerks: Office and Sales Workers in Philadelphia, 1870–1920*. Urbana and Chicago: University of Illinois Press, 2005.

Davies, Margery W. *Woman's Place Is at the Typewriter: Office Work and Office Workers, 1870–1930*. Philadelphia: Temple University Press, 1982.

DeVault, Ileen A. *Sons and Daughters of Labor: Class and Clerical Work in Turn-of-the-Century Pittsburgh*. Ithaca, N.Y.: Cornell University Press, 1990.

Fine, Lisa M. *The Souls of the Skyscraper: Female Clerical Workers in Chicago, 1870–1930*. Philadelphia: Temple University Press, 1990.

Srole, Carole. *Transcribing Class and Gender: Masculinity and Femininity in Nineteenth-Century Courts and Offices*. Ann Arbor: University of Michigan Press, 2010.

Ileen A. DeVault

CLOSED SHOP

One strategy by labor to achieve permanence and stability relied upon closed shops that required workers to be union members before firms were able to hire them. The closed shop also gave unions greater control over the supply of labor and improved their ability to discipline members. The 1947 Taft–Hartley Act, amending the 1935 National Labor Relations Act, prohibited the closed shop. Taft–Hartley permitted individual states to allow collective-bargaining agreements that required workers to be union members, but the requirement could apply only after a worker was hired.

In the nineteenth century, attempts to enforce closed shops were more common among skilled craft unions acting as hiring halls. When unions set their own qualifications for admission to trades, they controlled not only the quantity of labor available, but also its quality. The unions that successfully controlled entry into shops could achieve substantial power by dismissing or penalizing members. Such unions could unilaterally define their own rules without negotiating employment contracts. Their strength led to frequent attacks from employers, who sought open shops and the right to hire, fire, and train as they saw fit.

With labor's turn toward industrial unionization in the early twentieth century, unions contracted for security agreements comparable to those of a closed shop. At the turn of the twentieth century, the machinists and metalworking unions in particular became the targets of open-shop battles. By the 1920s, many employers united under the aegis of the National Association of Manufacturers to advance what they called the "American Plan" of nonunionized open shops. After World War II, rising union power—as evidenced in mass strikes—created an employer backlash that culminated in the Taft–Hartley law's elimination of the closed shop.

[*See also* Collective Bargaining; National Labor Relations (Wagner) Act; Open-Shop Movement; Repression of Unions; Right-to-Work Committees and Organizations, National; Right-to-Work Committees and Organizations, State Laws Related to; Taft–Hartley Act; *and* Union Shop.]

BIBLIOGRAPHY

Harris, Howell John. *Bloodless Victories: The Rise and Fall of the Open Shop in the Philadelphia Metal Trades, 1890–1940*. New York: Cambridge University Press, 2000.

Madsen, Chris. "Organizing a Wartime Shipyard: The Union Struggle for a Closed Shop at West Coast Shipbuilders Limited 1941–44." *Labour/Le Travail* 65 (Spring 2010): 75–108.

Daniel Jacoby

COLLECTIVE BARGAINING

"Collective bargaining" is a term used to describe several aspects of interaction between labor and management in the workplace. The term was originally coined by Beatrice Webb (née Potter) in her 1891 book *The Co-operative Movement in Great Britain*. Webb used this term as part of a larger discussion of working-class consumerism in Britain, which suggests that she considered collective bargaining to be primarily an economic activity. Webb believed that workers should work collectively to pursue their economic goals. She and her husband, Sidney Webb, further described the importance of collective bargaining in their 1897 book *Industrial Democracy*. The Webbs described collective bargaining as one method, along with trade union action and legal action, used by workers to further their collective aims. They also suggested that workers should rely on experts to represent them when dealing with employers. The Webbs theorized that if workers relied on rank-and-file representatives, they would be at a disadvantage in negotiating with employers who used the services of skilled negotiators.

Twentieth-Century Practices.

Although the term "collective bargaining" originated in Britain, it also became widely adopted by American trade unionists. Samuel Gompers, the longtime president of the American Federation of Labor and himself an immigrant cigar maker, strongly supported collective bargaining. In *Labor and the Employer*, Gompers argued that proper collective-bargaining procedures would lead to economic success for workers and their unions. Like Sidney and Beatrice Webb, Gompers insisted that workers should receive a greater share of the fruits of their productivity as an alternative to other, more radical forms of economic redistribution. Collective bargaining became a key part of the system of labor relations in most Western industrialized countries in the twentieth century, especially in English-speaking countries such as the United States, Britain, Australia, New Zealand, and Canada.

In the United States, collective bargaining was most clearly manifested in the negotiation of written collective agreements that delineated the terms of employment for unionized workers. Prior to the passage in 1935 of the National Labor Relations Act (NLRA), many employers were reluctant to engage in collective bargaining. The NLRA guaranteed that workers had the right to bargain collectively through unions of their own choosing and, more important, that employers had a legal obligation to bargain with unions that their employees had voluntarily chosen. The NLRA also created a new federal agency, the National Labor Relations Board (NLRB), to regulate industrial relations, conduct union-representation elections, and adjudicate disputes between unions and employers. From the 1940s onward, a vast bureaucracy related to labor relations gradually grew. Federal labor legislation—principally the

NLRA—governed the collective-bargaining rights of most unionized private-sector American workers. Federal public-sector workers did not gain collective-bargaining rights until the issuance of Executive Order 10988 by President John F. Kennedy in 1962, and similar bargaining rights were gradually extended to public-sector workers at the state and local levels. By the final quarter of the twentieth century a wide array of labor boards and laws across the United States served to implement the rules and procedures of collective bargaining.

Controversies.

Collective bargaining in the United States operates within a voluntarist framework through which unions and employers are encouraged to engage in collective bargaining but are not required to do so. Collective bargaining became a central feature of the post–World War II process of labor relations. Collective agreements not only governed wage rates, working conditions, and fringe benefits, but also included grievance and arbitration clauses that provided channels for employees to seek justice for work-related grievances. The amelioration of conflict acted as one of the key underlying principles of collective bargaining. Collective bargaining led to contracts that established a quasi-legal or constitutional form of workplace justice. It defined which forms of action by employers or employees were proper and hence contractually enforceable and which practices were improper and hence banned.

According to their critics on the left, such advocates for the effectiveness of collective bargaining as Sidney and Beatrice Webb, Samuel Gompers, and John R. Commons are conservative theorists of labor-movement action. In contrast, such Marxist labor theorists as Richard Hyman have criticized collective bargaining for preventing unions from challenging management prerogatives in the workplace. The actual results of collective bargaining in the United States from the 1940s to the 1970s—a period when collective bargaining reached its apogee—may be said to support the arguments of both collective bargaining's critics and its advocates. The immediate post–World War II decades witnessed substantial increases in union wages that enabled working-class families to enjoy more comfortable, stable, and secure lives. Among other benefits, union members covered by collective-bargaining agreements enjoyed better working conditions, more generous paid vacations, employer-financed health insurance, and cost-of-living (COLA) wage increases. American unions, however, rarely chose to challenge corporate business practices. During its heyday from the end of World War II into the 1970s, collective bargaining created a mini-empire of academics, attorneys, arbitrators, mediators, and other experts who studied and worked on various aspects of the collective-bargaining process.

Since the early 1980s, collective bargaining has faced a rising wave of attacks. Employers have increasingly rejected unions and the system of collective bargaining that came along with them. Indeed, by 2012 less than 7 percent of private-sector employees belonged to a union, and 90 percent were no longer covered by contracts negotiated through collective bargaining. Similarly, the federal legislation that governs industrial relations and collective bargaining has not been amended to reflect the changing nature of the American workplace. Employers and their allies have fought vigorously and successfully to defeat any and all legislative initiatives to strengthen unions and their right to bargain collectively. Collective bargaining as a concept and a practice originated in the late nineteenth century, brought workers economic gains in the immediate post–World War II decades, and was of diminishing importance and value by the early twenty-first century.

[See also **Antilabor Mobilization after 1945; Employee Representation Plans; Executive Order 10988; Industrial Democracy; Industrial Relations; Labor Movements; National Labor Relations Board; National Labor Relations (Wagner) Act; Taft–Hartley Act; Treaty of Detroit and Postwar Labor Accord; Voluntarism;** *and* **Yeshiva University, the NLRB, and Collective Bargaining.**]

BIBLIOGRAPHY

Commons, John R. *Industrial Goodwill.* New York: McGraw–Hill, 1919.

Gompers, Samuel. *Labor and the Employer.* Compiled and edited by Hayes Robbins. New York: E. P. Dutton, 1920.

Hyman, Richard. *Industrial Relations: A Marxist Introduction.* London: Macmillan, 1975.

Webb, Beatrice (Potter). *The Co-operative Movement in Great Britain.* London: Swan Sonnenschein, 1891.

Webb, Sidney, and Beatrice Webb. *Industrial Democracy.* London: Longmans, Green, 1897.

Jason Russell

COLORADO LABOR WARS (1903–1905)

Industrial conflict between the Western Federation of Miners (WFM) on one side and the gold-mine operators, local business owners, state government officials, national guardsmen, private detectives, and vigilantes on the other side erupted into open warfare between 1903 and 1905 in the mining district of Cripple Creek and Victor, Colorado. The conflict serves as a historical example of how a concerted, premeditated effort by business leaders allied with state officials could destroy a union stronghold. General Sherman Bell, who led the state militia during the conflict, described the militia's campaign against the WFM as "a military necessity, which recognizes no laws."

In 1894, Cripple Creek–Victor mine owners increased the workday from eight to ten hours without raising pay, precipitating a strike by the local union. The Populist governor of Colorado Davis Waite negotiated an agreement between owners and miners that transformed Cripple Creek into a union district: local trades unionized, union men served as local elected officials, and unions negotiated their members' wages and hours.

When the Republican governor James Peabody took office in 1902, he promised to protect the interests of Colorado businessmen. Mine owners formed the Cripple Creek Mine Owners' Association (CCMOA), and local businessmen created a Citizens' Alliance (CA). When in 1902 the Cripple Creek WFM local called a strike in support of neighboring smelter workers, the governor sent National Guard troops, financed by the CCMOA, under Sherman Bell to replace local government. The CCMOA then urged all district businessmen to fire union employees. As tensions mounted, the governor declared martial law in Teller County. The National Guard confiscated citizens' weapons and arrested union leaders, merchants who displayed union posters, and the staff of the *Victor Daily Record* for pro-union editorializing. The WFM secretary William D. "Big Bill" Haywood created a poster that intensified the enmity. It featured the U.S. flag with constitutional abuses against union men strewn across its stripes and the title: "Is Colorado in America?"

When a bomb exploded at a local railroad depot on 6 June 1904, killing thirteen and injuring six scab miners, the CCMOA and CA accused the union of responsibility for the incident. Next the CCMOA and CA organized a gathering of several thousand residents across the street from the Victor Miners' Union Hall to listen to antiunion speeches, encouraging them to kill or drive out every union man. The upshot was open warfare between mob members and national guardsmen and union members defending the Victor union hall. The guardsmen volleyed rifle shot after shot into the union hall, causing its defenders to surrender. The CCMOA and CA forces then wrecked the hall, looted the four WFM cooperative stores, and destroyed the office of the *Victor Record*. Union members were incarcerated in outdoor holding encampments known as bullpens, and General Bell tried more than fifteen hundred prisoners in military courts, offering them freedom in return for relinquishing their union cards. He summarily deported across state lines those who refused the bargain. Simultaneously, hooded men called "whitecaps" visited the home of the local WFM leader John Harper, whom they beat, robbed, and finally kidnapped.

Many union families unable to find work locally left the Cripple Creek District and Colorado. Some followed Haywood into the more radical Industrial Workers of the World, founded in 1905 in the aftermath of Colorado's labor wars. The Colorado labor war remained a symbol of union dedication when faced by an armed and determined alliance of businessmen and state officials. The bullet-shattered Victor Miners' Union Hall remained standing as a symbol of worker resistance.

[*See also* **Citizens' Committees and Alliances; Haywood, William D.; Industrial Workers of the World; Mining Industry; Repression of Unions; Strikes;** *and* **Western Federation of Miners.**]

BIBLIOGRAPHY

Blevins, Tim, et al., eds. *The Colorado Labor Wars, Cripple Creek, 1903–1904: A Centennial Commemoration.* Colorado Springs, Colo.: Pikes Peak Library District, 2006.

Jameson, Elizabeth. *All That Glitters: Class, Conflict, and Community in Cripple Creek.* Urbana: University of Illinois Press, 1998.

Langdon, Emma F. *The Cripple Creek Strike: A History of Industrial Wars in Colorado, 1903–4–5, Being a Complete and Concise History of the Efforts of Organized Capital to Crush Unionism.* Denver, Colo.: Great Western, 1904–1905. Available with other relevant materials at Save the Victor Miners' Union Hall website http://www.rebelgraphics.org/wfmhall/langdon00.html.

Rastall, Benjamin McKie. "The Labor History of the Cripple Creek District: A Study in Industrial Evolution." PhD diss., University of Wisconsin, Madison, 1908.

Suggs, George G., Jr. *Colorado's War on Militant Unionism: James H. Peabody and the Western Federation of Miners.* Norman: University of Oklahoma Press, 1991.

Katherine Scott Sturdevant

COMMISSION ON INDUSTRIAL RELATIONS

Among all Progressive Era investigating bodies, the Commission on Industrial Relations was arguably the most famous and influential. President William Howard Taft had formally requested that Congress establish the commission during his State of the Union address in February 1912. Taft and others were concerned by the growing violence of labor conflicts, and they hoped that an impartial, scientific investigation would avert more radical legislation. Therefore, he proposed a commission empowered to review all state and federal laws, investigate labor conditions, and make a series of public recommendations that would alleviate labor violence.

After Taft lost the 1912 presidential election, Woodrow Wilson successfully nominated the commission's nine members and shepherded it into existence. These nine members included representatives from labor, business, and the public. The labor representatives were Austin Garretson, leader of the Order of Railway Conductors; James O'Connell, former president of the International Association of Machinists; and John Brown Lennon, former president of the Journeyman Tailors' Union. The business representatives were Frederic Delano, railroad executive and uncle of Franklin D. Roosevelt; Harris Weinstock, owner of a department store; and Samuel Thurston Ballard, owner of a wheat refinery. Representing the public were Florence Harriman and Professor John R. Commons. Frank P. Walsh, a liberal attorney from Kansas City, Missouri, was appointed chairman.

Over the next several years, the commission heard 6 million words of testimony from more than seven hundred witnesses, including John D. Rockefeller Jr., Andrew Carnegie, Samuel Gompers, Louis D. Brandeis, Bill Haywood, and Clarence Darrow, as well as miners, farmers, textile workers, lumberjacks, economists, and women like Beulah Stewart, the wife of a Texas tenant farmer and mother of eleven children, who testified to the hard conditions in the cotton fields.

The commission ultimately produced a controversial eleven-volume final report, published in 1916, that called for a steeply graded inheritance tax, reformed land laws, curbs on the power of courts to invalidate legislative acts, and, most significantly, constitutional amendments to protect the rights of workers to organize and bargain collectively. Walsh and the three labor commissioners signed the final report, but the three employer members issued a separate statement, as did Harriman and Commons. The business community at large damned the report as inflammatory and biased, while both moderate and radical members of the labor movement hailed it as an indictment of working-class conditions and an argument for industrial democracy.

Following the publication of the final report, a number of bills were introduced in Congress to enact its recommendations. The Adamson Eight-Hour Act, for example, passed in 1916 after vigorous lobbying by Austin Garretson and the railroad brotherhoods, gave railway workers a reduced workday. Walsh later became cochairman of the War Labor Board, which followed many of the principles of the final report, including equal compensation for women and strong support for unions.

The Commission on Industrial Relations was significant in three other ways. First, the commission was an example of the Progressive impulse by business, labor, reformers, and government to collect and use economic data to address poverty. Second, the political alliances forged between labor and Democrats in the course of the commission's work helped form a path toward New Deal legislation. Finally, the remarkable range of witnesses that the commission heard brought working-class voices into Progressive political reform, providing an invaluable historical record of working people's experiences in that period.

[*See also* **Industrial Relations.**]

BIBLIOGRAPHY

Adams, Graham, Jr. *Age of Industrial Violence, 1910–15: The Activities and Findings of the United States Commission on Industrial Relations.* New York: Columbia University Press, 1966.

Furner, Mary O., and Barry Supple, eds. *The State and Economic Knowledge: The American and British Experiences.* Cambridge, U.K.: Cambridge University Press, 1990.

McCartin, Joseph A. *Labor's Great War: The Struggle for Industrial Democracy and the Origins of Modern American Labor Relations, 1912–1921.* Chapel Hill: University of North Carolina Press, 1997.

Stephanie Taylor

COMMODITY FUTURES MARKETS

"Commodity futures markets," or simply "futures markets," is the term given to financial markets in which what is traded are not actual commodities or financial instruments, but rather contracts for future delivery of commodities or financial instruments. These markets originally were established so that farmers could sell their crops to buyers at prices determined in the present but for delivery at some future date. This was called "when-arrived" trading.

The futures markets began before the Civil War in Chicago and New York City, trading contracts for agricultural commodities. The Chicago Board of Trade, established in 1848, was that city's first established futures market, although several decades passed before futures trading became well established. Markets were opened in other midwestern cities, including Saint Louis and Kansas City, as well as in New York. Other exchanges include the Kansas City Board of Trade (founded in 1856), the New York Mercantile Exchange (1882), and the Chicago Mercantile Exchange (1898). Exchanges tended to specialize in certain types of contracts. Originally the exchanges in the Midwest specialized in home-grown agricultural commodities, while those in New York specialized in commodities related to international trade. Over the years, contracts on a wide array of commodities were added, including precious metals, building supplies, livestock, agricultural by-products, heating oil, fuel oil, and financial instruments, among others.

Congress passed legislation in the 1920s and 1930s in an attempt to control the futures markets. In 1922, Congress enacted the Grain Futures Act, an attempt to control speculation in the grain futures markets. The legislation failed to achieve its aims, and in 1936 Congress responded by passing the Commodity Exchange Act. This law made price manipulation on the exchanges illegal and sought to curb excessive speculation and fraud. Further legislation became necessary because of the absence of a regulatory agency to police futures markets.

Established in 1974, the Commodity Futures Trading Commission regulates futures trades in the twenty-first century. The commission is responsible for overseeing trading on the various exchanges in much the same way that the Securities and Exchange Commission regulates securities trading on the stock exchanges.

After 2000 the futures exchanges began a move toward electronic trading of contracts; traditionally orders had been executed in the futures pits. The Chicago Board of Trade and the Chicago Mercantile Exchange, the two largest of the exchanges, merged in 2007.

[*See also* **Stock and Commodity Exchanges.**]

BIBLIOGRAPHY

Cowing, Cedric B. *Populists, Plungers, and Progressives: A Social History of Stock and Commodity Speculation, 1890–1936.* Princeton, N.J.: Princeton University Press, 1965.

Geisst, Charles R. *Wheels of Fortune: The History of Speculation from Scandal to Respectability.* Hoboken, N.J.: Wiley, 2002.

Charles Geisst

COMMUNICATIONS REVOLUTION

Nineteenth- and twentieth-century telegraphy and telephony, just like twenty-first-century emailing, are included in any list of revolutionary changes in communications. Opening up the definition of communications brings in, first, electronic media like radio and television and then recorded sound and cinema. The inclusion of traditional postal mailing and newspaper circulation in the history of communications results in an even broader definition, which pushes back the origins of the communications revolution to the eighteenth century and earlier. This makes the communications revolution no younger than industrial capital—and some historians even consider it as old as merchant capital. This understanding of the communications revolution has been reinforced since the later twentieth century by scholars who have observed that the whole of modern technology has been promoted by reference to a communications revolution. A series of transportation revolutions, from early-modern canals to late-modern spacecrafts, were idealized as means for revolutionary improvements in communications. Similarly, electric lighting was initially advertised as a revolution in communications.

Broadening the definition of "communications" also affects the definition of "revolution." The permanence of revolution becomes the feature that defines the history of communications, making it impossible to attach the communications revolution to any particular technology or event. A series of studies by economic historians have attempted to measure the exact impact of different communications technologies on various economic sectors. Pioneering studies quantified the importance of telegraphy to a railway-based economy. Labor historians have pointed to the dependence of the economy on communications by drawing attention to myriad invisible communications workers, from telegraph operators who transmitted messages electrically to telegraph messenger boys who rode bicycles to deliver these messages physically from and to the telegraph office. Forms and technologies of communication and those who deliver communications in diverse formats constantly evolve and suggest perpetual revolution.

[*See also* **Electricity and Electrification; Postal Services; Radio; Satellite Communications; Telegraph; Telephone; Television;** *and* **Transportation Revolution.**]

BIBLIOGRAPHY

Blok, Aad, and Greg Downey, eds. *Uncovering Labour in Information Revolutions, 1750–2000.*

Cambridge, U.K.: Cambridge University Press, 2003.

Downey, Greg. *Technology and Communication in American History*. Washington, D.C.: American Historical Association, 2011.

Lubar, Steven. *InfoCulture: The Smithsonian Book of Information Age Inventions*. Boston: Houghton Mifflin, 1993. An inclusive introduction to the history of communications, from the printed book to the computer.

Aristotle Tympas

COMMUNICATIONS WORKERS OF AMERICA

Established in 1947, by the early twenty-first century the Communications Workers of America (CWA) represented more than 700,000 American, Canadian, and Puerto Rican workers in the fields of telecommunications, broadcast media, transportation, manufacturing, health care, and other related sectors. The union's roots date back to 1938 when labor organizers founded the National Federation of Telephone Workers (NFTW) to represent employees of American Telephone and Telegraph (AT&T), local Bell affiliates (the Bell System), and independent telephone companies. Prior to the formation of the NFTW, in the early twentieth century the International Brotherhood of Electrical Workers (IBEW) had attempted to organize telephone workers. Initially, IBEW organizers focused more on securing employment opportunities for IBEW linemen in the growing telephone sector than on organizing existing employees of telephone companies. IBEW officials eventually began to assist unionization efforts within individual firms. World War I brought a one-year takeover by the federal government of the telephone industry but did not lead to wage increases or federal recognition of IBEW locals. Disgruntled IBEW locals struck against a number of Bell affiliates, most significantly New England Bell in April 1919. The strike led to a settlement with the federal government, but once AT&T and the Bell System regained control of their networks, company officials used coercive tactics and organized company unions to undermine the IBEW. Independent union membership in the telephone industry collapsed during the 1920s and remained depressed until the 1935 National Labor Relations Act forced AT&T and its Bell affiliates to restructure company unions as independent unions.

The restructuring process encouraged employees to organize the National Federation of Telephone Workers in 1938 to provide a national voice for the separate local telephone unions. The NFTW struggled to represent its organizationally and geographically diverse local affiliates during the 1940s as AT&T, the Bell System, and the independents refused to raise wages to put them in line with those earned by workers in comparable industries. Other unions, particularly the militant American Communications Association, an affiliate of the Congress of Industrial Organizations, began to raid NFTW locals. Some organizers within the NFTW began advocating for the creation of a more centralized national union. A series of successful strikes across the country in 1944 and 1945 coordinated by the NFTW's national office seemed to justify the goal of those who advocated a stronger national union.

In late 1946, NFTW organizers proposed a more powerful national union named the Communications Workers of America. Before the new union held its first meeting in 1947, however, the NFTW engaged in a system-wide strike against AT&T. The company diluted the strike's impact by negotiating separate agreements with individual NTFW affiliates. For the organizers of the CWA, the failure of the NFTW strike highlighted the ineffectiveness of that organization and confirmed the need for a national union that could present a united front against AT&T, the Bell System, and the independents.

The CWA gained strength during the 1950s and 1960s and by the mid-1970s achieved a major goal when the Bell System agreed to national bargaining with the union. The 1984 AT&T divestiture and the breakup of the Bell System into regional operating companies forced the CWA to negotiate separate contracts with the new regional firms. Successful strikes against AT&T and the regional operating companies secured expanded benefits for CWA members during the 1980s and 1990s. During the same period, the CWA began to incorporate other unions in communications, media, and transportation fields and to expand its presence into Canada and Puerto Rico. In the early twenty-first century the union faced renewed challenges in the telecommunications sector as regional operating companies both attempted to reduce benefits and slash the number of union workers in legacy landlines divisions and also employed nonunion workers in their expanding wireless and Internet divisions.

[*See also* **Communications Revolution; Radio;** *and* **Telephone.**]

BIBLIOGRAPHY

Bahr, Morton. *From the Telegraph to the Internet.* Washington, D.C.: National Press Books, 1998.

Brooks, Thomas R. *Communications Workers of America: The Story of a Union.* New York: Mason/Charter, 1977.

Communications Workers of America. http://www.cwa-union.org.

Palladino, Grace. *Dreams of Dignity, Workers of Vision: A History of the International Brotherhood of Electrical Workers.* Washington, D.C.: International Brotherhood of Electrical Workers, 1991.

Schacht, John N. *The Making of Telephone Unionism, 1920–1947.* New Brunswick, N.J.: Rutgers University Press, 1985.

Benjamin Schwantes

COMPANY UNIONS

Company unions have been a source of concern to the U.S. labor movement, which saw them as sham organizations and a threat to solidarity. They take a variety of forms. From the early twentieth century until 1935, employers, when faced with the threat of union organizing campaigns, encouraged the formation of unions that resembled bona fide unions but remained under management control. The term "company union" has also been associated with the employee representation plan (ERP), which also takes a variety of forms, the best known of which was the Rockefeller Plan, at the Colorado Fuel and Iron Company, that provided for joint committees of elected employee representatives without union representation. ERPs were the most pervasive form of company unionism, with surges of growth occurring during World War I and following the National Industrial Recovery Act of 1933, with employers on both occasions hoping to preempt union organization in the workplace. By 1935 when the National Labor Relations Act outlawed them, ERPs covered approximately two and a half million workers. Critics condemned ERPs for reducing workers' bargaining power and impeding economic recovery. Following the 1935 prohibition on ERPs, independent local unions, which do not affiliate to the broader labor movement and whose jurisdiction is limited to one company, have often functioned as company unions.

[*See also* **Employee Representation Plans; National Labor Relations (Wagner) Act;** *and* **Welfare Capitalism.**]

BIBLIOGRAPHY

Jacoby, Sanford. "A Road Not Taken: Independent Local Unions in the United States since 1935." In *Nonunion Employee Representation: History,*

Contemporary Practice, and Policy, edited by Bruce E. Kaufman and Daphne Gottlieb Taras, pp. 76–95. Armonk, N.Y.: M. E. Sharpe, 2000.

Patmore, Greg. "Employee Representation Plans in the United States, Canada, and Australia." *Labor* 3 (2006): 41–65.

Greg Patmore

COMPUTER MONITORING OF OFFICE WORKERS

Nineteenth-century commentators on the rise of the factory took note of surveillance as central to its genesis and expansion. In the *Philosophy of Manufactures* (1835), Andrew Ure observed that "when capital enlists science in her service, the refractory hand of labour will always be taught docility." In the twentieth century, machine-tool operations confronted a choice between computerized automation and so-called record playback, the latter leaving more control to workers on the shop floor. Management opted for computerized automation when they saw how it could augment centralized control.

In the 1980s, office workers welcomed the personal computer as a new tool allowing for enhanced autonomy and mastery of sophisticated tasks. It soon became the centerpiece of office labor and work life. Nevertheless, management recognized the new possibilities for monitoring workers, as reflected in the title of an article in *Industrial Engineering* (vol. 16, no. 1 [1984]): "Office Automation Provides Opportunity to Examine What Workers Actually Do." Surveillance soon increased through an array of domains and platforms: keystrokes, the content of telephone calls, email and web monitoring, cards, closed-circuit television (CCTV), GPS, pagers, radio-frequency identification (RFID), and biometrics.

In 1987 the U.S. Office of Technology Assessment commissioned a report, *The Electronic Supervisor: New Technologies, New Tensions*, that expressed concern about affronts to worker dignity and autonomy but affirmed that many of the surveillance activities remain legal under U.S. law. Some social scientists have tried to maintain a distinction between "monitoring" and "surveillance," with "surveillance" having more sinister and dystopian implications. The *Electronic Supervisor* observed that between 1940 and 1980 the U.S. clerical workforce expanded from 5 million to 20 million workers, with only 6.3 percent of these workers male. For feminist critics of enhanced monitoring capabilities, this social context raised the specter of predominantly male management invading the personal space of female employees.

The prevalence of computer monitoring of office workers is a subject for statistical speculation. The American Management Association (AMA) reported that the great upsurge of computer monitoring occurred in the late 1990s. Polling its membership of medium to large organizations, the AMA found that in the year 2000, 54 percent tracked the Internet connections of employees, and 38 percent stored and reviewed employee email, up from 15 percent just three years earlier. Proofprint and Forrester conducted a modest survey in 2006 and concluded that approximately one third of U.S. companies with more than a thousand employees hire people who inspect the email correspondence of workers to make sure that there are no rules violations. In 1999, Xerox fired forty employees for peering at pornographic websites, and in 2000 the *New York Times* fired twenty-three workers for sending what *BusinessWeek* (10 July 2000) called "off-color email." The AMA reported that 45 percent of surveyed companies disciplined workers for violations of company email policy.

In December 2007 the software goliath Microsoft filed a patent application for a "unique monitoring system" with wireless sensors that could allow management to monitor workers' "heart rate, galvanic skin response, EMG, brain signals, respiration rate, body temperature, movement, facial movements, facial expressions, and blood pressure." In 2009 the company followed up with a patent application for Legal Intercept, a tool for monitoring and recording Skype telephone calls via the Internet. Microsoft acquired Skype in May 2011 for $8.5 billion. These technologies for monitoring the physiological responses and communication activities of workers may portend the intensification of computer surveillance in the twenty-first century.

[*See also* **Clerical Workers; Labor Spies and Pinkertons;** *and* **Office Technology.**]

BIBLIOGRAPHY

Armstrong, Larry. "Someone to Watch over You." *BusinessWeek*, 10 July 2000, pp. 189–190. Available at http://www.businessweek.com/2000/00_28/b3689172.htm.
Ball, Kirstie. "Workplace Surveillance: An Overview." *Labor History* 51, no. 1 (2010): 87–106.
Lyon, David. *The Electronic Eye: The Rise of Surveillance Society.* Minneapolis: University of Minnesota Press, 1994.

John Trumpbour

CONGRESS OF INDUSTRIAL ORGANIZATIONS

John L. Lewis of the United Mine Workers (UMW) and other unionists created the Committee for Industrial Organization (CIO) in November 1935 as a means of encouraging industrial unionism within the American Federation of Labor (AFL).

The onset of the Great Depression, deteriorating workplace conditions, and the apparent support for collective bargaining evidenced by the first administration of Franklin D. Roosevelt triggered a wave of union activism. Coal miners and garment workers rebuilt unions that had atrophied in the 1920s and early 1930s. Thousands of workers new to the labor movement surged into AFL-affiliated unions. In 1934 mass strikes in the textile, auto parts, longshoring, and goods-hauling sectors gave vivid evidence of workers' unrest and of their desire for union representation. Lewis and other AFL leaders saw in this activism an opportunity to rebuild the labor movement and to extend it into the mass-production industries.

Formation. When the AFL's convention in November 1935 failed to adopt an aggressive program to recruit large numbers of industrial workers, Lewis, Sidney Hillman—the president of the Amalgamated Clothing Workers (ACW)—and other dissidents formed the Committee for Industrial Organization, designed to promote industrial unionism within the AFL. AFL leaders denounced this move, and in 1936 the AFL executive council suspended the UMW, the ACW, and its other affiliates that had launched the CIO. Meanwhile, however, thousands of workers, most notably those enrolled in AFL organizations in the auto, rubber, electrical-goods, and miscellaneous industrial sectors, embraced the CIO. Particularly notable was the action of the United Auto Workers (UAW), which was chartered by the AFL in 1935 but signed on with the CIO the next year.

Rank-and-file activism characterized the early CIO. In the winter of 1936 in Akron, Ohio, the center of the U.S. rubber-tire industry, the CIO and its cooperating unions dispatched organizers and financial resources to aid in a strike against the industry giant Goodyear. Later that year, the United Rubber Workers (URW), chartered by the AFL in 1935, announced its support for the CIO. In December 1936, autoworkers in Flint, Michigan, the site of a key General Motors (GM) complex, launched a sit-down strike. Assisted by CIO legal counsel, Lewis's high-profile public support, and state and federal authorities anxious to avoid violent confrontation, the fledgling UAW wrested a collective-bargaining contract from GM—the world's largest corporation—in February 1937. A month later, the U.S. Steel Company signed a contract with the CIO's newly created Steel Workers Organizing Committee (SWOC), bolstering the CIO's prestige and appeal. Victories in rubber, autos, and steel triggered a wave of general organizing and impelled the embryonic CIO to create the rudiments of an institutional structure.

From the outset, Lewis, Hillman, and other CIO leaders grasped the importance of politics to the success of their efforts. They openly identified with liberal candidates, most of them in the Democratic Party. In the summer and fall of 1936, UMW and other CIO field representatives campaigned for the Democratic ticket. Lewis contributed more than half a million dollars—an enormous sum in the deflationary 1930s—to the reelection of Roosevelt and the election of liberals to Congress and statehouses. Liberal victories paid off, as evidenced by the conciliatory role played by the Roosevelt administration and by the Michigan governor Frank Murphy during the Flint sit-down strike. The passage in July 1935 of the National Labor Relations Act (NLRA) and the appointment in 1936 of a special Senate subcommittee charged with investigating employers' abuses of workers' rights further attested to the importance of politics in labor's resurgence. Throughout the latter years of the decade, exposure of employer-instigated violence and espionage, along with support by the National Labor Relations Board (NLRB) for collective bargaining and industrial unionism, contributed significantly to the CIO's successes.

Inclusion of African Americans. The CIO evidenced particular concern about the role of African American workers in the industrial economy. Since its founding in 1890, the UMW had organized on a biracial basis, whereas a number of important AFL affiliates had either barred blacks from membership or relegated them to subordinate status. In the steel, meatpacking, and automobile industries, blacks played critical roles in the production process. Any union that claimed, as CIO affiliates did, to speak on behalf of industrial workers had to reach out to African Americans and overcome their legitimate skepticism about organized labor. Lewis and other CIO leaders, especially those associated with the Communist Party and other radical organizations, sought with some success to convince blacks that the CIO was breaking with the discriminatory practices associated with both the AFL and the powerful independent railroad brotherhoods. African American workers thus were at the forefront of the creation of a CIO union in the meatpacking industry. Allying themselves with civil rights organizations, notably the National Association for the Advancement of Colored People, UAW leaders overcame initial black skepticism in their eventually successful campaign to organize the Ford Motor Company and to incorporate thousands of black autoworkers into the union.

Despite the CIO's generally positive record on racial issues, however, its leaders and grassroots organizers often found it difficult to balance a response to black workers' concerns with the need to appeal to white majorities in the factories and shipyards. Strong in their support of civil rights measures, the CIO and its major affiliates sometimes faced criticism for neglecting the distinctive problems of black workers in the contracts that they signed and in the union's day-to-day activities. Racial issues were particularly acute during World War II, when manpower needs and the rhetoric of equality led to the promotion of black workers into jobs previously held only by whites. As white workers protested the hiring or upgrading of black workers, hate strikes erupted in CIO-organized facilities in Detroit, Baltimore, Philadelphia, Mobile, Alabama, and elsewhere. The national CIO and the unions most affected, notably the UAW, the Transport Workers Union (TWU), and the Marine and Shipbuilding Workers, disavowed these walkouts. Indeed, the UAW and the TWU broke hate strikers' picket lines and forced the firing of ringleaders. Racial tensions lingered, however, especially in the South, where Communist-led affiliates pressed aggressively for racial justice, while mainline CIO leaders, though never repudiating their support of civil rights, soft-pedaled the organization's racial liberalism lest ardent advocacy alienate whites.

Break with the AFL. After its spectacular early victories, the CIO suffered serious defeats. An aroused AFL used its long-established presence in industrial locales and employers' reluctant preference for its presumably more moderate brand of unionism to compete with the upstart CIO for membership in textiles, woodworking, aeronautics, pulp and paper, shipbuilding, and other sectors. In the auto, steel, farm-equipment, and rubber-tire industries, obdurate employers fought the CIO without quarter. The defeat of the so-called Little Steel strike, which culminated in the murder of eleven unionists on Memorial Day in 1937, and the Ford Motor Company's brutal assault on UAW organizers that same month stymied efforts to build upon earlier success. A deep economic recession, which began in mid-1937 and lasted more than eighteen months, also slowed CIO momentum, as did sharp internal conflict within the young UAW and URW. Even so, in 1938 the CIO formalized its break with the AFL, holding its first constitutional convention and adopting its permanent name, the Congress of Industrial Organizations, with Lewis continuing as president.

In the late 1930s and early 1940s, the Roosevelt administration's diplomatic and military response to deepening international crises powerfully affected the CIO. Lewis believed that Roosevelt was leading the country into a war that would entangle the labor movement in a repressive bureaucratic apparatus. In late October 1940 the CIO chief shocked laborites when, on a national radio hookup, he announced his support for the Republican presidential candidate Wendell Willkie and urged union members to turn their backs on Roosevelt. At the CIO's annual convention in December of that year, Lewis stepped down as the organization's president, turning the reins over to his long-term associate, the SWOC president Philip Murray. Lewis grew disdainful of his former allies in the CIO, criticizing their support of the Roosevelt administration's interventionist policies with respect to the war raging in Europe. By 1942 he had broken completely with the CIO.

Controversies over the role of CIO unions in the country's massive military buildup launched in 1938–1939 highlighted the role of Communists in the organization's early years. Communists had played an important role in early CIO organizing, especially in autos, steel, electrical appliances, food processing, meatpacking, and longshoring. After the Nazi–Soviet pact of August 1939, the Communist Party of the United States (CPUSA) abandoned its ardent support of military buildup and encouraged labor militancy—something that critics believed impeded national defense. The German attack on the Soviet Union in June 1941, however, triggered a sharp reversal of the CPUSA's position, with the CIO's party members and supporters now urging organized labor's full-scale enlistment in Roosevelt's defense-mobilization program. The pro-Soviet leaders of important CIO unions among West Coast longshoremen and electrical-goods workers were particularly vehement in urging the need to sacrifice for the U.S. war effort, especially since the Soviet Union bore the brunt of German aggression.

Participation in World War II and After.

The Japanese attack on Pearl Harbor on 7 December 1941 and the resultant entry of the United States into World War II posed both challenges and opportunities for the CIO. During the period of defense production, 1939–1941, the UAW, the SWOC, the URW, and the United Electrical Workers (UE) made major strides in organizing such large corporations as Ford, Republic Steel, International Harvester, Goodyear, and Westinghouse. CIO leaders believed that the tightened labor markets associated with expanded military production would bring an opportunity for wage increases. As strong supporters of the war effort, however, they opposed any interruption in production. Indeed, they quickly joined AFL leaders in issuing a no-strike pledge, promising to refrain from using organized labor's most effective weapon for the duration of the conflict. In January 1942, Roosevelt issued an executive order creating the National War Labor Board (NWLB), charged with resolving labor disputes while limiting inflationary wage settlements. Throughout the war, the generally union-friendly board encouraged the expansion of such so-called fringe benefits as pension provisions, in part to compensate workers for wage stagnation and in part to siphon off inflation-creating consumer buying power. The board's adoption of a so-called maintenance-of-membership policy in 1942 also benefited established unions, encouraging the vast influx of new workers into booming military-production factories to become union members.

Murray and the leaders of other CIO unions had to discourage rank-and-file activism, relying on their influence in the NWLB to gain favorable rulings. Extensive wartime strikes—the vast majority of them wildcat, or unauthorized, walkouts—attested to the difficulties that union leaders faced, making them, in the words of one critic, "managers of discontent" rather than bold advocates of their own members' concerns. On the whole, however, and despite a strike wave that peaked in the first half of 1944, CIO members approved of the no-strike pledge and compiled remarkable records of production and purchase of war bonds. Thanks to the wartime boom, a tight labor market, and the NWLB's maintenance-of-membership policy, CIO membership soared to nearly 5 million as the war ended.

After the war, the hopes of Murray and the UAW president Walter Reuther that organized labor would be able to play an increasingly active role in the organization and development of the American economy were thwarted by the aggressive reassertion of corporate prerogatives. Strikes in 1945–1946 in autos, steel, meatpacking, and other CIO-organized industries brought wage gains and made it clear that, unlike the situation after World War I, industrial unionism had become a permanent fixture of American life. Republican victories in the congressional elections of 1946, however, led to passage in 1947 of the Taft–Hartley Act, which amended the NLRA in a fashion designed to strengthen employers' ability to resist unionization. Meanwhile, the CIO's campaign to bring large-scale organization to the South, launched with much fanfare in 1946, failed.

Nonetheless, in the first postwar decade, CIO unions such as the UAW, the United Steelworkers of America (USWA, the SWOC's successor body), the UE, and the United Packinghouse Workers made major breakthroughs in negotiating provisions for wage increases, pension benefits, and medical insurance. Indeed, in these years CIO unions' contracts established new standards for two generations of American workers. In the nation's central industrial core, collective bargaining involving large corporations and CIO unions became routinized, evidencing little of the violence and obduracy that had prevailed previously, even when protracted strikes did occur.

Politics, Conflicts, and Merger with the AFL.

During the war, under the leadership of Hillman, the CIO executive board had created a political action committee, CIO-PAC, in an effort to expand and formalize the organization's hitherto ad hoc involvement in politics. Soliciting small monetary contributions from union members, CIO-PAC aggressively mobilized on behalf of Roosevelt's reelection in 1944. The disastrous results of the 1946 congressional elections encouraged Murray and other CIO leaders to expand this political arm further, and in 1948 CIO-PAC helped to mobilize blue-collar workers on behalf of the Democrat Harry Truman's upset victory. Thereafter it became an integral part of the Democratic Party's apparatus in key industrial states.

In 1949–1950, long-simmering ideological conflict led to the expulsion of eleven pro-Soviet affiliates. The support of the CIO's Communists and their allies for the Progressive Party's presidential candidate Henry Wallace in 1948 and their consistently pro-Soviet orientation on foreign-policy issues were decisive factors in the purge. Communists and their allies had played important roles in building CIO unions, and in such affiliates as the UE and the West Coast longshoremen's union they had compiled outstanding records in organizing and collective bargaining. Critics believed that the expulsion of these unions robbed the CIO of a key cadre of effective unionists. Murray, the UAW chief Walter Reuther, and other liberals and social democrats, however, held that those associated with the Stalinist CPUSA had long since forfeited any legitimate claim to association with the CIO.

Murray's death in 1952 brought other internal conflicts into the open. Of the thirty-odd CIO affiliates, only a few, most notably the UAW and the USWA, had achieved a significant and dynamic presence in their industries. With the Steelworkers hinting at abandonment of the CIO, Murray's successor Walter Reuther concluded that a merger with the older AFL represented the CIO's best hope of institutional survival. This merger took place in 1955. The AFL, which had twice the membership of the CIO, quickly became the dominant partner, and the former AFL chief George Meany, now chief of the merged AFL-CIO, emerged as organized labor's most influential public voice.

The CIO brought union organization and improved working conditions and living standards to millions of workers. It also integrated the labor movement into mainstream American liberal politics. Its inability to expand geographically and into white-collar and service sectors, however, limited its postwar effectiveness. Although its merger with the larger AFL in 1955 eliminated the CIO as an independent entity, leading affiliates such as the UAW, the USWA, and the Communications Workers of America remained powerful forces in the nation's collective-bargaining system. The CIO's early militancy, its support for civil rights, and its innovative approach to political action have left an enduring legacy.

[*See also* **American Federation of Labor; American Federation of Labor and Congress of Industrial Organizations; Automotive Industry; Great Depression (1929–1939); Hillman, Sidney; Iron and Steel Industry; Labor and Anti-Communism; Labor Movements; Lewis, John L.; Mass Production; No-Strike Pledge, World War I and World War II; Reuther, Walter;** *and* **Strikes.**]

BIBLIOGRAPHY

Bernstein, Irving. *Turbulent Years: A History of the American Worker, 1933–1941.* Boston: Houghton Mifflin, 1969.

Dubofsky, Melvyn, and Warren Van Tine. *John L. Lewis: A Biography*. New York: Quadrangle, 1977.

Foster, James Caldwell. *The Union Politic: The CIO Political Action Committee*. Columbia: University of Missouri Press, 1975.

Fraser, Steven. *Labor Will Rule: Sidney Hillman and the Rise of American Labor*. New York: Free Press, 1991.

Levenstein, Harvey A. *Communism, Anti-Communism, and the CIO*. Westport, Conn.: Greenwood Press, 1981.

Lichtenstein, Nelson. *Labor's War at Home: The CIO in World War II*. Cambridge, U.K.: Cambridge University Press, 1982.

Lichtenstein, Nelson. *The Most Dangerous Man in Detroit: Walter Reuther and the Fate of American Labor*. New York: Basic Books, 1995.

Zieger, Robert H. *The CIO, 1935–1955*. Chapel Hill: University of North Carolina Press, 1995.

Zieger, Robert H. *For Jobs and Freedom: Race and Labor in America since 1865*. Lexington: University Press of Kentucky, 2007.

Robert H. Zieger

CONSUMER CREDIT AND CREDIT CARDS

Consumer credit has existed for centuries. The Code of Hammurabi, from around 1700 BCE, contains the first written laws regarding consumer credit. Debtors had to repay amounts owed, and Hammurabi specified regulations for debtor–creditor relationships. The Old Testament prohibited charging interest to poor debtors, as well as taking advantage of others financially.

Consumer credit was used in ancient Greece; the Roman Empire; Gothic Catalonia, from which comes the first documented case of a European pawnbroker, from CE 1000; medieval Italy, which in the fifteenth century saw the first public pawnshops; and northern Europe during the Reformation. But consumer credit really expanded when it became popular in the United States in the twentieth century.

Consumer Credit in the United States. About 1910, American household finance underwent drastic changes because of consumers' use of credit. From a system that was chaotic, in poor repute, and undercapitalized came a new corporate system that was regulated by the state, heavily promoted, and eventually recognized as a legitimate part of American life. The Ford Motor Company issued credit so that consumers could purchase an expensive product, the automobile. Before World War II, however, Americans rarely used consumer debt. After the war, consumer spending rose rapidly, and soon it was accelerated by a dramatic increase in the number and use of credit cards. Consumer debt's stigma ended in the 1950s, and buying items such as cars and homes on credit gained widespread acceptance in American society. With the introduction of the Diners Club card in 1950, consumers purchased goods and services without cash. Other companies soon embraced the idea of extending consumer credit as a profitable, needed service. In the 1970s and 1980s, American consumers increasingly used credit cards to purchases necessities as well as luxuries. In the 1970s only 16 percent of Americans held credit cards, but by the twenty-first century, 70 percent of households used a major credit card.

The History of Credit Cards. Consumers have borrowed money since time immemorial, but the use of credit cards is relatively new. Issued by financial institutions, credit cards have a revolving credit line that enables holders to manage their funds more flexibly. Credit cards also offer holders the option of either paying their bill in full and thus avoiding interest charges or making monthly payments and thus incurring interest on the remaining balance. Some cards, however, require that balances be paid in full monthly.

Edward Bellamy's 1887 novel *Looking Backward* includes a description of a card that is considered a forerunner of the modern version. In the 1800s, merchants and financial intermediaries provided customers credit for agricultural and durable goods. In 1914, Western Union invented the first charge card by giving prominent customers a metal card, or "metal money," to defer payments on services without interest. In 1924 the General Petroleum Corporation issued metal cards to their employees, customers, and the general public for purchasing gasoline and repair services. In the late 1930s the American Telephone and Telegraph Company (AT&T) started the so-called Bell system credit card in response to the growing popularity of consumer credit. During World War II, all credit and charge cards were prohibited. With the war's end, the American credit-card industry grew enormously.

Businesses boomed in the postwar years as consumers wanted to purchase many costly commodities and appliances. In 1946, John Biggins of the Flatbush National Bank of Brooklyn, New York, invented the first bank credit card, called "Charge-it," which allowed area merchants to deposit sales slips in a bank that later billed customers. A link was established among banks, merchants, and customers to facilitate credit and purchases. The biggest development occurred in 1950 when Frank McNamara started the Diners Club credit card, allowing customers to purchase merchandise and restaurant meals on credit. The Diners Club card allowed businesspeople to pay for travel and entertainment without carrying cash. The card gained popularity in the 1950s and led American Express to issue its own charge card in 1958. In the same year, Bank of America introduced its first revolving credit card, BankAmericard, which allowed cardholders different payment options.

The credit-card industry continued to grow in the 1960s. In 1965, Bank of America signed licensing agreements with banks across the nation. For the first time, other banks could issue BankAmericards and participate through a common interchange transaction system. In 1966, fourteen U.S. banks formed the Inter-Bank Card Association to exchange card transaction information and to manage credit-card governance and regulation. Four California banks formed the Western States Bankcard Association in 1967 and introduced Master Charge, competing with BankAmericard. Consolidation in the credit-card industry occurred in 1969 when most independent bank charge cards converted to either BankAmericard or Master Charge.

The credit-card industry realized its need to expand into foreign markets, and in 1977 BankAmericard was renamed Visa. In 1979, Master Charge also changed its name, to MasterCard. With advanced technology, credit cards by 1979 used electronic processing that was managed with magnetic strips on the card's back and electronic dial-up terminals to process purchases. The new technology speeded transactions, increased processing, and reduced credit-card fraud.

The 1980s saw increased use of credit cards and thus higher profits for issuing companies. In 1989, Citibank ushered in a new era through its arrangement with American Airlines that introduced reward points. Now cardholders received awards and incentives for using their cards more. The new benefits came with increased fees for cardholders and thus higher revenues and profits for banks.

The economic crisis of 2008–2010 led consumers and government regulators to subject the credit-card industry to greater scrutiny. In December 2008 the Office of Thrift Supervision, the Federal Reserve Board, and the National Credit Union Administration adopted regulations to protect consumers from shady lending practices, regulating interest rates on current balances and forbidding rate changes during a cardholder's initial year. The regulations became effective in July 2010.

[*See also* **Bank of America; Consumer Culture; Consumer Movements; Financial and Banking Promotion and Regulation; Internet Commerce;** *and* **National City Bank (Citibank).**]

BIBLIOGRAPHY

Calder, Lendol. *Financing the American Dream: A Cultural History of Consumer Credit.* Princeton, N.J.: Princeton University Press, 1999.

Gelpi, Rosa-Maria, and François Julien-Labruyère. *The History of Consumer Credit: Doctrines and Practices.* Translated by Liam Gavin. New York: St. Martin's Press, 2000.

Arthur S. Guarino

CONSUMER CULTURE

The term "consumer culture" refers to societies in which the widespread consumption and production of goods is a central element of economic organization. The earliest signs of such cultures emerged during Britain's so-called consumer revolution in the eighteenth century, when increasing prosperity fostered demand for goods such as clothing, tableware, beer, tea, sugar, vases, razor strops, and more. Growing demand, in turn, spurred innovations in production and new techniques for marketing, including retail stores, advertisers, and more efficient communication and transportation.

Long-distance trade routes expanded Britain's "empire of goods" to incorporate the colonies as well. Exports to America grew eightfold between 1700 and 1773. Consumption spiked in the 1740s: colonial newspapers advertised additional English goods, and stores spread even into smaller villages. Per capita consumption rose 120 percent between 1750 and 1773 as newspapers began to carry advertisements for thousands of elaborately specific items, such as "Axminster carpets" and "Maid's Lamb Gloves."

Contrary to their reputation as self-sufficient yeomen, ordinary American farm families also acted as consumers, and frequently they purchased on credit. Women in particular benefited from readymade cloth, beer, and other goods that eased their daily household labors. Even poorer households began to acquire tables, chairs, beds, linens, tableware, and the like.

Native Americans also participated in the consumer experience. Various tribes trapped and traded beaver and otter pelts to the English and French in the early 1600s in return for metal tools, clothing, guns, alcohol, mirrors, and decorations and jewelry. By the middle of the 1700s, southeastern tribes were trading well over 100,000 pelts every season. As early as the 1650s, some three quarters of native artifacts were European. As one Montagnais hunter joked to a trader, "The Beaver does everything perfectly well, it makes kettles, hatchets, swords, knives, bread, in short it makes everything."

Their desire for consumer goods heightened colonists' dependence on Britain, especially during difficult economic times. The consumer credit that British merchants extended liberally encouraged overbuying and excessive personal debt. After 1764 the British government tried to raise revenue by levying new taxes on consumer goods—including on crucial items such as glass, paper, and paint that Americans could not produce themselves. To many colonists, the bonds of consumerism suddenly seemed to resemble a real bondage.

In response to the Stamp Act of 1765, the Townshend Act of 1767, and the Tea Act of 1773, rebellious colonists initiated nonimportation, meaning that merchants would refrain from purchasing British goods and that ordinary

Americans would refuse to consume those goods. When the Continental Congress met in September 1774, one of its first acts was to create nonimportation associations, a vast network of local communities charged with scrutinizing their neighbors' clothing, drinking, and other consumer habits. By using their power as consumers, colonial rebels tried to induce Britain to loosen imperial policy and allow the colonies more autonomy. When nonimportation failed, they resorted to open rebellion.

After the Revolutionary War, the consumer revolution continued apace in the new United States. Federal policies encouraged territorial expansion, and improvements in transport and communications expanded the domestic market for goods. Consumerism also continued to be both practically and symbolically important in American political struggles. As they expanded, consumer markets also changed in subtle but important ways. They became more impersonal and increasingly organized around a cash nexus. The ability to pay determined which goods could be purchased, and the goods acquired distinguished poorer from respectable middle-class and more ostentatious upper-class families. The continued expansion of consumer demand down to the Civil War increased the impact of anonymous, money-driven market relations that undermined traditional cultural hierarchies and made possible new ones that were based, in part, on styles of consumption.

A Nation of Consumers, 1865–1941.
Despite their expansion, consumer markets remained fragmented in the nineteenth century. There were no national manufacturers, nationally known brand names, widely promoted advertising campaigns, nor retailers with multiple outlets. This changed during the late nineteenth century when production capacity increased dramatically and railroads, telegraphs, and eventually the telephone made mass markets possible. In response, larger manufacturers and

retailers exploited economies of scale to expand their reach.

National companies that produced consumer goods developed strategies to connect directly with consumers. The most important was the brand name associated with a single, uniform prepackaged product, ready to buy in multiple stores. Brands such as Ivory Soap, Ford automobiles, and others were supported by national advertising campaigns, colorful labels, elaborate product lines and promotional gimmickry, trademarks, market research, franchise agreements, and more. The emerging national corporations generated their profits through mass production, mass marketing, and mass consumer purchasing that enabled them to sell a high volume of goods at low prices. The formula worked so well that leading companies became universally recognizable. Customer loyalty went to the manufacturer—say, the National Biscuit Company—rather than to the local merchant who peddled the product, enabling the rise of mail-order houses (e.g., Sears, Roebuck) and chain stores (e.g., Walgreens and A&P). By 1930, Montgomery Ward, a Sears competitor, was shipping more than 13,000 items per day from a catalog swollen to include 70,000 items on 1,200 pages.

Department stores, another central element of mass consumer culture, first appeared in the 1870s and spread to thousands of cities by the 1890s. Macy's, Wanamaker's, Marshall Field's, and other famous department stores built grand palaces of consumption that deployed light, color, and glass to dramatize goods and the pleasures they could bring. The new shop windows, elaborate display cases, commercial posters, electric signs, and other consumerist fanfare celebrated commodities so insistently that the labor that had produced the goods faded into the background, invisible to the buying public.

Advertising was central to the new consumer culture. The advertisers that emerged in the late nineteenth century developed an astonishing range of clever techniques to promote and differentiate products. Advertising evolved from text-heavy "reason-why" strategies to more effective image-laden emotional appeals. By 1919 large agencies such as J. Walter Thompson had their own wings for market research, and advertising had been permanently integrated into corporate marketing strategies.

The 1920s saw mass consumption reach new heights. Chain stores proliferated wildly, their growth fueled by an expansion of consumer credit in the form of installment buying. By decade's end, consumers were borrowing as much as $7 billion per year. Meanwhile, mass-culture forms such as movie theaters, Victrola record players, and radios expanded the reach of a unified, commercial national culture and provided advertisers with an easily accessible mass audience. In 1925, 50 million Americans went to see a movie every week—half the entire population. Many observers heralded the elimination of poverty and need as access to plentiful goods would soon be within reach of all Americans.

In fact, however, working-class families did not always have easy access to credit, nor did they earn enough to consume heedlessly by buying luxuries. National chain stores were seldom located in working-class neighborhoods, especially those dominated by newer immigrants and their children. Ethnic working people preferred to patronize local merchants who spoke their language, stocked the produce and goods that they preferred, and ran an informal tab for them. Not until the post–World War II years did working-class families, especially ethnic ones, participate more fully in the wonders of mass consumption.

African Americans, as a rule, were even more isolated from the mass consumer market than white ethnics were. They earned less, had smaller savings, and had less access to credit. African Americans rarely had the funds or access to capital that might enable them to own and operate small neighborhood stores as many ethnics did. Typically, in New York's Harlem and Bedford-Stuyvesant or Chicago's South Side "Black Belt," Jewish and Italian petty entrepreneurs operated the groceries, greengroceries, butcher shops, and clothing or department stores that served African American patrons, leading to all sorts of friction and sometimes open conflict.

The Consumerist Era, from 1941.   Consumption and its politics were central to the ways Americans experienced World War II. During the war, large corporations shut down the lines that mass-produced consumer goods and converted them to the production of military items. The federal government discouraged excessive consumption of scarce consumer goods by instituting mandatory rationing, especially limiting the ability of citizens to purchase gasoline, car tires, silk products, beef and pork, and sugar and coffee, among numerous other everyday items. Government campaigns urged citizens to invest their wartime earnings and savings in U.S. war bonds instead of seeking to acquire scarce goods on the black market. To restrain one's purchases and consumption became a patriotic obligation for the duration of the war.

After the war, however, the savings amassed by citizens and the demand for goods that had been restrained fueled a surge of mass consumption that was supported by federal policy and embraced by business and labor as a uniquely American "way of life," particularly in contrast to what was portrayed as the gray, dull, and choiceless monotony of Russian totalitarianism. In the five years after World War II, Americans purchased 20 million cars and refrigerators, 5.5 million electric stoves, and 12 million television sets. In the 1959 so-called Kitchen Debate with the Soviet premier Nikita Khrushchev, the U.S. vice president Richard

M. Nixon made the case overtly: America was freer because American housewives could choose to purchase more conveniences to make their lives easier.

Postwar consumerism took on distinctive forms, the most notable of which was the proliferation of homogenous and racially segregated spaces to live, shop, and recreate. Housing patterns lay at the heart of this: taking advantage of government subsidies, white Americans moved en masse to new suburbs. The rapidly growing and spreading suburbs were accessible by highway and insulated by wide cordons of parking lots from the urban fabric around them. Meanwhile, giant, enclosed, climate-controlled shopping malls beyond the borders of central cities—featuring the same buffer zone of highway exits and parking lots—replaced downtown department stores as new grand palaces of consumption. Smaller, unenclosed strip malls, also with ample parking, rapidly proliferated along primary suburban traffic arteries that also featured fast-food franchises such as McDonald's, Burger King, Wendy's, Arby's, and Taco Bell.

Access to the new palaces of consumption was profoundly unequal. The new spaces of consumerism were rigidly segregated by class and race: Levittown, New York, the first mass-produced postwar suburb, was the single-largest all-white community in the entire nation, and the shopping malls, chain restaurants, and other institutions that grew around it and other suburbs were essentially whites-only as well. Suburbs and consumer spaces were closely calibrated by economic class, too, with larger and more expensive houses linked to upscale shopping areas for the affluent.

The youth culture that was fueled by the offspring of the postwar baby boom and that blossomed in the 1960s reshaped consumer culture—and continued to do so into the twenty-first century. American businesses responded to such shifts in popular culture and

consumer preferences by shifting their marketing. Advertisers, for example, shifted to a more youthful, hipper style in the 1960s, heralded by the campaign for Volkswagen in 1959 that mocked Madison Avenue advertising and promised that buying from Volkswagen meant being liberated from conformity and manipulation. The "Pepsi Generation" campaign of 1961 celebrated youthful "revolution" in thinking and attitude. Even rebellious rock music quickly became a booming consumer niche and also came to provide the background music for some of the most successful ad campaigns. Eventually marketers hired "cool hunters" to discover and identify new, "authentic" trends as sources for new products.

The youth-marketing strategy was one part of a broader shift in the 1960s and 1970s to market segmentation, or selling products for particular demographic groups—a major change in a modern consumer culture that had been founded on national brands and advertising. Over the next half a century, market segmentation grew increasingly sophisticated, and it culminated when personal computers and the Internet enabled advertisers to target their appeals to individuals.

By the end of the 1960s, the old mail-order retail business that had transformed Sears, Roebuck and Montgomery Ward into giant enterprises was dying. Before the century ended, Montgomery Ward had died economically, and Sears operated primarily as an on-site department store that had great difficulty adjusting to new styles of consumption. By the early twenty-first century, personal computers, smartphones, and the Internet had re-created a form of mail-order business: consumers were able to access an endless array of goods online, place orders electronically, and have them delivered to their home by Federal Express or United Parcel Service. Individuals could also become their own merchandisers by advertising and selling goods on eBay or Craigslist.

The United States remains in the twenty-first century an economy driven by consumer spending. From President George W. Bush's 2002 appeal for Americans to support the war on terror by shopping, to President Barack Obama's John Maynard Keynes–inspired stimulus spending in 2009, consumerism has continued to be openly acknowledged as vital to the economy. Yet the patterns of consumption remain starkly class-based. Less-affluent citizens patronize Wal-Mart, Sam's Club, K-Mart, and Kohl's and dine out at McDonald's or Wendy's; more comfortable middle-class consumers patronize Target, Costco, Men's Wearhouse, and Macy's and dine out at Olive Garden, P. F. Chang's, or Red Lobster; the affluent patronize Saks Fifth Avenue, Nordstrom, Nieman-Marcus, and perhaps Tiffany, and they dine in the finest restaurants. The economic crisis of 2008 and the ensuing Great Recession, combined with the ever-increasing inequality among citizens, has led to hard economic times for businesses that sell to the vast majority of consumers and has led to great profits for those that sell to the affluent. The role of consumption and mass consumerism throughout American history reveals how much has been and remains at stake in the deceptively simple act of purchasing goods.

[*See also* **Advertising; Consumer Credit and Credit Cards; Department Stores; Mail-Order Houses; Mass Marketing; Mass Production; McDonald's; Shopping Centers and Malls; Transportation Revolution; Wal-Mart;** *and* **Wanamaker, John, and Wanamaker's.**]

BIBLIOGRAPHY

Avila, Eric. *Popular Culture in the Age of White Flight: Fear and Fantasy in Suburban Los Angeles.* Berkeley: University of California Press, 2004. A fascinating analysis of the post–World War II landscape of suburbia and mass amusements such as Disneyland and Dodgers Stadium.

Axtell, James. "The First Consumer Revolution." In *Consumer Society in American History: A Reader*, edited by Lawrence B. Glickman, pp. 85–99. Ithaca, N.Y.: Cornell University Press, 1999. Native Americans and the consumer culture.

Breen, T. H. *The Marketplace of Revolution: How Consumer Politics Shaped American Independence.* New York: Oxford University Press, 2004.

Cohen, Lizabeth. *A Consumers' Republic: The Politics of Mass Consumption in Postwar America.* New York: Alfred A. Knopf, 2003. A sweeping synthesis; the most important single work on the post–World War II era.

Cohen, Lizabeth. *Making a New Deal: Industrial Workers in Chicago, 1919–1939.* New York: Cambridge University Press, 1990. Examines how ethnic workers' engagement with consumer culture helped give rise to Depression-era industrial unionism.

Cross, Gary. *An All-Consuming Century: Why Commercialism Won in Modern America.* New York: Columbia University Press, 2000. An easily digestible survey of major trends, sharpened by a strong central argument.

De Grazia, Victoria. *Irresistible Empire: America's Advance through Twentieth-Century Europe.* Cambridge, Mass.: Belknap Press of Harvard University Press, 2005. A dense but rewarding look at the practical and cultural mechanics of Americanization as viewed from Europe.

Enstad, Nan. *Ladies of Labor, Girls of Adventure: Working Women, Popular Culture, and Labor Politics at the Turn of the Twentieth Century.* New York: Columbia University Press, 1999.

Enstad, Nan. "Popular Culture." In *A Companion to American Cultural History*, edited by Karen Halttunen, pp. 356–370. Malden, Mass.: Blackwell, 2008. A history of how historians have looked at the consumer goods that populate American popular culture.

Ewen, Stuart. *Captains of Consciousness: Advertising and the Social Roots of the Consumer Culture.* New York: McGraw–Hill, 1976. The classic, endlessly debunked but still provocative and indispensable account of how advertisers tricked Americans into a dependence on consumer goods.

Fox, Richard Wightman, and T. J. Jackson Lears, eds. *The Culture of Consumption: Critical Essays in*

American History, 1880–1980. New York: Pantheon Books, 1983. A pioneering book that helped establish the field of the history of consumer culture in the United States.

Franks, Thomas. *The Conquest of Cool: Business Culture, Counterculture, and the Rise of Hip Consumerism.* Chicago: University of Chicago Press, 1997. Argues that corporate marketers invented the counterculture even before hippies existed.

Glickman, Lawrence B. *Buying Power: A History of Consumer Activism in America.* Chicago: University of Chicago Press, 2009.

Glickman, Lawrence B. *A Living Wage: American Workers and the Making of the Consumer Society.* Ithaca, N.Y.: Cornell University Press, 1997.

Glickman, Lawrence B., ed. *Consumer Society in American History: A Reader.* Ithaca, N.Y.: Cornell University Press, 1999.

Kasson, John F. *Amusing the Million: Coney Island at the Turn of the Century.* New York: Hill and Wang, 1978.

Kelley, Robin D. G. "The Riddle of the Zoot: Malcolm Little and Black Cultural Politics during World War II." In his *Race Rebels: Culture, Politics, and the Black Working Class,* pp. 161–182. New York: Free Press, 1994.

Lears, T. J. Jackson. *Fables of Abundance: A Cultural History of Advertising in America.* New York: Basic Books, 1994.

Marchand, Roland. *Advertising the American Dream: Making Way for Modernity, 1920–1940.* Berkeley: University of California Press, 1985. A no-nonsense, well-illustrated history of the advertising profession.

Peiss, Kathy. *Cheap Amusements: Working Women and Leisure in Turn-of-the-Century New York.* Philadelphia: Temple University Press, 1986.

Rosenzweig, Roy. *Eight Hours for What We Will: Workers and Leisure in an Industrial City, 1870–1920.* New York: Cambridge University Press, 1983.

Sellers, Charles. *The Market Revolution: Jacksonian America, 1815–1846.* New York: Oxford University Press, 1991.

Von Eschen, Penny M. *Satchmo Blows Up the World: Jazz Ambassadors Play the Cold War.* Cambridge, Mass.: Harvard University Press, 2004.

Weems, Robert E., Jr. *Desegregating the Dollar: African American Consumerism in the Twentieth Century.* New York: New York University Press, 1998.

David Herzberg

CONSUMER MOVEMENTS

The modern consumer movement—organizations promoting the economic interests of consumers—arose during the Progressive Era. Yet it had antecedents in the United States that went as far back as the early nineteenth century when poorer urban dwellers sometimes took to the streets and even rioted to protest rising food prices. As trade unions developed and grew later in the century, the unions' members, their families, and their supporters also used their power as consumers to further union goals. Union members and their friends boycotted—that is, refused to patronize and purchase goods from—so-called unfair employers until the employers recognized and bargained with unions. Such boycotts proved especially effective against the producers and purveyors of such wares as cheap cigars, beer, work clothes, and work shoes, items consumed primarily by working people. Even as the modern consumer movement emerged early in the twentieth century, food protests persisted during periods of high inflation, and unions continued to use the boycott.

During the Progressive Era, middle-class and affluent citizens concerned about unsafe products and business monopolies used their buying power—by means of "white lists" of approved stores—journalistic exposés, and lobbying to press for government action. The first enduring consumer organization, the National Consumers League, was formed at the turn of the twentieth century. Led by Florence Kelley, the league sought both worker and consumer protections. The league's lobbying for consumer protections resulted in three landmark consumer laws: the Meat Inspection Act (1906), Pure Food and Drug Act (1906), and the Federal Trade Commission Act (1914).

A second wave of the consumer movement arose during the 1920s and 1930s when new technology spread from the factory to the American home. Technological progress brought branded products, typically produced by companies whose factories were hundreds or even thousands of miles away from the point of purchase. These packaged and often complex products were difficult for shoppers to evaluate. The resulting "impenetrable ignorance," a term used by Stuart Chase and Frederick J. Schlink in *Your Money's Worth: A Study in the Waste of the Consumer's Dollar* (1927), gave rise in 1936 to the Consumers Union, whose magazine *Consumer Reports* provides consumers with objective information based on rigorous product testing. By the early twenty-first century the Consumers Union boasted more than 7 million subscriptions and had spawned similar magazines in numerous countries.

The consumer movement's third and most activist wave took place during the 1960s and 1970s, a time of heightened social activism. The movement won the support of President John F. Kennedy, who in 1962 urged Congress to recognize the consumer's right to be safe, be informed, have meaningful marketplace choices, and be heard by government bodies in the formulation of consumer policy. The movement also created a celebrity in the person of a young lawyer, Ralph Nader. His book *Unsafe at Any Speed: The Designed-In Dangers of the American Automobile* (1965) detailed safety hazards plaguing the U.S. auto industry in general and the Corvair, produced by General Motors (GM), in particular. Using $425,000 that he won in an invasion-of-privacy suit against GM in 1970, Nader founded several consumer groups, led by Nader's Raiders, that pursued legal challenges to unsafe products and demanded greater govern-

ment protection for consumers. The formation in 1968 of the non-profit Consumer Federation of America as an umbrella organization for the movement and the formation in 1972 of the governmental Consumer Product Safety Commission attested to the movement's success but also to its reformist bent. Rather than threatening everyday business practices or capitalism, the movement aimed at correcting market imperfections and protecting vulnerable consumers. When the movement sought the ambitious goal of establishing a consumer protection agency within the federal government, the business community mobilized to defeat it in the late 1970s. One instance in which consumer purchasing power did present a direct threat to business in the 1960s was when Cesar Chavez, leader of the United Farm Workers, called for a consumer boycott of table grapes grown by producers who refused to recognize and bargain with the United Farm Workers. That call elicited a positive response among masses of affluent urban and suburban consumers.

The early twenty-first century saw a revival of the consumer movement, spurred by concerns regarding financial and medical privacy, as well as by mortgage lending practices. New organizations (e.g., the Electronic Privacy Information Center, the Center for Responsible Lending) and new federal legislation (e.g., the Fair and Accurate Credit Transactions Act of 2003, the Credit Card Accountability, Responsibility, and Disclosure Act of 2009) are products of this latest wave of movement activity. The movement's most notable feat, however, was the establishment of the Consumer Financial Protection Bureau (CFPB), with broad powers to regulate credit transactions, including mortgages. The successful campaign to establish the CFPB illustrated the consumer movement's continued relevance. It also illustrated the difficulty in making such an agency effective: in 2011, congressional Republicans refused to consent to President Barack Obama's appointment of a director for the CFPB unless the act that authorized the creation of the CFPB was amended to strip the new agency of much of its power. The whole episode, however, elevated Elizabeth Warren, the Harvard Law School professor who originally proposed the idea of the CFPB, to the status of crusader for the average consumer.

[*See also* Chavez, Cesar; Consumer Credit and Credit Cards; Federal Regulatory Agencies; Federal Trade Commission; Food and Diet; *Jungle, The*; Kelley, Florence; Mass Marketing; *and* Pure Food and Drug Act.]

BIBLIOGRAPHY

Cohen, Lizabeth. *A Consumers' Republic: The Politics of Mass Consumption in Postwar America*. New York: Alfred A. Knopf, 2003.
Glickman, Lawrence B. *Buying Power: A History of Consumer Activism in America*. Chicago: University of Chicago Press, 2009.
Hilton, Michael. *Prosperity for All: Consumer Activism in an Era of Globalization*. Ithaca, N.Y.: Cornell University Press, 2009.
Jacobs, Meg. *Pocketbook Politics: Economic Citizenship in Twentieth-Century America*. Princeton, N.J.: Princeton University Press, 2005.
Mayer, Robert N. *The Consumer Movement: Guardians of the Marketplace*. Boston: Twayne, 1989.

Robert N. Mayer

CONTAINERIZATION AND TRANSFORMATION OF SHIPPING

See Maritime Transport.

CONTRACT, SANCTITY OF

By the mid-eighteenth century, contracts had become a vital element in the growing market economy. The central premise of contract law was that the courts, absent unusual circumstances, were simply to enforce bargains freely made by private parties. Courts were to hold the parties to their agreement, not to review the substantive terms of contracts. Parties were expected to look out for their own interests. Aside from contracts' economic importance, reliance on contracts also strengthened individual autonomy. The triumph of contract marked a move away from a hierarchical society in which one's place was determined by birth and status.

In view of the crucial role of contracts in a market economy, stability of contractual arrangements was essential. Parties to commercial transactions had to be able to trust that the terms of contracts would be honored. It followed that lawmakers should not be able to retroactively alter contracts by rearranging the terms upon which the parties had agreed.

Yet in the troubled economic circumstances of post-Revolutionary America, state legislators were prone to interfere with existing contracts by enacting a host of laws calculated to assist debtors at the expense of creditors. To many political leaders, however, such laws were counterproductive and discouraged economic growth. Anxious to ensure the stability of contracts, the framers of the Constitution inserted language in Article I, section 10, providing: "No state shall . . . pass any . . . Law impairing the obligation of Contracts." It is significant that the framers saw contractual rights as sufficiently vital to warrant a specific ban on state abridgment. As Chief Justice Roger B. Taney explained in *Bronson v. Kinzie* (1843), the purpose of the contract clause "was to maintain the integrity of contracts, and to secure their faithful execution throughout this Union." Moreover, many state constitutions contained similar language designed to safeguard the security of contracts.

The Supreme Court gave a broad reading to the notion of "contract," holding that the contract clause encompassed not only agreements among private parties but also contracts to which a state was a party, such as land grants and corporate charters. Throughout the nineteenth century the Court frequently invoked the contract clause and extolled the virtue of contracts. "Contracts mark the progress of communities in civilization and prosperity," it proclaimed in *Farrington v. Tennessee* (1877). "They are the springs of business, trade, and commerce. Without them, society could not go on."

Still, there were limits to how far the contract clause protected the sanctity of contracts. Several factors were at work. First, the clause was confined to contractual impairments by state governments. Based on their experience, the Constitution's framers believed that the states were likely to be the primary source of interference with contracts. Congress, on the other hand, was free to rearrange contracts, and certainly it could authorize such a step through exercise of its bankruptcy power. Second, the contract clause safeguarded existing agreements from retroactive impairment but afforded no protection for the making of future agreements. These were subject to state economic regulations. Third, the Supreme Court itself limited the reach of the contract clause in several ways. The Court recognized a nebulous distinction between contractual rights and the remedies available to enforce those rights. States could alter the procedure for the enforcement of contracts so long as a substantive remedy remained. This was a fertile source of confusion and litigation. Even more significant, the Court ruled that state police power to safeguard the health, safety, and morals of the public trumped contractual arrangements. This gave the states room to override contractual provisions in the name of public interest.

The high regard for contractual stability that characterized the founding era and the nineteenth century waned after 1900. Scholars associated with the Progressive movement charged that unequal bargaining power often permitted one party effectively to dictate the terms of many contracts. Legislators increasingly intervened in the formation of contracts, first with respect to insurance contracts and after World War II through consumer-protection laws. As society gradually assigned less value to the protection of contracts, judicial interest in the contract clause waned. The clause received a near-fatal blow in *Home Building and Loan Association v. Blaisdell* (1934), a controversial decision that sustained a state moratorium on the foreclosure of mortgages. After the New Deal constitutional revolution of 1937, the contract clause faded into disuse. It has not been invoked by the Supreme Court since 1978. Despite legislative inroads and lack of significant constitutional support, the principle of sanctity of contract has proved remarkably durable. Contracts remain a key component in organizing economic relationships.

BIBLIOGRAPHY

Ely, James W., Jr. "The Protection of Contractual Rights: A Tale of Two Constitutional Provisions." *NYU Journal of Law and Liberty* 1 (2005): 370–403.

Friedman, Lawrence M. *Contract Law in America: A Social and Economic Case Study.* Madison: University of Wisconsin Press, 1965.

James W. Ely Jr.

COOPERATIVES

Cooperatives provide a means for workers and others to directly control the aspects of their lives relating to consumption and production. Although some cooperatives had existed before, the founder of the modern cooperative movement was the Welsh social reformer Robert Owen (1771–1858), who believed that cooperation rather than competition would create a prosperous and harmonious community. The best known of the early cooperative movements were the Rochdale consumer cooperatives, which date back to 1844 in England: following an unsuccessful strike, Rochdale flannel weavers helped start a movement to combat high prices and poor-quality food. The Rochdale consumer co-ops were founded on clear principles. These included the provision of capital by members at a fixed rate of interest; a dividend, or "divvy," based on profits, to be divided among members in proportion to the amount of purchases; and management to be based on democratic principles, with "one member, one vote." The cooperative movement manifested itself in other forms, including worker cooperatives and credit unions. Practical utopians, cooperativists believe that through collective action they can improve and even transform the market economy.

Interest in the notion of cooperation first appeared in the United States in the 1830s and ever since has tended to fluctuate. Surges occurred during the 1930s Depression and the 1960s, both times accompanying general economic and political disillusionment. Particular ethnic groups, such as the Finns in Minnesota and Wisconsin, were active promoters of cooperation. Efforts to form national cooperative associations include the Cooperative League of America, created in Brooklyn in 1915. Cooperatives' relationship with the labor movement also tended to fluctuate. An early example of the fledgling labor movement's interest in cooperation was the Working Men's Protective Union in Boston in 1845, a network of cooperatively owned stores and buying clubs. The American Federation of Labor (AFL) gave support to the cooperative movement at its 1896 convention, and in the late 1940s, against the background of rising prices, active support for the cooperative movement by the AFL and the Congress of Industrial Organizations peaked. Political controversy continued over whether co-ops should receive assistance through tax concessions and

direct financial assistance. During the 1930s Depression, credit unions fared well, and in recognition of this the federal government in 1934 enacted the Credit Union Act, which provided an opportunity for all citizens to organize credit unions. In 1978, Congress established the federally funded National Cooperative Bank to provide cheap finance to cooperatives. With the support of the administration of Ronald Reagan, this bank was privatized in 1981. Since the 1960s, though many retail cooperatives have collapsed in the face of competition from the profit sector, some survive by specifically focusing on organic foods and locally produced goods. Though the number of credit unions has also declined, credit unions have increased their membership.

[*See also* **Cooperatives and Worker Management; Utopian and Communitarian Movements;** *and* **Workers Self-Management.**]

BIBLIOGRAPHY

Keillor, Steven J. *Cooperative Commonwealth: Co-ops in Rural Minnesota, 1859–1939.* Saint Paul: Minnesota Historical Society Press, 2000.

Leikin, Steve. *The Practical Utopians: American Workers and the Cooperative Movement in the Gilded Age.* Detroit, Mich.: Wayne State University Press, 2005.

Parker, Florence E. *The First 125 Years: A History of the Distributive and Service Cooperation in the United States, 1829–1954.* Chicago: Cooperative League of the U.S.A., 1956.

Greg Patmore

COOPERATIVES AND WORKER MANAGEMENT

Producer cooperatives, also known as industrial cooperatives or worker cooperatives, may be considered an advanced form of worker participation. Producer cooperatives form part of a broader cooperative movement that includes consumer cooperatives and credit unions. Though there is no generally accepted definition of producer cooperatives, there are a number of characteristics on which most commentators would agree. The enterprise is autonomous, and workers are able to become members of the enterprise usually through nominal holdings of share capital. There are formal provisions that exist for the direct and indirect participation by worker members in all management levels of the enterprise. Workers should receive a share of the income after the payment of material costs, and the cooperative principle of one vote for each member applies. There are variations in the model. Membership of traditional French producer cooperatives is not confined to current workers. In other cases, such as the plywood cooperatives of the Pacific Northwest, not all workers were members. The link between ownership and employment can break down if the cooperative hires nonmember staff to meet increases in demand for its products.

Divergent views concerning producer cooperatives existed within the U.S. trade union movement and among socialists in the last half of the nineteenth century. William Sylvis, president of the Iron Molders' International Union, encouraged molders to set up self-governing producers' cooperatives in the late 1860s. The Knights of Labor tried unsuccessfully through its Cooperative Department to finance and establish worker cooperatives. Socialists and syndicalists pointed toward a so-called cooperative commonwealth as the answer to the oppression of a capitalist society, a vision that implied workers' control on the workshop floor and in the ownership of the enterprise.

Samuel Gompers, the president of the American Federation of Labor (AFL) from 1886 to 1924, along with craft unions, generally rejected the radicals' arguments and claimed that workers could obtain a voice in the workplace and ameliorate the worst conditions of capitalism through organizing into trade unions. Unions' benefit plans would protect workers from misfortunes such as illness and unemployment, while standardized wages and conditions negotiated with employers through collective bargaining would prevent workers from competing against each other. With the defeat in 1893–1895 of those proposing socialist political action within the AFL, collective bargaining became the dominant means by which organized labor believed that it could achieve industrial democracy. This view extended beyond the AFL to younger economists, such as John R. Commons, who were influenced by the writings of Sidney and Beatrice Webb, particularly their book *Industrial Democracy* (1897). The Webbs were also critical of the long-term viability of producer cooperatives. They doubted that workers would be able to exercise self-discipline in regard to production output and quality. They also believed that the workers in producer cooperatives did not have a requisite knowledge of the market and could not change existing work practices to meet shifting market needs. Similar views that trade unions rather than producer cooperatives gave workers a share in the control of the enterprise can be found in the report of the Industrial Commission appointed in 1898 by President William McKinley and the Congress, as well as in reports by the National Civic Federation.

Despite the preference of organized labor for collective bargaining, the United States has had a rich and broad experience with producer cooperatives. Derek Jones has estimated that from 1840 to 1979 at least 785 producer cooperatives were formed. Two notable periods were the 1880s and the 1930s. The first period featured the organizing efforts and founding of the Knights of Labor, and the second reflected the hardships of the Great Depression, with workers forming self-help production cooperatives. From 1931 to 1938 more than half a million families affiliated with 600 self-help organizations in thirty-six states, of which 250 were productive associations. These cooperatives received almost $5 million in funding from state and federal governments for their production activities. In California these self-help cooperatives were involved in a broad range of activities, including baking, canning, lumbering, and soap making. With the cessation of state aid in California on 1 January 1938, the Californian self-help cooperatives found it difficult to continue, and many seem to have disappeared before the end of World War II.

Since World War II, interest in producer cooperatives has fluctuated. A surge of interest accompanied the protest movements of the 1960s and 1970s: worker cooperatives reached their peak in 1979 with approximately seventeen thousand members. Particularly notable in size were the plywood cooperatives of the Pacific Northwest and the Hoedads Reforestation Cooperative in Eugene, Oregon, which had three hundred members. An adverse political and economic climate weakened the producer cooperatives in the 1980s.

Since then, several new initiatives have developed. The Network of Bay Area Worker Cooperatives in San Francisco, which has a high concentration of producer cooperatives, was founded in 1994 to bring together existing producer cooperatives and to promote new ones. The United States Federation of Worker Cooperatives was formed in 2004 to promote productive cooperatives nationally. An initiative announced in October 2009 involves collaboration between the United Steelworkers and the Mondragon cooperative movement in Spain, with the goal of establishing manufacturing cooperatives in Canada and the United States. According to estimates, however, the early twenty-first-century United States still had only approximately three hundred worker cooperatives.

[*See also* Collective Bargaining; Cooperatives; Industrial Democracy; Labor Movements; Utopian and Communitarian Movements; *and* Workers Self-Management.]

BIBLIOGRAPHY

Curl, John. *For All the People: Uncovering the Hidden History of Cooperation, Cooperative Movements, and Communalism in America*. Oakland, Calif.: PM Press, 2009.

Jones, Derek C. "American Producer Cooperatives and Employee-Owned Firms: A Historical Perspective." In *Worker Cooperatives in America*, edited by Robert Jackall and Henry M. Levin, pp. 37–56. Berkeley: University of California Press, 1984.

Jones, Derek C., and Donald J. Schneider. "Self-Help Production Cooperatives: Government-Administered Cooperatives during the Depression." In *Worker Cooperatives in America*, edited by Robert Jackall and Henry M. Levin, pp. 57–84. Berkeley: University of California Press, 1984.

Leikin, Steve. *The Practical Utopians: American Workers and the Cooperative Movement in the Gilded Age*. Detroit, Mich.: Wayne State University Press, 2005.

Markey, Raymond, Nicola Balnave, and Greg Patmore. "Worker Directors and Worker Ownership/Cooperatives." In *The Oxford Handbook of Participation in Organizations*, edited by Adrian Wilkinson, Paul J. Gollan, Mick Marchington, and David Lewin, pp. 237–257. Oxford: Oxford University Press, 2010.

Greg Patmore

CORN, HYBRID

In the early twentieth century, corn was the dominant field crop in the United States and a major focus of plant-breeding research efforts. Those efforts yielded the first commercially viable hybrid variety when Henry A. Wallace introduced the hybrid that he named "Copper

Cross" in 1924. By 1926, Wallace founded the Hi-Bred Corn Company, later known as the Pioneer Hi-Bred Corn Company, the first company to produce and sell hybrid seed corn. (Wallace went on to become secretary of agriculture, vice president, and Progressive Party presidential candidate.) Several new firms began production within a few years. Hybrid-corn cultivation expanded from about 0.1 percent of planted acreage in 1933 to 96.3 percent by 1960. Hence within a thirty-year span, farmers in the United States had almost completely abandoned the kind of open-pollinated varieties that had been cultivated in the Americas for thousands of years and that still account for most corn planted around the world. Pioneer Hi-Bred, owned by DuPont since the late 1990s, is the second-largest seed company in the world, behind Monsanto.

Hybrids are the result of cross-breeding different varieties of inbred, or self-pollinated, lines of corn. The first generation of hybrid plants, referred to as F1, exhibits what is called "hybrid vigor." That is, plants of this generation have greater yield potential than either parent plant. Hybrids may also exhibit other desirable qualities, such as drought resistance. The seeds of F1 hybrid plants do not "come true." That is, yields decline dramatically with the second generation, making the seeds of the first-generation plants virtually worthless. This characteristic is referred to as a "genetically closed pedigree." For this reason, farmers must return to the seed company every year to purchase new hybrid seeds and the increased yields or other characteristics they offer.

The rapid adoption of hybrid corn by U.S. farmers following its commercial introduction was accompanied by a remarkable increase in corn yields per acre, from an average of 20 bushels per acre in 1930 to an average of more than 150 bushels per acre in 2010. This increase followed a period of relative stagnation in corn yields, a period dating back at least to when official measurement began in 1866. The adoption and improvement of hybrid varieties is commonly credited with this achievement, but this perspective has been criticized for being overly simplistic in overlooking the complex synergies among the chemical, biological, and mechanical technologies being adopted nearly simultaneously. For example, realizing the full yield potential of hybrids relied upon the application of synthetic fertilizer, as well as the mechanization of planting equipment.

Zvi Griliches based his famous model of technological diffusion on the case of hybrid corn, assuming that hybrid corn represented a superior technology. There is disagreement about whether this presumption is true, as well as about whether farmers were the unambiguous beneficiaries. The biologists Jean-Pierre Berlan and R. C. Lewontin, for example, argue that the choice of hybrid technologies was motivated by the superior profit potential for commercial seed companies of hybridization over other breeding techniques. Similarly, Richard Sutch points to the influence of a sustained propaganda campaign encouraging adoption of hybrid corn. Deborah Fitzgerald describes the ways in which adoption of hybrid corn resulted in the deskilling of farmers.

[*See also* **Agriculture,** *subentries on* **The Golden Age (1890 to 1920)** *and* **Since 1920; Corporate Agriculture;** *and* **Grains.**]

BIBLIOGRAPHY

Berlan, Jean-Pierre, and R. C. Lewontin. "The Political Economy of Hybrid Corn." *Monthly Review,* July–August 1986. Available at http://libcom.org/library/political-economy-hybrid-corn.

Fitzgerald, Deborah. "Farmers Deskilled: Hybrid Corn and Farmers' Work." *Technology and Culture* 34 (1993): 324–343.

Griliches, Zvi. "Hybrid Corn: An Explotation in the Economics of Technological Change." *Econometrica* 25:4 (1957): 501–522.

Runge, C. Ford. "King Corn: The History, Trade, and Environmental Consequences of Corn (Maize) Production in the United States." World Wildlife Fund, September 2002. Available at http://www.worldwildlife.org/what/globalmarkets/agriculture/WWFBinaryitem7205.pdf.

Sutch, Richard C. "Henry Agard Wallace, the Iowa Corn Yield Tests, and the Adoption of Hybrid Corn." National Bureau of Economic Research, Working Paper 14141, June 2008. Available at http://www.nber.org/papers/w14141.

Elizabeth A. Ramey

CORPORATE AGRICULTURE

"Corporate agriculture" refers to the role of corporations in the food and agricultural system. Non-family corporate farms account for no more than 2 percent of all farms in the United States, so the term most often applies to related stages of the food supply chain, including the production of seeds, agrochemicals, machinery, and other inputs, as well as storage, transportation, marketing, processing, and retailing.

Since European settlement, farming in the United States has been largely commercially oriented, so farms have long been reliant on other enterprises for storing, transporting, and marketing their produce to distant populations. Discontent over the unequal balance of economic power between farmers and merchants, creditors, and railroads fueled the fury of late nineteenth-century Populists such as Mary Elizabeth Lease, who is famously said to have exhorted farmers to "raise less corn and more hell." The issue of corporate power in agriculture has remained, and her call to arms remains standard in twenty-first-century critiques of corporate agriculture.

The industrialization of agriculture by the early twentieth century resulted in the increased role of agribusinesses that produced and supplied inputs such as seed, fuel, machinery, fertilizers, and pesticides. For example, the purchase of a tractor to replace horsepower necessitated the further purchase of fuel and fertilizer to substitute for hay, oats, and manure, all of which, including the horses, had been previously produced on farms. Corporate consolidation through horizontal and vertical integration and the resulting trend toward fewer, larger enterprises along the food supply chain intensified through the twentieth century. Horizontal integration occurs when a firm expands within the same stage of production. For example, in 1989, Tyson Foods, Inc., solidified its position as the largest poultry processor in the United States by merging with a leading competitor, Holly Farms. Vertical integration occurs when a single firm takes over several stages in the production process. For example, in addition to processing poultry, Tyson Foods operates hatcheries, feed mills, and transportation facilities, thus undertaking nearly every stage along the poultry production process with the exception of raising chickens, which is contracted out to farmer-growers.

Though the poultry industry is one of the most integrated, these trends are by no means confined to this area of agriculture. One measure of market structure is the four-firm concentration ratio, or the percent of the market share controlled by the top four firms. The four largest processors of the major agricultural commodities including beef, pork, broilers, soybeans, corn, and wheat account for between 55 and 85 percent of U.S. production. Many economists consider any number above 40 percent to indicate that the largest firms have the ability to exert influence in the market, unlike in a competitive system. For this reason, the trend toward increased corporate consolidation and concentration is controversial. Proponents point to the increased efficiency and lower cost of a streamlined food chain, while opponents blame the trend for the disappearance of family farms, as well as for a general tendency to promote profitability over other values, including food safety, environmental quality, and vibrant local rural economies. Several states have enacted laws against corporate farming in response to these concerns.

[See also Corn, Hybrid; Factory Farming; Family Farm; Farm Machinery; Livestock Industry; Subsidies, Agricultural; and Vertical Integration, Economies of Scale, and Firm Size.]

BIBLIOGRAPHY

Heffernan, William D. "Concentration of Ownership and Control in Agriculture." In *Hungry for Profit: The Agribusiness Threat to Farmers, Food, and the Environment*, edited by Fred Magdoff, John Bellamy Foster, and Frederick H. Buttel, pp. 61–75. New York: Monthly Review Press, 2000.

Hendrickson, Mary. "Consolidation in the Food System." Food Circles Networking Project. University of Missouri Extension. http://www.foodcircles.missouri.edu/consol.htm.

Lamb, Russell L. "The New Farm Economy." *Regulation* 26, no. 4 (Winter 2003–2004): 10–15.

Striffler, Steve. *Chicken: The Dangerous Transformation of America's Favorite Food*. New Haven, Conn.: Yale University Press, 2005.

Elizabeth A. Ramey

CORPORATIONS, MODERN

See **Berle, Adolf, and Gardiner Means and the Modern Corporation.**

CORPORATISM

The term "corporatism" refers both to a distinctive institutional structure and to a body of political thought. Its central characteristic is a system of governance exercised through an established set of private associations linking business, labor, agriculture, and other functional groups with each other and with the state for purposes of achieving political stability and harmonious economic and social development. In most versions of corporatism, business, labor, agricultural, and professional societies have representation in joint councils that share power with public agencies and theoretically serve all legitimate interests.

Modern corporatist thought, originating in response to nineteenth-century liberalism and socialism, called in essence for modernized guilds and estates that could re-create a harmonious moral order grounded in organic social relationships. Its first theorists were primarily Roman Catholics and aristocrats. By the end of World War I, however, secular, laboristic, and technocratic versions had appeared as well, some of whose advocates discerned a modern corporatism in the institutional machinery produced by war mobilization. Subsequently, fascist theorists in Europe urged that the state itself be turned into a corporative apparatus, but efforts purporting to do this, notably in Italy and Germany, were mostly a camouflage for dictatorships.

Fascist-style corporatism had little appeal in liberal democracies. But new forms of governance through state–society partnerships did attract supporters, who produced designs for a corporative apparatus operating alongside the liberal state. In the United States, where reformers and businesspeople desired to remedy market failures while also minimizing the expansion of government, the result was a so-called Progressivism that stressed public-spirited private "associational action" rather than expanded public administration. Such was the approach advocated by the National Civic Federation, founded in 1900, and later by Herbert Hoover, who, as secretary of commerce in 1921–1928 and then as president in 1929–1933, sought to establish an associational structure that would make state bureaucratic growth unnecessary.

The United States came closest to being "corporatized" during the Great Depression of the 1930s, when President Franklin Delano Roosevelt's initial alternative to a failed Hooverism, the National Recovery Administration (NRA), became a more coercive associationalism under which the state would force noncooperators into line. In practice, however, the NRA worked badly, and following its invalidation by the Supreme Court in 1935, the New Deal moved toward the creation of an enlarged welfare and regulatory state as more appropriate to liberal economic governance. Only in a few select industries and in special cases like defense mobilization did the Roosevelt administration's flirtation with corporatist solutions continue.

Still, World War II and the postwar recovery undermined antibusiness liberalism, and associationalism again won support as the best way to meet economic and social needs without undue expansion of government. A limited corporatism found new champions in the war-spawned Committee for Economic Development and a new array of government-established industrial councils. It was also central to the vision of Dwight D. Eisenhower's administration of a "corporate commonwealth" working to curb "socialism" by entrusting a share of the nation's governance to responsible wielders of private economic power. During the 1950s, America did not erect the corporatist institutions that were helping to guide European economic development, yet even in the United States, the "cooperative mode" then in vogue meant an enlarged role for private organizations.

In the 1960s and 1970s, new critiques of the political economy altered the functions of both the federal government and the private inter-mediaries sharing in national governance. Still, some critics alleged that the new arrangements failed to achieve the balance between planning and freedom that highly developed capitalist economies required. An articulate group of so-called reindustrializers and advocates of industrial policy argued that the United States needed its own version of the corporatist machinery that was achieving such a balance abroad. Moreover, a growing body of academic theory held that corporatism was evolving spontaneously in advanced capitalist societies everywhere and could take forms compatible with liberal-democratic values.

In the 1980s and 1990s, agitation for making America more "competitive" through corporatist policies continued but enjoyed little success. Serious presidential support ended with Ronald Reagan's inauguration, and Americans repeatedly showed their unwillingness to embrace corporatist forms of state building. In the polity at large, corporatism encountered potent opposition from populist, republican, and entrepreneurial forces that invoked historical experience and the persisting divisiveness of government, business, and labor as reasons why joint public–private planning could never work in the United States. Limited forms of corporatism did exist, however, in state-level development commissions and in partnerships for technical research.

Corporatism has been more at home in western Europe, Latin America, and Asia than in the United States. But variations of it entered into twentieth-century American political discourse, and recurring attempts at corporatization left an institutional residue and proved useful for certain public regulatory and promotional tasks.

[*See also* **Capitalism; Economic Development; Economic Theories and Thought; Industrial Policy, Theory and Practice of; National Industrial Recovery Act and**

National Recovery Administration; *and* New Deal and Institutional Economics.]

BIBLIOGRAPHY

Gerber, Larry G. "Corporatism and State Theory: A Review Essay for Historians." *Social Science History* 19 (Autumn 1995): 313–332.

Golob, Eugene O. *The "Isms": A History and Evaluation.* New York: Harper, 1954.

Griffith, Robert. "Dwight D. Eisenhower and the Corporate Commonwealth." *American Historical Review* 87 (February 1982): 87–122.

Hawley, Ellis W. "Society and Corporate Statism." In *Encyclopedia of American Social History,* edited by Mary Kupiec Cayton, Elliott J. Gorn, and Peter W. Williams, pp. 621–636. New York: Charles Scribner's Sons, 1993.

Schmitter, Philippe C., and Gerhard Lehmbruch, eds. *Trends toward Corporatist Intermediation.* London: Sage, 1979.

Weinstein, James. *The Corporate Ideal in the Liberal State, 1900–1918.* Boston: Beacon, 1968.

Williamson, Peter J. *Corporatism in Perspective: An Introductory Guide to Corporatist Theory.* London: Sage, 1989.

Ellis W. Hawley

COTTON INDUSTRY

Cotton, the world's chief natural fiber for textile manufacturing and a principal ingredient in a variety of products including foods and building materials, has figured prominently in American history. It played an important role in the growth of slavery in the American South and has been a major export for the United States, particularly in the era before the Civil War. Since cotton requires semitropical growing conditions, it was grown exclusively in the southern states until the twentieth century, when it started expanding westward into Arizona, California, the Texas High Plains, and New Mexico.

The settlers at Jamestown brought cottonseed to the New World but were unable to produce the fiber in significant quantities. The lack of a technology to separate the seed from the lint retarded production. Planters along the southeastern tidewater belt grew small amounts of Sea Island cotton, a long-staple variety, but there was not enough for economic significance. When Eli Whitney invented the cotton gin in 1793, cotton farming became economically feasible because farmers and planters could grow so-called upland varieties in large quantities and supply the modernized textile industry in Europe, particularly in Britain, the world leader in cotton-textile production. Cotton became so lucrative that it was called "white gold," and settlers and planters spread across the South seeking fertile land. Planters used slaves for the intensive hand labor essential in cultivating the crop, and cotton growing became synonymous with slavery. The South produced much of the cotton that went into British and European textiles, and cotton thus brought much wealth to the region.

The Civil War ended slavery but not cotton production. Indeed, cotton acreage increased, and by 1900 the U.S. production reached more than 10 million bales, twice the number produced in 1860. Cotton still created prosperity for large-scale farmers, but smaller, self-sufficient farmers also typically devoted some acres to cotton as a meager source of cash. Tenants and sharecroppers fared even worse: they generally owned no land and depended on large-scale planters. As world production increased in the late nineteenth century, cotton prices declined and profits became harder to achieve, even for many large landowners. Adding to growers' woes, the boll weevil, a destructive boring beetle, migrated from Mexico to Texas in the 1890s and gradually spread across the Cotton Belt. Insecticides and other control methods alleviated insect damage, but boll weevil depredations remained a chronic problem.

The profitability of cotton worsened after World War I as U.S. production increased owing to improved varieties and cultivation practices. By 1932 world production surpassed 23 million bales, of which the U.S. portion was 13 million, glutting the market. The price for American cotton fell below 10 cents per pound, the lowest since the 1890s, and growers suffered hardship. Producers of other agricultural staples such as wheat and corn also faced saturated markets, but the severity of the economic depression in southern cotton-growing areas created the greatest distress. To alleviate these conditions the Agricultural Adjustment Act of 1933 offered subsidized cotton prices in exchange for mandatory crop reduction to limit supply. Surpluses persisted, however, because of greater foreign production and the increased use of synthetics in textile manufacturing.

Post–World War II changes transformed the cotton industry. Acreage expanded into the West. Mechanization displaced great numbers of cotton laborers and sharecroppers to the North and West. The number of cotton farmers fell, from more than a million in 1945 to approximately thirty thousand by 2000. Yet total U.S. production at the end of the twentieth century remained high because of improved seed genetics and machinery, the expansion of irrigation, and new technologies to control the boll weevil and other harmful insects.

By the twenty-first century a major shift had occurred in the world cotton trade. In 1945 about a dozen countries supplied the world market, producing 21.41 million bales, with the United States furnishing about half of the total. In 2005 more than one hundred countries grew cotton, and China was the largest producer. Total world output that year reached 116.6 million bales, with the United States accounting for 23.89 million bales. And with the decline of the domestic textile industry, American growers depended more than ever on the foreign market: in 2010 more than 80 percent of the annual crop was exported. This development threw growers into the competitive global market and made them operate at the highest level of efficiency. They also faced the steady erosion of the world cotton market by synthetic fibers such as polyester. The U.S. industry fought diligently to hold its place and supported trade agreements such as the World Trade Organization (WTO), the North American Free Trade Agreement (NAFTA), and the Dominican Republic–Central America Free Trade Agreement (DR-CAFTA). In 2002 the cotton trade became embroiled in international disputes when Brazil charged that U.S. subsidies held down the world price of cotton. Other countries claimed that the subsidies accounted for the poverty of African farmers. The WTO's striking down of a principal feature of the U.S. cotton program known as Step 2 demonstrated the importance of geopolitical and global perspectives for the cotton industry. The king of fibers continued to follow the laws of supply and demand that made price fluctuations and risk features of cotton farming.

[*See also* **Agriculture; Cotton Trade, Antebellum Era; Sharecropping and Tenancy; Slavery; Textile Industry;** *and* **Trade Policy, Federal.**]

BIBLIOGRAPHY

Brown, D. Clayton. *King Cotton in Modern America: A Cultural, Political, and Economic History since 1945.* Jackson: University Press of Mississippi, 2011.

Brown, Harry Bates. *Cotton: History, Species, Varieties, Morphology, Breeding, Culture, Diseases, Marketing, and Uses.* 2d ed. New York: McGraw–Hill, 1938.

Fite, Gilbert C. *Cotton Fields No More: Southern Agriculture, 1865–1980.* Lexington: University Press of Kentucky, 1984.

Smith, C. Wayne, and J. Tom Cothren, eds. *Cotton: Origin, History, Technology, and Production.* New York: John Wiley & Sons, 1999.

D. Clayton Brown

COTTON TRADE, ANTEBELLUM ERA

Because of the lack of technology for separating the cottonseed from the lint, cotton had little commercial significance in the Colonial Era. When Eli Whitney invented the cotton gin in 1793, total production amounted to just 10,000 bales. By 1800, however, production had climbed to 73,000 bales—and it continued to rise until no other product equaled the importance of cotton during the antebellum era. Cotton was the principal crop of the southern states and the major export of the United States, and a cotton-based empire, the "cotton kingdom," stretched across the South. This natural fiber fueled not only the economy of the United States but also the Industrial Revolution of Britain. By 1861, U.S. production reached 4,491,000 bales, with approximately 4 million exported.

Cotton had a serious drawback. Slaves were used on plantations to provide the menial labor involved in growing and harvesting the crop. Black labor and white cotton went hand in hand, so as settlers migrated in a westward direction across the South, slavery expanded. A plantation economy, reliant on captive labor, took over the region. Cotton generated wealth for planters, and small landowners raised a few bales each year as a meager source of cash. As opposition to slavery grew, however, many Americans saw plantations as work camps in which forced laborers lived under brutal conditions. This development gave cotton a peculiar identity not associated with other crops.

Cotton became more than an agricultural crop: it permeated southern life, driving both social and commercial activity. Large-scale planters stood at the top of the agricultural ladder, and many even came to embrace the ideology of the French physiocrats, who insisted that all value rested in land. The South thus neglected industrialization, the planters feeling justified and content to rest the region's well-being on plantation agriculture. With the passage of time, this rigid view became embedded in the antebellum South, giving rise to the growth of southern sectionalism: the South, having a cotton-based culture, saw itself and was seen as a distinct region with an identifiable culture that was based on slavery and one-crop farming. To meet the increasing criticisms of slavery, southerners became defensive and determined to protect the status quo, convinced that because of cotton's economic importance, it was indispensible to both the American and the European economies.

In 1855, David Christy, a Cincinnati journalist opposed to slavery, wrote *Cotton Is King.* Southern interests began to use the term "King Cotton" to express their devotion to the fiber, and when in 1858 the South Carolina senator James Hammond in a Senate speech warned antislavery adherents, "you dare not make war on cotton . . . Cotton is king," the term became well known. The emphasis on cotton hurt the South during the Civil War: the region lacked the industrial capacity to sustain a long war against the more economically developed North. During the war the South placed an embargo on the sale of cotton to Britain and Europe, hoping to make them come to the assistance of the Confederacy, but this effort, dubbed "King Cotton diplomacy," failed. After the war, cotton production resumed—indeed, total output eventually surpassed that of the antebellum era—but it relied on contract farming, or sharecropping, instead of slavery. Industrialization began moving forward in the South, and cotton no longer single-handedly dominated the region.

[*See also* **Agriculture,** *subentry on* **1770 to 1890; Cotton Industry;** *and* **Slavery.**]

BIBLIOGRAPHY

Cohn, David L. *The Life and Times of King Cotton.* New York: Oxford University Press, 1956.

Dattel, Gene. *Cotton and Race in the Making of America: The Human Costs of Economic Power.* Chicago: Ivan R. Dee, 2009.

Gray, Lewis Cecil. *History of Agriculture in the Southern United States to 1860.* 2 vols. Washington, D.C.: Carnegie Institution, 1933.

D. Clayton Brown

COWBOYS

The American cowboy descended from the Spanish and Mexican vaquero, who evolved in New Spain after the arrival of cattle in the Western Hemisphere. As cattle ranching spread northward into California and Texas, Americans adopted the tools and techniques of the vaquero. Texas cowboys watched over cattle, branded them, and rounded them up before herding them to markets first in New Orleans and by the 1850s northward to Missouri and beyond. As railroads pushed westward following the Civil War and the demand for beef increased in the East, Texas cowboys began to drive cattle herds north to railheads in Kansas and later Nebraska. By the late 1870s, cowboys, including many of African American and Hispanic descent, were found in cattle-raising regions throughout the West. After the invention of barbed wire and the fencing of ranches, the cowboy became a hired man on horseback, repairing fences, doctoring cattle, and participating in cattle-branding roundups. By 1900 the golden age of the American cowboy was over.

Compared to his counterpart south of the Rio Grande, the American cowboy played a regional and relatively short-lived role. Yet he found his place in the history and mythology of the West, celebrated for fairness, justice, and courage, as exemplified by the hero of Owen Wister's enduring novel *The Virginian* (1902). Dime novels, folk songs, motion pictures, television series, and the fashion and advertising industries all helped to create the mythic version of the American cowboy that survives today.

[*See also* **Cattlemen's Associations.**]

BIBLIOGRAPHY

Dary, David. *Cowboy Culture: A Saga of Five Centuries.* New York: Alfred A. Knopf, 1981.

David Dary

COXEY'S ARMY

Coxey's Army, a collection of the unemployed from around the United States, traveled to Washington, D.C., in 1894 to promote the idea that the federal government bore responsibility for the economic well-being of its citizens. Led by the wealthy Ohio quarry owner Jacob S. Coxey, the crusade emerged in response to a severe economic depression. Coxey wanted the government to hire men to improve roads, thereby providing much-needed jobs. The marchers, about five thousand men and a few women in thirteen contingents, came from every section of the United States. The influence of the marchers extended to all those who provided food and aid along the way. Coxey's Army chipped away at the popular belief that poverty and unemployment were mainly the result of individual weakness and laziness. Towns and cities that initially feared the arrival of bums and criminals soon recognized the marchers as ordinary Americans.

The marchers aimed to gather at the U.S. Capitol on 1 May, International Workers' Day.

Only a few contingents arrived by the appointed date—and they were met by an unfriendly welcome by the federal government. Police arrested Coxey as he attempted to speak at the U.S. Capitol. Sentenced to twenty days in jail for trampling the Capitol's grass, Coxey saw his movement quickly collapse as a result of government harassment at the federal and state levels. Many marchers who never made it to Washington were imprisoned by state governments on vagrancy charges. By the early months of 1895, most people associated with the crusade had disappeared into the obscurity whence they had come.

[*See also* **Depressions, Economic; Poverty;** *and* **Unemployment.**]

BIBLIOGRAPHY

Schwantes, Carlos A. *Coxey's Army: An American Odyssey.* Lincoln: University of Nebraska Press, 1985.

Caryn E. Neumann

CRÉDIT MOBILIER

Crédit Mobilier was a construction company created by the builders of the Union Pacific Railroad, the corporation chartered by Congress in 1864 to lay rails westward from Omaha, Nebraska, to join a railway built eastward from Oakland, California, by the Central Pacific Railroad. Because both railroads were constructed in advance of demand for passenger and freight service, no immediate profit was likely to be made. Federal subsidies in the form of land grants and government bonds covered the basic costs of construction, but the Union Pacific entrepreneurs sought a surer means to turn a quick profit. To do so, they established a subsidiary, Crédit Mobilier, to serve as the construction company responsible for building the railroad. Crédit Mobilier, in turn, charged the Union Pacific excessive fees for construction costs, hence generating substantial profits. To shield the subterfuge from congressional oversight and investigation, the railroad entrepreneurs worked with Representative Oakes Ames of Massachusetts to distribute shares in Crédit Mobilier to numerous other federal legislators. The bribed legislators who obtained their stock at a discount could either enjoy the dividends that resulted from the company's high profits or sell their shares at a price far higher than they had paid. The scheme worked successfully for nearly five years until a leak to a New York City newspaper during the election of 1872 revealed the sordid details and led to a congressional investigation. The probe found at least thirty members of Congress complicit in the corruption, including a future president, James A. Garfield.

[*See also* **Railroad Land Grants** *and* **Railroads.**]

BIBLIOGRAPHY

Ambrose, Stephen E. *Nothing like It in the World: The Men Who Built the Transcontinental Railroad, 1863–1869.* New York: Simon and Schuster, 2000.
White, Richard. *Railroaded: The Transcontinentals and the Making of Modern America.* New York: W. W. Norton and Company, 2011.

Melvyn Dubofsky

D

DAIRY INDUSTRY AND DAIRY PRODUCTS

Dairying in North America began with the earliest European invasions. Spaniards brought cattle to Veracruz (Mexico) in 1525; English cattle reached Jamestown in 1611.

Colonial Era and Nineteenth Century.

The dairy, including butter churning and cheese pressing, remained women's work from colonial times well into the nineteenth century, long after commercial sales flourished in the public markets of seaports and river towns. Dairying acquired more than local significance in parts of New York, Pennsylvania, and New England when farmers could no longer compete with wheat shipped by canals and railroads from newly settled lands farther west. Dairy farming eventually took hold in part of the Old Northwest as wheat culture followed the westward-moving frontier beyond the Mississippi valley.

From the 1850s, cheese making was reorganized into small "factory" associations in which the more adept cheese makers, both women and men, could work on greater volumes of milk gathered from neighboring farms. By the early 1900s, almost all cheese was made in factories, and Wisconsin had displaced New York as the banner cheese state. Butter making lingered on farms until the 1880s when, despite the threats from oleomargarine, Gustaf de Laval's steam-driven cream separator from Sweden first led to an expansion of cooperative creamery associations and large-scale "centralizer" plants, especially in the Middle West. Not before World War I did creameries supply more than half the nation's huge butter output, with Minnesota the banner state. Gail Borden patented condensed milk (concentrated and sterilized under heat in a vacuum pan) in 1856, and by 1899 twenty-four condenseries were manufacturing condensed and evaporated milk countrywide. By that time sanitary bottling procedures and pasteurization techniques (partial sterilization by heat) were making milk products safer and thus were ending the dreadful sequence of nineteenth-century urban epidemics associated with tainted milk.

Dairy farming remained a seasonal and, California excepted, a family enterprise. More-ample feed and better cow barns increased milk yields somewhat, but the so-called dairy quality of the stock improved little before importations of Shorthorns, Ayrshires, Holstein–Friesians, and Channel Islands breeds after the mid-nineteenth century. Under competitive pressures to preserve the fertility of their soil and to raise the return on its use, dairymen sought a more balanced crop program and a more nutrient-rich diet—including, from the 1880s, unripened maize, alfalfa, and clover preserved in airtight silos—in order to extend lactation further into the winter months. The Babcock test, developed in 1890 by Stephen M. Babcock at the University of Wisconsin, provided a more accurate test of milk quality based on butterfat content and stimulated cooperative herd improvement through selective breeding; official animal testing and disease-eradication programs, especially for bovine tuberculosis, followed under sponsorship of state agricultural colleges. By the middle of the nineteenth century, annual milk yields per cow had nearly doubled, averaging 3,883 pounds by 1900.

Technical advances in milk processing and distribution brought hand separators, milking machines, cooling equipment, and storage tanks to commercial dairy farms, while refrigerated tank trucks and glass-lined railcars by the 1930s carried milk to processing plants and profitable metropolitan markets. Ice cream, offered by confectioners in New York City and Philadelphia in the 1770s, was first manufactured for wholesale delivery in Baltimore in 1851 and gained popularity after the introduction of waffle cones at the Louisiana Purchase Exposition in Saint Louis, Missouri, in 1904. The recovery of U.S. cheese production from the loss of lucrative foreign markets—which occurred following the export of substandard "skim" and "filled" cheese—was facilitated from the late 1890s by the regulatory enforcement of state dairy and food commissions and by laboratory investigations of enzyme action in the "cold curing" of natural cheddar-type cheese. It was the introduction of J. L. Kraft's patented processed cheese in Chicago after 1916, however, that changed the United States into a nation of cheese eaters.

Twentieth-Century Developments. The thrust of technological development in dairying, as in other industries, has been toward continuous production for mass markets and away from batch and bulk operations. From the 1920s, when dairying was already a $4 billion industry, such tendencies were driven by the imperatives of big business toward growth and restructuring. Private bankers determined that mergers and acquisitions, rather than direct investments, were the most economical modes of expansion. Thus in 1923 the National Dairy Products Company set off a merger mania in the dairy industry by absorbing the small margins of independent wholesalers; soon the company displaced the Borden Company as the largest dairy corporation in capitalization and sales. Between 1921 and 1948, eight large dairy corporations emerged, while thousands of local mergers occurred among smaller corporations. More than five hundred of these local mergers involved cooperatives exempted from federal antitrust legislation by the Capper–Volstead Act of 1922. The agricultural crises of the 1930s eventually brought the dairy industry federal price supports and cartel-like agreements to equalize prices paid to producers of milk used for either fluid or manufacturing purposes.

After 1900 the number of farms with dairy cattle barely increased, but many had become specialized dairy enterprises. From the 1930s, innovations in cattle breeding and feeding, including artificial insemination by proven sires and commercial availability of hybrid-corn seed (maize), continuously raised milk output, but it was the genetically engineered capacity rather than the scientifically enhanced rations that accounts for spiraling milk yields. By 1980, high-yield, low-fat Holsteins constituted 80 percent of the national herd. By 1995 the herd, comprising only 9.46 million cows, averaged 16,451 pounds of milk per head; by contrast, the peak herd, of 27.7 million in 1945, averaged but 4,375 pounds per head.

Although by the end of the twentieth century, mechanization and the purchase of feed and specialized services had reduced the intensive labor of farm families, more than 80 percent of dairy farms in the 1990s continued to be held by family or individual proprietors, 15.5 percent were partnerships that included family members, and 3.5 percent were family corporations. The trend in milk production, as in other agricultural sectors, was toward fewer but larger operations; only 6 percent of all farms reported milk animals in 1992, with California now the largest milk producer.

The post–World War II popularity of store sales of ice cream (earlier a soda-fountain item), the rise of Italian-style cheese pizza, and the conversion of yogurt from a health food into a fruit-flavored dessert, as well as such marketing novelties as prepackaged sliced natural cheese—introduced by Kraft in the 1950s—all boosted dairy consumption. Most fluid milk, along with an array of branded and packaged dairy products, was now retailed in self-service supermar-

kets or convenience stores in wax paper cartons (1930s) or molded plastic jugs (1960s). Home deliveries had virtually disappeared.

On the manufacturing and marketing sides of dairying, the process of consolidation intensified in the 1970s when the industry, now a business worth $20 billion, became a target of Wall Street mergers, acquisitions, and divestitures in which giant food corporations took over divisions of large dairy conglomerates. By the 1990s, transnational food conglomerates such as Philip Morris, Unilever, Nestlé, Con Agra, and Groupe Danone S.A. were major players in the dairy industry, which, however, represented only a fraction of their total food sales. The huge Minnesota-based Land O'Lakes, founded in 1921, and other regional cooperatives, in contrast, selling chiefly bulk milk and low-branded dairy goods, had meanwhile raised their market share to 42 percent of corporate sales.

In 1996 the federal government began a phased termination of dairy price supports and greatly reduced milk marketing regulations with a view to lowering the public costs of handling vast milk surpluses in a deregulated market environment. The Agricultural Improvement and Reform Act of 1996 retained the restrictions on dairy imports permitted under the General Agreement on Tariffs and Trade (GATT), while seeking to promote maximum allowable exports of U.S. dairy products to global markets. Such changes introduced a higher degree of price volatility in domestic markets, in which dairymen already faced a perilous future because of changing consumption patterns related to health and dietary concerns—per capita consumption of all dairy products fell from a peak of 838 pounds milk equivalent in 1931 to barely 517 pounds by 1994, with butter the principal victim—and public uneasiness over the genetic manipulation of cattle and the increased use of antibiotics and bovine somatropin growth hormone (BGH).

By the end of the twentieth century and the onset of a new millennium, innovation continued in the dairy industry. Growing concerns about genetically altered livestock and the use of chemicals and antibiotics to treat animal feed and dairy cattle led more-affluent consumers to seek organically produced, chemical-free dairy products. Similar concerns also led consumers to favor locally produced dairy products over those marketed by national and transnational enterprises. Dairy farmers responded to such consumer demand by producing and marketing organic dairy products. Such innovative retail grocery chains as Whole Foods had enormous success in stocking and selling organic dairy products to affluent consumers. A similar trend developed in cheese making when consumers developed a taste for expensive, craft-produced specialty cheeses in preference to the mass-produced generic cheeses marketed by such companies as Kraft Foods. By the 2000s the market for organic dairy products had grown so profitable that their production and marketing spread from smaller specialty producers and niche retailers to major national dairy enterprises and to such mass-market retailers as Kroger, Albertsons, and Safeway.

[See also Agriculture; Cooperatives; Corporate Agriculture; Factory Farming; Family Farm; Food and Diet; Marketing Cooperatives; and Subsidies, Agricultural.]

BIBLIOGRAPHY

Lampard, Eric E. Rise of the Dairy Industry in Wisconsin: A Study in Agricultural Change, 1820–1920. Madison: State Historical Society of Wisconsin, 1963.

Manchester, Alden C., and Don P. Blayney. Structure of Dairy Markets: Past, Present, Future. Washington, D.C.: U.S. Department of Agriculture, Economic Research Service, 1997.

McMurry, Sally. Transforming Rural Life: Dairying Families and Agricultural Change, 1820–1885. Baltimore: Johns Hopkins University Press, 1995.

Perloff, Harvey S., et al. Regions, Resources, and Economic Growth. Baltimore: Johns Hopkins University Press for Resources for the Future, 1960.

Selitzer, Ralph. Dairy Industry in America. New York: Magazines for Industry, 1976.

Eric E. Lampard

DANBURY HATTERS' CASE

In response to popular support for legislation to limit the anticompetitive conduct of large corporations, Congress in 1890 passed, with only one dissenting vote, the Sherman Antitrust Act, which prohibited "monopolies or attempts to monopolize" and "contracts, combinations, or conspiracies in restraint of trade" in interstate and foreign commerce. Twelve years later, in 1902, the hat-factory owner Dietrich Loewe used the Sherman Act to sue the United Hatters of North America (UHU) over a boycott that it had organized against Loewe's company in retaliation for the company's refusal to employ only union members. In its defense, the union argued that the legislative history of the Sherman Act showed that it was directed against business entities, not membership organizations like trade unions, and that under the case of United States v. E. C. Knight (1895), in which the Supreme Court had exempted the local activities of the nationwide Sugar Trust from the Sherman Act's scope, only the interstate actions of the union could be considered. The case, Loewe v. Lawlor, reached the Supreme Court in 1908, and Chief Justice Melville Fuller, writing for a unanimous Court, held that the Sherman Act did not explicitly exempt labor unions from its scope and that the Court would not exempt the local activities of the union as it had done for corporations in E. C. Knight.

This case created the specter of corporate lawsuits against striking or boycotting unions, which faced potentially crippling treble damages under the Sherman Act. The labor movement soon persuaded Congress to pass a labor exemption as part of the Clayton Antitrust Act (1914), but the Court remained intransigent, as demonstrated in its decision in *Duplex v. Deering* (1921), and the issue was not entirely resolved until Congress passed the Norris–LaGuardia Act in 1932 and the Court affirmed the exemption in *United States v. Hutcheson* (1941).

[*See also* **American Anti-Boycott Association; Antitrust Legislation; Clayton Antitrust Act; Norris–LaGuardia Act; Repression of Unions; Strikes;** *and* **United States v. E. C. Knight.**]

BIBLIOGRAPHY

Forbath, William E. *Law and the Shaping of the American Labor Movement.* Cambridge, Mass.: Harvard University Press, 1991.

Matthew S. R. Bewig

DAVIS–BACON ACT

Passed during the depths of the Great Depression in 1931, the Davis–Bacon Act for the first time provided federal regulation of minimum wages for some private-sector workers. Sponsored by two Republicans, Congressman Robert L. Bacon of New York and Senator James J. Davis of Pennsylvania, and signed into law by President Herbert C. Hoover, the bill provided that wages paid on federally funded construction projects would not undercut the "prevailing wage" in a community. Although the act did not, as some critics alleged, require that contractors employ union labor, in practice it functioned to protect the wages of unionized construction workers from the downward pressure created by mass unemployment, for the "prevailing wages" determined by the U.S. Department of Labor tended to conform with the wages earned by union workers. At its passage, and for decades thereafter, the act enjoyed bipartisan support and was seen as a force for stabilizing wages in the construction industry. Many states adopted similar laws, dubbed "little Davis–Bacon acts." In 1964 the formulas used to calculate the prevailing wage were adjusted to include data on fringe benefits.

By the early 1970s, however, contractors—through organizations such as the Associated Builders and Contractors and the Construction Users Anti-Inflation Roundtable (later called the Business Roundtable)—began calling for the repeal of Davis–Bacon. They alleged that the act contributed to inflation and higher taxes. Repeated well-financed attempts to repeal the act failed in part because organized labor united its political allies to rebuff such attempts. Still, by the early twenty-first century, the act no longer worked so well to protect construction unions from the threat of nonunion labor, for multiple forces had conspired to drive unionization rates down in the building trades.

[*See also* **Antilabor Mobilization after 1945; Business Roundtable; Inflation and Deflation;** *and* **Wages, Real and Nominal.**]

BIBLIOGRAPHY

Palladino, Grace. *Skilled Hands, Strong Spirits: A Century of Building Trades History.* Ithaca, N.Y.: Cornell University Press, 2005.

Thieblot, Armand J., Jr. *The Davis–Bacon Act.* Philadelphia: Industrial Research Unit, Wharton School, University of Pennsylvania, 1975.

Walsch, Christopher N., ed. *The Davis–Bacon Act: Background, Issues, Evolution.* New York: Nova Science, 2011.

Joseph A. McCartin

DEBS, EUGENE V.

(1855–1926), labor leader, socialist, and presidential candidate. The son of Alsatian immigrants, Eugene Victor Debs became a railroad worker at age fourteen in his native Terre Haute, Indiana. After four years as a railway fireman, he took a job as a clerk but remained active in the Brotherhood of Locomotive Firemen, becoming its secretary-treasurer and editor of its journal. In 1893 he broke with the craft-union tradition by helping found the American Railway Union, which organized both skilled and unskilled workers. The following year, he led a boycott of the Pullman Palace Car Company; the strike tied up the nation's railroad system but ultimately failed.

After six months in jail for his role in the Pullman boycott, Debs began a career as a lecturer and journalist. Embracing socialism, he ran as the Socialist Party's candidate for president five times, beginning in 1900. His best showing came in 1912 when he won nearly 6 percent of the popular vote. In 1905, Debs helped found the Industrial Workers of the World, a radical alternative to the American Federation of Labor. Debs served two years in prison (1919–1921) for a 1918 speech denouncing the federal government's repressive wartime policies. Even behind bars, he polled nearly 920,000 votes in the 1920 presidential election. Afterward, he returned to Terre Haute, still committed to socialism but hampered by bad health.

Debs looms large in American labor history as an eloquent spokesperson for workers' rights and an early advocate of industrial unionism. Later he became the most influential socialist in the nation's history. A spellbinding orator, he used the language of Christianity and American radicalism to argue for revolutionary change, widening socialism's appeal beyond the immigrant circles in which it first won favor. Even after government repression and factionalism crippled the Socialist Party, Debs remained a popular symbol of dissent and egalitarianism.

[*See also* **Industrial Workers of the World; Labor Leaders; Labor Movements; Pullman Strike; Radicalism and Workers; Railroad Brotherhoods; Socialism and American Exceptionalism;** *and* **Strikes.**]

BIBLIOGRAPHY

Ginger, Ray. *The Bending Cross: A Biography of Eugene Victor Debs.* New Brunswick, N.J.: Rutgers University Press, 1949.
Salvatore, Nick. *Eugene V. Debs: Citizen and Socialist.* Urbana: University of Illinois Press, 1982.

Joshua B. Freeman

DEPARTMENT STORES

Between 1850 and 1890, urban growth spawned giant emporiums that sold vast arrays of merchandise at fixed prices and provided services and amenities that encouraged customers to linger and browse. Rowland H. Macy in New York City (1858), John Wanamaker in Philadelphia (1861), and Marshall Field in Chicago (1865) led this retailing revolution. During their golden age between 1890 and 1940, department stores supplanted small specialized shops in cities large and small. Elaborate store buildings attracted the public with their sheer size, luxurious appointments, and technological innovations. Highly successful as both businesses and cultural institutions, department stores nonetheless wrestled with troubling contradictions.

Resisting the corporate merger movements of the late nineteenth and early twentieth centuries, they tended to remain locally oriented, family-identified businesses loosely linked through buying and information-sharing groups, as well as trade associations such as the National Retail Dry Goods Association (1911) and the Retail Research Association (1916). Even when department stores merged, as in the formation of Federated Department Stores in 1929, separate stores retained their individual identities and management autonomy. Attractive, ever-changing merchandise and attentive services combined with functional structures and management innovations, such as systematic data gathering, to make department stores enormously profitable.

Persistent operating problems nevertheless shadowed the giant stores' successes. Buyers who headed merchandise departments insisted that their expertise required autonomy, but the stores' functional organization challenged the buyers' authority by subordinating them to managers in charge of service, merchandising, advertising, and accounting. Although close supervision hampered buyers' abilities to respond to fashion trends and customer demand, loose control threatened the store's overall image and financial health. Time-and-motion studies and employee bonuses enhanced efficiency, but efficiency sometimes undermined customer service. Statistical data failed to enhance predictability and regularity, as the flow of customers fluctuated wildly according to hour, day of the week, season, and weather.

Class and gender differences created other tensions. Male managers struggled to control the behavior of salesclerks and customers, who were predominantly female. Working-class saleswomen, hired as cheap labor yet expected to sell skillfully, might offend or ignore upper-class customers. Wealthy female customers used their class prerogatives to push stores into expensive and wasteful practices. Department stores appealed primarily to an affluent minority, but their heavy fixed operating costs compelled them to court working-class consumers in price-segregated departments and bargain

basements. Sensual appeals encouraged customers to buy but also seduced some into shoplifting or reckless overuse of credit.

The combination of internal contradictions and the decay of central cities after World War II weakened the department store as the flagship institution in the twentieth century's consumer culture. Self-service replaced skilled selling. Suburban branch stores, rare and small before 1940, proliferated and even eclipsed downtown stores. Beginning in the 1980s, a rash of mergers, bankruptcies, and closings undermined department stores' power as local institutions. Specialty stores, mall-based chains, discount stores, and catalog merchants grabbed greater market share. Dethroned from their former glory, department stores nonetheless maintained a prominent presence in major metropolises and in upscale shopping centers and malls in more-affluent suburban areas. The economic crisis and contraction that afflicted the economy beginning in 2008 hit department stores that catered to lower-income consumers especially hard and forced many into bankruptcy. Yet such upscale department stores as Nordstrom, Saks Fifth Avenue, Nieman-Marcus, and Bloomingdale's flourished in an economy in which the disposable income available to the wealthy expanded extraordinarily. The better-managed department stores also proved adept at marketing their wares online, thus competing with more-specialized Internet marketers, or "e-tailers," and maintaining some of their former economic and cultural authority. The spread of smartphones and tablets such as iPads made comparison shopping and online purchasing more common, and department stores had to adapt to survive.

[*See also* **Consumer Credit and Credit Cards; Consumer Culture; Internet Commerce; Shopping Centers and Malls; Wanamaker, John, and Wanamaker's;** *and* **Women Workers.**]

BIBLIOGRAPHY

Benson, Susan Porter. *Counter Cultures: Saleswomen, Managers, and Customers in American Department Stores, 1890–1940*. Urbana: University of Illinois Press, 1986.

Leach, William. *Land of Desire: Merchants, Power, and the Rise of a New American Culture*. New York: Pantheon Books, 1993.

Susan Porter Benson

DEPRESSIONS, ECONOMIC

Depressions are sustained troughs in the business cycle characterized by declines in output, employment, income, and trade. Their spreading effects can be traced through declining prices, profits, interest rates, wages, consumer spending, and capital investment. Depressions date from the earliest years of American history, but the paucity of data precludes evaluation of them in the Colonial Era. Before 1815, depressions were caused primarily by exogenous shocks, that is, by forces external to the economy, such as wars, widespread crop failures, or other disasters. With the growth of capitalism, however, depressions became more pervasive, in part because the market held sway over more economic production and exchange, and in part because of the dramatic increase in capital formation that accompanied economic development and industrialization. Though economists agree on the correlation between business cycles and capitalism, they are unable to offer a simple, consistent explanation as to why depressions occur.

The United States experienced depressions after the onset of severe economic contractions in 1818–1819, 1836–1837, 1856–1857, 1872–1873, 1884–1885, 1892–1893, 1920–1921, 1929–1933, and 1937–1938. Though most of these contractions began with stock market panics or banking crises, these events did not determine either the severity or the length of the contraction: each depression had its own unique history.

Depressions draw attention because of their pervasive effect upon the economy, politics, and society. First of all, unemployment and the decline in income create human misery. As the economy matured, the urban unemployed found it increasingly difficult to supplement the family's income, since they could no longer fish, hunt, or garden to fill the family's larder. Part-time jobs for the breadwinner or the breadwinner's family disappeared. With modest savings, families quickly faced destitution. Even for those retaining jobs, the decline in prices led to a demand for wage cuts. Labor unions faced insurmountable challenges. If workers resisted wage cuts and went on strike, firms could hire replacements from the mass of the unemployed. Deprived of effective economic means of protest, workers and their allies increasingly sought political solutions.

Business enterprises suffered during extended downturns as well. Not only did they postpone new investments in plants and equipment, but they also faced the prospect of substantial losses. In the early nineteenth century, industrial firms confronted depressions by suspending activity. But by the end of the century, the mass-production industries, such as steel, oil, and cigarettes, changed tactics: rather than reduce production and maintain prices, they slashed prices and maintained production. This ignited competitive wars that were often resolved by mergers and other anticompetitive activities. For banks, depressions presented some of the most daunting challenges. Savings tended to flow out, while repayments on loans slowed. Banks cut back on lending, making it even more difficult for businesses to survive. Deprived of working capital—short-term loans to cover raw materials, wages, and goods in transit—firms went bankrupt.

Antebellum Era. Though the antebellum era witnessed severe business cycles, especially in the late 1810s, the 1830s, and the 1850s, only the downturn of the 1830s and early 1840s has attracted much scholarly attention. Even here, considerable debate exists as to the extent of the decline in production. Part of the difficulty in describing the effects of the antebellum depressions lies in the fact that the economy was not fully integrated. For example, the Panic of 1857 brought hard times in the North, while the southern cotton industry enjoyed unprecedented prosperity. Second, the economy remained flexible: it could adjust quickly to price declines. This can be seen in the Panic of 1819. Despite a sudden and sharp decline in output and prices, a wave of bankruptcies, and widespread unemployment, recovery came quickly after 1822 as wages and interest rates adjusted to the price shock.

The depression of 1839–1843 had its origins in international trade and investment. Rapid increases in British investment in the United States encouraged a boom in the mid-1830s. As British silver flowed into the United States, it was deposited in banks, which then increased their lending. Prices soared. But in 1836 the British government raised interest rates, making British investment more attractive than American, and silver flowed back to England. This caused the short-lived Panic of 1837. The economy recovered briefly, but with the Panic of 1839—which again was abetted by rising British interest rates—prices did not bounce back. Indeed, they fell some 46 percent between 1839 and 1843. But output actually rose 16 percent during this period, leading some experts to argue that this was not a depression.

Nevertheless, the monetary contraction of 1839–1843 wrought considerable havoc on individuals and their governments. Seeking relief from creditors, debtors, particularly landowners, turned to their state legislatures. Relief came in the form of stay laws, restrictions upon forced sales, and freedom from attachment for debt for certain classes of property. In the cities, thousands were thrown out of work. Workers' trade unions, having grown rapidly in good times, disappeared. Aside from some outdoor relief, cities did little to address the needs of the poor. Governments were reluctant to become involved in relief, and even had they wanted to, their finances were in disarray. Revenues dried up, leaving cities to impose wage cuts, lay off employees, and seek additional loans. States fared even worse. In the 1830s, states, especially in the mid-Atlantic and Midwest, had undertaken huge debts to build canals and railroads. By the 1840s, many were on the edge of bankruptcy. In the wave of constitutional revision after the depression, more than half of the states wrote into their constitutions prohibitions against further debt for internal improvements.

From 1873 to 1896. Some historians have described the period from 1873 to 1896 as the long depression, but this is inaccurate. Though prices did fall during this period, output rose on average 4 percent a year. Each decade, however, brought a sharp economic contraction, or depression: in 1873–1879 (the longest in American history), 1882–1885, and 1893–1896. The first two had their origins in the collapse of railroad booms. After the Civil War, the nation constructed thousands of miles of railroads. In a race to get the most profitable routes and feeders, railroads sold billions of dollars worth of bonds and stocks. When they discovered that their profit estimates had been too high, they could not pay their debts on the bonds or dividends on their stocks. This led to a financial panic. Banks curtailed credit, and foreigners stopped buying American assets. Prices fell some 25 percent, creating havoc for industrial workers and farmers. In the depression of the 1870s, unemployment in construction and manufacturing climbed to perhaps 10 percent, while those who kept their jobs faced wage cuts. In farming, by the mid-1880s, wheat sold for sixty-four cents a bushel, half its normal price. Debt-burdened farmers in newly settled areas faced bankruptcy. Nonfarming businesses that depended upon railroads, construction, and agriculture failed. At the bottom of the depression in the 1870s and again in the 1880s, some ten thousand firms filed for bankruptcy, citing liabilities of almost a quarter of a billion dollars.

Widespread hardship brought demands for relief. Cities again expanded their soup kitchens. Charity organization societies formed in some twenty-five cities to coordinate relief. But many leaders worried that such assistance would undermine citizens' self-reliance. Most assistance came in the form of helping the unemployed find work through employment exchanges or public works projects. In 1894 a group of some five hundred jobless workers, organized by Jacob S. Coxey of Massillon, Ohio, marched to Washington, D.C., in support of Coxey's bold but not revolutionary demand: the creation of $500 million in paper money by the federal government to be distributed to the states so that they could hire the unemployed to build roads. Though Coxey's plan failed, the cycle of repeated depressions led to a growing discontent with laissez-faire policies. Religious leaders and intellectuals, in particular, insisted that the government become more deeply involved in ensuring the material well-being of its citizens.

Facing wage cuts and layoffs, workers responded with waves of strikes. The most dramatic took place in the railroad industry, which had sought economies in the wake of bankruptcy. In July 1877, workers staged major strikes against the trans-Appalachian railroads. Violence erupted in several places, but the bloodiest battles occurred in Pittsburgh, Pennsylvania, taking the lives of some fifty civilians and five militiamen. Again in 1894, workers struck Chicago's Pullman Company when it announced wage cuts and layoffs. Eugene V. Debs led his American Railway Union in a sympathetic boycott, refusing to pull Pullman cars. Fourteen thousand state and federal troops were called out by the administration of Grover Cleveland, and the Justice Department issued an injunction against Debs. Again violence ensued: in Chicago, twenty were killed, and thousands of railroad cars were destroyed. The workers lost, as they usually did in the major strikes, and their unions witnessed precipitous declines in membership.

Finally, the depressions of the late nineteenth century had political consequences. Although farmers and workers lobbied for a number of reforms, the most pressing issue was the money supply. After the Civil War, the United States slowly moved toward adoption of a gold standard of monetary valuation. This required bringing down wartime inflation, and then, as gold discoveries lagged behind the pace of economic growth, prices fell still further. In 1893 a financial panic occurred when foreign investors and American businessmen liquidated their paper assets and demanded gold. Facing huge drains, banks curtailed credit, the economy slowed, unemployment mounted, and the depression of the mid-1890s settled in. Many demanded relief through the coinage of silver, which, by increasing the monetary supply, would cause prices to rise and hasten recovery. Others argued that in a growing global economy, the nation must adhere to a gold standard. The monetary issue reached its climax in the presidential election of 1896, when the Republican "goldbug" William McKinley decisively defeated the Populist and Democratic "free silver" candidate, William Jennings Bryan. Radicalism had been repudiated; political power had been consolidated in the hands of the more prosperous.

The Great Depression. The twentieth century experienced two depressions, both closely associated with public policy. The first occurred in 1920–1921. After World War I, with strong consumer demand from Europe and at home, U.S. firms maintained high levels of production and even increased inventories. But a sudden contraction in demand, as the U.S. government slashed spending and European production recovered, burst this speculative inventory bubble. The real gross national product fell some 6 percent, unemployment spiked to 12 percent, and wholesale prices fell 37 percent. Prices returned to prewar levels by July 1921, however, and the economy began to rebound.

The Great Depression, which began in 1929, did not witness such rapid recovery. Indeed, it proved to be the worst depression in American history. The real gross national product fell 30 percent, prices fell 23 percent, net investment became negative (that is, new capital investment did not equal the depreciation of the existing stock of capital), and unemployment became a fact of life for 24 percent and more of the labor force. Recovery from such an economic catastrophe was slow and difficult. The gross national product did not return to 1929 levels until 1937, and then in 1937–1938 the economy experienced a depression within a depression. Unemployment remained high. As late as 1941, even as the war in Europe stimulated the U.S. economy, more than 10 percent of Americans were still seeking work.

The causes of the Great Depression remain a matter of intense debate. Most scholars argue that a combination of factors led to the downturn in 1929, including changes in Federal Reserve policy, a decline in consumption, and diminished investment. The 1929 stock market crash did not cause the depression, but stock speculation on Wall Street had encouraged the Federal Reserve to raise interest rates. Losses in the stock market diminished consumer spending by investors, while poor harvests and low agricultural prices restrained farm spending.

After record years of residential construction, investment peaked in 1926 but fell thereafter, dropping to one half its 1926 level by 1929. What made this depression so devastating, however, was not the downturn in 1929, but the great skid thereafter, as the economy declined at an accelerating rate into 1933.

Economists have highlighted the international nature of the depression of the 1930s and the role of the gold standard in spreading its misery. During World War I, most nations had gone off gold; that is, they would not redeem their currency for gold at the prewar rate. During the 1920s the leading industrial nations returned to the gold standard. However, the system suffered from serious flaws. Among the most important was that the United States and France held a disproportionate share of the world's gold, reducing the flexibility of other nations. To remain on the gold standard when faced with demands for their gold, these nations would have to raise interest rates, slowing their economies and creating unemployment. In an era of mass politics this proved impossible, and nations began to abandon the gold standard, culminating with Great Britain and the British Commonwealth nations in 1931. Recovery generally came quickly to nations that devalued their currencies.

The United States, however, remained committed to the gold standard, and as other countries devalued, Americans faced tremendous pressure. Offered the choice of American goods or American gold, holders of U.S. dollars preferred gold, believing that the United States would not stay on the gold standard forever. This constrained the Federal Reserve System. It could not expand the monetary supply, since this would increase the potential claims on its gold stocks. Instead, to conserve what gold it had, the Federal Reserve raised interest rates, driving the economy deeper into depression.

Recovery began when Franklin Delano Roosevelt became president in March 1933.

Though depressions usually brought a change in presidential administrations, Roosevelt won in a landslide and used this mandate to secure passage of an amazing slate of legislation during his first hundred days. Most important, he devalued the dollar, increasing the value of gold from slightly more than $20 to $35 an ounce. At these prices, and with political unrest rising in Europe, gold flowed into the United States. Since the money stock in the United States was a function of gold holdings, the money supply grew rapidly, increasing by some 11 or 12 percent a year until 1937. As their reserves grew, banks were encouraged to lend, businesses to build inventories, and consumers to spend in anticipation of further price increases.

But given the depth of the depression, the public demanded more than monetary measures. The New Deal, the label given to Roosevelt's policies between 1933 and 1938, brought a host of programs that altered fundamentally the relationship between the government and the economy. Among the most important programs were regulation of securities, trucking, banking, and utilities; federal deposit insurance; agricultural price supports; minimum-wage and maximum-hours legislation; collective bargaining for unions; Social Security; unemployment insurance; and public housing. The federal government matched state spending (on a ratio of 1 to 1 or 2 to 1, depending on the program) for relief, assistance to the elderly and disabled, and destitute mothers with dependent children.

In 1937 the federal government's decision to increase required bank reserves and to cut spending, coupled with the withholding of Social Security taxes from workers' paychecks, again sent the economy into depression. The stock market fell 50 percent, industrial production fell 38 percent, and the number of unemployed doubled. The government immediately shifted course, increasing bank reserves and undertaking more spending on public works and work relief. Though Keynesianism was not adopted as explicit policy until after World War II, the 1937–1938 debacle proved that government would no longer stand by while the economy sank.

After World War II. From World War II to the end of the twentieth century, the United States did not experience a depression. The business cycle did not disappear, however, as the era witnessed a number of recessions. Growth slowed noticeably in 1954–1955, 1957–1958, 1960–1961, 1969–1970, 1974–1975, 1980–1982, and 1990–1992. The sources of these recessions varied, but all were mercifully brief, thanks in some measure to government policy. First of all, government spending soared in this era, rising from one fifth to two fifths of the gross national product between 1940 and 1990. Further, after the war, government activities had a much greater effect upon the level of economic activity. Specifically, fiscal policy worked to moderate economic cycles through automatic stabilizers. When the economy moved into recession, government tax revenues fell, while its expenditures rose. The resulting fiscal deficit stimulated economic recovery.

In the early 1960s, Democratic Party policy makers moved beyond these built-in countercyclical effects. Embracing Keynesian economics in 1963, President John F. Kennedy assumed explicit responsibility for macroeconomic performance. The Kennedy tax cuts, passed shortly after his assassination, consciously produced a government budget deficit designed to stimulate the economy and prevent an anticipated recession. The Republican Party, by contrast, led by President Ronald Reagan in the 1980s, tried to reduce the federal government's role. Explicitly repudiating Keynesian economics, Reagan's advisers sought to slash government by means of tax and spending cuts and to reassert the primacy of markets in determining the pace and pattern of economic activity. But although the Reagan administration secured modest tax cuts, spending soared, producing huge fiscal deficits. As Keynesians would have predicted, this brought a sturdy if not spectacular recovery from the 1980–1982 recession. And much to the chagrin of Reaganites, Americans still expected the government to take responsibility for macroeconomic performance. When President George H. W. Bush called for fiscal restraint and higher taxes during a recession, he was voted out of office in 1992.

Following a stuttering recovery from the economic impact of the terrorist attacks of 11 September 2001, the first depression of the twenty-first century was signaled by the collapse of inflated commodity and housing markets in autumn 2008. A speculative bubble made up of mortgage-backed securities burst, triggering a financial crisis as commercial and investment banks suffered staggering losses. This forced a series of high-profile bankruptcies and takeovers before the U.S. government intervened to avert a complete meltdown. Eighteen months of recession followed, and unemployment rose above 10 percent, to the highest level since the 1940s. This downturn was not confined to the United States: repercussions were felt worldwide. The causes of the depression are the subject of continuing academic and political discussion.

[*See also* **Business Cycles; Capitalism; Economic Development; Federal Reserve System; Financial Crises, 1980s–2010; Free Silver and Bimetallism; Gold Standard; Great Depression (1929–1939); Great Recession of 2008 and After; Inflation and Deflation; Keynesian Economics; Laissez-Faire and Classical Economics; Long Swings and Cycles in Economic Growth; Monetarism; Monetary Policy, Federal; Stock Market Crash of 1929;** *and* **Unemployment.**]

BIBLIOGRAPHY

Chandler, Lester V. *America's Greatest Depression, 1929–1941*. New York: Harper & Row, 1970.

Eichengreen, Barry. *Golden Fetters: The Gold Standard and the Great Depression, 1919–1939*. New York: Oxford University Press, 1992.

Fels, Rendigs. *American Business Cycles, 1865–1897*. Chapel Hill: University of North Carolina Press, 1959.

Glasner, David, ed. *Business Cycles and Depressions*. New York: Garland, 1997.

Rezneck, Samuel. *Business Depressions and Financial Panics: Essays in American Business and Economic History*. New York: Greenwood, 1968.

Spulber, Nicolas. *Managing the American Economy, from Roosevelt to Reagan*. Bloomington: Indiana University Press, 1989.

Temin, Peter. *The Jacksonian Economy*. New York: W. W. Norton and Company, 1969.

Temin, Peter. *Lessons from the Great Depression*. Cambridge, Mass.: MIT Press, 1989.

Diane Lindstrom; updated by
Patrick M. Dixon

DEREGULATION, FINANCIAL

The financial system is designed to transform surplus savings into productive investment in the commercial and consumer sectors. Ideally, through this intermediation process, finance fosters sustainable economic growth. Financial services include banking, nonbank lending, investment advice and management, securities underwriting, dealing and trading, brokerage services, mutual funds, hedge funds, private equity, insurance, and real estate. Also within the financial system's scope are such activities as debt collection, appraisal, and custody of financial assets.

Tension between Regulation and Deregulation.

Throughout United States history, tension has existed between efforts to limit financial speculation, its excesses, and its abuses and a desire to allow it to operate free from government constraints. The rationale for limiting government regulation and oversight resides in the claim that self-regulation and self-policing by the private sector will be more effective and less burdensome. Additionally, the advocates of financial deregulation argue that regulation increases the cost and reduces the availability of credit for businesses and consumers.

These differing aims of regulation and deregulation have produced legislation and rule-making, often in a cyclical manner. After a major financial panic, laws are enacted and regulations promulgated that attempt to protect the public from the contagion that a collapse of banks and other financial firms spreads. As time passes and memories fade as the economy expands, regulators begin to relax the government restrictions through exemptions and repeals. When another crisis erupts, the public again favors government regulation. The 2010 restoration of regulation through the Dodd–Frank Wall Street Reform and Consumer Protection Act appears at best mild and incomplete and at worst counterproductive. Either way, both those who approve and those who disapprove of the legislation agree that it likely would not prevent another, even more severe, financial crisis than that of 2008.

Largely owing to mergers and acquisitions spawned by deregulation, finance has grown significantly relative to gross domestic product (GDP) in the late twentieth and early twenty-first centuries. According to Simon Johnson, former chief economist of the International Monetary Fund, prior to the onset of the late 2000s financial crisis, the financial sector accounted for 40 percent of total corporate profits in the United States and represented about 7 to 8 percent of GDP. The power that this sector wields over public policy has also increased. The concentration of wealth in a small number of financial firms perpetuates a cycle

of regulatory capture, leniency, financial-firm failures, and taxpayer bailouts.

"Deregulation of the financial sector" refers to both acts and omissions of Congress and of federal regulatory authorities in a roughly thirty-year period between the 1980s and the early 2000s. During this period, public officials ignored risky innovation and the growth of the shadow banking sector and dismantled regulations dating back to the New Deal era. Many experts identified the unraveling of the New Deal regulatory measures as either a root cause or a significant accelerator of the Great Recession of 2007 and the Panic of 2008.

Two examples of deregulation from the early 1980s that facilitated the financial crisis were the Depository Institutions Deregulation and Monetary Control Act of 1980 and the Alternative Mortgage Transaction Parity Act of 1982. The 1980 act removed most state restrictions on how much interest home-buying borrowers could be charged on their mortgage loan. The 1982 act permitted risky products such as adjustable-rate mortgages and negatively amortizing loans. The two acts created the conditions for the first wave of subprime mortgage lending in the late 1990s, as well as the risky underwriting practices that flourished beginning in 2002. Although Congress passed the Home Ownership and Equity Protection Act of 1994 that paved the way for the Federal Reserve to protect borrowers, the Fed's chairman, Alan Greenspan, declined to implement it. Another example of financial deregulation that enabled the late 2000s financial crisis is the Commodity Futures Modernization Act of 2000, which prohibited the regulation of credit default swaps as insurance or gambling.

Repeal of Glass–Steagall. One of the most frequently cited examples of deregulation was the repeal of the Banking Act of 1933, known better as the Glass–Steagall Act. It had been enacted in response to the observation that the merger of investment and commercial banking in the 1920s "produced a wave of speculative financings, an unsustainable economic boom, and the distribution of high-risk securities that inflicted massive losses on unsophisticated investors" (Wilmarth, 2007, p. 98). Glass–Steagall created a wall between commercial banking (taking deposits and making loans) and investment banking (underwriting and trading securities). Financial firms that engaged in both activities within a single holding company were required to divest. Separate entities had to house these distinct businesses. Commercial banks gained access to federal deposit insurance and also to liquidity support from the Federal Reserve. Congress determined that commercial banks should not be able to speculate or take excessive risks, the losses of which would be borne by taxpayers.

In the late 1980s through the 1990s, regulators began to break down the regulatory wall. For example, in 1989, the Federal Reserve Board allowed bank holding companies to use special subsidiaries to underwrite equity and debt securities within certain limits. By 1996, however, the Fed had loosened restrictions on these subsidiaries, and they posed a competitive threat to securities firms. By 1999, three of the forty-five banks with such special subsidiaries—Citigroup, JPMorgan Chase, and Bank of America—were among the top ten underwriters of U.S. securities. Another act that helped commercial banks was the Riegle–Neal Interstate Banking and Branching Efficiency Act of 1994, which permitted bank holding companies to purchase banks throughout the country and to open branches in multiple states. An enormous consolidation of commercial banks followed.

To respond to the threat posed by the expansion of commercial banks, the investment banks began to acquire thrifts and industrial loan companies. Though these were not commercial banks, they did hold deposits that investment banks were able to use to fund the asset side of their balance sheet—extending loans and purchasing and trading bonds. Bankers, however, wanted to eradicate the financial regulatory system. They came close to achieving that end in 1998 when the Federal Reserve permitted Citicorp to merge with Travelers Insurance. Shortly thereafter, Congress repealed almost all that was left of Glass–Steagall through the enactment of the Financial Services Modernization Act of 1999, also known as the Gramm–Leach–Bliley Act. This law provided the basis for the creation of holding companies through which universal banks could engage in commercial banking, investment banking, and insurance underwriting.

Deregulation brought a wave of so-called megamergers. According to the report of the Financial Crisis Inquiry Commission (FCIC), between 1990 and 2005, the ten largest banks grew from holding "25% of the industry's assets to 55%" (2011, p. 53). Critics contended that the size of the new megabanks and the diversity of businesses within them would prove unmanageable, owing to quick growth absent effective internal risk-management systems and corresponding government supervision. Some scholars attributed the debacles at Enron and WorldCom to the competitive pressures fostered by the rise of universal banks. And policy makers and some bankers believed that the repeal of Glass–Steagall contributed to the depth of the crisis. The former chief executive of Citigroup, John Reed, told the FCIC that "the compartmentalization that was created by Glass–Steagall would be a positive factor" and would possibly prevent the financial system from a "catastrophic failure" (FCIC, 2011, p. 55). The Dodd–Frank Act made an attempt to restore some of the separation between utility and investment banking through what became known as the "Volcker Rule."

[*See also* **Economic Deregulation and the Carter Administration; Financial and Banking Promotion and Regulation; Financial Crises, 1980s–2010; Glass–Steagall, Repeal of; Great**

Recession of 2008 and After; New Deal Banking Regulation; *and* Shadow Banking System.]

BIBLIOGRAPHY

Baxter, Lawrence G. "How 'Big' Became Bad: America's Underage Fling with Universal Banks." Duke Law Working Papers, Paper 17 (2010). Available at http://scholarship.law.duke.edu/working_papers/17.

Financial Crisis Inquiry Commission. *The Financial Crisis Inquiry Report: Final Report of the National Commission on the Causes of the Financial and Economic Crisis in the United States.* New York: Public Affairs, 2011.

Johnson, Simon. "The Nature of Modern Finance." Baseline Scenario, 1 October 2009. Available at http://baselinescenario.com/2009/09/01/the-nature-of-modern-finance.

McCoy, Patricia, Andrey D. Pavlov, and Susan M. Wachter. "Systemic Risk through Securitization: The Result of Deregulation and Regulatory Failure." *Connecticut Law Review* 41 (May 2009): 493–532.

Stigler, George J. "The Theory of Economic Regulation." *Bell Journal of Economics and Management Science* 2 (Spring 1971): 3–21.

Stout, Lynn A. "How Deregulating Derivatives Led to Disaster, and Why Re-Regulating Them Can Prevent Another." *Lombard Street* 1, no. 7 (2009): 4–9. Available at http://papers.ssrn.com/sol3/Delivery.cfm?abstractid=1432654.

Wilmarth, Arthur E., Jr. "Conflicts of Interest and Corporate Governance Failures at Universal Banks during the Stock Market Boom of the 1990s: The Cases of Enron and WorldCom." In *Corporate Governance in Banking: A Global Perspective*, edited by Benton E. Gup, pp. 97–133. Cheltenham, U.K.: Edward Elgar, 2007.

Jennifer Taub

DESKILLING

The process of deskilling basically involves the segmentation and simplification of the tasks required to manufacture goods or provide services. Deskilling decreases the costs of labor by rendering workers interchangeable, ultimately concentrating within management all control over the direction of production. Deskilling has occurred across the economy, transforming manual and nonmanual work, as well as the lives of blue- and white-collar workers.

Early American craftspeople learned such trades as shoemaking by being apprenticed to masters who possessed an intimate knowledge of every step of the production process. Master craftsmen were both managers and workers, setting the pace of production, managing the distribution of complex tasks within their shops, and controlling the number of apprentices allowed to enter into the trades. Most production in the early eighteenth century was based on the craft model—home or small-shop production distinguished by a relative lack of specialization—but a few master craftsmen and entrepreneurs began to experiment with segmenting and simplifying the production process.

Masters and factory owners broke down what appeared to be the continuous and fluid application of knowledge and manual dexterity into separate, discrete, and more easily mastered steps, and then they distributed the separate tasks of production among less-trained journeymen and apprentices, who relied upon increasingly sophisticated tools and machines. Shoemakers, for example, began to organize their shops not around the completion of pairs of shoes by individual craftsmen but around the separate components of the finished shoe: one worker might specialize in soles, another uppers, yet another heels, and others final assembly of the parts. In the emergent textile factories, spinning and weaving machines transformed craftspeople into machine tenders—employees who were able to load cotton or thread and service machines, but who were unable to spin thread or weave cloth.

By the mid-nineteenth century, increasing urbanization, a burgeoning population, and improvements in transportation transformed local markets into regional and then national markets, enabling the productive capacity of machines to be more fully exploited. Machine production began to dominate manufacturing. Production moved to workshops and factories, deserting homes or small shops, and companies became larger, concentrating power over work processes in the hands of managers rather than craftspeople. By the turn of the twentieth century the United States had become a mature industrial economy, and the tasks of production had grown more specialized; few workers knew much more than the discrete processes for which they were responsible on factory floors.

Efficiency experts inspired by the work of Frederick Winslow Taylor turned to managing even the minutest detail of a worker's daily regime in their attempt to routinize every detail of production. By the 1920s Henry Ford seemed to have perfected the transformation of work by combining the moving assembly line, interchangeable parts, and masses of less-skilled manpower: engaged in strenuous, tiresome, monotonous, and repetitive work, workers in such a system could produce his Model T Ford in about two hours, supplying millions of automobiles to a growing mass market. World War II accelerated the concentration of skill in machines and management, and by the 1960s and 1970s the skills once possessed by workers had been built into increasingly complex machines, robots, and computers that could simplify and rationalize the work of white-collar and service employees as well as factory workers.

[*See also* **American System of Manufacturing and Interchangeable Parts; Apprenticeship Systems; Artisanal Labor; Factory System; Ford, Henry, and Fordism; Industrialization and Deindustrialization; Mass Production; Productivity; Scientific Management;** *and* **Vertical Integration, Economies of Scale, and Firm Size.**]

BIBLIOGRAPHY

Braverman, Harry. *Labor and Monopoly Capital: The Degradation of Work in the Twentieth Century.* New York: Monthly Review Press, 1974.

Laurie, Bruce. *Artisans into Workers: Labor in Nineteenth-Century America.* New York: Hill and Wang, 1989.

Montgomery, David. *Workers' Control in America: Studies in the History of Work, Technology, and Labor Struggles.* New York: Cambridge University Press, 1979.

Vickers, Daniel. *Farmers and Fishermen: Two Centuries of Work in Essex County, Massachusetts, 1630–1850.* Chapel Hill: University of North Carolina Press for the Institute of Early American History and Culture, Williamsburg, Va., 1994.

Gerald Ronning

DOCKWORKERS' UNIONS, MULTIRACIAL

Dockworkers and their unions have experienced a turbulent history. As early as the colonial period, more respectable citizens perceived dockworkers as dangerous and volatile individuals. Throughout the nineteenth century, dockworkers struggled to gain a union foothold on the country's docks. By the late nineteenth century, dockworkers in New York City at last established one. Using a form of ethnic and racial solidarity, the Irish and the Italians came to dominate New York's piers. The Irish seized control of the docks on Manhattan's west side, while the Italians dominated in Brooklyn, Staten Island, and the Lower East Side. In 1895 they organized the International Longshoremen's Association (ILA), a union that ostracized African American longshoremen.

Prior to the Civil War, African Americans played a large role on New York's docks, but after a series of hate strikes in the late nineteenth century, white unionists removed blacks from nearly all the city's docks. Only on certain piers that handled filthy cargoes, such as bananas, did African Americans remain. The ILA expanded its area of operations to the Great Lakes, the Gulf coast, and the Pacific coast. Though in New York and in Pacific coast ports the ILA excluded blacks, in other ports, those where a large of number of blacks labored, a different phenomenon occurred. In New Orleans, for example, white and black dockworkers came to an arrangement whereby separate union locals formed around the different cargoes that the workers handled. New Orleans's form of biracialism, as Eric Arnesen put it, entailed a unique racial solidarity. Such racial inclusiveness enabled the New Orleans dockworkers to present a united front. In other regions of the country, race relations were less harmonious. On the West Coast, for example, the ILA did little to protect black and Filipino longshoremen. On the East Coast the ILA under the leadership of Joe Ryan, president from 1927 to 1953, followed the customary practice of allowing black and Hispanic longshoremen jobs only as banana carriers or extras for work gangs. The shape-up system, in which dockworkers stood around a hiring boss in a circle waiting to be selected for work, ensured that only (white) favorites were chosen. Such a system, Bruce Nelson (2001) has argued, excluded militant dockworkers from regular work, and it offered minority longshoremen only an occasional turn at work.

In more recent studies of New York's dockworkers, Colin Davis (2002) has highlighted how black union locals in Brooklyn and New Jersey offered a semblance of protection to members. Some minority dockworkers boldly protested their discriminatory treatment. Several appealed to the New York State Commission against Discrimination (SCAD) for redress. The commission's ruling in several cases compelled employers and union officials to pay financial penalties and to open the docks to greater minority participation. On the West Coast, in contrast, the ILWU welcomed the membership of nonwhite waterfront workers, and its organization of workers on sugar and pineapple plantations in Hawai'i attracted an Asian and Polynesian membership, solidifying a union presence on the Hawaiian Islands.

[*See also* **Longshoremen and Longshoremen's Unions** *and* **Racism.**]

BIBLIOGRAPHY

Arnesen, Eric. *Waterfront Workers of New Orleans: Race, Class, and Politics, 1863–1923*. New York: Oxford University Press, 1991.

Connolly, Michael C. *Seated by the Sea: The Maritime History of Portland, Maine, and Its Irish Longshoremen*. Gainesville: University Press of Florida, 2010.

Davis, Colin. " 'Shape or Fight?' New York's Black Longshoremen, 1945–1961." *International Labor and Working-Class History* 62 (Fall 2002): 143–163.

Davis, Colin. *Waterfront Revolts: New York and London Dockworkers, 1946–61*. Urbana: University of Illinois Press, 2003.

Nelson, Bruce. *Divided We Stand: American Workers and the Struggle for Black Equality*. Princeton, N.J.: Princeton University Press, 2001.

Colin J. Davis

DODGE REVOLUTIONARY UNION MOVEMENT

The Dodge Revolutionary Union Movement (DRUM) was the first of a succession of groups that originated among black nationalists and white revolutionaries in the late 1960s and early 1970s. Although they were embedded in the industrial unionism of the United Auto Workers, DRUM's leaders claimed to practice a Marxist–Leninist approach to labor action.

DRUM used wildcat, or unauthorized, strikes and rank-and-file activism to call attention to poor working conditions in assembly plants, institutional racism in union locals, and the need to integrate black workers more fully within organized labor and the auto industry.

DRUM was founded after a May 1968 wildcat strike at the Dodge Main plant in Hamtramck, Michigan, a politically autonomous Polish American enclave within Detroit. Its creation inspired similar movements nationwide among various laborers, and in 1969 it became part of the League of Revolutionary Black Workers. DRUM was most notable for bringing attention to increasingly hazardous work conditions in auto assembly plants, especially those operated by the Chrysler Corporation.

DRUM focused on uniting what was at the time an expanding workforce of African American autoworkers. The goal was to organize all autoworkers in a new entity that would supplant the United Auto Workers—which, DRUM's leaders charged, was more attuned to the needs of auto manufacturers than to the needs of autoworkers. DRUM also promoted civil rights more aggressively than did the moderate Trade Union Leadership Conference, and it articulated revolutionary principles that it sought to inculcate in black communities. Despite their activism, DRUM members failed to win elections for leadership positions in the United Auto Workers, and the organization collapsed by 1973 amid bitter opposition from automakers, the union, and law enforcement.

[*See also* **African American Labor Organizations; Automotive Industry; Racism;** *and* **United Auto Workers.**]

BIBLIOGRAPHY

Georgakas, Dan, and Marvin Surkin. *Detroit, I Do Mind Dying: A Study in Urban Revolution.* New York: St. Martin's Press, 1975.

Geschwender, James A. *Class, Race, and Worker Insurgency: The League of Revolutionary Black Workers.* Cambridge, U.K.: Cambridge University Press, 1977.

Thompson, Heather Ann. *Whose Detroit? Politics, Labor, and Race in a Modern American City.* Ithaca, N.Y.: Cornell University Press, 2001.

James C. Benton

DOMESTIC LABOR

Since the Colonial Era, domestic labor has been a significant contributor to economic production and development in America. Though domestic labor encompasses a wide range of market and nonmarket activities, this article will focus on three major productive elements: household manufactures for home consumption; industrial outwork, a form of wage labor conducted in the home; and independent production within the home for sale in wider commodity markets.

From Rural Areas to Urban. Household manufactures for home consumption prevailed as a system of domestic labor in rural areas prior to the era of industrialization. With the emergence of mechanized textile, shoe, and garment production after 1830, household manufactures declined steadily. With the growth of the factory system in the nineteenth century, initially concentrated in New England and the mid-Atlantic states, household manufactures declined in those regions, while remaining substantial in the South and Middle West. The rapid expansion of commercial markets for items previously produced within the home substantially reduced household manufacturing across the United States. American families after World War II rarely produced goods at home for their own consumption.

Independent production within the home for sale in broader markets declined at the same time. Such independent production was more commonly concentrated in cities than in rural areas. In the first half of the nineteenth century, independent male weavers or shoemakers often worked in their own homes, drawing upon the unpaid labor of family members for certain steps in the production process. Women dressmakers and laundry workers also brought work home and commonly sold their services to a varied clientele. Technological developments and the steady commodification of goods and services undermined independent production within the home. Increasingly individuals who performed such work at home were displaced by wageworkers employed in urban factories and shops that took advantage of machinery or economies of scale to undersell homeworkers.

Industrial outwork, by contrast, has had a much longer and more significant history. For almost 150 years, a substantial share of industrial wage-work was performed in workers' homes. From the emergence of the first factories in the 1790s until the passage of the Fair Labor Standards Act in 1938, employers found it economical to distribute work to be performed outside factories or workshops. Rural and urban residents alike were drawn into a system of dispersed contracting out, earning wages for domestic labor performed with raw materials owned by their employers and producing goods for sale in distant markets.

Industrial outwork flourished initially in rural communities: wives and daughters in farming families supplemented farm income by laboring for textile mills, storekeepers, or middlemen who distributed raw materials throughout the countryside and sold the finished cloth, hats, and shoes in widely dispersed markets. The first water-powered cotton spinning mills typically expanded production by putting out yarn to be woven by members of farming families. Handloom weaving on an outwork basis

grew significantly in New England in the early nineteenth century, but it declined after the mid-1820s with the adoption of the power loom. Farm women turned to braided straw hats and palm-leaf hats as an outwork occupation, and by 1837 more than fifty thousand women and children were employed on a part-time basis in Massachusetts alone. At about the same time, farm women also worked at binding and stitching shoe uppers. By midcentury a decentralized hybrid system had developed: much of shoe binding was done by women in their own homes, while male artisans working in small urban shops did the shoemaking itself. Domestic labor in boot and shoe manufacturing declined sharply after the Civil War with the fuller mechanization of shoemaking and the adoption of steam power in urban factories.

In the Gilded Age the garment industry became the leading employer of homeworkers. In Boston, for instance, clothing manufacturers put cut goods into rural communities; by 1870, Boston employers paid some $2 million in wages to a workforce of about fifty thousand New England farm women. By then, however, urban homework in the garment industry dwarfed its rural cousin. In Boston, New York City, and Philadelphia, home employment in the needle trades came to be known as the "sweating" system, as women and children in urban immigrant families earned meager wages from employers whose exploitative practices led them to be known as "sweaters." By the early twentieth century, the impoverishment of immigrant families and the squalid conditions within which they worked and lived attracted the concern of Progressive Era reformers, who lobbied to outlaw tenement-house production and child labor in manufacturing.

Regulation and Deregulation. Whereas in the antebellum era rural outwork had been a part-time occupation for members of farming families, its later urban counterpart was full-time and highly exploitative, depending on a system of underpaid subcontracting that forced workers to put in long hours during peak seasons simply to survive. The low wages and long hours of homeworkers, in turn, undermined wages and employment in factories and workshops. State and local efforts to regulate or outlaw homework were typically stymied by court rulings: the U.S. Supreme Court's decision in *Lochner v. New York* (1905), for example, protected workers' putative right to "freedom of contract" under the Fourteenth Amendment. Only when Congress enacted the Fair Labor Standards Act in the New Deal era did industrial outwork become largely unprofitable. Afterward, the federal government's enforcement of wage and hours regulations on homeworkers and the outright ban of homework in a number of industries sharply limited these practices.

Industrial outwork, though exploitative, has nonetheless had a certain appeal for individuals and families that have sought to work within its bounds. In an economic system in which the wages of male household heads were—and often still are—insufficient to support a family, outwork permitted the employment of children and married women to supplement family income. Homework has also permitted women homemakers to combine housekeeping, cooking, and child rearing with wage-earning activities. Homework has had a certain logic for urban immigrant families in the United States since the early twentieth century, but it has been a logic based on the inadequacy of state regulation of wages and hours of labor.

At the end of the twentieth century industrial outwork made a comeback with the growth of an underground, largely immigrant economy in the garment trades of New York, Los Angeles, and other large cities. In the 1980s the administration of Ronald Reagan rescinded the laws against homework in several industries and cut back on regulatory enforcement. These steps, coupled with the growth of telecommuting among white-collar clerical workers, led to a resurgence of homework. Whether this form of domestic labor will see continued growth depends on future technological changes and legal struggles. Homework, then, is an issue that refuses to go away.

[*See also* **Child Labor; Factory and Hours Laws; Freedom of Contract; Homework; Labor Markets; Textile Industry;** *and* **Women Workers.**]

BIBLIOGRAPHY

Boris, Eileen. *Home to Work: Motherhood and the Politics of Industrial Homework in the United States.* Cambridge, U.K.: Cambridge University Press, 1994.

Boris, Eileen, and Cynthia R. Daniels, eds. *Homework: Historical and Contemporary Perspectives on Paid Labor at Home.* Urbana: University of Illinois Press, 1989.

Dublin, Thomas. "Rural Putting-Out Work in Early Nineteenth-Century New England: Women and the Transition to Capitalism in the Countryside." *New England Quarterly* 64 (1991): 531–573.

Dublin, Thomas. *Transforming Women's Work: New England Lives in the Industrial Revolution.* Ithaca, N.Y.: Cornell University Press, 1994.

Nobles, Gregory. "Merchant Middlemen in the Outwork Network of Rural New England." In *Merchant Credit and Labour Strategies in Historical Perspective,* edited by Rosemary E. Ommer, pp. 333–347. Fredericton, New Brunswick: Acadiensis Press, 1990.

Tryon, Rolla Milton. *Household Manufactures in the United States, 1640–1860: A Study in Industrial History.* Chicago: University of Chicago Press, 1917.

Thomas Dublin

DUKE, JAMES

(1856–1925), manufacturer of tobacco products and philanthropist. James Buchanan "Buck"

Duke, the son of Washington Duke and Artelia Roney Duke, was born on the family's farm in Orange County, North Carolina. After the Civil War, Washington Duke and his sons began manufacturing and selling smoking tobacco under the brand name "Pro Bono Publico." The family moved to nearby Durham and opened a factory. Under James's leadership, the company began making hand-rolled cigarettes in New York. Securing exclusive rights to the Bonsack cigarette-making machine in 1885, the firm soon gained dominance in the industry. Duke's imaginative advertising enlarged markets for his mass-produced cigarettes, but his real genius lay in creating a corporate structure that integrated purchasing, manufacturing, marketing, and distribution. Organizing the American Tobacco Company (ATC)—known to its detractors as the "American Tobacco Trust"—in 1890, he consolidated control over the entire tobacco industry. Ruthlessly cutting prices to undermine competitors, the ATC and its affiliates dominated the production of cigarettes, pipe tobacco, snuff, chewing tobacco, and every tobacco product except cigars. The ATC became so dominant that the U.S. Supreme Court ordered its dissolution in 1911 under antitrust legislation.

James Duke increasingly devoted himself to Duke Power Company, which figured prominently in the industrialization of the Carolina Piedmont region. He also became involved in philanthropic causes, primarily the Methodist Church and Trinity College, which moved from Randolph County, North Carolina, to Durham in 1892. Creating the family philanthropic foundation, the Duke Endowment, in 1924, Duke specified that its annual income be distributed among colleges, hospitals, and orphanages in North and South Carolina. The endowment provided for the transformation of Trinity College into Duke University.

[*See also* **Tobacco Industry.**]

BIBLIOGRAPHY

Durden, Robert F. *The Dukes of Durham, 1865–1929.* Durham, N.C.: Duke University Press, 1975.

Durden, Robert F. *The Launching of Duke University, 1924–1949.* Durham, N.C.: Duke University Press, 1993.

Robert Korstad

DUST BOWL ERA AND FARM CRISIS

The farm crisis of the 1920s and 1930s was born out of more than sixty years of federal policy promoting the intense cultivation of land, stretching as far back as the Homestead Act (1862). Yet it was more acutely the result of the boom in export prices that accompanied World War I, along with the encouragement of the administration of Woodrow Wilson—exemplified by the slogan, "food will win the war."

Answering this call, farmers pushed forward into new and previously unbroken lands, expanding their properties and taking advantage of the new wave of agricultural machinery that was transforming their vocation. The postwar recovery of western European and Soviet agricultural production, along with the expansion of operations in countries like Argentina, Australia, and Canada, crowded out American exports and drove international commodity values sharply downward. Unable to fulfill their recently acquired debt obligations with these diminishing returns, America's farmers, particularly those producing crops such as wheat and cotton, faced an economic crisis several years before the onset of the Great Depression.

The Dust Bowl was the most dramatic consequence of the farmers' drive to plow substandard lands in the Southwest and plant seed in ground that was better suited for other techniques, if not other purposes altogether. The destruction of plains grasses and sod loosened vast amounts of topsoil, and when in the early 1930s this combined with droughts, the result was a series of colossal dust storms, ultimately forcing a significant minority of migrants to abandon their farms in search of economic opportunities elsewhere, most famously in California.

[*See also* Agriculture, *subentry on* Since 1920, *and* Great Depression (1929–1939).]

BIBLIOGRAPHY

Hamilton, David E. *From New Day to New Deal: American Farm Policy from Hoover to Roosevelt, 1928–1933.* Chapel Hill: University of North Carolina Press, 1991.

Hurt, R. Douglas. *The Dust Bowl: An Agricultural and Social History.* Chicago: Nelson–Hall, 1981.

Rochester, Anna. *Why Farmers Are Poor: The Agricultural Crisis in the United States.* New York: International Publishers, 1940.

Worster, Donald. *Dust Bowl: The Southern Plains in the 1930s.* New York: Oxford University Press, 1979.

Patrick M. Dixon

E

ECONOMIC DEREGULATION AND THE CARTER ADMINISTRATION

James Earl "Jimmy" Carter took office in January 1977 at a moment of economic stagnation, persistent unemployment, and rising inflation. By then it was clear that a quarter of a century of rising productivity, increasing incomes, and low unemployment had come to an end for the world's dominant industrial nations. Keynesian economic policies that used fiscal and monetary tools to regulate the economy and maintain relatively full employment no longer seemed to work effectively. Carter had inherited an economic recession and what then were unacceptable levels of unemployment. Worse yet, the policies of the Organization of Petroleum Exporting Countries (OPEC) increased oil prices, raising production and distribution costs and thus threatening to worsen inflation. The Carter administration sought to devise an economic policy that would stimulate employment without generating runaway inflation.

Internally the administration remained split between economic advisers, who stressed the need to balance the federal budget and to tighten monetary policy in order to combat inflation, and social and political advisers, who argued for stimulating the economy in order to reduce unemployment. Initially the advocates of economic stimulus won the day, although Carter himself remained committed to budgetary restraint and receptive to the policy prescriptions offered by his economic advisers. Stimulus did reduce unemployment but seemed to unleash inflation, doing great damage to the political prospects of both Carter and the

Democratic Party. The combination of inflation, economic rigidity, and less-than-full employment resulted in the coinage of the term "stagflation." As inflation rose into double digits and interest rates soared to 18 percent and even higher in some circumstances, Americans found it harder to finance mortgages or to purchase new automobiles, further limiting economic growth.

The persistence of inflation and growing concerns about stagflation increased the influence within the administration of such advisers as Charles Schultze, the chair of the Council of Economic Advisers, and Alfred Kahn, whom Carter appointed as his special adviser on inflation. Both Schultze and Kahn reinforced Carter's belief in budgetary restraint and managing federal expenditures wisely and frugally. All three men realized that the United States could do little about OPEC's impact on global oil prices—Carter did try to encourage fuel conservation and alternatives to oil—but Schultze and Kahn thought that smarter governmental policies might lead to lower inflation. They had come to believe that federal regulatory policies created economic inefficiencies that led to prices higher than free markets would tolerate. Schultze and Kahn also agreed that the government's encouragement of trade unionism and its failure to restrain union leaders resulted in wage rises that stoked inflation, harmed nonunion workers, and damaged consumers. They were sure that in the trucking and airline industries, government regulations and union power created informal cartels that maintained freight rates, airline fares, and wages above competitive market levels. Kahn especially gained repute as an advocate of economic deregulation. His economic analyses led to the deregulation of trucking and the airlines. And his policy prescriptions seemed to work when truck freight charges declined as nonunion carriers stole market share from unionized firms; likewise, competition among airlines intensified and

passenger fares fell. Both economic advisers also recommended that Carter take a harder line with the leaders of such unions as the United Auto Workers and the United Steelworkers. Kahn said bluntly: "I'd love the Teamsters to be worse off. I'd love the automobile workers to be worse off." In his own words, "those unemployed auto workers are being screwed by the employed automobile workers." Or in Schultze's piquant comment: "Whenever big management and big labor get together, they normally . . . screw the public."

Schultze, Kahn, and ultimately Carter advocated what soon came to be characterized as neoliberalism, the belief that so-called free markets operated in the general interest. Whenever government regulations and union power interfered with the workings of the market, consumers suffered through poorer service and higher prices. Liberating industries and markets from regulation would unleash entrepreneurialism and innovation, improving products, bettering services, and lowering prices. "Government cannot eliminate poverty or provide a bountiful economy or reduce inflation or save our cities or cure illiteracy or provide energy," echoed Carter. His words were only a short step from Ronald Reagan's aphorism, "Government is not the solution to our problem; government is the problem." The politics of anti-Keynesian budget restraint, liberation of the market, union bashing, and idolization of so-called job creators had come to fruition before Reagan and the Republicans took over the White House in 1981.

Perhaps the ultimate irony for Carter and his administration was that deregulation and neoliberalism alone failed to end stagflation. Instead Carter fought inflation by appointing Paul Volcker as chair of the Federal Reserve Board, a position from which Volcker tightened monetary policy by raising interest rates to historically high levels, constricting economic growth and employment, a policy that likely cost Carter and the Democrats victory in the

1980 election. Volcker continued his tight-money policies in the opening year of the Reagan administration, producing in 1981–1982 the highest level of unemployment since the Great Depression. Such policies cured inflation, thus setting the stage for further advances in deregulation, union bashing, sanctification of the free market, and a Republican Party version of military Keynesianism.

[*See also* **Deregulation, Financial; Inflation and Deflation; Keynesian Economics; Labor Movement, Decline of the; Monetary Policy, Federal; Neoliberalism as Public Economic Policy; Stagflation; Unemployment;** *and* **Volcker, Paul.**]

BIBLIOGRAPHY

Dubofsky, Melvyn. "Jimmy Carter and the End of the Politics of Productivity." In *The Carter Presidency: Policy Choices in the Post–New Deal Era*, edited by Gary M. Fink and Hugh Davis Graham, pp. 95–116. Lawrence: University Press of Kansas, 1998.

Kaufman, Burton I. *The Presidency of James Earl Carter, Jr.* Lawrence: University Press of Kansas, 1993.

Schulman, Bruce J. "Slouching toward the Supply Side: Jimmy Carter and the New American Political Economy." In *The Carter Presidency: Policy Choices in the Post–New Deal Era*, edited by Gary M. Fink and Hugh Davis Graham, pp. 51–71. Lawrence: University Press of Kansas, 1998.

Stein, Judith. *Pivotal Decade: How the United States Traded Factories for Finance in the Seventies.* New Haven, Conn.: Yale University Press, 2010.

Melvyn Dubofsky

ECONOMIC DEVELOPMENT

Economists define "economic development" as a sustained increase in per capita income. Though this definition is a good starting point, historians generally conceive economic development as a broader set of social and political changes. In the context of U.S. history, those changes include the settlement of a capacious frontier, the growth of large cities, a vast influx of immigrants, and the rapid spread of new technology. The complexity of these changes notwithstanding, the course of U.S. development can be traced through three major periods: the extensive growth of the colonial and revolutionary periods, the expansion of commerce during the first half of the nineteenth century, and the emergence of so-called managerial capitalism after the Civil War.

The Colonial and Revolutionary Periods. The economy of colonial America grew rapidly because of sustained population growth and profitable cultivation of staple crops. Massive free and unfree immigration from Europe and Africa—coupled with a moderate climate, relatively high nutritional levels, and high fertility rates—resulted in extraordinarily rapid population growth. Between 1650 and 1770 the population of Britain's mainland North American colonies increased from 55,000 to more than 2.2 million. Most colonists participated in a vibrant agricultural economy. High prices for wheat and tobacco—British North America's two main staples—encouraged the particularly rapid settlement of the middle and southern colonies in the eighteenth century. White colonists in the slave South—benefiting from slave labor and high staple prices—ranked as the wealthiest of the colonists.

Rapid population growth produced substantial economic development. Because no sweeping technological or organizational advances dramatically stimulated productivity, per capita income grew quite modestly by modern standards, increasing anywhere from 0.3 to 0.6 percent per year. Yet colonists built an increasingly sophisticated commercial infrastructure that resulted in the growth of towns and cities. Such development was particularly important in New England and the middle colonies, where cities became major market centers. By 1770 such cities as Boston, New York, and Philadelphia provided an impressive array of mercantile services that induced future economic growth.

Government policy, both in Britain and in the colonies, also aided colonial development. Unlike France or Spain, Britain did not seek to regulate overseas migration, thus abetting the population explosion in the North American colonies. British mercantilist policies, designed to further the interests of the imperial center, sometimes impeded colonial trade with other nations. Colonists, however, successfully evaded the most onerous regulations, while the British mercantile system enabled American merchants to export grains, lumber, livestock, and other goods. The Revolutionary War, in fact, initially had devastating economic consequences because American merchants lost many of the trading privileges that they had enjoyed under the British Empire.

Expansion of Commerce between the Revolution and the Civil War.

Most export agriculture in the colonial and revolutionary periods was confined to areas with access to water transportation. Transporting bulky crops over the nation's rutted and muddy roads was prohibitively expensive. In the period 1800–1820, private turnpike companies—which improved roads in order to collect tolls—alleviated the worst problems of overland transport, but grains and other bulky commodities remained too expensive to ship over roads. Hence proponents of economic development avidly improved rivers and built canals to extend the nation's system of waterways. The Erie Canal, completed in 1825, was by far the most important of these improvements. Built through the gently rolling landscape of upstate New York, the Erie Canal connected the Great Lakes to the Hudson River. It transformed such cities as Buffalo, Rochester, and Syracuse into major transport, mercantile, and manufacturing hubs. Canal systems in Ohio and other midwestern states extended the reach of the Erie system, providing farmers throughout the Middle West with an all-water connection to New York City. The steamboat, meanwhile, facilitated trade on the Mississippi and Ohio River systems, providing yet another avenue of commerce.

Steam power soon had an even larger impact when applied to overland carriage. Areas in which water transportation was either unavailable or prohibitively expensive turned to the railroad. First built in the late 1820s, railroads rapidly spread across the county. By 1860, Americans had built approximately thirty thousand miles of track, with four separate roads penetrating the Appalachian Mountain barrier. Railroads not only accelerated the growth of cities on the Eastern Seaboard, but also transformed Pittsburgh, Chicago, and other midwestern cities into major marketing and manufacturing centers.

Although historians have discarded the view that the railroad single-handedly accounted for American industrialization, it nevertheless contributed to the dramatic expansion of commerce in everyday life. In the North and Midwest, the expansion of the railroad network created a self-reinforcing cycle of growth. As transportation improved, farmers produced more grains, dairy products, and other produce for urban centers. With more cash to spend on consumer goods, farm families demanded textiles, shoes, furniture, and other manufactured products. Manufacturers and merchants, responding to the larger agrarian market, increased their output and improved productivity. Firms producing such goods as readymade apparel, hats and caps, and boots and shoes, for example, increased productivity through specialization and greater division of labor.

Incremental technological advances—usually the result of tinkering by rather ordinary mechanics—further increased manufacturing productivity.

The South lagged far behind in inventive activity and other measures of economic development. Its slave-based economy, to be sure, produced enormous profits for many planters and farmers. The southern economy did especially well in the 1850s when the price of cotton, tobacco, and other staples soared. Yet in almost every other measure of development—urbanization rates, inventive activity, manufacturing output, population growth—the North far outstripped the South. As the Civil War approached, the regional disparities grew. In 1860 the value of manufactured goods produced in New York City alone exceeded the combined production of the eleven southern states that formed the Confederacy. Underlying the South's failure was a lack of adequate demand to spur industrialization. Plantation slavery restrained population growth among free farmers, and an unequal distribution of rural income undermined the earnings and consumption habits of farm families that had provided northern entrepreneurs with lucrative markets. However profitable it was to southern planters, slavery seriously impeded southern industrial development.

The limitations of southern development notwithstanding, the U.S. economy grew impressively between 1800 and 1860. Historians debate to what extent federal and state government action contributed to this remarkable economic expansion. State governments frequently intervened in the economy in the early nineteenth century, especially when, as in New York and Pennsylvania, they operated their own canal systems. Although New York's Erie Canal succeeded, most other state-owned canals failed. State and federal governments provided engineering expertise, land grants, and other subsidies to the railroads, but private investors supplied most of the capital. The most important government intervention was enforcing a stable set of property rights, including a patent system, that encouraged economic expansion and technological innovation. State governments made it easier for entrepreneurs to obtain corporate charters for banks, factories, and other enterprises, while the federal courts protected interstate commerce and used law to validate corporate charters and contracts. With a strong legal foundation in place, national markets and national enterprises came to dominate the economy.

Managerial Capitalism and the Modern Economy.
The post–Civil War expansion of the railroad network—including the construction of the first transcontinental lines—enabled entrepreneurs to establish national corporations. Though a few large firms had flourished earlier during the market revolution, especially in the New England textile industry, these firms paled compared to the corporate giants of the late nineteenth and early twentieth centuries. By 1910, Standard Oil, U.S. Steel, Armour and Co., and the American Tobacco Company were among the firms with assets in excess of $200 million. Another round of technological change soon added such newer businesses as Ford Motor Company and General Motors to the list of industrial giants. These enterprises tended to be capital-intensive, using their large size to forge substantial economies of scale. Technological advances became even more important. Many large firms organized research divisions and departments that institutionalized technological change.

Borrowing from the experience of the railroads, these large industrial firms also developed complex administrative bureaucracies heavily stocked with middle managers and upper-echelon executives. Entrepreneurs such as John D. Rockefeller and Andrew Carnegie used these new administrative forms to ascertain precise production costs, enabling them to identify and then to eliminate expensive bottlenecks. Rockefeller's Standard Oil Company in particular ruthlessly cut production costs, enabling the company to buy out or destroy less efficient competitors. By 1890, Standard Oil—which owned 20,000 oil wells, 4,000 miles of pipeline, and 5,000 specialty railroad cars—controlled more than 90 percent of the American oil and kerosene market. Whereas large corporations tended to dominate industries with relatively homogenous output (oil, steel, and tobacco), smaller firms thrived in sectors that produced specialty goods, ranging from complex machinery to such consumer goods as furniture. By the early twentieth century, America's combination of large and small firms encouraged the birth of new industries, including automobiles and electrical manufacturing.

Mass production made the marketing and distribution of consumer goods extraordinarily important. To ensure a constant demand for their products, businesses invested heavily in advertising, first in print publications and later on radio and television. Innovative retailers devised new ways of selling both basic necessities and luxury goods. Department stores, fashionable retail districts, and, eventually, supermarkets, as well as shopping centers and malls, indelibly shaped the American landscape. By the early twentieth century, a number of firms expanded the scale of consumer borrowing, especially through installment plans, and this allowed a broad range of families to purchase automobiles and other consumer durables.

By 1900 the United States possessed the basic elements of a developed economy: growing per capita income, rapidly evolving technologies, increasingly efficient industrial producers, and sophisticated marketing and distribution channels. Although certain regions of the country—most notably Appalachia and other parts of the South—continued to lag, rapid economic development made the United

States the world's largest economy for much of the twentieth century and laid the material foundations for what the publisher Henry Luce called the "American century."

The advent of the desktop computer in the 1980s and of the Internet and World Wide Web in the 1990s opened a new era of U.S. economic development. The so-called information age also exemplified many of the same characteristics of earlier changes, including the rapid adaptation of new technologies; a complex mix of both large corporations (including giants such as Microsoft and Intel) and smaller, more flexible firms; and attitudes and regulations generally favorable to free enterprise and hostile to government regulation. The information age hastened the process of economic globalization as the speed of communications obliterated space and time. It became far easier for U.S. industrial enterprises to invest in operations overseas where they might locate a productive yet far cheaper labor force. Given the ease and speed of market transactions, U.S. manufacturers and retailers could also subcontract production and supply to cheaper-labor foreign enterprises. Many of the new technologies also increased productive efficiency so greatly that industrial enterprises could reduce their labor forces while lowering their unit costs of production and increasing profitability. Not only did industrial enterprises lower their costs of production through technological innovation, but in response to cheaper overseas labor they weakened unions and lowered wages domestically.

For a time from the late 1970s into the early twenty-first century, a consensus formed among public-policy makers that deregulation of the economy, lower taxes, and greater reliance on private markets, ideas that fell under the rubric of neoliberalism, would best foster economic development. The triumph of neoliberalism propelled the financial sector to a dominant position in the economy. Where once mass production and professionally managed corporate oligopolies characterized economic development, by the year 2000 giant banks with international operations, traders in the stock and commodities markets, venture capitalists, and hedge-fund managers appeared to be the new generators of economic development. Yet the altered economy also raised new questions. Would the rapid transmission of information make global markets the driving force of continued growth? Would the new information technologies transform consumer culture? How would new technologies affect the managerial structure of "old economy" stalwarts such as the steel, automotive, and chemical industries?

The economic crisis of 2008–2010—brought on largely by neoliberal policies that led banks and other financial institutions to engage in risky and ultimately destructive investments— brought back into play older American suspicions about bankers and businesspeople. Throughout U.S. history, despite widespread support of economic development, many Americans have nevertheless feared that the growing power of big business might subvert democracy. These fears, coupled with deep swings in the business cycle, have created influential political movements, especially in the Populist, Progressive, and New Deal eras, that raised important questions about economic development. Should the federal government encourage certain industries with tariffs and other subsidies? Should state and federal governments dissolve or regulate corporations that threaten to become monopolies? How should government mediate conflicts among labor, business, and consumers? What kinds and levels of taxation best encourage economic development while also promoting other social goods?

Because economic development is so complicated, scholars continue to debate the ultimate source of U.S. success. Some stress the availability of such abundant natural resources as fertile soils and rich supplies of iron, coal, and oil. Others underscore the emergence of a national, integrated market that encompassed most of North America. Whereas political and geographic barriers hindered development elsewhere, these scholars argue, U.S. businesses grew in tandem with an expanding home market. Finally, many scholars have emphasized the importance of distinctive American cultural and political attitudes, including a devotion to private property and free enterprise and a corresponding suspicion of economic regulation that might hinder business success. The economic contraction of 2008–2010, which affected economies around the globe, revived memories of the last global economic crisis of comparable proportions, the Great Depression of the 1930s. As happened in the 1930s, once again after 2008 economists, politicians, government officials, businesspeople, and citizens questioned conventional wisdom about economic development. Debate raged about how to promote economic development without producing the glaring and growing economic inequality that came to characterize the United States between 1980 and 2012. Clearly the history of economic development remains unfinished, and its impact remains in dispute, as it continues to influence society, politics, and culture.

[See also Business Growth and Decline; Canals and Waterways; Economic Growth and Income Patterns; Globalization; Industrialization and Deindustrialization; Industrial Policy, Theory and Practice of; Labor Productivity Growth; Neoliberalism; Productivity; Railroads; Technology; Transportation Revolution; and Vertical Integration, Economies of Scale, and Firm Size.]

BIBLIOGRAPHY

Balleisen, Edward J. *Navigating Failure: Bankruptcy and Commercial Society in Antebellum America.*

Chapel Hill: University of North Carolina Press, 2001.

Bruchey, Stuart. *Enterprise: The Dynamic Economy of a Free People*. Cambridge, Mass.: Harvard University Press, 1990.

Chandler, Alfred D., Jr. *The Visible Hand: The Managerial Revolution in American Business*. Cambridge, Mass.: Belknap Press of Harvard University Press, 1977.

Engerman, Stanley L., and Robert E. Gallman, eds. *The Cambridge Economic History of the United States*. Vol. 1, *The Colonial Period*. Cambridge, U.K.: Cambridge University Press, 1996.

Fogel, William Robert. *Without Consent or Contract: The Rise and Fall of American Slavery*. New York: W. W. Norton and Company, 1989.

Lindstrom, Diane. *Economic Development in the Philadelphia Region, 1810–1850*. New York: Columbia University Press, 1978.

McCusker, John J., and Russell R. Menard. *The Economy of British America, 1607–1789*. Chapel Hill: University of North Carolina Press for the Institute of Early American History and Culture, Williamsburg, Va., 1985.

Scranton, Philip. *Endless Novelty: Specialty Production and American Industrialization, 1865–1925*. Princeton, N.J.: Princeton University Press, 1997.

Taylor, George Rogers. *The Transportation Revolution, 1815–1860*. New York: Rinehart, 1951.

John Majewski

ECONOMIC GROWTH AND INCOME PATTERNS

Growth is the dominant paradigm that economists use to understand long-term economic improvement. The term generally refers to intensive growth, broadly defined as the material increase in standard of living or wealth per person, as opposed to extensive growth, the absolute increase in land, population, or aggregate wealth. The United States economy has, on average, grown at a rate of 1.6 percent a year since 1840, and it grew at a slower rate of roughly 1 percent during the preceding 250 years; both of these percentages are based on the analysis of North, Anderson, and Hill (1983) and refer to increases in real per capita income. Throughout its history, income inequality in the United States has varied widely: analyses by historians in the early twenty-first century have identified a narrowing of inequality during the middle part of the twentieth century and an expansion since 1970. Because historians generally agree that most countries in the world had similarly sized economies and standards of living in 1700, there is fierce debate about the causes of the growth that has created the twenty-first century's vastly different economies.

U.S. Economic Growth through History.

Estimating the United States' economic growth for the colonial period is difficult, largely because there is little reliable macroeconomic data for the period. Consequently, a key method of estimating colonial growth takes the economy's size in 1840 and projects backward using the nineteenth century's average growth rate. Yet if this projection were accurate, the colonial economy would have had to have been much smaller than it appears, indicating that actual growth must have been substantially slower than that of the later period. Nevertheless, from the seventeenth into the mid-eighteenth century, the standard of living appears to have increased, with material possessions increasing in quality and quantity. The Revolutionary period, from about 1774 to 1793, saw a great deal of economic dislocation; the economy was roughly the same size in 1793 as it had been twenty years earlier. Between 1790 and 1840, the economy grew slowly but unevenly, with years of success preceding or following years of tepid growth or contraction. An estimate of 1 percent growth for the colonial and early republic periods appears appropriate.

From roughly 1840 onward, the American economy's growth accelerated. Because the Census Bureau began compiling statistics on agriculture and industry in 1840, the data on this period is also more reliable. As a result of market integration in the earlier part of the century and expanded international capital flows and infrastructural improvement in the middle and later parts of the century, the American economy grew rapidly. Yet this growth was not uniform: violent and prolonged panics occurred in 1819, 1837, 1839, 1857, 1873, and 1893. Nevertheless, the overall growth rate was high, and this trend continued into the twentieth century. Despite massive dislocations around World War I, the Great Depression, and World War II, high average growth remained through the 1970s. Though it appears that growth has slowed somewhat since then, this might not mean a fundamental shift in long-run prospects.

Explaining the origins of growth has proved complicated; answers have variously traced the interplay among technology, institutions, and geography. Rapid economic growth in the late nineteenth-century United States, for example, is often explained by the spread of a new technology—the railroad—that created a transcontinental market, the funding of which necessitated the development of new institutions for business organization and the allocation of capital. Yet scholars have sharply divergent views of the relative importance of these various factors: some emphasize accidents of geography, and others emphasize cultural practices that they believe were key to creating a growth-friendly climate.

Similarly, the relationship between inequality and growth is complex: some accounts assert that higher inequality accelerated capital formation and investment, spurring economic growth, while other accounts posit that relative equality enabled the formation of the mass consumer markets necessary to take advantage of technological improvements in mass production and infrastructure. Engerman and Sokoloff (1994) take the latter position, arguing that compared to the plantation systems of the American South and the Caribbean, the settlement patterns and geographic factors in places like Canada and the northern United States promoted more egalitarian social and political regimes. This relative social equality in turn enabled the particular technological changes of the nineteenth century—mass production and infrastructure improvements—to spur rapid growth. Though their account is only one of many, it is emblematic of a literature tracing the interplay among technology, geography, institutions, and growth.

Income Patterns. In the colonial period and early nineteenth century, income distribution was more equal, in part because economic growth was just starting to accelerate. Slavery, however, meant that not only were a significant number of Americans held in bondage and unable to better their material circumstances, but a wealth divide existed in plantation regions between people who possessed large amounts of capital in the form of slaves and people who did not. For the same reason that economic growth before 1840 is difficult to measure, there is little quantitative work on income inequality in that period. Nevertheless, an account based on the pioneering work of Simon Kuznets (1955) appears accurate: early industrialization increased inequality during the mid- to late nineteenth century, but inequality narrowed during the early twentieth century as the economy more broadly shared the gains in industrial productivity.

Yet more recent work has suggested that this trend has changed: wealth inequality has widened since 1970. Following World War II, when the wealthiest tenth's share of national wealth dropped from roughly 40–45 percent to closer to 30 percent, their share of the national wealth remained stable through the 1970s. Piketty and Saez (2003) argue that this was a result of progressive tax and inheritance policies, which began changing in the 1970s. Since then, the top tenth's share of wealth has increased and may come to exceed its twentieth-century high, which occurred during the interwar period. In contrast with other studies, many of which are based on Kuznets's study of the relationship between industrialization and income patterns, Piketty and Saez use comparisons between the United States and France—which had similar technological experiences but radically different social policies and divergent income distributions—to argue that social norms and policy play a critical role in income distribution.

[*See also* **Business Cycles; Business Growth and Decline; Economic Theories and Thought;** *and* **Long Swings and Cycles in Economic Growth.**]

BIBLIOGRAPHY

Acemoglu, Daron. "Introduction to Economic Growth." *Journal of Economic Theory* 147, no. 2 (March 2012): 545–550.

Engerman, Stanley L., and Kenneth L. Sokoloff. "Factor Endowments, Institutions, and Differential Paths of Growth among New World Economies: A View from Economic Historians of the United States." NBER Historical Working Paper no. 66, December 1994. http://www.nber.org/papers/h0066.

Kuznets, Simon. "Economic Growth and Income Inequality." *American Economic Review* 45, no. 1 (March 1955): 1–28.

North, Douglass C., with Terry L. Anderson and Peter J. Hill. *Growth and Welfare in the American Past: A New Economic History.* 3d ed. Englewood Cliffs, N.J.: Prentice Hall, 1983.

Piketty, Thomas, and Emmanuel Saez. "Income Inequality in the United States, 1913–1998." *Quarterly Journal of Economics* 118, no. 1 (February 2003): 1–39.

Joshua Specht

ECONOMIC REGULATION

The objectives of economic regulation are usually mixed: to achieve an appropriate balance between efficiency and equity, to steer acquisitive human urges into productive channels, and to strike reasonable trade-offs between economic growth and environmental protection. The United States has had an uneven history of regulation, one that was relatively good in comparison to those of many other countries. For most of its history, the United States featured the world's most entrepreneurially "free" economy, the one with the least amount of public regulation. Such generalizations, however, disguise a more complex reality.

In the Colonial Era, religious considerations limited entrepreneurial impulses, yet the spread of a pervasive market economy in the eighteenth and nineteenth centuries worked a dramatic change. Although such old customs as the "just price" (the maximum allowable price for a basic necessity) ended, that did not preclude all regulation. The developing American capitalist economy still required a strong regulatory framework. Commercial transactions depended on a system of contract law enforced through courts. Other public and private regulatory mechanisms were essential as well.

The Monetary System and the Capital Markets. All cash-and-credit economies, including the American one, also require a monetary authority—typically a central bank—to regulate the supply and value of money. In colonial America, banks were almost nonexistent, but after independence Alexander Hamilton's First Bank of the United States (1791–1811) served some functions of a central bank until its twenty-year charter expired and was not renewed. The Second Bank of the United States (1816–1836) was even more successful, but it, too, fell victim to politics, and its charter was not renewed. Thereafter, the United States had no central bank until the creation of the Federal Reserve System (the Fed) in 1913. During those three generations, the government generally maintained the gold standard, state authorities regulated banking haphazardly, and the nation experienced a chronically deficient money supply. All these conditions changed under the Federal Reserve System. By the 1930s the Fed, assisted by other bodies and officials such as state banking commissions and the Comptroller of the Currency, had become a modern regulatory agency overseeing the monetary system.

The nation's securities (stock and bond) markets, which developed during the nineteenth century and then blossomed in the twentieth, have benefited from one of the world's most modern and effective regulatory systems. A series of laws passed during the 1930s—including the Securities Act of 1933, the Securities Exchange Act of 1934, the Public Utility Holding Company Act of 1935, and the Trust Indenture Act of 1939—created a system in which regulation was overseen by the Securities and Exchange Commission (SEC) and the federal courts but was implemented largely through third parties. These included hundreds of thousands of private lawyers and accountants, officials of the New York Stock Exchange and other exchanges, plus the National Association of Securities Dealers (NASD).

During the administration of the Democratic president Bill Clinton, Congress weakened the regulations of the financial sector that had been instituted during the New Deal, most especially by repealing the Glass–Steagall Act, which had separated commercial and investment banking. At the same time, the SEC loosened its regulation of the financial markets and stock exchanges. The economic crisis and recession of 2008–2010, which many blamed on the reforms that had loosened regulation of the financial and banking sectors, led to renewed demands for stricter federal regulation. In 2009 and 2010 the Democratic administration of Barack Obama, with the support of a Democratic congressional majority, tried to do just that. Tighter regulation of banking and finance was reinstituted, and a new agency, the Consumer Financial Protection Bureau, was created to protect consumers from financial and economic market fraud. The SEC was given additional funding to enable it to strengthen its regulation of financial markets. The 2010 congressional elections, however, returned Republicans to majority control of the House of Representatives, and immediately they sought to eviscerate the new regulatory regime and its bureau. Thus in the twenty-first century the ability of the federal government to regulate the financial sector remained hotly contested.

Labor Markets and Conditions of Work.
Efficient, equitable, and flexible labor markets require systematic wage scales, rules for the number of hours and days to be worked, and numerous other regulations. In America, some of these had long been enforced through apprenticeship systems. With industrialization, however, the exploitation of factory labor became commonplace, and it lasted for many decades. During the Progressive Era, most states instituted workers' compensation laws, and some enacted unemployment insurance, but effective national resolution of the labor question awaited the New Deal era. The National Labor Relations Act of 1935 gave organized labor the power to bargain collectively; other laws passed during the 1930s ended child labor, set maximum hours, and established minimum wages.

By the 1990s, antidiscrimination laws designed to protect women, minorities, the handicapped, and others brought additional regulation to the labor market. Then and during the next two decades, however, minimum-wage levels failed to keep up with price inflation, employers increasingly violated wage and hours standards, and the industrial-relations reforms of the New Deal had come to prove more useful to employers than to employees. By the twenty-first century, more than ever, American laws granted fewer benefits to workers than did laws in other countries, especially in western Europe, where employees enjoyed greater job security, longer paid vacations, and generous family benefits.

Product Markets and Competition.

The United States has always had one of the world's most intensely competitive economies. There are many reasons why. For one thing, the entrepreneurial spirit of its ethnically mixed population has been remarkably vigorous. Also, for the first 150 years of the nation's history, few countervailing forces existed to challenge business interests. The United States had no strong guild tradition, no established church, no hereditary aristocracy, and no powerful peacetime military. Until the mid-twentieth century, it had only a minuscule government. All these conditions interacted to intensify business competition.

With the rise of so-called big business in the 1870s and 1880s, state legislatures responded by enacting antitrust legislation. In 1890, Congress passed the landmark Sherman Antitrust Act, which outlawed cartels and monopolies. Since then, the Sherman Act, in combination with the Federal Trade Commission Act and the Clayton Antitrust Act (both passed in 1914), has had mixed results. But on balance, economists conclude that these antitrust measures have increased the level of competition within the American economy. Perhaps the truest index of the effectiveness of U.S. antitrust laws has been their widespread emulation by other nations since World War II.

The Economic Infrastructure.

Active economic regulation has been most conspicu-ous in the areas of transportation, electric utilities, and telecommunications, where conventional competition seemed inadequate to achieve its usual function of automatically regulating prices and quality. The years from the 1870s through the New Deal saw a proliferation of state and federal commissions charged with regulating these industries. First railroads, then gas and electric utilities, streetcars, pipelines, telephones, trucking, and finally airlines came under regulation by public commissions, which oversaw prices and sometimes actually set them. Almost every state established a railroad and utility commission. The most prominent federal agencies were the Interstate Commerce Commission (established in 1887), which regulated first railroads, then pipelines and trucking; the Federal Power Commission (established in 1920, strengthened in 1930, and in the 1980s renamed the Federal Energy Regulatory Commission), which regulated gas and electric utilities; the Federal Communications Commission (established in 1934), which regulated radio, telephones, and television; and the Civil Aeronautics Board (established in 1938), which regulated airlines. This complex regulatory structure proved controversial, however, in part because the "cost-plus" formula employed by regulators in some of these agencies provided little incentive for efficiency for cost cutting, and in part because some of the industries regulated (trucking, for example) had few of the "natural monopoly" characteristics of early railroads and electric utilities. During the years after World War II, and particularly after the economic downturn of the 1970s, the cost-plus type of economic regulation began to be discredited.

Deregulation.

The deregulation movement began in a serious way during the presidential administration of Jimmy Carter. It rapidly gathered force in many industries and spread to other countries as well. During the

1980s, the election of such free-market-oriented politicians as Ronald Reagan in the United States, Margaret Thatcher in the United Kingdom, and Helmut Kohl in Germany underscored the apparent popularity of deregulation. Privatization schemes, moreover, marched alongside deregulation, as governments in Great Britain, Germany, Japan, and several other countries sold nationalized industries to private investors. In the United States, privatization often meant spinning off what had been public functions, such as garbage collection, to private contractors. Meanwhile, deregulation in the federal government included the outright abolition of several agencies, such as the Civil Aeronautics Board and the Interstate Commerce Commission. By the early twenty-first century some of the industries that once were regulated—railroads, trucking, airlines, radio, and television—were largely unregulated, and others, such as electric power and telephones, had been effectively deregulated.

Even earlier, as if to underscore the apparent triumph of free-market economics, the collapse of socialist economies and the breakup of the Soviet bloc at the end of the 1980s seemed to complete the cycle of deregulation and privatization. This development, coupled with the superior growth performance—at first—of capitalist economies, seemed to demonstrate the virtues of minimal regulation. The economic crisis that began in 2008, however, raised grave doubts about the superiority of deregulation and privatization.

Assessment.   By the second decade of the twenty-first century it could clearly be seen to be a mistake to pronounce an end to the need for economic regulation, let alone regulation applying to health, safety, and the environment.

Still, the United States has regulated its economy less than most industrialized countries have done, although it has created large numbers of regulatory agencies. Second, the onset of regulation in America was usually associated with periods of political reform: the Progressive Era, the New Deal, and the New Frontier and Great Society era of the 1960s. Finally, and paradoxically, the enactment of laws related to consumer protection, health and safety, and the environment accelerated during the 1970s and 1980s, an era of economic deregulation. Regulatory bodies such as the Environmental Protection Agency (1970), the Occupational Safety and Health Administration (1970), and the Consumer Product Safety Commission (1972) were created through laws passed during the administration of Richard M. Nixon. These latter laws differed from traditional economic regulation despite their powerful economic impacts. In some respects they resembled Progressive Era legislation such as the Pure Food and Drug Act and the Meat Inspection Act (both passed in 1906) and similar measures having to do with forestry and other environmental concerns. They represented a nonpartisan consensus that people and the environment must be protected from the excesses of the unfettered market. By the second decade of the twenty-first century, however, that consensus had collapsed as significant elements in the business community, libertarian groups, and a united Republican Party fought for looser regulation of the environment and more freedom for mining, oil, natural gas, and pharmaceutical companies.

[*See also* **Antitrust Legislation; Bank of the United States, First and Second; Deregulation, Financial; Economic Deregulation and the Carter Administration; Environmental Regulations; Factory and Hours Laws; Federal Regulatory Agencies; Federal Reserve System; Financial and Banking Promotion and Regulation; Glass–Steagall, Repeal of; Great Society; Industrial Policy, Theory and Practice of; Monetary Policy, Federal; New Deal and Institutional Economics; New Deal Banking**

Regulation; New Deal Corporate Regulation; New Frontier; Public Utility Holding Company Act; Securities and Exchange Commission; State Regulatory Laws; *and* Wartime Economic Regulation.]

BIBLIOGRAPHY

Breyer, Stephen. *Regulation and Its Reform.* Cambridge, Mass.: Harvard University Press, 1982.

Derthick, Martha, and Paul J. Quirk. *The Politics of Deregulation.* Washington, D.C.: Brookings Institution, 1985.

Hawley, Ellis W. *The New Deal and the Problem of Monopoly: A Study in Economic Ambivalence.* Princeton, N.J.: Princeton University Press, 1966.

Hughes, Jonathan R. T. *Social Control in the Colonial Economy.* Charlottesville: University Press of Virginia, 1976.

Kahn, Alfred E. *The Economics of Regulation: Principles and Institutions.* 2 vols. New York: Wiley, 1970–1971.

Keller, Morton. *Regulating a New Economy: Public Policy and Economic Change in America, 1900–1933.* Cambridge, Mass.: Harvard University Press, 1990.

McCraw, Thomas K. *Prophets of Regulation: Charles Francis Adams, Louis D. Brandeis, James M. Landis, Alfred E. Kahn.* Cambridge, Mass.: Belknap Press of Harvard University Press, 1984.

Vietor, Richard H. K. *Contrived Competition: Regulation and Deregulation in America.* Cambridge, Mass.: Belknap Press of Harvard University Press, 1994.

Wilson, James Q., ed. *The Politics of Regulation.* New York: Basic Books, 1980.

Thomas K. McCraw

ECONOMIC THEORIES AND THOUGHT

Writings about economic matters developed in the United States before the emergence of an academic discipline devoted to political economy and economics. As in Britain, U.S. authors devoted an extensive pamphlet literature to the advocacy of economic policies and actions, most particularly as related to monetary issues, employment, and international trade.

Economic Thought in the Early Republic.
Despite the early influence of Adam Smith's *The Wealth of Nations* (1776), Smith's major policies did not become the basis for the organization of the U.S. economy after independence. Instead the programs associated with Alexander Hamilton introduced a system of mercantilism, discarding free trade in favor of tariff protection for manufactured goods. The U.S. Constitution and related legislation defined the government's power over monetary and banking issues, immigration, and land distribution. Differences between the Hamiltonians and the more agrarian followers of Thomas Jefferson on economic policy seem minor compared to their general acceptance of Smithian principles about individualism, choice, and markets. Although economic arguments about the path of economic growth and the distribution of income remained central in the early national era, no discipline emerged in the United States that could be described as economics.

Prior to 1820, colleges subsumed "political economy," as it was generally called until about 1900, into their concern with moral philosophy and the moral study of social problems. The central readings were based on treatises written by Europeans, whether British, such as Adam Smith and John Ramsay McCulloch, or, more important in the first half of the nineteenth century, the Frenchman Jean-Baptiste Say. American editions of European texts often used footnotes to describe how American conditions differed. These references, along with the emerging school of American writers of texts or monographs on economics, substantially revised British economic theory. Few American economists believed in the accuracy of the pessimistic theories about population growth and land rents associated with Thomas Malthus and David Ricardo. American economics reflected the seemingly unlimited amount of land available in the United States and thus evinced a greater optimism concerning the effects of population growth on land rent. Perhaps the most sophisticated of these optimists was the Pennsylvanian Henry Charles Carey, who followed his father Matthew Carey by advocating protective tariffs and using the American experience to invert the principles of Ricardian rent. Carey argued that population density and urbanization offered significant economic returns, presenting a case for reducing the pace of western migration in order to encourage the development of cities and manufacturing industries.

The Elements of Political Economy (1837), by Reverend Francis Wayland, president of Brown University, was the first influential economics textbook published in the United States. Wayland regarded political economy as basically an extension of Christian moral philosophy, which aimed to influence social action by its impact on popular audiences. Though Wayland exemplified the predominant approach down to the Civil War, there was also a Pennsylvania school of protectionists and a southern school, exemplified by Thomas Cooper, that extolled free trade, anticapitalism, and—under certain conditions of land availability and climate—slavery.

Economics as a University-Based Discipline.

The professionalization of economics as an academic subject came in the last third of the nineteenth century, under the influence of scholars who had studied in Germany, often with members of the German historical school. These scholars, the most important of whom in influencing the direction taken by economists was Richard T. Ely of Johns Hopkins University

and, after 1892, the University of Wisconsin, maintained the antebellum interest in social reform, which they now based on Christian socialism. They also maintained the goal of educating the masses, and often they involved themselves in nonacademic organizations to reach a wider audience. When the American Economic Association was formed in 1885, with Francis A. Walker of the Massachusetts Institute of Technology as president and Ely as secretary, its founders attempted to broaden the membership to include businessmen, government officials, and other members of the public. Though more professional economists emphasized empirical research, most aimed the research to advance social reforms that they advocated.

In the late nineteenth century, many colleges and universities introduced programs in economics. Subsequently, programs in political science (government) emerged as a separate academic discipline. Academic journals devoted to economics appeared in the 1880s. An increasing concern with empirical research, theory, and scientific approaches did not mean a loss of interest in social reform, but rather a shift in the strategy of influencing public policy toward bringing the presumed expertise of the academic economists to bear upon public officials. Economists now served in government regulatory agencies, testified before legislative and investigative bodies, and designed state and municipal tax structures. In the years before World War I, academic economists were central in the drafting of the Federal Reserve System, tariff policy and its implementation, and other forms of national economic regulation. At the state level, the University of Wisconsin economist John R. Commons promoted the so-called Wisconsin Idea, by which economists and other specialists would work with legislators in the shaping of public policy. World War I saw an expanded use of economists in the national government, particularly at the War Industries Board.

In the first three decades of the twentieth century the discipline of economics assumed its present shape. Economics became mainly an academic discipline, with teaching and research primarily at colleges and universities—although, as befit a field dealing with real-world issues, a nonacademic fringe of policy advocates always existed. Economists developed a standard corpus of microeconomic theory, first in prose, then geometrically, and later mathematically. They gave more attention to collecting empirical and quantitative data concerning the economy, a trend boosted by the formation of the National Bureau of Economic Research (NBER) in 1920, under the leadership of Edwin F. Gay, a Harvard economic historian. Its director of research, the Columbia University economist Wesley C. Mitchell, whose major research focused on the economic problem of the business cycle, led the NBER to collect and analyze large bodies of quantitative data. Despite a new emphasis on theoretical and empirical matters, economists still sought to influence public policy by demonstrating their importance to political elites. Economists often participated in government economic commissions in the 1920s.

The Keynesian Revolution. The Great Depression of the 1930s led to some disillusionment with the standard economic models, particularly when the decline persisted for longer than had earlier economic downturns. Thus the analysis of the British economist John Maynard Keynes attracted considerable attention, and under the influence of the Harvard economist Alvin Hansen and his students, including Paul Samuelson, Keynesianism dominated macroeconomic theory in the 1940s and 1950s. Keynes modified the standard classical model, but more important for policy purposes, he presented an argument for an activist government role in the economy, including the use of government tax and expenditure changes to influence the economy. It is unclear whether or not Keynes actually influenced U.S. economic policy in the 1930s, but the so-called Keynesian revolution clearly had a major impact upon the discipline.

The interest in using the government as an active agent in influencing the economy placed a premium on the acquisition of reliable information about economic conditions. Though data of various types had long been collected by government agencies and as part of the decennial censuses, the 1930s saw the beginnings of the government's collection of monthly data on unemployment and prices and also of quarterly data on national income and output. Though the concept of national income was long known, and several American writers presented estimates in the nineteenth century, only with the work of Simon Kuznets in the 1930s was the concept clarified and detailed methods of implementation and measurement devised. The government's measures of national income subsequently featured in wartime debates about military mobilization. The 1930s thus saw a marked increase in the number of government regulatory agencies and organizations for statistical collection, often using economists, a tendency further accelerated during World War II. Economists continued the time-honored tradition of disagreeing with each other, at times causing negative public and political reactions. Some criticized economists for being too certain about their arguments, while others, like President Harry S. Truman, expressed frustration over economists' equivocation, preferring what he referred to as "a one-armed economist"—that is, one who would never say "on the other hand."

At the end of World War II, reflecting Keynesian influence, Congress passed the Employment Act of 1946, which included a provision for a Council of Economic Advisers to collect and prepare data for the president and issue an annual economic report. The precise nature and impact of this council has changed over time, reflecting political and personal factors, but it did make economists—who in most cases served only briefly, on leave from academic positions—central to policy debates and, over time, led to more positions for economists in government agencies. Although microeconomic theory continued to become more mathematical and abstract, in the years after 1950 economists and economic knowledge became more highly valued by business, governments, and international agencies, and economics came to play a role in the study of political science and law. Under the theoretical and empirical critiques of Milton Friedman and others, especially at the University of Chicago, macroeconomics shifted away from the Keynesianism of the 1950s toward a focus on monetary forces and the ability of markets to adapt to changing conditions.

Dominance of the Chicago School.
From the 1980s to 2008, the theories associated with Friedman and the Chicago school of economics replaced the Keynesianism that dominated economics and public policy from World War II into the 1970s. As President Ronald Reagan said so often, government was the problem, not the solution. Better that free markets, not government bureaucrats, decide the allocation of resources and the actions of producers and consumers. All that government need do, primarily through the Federal Reserve Board, was pursue a monetary policy that promoted economic growth without unleashing inflation; the markets would take care of the rest. The prevailing economic credo asserted that government regulation of business undermined confidence and investment, thus sacrificing jobs. Lowering progressive taxes on the wealthy and cutting taxes on dividends and capital gains would lead to greater investment, more rapid economic growth, and the creation of jobs. Economists who still subscribed to Keynesian principles might carp from the sidelines, but they had little influence on public policy and diminished influence among academic economists. And in the United States, unlike in many other nations, Marxist and social democratic economists were few in number and widely ignored.

The economic crisis of 2008–2010 brought the theories of the Chicago school and free-market advocates into some disrepute. Keynesianism staged a revival of sorts as many economists urged strong government action to combat the crisis, restore economic growth, and reduce unemployment. A reaction also developed against the free market and against low tax policies that critics alleged produced the enormous inequality that had come to characterize the American economy. Thus despite heated and revived disagreements among economists about theory and policy, economics will continue to influence public policy and adjust its principles according to both what has been established as basic empirical reality and also what changed conditions might demand.

[*See also* **American Economic Association and the New Economics; Behavioral Economics; Berle, Adolf, and Gardiner Means and the Modern Corporation; Business Cycles; Capitalism; Friedman, Milton, and the Chicago School of Economics; Gallatin, Albert, and Economic Development; Hamilton, Alexander, and Economic Development; Institutional and Historical Economics; Keynesian Economics; Laissez-Faire and Classical Economics; Long Swings and Cycles in Economic Growth; Marxian Economics; Mercantilism; Monetarism; National Bureau of Economic Research; Neoclassical Economics; Neoliberalism as Public Economic Policy; New Deal and Institutional Economics; New Left Economics; Okun, Arthur, and Inequality; Supply-Side Economics; Technocracy; *and* Wisconsin School of Economics.**]

BIBLIOGRAPHY

Barber, William J. *Designs within Disorder: Franklin D. Roosevelt, the Economists, and the Shaping of*

American Economic Policy, 1933–1945. Cambridge, U.K.: Cambridge University Press, 1996.

Barber, William J. *From New Era to New Deal: Herbert Hoover, the Economists, and American Economic Policy, 1921–1933.* Cambridge, U.K.: Cambridge University Press, 1985.

Barber, William J., ed. *Breaking the Academic Mould: Economists and American Higher Learning in the Nineteenth Century.* Middletown, Conn.: Wesleyan University Press, 1988.

Church, Robert L. "Economists as Experts: The Rise of an Academic Profession in America 1870–1917." In *The University in Society*, edited by Lawrence Stone, vol. 2, pp. 571–609. Princeton, N.J.: Princeton University Press, 1974.

Conkin, Paul K. *Prophets of Prosperity: America's First Political Economists.* Bloomington: Indiana University Press, 1980.

Dorfman, Joseph. *The Economic Mind in American Civilization.* 5 vols. New York: Viking, 1946–1959.

Furner, Mary O. *Advocacy and Objectivity: A Crisis in the Professionalization of American Political Science, 1865–1905.* New ed. New Brunswick, N.J.: Transaction, 2011.

Furner, Mary O., and Barry Supple, eds. *The State and Economic Knowledge: The American and British Experiences.* Cambridge, U.K.: Cambridge University Press, 1990.

O'Connor, Michael Joseph Lalor. *Origins of Academic Economics in the United States.* New York: Columbia University Press, 1944.

Parrish, John B. "Rise of Economics as an Academic Discipline: The Formative Years to 1900." *Southern Economic Journal* 34 (July 1967): 1–16.

Stein, Herbert S. *The Fiscal Revolution in America.* Chicago: University of Chicago Press, 1969.

Stanley L. Engerman

EDUCATION AND HUMAN CAPITAL

Despite its late start, the United States rapidly came to lead the rest of the world in the educational attainment of its population. Many scholars attribute the nation's exceptional economic success to its high level of investment in education. By the standard of per capita primary-school enrollment, the United States was the best-educated nation in the world by the 1840s. Scholars have debated the factors driving the rapid growth of the American school system: some, such as Nancy Beadie, have emphasized the private provision of education in response to market forces, whereas others, such as Peter Lindert, have emphasized strong local support for tax-funded public education. Relative to other nations, schooling in the United States was from its earliest years highly decentralized in both its funding and its decision making. Decentralization may have contributed to the system's rapid growth, through the greater willingness of relatively homogenous small communities to fund the education of their children. Most scholars agree that by the middle of the nineteenth century, U.S. schooling rates were exceptionally high by world standards, primarily thanks to the broad diffusion of locally controlled, tax-funded public schools.

In the twentieth century, the United States widened its lead in education through the expansion of secondary and higher (tertiary) education. Technological change had created demand for a literate and numerate labor force, accelerating the spread of secondary education. The so-called high school movement took off so rapidly in the early decades of the century that by 1940 the majority of American youth had completed high school. Increased secondary-school completion rates fed higher rates of college attendance. The 1944 Servicemen's Readjustment Act and the 1952 Veterans' Readjustment Act—better known as the GI Bills—that funded college for World War II and Korean War veterans also significantly broadened access to higher education. Twentieth-century growth in the demand for college education was met by the expansion of the public sector of the higher-education system relative to the private sector.

By comparison with European educational systems, the U.S. educational system was quite egalitarian from the outset, emphasizing the broad provision of a common level of education. An unfortunate exception, however, was the denial of education to African Americans. One of the earliest laws in the colonies, the 1740 South Carolina slave code, explicitly prohibited the education of slaves. The legacy of slavery outlasted abolition: separate education by race was legally required in all of the southern states until the mid-twentieth century. Only with the 1954 Supreme Court decision in *Brown v. Board of Education* and the passage of the 1964 Civil Rights Act did the nation take a clear stance regarding the unconstitutionality of de jure racial segregation.

With regard to women, coeducation by gender was the norm in primary and secondary education from early in the nation's history. The exception was higher education, where many of the nation's most elite universities remained single-sex and where men significantly outnumbered women until the late 1960s. During the 1960s and 1970s, the most prominent men's universities opened their doors to women, and women's overall enrollment in college and professional schools rose sharply. By the 1980s, women's enrollment in higher education exceeded that of men. Women's increased participation in higher education reflected and reinforced their increased participation in the labor force.

[*See also* **Worker Colleges and Education.**]

BIBLIOGRAPHY

Beadie, Nancy. *Education and the Creation of Capital in the Early American Republic.* Cambridge, U.K.: Cambridge University Press, 2010. A case study of the development of the first schools in Lima, New York, which illustrates the economic, political, religious and social dynamics of the early development of a school system.

Goldin, Claudia, and Lawrence F. Katz. *The Race between Education and Technology.* Cambridge, Mass.: Belknap Press of Harvard University Press, 2008. A definitive economic history of American education.

Lindert, Peter H. *Growing Public: Social Spending and Economic Growth since the Early Eighteenth Century.* Cambridge, U.K.: Cambridge University Press, 2004. An international comparison of public education and its funding.

Stacey M. Jones

EIGHT-HOUR DAY

Modern industrialism itself generates the notion of limiting the workday by law or contract, because industrialism separates workplaces from households and their rhythms and uses clock time to demarcate wage labor from other parts of daily life. By the 1840s, labor movements promoted a ten-hour standard. Shifts of twelve hours were then commonplace. In textiles and many other trades, workdays extended sixteen hours. Bakers and brewers regularly worked hundred-hour weeks until the late 1800s.

After the Civil War a Boston machinist, Ira Steward, and the National Labor Union popularized eight hours, a commonsense division of the day into three parts: eight hours each for work, rest, and leisure and other forms of personal activity. Arguments were humanitarian and political: all citizens in a democratic society needed time and energy to improve their minds and engage in civic affairs. By 1868, eight states and the federal government passed eight-hour laws, but the laws had numerous loopholes and weak enforcement provisions. In Chicago on 1 May in 1867 and 1886, workers popularized May Day as their holiday by staging massive rallies for the eight-hour day. The infamous Haymarket bombing three days after that second rally briefly discredited the movement for eight-hour legislation. Unions in the American Federation of Labor (AFL) sought instead to secure eight- or-nine-hour workdays through negotiation with employers in construction, mining, machine shops, printing, and other highly organized crafts. This contributed to a downward trend in hours from an average of sixty a week in 1890 to fifty-five in 1915. Yet shifts of twelve hours or more remained common, and not just in obscure canneries and sweatshops. Once unions were driven from the steel industry during the 1890s, U.S. Steel vigorously defended its twelve-hour day and seven-day week.

The U.S. Supreme Court overturned ten-hour legislation for bakery workers in *Lochner v. New York* (1905) but sustained such legislation for women in *Muller v. Oregon* (1908). By 1908 the Democratic Party wrote the eight-hour day into its platform. Reform-minded businesses behind the National Civic Federation offered tepid support for shorter hours. The conservative National Association of Manufacturers resisted even such halfhearted support. In 1914, Henry Ford conspicuously implemented an eight-hour day. Congress extended it to interstate railroad workers in the 1916 Adamson Act. In upholding this law a year later, the Supreme Court recognized Congress's authority to limit working hours for employees directly engaged in interstate commerce.

During World War I, potential labor shortages enabled the AFL to push the issue. To avoid strikes and maintain production, the National War Labor Board pressured employers to shorten the workday. By 1919 the average workweek decreased to fifty-one hours. Yet numerous industries retained long workdays, a central point of contention during the angry strike wave of 1919. Adverse public opinion finally forced U.S. Steel to adopt eight-hour shifts in 1923. By the onset of the Great Depression, more than 45 percent of industrial workers labored at most forty-eight hours per week, and nearly 77 percent

labored at most fifty-four hours. The New Deal's work-sharing proposals and unionization drives culminated in the Fair Labor Standards Act of 1938, which with exceptions—for example, retail and agricultural workers—mandated a standard of eight hours and time-and-a-half pay for overtime.

[*See also* Adamson Act; Factory and Hours Laws; Fair Labor Standards Act; Five-Dollar Day; *Lochner v. New York*; *Muller v. Oregon, and* Strikes.]

BIBLIOGRAPHY

Currarino, Rosanne. "'To Taste of Life's Sweets': The Eight-Hour Movement and the Origins of Modern Liberalism." *Labor's Heritage* 12 (2004): 22–33.

Grossman, Jonathan. "Fair Labor Standards Act of 1938: Maximum Struggle for a Minimum Wage." *Monthly Labor Review* 101 (1978): 22–30.

Roediger, David, and Philip S. Foner. *Our Own Time: A History of American Labor and the Working Day*. New York: Greenwood, 1989.

Alan Lessoff

ELECTRICITY AND ELECTRIFICATION

Electricity—so named by the Englishman William Gilbert around 1600—was known since ancient times in the form of static electricity, which can be induced by rubbing amber, for example. From the seventeenth century onward, such scientists as Robert Boyle, Henry Cavendish, Alessandro Volta, G. S. Ohm, and the American Benjamin Franklin added to electrical knowledge. Franklin, whose *Experiments and Observations on Electricity* (1751–1753) won international attention, is best remembered for his 1752 experiment with a kite and a key in a thunderstorm, which demonstrated that lightning is an electrical discharge. By the early nineteenth century, Michael Faraday and other scientists were developing techniques of generating electricity. Working independently of Faraday, the American Joseph Henry began research on electromagnetism in 1827. Henry constructed an electromagnetic motor in 1829 and later discovered electrical induction, crucial to generating power, and demonstrated the oscillatory nature of electrical discharges.

Practical applications came slowly and piecemeal, long before anyone conceived of electrification as a universalizing process. Most early electrical technologies, including fire-alarm systems, railway signaling, burglar alarms, doorbells, servant-calling systems, and the telephone, were modifications of the telegraph (1838). These devices relied on batteries to supply a modest direct current. A much more powerful current was needed for practical lighting, heating, electroplating, and electric motors. Such applications developed only after about 1875, when improved generators and dynamos became available. After 1878, arc lighting, a powerful but crude form of illumination, drew crowds to demonstrations in city centers and expositions. Large cities quickly adopted lights for streets and public places such as theaters and department stores. Once Thomas Edison's firm installed incandescent lighting systems across the country, beginning in New York City in 1881, however, most indoor sites and street-lighting companies chose his technology. Edison and his assistants developed not only a practical incandescent lightbulb (1879), but also the now familiar system of wiring, wall switches, sockets, meters, insulated transmission lines, and central power plants. Edison designed this distribution system to compete with gaslight on price, while offering brighter and safer illumination. Rapidly adopted by the wealthy for fashionable indoor venues, including theaters, clubs, expensive homes, and the New York Stock Exchange, electric lighting became a prestigious and sought-after form of illumination.

Initially electrical technology had a separate energy source, as well as different financial backers. Lighting utilities, factories, and street-car lines maintained their own power plants and delivery systems, with no uniform standards for wiring or current. The private systems installed by hotels, skyscrapers, and large private homes in the 1880s were incompatible with one another, but they did have the advantage of not requiring overhead wires—which soon became so numerous in the major cities as to constitute a public nuisance—or costly underground conduits. This pattern of development merely continued the earlier piecemeal commercialization of electricity.

Commercial Development and Standardization.

The electrical industry was the most dynamic sector of the economy between 1875 and 1900, growing into a $200-million-a-year industry with the backing of farsighted investors like J. P. Morgan, who financed Edison's work. Once commercial development began, a flurry of mergers reduced the field from fifteen competitors in 1885 to only General Electric and Westinghouse in 1892. Railroads, once America's largest corporations, were now a mature industry, in contrast to the rapidly expanding electric traction companies, local utilities, and equipment manufacturers that collectively exemplified the spread of managerial capitalism (as opposed to partnerships and family firms). From its inception, the electrical industry also relied heavily on scientific research and development, a fact formalized when General Electric founded the first corporate research laboratory in 1900.

Electric trolleys, eagerly sought by burgeoning cities to replace dirty, slow horsecars, became practical after 1887 when Frank Sprague's new motor proved itself in hilly Richmond, Virginia. By 1890, two hundred cities had ordered similar systems. By 1902, $2 billion had been invested in electric railways, and a typical urban family of four spent about $50 a year on fares.

Electricity spread into factories with equal speed, starting with lighting in textile and flour mills. From a worker's point of view, incandescent lighting improved visibility and reduced pollution and the danger of fire, but it also made possible round-the-clock shifts. Furthermore, as electric motors and cranes provided more horsepower for production, they brought radical changes in the construction and layout of factories, most strikingly in Henry Ford's assembly line (1912), an innovation partly anticipated by Edison's experiments with automating iron mining in the 1890s. The assembly line was literally impossible in any complex industry before electricity freed machines from fixed, steam-driven overhead drive shafts.

As electrical systems spread throughout the industrial, commercial, and residential worlds, utilities improved the technologies for generating power and achieved economies of scale. They began to sell current and service so cheaply that the myriad small plants could no longer compete. Samuel Insull of Chicago early grasped the importance of consolidating power production and maximizing consumption. Insull convinced traction companies and factories to abandon their power plants and to purchase electricity from him. Through astute marketing he created one of the world's largest electrical utilities. As others copied his methods, holding companies created regional power companies and linked the many local systems into a national power grid. Private companies proved more agile in the consolidation process, for they possessed readier access to capital and had fewer jurisdictional problems than government-run utilities did, and by the 1920s they owned all but a fraction of national generating capacity.

Between the 1880s and the 1940s the spread of electrification, first in cities and towns and then in rural areas, provided a major economic stimulus and transformed everyday life. An array of electric appliances—from fans and mixers to vacuum cleaners, refrigerators, and washing machines—eased domestic labor for middle-class housewives, while a different form of electric power, the storage battery, was crucial to automotive technology. Electricity made possible not only the automotive and aviation industries, but also the new mass media—radio, films, and recordings—as well as night baseball, introduced in Cincinnati, Ohio, in 1935.

During the Depression of the 1930s, the federal government promoted public utilities, in part to create a yardstick to measure the price and performance of private power companies. The government built a system of dams on the Tennessee River—administered by the Tennessee Valley Authority (TVA), which sold power to rural cooperatives—as well as systems of dams on the Colorado and Columbia Rivers. Because private power had generally ignored farmers, only 10 percent of whom had electricity as late as 1935, President Franklin Delano Roosevelt in 1935 established the Rural Electrification Administration (REA) to bring power to this neglected sector of the nation. Rural electrification spread comparatively slowly in the South and Middle West, where customers were widely dispersed, but more rapidly in the arid West, where farmers wanted electric pumps for irrigation, and in areas served by interurban trolleys. The REA and the TVA organized cooperatives and made available loans and technical expertise. By 1945, thanks to the New Deal, most of America was electrified. Electricity had important military applications as well, playing a crucial role in World War II and the Cold War era—for example, in the development of radar, rocketry, and the mainframe computers essential to ballistic missiles and space technology.

Changes beyond the Functional. Electric lighting dominated public spaces and changed the culture in ways that went far beyond the functional. American cities became the most intensively lighted in the world, not least because of the spread of electric advertising. Spurred by the marketing campaigns of Westinghouse, General Electric, and the utilities, the illuminated skyline became a source of civic pride. Even small cities aspired to emulate New York City's "Great White Way," where millions of flashing bulbs in Times Square and the theater district created a scintillating artificial environment. Nightlife expanded as hundreds of brightly lit amusement parks emerged as early as the 1890s, followed by stadiums and other outdoor venues.

As early as 1903, American cities were far more brightly lit than their European counterparts: Chicago, New York, and Boston had three to five times as many electric lights per inhabitant as Paris, London, and Berlin. This indicated more than prosperity and wealth. Levels and methods of lighting varied from culture to culture, and what was considered dramatic and necessary in the United States often seemed a violation of tradition elsewhere. Many European communities continued throughout the twentieth century to resist electric signs and spectacular advertising displays. At the 1994 Winter Olympics in Lillehammer, Norway, for example, the city council refused corporate sponsors the right to erect illuminated signs.

Once American families acquired electrical lighting, they had less reason to cluster at night around the hearth, giving rise to a pattern of dispersed privacy. With power available at the flick of a switch, consumers ceased to associate lighting with physical work such as hauling wood and ashes or cleaning lamps. Electricity also extended the range of usable space. Domestic activity after sunset was no longer confined to the hearth and the range of the kerosene lamp. In commerce, immense department stores, office buildings, and eventually malls could be built with adequate illumination far from any natural light source.

In industry, the flexibility of electrical power permitted the rearrangement of the work flow, and the expansion of the electrical grid made it possible to locate a factory virtually anywhere, without regard for proximity to coal supplies or waterpower. Further, because not only factories but also shops, homes, and businesses could spring up wherever the grid reached, electrification facilitated urban deconcentration. By the 1930s this trend was being assisted by the development of air-conditioning and climate control, and later it was assisted by computers and the electrical transmission of information.

But if electrification homogenized space, delivering light, power, climate control, and information to any site, it also facilitated the concentration of people in cities. Indeed, night satellite photographs of the United States reveal the location of thousands of cities as intense blobs of light. Electricity, a scientific curiosity in 1800 and still a novelty for the rich in 1880, had become indispensable by the mid-twentieth century and beyond.

Although electricity remained indispensable as the twentieth century passed into the twenty-first century, the steady growth of its use raised critical environmental concerns. Utilities commonly produced electricity by burning soft coal, a process that spewed greenhouse gases into the atmosphere and contributed to global warming. To limit utilities' tendency to worsen pollution, the federal Environmental Protection Agency, acting on congressional legislation, issued rules requiring power companies to install expensive new equipment at existing plants in order to reduce toxic emissions, or else to build new plants that had equipment that reduced such emissions. Because these rules increased substantially the cost of electricity generation, utilities fought their implementation—and they had some success. By and large, however, utilities responded to environmental concerns by switching from coal to natural gas, a cleaner, less-polluting resource, especially as the supply of gas rose and its price dropped. The use of waterpower and solar power, clean and sustainable alternatives to coal and natural gas, also expanded.

Electricity also found a new, old use in its application to powering automobiles. Here, too, concern about the environment and the fact that gas-powered internal combustion engines were a major contributor to the release of greenhouse gases led automobile companies to produce hybrid cars that used both gas engines and electric batteries and also to experiment with and begin to produce all-electric automobiles. Although hybrids and all-electric cars were far more expensive than internal combustion models and lacked the range in mileage of gas-powered vehicles, federal tax rebates partly subsidized their cost for consumers who were eager to play their role as environmentalists. Because modern societies and economies cannot function without the ready availability of electricity, its continued generation poses environmental, political, and social concerns and conflicts.

[*See also* **Automotive Industry; Communications Revolution; General Electric; Household Technology and Domestic Labor; Hydroelectric Power; Insull, Samuel; New Deal and Institutional Economics; Renewable Energy and Climate Change; Technology; Tennessee Valley Authority;** *and* **Westinghouse, George.**]

BIBLIOGRAPHY

Hughes, Thomas P. *Networks of Power: Electrification in Western Society, 1880–1930*. Baltimore: Johns Hopkins University Press, 1983.

Nye, David E. *Electrifying America: Social Meanings of a New Technology, 1880–1940*. Cambridge, Mass.: MIT Press, 1990.

Platt, Harold L. *The Electric City: Energy and the Growth of the Chicago Area, 1880–1930*. Chicago: University of Chicago Press, 1991.

Rose, Mark H. *Cities of Light and Heat: Domesticating Gas and Electricity in Urban America*. University Park: Pennsylvania State University Press, 1995.

Rudolph, Richard, and Scott Ridley. *Power Struggle: The Hundred-Year War over Electricity*. New York: Harper & Row, 1986.

Tobey, Ronald C. *Technology as Freedom: The New Deal and the Electrical Modernization of the American Home*. Berkeley: University of California Press, 1996.

David E. Nye

EMPLOYEE FREE CHOICE ACT

From 2005 to 2010, unions and progressives sought passage of the Employee Free Choice Act (EFCA), which would have marked the first significant change in federal labor law in sixty years.

The bill originated from the recognition that federal labor law was in urgent need of reform. Polling suggested that although more than 40 million nonunion workers wished that they were represented by a union, less than 100,000 employees a year were succeeding at creating new unions through the process run by the National Labor Relations Board. This discrepancy had two primary causes: the undemocratic nature of election procedures—which resemble those of totalitarian ruling parties in foreign regimes whose elections the U.S. government condemns as illegitimate—and the fact that the penalty for employers who violate federal labor law is extremely slight, with no provision for punitive damages.

The EFCA proposed three changes: a mandate that employers recognize unions whenever a majority of employees present verified signed statements indicating their desire to bargain collectively; increased penalties for lawbreaking; and third-party arbitration whenever employees and employers are unable to agree on terms for a first contract.

The EFCA was the object of visceral and extremely well-funded corporate opposition. It passed the House of Representatives in 2007 but died in the Senate after President George W. Bush threatened a veto. The election of Barack Obama in 2008 revived the bill. But in 2009, every Senate Republican opposed the bill, and when Democrats lost their filibuster-proof majority in late 2009, the bill was doomed.

[*See also* **National Labor Relations Board; Repression of Unions;** *and* **Unionization Rates.**]

BIBLIOGRAPHY

Bronfenbrenner, Kate. "No Holds Barred: The Intensification of Employer Opposition to Organizing." Economic Policy Institute Briefing Paper no. 235, 20 May 2009. Available at http://www.epi.org/publication/bp235.

Lafer, Gordon. "What's More Democratic Than a Secret Ballot? The Case for Majority Sign-Up." *WorkingUSA: The Journal of Labor and Society* 11 (March 2008): 71–98.

Gordon Lafer

EMPLOYEE REPRESENTATION PLANS

Employee representation plans (ERPs) were organizations created by companies in order to give some of the rights and bargaining abilities associated with independent unions to unrepresented workers without the companies' having to recognize such independent unions. Supporters of organized labor often referred to ERPs as "company unions," but that term does not describe all such organizations accurately. To understand the difference, it is best to think of a sliding scale with independent unions on one side and employer-dominated company unions on the other. Employee representation plans fell somewhere in the middle, because these arrangements often made important concessions to workers and sometimes even stimulated the growth of independent unions in the workplace. This distinction became irrelevant in 1935, however, when Section 8(a)(2) of the National Labor Relations Act outlawed employer-dominated labor organizations of all kinds, no matter how benevolent such an organization might be.

Determining the first employee representation plan is an impossible task. The first ERP to attract national attention, however, was the Rockefeller Plan at the Colorado Fuel and Iron Company (CF&I). This plan was written by a future prime minister of Canada, W. L. Mackenzie King, at the behest of John D. Rockefeller Jr. Rockefeller had been blamed for the Ludlow massacre of April 1914—in which striking miners at Ludlow, Colorado, were attacked, and a number were killed, by the Colorado National Guard—and to prevent future tragedies, he wanted to give CF&I miners some voice over their terms and conditions of employment: then, he hoped, they would not have to turn to the United Mine Workers of America for assistance. Unlike the authoritarian company unions of the 1930s, Rockefeller's organization ceded real power to CF&I workers. For instance, disgruntled miners often reversed their own firing by turning to the ERP and even appealed their cases beyond the president of the company to an outside state agency.

The Rockefeller Plan was an important precedent for employee representation plans mandated by the National War Labor Board (NWLB) during World War I. An important part of the NWLB's mission was to maintain the peace in factories with government contracts so that labor strife did not harm the war effort. The NWLB called these organizations "shop committees," and it mandated the creation of these organizations 125 times during its brief existence. In some cases, as in the munitions plants of Bridgeport, Connecticut, previously nonunion employers agreed to abide by the NWLB's order, and workers used shop committees to organize and win important concessions. In other cases, most notably at the Bethlehem Steel Company in Pennsylvania, management stalled long enough to prevent independent ERPs from taking shape. Either way, the existence of a war emergency played a vital role in the creation of employee representation plans because it meant that a government board existed to guarantee whatever rights workers enjoyed under these organizations. Indeed, NWLB representatives were often on-site watching ERPs function. Once the war ended, many of these government-mandated ERPs morphed into company unions or simply disappeared.

With the election of Franklin D. Roosevelt as president and the passage of new legislation related to labor organizing, employee representation plans made a comeback as a way for companies to fulfill the letter of the law without having to recognize an independent union. Roosevelt himself undercut the weak language of the National Industrial Recovery Act (NIRA), suggesting that the government would not force anyone to join or recognize a union. As a result, approximately 2.5 million American workers were represented by some form of ERP by early 1935. The National Labor Relations Act of 1935 (NLRA) was much more explicit than the NIRA, making it illegal for an employer "to dominate or interfere with the formation or administration of any labor organization or contribute financial or other support to it." Many employers ignored the provisions of the act, expecting it to be invalidated by the Supreme Court. Once the Supreme Court, through its decision in 1937 in *National Labor*

Relations Board v. Jones & Laughlin Steel Corp., gave its approval to the NLRA, the National Labor Relations Board rightfully invalidated many company unions under Section 8(a)(2) of the law.

Some employee representation plans escaped this fate by transforming themselves into independent labor unions not affiliated with national organizations. They could do so only when management willingly gave them autonomy sufficient to survive NLRB scrutiny. One prominent example was the ERP at Thompson Products, ruled a "company union" by the NLRB in 1942, prompting management eventually to sever its ties with the union. The newly independent organization proved popular enough to resist repeated organizing attempts by the United Auto Workers. Other ERPs or company unions of this era were captured from within by union partisans. This happened most prominently at United States Steel in 1937. Members of the Steel Workers Organizing Committee (SWOC) captured the ERP. In and out of meetings, they argued that every concession that management made happened only because of the existence of their union-organizing campaign. This strategy proved so successful that U.S. Steel recognized the SWOC without a strike or a legal mandate to do so.

Though some organizations that share a few traits with employee representation plans exist in twenty-first-century American factories, most are not nearly as powerful or useful as the liberal-minded ERPs of the pre–National Labor Relations Act era. In 1989 the NLRB ruled on the legality of joint labor-management action committees at the electrical parts manufacturer Electromation, Inc. The Teamsters filed an NLRB complaint against these committees, charging that they violated Section 8(a)(2) of the NLRA. The NLRB upheld a law judge's ruling that the committees were "labor organizations" and ordered them disbanded because they created an illusion of collective bargaining where real collective bargaining did not exist. As a result of this reasoning, half measures are not acceptable in the American workplace. Workers are left with two choices: join an independent union or have no representation at all. Many other countries, including Canada, Germany, and Australia, continue to permit employee representation plans, and they play a major role in their industrial relations systems.

[*See also* **Company Unions; National Labor Relations Board;** *National Labor Relations Board v. Jones & Laughlin Steel Corp.*; **National Labor Relations (Wagner) Act; National War Labor Board, World War I;** *and* **Welfare Capitalism.**]

BIBLIOGRAPHY

Jacoby, Sanford M. *Modern Manors: Welfare Capitalism since the New Deal.* Princeton, N.J.: Princeton University Press, 1997.

Kaufman, Bruce E., and Daphne Gottlieb Taras, eds. *Nonunion Employee Representation: History, Contemporary Practice, and Policy.* Armonk, N.Y.: M. E. Sharpe, 2000.

McCartin, Joseph A. *Labor's Great War: The Struggle for Industrial Democracy and the Origins of Modern American Labor Relations, 1912–1921.* Chapel Hill: University of North Carolina Press, 1997.

Jonathan Rees

EMPLOYMENT ACT OF 1946

The Employment Act of 1946 created the Council of Economic Advisers as part of the White House staff, whose duty was to "formulate and recommend national economic policy" that would further the national goal of "full employment, production, and purchasing power." It reflected the conviction of many liberal policy makers that the greatest economic danger facing the United States after the war was a return to mass unemployment and that the surest way to avoid such a catastrophe was through economic growth. But the law provided no effective tools for achieving its goals, and its supporters soon became disillusioned.

The idea for the bill emerged from the National Resources Planning Board, the New Deal's official planning agency, which in the early 1940s promoted the idea of full employment. The bill also reflected President Franklin Delano Roosevelt's call in 1944 for an "economic bill of rights," which included "the right to a useful and remunerative job." Progressive labor and farm groups were also actively lobbying for legislation to promote government-guaranteed full employment, as were leading Keynesian economists. When the bill was introduced in Congress in January 1945, it was titled the Full Employment Bill; it called for the president to adopt economic policies that would create jobs for all who wanted them. The government would spend money on job-creation programs if the private sector appeared unlikely to generate enough employment. President Harry S. Truman supported the bill after Roosevelt's death in April 1945, as did most congressional New Dealers.

But by 1946, too few New Dealers remained in Congress to enact the original bill. After strenuous opposition from employers, who feared that a full-employment economy would drive up their labor costs, conservatives in Congress so diluted the legislation that many of its early supporters dismissed it as meaningless rhetoric. The phrase "full employment," which had resonated so strongly among liberals in the 1940s, disappeared from both the title and the body of the bill, as did all the specific policy requirements that were to have given the phrase meaning. But the Council of Economic Advisers created by the act did at times influence presidents to choose policies that promoted economic growth. Though the Employment Act did not guarantee full employment, it did help make fiscal policy an important lever of economic planning in the postwar era.

[*See also* **Keynesian Economics; New Deal and Institutional Economics;** *and* **Unemployment.**]

BIBLIOGRAPHY

Bailey, Stephen K. *Congress Makes a Law: The Story behind the Employment Act of 1946.* New York: Columbia University Press, 1950.

Alan Brinkley

EMPLOYMENT-AT-WILL

In the United States, as opposed to European legal systems, the standard employment contract is "at will." Under this rule, employers and employees are free to change the terms of the contract or to terminate it at any time. The most famous statement of the at-will rule dates back to 1884. Deciding the case of a railroad that threatened its employees with dismissal if they did not buy from company stores, the Tennessee Supreme Court noted that employers "may dismiss their employees at will, be they many or few, for good cause, for no cause, or even for cause morally wrong, without being thereby guilty of legal wrong." The important principle here is that of mutuality. As the court explained, it "is a right which an employee may exercise in the same way . . . as the employer. He may refuse employment from a man or company that trades with an obnoxious person, or does other things which he dislikes."

In the late nineteenth century, the United States was in the midst of the Industrial Revolution, and economic liberalism—the faith in an unregulated free market—had become the dominant ideology of the nation. The at-will

rule was part of a political and legal framework designed to foster economic development. On the one hand, it was liberating for workers because they were no longer bound by the strict rules of the old master and servant regime, which allowed employers to forfeit wages if workers quit before the end of a one-year contract. On the other hand, courts often invoked the at-will rule to block attempts to regulate capitalism. In the 1905 case *Lochner v. New York*, the Supreme Court famously ruled that the state of New York violated workers' freedom of contract when it adopted a law limiting the working hours of bakers to sixty a week.

The twentieth century brought serious limitations to the at-will rule and its use. First, corporations developed personnel policies to promote employee attachment. To maintain a stable workforce, they offered job security and encouraged the employees' loyalty through internal promotions. During the New Deal, the federal government created serious exceptions to the rule by adopting laws that encouraged unionism, mandated minimum wages, and fixed maximum numbers of working hours. Later, Title VII of the 1964 Civil Rights Act further limited the freedom of employers by requiring them to treat all their employees equally, regardless of race and gender. Since then, a number of courts and legislatures have extended workers some form of protection against arbitrary dismissals.

In the economic context of the twenty-first century, the at-will rule has regained much of its interest for employers, who have come to put a premium on flexibility and short-term employment relationships and no longer offer promises of job security. Rather, they have increasingly resorted to temporary workers, independent contractors, and on-call workers. Employers have also proved increasingly hostile to unionism. As a result, the collective-bargaining contract, one of the main alternatives to at-will contracts, has become increasingly rare.

[*See also* Collective Bargaining; Freedom of Contract; *Lochner v. New York; and* Master and Servant Law.]

BIBLIOGRAPHY

Muhl, Charles J. "The Employment at Will Doctrine: Three Major Exceptions." *Monthly Labor Review* 124, no. 1 (January 2001): 3–11.

Orren, Karen. *Belated Feudalism: Labor, the Law, and Liberal Development in the United States.* Cambridge, U.K., and New York: Cambridge University Press, 1991.

Stone, Kathryn Van Wezel. "Revisiting the At-Will Employment Doctrine: Imposed Terms, Implied Terms, and the Normative World of the Workplace." *Industrial Law Journal* 36, no. 1 (2007): 84–101.

Jean-Christian Vinel

ENERGY CRISES, LATE TWENTIETH CENTURY

The energy crisis of the 1970s damaged the American economy and decisively affected presidential politics. Retaliating for Western support of Israel in the October 1973 war in the Middle East, Arab members of the Organization of Petroleum Exporting Countries (OPEC) temporarily barred oil sales to the United States and dramatically raised prices for all customers. In six months the price of a barrel of crude oil soared from $3 to $18. President Richard M. Nixon advocated conservation and development of domestic energy sources, and he also signed legislation controlling the prices charged by domestic oil producers. In 1975, Congress rejected President Gerald Ford's proposal to decontrol domestic oil and natural gas to increase supply. Rising energy prices contributed to the economic "stagflation" that cost Ford the 1976 election.

Although President Jimmy Carter called the energy crisis the "moral equivalent of war," Americans remained divided on the causes and cure of the problem. In 1978, Carter secured legislation that fostered conservation and decontrolled the price of some domestic natural gas. The Iranian revolution allowed OPEC again to raise prices rapidly in 1979. As stagflation worsened and lines of angry motorists formed at gas stations, Carter diagnosed a "crisis of confidence" and urged citizens to build their character by coping with austerity. Ridiculed as a prophet of "malaise" and blamed for the sagging economy, Carter lost to Ronald Reagan in 1980. During the early 1980s, conservation, an international recession, and development of new fuel sources brought down energy prices. As memories of the crisis faded, the United States steadily increased its dependence on imported petroleum.

Because of the United States' growing reliance on imported oil, the unsettled political environment of the Middle East throughout the closing decades of the twentieth century and into the twenty-first raised the specter of another oil crisis with escalating fuel prices at the pump and rising energy costs. To combat overreliance on unreliable foreign sources of petroleum, Democratic administrations tended to promote conservation and wiser use of energy resources, whereas Republicans favored easing domestic restraints—for instance, through deregulating the coal, oil, and natural gas industries—and promoting the expansion of domestic drilling and mining. Even the administration of a Democrat, Barack Obama, encouraged increases in the domestic production of energy. The twenty-first century also saw technological innovations in drilling for domestic oil and natural gas: associated with the technique of hydrofracturing, popularly known as "fracking," these innovations created an energy boom in North Dakota and in the Marcellus shale formation of southeastern Ohio, large parts of Pennsylvania, and the Southern Tier of New York State. The boom resulted in falling prices for natural gas and its increasing substitution for oil in the production of energy.

The rise in drilling for oil and natural gas, and especially in the use of fracking, led to increased conflict between energy producers and environmentalists. Environmentalists insisted that fracking imperiled water supplies and threatened other environmental damage and also insisted that expansion of carbon-based energy sources worsened climate change. The continued reliance of the United States on oil imported from turbulent overseas sources and the potential threat to the environment and climate posed by expanded domestic production of carboniferous products meant that energy crises remained a persistent threat for the future.

[*See also* **Economic Deregulation and the Carter Administration; Environmental Regulations; Mining Industry; Petroleum Industry; Renewable Energy and Climate Change;** *and* **Stagflation.**]

BIBLIOGRAPHY

Goodwin, Craufurd D., ed. *Energy Policy in Perspective: Today's Problems, Yesterday's Solutions.* Washington, D.C.: Brookings Institution, 1981.

Tugwell, Franklin. *The Energy Crisis and the American Political Economy: Politics and Markets in the Management of Natural Resources.* Stanford, Calif.: Stanford University Press, 1988.

Leo P. Ribuffo

ENVIRONMENTAL REGULATIONS

Environmental regulation began in the mid-nineteenth century as a pragmatic response to urbanization and industrialization. Visibility and public perceptions were and are key factors in explaining the growth of regulation. Thus, nineteenth-century communities were reasonably successful in reducing contaminated drinking water, less effective in controlling smoke and other air pollutants, and almost wholly ineffective in addressing industrial pollution, notably discharges into river and lakes. Progressive reformers in the early twentieth century extended these initiatives, campaigning against a variety of environmental hazards, but usually in association with broader efforts to improve public health and reform urban government. No regional or national environmental organizations emerged to coordinate or extend these efforts.

A parallel awakening to the often corrupt administration of federally owned lands led to complementary innovations. Responding to widespread abuses, Congress adopted piecemeal reforms, creating national parks, for example, and giving the president the power to set aside forested areas and national monuments. These measures became the basis for an organized conservation movement during the presidency of Theodore Roosevelt. With Roosevelt's support, the chief forester, Gifford Pinchot, introduced systematic natural-resource management based on the regulated use of public resources. By the 1920s, conservation activism had given rise to powerful regional organizations devoted to wildlife protection and outdoor recreation.

The post-1940 economic boom created a host of new environmental issues and led to the most dramatic initiatives in the history of American environmental regulation. The challenges were both quantitative—a larger population, increased production—and qualitative—new scientific and technological discoveries. Science contributed to the problems but also to the public's perception of environmental degradation and the search for solutions. Ecology, emphasizing the interrelatedness of living things, provided the intellectual foundation for a more holistic view of environmental issues. And the seriousness of the problems was brilliantly dramatized by scientists, notably Rachel Carson, whose 1962 book *Silent Spring* exposed the perils of pesticide use. By the mid-1960s, most conservation organizations had added pollution issues to their policy agendas, and many new groups had appeared. Earth Day, 22 April 1970, is generally viewed as a turning point in the mobilization of public support for new regulatory measures.

In the 1950s and early 1960s, states and some cities had taken the lead in restricting environmentally harmful activities. Congress became more active in the mid-1960s, creating new air and water regulations. Responding to mounting public pressure, it adopted landmark regulatory laws in the early 1970s, including the National Environmental Policy Act (1970), the Clean Air Act (1970), the Clean Water Act (1972), and the Endangered Species Act (1973), and President Richard M. Nixon took the first steps toward creating a national environmental regulatory body, the Environmental Protection Agency (EPA). Altogether, Congress enacted twenty-two major environmental laws between 1964 and 1980. Half were aimed at reducing pollution and restoring areas degraded by industrial activity; half were conservation measures that redefined and expanded the activities of federal conservation agencies.

Despite popular support for environmental regulation, most of these measures were controversial and adopted only after extended campaigns. Opponents of environmental regulation seemed to regain the upper hand in 1980 with the election of Ronald Reagan, but after unpopular efforts to reduce regulation and sabotage the EPA, Reagan retreated and was content simply to thwart additional initiatives. In the following decades, political gridlock prevented major changes in the status quo, though the details of environmental regulations were subject to continuous battles. In the meantime the EPA became the largest and arguably the most effective federal regulatory agency. It set standards and maintained a large research staff. Most actual enforcement was undertaken through state-level agencies.

By the mid-1990s the major concerns of the 1970s and 1980s, such as air and water pollution, toxics, and mine reclamation, were increasingly overshadowed by two new concerns: global warming and an accelerating decline in biodiversity. Because both were known primarily through scientists' studies and had yet to result in obvious crises, environmental leaders had difficulty mobilizing support for remedial measures. By 2011, Congress had only begun to address these issues, and it had done so with relatively mild regulations such as increased fuel-economy standards for automobiles and additions to the roster of endangered species.

[*See also* **Federal Regulatory Agencies; Public Land Policy;** *and* **Renewable Energy and Climate Change.**]

BIBLIOGRAPHY

Andrews, Richard N. L. *Managing the Environment, Managing Ourselves: A History of American Environmental Policy.* New Haven, Conn.: Yale University Press, 1999.

Klyza, Christopher McGrory, and David J. Sousa. *American Environmental Policy, 1990–2006: Beyond Gridlock.* Cambridge, Mass.: MIT Press, 2008.

Daniel Nelson

EQUAL PAY ACT

Signed into law by President John F. Kennedy in 1963, the Equal Pay Act (EPA) required that men and women in the same workplace be paid the same wages for jobs requiring substantially equal skill, effort, and responsibility under similar working conditions. As part of the Fair Labor Standards Act of 1938, the EPA excluded many employees, including domestic workers.

During the post–World War II period, working-class women protested dismissals when men returned from war, challenged job segregation, and used leadership roles in unions to influence collective bargaining. Their gender-equity agenda included revaluing—and ending wage discrimination in—women's jobs, securing a living wage, protecting excluded groups, and promoting shorter hours, maternity leave, and child care. They also used governmental channels and pressed for legislation. The labor organizer and union lobbyist Esther Peterson served as the head of the Women's Bureau of the Department of Labor under President Kennedy. Labor women were also instrumental on Kennedy's 1961 President's Commission on the Status of Women.

Rather than seek access to traditionally male blue-collar jobs, labor feminists sought pay equity to raise the wages of traditionally female jobs. A telephone operator did not want to be required to switch to a telephone-line repair job in order to earn comparable wages. Labor feminists thus found themselves at odds with middle-class feminists, who preferred an equal-rights amendment and access to men's professional jobs. Union women and labor feminists like Peterson played a crucial role in getting the EPA passed in 1963. Critics argued that the EPA would not reach women in exempted occupations, that there were no "equal" male jobs for comparison because most women worked in segregated occupations, and that the EPA protected men's jobs by preventing women from under-cutting their wages. Indeed, the EPA barely touched labor women's ultimate goal: equal pay for men and women in jobs requiring comparable levels of skill.

Nevertheless, the EPA was a huge achievement in 1963. Passed without the help of a widespread social movement and in an atmosphere not conducive to women's progress, it required patience and compromise. Passage of the act was a small but important first step that gave women a leading role in the fight for equality. Moreover, it brought equal-rights and labor feminists together politically, despite their different goals. Middle-class women wanted to recognize the value of women's work, and working-class women sought workplace protections while affirming traditional roles. The EPA brought gender inequality in the workplace into the public debate, laying the foundation for the resurgence of the feminist movement in the late 1960s.

Although the feminist movement brought many women into the workforce, it could not eliminate the gender wage gap. In the early 1980s, women pressed for the next step, equal pay for jobs requiring substantially the same, though not identical, skills and responsibility—what was labeled "comparable worth." Lacking support from the administration of Ronald Reagan, advocates turned to the courts and unions. In June 1981 the U.S. Supreme Court ruled that women could compare their pay to that of men holding different jobs, but it did not fully endorse the concept of comparable worth. In September 1983 the American Federation of State, County, and Municipal Employees won a lawsuit against Washington State, which was ordered both to pay $800 million, including retroactive wages, for fifteen thousand workers, and also to establish increased wage scales. Union attorneys applied the same strategies in lawsuits against other large public employers. Minnesota instituted a $42 million plan for state employees and instructed local governments to integrate comparable worth into salary scales by 1987. Despite significant inroads in public-sector jobs, however, comparable worth fizzled as the rise of conservatism and backlash against the women's movement made it difficult to capitalize on early successes. Corporate America resisted any interference with market forces in setting wages.

[*See also* **Fair Labor Standards Act; 9to5 and Women Office Workers;** *and* **Women Workers.**]

BIBLIOGRAPHY

Cobble, Dorothy Sue. *The Other Women's Movement: Workplace Justice and Social Rights in Modern America.* Princeton, N.J.: Princeton University Press, 2004.

Deslippe, Dennis A. *Rights, Not Roses: Unions and the Rise of Working-Class Feminism, 1945–80.* Urbana and Chicago: University of Illinois Press, 2000.

Gabin, Nancy F. *Feminism in the Labor Movement: Women and the United Auto Workers, 1935–1975.* Ithaca, N.Y.: Cornell University Press, 1990.

Kessler-Harris, Alice. *A Woman's Wage: Historical Meanings and Social Consequences.* Lexington: University Press of Kentucky, 1990.

Peterson, Esther, with Winifred Conkling. *Restless: The Memoirs of Labor and Consumer Activist Esther Peterson.* Washington, D.C.: Caring, 1995.

Emily Zuckerman

ERDMAN ACT

Passed by Congress in 1898 and signed into law by President Grover Cleveland, the Erdman Act represented a major turning point in railroad labor relations and an early precedent for government intervention to protect certain basic rights of wage earners in the private sector. The roots of the legislation lay in the little-used Arbitration Act of 1888 and in the rising levels of railroad labor conflict during the 1880s and early 1890s. The formation of the American Railway Union (ARU) and the Pullman strike and boycott that crippled the American economy from Chicago westward for three weeks in late June and July 1894 precipitated new thinking on railroad labor relations.

The architect of the government's intervention to halt the Pullman strike was the former railroad corporation counsel and attorney general of the United States, Richard J. Olney. He authored and became the driving force behind the passage of the Erdman Act, even as he vigorously pursued the prosecution of the ARU leaders, including Eugene V. Debs, for contempt of court during the strike. The U.S. Strike Commission argued for recognizing the railroad brotherhoods "to conserve their usefulness" and "increase their responsibility." Olney himself sought a means by which "ever recurring controversies" between railroad labor and capital might be "adjusted and terminated." Olney's bill, despite a tortuous legislative history between 1895 and 1898, passed with provisions that established machinery for the voluntary arbitration of railroad labor disputes that would be fully enforced by the federal government. Further, it prohibited the practice of blacklisting and the use of yellow-dog contracts to prevent workers from joining unions, and it restricted railroad companies from interfering in other ways with the right of their workers to unionize.

The conservative railroad brotherhoods strongly supported the legislation. Though strikes in the railroad industry persisted and the Erdman Act had limited application, an era of relative labor peace, at least between the operating trades and the major rail lines, ensued. Government efforts to ensure labor peace on the railroads continued in the twentieth century with legislation improving the arbitration process (Newlands Act, 1913), mandating the eight-hour day in the industry (Adamson Act, 1916), and guaranteeing collective-bargaining rights in return for mandatory arbitration (Railway Labor Act, 1926.)

[*See also* Adamson Act; Eight-Hour Day; Railroad Brotherhoods; Railroads; *and* Railway Labor Act.]

BIBLIOGRAPHY

Eggert, Gerald G. *Railroad Labor Disputes: The Beginnings of Federal Strike Policy.* Ann Arbor: University of Michigan Press, 1967.

Eggert, Gerald G. *Richard J. Olney: Evolution of a Statesman.* University Park: Pennsylvania State University Press, 1974.

Huibregtse, Jon R. *American Railroad Labor and the Genesis of the New Deal, 1919–1935.* Gainesville: University Press of Florida, 2010.

Lecht, Leonard A. *Experience under Railway Labor Legislation.* New York: Columbia University Press, 1954.

Stromquist, Shelton. *A Generation of Boomers: The Pattern of Railroad Labor Conflict in Nineteenth-Century America.* Urbana: University of Illinois Press, 1987.

Shelton Stromquist

EXECUTIVE ORDER 10988

President John F. Kennedy issued Executive Order 10988 on 17 January 1962, legalizing collective bargaining for most of the federal workforce. The order was the product of recommendations by the Task Force on Employee–Management Relations, created by Kennedy in June 1961 in response to mounting militancy among federal workers, particularly in the Post Office. Built on the premise that "the efficient administration of the Government and the well-being of employees require that orderly and constructive relationships be maintained between employee organizations and management officials," Executive Order 10988 formally introduced collective bargaining into federal employment. The order established a three-tier system of recognition that granted unions exclusive, formal, or informal status depending on their level of support within a given bargaining unit.

The system of collective bargaining created by Executive Order 10988 was more limited than that prevailing in the private sector. Most important, recognition was denied to organizations that asserted the right to strike, and wages and salaries were excluded from the scope of bargaining. Agreements had to include a strong management-rights provision. Binding arbitration was prohibited. Finally, the order applied to only certain groups of workers, specifically excluding employees of the security services.

In spite of these limitations, the order proved critical in reinforcing and legitimizing the growth of public-sector unionism at all levels of government. Prior to 1962, barely 10 percent of the nation's public employees were unionized. Within four years, nearly a million federal workers were covered by a union contract. By the mid-1970s, twenty-four states had general bargaining laws for public employees. By 2010, public-sector unions had a majority of all union members.

[*See also* Collective Bargaining.]

BIBLIOGRAPHY

Hart, Wilson R. "The U.S. Civil Service Learns to Live with Executive Order 10,988: An Interim Appraisal." *Industrial and Labor Relations Review* 17, no. 2 (January 1964): 203–220.

Slater, Joseph C. *Public Workers: Government Employee Unions, the Law, and the State, 1900–1962.* Ithaca, N.Y.: ILR Press, 2004.

Joseph E. Hower

F

FACTORY AND HOURS LAWS

Factory and hours legislation in the United States developed over a century and a half in response to workers' and reformers' activism. The ten-hours movement of the 1830s had only limited legislative success—an 1840 federal law that established a ten-hour day for workers on federal projects, and an 1852 Ohio law that limited women's hours—but it laid the groundwork for the eight-hour-day movement that began in the 1870s. By then, pressure from organized labor led many states to create bureaus of labor statistics, beginning with Massachusetts in 1869. Continued pressure from labor led to publication of statistics on industrial accidents, illnesses, and dangerous and unhealthy working conditions, which built public support for protective laws. By 1890 more than twenty states had passed some form of factory safety laws, including nine that provided for factory inspectors. The laws' effectiveness, however, varied widely owing to the weak enforcement provisions of many of these laws, legislators' inability or unwillingness to amend laws to account for rapid technological change, and shifts in political leadership.

Growing judicial support for the "liberty of contract" reading of the Fourteenth Amendment further undermined efforts to establish legal protections for factory workers, particularly with respect to hours and wages. In 1895 the New York Bakeshop Act included a provision that no bakery employee could work more than ten hours a day or sixty hours a week.

The U.S. Supreme Court's 1905 decision in *Lochner v. New York* ruled that the law violated the liberty of contract of both the employer and employees. Thereafter advocates of maximum-hours legislation, led by the National Consumers League and the Women's Trade Union League, sought hours laws for women and children only, arguing that women's and children's disadvantages in the labor market, dependent political status, and physical differences from men legitimized their special protection by the state. These activists hoped that gender-based laws would build a legal foundation to establish regulatory laws for male adult workers as well. In its 1908 decision in *Muller v. Oregon*, the U.S. Supreme Court affirmed that the Oregon maximum-hours law for women was a legitimate exercise of the state's police power. By 1919 forty states and the District of Columbia had passed some form of maximum-hours law for women and children. A significant exception to the gender and age limits of Progressive Era hours laws was the federal Adamson Act of 1916, which established an eight-hour day for operating railway workers, with time-and-a-half pay for overtime.

A number of states also passed tougher factory safety and health laws during the Progressive Era, often in response to particularly horrifying accidents, such as the fire at the New York City factory of the Triangle Shirtwaist Company in 1911. Over the next four years the New York Factory Investigating Commission (NYFIC), which the legislature created in response to the fire, did the most extensive investigation of working conditions to date and succeeded in getting most of its recommendations enacted into law.

During the Great Depression, advocates of federal labor legislation built on this earlier work at the state level. The Fair Labor Standards Act (FLSA) of 1938 established a maximum workweek of forty hours, with time-and-a-half pay for overtime, as well as a federal minimum wage and a ban on child labor. The original FLSA excluded workers in many occupations; though it has been amended to include additional workers in the intervening decades, the law remains less than universal. Efforts toward comprehensive federal workplace safety and health legislation took considerably longer, culminating in the Occupational Safety and Health Act of 1970.

[*See also* **Adamson Act; Child Labor; Eight-Hour Day; Fair Labor Standards Act; Freedom of Contract; Living-Wage Campaigns;** *Muller v. Oregon*; **Occupational Diseases and Hazards; Occupational Safety and Health Administration; Triangle Shirtwaist Company Fire;** *and* **Women Workers.**]

BIBLIOGRAPHY

MacLaury, Judson. "Government Regulation of Workers' Safety and Health, 1877–1917." U.S. Department of Labor. http://www.dol.gov/oasam/programs/history/mono-regsafeintrotoc.htm.

Rogers, Donald Wayne. *Making Capitalism Safe: Work Safety and Health Regulation in America, 1880–1940.* Urbana: University of Illinois Press, 2009.

Sklar, Kathryn Kish. "Two Political Cultures in the Progressive Era: The National Consumers' League and the American Association for Labor Legislation." In *U.S. History as Women's History: New Feminist Essays*, edited by Linda K. Kerber, Alice Kessler-Harris, and Kathryn Kish Sklar. Chapel Hill: University of North Carolina Press, 1995.

Laura Murphy

FACTORY FARMING

"Factory farming" refers to the industrial model of agricultural organization that developed in the United States across the twentieth century.

Development. After beginning with the mechanization of wheat farms in the Dakotas, California, and the Great Plains early in the twentieth century, industrialization soon spread to other crops, including corn, fruits, vegetables, and even animals. It involved the application of industrial logic to farm production: farmers were encouraged to apply the methods of factory production and scientific management, such as those modeled by Henry Ford, to their farms. This resulted in the rise of large-scale, specialized farms that mass-produced standardized products rapidly and with less need for skilled labor (or labor of any kind) thanks to mechanization and the adoption of other new technologies embodied in purchased inputs.

Industrialization was accompanied by transformations in the act of farming, as well as in the broader agricultural system. Not only did farms come to look and act more like factories, but various production processes also moved off the farm and into industrial factories. The development and adoption of new mechanical, biological, and chemical technologies in farm production played a prominent role in these transformations and meant that farmers increasingly purchased inputs that substituted for those previously produced on the farm. Tractors, trucks, and combines rapidly replaced horses and mules. This required the increased use of purchased chemical fertilizers to replace manure. Purchased hybrid seeds replaced open-pollinated, self-reproducing varieties that farmers could breed and save themselves. Increasing uniformity and density of hybrid crops required the purchase of chemicals to control weeds and other pests. By the late 1960s the basic elements of the twenty-first century's model of industrial agriculture had been widely adopted. In its issue for 9 March 1959, *Time* magazine hailed the new "pushbutton cornucopia," observing optimistically that the same "assembly line techniques" applied in industry could be applied in agriculture as well.

Farmers not only adopted new ideas and practices, but also entered a new configuration of relationships with capitalist corporations and related concerns, including creditors. The modern industrial farmer is surrounded by a vast array of commercial and industrial enterprises supplying inputs, as well as transporting, processing, packaging, and marketing the outputs of that production. This array of commercial and industrial interests with a stake in farm production is variously referred to as "agribusiness," the "agrifood system," or "the industrial agriculture complex." The agribusiness industry is populated by relatively few national and international firms such as Cargill, Archer Daniels Midland, Monsanto, and Tyson Foods, Inc.

By the 1960s, agribusiness was capturing more of gross farm income, leaving a declining share for farmers themselves. By the early twenty-first century the farm share of the average food dollar stood at about 16 cents, compared to around 40 cents in 1900. Just as the process of industrialization has resulted in the increased role of nonfarm links in the commodity food chain, it has also been accompanied by a decline in the number of farms, from a peak of nearly 7 million in 1935 to just over 2 million in 2011. Though the number of farms has fallen, average farm size has increased from 147 acres in 1900 to more than 400 acres in 2011.

Controversy. Whereas early discussions of factory farming were dominated by its boosters, who focused on the benefits in terms of increased efficiency, productivity, and predictability with less heavy manual labor, by the twenty-first century the term had become fraught with controversy. A thorough review of the relevant discussions is beyond the scope of this article, but a few overarching themes and representative scholars may be summarized.

A first area of critique focuses on the ways that agribusiness has wrested control over the production process from farmers, who are viewed as having formerly enjoyed a considerable degree of autonomy and managerial authority over their farming operations. For example, the agricultural historian Willard Cochrane refers to the intense competitive pressure on farmers continually to adopt new technologies, often going into debt to do so, as the "technology treadmill," implying the loss of control, the continued struggle to keep up, and the difficulty of jumping off once the process has begun. In a related aspect of this critique, some scholars question the impacts of the "inverted hourglass" structure of agricultural markets, with millions of farmers sandwiched between the few multinational behemoths that sell farm inputs and buy outputs. Sometimes the same firm sells several inputs, provides credit, and markets farmers' products, too. From the perspective of critics, this market structure places farmers at the mercy of agribusiness giants that have potentially substantial market power to create a "price squeeze" by charging farmers more for the products they buy and paying less for the products they sell. The work of the rural sociologist William Heffernan and the so-called Missouri school exemplify this approach. Finally, some scholars point to the deskilling and routinization of farmers' work as dehumanizing and alienating. The biologist Richard Lewontin calls this process "proletarianization." All of these approaches juxtapose the twenty-first century's dependent, cog-in-the-machine factory farmers with their almost legendary preindustrial counterparts, the representatives of rugged individualism, practical wisdom, and autonomy.

A second area of critique includes ethical and environmental considerations, especially those pertaining to the application of industrial logic to the production of livestock such as chickens, cattle, and hogs. Factory animal farms are often referred to as "concentrated animal feeding operations," or CAFOs. They are animal feedlots

that concentrate large numbers of animals in relatively small spaces, often indoors. Genetic engineering of animals, specially formulated feed, vitamin supplements, and medications, especially antibiotics, have allowed producers to overcome the natural constraints to animal growth under these conditions so that animals can mature more quickly and at lower economic cost. Some critics object on ethical grounds to the treatment of animals as machines, viewing the unnatural, assembly-line conditions as a form of animal cruelty. Peter Singer is a well-known critic in this regard. Others focus on the environmental impacts, including air and water pollution, as well as food safety and hazards to human health, arising from these operations. Michael Pollan provides an accessible account of these issues in *The Omnivore's Dilemma* (2006).

[*See also* **Agricultural Extension and Education; Agricultural Workers; Agriculture,** *subentry on* **Since 1920; Corn, Hybrid; Corporate Agriculture; Deskilling; Family Farm; Farm Machinery; Grain Processing; Industrialization and Deindustrialization; Meatpacking and Meat-Processing Industry;** *and* **Proletarianization.**]

BIBLIOGRAPHY

Cochrane, Willard W. *The Development of American Agriculture: A Historical Analysis*. 2d ed. Minneapolis: University of Minnesota Press, 1993.

Fitzgerald, Deborah. *Every Farm a Factory: The Industrial Ideal in American Agriculture*. New Haven, Conn.: Yale University Press, 2003.

Hendrickson, Mary. "Consolidation in the Food System." Food Circles Networking Project. University of Missouri Extension. http://www.foodcircles.missouri.edu/consol.htm.

Lavin, Chad. "Factory Farms in a Consumer Society." *American Studies* 50 (2009): 71–92.

Lewontin, R.C. "The Maturing of Capitalist Agriculture: Farmer as Proletarian." *Monthly Review* 50 (July 1998).

Pollan, Michael. *The Omnivore's Dilemma: A Natural History of Four Meals.* New York and London: Penguin Press, 2006.

Elizabeth A. Ramey

FACTORY SYSTEM

The shift of manufacturing from hand to machine processes was a central element of the Industrial Revolution that transformed the early modern economy and contributed to the emergence of modern industrial capitalism. The coming of the modern factory led to a tremendous increase in labor productivity, which contributed, in turn, to a rising standard of living, an increasingly complex division of labor, growing agricultural production, and a massive rural-to-urban population shift. It is no exaggeration to characterize the factory system as the major contributor to this interrelated complex of changes that distinguishes modern society.

The factory system in the United States emerged with the growth of the cotton-textile industry in New England after the Revolutionary War. Customarily historians identify the cotton-spinning mill of Almy, Brown, and Slater that was established in Pawtucket, Rhode Island, in 1790 as the first permanent factory in the new nation. Samuel Slater, a former apprentice in the mill of Jedidiah Strutt in Derbyshire, England, immigrated to the United States in 1789 with an extensive knowledge of English carding and spinning machinery. In Pawtucket, with the financial backing of two Providence merchants, William Almy and Smith Brown, he constructed the requisite machinery and set a small spinning mill in operation in December 1790. Rhode Island, eastern Connecticut, and southern Massachusetts dominated early cotton-textile manufacturing in the United States. The reconstruction of a power loom at the Boston Manufacturing Company in Waltham, Massachusetts, in 1813 by a group of investors—subsequently called by historians the "Boston Associates"—set the stage for further expansion of the industry, with the emergence of a vertically integrated system that combined all stages of the production process at a single site.

Before 1850, textiles were the single major consumer commodity successfully produced within a factory setting. The Waltham–Lowell-type mills of northern New England realized the full potential of factory production. In Lowell, for instance, by 1850, ten large mill complexes, with assets valued at $12 million, employed more than ten thousand operatives producing a million yards of cloth weekly. With a population of some thirty-three thousand, Lowell was Massachusetts's second-largest city and the leading factory town in the country. By 1850, textiles manufactured in New England and the Philadelphia region clothed virtually the entire nation. Only on isolated frontiers might homespun fabrics still be found; only among urban elites did imported textiles have a substantial market.

Factory production soon spread to other sectors of the economy. By the mid-nineteenth century, shoemaking and garment manufacture were increasingly concentrated in urban factories. After the Civil War, the iron and steel industry emerged as the leader of the Second Industrial Revolution, which shifted production from light consumer goods to heavy industry. Whereas textile, shoe, and garment manufacturing were localized operations, by the turn of the twentieth century steel production created new national corporate enterprises. Buying up deposits of coal and iron ore, purchasing railroads and steamship lines, and merging with potential competitors, steel magnates such as Henry Clay Frick and Andrew Carnegie built and administered fortunes that dwarfed those of the antebellum New England cotton-mill owners.

Given the economies of factory production, corporate managers sought to systematize factory operations to maximize their returns. The principles of scientific management espoused by Frederick W. Taylor in the Progressive Era captured the new imperatives. In the meatpacking, automotive, rubber, and electrical industries, new ways of organizing production emerged to take advantage of mechanization and increase the productivity of labor. As workers lost control of the work process in the modern factory, their unions bargained for increased wages, offering American workers by the mid-twentieth century the highest standard of living in the world. Referring to feelings of powerlessness and purposelessness among factory workers in the post–World War II decades, some sociologists discerned a growing sense of alienation. Radical social critics questioned whether labor's new contract was a pact with the devil.

By the end of the twentieth century the continuing growth of factory productivity had transformed the American economy in still other ways, resulting in a sharp decline in manufacturing jobs and the growth of a newly dominant service sector. Financial and information services increasingly constituted the growth sectors of the nation's economy. Unions, traditionally strongest in the manufacturing sector, experienced dramatic declines in membership and economic and political power—yet another consequence of the ongoing global transformation of factory production. What role the factory will continue to play in a postindustrial world economy remains an open question.

[*See also* **American System of Manufacturing and Interchangeable Parts; Deskilling; Industrialization and Deindustrialization; Labor Productivity Growth; Lowell System; Mass Production; Productivity; Proletarianization; Scientific Management; Technology; Textile Industry; Vertical Integration, Economies of Scale, and Firm Size;** *and* **Work.**]

BIBLIOGRAPHY

Bluestone, Barry, and Bennett Harrison. *The Deindustrialization of America: Plant Closings, Community Abandonment, and the Dismantling of Basic Industry*. New York: Basic Books, 1982.

Braverman, Harry. *Labor and Monopoly Capital: The Degradation of Work in the Twentieth Century*. New York: Monthly Review Press, 1974.

Dawley, Alan. *Class and Community: The Industrial Revolution in Lynn*. Cambridge, Mass.: Harvard University Press, 1976.

Dublin, Thomas. *Women at Work: The Transformation of Work and Community in Lowell, Massachusetts, 1826–1860*. New York: Columbia University Press, 1979.

Licht, Walter. *Industrializing America: The Nineteenth Century*. Baltimore: Johns Hopkins University Press, 1995.

Thomas Dublin

FAIR DEAL

The Fair Deal was President Harry Truman's attempt, through both new programs and expansion of New Deal efforts, to create a social democratic welfare system comparable to those under development in western Europe in the 1940s.

Truman, from 1945 on, pursued initiatives on a variety of fronts, including civil rights (the desegregation of the military), expansion of Social Security, increased aid to education, full-employment policies, higher minimum wage, national health care, and low-cost housing. These various programs derived from Truman's sincere beliefs, Keynesian economic advice, and a politician's sense of his political base.

The opposition to Fair Deal initiatives proved formidable. Republicans in Congress considered the initiatives a form of so-called creeping socialism. The American Medical Association spread fear concerning national health initiatives. Southern Democrats in Congress opposed universal social programs that would undermine white supremacy in southern labor and political systems. Many unions preferred, and gained access to, private health and pension benefits through collective bargaining rather than through federal programs. Finally, civilian spending ultimately took a back seat to military and economic programs associated with the Cold War.

The long-term legacy of the few implemented Fair Deal initiatives was mixed. The expansion of Social Security, for instance, helped raise the standard of living for many Americans. Successful desegregation of the military set the stage for federal intervention in civil rights. National health care remained a Democratic priority for decades, was partially realized in Medicare and Medicaid, and was finally passed for nearly all citizens in 2010. The compromises that brought forth the Housing Act of 1949, however, yielded institutional, class-segregated public-housing projects that gave low-cost housing a poor reputation for decades.

[*See also* **Employment Act of 1946.**]

BIBLIOGRAPHY

Bell, Jonathan. *The Liberal State on Trial: The Cold War and American Politics in the Truman Years.* New York: Columbia University Press, 2004.

Hamby, Alonzo L., ed. *Harry S. Truman and the Fair Deal.* Lexington Mass.: D. C. Heath, 1974.

Klein, Jennifer. "The Politics of Economic Security: Employee Benefits and the Privatization of New Deal Liberalism." *Journal of Policy History* 16, no. 1 (2004): 34–65.

Poen, Monte M. *Harry S. Truman versus the Medical Lobby: The Genesis of Medicare.* Columbia: University of Missouri Press, 1979.

Nicholas D. Bloom

FAIR EMPLOYMENT PRACTICES COMMITTEE

In June 1941, President Franklin Delano Roosevelt reluctantly created the Fair Employment Practices Committee (FEPC) to forestall a mass demonstration planned by the black labor leader A. Philip Randolph to protest discrimination and segregation in defense industries. Executive Order 8802 authorized the FEPC to investigate job discrimination in war industries and federal agencies. Led by Lawrence Cramer and the black Chicago alderman Earl B. Dickerson, the committee and its interracial, interethnic staff, including appointees from business and labor, examined complaints of discrimination and held hearings. Howls of protest, particularly from southern politicians and editors, soon led Roosevelt to abolish the original committee.

The FEPC enjoyed strong support among blacks, liberals, religious groups, and labor unions, however, and in May 1943 Roosevelt created a new FEPC. The staff at the Washington headquarters, headed by the black law school dean George M. Johnson, oversaw thirteen regional offices. Significantly, the agency became the first in U.S. history to appoint blacks to policy-making positions. Dealing with other agencies often cool and even hostile toward its goals, the FEPC exposed the subterfuges used by private and federal employers to deny war-related jobs and upgrading to minorities. But the FEPC had little real power. By summer 1946, relentless congressional opposition led to its dismantling.

Many historians credit wartime labor shortages, not the parsimoniously funded FEPC, for decreasing job discrimination. Others, however, cite the FEPC for establishing the principle that job bias constituted a denial of civil rights. Blacks indeed used the FEPC in tight labor markets to open up work opportunities, and in some regions the agency placed qualified minorities in skilled trades and professions ordinarily closed to them. In some ways a precursor of the postwar civil rights movement, the FEPC has great symbolic and long-term significance.

[*See also* **Racism; Randolph, A. Philip;** *and* **Wartime Economic Regulation.**]

BIBLIOGRAPHY

Neuchterlein, James A. "The Politics of Civil Rights: The FEPC, 1941–46." *Prologue* 10, no. 3 (1978): 171–191.
Reed, Merl E. *Seedtime for the Modern Civil Rights Movement: The President's Committee on Fair Employment Practice, 1941–1946.* Baton Rouge: Louisiana State University Press, 1991.

Merl E. Reed

FAIR HOUSING ACT

The United States Fair Housing Act of 1968 prohibited discrimination based on race, color, sex, familial status, and religion in the sale or rental of housing. Passed as an amendment to the Civil Rights Act of 1964, the measure was the first comprehensive federal open-housing law. Its enactment came in the wake of civil disorders that had torn through ghettoized African American neighborhoods in the mid-1960s, revealing deep racial and economic inequities that had not been remedied by federal civil rights or antipoverty programs. Though the Supreme Court had deemed housing discrimination unconstitutional in its *Shelley v. Kraemer* decision in 1948, the absence of enforcement mechanisms allowed sellers in the private housing market to continue both formal and informal exclusionary practices, from racially restrictive homeowners' covenants to violence.

Although the Fair Housing Act was intended to deliver on the promise of *Shelley*, it lost most of its enforcement power as it passed through a divided Congress. Real estate interests adopted new tactics, such as steering minorities away from exclusive communities, to circumvent its provisions. Not until 1988 did amendments to the act increase the federal government's capacity to enforce its provisions. Civil rights advocates continue to criticize the act because its implementation relies not on the government's systematically enforcing antidiscrimination, but on individuals' bringing complaints before federal agencies. Although a landmark in the history of federal intervention in private markets in the name of equal rights, the act has failed to eliminate housing discrimination.

[*See also* **Federal Housing Administration; Great Society;** *and* **Racism.**]

BIBLIOGRAPHY

Massey, Douglas S., and Nancy A. Denton. *American Apartheid: Segregation and the Making of the Underclass.* Cambridge, Mass.: Harvard University Press, 1993.
Sugrue, Thomas J. *Sweet Land of Liberty: The Forgotten Struggle for Civil Rights in the North.* New York: Random House, 2008.

Margaret O'Mara

FAIR LABOR STANDARDS ACT

The Fair Labor Standards Act (FLSA) of 1938 established a federal minimum wage, required overtime pay for hours worked beyond a federally mandated maximum, and banned child labor from the production of goods involved in interstate commerce. The law applied to all industries engaged in interstate commerce but excluded agricultural and domestic workers.

The long battle in Congress that preceded its passage reflected declining congressional support for labor legislation, especially among southern Democrats, as well as resistance from the American Federation of Labor. President Franklin D. Roosevelt signed the Fair Labor Standards Act into law in June 1938 as the last major piece of New Deal labor legislation.

Provisions and Background. The FLSA set the initial hourly minimum wage at 25 cents and set forty-four hours as the standard full-time workweek. The law did not limit the number of hours that employees might be required to work, but it required that employers pay those who worked more than the federal maximum time-and-a-half for each additional hour. The law stipulated that the minimum wage would rise to 30 cents an hour in the second year and to 40 cents by the seventh year. Similarly, within three years the standard workweek would drop to forty hours. The law failed, however, to index the minimum wage to inflation: Congress would have to approve increases to the minimum wage. The FLSA also created the Wage and Hour Division of the U.S. Department of Labor to implement, administer, and enforce the new law. When the law went into effect in October 1938, the Department of Labor estimated that the FLSA covered about one fifth of American workers. Of those 11 million workers, the minimum wage of 25 cents would immediately raise wages for about 300,000 people, and the maximum workweek of forty-four hours would entitle 1.4 million workers to overtime pay.

The FLSA represented the culmination of decades of work by activists involved in state-level campaigns for minimum-wage and maximum-hours legislation. Secretary of Labor Frances Perkins was the strongest link between the state and federal efforts. Perkins was a veteran of the National Consumers League, which led the early twentieth-century movement for protective legislation, and one of her highest legislative priorities was a federal law related to wages and hours. Such a law became a possibility when in 1937 the Supreme Court upheld the constitutionality of a Washington State minimum-wage law: the Court's ruling in the case, *West Coast Hotel v. Parrish*, struck a blow to the doctrine of liberty of contract that had hindered the living-wage movement for decades. The Court upheld the constitutionality of the FLSA in 1941 in *United States v. Darby* and *OPP Cotton Mills, Inc., et al. v. Administrator of Wage and Hour Division of Department of Labor*.

The minimum-wage provision of the Fair Labor Standards Act did not establish a living wage for American workers. Estimates of the cost of living in 1938 indicate that the FLSA failed to mandate a wage that could comfortably support a family of four. In addition, many agricultural and domestic workers, as well as those who worked in intrastate industries, were excluded from coverage. The federal minimum wage reached its real-wage peak in 1968, when it approximated 90 percent of the federal poverty level.

Amendments through the Years. Congress repeatedly amended the FLSA to include workers in additional occupations and to increase the minimum wage. In 1949 the amendments raised the minimum hourly rate to 75 cents, covered air-transport workers, and authorized the wage and hour administrator to regulate industrial homework. The hourly rate rose in 1955 to $1 and rose again in 1961, to $1.15, when the act also incorporated many retail workers. The 1963 Equal Pay Act amended the FLSA to require equal wages for women and men doing the same work. In 1966 the FLSA's coverage of retail workers expanded to include smaller establishments, as well as workers in public schools, laundries, nursing homes, and the construction industry. The 1966 amendments also extended coverage to agricultural workers who worked on larger farms, but the wage rates for these workers was lower. In 1974 many domestic workers and public-sector workers achieved FLSA protection—though the Supreme Court later qualified the terms of the public-sector workers' inclusion, first in 1976 and again in 1985. By 1977 the hourly minimum wage had risen to $2.30, and that year's amendments established a uniform minimum-wage rate for all covered workers. By 1981 the hourly minimum wage was $3.35. Additional amendments that year allowed ten- and eleven-year-olds to do agricultural work and ended the overtime exemptions for service workers in hotels, motels, and restaurants. The FLSA amendments of 1989 eliminated exemptions for small retail businesses, raised the minimum wage to $4.25 by 1991, established an 85 percent training wage (this provision expired in 1993), and authorized civil monetary penalties for "willful or repeated" violations of the law. In 1996, Congress raised the minimum wage to $5.15, with a ninety-day exemption for new employees under the age of twenty. Tipped employees could be paid as little as $2.13 an hour, so long as their tips brought them up to the regular minimum of $5.15. The FLSA amendments of 2007 raised the statutory minimum wage in stages to $7.25 by July 2009 and raised the minimum wages in the Commonwealth of the Northern Mariana Islands and American Samoa in stages that would eventually bring rates up to the federal standard.

Though the FLSA did not establish a federal living-wage standard, it did establish in law the principle that the federal government is responsible for regulating wage rates when market forces threaten to create poverty-level wages, and it prohibited the employment in most occupations of children under the age of sixteen. Although the FLSA never set absolute limits on U.S. workers' hours of labor, its overtime-pay requirement created a strong monetary incentive for employers to limit the workweek and thus helped to establish the cultural norm of the forty-hour workweek.

[*See also* **Child Labor; Eight-Hour Day; Equal Pay Act; Factory and Hours Laws; Living-Wage Campaigns; New Deal Corporate Regulation; Perkins, Frances; Poverty; Wages, Real and Nominal;** *and* **West Coast Hotel v. Parrish.**]

BIBLIOGRAPHY

Grossman, Jonathan. "The Fair Labor Standards Act of 1938: Maximum Struggle for a Minimum Wage." *Monthly Labor Review* 101, no. 6 (June 1978): 22–30.

"History of Changes to the Minimum Wage Law." Adapted from *Minimum Wage and Maximum Hours Standards under the Fair Labor Standards Act,* 1988 Report to the Congress under Section 4(d)(1) of the FLSA. http://www.dol.gov/whd/minwage/coverage.htm.

Paulsen, George E. *A Living Wage for the Forgotten Man: The Quest for Fair Labor Standards, 1933–1941.* Selinsgrove, Pa.: Susquehanna University Press, 1996.

Storrs, Landon R. Y. *Civilizing Capitalism: The National Consumers' League, Women's Activism, and Labor Standards in the New Deal Era.* Chapel Hill: University of North Carolina Press, 2000.

Laura Murphy

FAMILY FARM

U.S. agriculture has historically displayed a rich variety of organizational forms, including the communal village plots of some Native American communities, the feudal Dutch patroonships along the Hudson River during the colonial period, the slave plantations of the South until the Civil War, and the complex sharecropping system that grew to replace slavery, as well as the massive capitalist ranches that arose on the western prairie during the late nineteenth century. One enduring and often romanticized form has been that of the family farm, which is often touted as a quintessentially American institution.

It was the independent yeoman family farmer who served as the foundation for Thomas Jefferson's vision of democracy in America. In *Notes on the State of Virginia*, which he first published in 1784, Jefferson wrote, "Those who labour in the earth are the chosen people of God . . . whose breasts he has made his peculiar deposit for substantial and genuine virtue." Popular folklore is filled with images of the farmer and his family who, armed with the virtues of "rugged individualism," hard work, and ingenuity, forged westward with the frontier and held the line for "civilization" under the banner of Manifest Destiny. In his famous "Cross of Gold" speech at the 1896 Democratic convention in Chicago, the dark-horse candidate William Jennings Bryan invoked "those hardy pioneers who braved all the dangers of the wilderness, who have made the desert to blossom as the rose—those pioneers away out there, rearing their children near to nature's heart, where they can mingle their voices with the voices of the birds." By the end of the speech, Bryan won not only a standing ovation, but also his party's presidential nomination. Still culturally iconic and politically influential in the twenty-first century, in many ways the family farm remains a mainstay of U.S. agriculture, although not necessarily in the guise of the idyllic places that once formed the basis of the rural economy and society and that continue to live on in Americans' cultural imagination.

According to the U.S. Department of Agriculture (USDA), about 98 percent of the nation's 2.2 million farms are family farms, defined simply as those for which the majority ownership and control of the business resides with a group of related individuals. The single term disguises the wide variation in characteristics of family farms. Most farms are small family farms, with annual sales of less than $250,000, but family farms range in annual sales from $1,000 to more than $500,000. Average farm acreage ranges from fifty-eight to more than one thousand. In addition, family farms vary considerably in their economic situation. Unable to survive solely on farm income, most small farm households rely on a main occupation other than farming. In fact, most small farms report a loss from farming. Although on average, family farm households report a median income that is greater than that of all U.S. households, only large family farms report such a high average income from farming only. The great majority depend on income from off-farm activities. Larger family farms, along with nonfamily farms, account for only 12 percent of farms but 84 percent of production.

[*See also* **Agricultural Workers; Agriculture; *and* Corporate Agriculture.**]

BIBLIOGRAPHY

Hoppe, Robert A., and David E. Banker. "Structure and Finances of U.S. Farms: Family Farm Report, 2010 Edition." United States Department of Agriculture Economic Research Service, Economic Information Bulletin no. 66, July 2010. Available at http://www.ers.usda.gov/publications/eib66.

Hoppe, Robert A., David E. Banker, and James M. MacDonald. "America's Diverse Family Farms, 2010 Edition." United States Department of Agriculture Economic Research Service, Economic Information Bulletin no. 67, July 2010. Available at http://www.ers.usda.gov/publications/eib67.

Elizabeth A. Ramey

FARM BUREAU FEDERATION

Through the 1910s county agents working for the Department of Agriculture's extension service organized Farm Bureaus on a county and then on a federated state basis. Their purpose was to promote cooperativism and disseminate scientific agricultural techniques to farmers. In 1919 the state federations were organized into a nationwide unit, the American Farm Bureau Federation (AFBF). From its origins the government supported the expansion of the AFBF as a bulwark against Bolshevism and other threatening ideologies. The AFBF's natural constituency was thus wealthier farmers who had the capital required to develop their farms with modern methods and who felt most endangered by radicalism. Even as it evolved in its policy prescriptions, the AFBF did not deviate from its close alliance with landowners and agribusiness, nor from its bureaucratic, rather than democratic, form of self-government.

During the 1920s and 1930s the Farm Bureau grew to become America's largest agricultural organization. Its membership swelled because it also admitted nonfarming rural people, who were often eager to benefit from the provision of competitive insurance rates and other services that were not common in the hinterlands. Though the AFBF supported the never-passed McNary–Haugen farm-relief bill in the 1920s and then went on to become an early supporter of the Agricultural Adjustment Administration during the Depression, in the postwar period it was best known for its advocacy of a wide range of conservative positions relating to farming and nonfarming issues alike. Most notable was its support for free markets, which led it to propose the reduction of support payments to farmers, as well as to oppose the organization of farmworkers, while actively seeking to break the grape boycott led by the United Farm Workers in the 1960s.

[*See also* **Agricultural Extension and Education; Agriculture,** *subentry on* **Since 1920; Brannan Plan; Cooperatives; Corporate Agriculture; McNary–Haugen Bill;** *and* **Subsidies, Agricultural.**]

BIBLIOGRAPHY

Berger, Samuel R. *Dollar Harvest: The Story of the Farm Bureau.* Lexington, Mass.: Heath Lexington Books, 1971.

Campbell, Christiana McFadyen. *The Farm Bureau and the New Deal: A Study of Making of National Farm Policy, 1933–40.* Urbana: University of Illinois Press, 1962.

McConnell, Grant. *The Decline of Agrarian Democracy.* Berkeley: University of California Press, 1953.

Patrick M. Dixon

FARM MACHINERY

American farmers first used mechanized equipment during the Revolutionary War, when some farmers adopted grain drills (seed-planting devices) based on English designs. A successful American innovation did not occur until 1841, however, when Moses and Samuel Pennock of Pennsylvania significantly improved the design of this implement to facilitate more-uniform planting of seed. American farmers continued to plant corn with a hoe until 1853 when George Brown of Illinois marketed a two-row, horse-drawn corn planter.

In 1833, Obed Hussey patented the first successful reaper for small grains. This device consisted of an oscillating sickle bar and a platform to catch the cut stalks. The next year, Cyrus McCormick of Virginia patented a reaper that included a reel to help catch and hold the stalks against an improved cutter bar. In 1854 the firm of Seymour and Morgan of Brockport, New York, marketed the first commercially successful self-raking reaper, which automatically removed the stalks from the platform. By 1860 the reaper had spread across the Middle West, and the McCormick factory in Chicago had become one of the nation's great manufacturers of farm machinery. Although a machine designed to cut grain and bind sheaves with wire was patented in 1856, farmers disliked wire, in part because they could not easily dispose of it at threshing time. In 1880, twine binders began to replace wire binders after John Appleby of Wisconsin developed a mechanism for tying a knot in twine wrapped around a sheaf of grain. Reapers and binders enabled farmers to harvest from ten to twenty acres of grain per day, depending on field conditions, with far less labor than that required to cut the grain with a scythe and rake and bind the sheaves by hand. The next significant increase in daily harvested acreage and decrease in the labor needed at harvest and threshing time came with the adoption of the tractor-powered combine harvester–thresher—the "combine"—during the 1920s.

During the twentieth century, tractors powered by internal combustion engines became the most important and widely adopted agricultural implement in American history. In 1918, Henry Ford marketed the first affordable farm tractor, the Fordson. Six years later, the International Harvester Company (successor to the McCormick Harvesting Machine Company) introduced the Farmall, a tricycle-designed tractor that met the needs of small-scale, row-crop farmers.

The cotton picker, developed in the early 1940s, became the most important twentieth-century farm machine for a specific, regional crop. Before the International Harvester Company manufactured the first commercially successful cotton picker in 1942, however, scientists had to modify the cotton plant to eliminate foliage and ensure uniform ripening. The cotton picker initially proved most suitable for large-scale operations in California, but in time it supplanted handpickers in the South as well.

These and other forms of agricultural machinery enabled farmers to reduce labor costs and increase production, which contributed to lower agricultural and food prices. Farm machinery also eased the drudgery of farm work, but it necessitated an increase in farm size and capital investment and thus caused a corresponding decrease in the number of farms, farmworkers, and agricultural families.

[*See also* **Agricultural Workers; Agriculture; Cotton Industry; Factory Farming; Family Farm; Grain Processing; Labor Productivity Growth;** *and* **Technology.**]

BIBLIOGRAPHY

Hurt, R. Douglas. *American Agriculture: A Brief History.* Ames: Iowa State University Press, 1994.
Williams, Robert C. *Fordson, Farmall, and Poppin' Johnny: A History of the Farm Tractor and Its Impact on America.* Urbana: University of Illinois Press, 1987.

R. Douglas Hurt

FEDERAL COMMUNICATIONS COMMISSION

The Federal Communications Commission (FCC), created by the Federal Communications Act of 1934, assumed all federal oversight of broadcasting, telephone, and telegraph services. Under the initial terms of the act, the president appointed seven commissioners to seven-year terms; in 1982, Congress reduced the number of commissioners to five, serving five-year terms.

Congress gave the FCC limited powers and scant funding. Like the Federal Radio Commission, which regulated broadcasting from 1927 to 1934, the FCC awarded radio licenses in ways that favored commercial over noncommercial broadcasters and punished only the most irresponsible behavior. The lethargy ended with the chairmanship from 1939 to

1944 of James Lawrence Fly. Under Fly, the commission forced the National Broadcasting Company to sell one of its two networks.

The Fly years proved exceptional. In the 1950s the agency bungled its greatest postwar challenge: television. The FCC awarded TV licenses without consistent criteria except to reaffirm the dominance of two networks, NBC and CBS, at the expense of commercial and noncommercial rivals. In the 1960s the commission adopted rules inhibiting the diffusion of cable TV systems, fearing that they would undermine individual stations in smaller markets. For decades, FCC regulations similarly reinforced the monopolistic control of the American Telephone and Telegraph Company (AT&T) over the telephone industry, inhibiting competition and innovation. A 1982 district court ruling broke up AT&T.

Several key court decisions in the 1970s freed the cable industry. By then the FCC itself had started to deregulate broadcasting. Congress strongly encouraged this tendency with the 1996 Telecommunications Act, which greatly relaxed rules limiting the number of licenses that an individual or corporation could own. In the next decade, the commission's attempts to maintain some limits on ownership were usually overturned by the courts, which also rejected the commission's efforts to punish stations for indecent content.

[*See also* **Federal Regulatory Agencies; Radio; Satellite Communications; Telegraph; Telephone;** *and* **Television.**]

BIBLIOGRAPHY

Horowitz, Robert Britt. *The Irony of Regulatory Reform: The Deregulation of American Telecommunications.* New York: Oxford University Press, 1989.

Zarkin, Kimberly A., and Michael J. Zarkin. *The Federal Communications Commission: Front Line in the Culture and Regulation Wars.* Westport, Conn.: Greenwood Press, 2006.

James L. Baughman

FEDERAL DEPOSIT INSURANCE CORPORATION

The Federal Deposit Insurance Corporation (FDIC) was established in a provision of the Banking Act of 16 June 1933, a law better known as Glass–Steagall. The efficient cause of the FDIC was that some five thousand bank failures had occurred since the onset of the Great Depression in 1929. The FDIC, as implemented, guaranteed bank customers their first $2,500 in deposits at any member institution. This sum was increased periodically over the years, beginning with its doubling in 1934. Assessments levied on banks insured deposits, along with credit support from the U.S. Treasury and the Federal Reserve that provided the initial capitalization of the FDIC.

Six weeks prior to the passage of Glass–Steagall, President Franklin Delano Roosevelt issued an executive order prohibiting the private ownership of gold. A chief reason that bank depositors had been making cash withdrawals en masse since 1929 was the fear that banks would be unable to redeem deposits and a common suspicion that the official price of gold would soon rise significantly—which did indeed happen in 1934. Thus the issuance of the executive order in May was a necessary step so as to ensure that the FDIC would not be overwhelmed with business after it was chartered in June. Indeed, the number of bank failures requiring disbursements from the FDIC over its first seven years, through 1941, was only 370, a far cry from the record number of banks that failed during the early Great Depression years.

In the 1950s and 1960s the FDIC was relatively inactive, treating comparatively so few failures that at one point an overseer in Congress wondered if this indicated an unhealthy lack of competition in the banking system. The FDIC acted to limit bank competition and thus risk to depositors. It did so primarily by regulating interest rates. The FDIC denied member banks the power to offer interest on checking-account deposits, and it capped interest on savings accounts. Banks could not compete with each other by attracting depositors with higher interest rates.

It was precisely its policy on interest that played into the extreme volatility that the banking system, and thus the FDIC, experienced in the 1970s and 1980s. When inflation rose upward of 10 percent annually in the 1970s, it became untenable for depositors to keep assets in no-interest or capped-interest accounts. Yet as deposits fled for inflation hedges outside the banking system—such as commodities and money-market accounts—providers of the hedges in turn presented large sums ("petrodollars") for deposit. This raised the ratio of aggregate deposits to insured deposits and led to uncommon risk taking by banks. The FDIC had to cover large failures, such as that of Penn Square in 1982. As larger numbers of banks failed, the FDIC had to act not only as an insurer but also as a receiver of such banks.

In 1991 the FDIC swallowed the residue of a partner, the Federal Savings and Loan Insurance Corporation, which had served the residential housing market and been hit even harder by the inflation of the previous decades. The FDIC contribution to the bailouts that followed the financial crisis of 2008 was to raise the depositor guarantee from $100,000 to $250,000.

[See also **Financial and Banking Promotion and Regulation; Inflation and Deflation;** and **New Deal Banking Regulation.**]

Brian Domitrovic

FEDERAL HOUSING ADMINISTRATION

Congress created the Federal Housing Administration (FHA) under the National Housing Act of 1934 as a means to insure mortgages made by private lenders to homeowners. The agency was a response to the Great Depression and the economic crisis that had decimated both the housing and the banking sectors. Its creators hoped that the FHA would (1) expand homeownership, (2) strengthen banks and other lending institutions, and (3) provide a stimulus for employment in the home-building industry.

Prior to the 1930s, most mortgages were for short terms—around five years—with the principal due in full at the end of the term of the mortgage. Most borrowers were unable to pay off the mortgage and had to refinance. During the Depression, however, it became difficult to refinance mortgages, and many homeowners lost their homes to foreclosure. Banks were saddled with bad loans. The real estate market crashed, and mortgage lending dried up. The FHA intended to use the federal government to stimulate private markets. The FHA built no homes and provided no loans. Instead, it insured mortgages made by private lenders, thus helping to restore confidence in the mortgage market and stimulate lending.

In doing so, the FHA, along with the Home Owners' Loan Corporation, helped to revolutionize the mortgage market in the United States. Now home buyers could access long-term twenty-year mortgages—within a few years, that was extended to thirty years—that would be fully repaid at the end of the loan. These new, self-amortizing mortgages also required smaller down payments from homeowners, usually 20 percent or less. The government mortgage guarantee also helped lower interest rates for such loans. In short, FHA mortgage insurance helped reduce the risks of lending, made such lending more predictable, and thereby increased the supply of credit. The FHA also had its intended effect on the construction industry. With more credit available, new housing starts increased from 332,000 in 1937 to 619,000 in 1941.

Only lenders who met strict underwriting criteria set by the agency could make FHA-insured loans. Even more important, the FHA set minimum property standards for housing that it would insure. Home builders, home buyers, lenders, and home-improvement companies now had clear written guidelines that set out basic standards for housing. Such standards were enforced by on-site inspections, and they soon became the industry norm, even for loans not backed by the FHA.

By 1943 the FHA was insuring 80 percent of all new housing units. The Servicemen's Readjustment Act of 1944, better known as the GI Bill, also provided housing assistance to America's veterans. The FHA and the GI Bill boosted homeownership rates from 43 percent in 1940 to 62 percent in 1960. By the 1950s the private mortgage insurance (PMI) market had grown and FHA-backed mortgages had declined. By 1970, roughly 25 percent of mortgages were backed by the FHA.

Despite its successes, the FHA came under criticism. Critics charged that the FHA favored single-family, detached homes outside the city, thereby both fueling the postwar suburban boom and undermining urban neighborhoods. Others criticized FHA underwriting principles that discouraged lending in neighborhoods populated by African Americans. FHA policies made it much easier and cheaper to borrow money for homes in predominantly white suburbs than to borrow money for homes in densely populated, racially diverse urban neighborhoods. The FHA not only made lending in urban areas more difficult, but also was not shy about tying its decisions to race and ethnicity. Yet homeownership rates among African Americans, although lagging far behind those of whites, still increased steadily in the postwar years, from 23 percent in 1940 to 38 percent in 1960.

With the creation of the Department of Housing and Urban Development (HUD) in 1965, the FHA came under the authority of the new cabinet department. The FHA now implemented policies to help expand homeownership to low-income Americans and racial minorities. In the wake of the urban riots of the 1960s, the FHA extended heavily subsidized FHA-insured mortgages with a nominal down payment to low-income urban residents. Because of the program's ineffective administration, it fell prey to corrupt appraisers, as well as to speculators and real estate agents engaged in "blockbusting" of white neighborhoods. The number of foreclosures rose, and many urban neighborhoods suffered, leading to the program's cancellation. Still unresolved was how to increase lending in urban neighborhoods, especially those that were poor and populated mainly by minorities.

After the 1960s, however, the FHA assumed a less important part in the overall housing market. By 1993, FHA-backed mortgages had fallen to around 8 percent of the total market. But in 2008, as credit markets began to tighten, the FHA began insuring an increasing number of mortgages, often with down payments of only 3.5 percent. In the ensuing economic crisis, which hit the housing market hard, defaults on FHA-backed mortgages increased, putting great stress on FHA finances. Although the FHA tightened its loan standards marginally, it chose not to exacerbate an already weak real estate market by tightening credit excessively. By 2011 the housing market had yet to fully recover, and government housing policy remained the subject of hot debate.

[*See also* **Fair Housing Act; GI Bill; Home Owners' Loan Corporation; Poverty;** *and* **Racism.**]

BIBLIOGRAPHY

Jackson, Kenneth T. *Crabgrass Frontier: The Suburbanization of the United States.* New York: Oxford University Press, 1985.

Vincent J. Cannato

FEDERAL MEDIATION AND CONCILIATION SERVICE

The Federal Mediation and Conciliation Service (FMCS) is an independent agency of the federal government responsible for mediating disputes between labor unions and employers. Counting the time of its predecessor, the United States Conciliation Service (USCS), the FMCS has provided mediation services for a hundred years, making it arguably the oldest full-time, and continuing, mediation organization in the world.

This government role of mediation was created by the 1913 act that established the U.S. Department of Labor (DOL). The act provided that the secretary of labor "shall have the power to act as mediator and to appoint commissioners of conciliation in labor disputes."

During 1913–1914 the DOL mediated only 33 cases, but with World War I the caseload grew to 1,217 in 1918 and 1,789 in 1919. When the war ended, patriotic cooperation among labor, management, and government ended as well. The 1920s and the first half of the 1930s witnessed a significant decline in union membership, opportunities to negotiate with employers, and the need for mediation. New Deal legislation in the mid-1930s established collective-bargaining rights, thus enabling a growth in union membership and an increasing need for mediation assistance. During the 1940s, World War II caused a major increase in USCS mediation: the caseload averaged 13,000 per year.

Given the pent-up civilian demands for goods and income, the winter of 1945–1946 witnessed more strikes than ever before or since in U.S. history. The following year, through the Taft–Hartley Act, a newly elected Republican Congress amended the New Deal legislation of 1935, removing the mediation function from the DOL and placing it in the newly created independent FMCS.

On 20 August 1947 the FMCS began with the staff and offices of the defunct USCS. Only two major changes were made. First, staff mediators would no longer act as arbitrators. In their place, the FMCS created a roster of qualified private arbitrators who were available to disputants. Second, the technical services division was eliminated, and thus its work on time-and-motion studies was ceded to the private sector.

The next thirty years are often referred to as the golden years of collective bargaining and mediation. The bargaining parties, often with nearly equal strength, readily used mediation when needed. The FMCS improved the quality of its staff through recruiting and training, encouraged earlier intervention into disputes, and emphasized preventive mediation programs to improve parties' relationships. As economic growth proceeded apace, wages, hours, and working conditions also improved.

By the late 1970s, foreign competition and the shifting of manufacturing overseas began to accelerate. By the 1980s, abandoned factory sites in states between Pennsylvania and Minnesota gave rise to the region's nickname "Rust Belt." As a result, the work of the mediators changed. Whereas earlier, mediation had typically resulted in improved wages and benefits, now mediation involved givebacks by unions of hard-won contractual conditions. Most mediators struggled to adapt to their new role.

The number of FMCS mediators declined from its high in the early 1970s to half that by the mid-1990s. A comparable decline occurred in union membership and in the number of collective-bargaining agreements, mediation cases, and strikes.

Faced with a declining workload, the FMCS shifted its attention to other areas of conflict, such as grievance mediation, dispute mediation related to nonunion employment, domestic and overseas training and consulting in alternative dispute resolution (ADR), and other work for which it demanded reimbursement.

[*See also* **Collective Bargaining; Federal Regulatory Agencies; Industrial Relations; Labor Movement, Decline of the; National Labor Relations Board; National War Labor Board, World War I; National War Labor Board, World War II; No-Strike Pledge, World War I and World War II; President's Mediation Commission (1917); Strikes;** *and* **Taft–Hartley Act.**]

Jerome T. Barrett

FEDERAL REGULATORY AGENCIES

The first federal regulatory agency was the Interstate Commerce Commission (ICC). Created in 1887 after decades of controversy over the so-called railroad problem, the ICC in many ways served as a model for future agencies. Like the ICC, the other agencies were established by Congress in response to crises in particular industries (or, occasionally, across industries). Staffed with persons thought to be experts and bipartisan or nonpartisan by law, most were nevertheless plagued by continual controversy.

The ICC found its power limited by the federal courts. In a pattern repeated later with other regulatory commissions, Congress then proceeded to strengthen the original Interstate Commerce Act through a series of laws passed between 1903 and 1940 that, in effect, gave the commission de facto rate-making authority for railroads, pipelines, trucks, and barges. The ICC's staff evolved complicated standards to set rates for passengers and freight carried by diverse modes of transportation over different routes. Its primary principle sought to assure transportation companies a "fair rate of return" on the "fair value of property used and useful" in performing their services. This seemingly simple idea involved the ICC in arbitrary estimates, dubious valuation schemes to determine the "rate base," and unworkable attempts to allocate traffic "fairly" among various modes of transportation.

In reality, American capitalism proved too fluid and complex to lend itself to minute regulatory control as developed by the ICC, and industries under ICC supervision tended to stagnate because entrepreneurial opportunity was too constricted. Not until the deregulation movement of the 1980s and 1990s did some ICC-regulated industries again become vibrant parts of the national economy, by which time the ICC itself had been abolished by Congress.

Economic Regulation. Meanwhile Congress had created nine other federal regulatory agencies to address different areas of the economy. Five agencies were given primarily economic functions, and four were assigned social or environmental regulatory duties. The five economic agencies are:

1. The Federal Trade Commission (FTC), created in 1914 and assigned the ambiguous task of maximizing competition in business. The FTC's biggest successes came in presenting to Congress detailed industry studies that prompted important legislation such as the Public Utility Holding Company Act of 1935 and several laws restricting the fixing of retail prices.

2. The Federal Power Commission (FPC), created in 1920, strengthened in 1930 and 1935, and in the 1980s renamed the Federal Energy Regulatory Commission. The dyna-

mism of the energy sector overwhelmed this agency, and by the 1950s it could not manage its huge caseload effectively. Beginning in the 1960s and culminating with congressional deregulation of natural gas during the 1980s, a series of reforms alleviated the impossible pressures under which the FPC worked.

3. The Federal Communications Commission (FCC), created in 1934 with jurisdiction over radio, interstate telephone communication, and later television. The FCC was plagued by a fundamental lack of clarity about its proper functions. In the broadcasting industry, should it promote growth? Should it censor content? Should it take the draconian step of rescinding the licenses of wayward stations? As for the telephone industry, how could the FCC effectively regulate the monopolistic American Telephone and Telegraph Company (AT&T), which was—until the divestiture of regional operating companies in 1984, under pressure from antitrust authorities—America's largest single business firm? The FCC never successfully resolved these questions.

4. The Securities and Exchange Commission (SEC), created in 1934 and assigned the task of reviving and policing the nation's Depression-battered capital markets. Compared to other agencies, the SEC achieved remarkable success. It did so by working through allies in the private sector—especially lawyers, accountants, and officials of organized exchanges—whose interests were aligned by statutes and rulings with the goals that the SEC defined as best for the industry and the public.

5. The Civil Aeronautics Board (CAB), created in 1938 and abolished during the 1980s. The CAB restricted entry into the airline industry, allocated the routes that companies flew, standardized prices along these routes, and in general supervised a cartel. Although efforts to determine a fair rate of return made some sense for such so-called natural-monopoly industries as railroads and electric utilities, it did not make

sense for the airline industry, in which entry was easy, competition keen, and business flexibility high.

Social and Environmental Regulation. The four social and environmental regulatory agencies reflected the heightened attention to civil rights and environmental and consumer issues in the 1960s and 1970s. These agencies are:

1. The Equal Employment Opportunity Commission (EEOC), created in 1964 and charged with administering Title VII of the Civil Rights Act of that year. The EEOC coordinates federal efforts at affirmative action for the employment of women and minorities. It investigates charges of violation, promotes awareness of the law, and publishes statistical reports on employment patterns.

2. The Environmental Protection Agency (EPA), created in 1970 and granted a broad range of responsibilities for the control of air and water pollution and the cleanup of hazardous waste sites. As the largest of all federal regulatory agencies measured by both size of budget and number of employees (more than ten thousand by 1980), the EPA has formidable powers.

3. The Occupational Safety and Health Administration (OSHA), created in 1970, headed by an assistant secretary of labor and charged with developing regulations for workplace safety. OSHA's effectiveness suffered from the difficulty of conducting a sufficient number of inspections at the nation's millions of worksites.

4. The Consumer Product Safety Commission, created in 1972 to enforce safety standards on potentially dangerous items such as hand tools, lawnmowers, flammable clothing, and children's toys. Its rules are often cited in product liability suits brought by private parties.

In addition to these major regulatory agencies, many other government bodies, including the National Highway Traffic Safety Administration, the Federal Aviation Administration, the Food and Drug Administration, the National Labor Relations Board, the Nuclear Regulatory Commission, and the Federal Reserve Board, also have important regulatory responsibilities.

Resistance to Regulation. As the twentieth century ended, however, political resistance to federal regulatory agencies grew. Critics on both the left and the right charged that too often such agencies were "captured" by the industries or economic sectors that they were authorized to regulate. Thus the agencies restricted competition, hindered innovation, and cost consumers. Critics concentrated in the business community and the Republican Party charged that regulations issued too frequently and carelessly hampered business, raised costs, and stifled economic growth. They cited how the abolition of the ICC and the CAB resulted in the revitalization of the railroads, lower-cost trucking, and greater air-passenger traffic at reduced fares, thus contributing to a more competitive economy. During the administration of President George W. Bush (2001–2009) the regulatory agencies issued fewer rules and loosened existing ones. Even earlier, during the administration of Bill Clinton, Congress had weakened New Deal regulations governing the banking and financial sector, leading, perhaps, to the SEC's diluting its own restraints on those sectors.

The economic crisis and recession of 2008–2010, which many blamed on the loosening of existing federal economic regulations—especially those related to the financial and banking sectors—led to renewed demands for stricter federal regulation. In 2009 and 2010 the Democratic presidential administration and Democratic congressional majority tried to answer those demands. Tighter regulation of banking and finance was reinstituted, and a new agency, the Consumer Financial Protection Bureau, was created to protect consumers from financial and economic market fraud. The SEC was given additional funding to enable it to strengthen its regulation of financial markets. The 2010 congressional elections, however, returned Republicans to majority control of the House of Representatives, and immediately they sought to eviscerate the new regulatory regime and its bureau. Thus in the twenty-first century the role of federal regulatory agencies remained hotly contested.

[*See also* **Antitrust Legislation; Deregulation, Financial; Economic Deregulation and the Carter Administration; Environmental Regulations; Federal Communications Commission; Federal Trade Commission; Financial and Banking Promotion and Regulation; National Labor Relations Board; New Deal Banking Regulation; New Deal Corporate Regulation; Occupational Safety and Health Administration; Public Utility Holding Company Act; Securities and Exchange Commission; State Regulatory Laws; Technocracy;** *and* **Title VII.**]

BIBLIOGRAPHY

Bernstein, Marver H. *Regulating Business by Independent Commission.* Princeton, N.J.: Princeton University Press, 1955.

Hoogenboom, Ari, and Olive Hoogenboom. *A History of the ICC: From Panacea to Palliative.* New York: W. W. Norton and Company, 1976.

McCraw, Thomas K. *Prophets of Regulation: Charles Francis Adams, Louis D. Brandeis, James M. Landis, Alfred E. Kahn.* Cambridge, Mass.: Belknap Press of Harvard University Press, 1984.

Rosenbaum, Walter A. *Environmental Politics and Policy.* 7th ed. Washington, D.C.: CQ Press, 2008.

Vogel, David. "The New 'Social' Regulation in Historical and Comparative Perspective." In *Regulation in Perspective: Historical Essays*, edited by Thomas K. McCraw, pp. 155–185. Boston: Division of Research, Graduate School of Business Administration, Harvard University, 1981.

Wilson, James Q., ed. *The Politics of Regulation*. New York: Basic Books, 1980.

Thomas K. McCraw

FEDERAL RESERVE ACT

The Federal Reserve Act (1913) had its origins in the Panic of 1907, when the collapse of several loosely managed trust companies sparked a general financial crisis. Depositors frightened by the collapse of trust companies withdrew money from banks, which then called in loans and dumped securities on the market, contributing to a serious recession. The financier J. P. Morgan saved the day, using a fund created by bankers and the federal government to prop up threatened but basically sound financial institutions.

The crisis illuminated severe weaknesses in the American banking system. National banks around the country issued currency backed with U.S. government bonds. They kept their reserves either in cash or on deposit in several designated money-center banks. The system produced an inelastic currency: because it was tied to the availability of U.S. Treasury bonds, it could not expand with the economy. The problem became particularly acute at harvesttime, when the demand for money rose as farmers sold their crops. Moreover, because reserves were dispersed throughout the system, mobilizing them during a crisis proved extremely difficult.

The panic inspired Congress in 1908 to create the National Monetary Commission, chaired by Senator Nelson Aldrich of Rhode Island, to study banking reform. A Republican stalwart with personal ties to the John D. Rockefeller family, Aldrich was in no sense a Progressive, yet in this case he was open to change. His commission toured Europe studying continental financial arrangements, but Aldrich made his most important contact in New York. There he met Paul Warburg, a member of the noted German Jewish banking family and a partner at Kuhn, Loeb, who combined strong civic responsibility with wide financial experience.

In late 1910, Aldrich, Warburg, and several other leading bankers met secretly to hammer out a plan to create a central bank that would be similar to those in Europe, but more decentralized. The group recommended the creation of fifteen regional banks, controlled by local bankers, to handle the issuance of currency. These institutions would issue money in exchange for either gold or "real bills"—short-term commercial paper backed by goods (inventories, for example). Such a currency would be "elastic," that is, able to expand with the economy. The regional banks would also hold the reserves of financial institutions in their region, permitting a concerted response to any crisis. Over the regional banks would stand a central board composed largely of representatives of business and finance but also including a few government appointees. Aldrich formally submitted the plan to Congress in January 1911.

Although Aldrich's proposals remained stalled in Congress for almost two years, the election of Woodrow Wilson in 1912 opened the way for financial reform. In December 1912, even before Wilson's inauguration, Senator Carter Glass of Virginia, chairman of the Senate Banking Committee, put forward his own plan. It closely resembled Aldrich's, except that Glass, a states' rights Democrat, sharply restricted the authority of the central board.

Glass quickly secured Wilson's support, but his plan horrified most congressional Progressives. Deeply suspicious of bankers, who they believed manipulated the financial system for their own ends, Progressives feared that Glass's measure would increase bankers' power. Fortunately, Wilson, who knew little about finance and had few convictions on the subject, made enough concessions to win over Progressive critics. In a key concession, Wilson agreed to strengthen the authority of the central board and to make all of its members presidential appointees, giving Washington a predominant voice in the new system.

The financial community opposed the final version of the bill, which it feared gave the federal government too much authority over the nation's banking system. As a result, Progressives rallied around the measure and gave the proposal a radical aura that it did not entirely merit. The bill, authorizing the creation of twelve regional banks and the Federal Reserve Board in Washington, became law in 1913. The Federal Reserve Act had one serious weakness, not rectified until the 1930s: it did not define precisely the relationship between the regional banks and the central board. Nevertheless, the Federal Reserve Act gave the United States a central bank able to pursue consistent monetary policies.

[*See also* **Federal Reserve System; Financial and Banking Promotion and Regulation;** *and* **Monetary Policy, Federal.**]

BIBLIOGRAPHY

Chernow, Ron. *The House of Morgan: An American Banking Dynasty and the Rise of Modern Finance.* New York: Monthly Review Press, 1990.

Chernow, Ron. *The Warburgs: The Twentieth-Century Odyssey of a Remarkable Jewish Family.* New York: Random House, 1993.

Link, Arthur S. *Woodrow Wilson and the Progressive Era, 1910–1917.* New York: Harper & Brothers, 1954.

West, Robert Craig. *Banking Reform and the Federal Reserve, 1863–1923.* Ithaca, N.Y.: Cornell University Press, 1977.

Wyatt C. Wells

FEDERAL RESERVE SYSTEM

Congress created the Federal Reserve System, the central bank of the United States, in 1913. The system consisted of twelve regional banks and the Federal Reserve Board in Washington, D.C., which had ill-defined powers of oversight. Lawmakers expected the system to regulate the supply of money and credit (monetary policy), mitigating the effects of the business cycle; to oversee, in concert with other federal and state agencies, the operations of commercial banks; and to carry out the government's international financial transactions. Ideally, the system's decentralized structure would reduce the influence of New York City banks over the nation's credit system.

During World War I, the Federal Reserve financed government deficits by expanding the money supply, and it broke the postwar inflation by raising interest rates and sharply restricting credit. In the 1930s, however, the shortcomings of the Federal Reserve's decentralized structure became apparent. During the Great Depression, infighting between the regional banks and the central board prevented a coordinated response to the crisis. Incoherent monetary policy permitted the money supply to contract by a third, contributing mightily to the catastrophe.

Accordingly, President Franklin Delano Roosevelt and Marriner Eccles, his appointee as chair of the Federal Reserve Board, initiated reforms. Eccles persuaded Congress to enact new legislation confirming the board's authority over the regional banks, solidifying the position of its chair, and vesting in the Open

Market Committee—a group consisting of members of the Federal Reserve Board and the presidents of the regional banks—control over monetary policy.

Despite its new organization, the Federal Reserve soon fell under the influence of the Treasury Department. Throughout World War II and for many years after, the central bank at the behest of the Treasury "pegged" long-term interest rates at a low level, permitting Washington to finance its debt cheaply. This policy became controversial after 1945 because, by accommodating every demand for credit, it threatened to fuel inflation. Surging prices during the Korean War forced the Treasury to relent and grant the Federal Reserve the authority to set interest rates as it saw fit. The subsequent increase in the cost of money, engineered by the central bank, helped stabilize prices.

Over the next twenty years, the Federal Reserve exercised its newfound autonomy carefully, following policies described as "leaning against the wind." Put simply, during recessions it cut interest rates to stimulate production, and when inflation threatened, it increased rates to cool demand. But the so-called stagflation of the 1970s—simultaneous inflation and recession—stymied the central bank. After years of vacillating between expansion and contraction, the Federal Reserve in 1979 under its chair Paul Volcker embraced a policy of fierce monetary stringency, driving interest rates to near 20 percent and triggering the worst recession since the 1930s. Hard times inspired calls for reforms to make the Federal Reserve more responsive to elected officials. Economic recovery after 1983, however, coupled with stable, low inflation, bore out the wisdom of Volcker's policy and garnered the Federal Reserve immense prestige. Subsequently, the central bank followed policies designed primarily to keep prices stable. Under the leadership of Alan Greenspan, the Federal Reserve continued this policy through the long boom of the 1990s.

The Greenspan Federal Reserve approach to monetary policy collapsed with the economic crisis of 2008–2010. The board's relatively loose money policies, enabled by an era of moderate inflation, unleashed a debt-financed boom in real estate that was based on inflated housing values and cheap, poorly secured mortgages. When the real estate bubble burst, the entire economy went with it, causing even Greenspan to admit that economic markets were neither self-regulating nor tending toward equilibrium. His successor as chair of the Federal Reserve Board, Ben Bernanke, an academic economist and student of U.S. monetary policy during the Great Depression, acted firmly to combat the economic crisis and contraction of 2008–2010. Under Bernanke's leadership, the board cut interest rates, aggressively purchased U.S. bonds, and generously supported crisis-ridden private banks. By 2012 short-term interest rates were near zero—in fact, practically negative in real terms—and long-term rates remained extraordinarily low by historical standards. The board succeeded in limiting the duration and impact of the economic crisis without setting off inflation. Nevertheless, the Bernanke board found it difficult to pursue the other part of the board's dual mandate: to restrain inflation while combating unemployment. Inflation remained tame, but unemployment stayed high.

[*See also* **Federal Reserve Act; Financial and Banking Promotion and Regulation; Inflation and Deflation; Monetarism; Monetary Policy, Federal; Stagflation; Unemployment;** *and* **Volcker, Paul.**]

BIBLIOGRAPHY

Kettl, Donald F. *Leadership at the Fed*. New Haven, Conn.: Yale University Press, 1986.

Woolley, John T. *Monetary Politics: The Federal Reserve and the Politics of Monetary Policy.* Cambridge, U.K.: Cambridge University Press, 1984.

Wyatt C. Wells

FEDERAL TRADE COMMISSION

An independent federal regulatory agency created in 1914, the Federal Trade Commission (FTC) was part of an antitrust settlement that included the Clayton Antitrust Act and congressional acceptance of a judicial "rule of reason," which tolerated aspects of business concentration. Consisting of five appointed commissioners, the agency inherited the investigatory powers of the earlier Bureau of Corporations and became the administrator of regulatory legislation outlawing "unfair methods of competition." Subsequently the FTC also became the administrator of laws under which it supervised export associations and enforced restraints on price discrimination, deceptive advertising, proposed mergers, and certain labeling, lending, packaging, and warranty practices. In the 1990s it became concerned, too, with telemarketing fraud and abuses by funeral homes, and in 2007 it was given authority to investigate and punish the artificial inflation of energy prices.

The FTC's creation was supported both by antimonopolists seeking to halt the "unfair competition" involved in trust building and by businessmen seeking "fairness" as a basis for greater order and stability. Differing definitions of "fairness" could serve differing ends, however, and in practice the FTC pursued contradictory policies. At times it fought industrial concentration, most notably in its investigations of the electrical power, iron and steel, and cement industries in the 1930s and in its ac-

tions against so-called shared monopoly in the 1970s. But at other times, especially under the chairmen William E. Humphrey (1925–1933), Edward F. Howrey (1953–1955), and James C. Miller (1981–1985), it sponsored corporate collaboration and business-stabilization schemes. In addition, its rulings tended to be more concerned with protecting complaining competitors than with encouraging competitive markets, especially in its enforcement of the Robinson–Patman Anti–Price Discrimination Act (1936), which from 1945 to 1965 generated nearly 70 percent of the FTC's regulatory orders.

Historians generally regard the FTC as one of the least successful of America's regulatory commissions. It has shown political staying power and conducted investigations of lasting importance for industrial policy. But more often it has been characterized by contradictory impulses, unstable policies and standards, persistent organizational problems, and the squandering of its resources on relatively inconsequential matters.

[*See also* **Antitrust Legislation; Clayton Antitrust Act; Consumer Movements;** *and* **Federal Regulatory Agencies.**]

BIBLIOGRAPHY

Harris, Richard A., and Sidney M. Milkis. *The Politics of Regulatory Change: A Tale of Two Agencies.* 2d ed. New York: Oxford University Press, 1996.
Katzmann, Robert A. *Regulatory Bureaucracy: The Federal Trade Commission and Antitrust Policy.* Cambridge, Mass.: MIT Press, 1980.
Stone, Alan. *Economic Regulation and the Public Interest: The Federal Trade Commission in Theory and Practice.* Ithaca, N.Y.: Cornell University Press, 1977.

Ellis W. Hawley

FEDERATION OF ORGANIZED TRADES AND LABOR UNIONS

Formed at a meeting of more than one hundred union leaders in Pittsburgh, Pennsylvania, on 15 November 1881, the Federation of Organized Trades and Labor Unions of the United States and Canada (FOTLU) served as the basis for the formation five years later of the most durable labor organization in North American history, the American Federation of Labor.

The impetus for the FOTLU's formation came from the leaders of trade unions who had become disaffected with the largest labor organization of that time, the Knights of Labor, with which most were then affiliated. The trade unionists believed that their power was diluted by the Knights' structure, which included workers from a wide variety of occupations and varying skills who were organized in mixed local and regional assemblies. As skilled craft unionists, the FOTLU founders believed that they needed an organization through which they could aid each other in an effort to establish greater control over the labor markets that their members sought to organize.

John Jarrett of the Amalgamated Association of Iron, Steel, and Tin Workers chaired the founding meeting of the FOTLU. Samuel Gompers of the Cigar Makers' International Union chaired the FOTLU's organizing committee. Equally influential among the leadership was P. J. McGuire, of the recently established United Brotherhood of Carpenters. Of the three, it was Gompers who most influenced the vision of the new organization.

Initially the FOTLU focused on a legislative agenda that included laws abolishing child and convict labor, establishing an eight-hour workday and a national bureau of labor statistics, and restricting immigration. Later that agenda was expanded to include the establishment of a national holiday celebrating labor. Although a bureau of labor statistics was created in the Interior Department in 1884, the other initiatives proved more difficult to advance, and the FOTLU lost momentum as membership in the Knights of Labor surged between 1884 and 1886. Relations between the Knights and the FOTLU, whose memberships overlapped to a significant degree and which increasingly regarded each other as rivals, grew acrimonious.

A national wave of strikes to win the eight-hour workday, launched on 1 May 1886, provided the spark for the reinvigoration of the FOTLU, simultaneously demonstrating the power of trade union action and sidelining the Knights. The strikes erupted after the federal government failed to enact an eight-hour law demanded by the FOTLU, but hundreds of thousands of workers, many of whom were not in trade unions, joined the walkouts, including many Knights. The strikes in Chicago were fiercely contested and led to the Haymarket riot of 4 May 1886, during which anarchist activists were accused of hurling a dynamite bomb into the ranks of the police. In the panic that followed Haymarket, the Knights stumbled, losing a massive strike against the Missouri Pacific and the Southern Pacific railroads; the organization never recovered from this defeat. The trade unions, meanwhile, succeeded in reducing the workday in many workplaces through their walkout.

By the fall of 1886, relations between the Knights and the trade unions were irreparably ruptured. Thus on 8 December 1886 the executive committee of the FOTLU met in Columbus, Ohio, with representatives of thirteen national unions and a dozen citywide federations and local unions, dissolved itself, and reconstituted the assembled organizations into a new entity, the American Federation of Labor, with Gompers as its first president.

[*See also* **American Federation of Labor; Bureau of Labor Statistics; Eight-Hour**

Day; Gompers, Samuel; Haymarket Affair; Knights of Labor; *and* Labor Movements.]

BIBLIOGRAPHY

Commons, John R., et al. *History of Labour in the United States.* 4 vols. Vol. 2. New York: Macmillan, 1918.

Green, James. *Death in the Haymarket: A Story of Chicago, the First Labor Movement, and the Bombing That Divided Gilded Age America.* New York: Pantheon Books, 2006.

Kaufman, Stuart. *Samuel Gompers and the Origins of the American Federation of Labor, 1848–1898.* Westport, Conn.: Greenwood Press, 1973.

Joseph A. McCartin

FILM AND LABOR

From the opening of the first nickelodeon in 1905, movies have helped shape the ways in which Americans have thought about labor and working-class life. Although most silent films were innocuous love stories and action tales, a significant number focused on the central problems of workers' lives—low wages, poor working conditions, unemployment—and how they responded to those problems—strikes, unions, radical politics. Class-conscious filmmakers on both the left and the right transformed labor-capital struggles that were previously hidden from public sight into highly visible parts of a new public sphere. Tragedies of the 1910s such as the fire at the Triangle Shirtwaist Company, the Ludlow massacre, and the Pennsylvania coal wars were re-created and reinterpreted on the screen for millions of viewers to see. By 1910, movies about class struggle had grown so numerous that reviewers began speaking of a new genre of "labor-capital" films.

Although commercial companies produced the bulk of these films, the minimal demands of technical expertise and the low cost of production allowed groups that are no longer usually associated with Hollywood—from socialists and militant trade unionists on the left to the National Association of Manufacturers and the American Bankers Association on the right—to make films aimed at advancing their cause. Union and radical productions such as *A Martyr to His Cause* (1911), *From Dusk to Dawn* (1913), and *What Is to Be Done?* (1914) depicted labor and socialist struggles in a positive light and offered viewers viable alternatives to capitalism and capitalist politics. Business organizations parried these visual claims by making movies—*The Crime of Carelessness* and *The Workman's Lesson* (both 1912)—that denigrated unions and showed the extraordinary efforts that employers had undertaken on behalf of employees.

Studios and Conservatism. The outbreak of World War I precipitated dramatic changes in the evolution of the American movie industry and the ideological content of its films. By the beginning of the 1920s the early years' geographically scattered array of small and medium producers, distributors, and exhibitors was supplanted by an increasingly oligarchic, vertically integrated studio system centered in Los Angeles and financed by some of the largest industrial and financial institutions in the nation.

Looking to increase profits rather than solve labor problems, studios and exhibition chains built luxurious movie palaces aimed at attracting a broader range of middle-class and wealthy Americans. As studios attempted to increase profits by luring more middle- and upper-class viewers into these plush new theaters, films emphasizing class conflict were superseded by lavish productions—such as *Saturday Night* (1922) and *Orchids and Ermine* (1927)—that blurred traditional class distinctions, hailed the virtues of class harmony, and focused on the good-natured and often romantic interactions between the classes. Magnificent mansions, fashionable hotels, and exotic nightclubs where the moneyed set amused themselves supplanted the factory and tenement settings so popular in prewar films. Working-class film companies such as Labor Film Services, the Federation Film Corporation, the American Federation of Labor, and International Workers Aid turned out movies about class conflict and exploitation—*The Contrast* (1921), *The New Disciple* (1921), *Labor's Reward* (1925), and *The Passaic Textile Strike* (1926)—but these independent productions grew fewer in number and rarely appeared in the studio-owned first-run theaters that gave movies their greatest visibility and profits.

The rise of talking pictures in the late 1920s signaled a new era in American film. Over the next several decades, the corporate studios that dominated Hollywood turned out conservative labor-capital films—from *Black Fury* (1935) to *Reaching for the Sun* (1941) to *Slaughter on Tenth Avenue* (1957)—that rarely offered insights into the underlying causes of class conflict. Audiences saw lots of angry workers but little of the daily frustrations and injustices that led people to risk losing their jobs and savings in order to protest. Working people were repeatedly depicted as easily manipulated by union leaders, outside agitators, and ever-present Reds. Indeed, *Racket Busters* (1938) and *On the Waterfront* (1954) depicted unions as mob-infested organizations that did little good for the average worker.

Not all films were hostile to labor. Some studios and independent producers offered sympathetic depictions of the injustices that workers suffered at the hands of employers, police, judges, and politicians. Yet despite their liberal bent, films such as *Our Daily Bread* (1934), *Modern Times* (1936), *The Grapes of Wrath* (1940), *The Whistle at Eaton Falls* (1951), and *The Garment Jungle* (1957) empathized with the plight of individuals but not with their efforts at collective action. Class

problems were still portrayed in terms of corrupt individuals rather than a corrupt system.

Activism. Oppositional filmmaking during the early decades of the sound era came largely from independent groups that turned out left-liberal and radical productions such as *Millions of Us* (1936), *People of the Cumberland* (1937), *Native Land* (1947), and *Salt of the Earth* (1954)—productions that offered viewers stories of strikes, unions, and demonstrations that they were unlikely to see in more mainstream productions. During the late 1940s and early 1950s, unions endeavored to reach mass audiences by making nontheatrical films that were shown in schools, churches, synagogues, civic organizations, and union halls—films such as *Union at Work* (1949), *With These Hands* (1950), and *We the People* (1959).

The social and political activism of the 1960s and 1970s inspired Hollywood to turn out a small number of features, such as *The Front* (1976), *Norma Rae* (1979), *Reds* (1981), *Silkwood* (1983), and *Matewan* (1987), that, taken collectively, attacked Red-baiters and offered unabashedly positive portrayals of unions, labor organizers, and radicals. Audiences of this period also got to see documentaries—*Union Maids* (1976), *Harlan County, U.S.A.* (1976), *The Wobblies* (1979), *American Dream* (1989), and *Roger and Me* (1989)—that offered moving accounts of working-class resistance to corporate greed. However, an even greater number of studio feature films presented millions of Americans with disparaging visions of working-class organizations, their leaders, and their goals. *F.I.S.T.* (1978), *Blue Collar* (1978), and *Hoffa* (1992) perpetuated ideas of the union-mob connection and took hostile swipes at unions, strikes, and organizing efforts.

Since around the turn of the twenty-first century, filmmakers have turned to exploring the myriad problems faced by a new generation of immigrant workers. Like *Salt of the Earth*,

Real Women Have Curves (2002) and *Bread and Roses* (2000) examine the complex interconnections of class, ethnicity, race, and gender and the ways in which those identities shape working-class life and struggles. The globalization of Hollywood makes it likely that an increasing number of films will be made about the problems of immigrant workers. If the past is any guide, however, the vast majority of these productions will focus on the plight of individuals and not on the system that caused their problems in the first place.

[*See also* **Advertising.**]

BIBLIOGRAPHY

Bodnar, John E. *Blue-Collar Hollywood: Liberalism, Democracy, and Working People in American Film.* Baltimore: John Hopkins University Press, 2003.

Booker, M. Keith. *Film and the American Left: A Research Guide.* Westport, Conn.: Greenwood Press, 1999.

Brownlow, Kevin. *Behind the Mask of Innocence, Sex, Violence, Prejudice, Crime: Films of Social Conscience in the Silent Era.* Berkeley: University of California Press, 1992.

Ross, Steven J. *Working-Class Hollywood: Silent Film and the Shaping of Class in America.* Princeton, N.J.: Princeton University Press, 1998.

Stead, Peter. *Film and the Working Class: The Feature Film in British and American Society.* London and New York: Routledge, 1989.

Zaniello, Tom. *Working Stiffs, Union Maids, Reds, and Riffraff: An Expanded Guide to Films about Labor.* Ithaca, N.Y.: ILR Press, 2003.

Steven J. Ross

FINANCIAL AND BANKING PROMOTION AND REGULATION

Throughout U.S. history, the federal government has engaged in financial and banking promotion and regulation to further particular political, economic, and social policies. Some of the most significant promotional acts include creating a central bank and establishing deposit insurance.

The creation of a central bank to issue uniform currency, regulate the money supply, and act as lender of last resort to banking institutions was the first feature of banking promotion by the federal government. The initial attempt predated the nation's founding. In 1781 the Continental Congress created the Bank of North America (BNA) to help finance the Revolutionary War. A year later, the BNA stopped being a creature of central government when it received a charter from the state of Pennsylvania.

In 1790, Alexander Hamilton, the secretary of the treasury, recommended to the U.S. Congress that it charter a national bank that would be majority-owned by shareholders. Such a bank would be modeled after central banks abroad and would support trade and industry, foster economic development, and manage the federal government's funds. The plan included requiring owners to purchase shares, using, in large part, government bonds, thereby creating a demand for those instruments and improving the government's credit rating. Supporting Hamilton's plan, a year later Congress established the First Bank of the United States. The charter expired in twenty years and was not renewed. The Second Bank of the United States was established in 1816 and stayed in existence only until 1836.

In 1913, with the Federal Reserve Act, Congress established what continues to be the United States' central bank, the Federal Reserve System (the Fed). The lender-of-last-resort role includes the capacity to purchase assets from banks—or to make loans to banks against such assets—that may be depressed in value, thus establishing a price floor and also providing needed funds in the form of Federal Reserve

Notes (U.S. currency, whether paper or electronic) to a bank facing a liquidity crisis owing to depositor withdrawals or an inability to roll over financing for short-term debts.

The next important tool to promote banking was government-backed deposit insurance. Even with the Fed in place, depositors lacked confidence that their money would be returned if a bank failed. During the Great Depression, when many banking institutions did fail, legislation was passed in 1933 and 1934 to provide deposit insurance for accounts at both commercial banks and thrifts. This was a boost to banking because it solved the confidence problem: now the federal government was a guarantor of qualifying deposit accounts up to a dollar limit. Though the Deposit Insurance Fund (DIF) is financed with assessments on depository institutions, the amount in the DIF is less than total insured deposits. Thus deposit insurance is a taxpayer-backed safety net.

With such insurance, depositors are less prone to run on a bank when they fear either the mismanagement of a particular bank or the decline in value of the assets in which the bank has invested deposits. Given the absence of an incentive for depositors to monitor bank activities, combined with lender-of-last-resort financing through the Fed, banks may choose to act more recklessly than they would without such protections. Accordingly, an essential part of banking regulation is the power of the government to ensure the safety and soundness of banking operations. With these concerns in mind, Congress passed the Dodd–Frank Wall Street Reform and Consumer Protection Act of 2010, which attempts to prohibit financial institutions that have access to deposit insurance and Fed funding from engaging in certain risky practices.

[*See also* **Bank of the United States, First and Second; Deregulation, Financial; Federal Deposit Insurance Corporation; Federal Regulatory Agencies; Federal Reserve System; Glass–Steagall, Repeal of; Hamilton, Alexander, and Economic Development; Monetary Policy, Federal; National Banking System (1863); New Deal Banking Regulation;** *and* **Shadow Banking System.**]

BIBLIOGRAPHY

Carnell, Richard Scott, Jonathan R. Macey, and Geoffrey P. Miller. *The Law of Banking and Financial Institutions.* 4th ed. Austin, Tex.: Wolters Kluwer Law & Business, 2009.

Ferguson, Niall. *The Ascent of Money: A Financial History of the World.* New York: Penguin Press, 2008.

Johnson, Simon, and James Kwak. *13 Bankers: The Wall Street Takeover and the Next Financial Meltdown.* New York: Pantheon, 2010.

Moulton, R. K. *Legislative and Documentary History of the Banks of the United States from the Time of Establishing the Bank of North America, 1781, to October 1834.* New York: Carvill, 1834.

Jennifer Taub

FINANCIAL CRISES, 1980s–2010

The collapse of Bear Stearns in March 2008 marked the start of the worst U.S. financial crisis since the Great Depression of the 1930s. Yet the economic crisis actually dated to December 2007 when the gross domestic product (GDP) started to fall. Despite disagreement among economists about its causes, all agree that the recession of 2008–2012 was the most severe since the 1930s. The GDP fell for more than a year, until June 2009, much longer than for any downturn since the Great Depression. The recovery, furthermore, has been sluggish: the GDP began to grow at about 2.8 percent since June 2009, but this rate is only about half the rate of growth compared to previous recoveries. More than 2 million homeowners lost their homes, and by the end of 2010, 29.8 million people continued to be out of work or partially unemployed.

The crisis came after three decades of neoliberal policy that, ironically, replicated the free-market policies that had led to the Great Depression. Terrified by the Great Depression, policy makers during the 1930s recognized the failure of free-market polices and acted proactively to intervene in the economy. This tendency was strengthened by fear of the world revolutionary movement against capitalism; capital compromised with labor by yielding some power to collective bargaining and accepting progressive taxation, strict regulation of both financial and nonfinancial sectors, significant government expenditure for public education and health systems, and active fiscal and monetary policies to limit unemployment. This was the so-called Keynesian policy package that marked the golden age of capitalism that lasted from World War II to the mid-1970s.

Contraction and Neoliberalism.

By the 1970s, however, the favorable domestic and international conditions of the postwar era when the United States dominated world capitalism had begun to change. An era of contraction began as the U.S. economy started to slow and slip into repeated recessions. Competition from European and Japanese competitors, the decision by the Organization of Petroleum Exporting Countries (OPEC) to raise oil prices, the Vietnam War, and rising labor unrest all squeezed corporate profits and contributed to the stagflation of the 1970s. However, instead of realizing the limitations of capitalism, the policy makers, backed by conservative economists and others tired of compromising with pressure from the discontented, attributed the recession to the excessive power of trade unions and frequent government intervention in the economy. Their solution was to unleash capitalism and practice a free-market ideology and the trickle-down theory, implementing what became known as "neoliberalism."

The defeat of proposals by the administration of Jimmy Carter for a consumer protection agency, reform of labor law, and progressive tax reform, along with the passage in 1978 of Proposition 13 in California, initiated the full retreat from the postwar labor accord. Proposition 13 did more than lower and limit Californians' property taxes: it sparked an ideological campaign that identified government as the problem and that has remained influential ever since. In the thrall of neoliberalism, both Republicans and Democrats weakened organized labor to the benefit of the corporate and financial and political sectors. Typical neoliberal policies include privatizing existing public services, attacking unions, deregulating banking, freeing corporations to outsource production internationally, cutting taxes for the wealthy, and focusing attention on inflation rather than on unemployment.

Neoliberal policies promised to bring shared prosperity based on the trickle-down theory: if the wealthiest 1 percent flourished, then their investments and innovations would lead to such rapid economic growth that the benefits would trickle down to everyone else. What happened was the opposite. Though the top 1 percent's share of national income had fallen to 9 percent by the mid-1970s, it increased steadily during the 1980s and 1990s. Even while wages stagnated for most people, the top 1 percent's share of all income rose to 14 percent in 1991 and 21.5 percent in 2000. The income of the top 1 percent of households increased 10.1 percent per year from 2002 to 2007—even while the bottom 90 percent saw their real incomes grow by just 0.8 percent per year.

Economic inequality led to stagnating consumer demand. To stimulate the economy after the recession of 2000–2002, the Federal Reserve lowered interest rates: the federal funds rate averaged 5.1 percent during 1990s but was cut to 1.4 percent from 2002 to 2004 and remained low into 2007. Cheap credit stimulated home buying and consumption more than it stimulated domestic investment, however, because capital's freedom to outsource production meant that it continued to invest abroad.

Deregulation. The wave of financial deregulation that started during the administration of Jimmy Carter in the 1970s peaked with the passage of the Financial Services Modernization (Gramm–Leach–Bliley) Act in 1999 and the Commodity Futures Modernization Act (CFMA) in 2000. The Gramm–Leach–Bliley Act repealed parts of the Glass–Steagall Act to allow the merger of commercial banks, investment banks, and insurance companies, regardless of conflicts of interest and the danger of their being "too big to fail." The CFMA further limited oversight and regulation of the trading of complicated financial derivatives.

Policy makers were forewarned of the dangers of financial market deregulation. At least three relatively recent examples preceded the financial crisis of 2008–2009 and might have been taken as lessons about the dangers of financial deregulation, a key policy of the neoliberal package. Savings and loan banks (S&Ls) were deregulated in the 1980s and were allowed to invest in commercial real estate and other high-risk financial projects. When real estate prices fell in the 1980s, more than one thousand S&Ls failed. Despite this history, when the stock market boomed in the late 1990s and during the housing bubble at the turn of the millennium, many economists, including the Federal Reserve chairman at the time, Alan Greenspan, denied that a bubble existed; they refused to intervene and insisted that rising prices—inflation-adjusted housing prices rose by 85 percent from 1997 to 2006—reflected rising real values and the sector's excellent performance.

At the dawn of the 2008–2009 crisis, household mortgage debt had increased to 140 percent of after-tax personal income. When the asset bubble collapsed, as it had to, banks were caught holding trillions of dollars in exotic and bankrupt mortgage-backed assets. Most ordinary citizens and consumers could not continue borrowing but had to start repaying their debts, leading to the collapse of debt-sustained demand—as well as of the imagined free-market economy.

Policy makers intervened immediately. The Federal Reserve pushed the interest rate to virtually zero by the beginning of 2009, yet loose monetary policy failed to revive an economy suffering from severe consumer uncertainty. The 2008 Troubled Assets Relief Program (TARP) stabilized the banking sector at the price of maintaining the influence of the too-big-to-fail financial institutions. It also triggered the Occupy Wall Street (OWS) movement, putatively contrasting the 99 percent against the 1 percent. The fiscal stimulus in the 2009 American Recovery and Reinvestment Act (ARRA) aimed at the right economic maladies but was too small to revitalize a deeply depressed economy. The Dodd–Frank Act of 2010 sought to regulate financial institutions but lacked clear standards and left financial institutions with too much influence and power. At the end of 2012, the economy remained plagued by slack consumer demand, substantial unemployment, and an excess of foreclosed housing stock.

[*See also* **Depressions, Economic; Deregulation, Financial; Economic Deregulation and the Carter Administration; Glass–Steagall, Repeal of; Keynesian Economics; Monetary Policy, Federal; Neoliberalism; Neoliberalism as Public Economic Policy; New Deal Banking Regulation; Stagflation;** *and* **Supply-Side Economics.**]

BIBLIOGRAPHY

Baker, Dean. *Plunder and Blunder: The Rise and Fall of the Bubble Economy.* Sausalito, Calif.: PoliPointPress, 2009.

Center for Popular Economics. *Economics for the 99%*. Center for Popular Economics, 2012. http://www.populareconomics.org/wp-content/uploads/2012/06/Economics_99_Percent_for_web1.pdf.

MacEwan, Arthur, and John A. Miller. *Economic Collapse, Economic Change: Getting to the Roots of the Crisis*. Armonk, N.Y.: M. E. Sharpe, 2011.

Palley, Thomas I. *From Financial Crisis to Stagnation: The Destruction of Shared Prosperity and the Role of Economics*. New York: Cambridge University Press, 2012.

Stiglitz, Joseph E. *Freefall: America, Free Markets, and the Sinking of the World Economy*. New York: W. W. Norton and Company, 2010.

Ying Chen

FIRESTONE, HARVEY

(1868–1938), industrialist and corporate executive. Harvey Firestone was born near Columbiana, Ohio, to a well-to-do farm family. After graduating from high school in 1887, he held several clerical jobs, most notably with his uncle's Columbus Buggy Company. Firestone became interested in rubber carriage tires and developed a profitable tire dealership. In 1900 he moved to Akron, Ohio, the emerging center of the tire industry, to manufacture tires. Firestone quickly established his firm as an important producer of carriage, bicycle, and, increasingly, automobile tires. In 1905 the Firestone Tire and Rubber Company obtained a large order from the Ford Motor Company for its new Model T. From that time the company grew rapidly. By 1920, Firestone had become one of the best-known American industrialists.

In the 1920s and 1930s Firestone transformed his company into a vertically integrated corporation that participated in all aspects of tire production and distribution. He developed rubber plantations overseas, textile plants, specialized factories, a full line of tire-oriented products,

retail stores, and a worldwide marketing organization. Firestone scorned growth through mergers with competing companies; instead, he emphasized his own brand-name products, which he promoted relentlessly through advertising and public relations activities, such as camping trips with Thomas Edison, Henry Ford, and other notables. Despite his company's growing size, Firestone insisted on personal control and family management and opposed labor unions. His five sons all became Firestone executives and played important roles in the firm until the 1970s.

[*See also* **Vertical Integration, Economies of Scale, and Firm Size.**]

BIBLIOGRAPHY

Lief, Alfred. *The Firestone Story: A History of the Firestone Tire and Rubber Company*. New York: Whittlesey House, 1951.

Lief, Alfred. *Harvey Firestone, Free Man of Enterprise*. New York: McGraw-Hill, 1951.

Daniel Nelson

FISHERIES

From Native American subsistence to global markets, fisheries loom large in American history. Ancient weir sites under Boston Harbor and along the northwest coast and huge bone deposits at The Dalles in Oregon offer evidence that North Americans have fished intensively for more than nine thousand years. European cod fishermen venturing into the northwestern Atlantic in the 1480s soon came ashore in Newfoundland, Acadia, and New England, establishing some of the earliest permanent settlements. By the 1700s, fishers caught Atlantic salmon, lobsters, and cod; indeed, control of the cod fisheries figured in the era's diplomacy and imperials wars.

Evolving technologies have included aboriginal spears, nets, weirs, and European purse seines. The salmon fisheries' adoption of pound nets and fish wheels in the 1870s and the introduction of the otter trawl in 1905 increased catches. Early Europeans cured cod by salting the wet fish on shipboard, but by the later 1500s they were drying and salting fish on shore. Canning emerged in the mid-1800s, freezing late in the century. In the 1940s, giant factory-trawlers combined both operations.

The history of fisheries varies by region. In New England, freshwater species began to disappear after 1800 as agriculture, urbanization, and manufacturing altered their habitats, but offshore fishing and whaling remained economic mainstays. In the twentieth century, cod, striped bass, tuna, and marlin were the principal commercial fish, while anglers prized eastern trout and Atlantic salmon. Along the middle and south Atlantic coast, Chesapeake Bay, and the Gulf coast, crabs, oysters, striped bass, and shrimp were important, with Indians, African slaves, and poor whites the primary laborers. Anglers coveted warm-water fish such as bass and bonefish.

Fisheries also arose on inland rivers and lakes—including the Mississippi, Illinois, and Nipigon Rivers, the Great Lakes, and Lake Winnipeg—sustaining major industries and communities until habitat destruction undermined them in the late nineteenth and twentieth centuries. Market species included catfish, whitefish, pike, and sturgeon; anglers favored trout and bass. Late twentieth-century fish culturists created Pacific salmon fisheries, but pollution prevented these stocks from becoming important food sources.

On the West Coast, aboriginal societies caught salmon, eulachon, shellfish, and pinnipeds, while nineteenth-century European Americans pursued Pacific salmon, fur seals, and whales. Commercial fishers in Alaska formed communities that often preceded formal government. Indians, although important laborers initially, had by 1900 been displaced by southern Europeans, Scandinavians, and Asians. In the twentieth century, offshore fleets depleted salmon, halibut, whale, sardine, crab, pollack, and groundfish stocks. Anglers, meanwhile, fished for trout, stocked exotic species, and fought to control salmon and steelhead streams.

Fishery management and regulation were initially local prerogatives. In the Colonial Era, towns such as Concord, Massachusetts, set rules and sanctioned monopolies to conserve shad. State fish commissions did not appear until the 1860s. When the first federal fish commissioner tried in 1871 to resolve a conflict in New England over declining scup stocks, the states were ill-equipped to deal with the issue and the commissioner gave up. Only in Alaska, or when negotiating fishing treaties with Indians and other nations, did federal officials play a primary role, and even here states often contested their power. To avoid regulations, Americans relied on technical solutions such as hatcheries and fishways. When regulations proved unavoidable, they typically fell most heavily on the more marginal members of society.

On both the East Coast and the West Coast, unions had some success organizing fishermen. On the East Coast, most notably New York City and the Massachusetts ports of Gloucester, New Bedford, and Boston, the Atlantic Fishermen's Union (AFU) organized deep-sea fishermen or trawlermen. By the 1950s these ports were organized. Besides acting as a traditional trade union, the AFU was, like its counterparts on the West Coast, very much interested in protecting the surrounding fishery. The AFU then combined its trade union direction with an environmental appreciation of fish stocks and their role in guaranteeing work.

[*See also* **Environmental Regulations** *and* **Maritime Transport**.]

BIBLIOGRAPHY

Davis, Colin. "The Politics of Inclusion and Exclusion: A Transnational Comparison of Fishery Regulation in the USA and GB, 1960–1977." *Studia Atlantica* 13 (2009): 93–104.

Davis, Colin. "Transatlantic Danger: Work and Death among U.S. and British Trawlermen, 1960–1974." *International Journal of Maritime History* 21 (June 2009):153–174.

Innis, Harold A. *The Cod Fisheries: The History of an International Economy.* Rev. ed. Toronto: University of Toronto Press, 1954.

McEvoy, Arthur F. *The Fisherman's Problem: Ecology and Law in the California Fisheries, 1850–1980.* Cambridge, U.K., and New York: Cambridge University Press, 1986.

Taylor, Joseph E., III *Making Salmon: An Environmental History of the Northwest Fisheries Crisis.* Seattle: University of Washington Press, 1999.

Colin J. Davis

FIVE-DOLLAR DAY

The Five-Dollar Day was a minimum-wage scheme instituted by Henry Ford in 1914 to address the problems of high employee turnover and absenteeism. Ford and his business manager James Couzens decided that high pay could attract workers, maintain loyalty, and increase productivity. In addition, high wages could serve to undermine potential unionization efforts. Coupled with a reduction to an eight-hour day and the addition of a third shift, the change brought workers flooding to Ford's gates, despite the grueling production pace demanded. The plan succeeded: within a year, turnover and absences had slowed to a trickle.

Ford explained the move as profit sharing—and given that his was the most profitable automobile company at the time, he could easily afford nearly to double the firm's minimum wage. The move was widely hailed by workers' advocates, such as the American Federation of Labor's Samuel Gompers, as a sign of progressive business practices. Others rightly pointed out that this wage was available only at the whim of the manufacturer and could as easily be taken away. Ford's counterparts at other auto companies looked at his soaring profits and declared that he was competing unfairly. Some business critics argued that Ford was giving workers exorbitant wages that they were ill-equipped to handle and that they would misspend. Ford countered that without good wages, workers could not buy Ford products.

Workers soon learned that the new wage plan was not actually available to all. First, employees had to be employed by the company for six months to be eligible. Second, the plan excluded unmarried women and men without families. Third, the company determined eligibility based on its preferred standards of personal conduct. Ford dispatched his sociological department to evaluate and monitor those considered worthy of the Five-Dollar Day. Its standards included not using alcohol, maintaining a clean home, having a savings account, and generally showing good moral character. The department used home visits and other observations to make its determinations. All these criteria were intended to evaluate the reliability of a given employee. Workers could be removed from the program for drunkenness, gambling, domestic violence, or other immoral conduct. If workers resented the paternalism, they appreciated the wage.

The sociological department fit into the trend of scientific social work that became common during the Progressive Era. Whether in settlement houses or other social-work settings, a common goal of reformers was the so-called uplift of the poor and immigrant population. A major goal of that uplift was the assimilation—or "Americanization"—of immigrants. Ford's sociological department strove to Americanize the foreign-born employees who predominated at Ford, thus making them better workers.

The program lasted until 1920, when Ford dropped the sociological department as being impractical and too intrusive in his workers' lives. And with profits down in the recession of 1920–1921, the Five-Dollar Day was too costly, so the company returned to a more traditional bonus system to promote loyalty and productivity.

[*See also* **Automotive Industry; Eight-Hour Day; Ford, Henry, and Fordism;** *and* **Welfare Capitalism.**]

BIBLIOGRAPHY

Batchelor, Ray. *Henry Ford: Mass Production, Modernism, and Design.* Manchester, U.K., and New York: Manchester University Press, 1994.

Meyer, Stephen, III. *The Five Dollar Day: Labor Management and Social Control in the Ford Motor Company, 1908–1921.* Albany, N.Y.: State University of New York Press, 1981.

Watts, Steven. *The People's Tycoon: Henry Ford and the American Century.* New York: Alfred A. Knopf, 2005.

Elizabeth Jozwiak

FLETCHER, BEN

(1890–1949), African American labor leader. Benjamin Harrison Fletcher was the most important African American labor leader in the most influential radical union of the early 1900s, the Industrial Workers of the World (IWW), nicknamed the Wobblies. Though largely forgotten, he helped lead a militant, interracial, multiethnic union that dominated the Philadelphia waterfront for a decade.

Born in Philadelphia, Fletcher joined the IWW in 1912. It is unknown how he became radicalized, but presumably he heard street speakers in his diverse, working-class South Philadelphia neighborhood. Fletcher became the most prominent leader in Local 8, the Wobblies' branch of Philadelphia longshoremen, chartered in 1913. In Local 8, thousands of African Americans belonged to an organization that also included Irish Americans, Poles, and Lithuanians. Quite unlike most other labor organizations or nongovernmental institutions in the early twentieth century, the union integrated work gangs, meetings, parties, and leadership posts.

During World War I, Philadelphia was among the nation's most important ports, and the government targeted the IWW. Fletcher was the sole African American among the hundred Wobblies convicted of espionage and sedition in 1918. Though no evidence was brought against him specifically, Fletcher received a sentence of ten years in prison and a $30,000 fine. Fletcher served nearly three years before his sentence was commuted in 1922.

Fletcher remained firmly committed to the Wobblies, though he never again played a major role. He spent the last years of his life living with his wife in Brooklyn, New York City. Local 8 stood at the pinnacle of interracial equality in its era, an accomplishment that proved to Fletcher that the IWW could overcome racism, empower workers, and usher in a socialist society.

[*See also* **Dockworkers' Unions, Multiracial; Industrial Workers of the World; Labor Leaders; Longshoremen and Longshoremen's Unions;** *and* **Racism.**]

BIBLIOGRAPHY

Cole, Peter. *Ben Fletcher: The Life and Times of a Black Wobbly, Including Fellow Worker Fletcher's Writings and Speeches.* Chicago: Charles H. Kerr, 2007.

Cole, Peter. *Wobblies on the Waterfront: Interracial Unionism in Progressive-Era Philadelphia.* Urbana: University of Illinois Press, 2007.

Seraile, William. "Ben Fletcher, I.W.W. Organizer." *Pennsylvania History* 46, no. 3 (July 1979): 212–232.

Peter Cole

FLINT GENERAL MOTORS STRIKE

The sit-down strike of 1936–1937 pitted General Motors (GM), the world's largest manufacturing corporation, against the fledgling United Auto Workers of America (UAW). After GM refused a UAW request for a conference to discuss outstanding grievances, a small group of workers, adopting a tactic that the UAW had first used in November 1936, occupied the Fisher Body plant in Cleveland, Ohio, on 28 December 1936. Two days later, strikers occupied the two Fisher Body plants in Flint, Michigan, the heart of the GM empire. Eventually the strike spread to GM plants nationwide, idling 136,000 workers.

GM secured a court injunction on 2 January 1937 that ordered the sit-downers to evacuate the two Flint plants. The union ignored the injunction, and Michigan's governor, Frank Murphy, delayed its enforcement. Flint police made a futile effort on 11 January to dislodge the strikers in the No. 2 plant. Responding to the request of Flint officials, Murphy then sent the Michigan National Guard to Flint to preserve order but not to take sides. While the sit-down strikers carefully protected company property, wives and others on the outside supplied food and otherwise supported the cause. In a daring maneuver on 1 February, the UAW enlarged the strike by seizing the Chevrolet No. 4 plant, the sole producer of engines for Chevrolet cars.

Governor Murphy played the crucial role in resolving the dispute. The strike ended on 11 February when GM agreed to recognize the UAW as the bargaining agency for its GM members. Arguably the twentieth century's most important labor conflict, the GM sit-down proved a boon not only to the UAW but to mass-production unionism in general during the 1930s.

[*See also* Automotive Industry; General Motors Strike (1945); Strikes; *and* United Auto Workers.]

BIBLIOGRAPHY

Fine, Sidney. *Sit-Down: The General Motors Strike of 1936–1937*. Ann Arbor: University of Michigan Press, 1969.

Kraus, Henry. *The Many and the Few: A Chronicle of the Dynamic Auto Workers*. Los Angeles: Plantin Press, 1947.

Sidney Fine

FLYNN, E. G.

(1890–1964), labor activist. Born in 1890 in Concord, New Hampshire, Elizabeth Gurley Flynn was the oldest of the four children of Tom Flynn and Annie Gurley. Poverty forced her family to move several times before they finally settled in the South Bronx, New York, in 1900. Flynn's radicalism was nurtured by the poverty and political inclinations of her family. Her father was an active socialist and Irish nationalist; her mother was a strong advocate of women's rights.

Flynn became a gifted orator at an early age. In 1904 she won a school medal for her advocacy of women's suffrage, and two years later she spoke on women and socialism at the Harlem Socialist Club. The same year, 1906, Flynn joined the Industrial Workers of the World (IWW, or Wobblies), leaving school in 1907 to serve as a delegate to that year's Chicago IWW convention.

Flynn played a prominent role in the free-speech fights called by the IWW in Missoula, Montana, in 1908 and in Spokane, Washington, in 1909. She stirred workers during industrial struggles at the textile mills of Lawrence, Massachusetts, in 1912; at the silk mills of Paterson, New Jersey, in 1913; and on the Mesabi iron range in northern Minnesota in 1916. Her work for the IWW inspired the Wobbly organizer and songwriter Joe Hill, who composed "The Rebel Girl" in her honor.

In September 1917, Flynn was one of 166 IWW members and the only woman indicted by a federal grand jury in Chicago for violating the Espionage Act. Rather than participate in a mass trial, Flynn, along with her lover and close political associate, the Italian anarchist Carlo Tresca, moved for severance, that is, a separate trial. Flynn herself wrote a letter to President Woodrow Wilson seeking sympathy and disavowing any connection to the IWW. The severance motion succeeded.

The trial ended Flynn's formal association with the IWW, and she devoted herself to civil liberties work during the interwar years. In 1918 she founded the Workers' Defense Union, a coalition of more than 170 labor, socialist, and radical organizations, to seek amnesty for political prisoners and others imprisoned because of their participation in the labor movement. She was a founding member of the American Civil Liberties Union in 1920 and served on the executive board of the American Fund for Public Service, also known as the Garland Fund, a philanthropic organization that abetted radical undertakings. Through her civil liberties work, Flynn championed the rights of hundreds of mostly unknown workers, including the Italian anarchists Nicola Sacco and Bartolomeo Vanzetti.

Her efforts on behalf of civil liberties and strikers during the 1920s undermined her health, and from 1926 to 1936 Flynn convalesced in Oregon at the home of her friend Dr.

Marie Equi, a former IWW activist and birth control advocate. Flynn joined the Communist Party USA (CPUSA) in 1936 and began writing a column in the party's *Daily Worker* about women's issues. An open Communist, she was nevertheless reelected to the executive committee of the ACLU in 1939. Flynn's continued support of CPUSA policy and the 1939 Hitler–Stalin pact, however, led the ACLU to remove her from office and membership in 1940 after a highly controversial trial. The ACLU reinstated her posthumously in 1976.

During the war years, Flynn supported CPUSA policy and rose steadily through the party's ranks, gaining election to the Central Committee in 1941. When top party leaders were arrested in 1948 for violating the Smith Act, Flynn chaired the Smith Act Defense Committee. In 1951 she was one of twenty-three Communist leaders targeted in a second round of Smith Act indictments. All the defendants were found guilty. On 11 January 1955, at sixty-four years old, she went to Alderson Federal Reformatory for Women in West Virginia to serve a twenty-eight-month sentence. In 1961 she became the first female chair of the CPUSA, a position that she held until her death in Moscow in September 1964.

[*See also* **Industrial Workers of the World** *and* **Labor and Anti-Communism.**]

BIBLIOGRAPHY

Baxandall, Rosalyn Fraad, ed. *Words on Fire: The Life and Writing of Elizabeth Gurley Flynn.* New Brunswick, N.J.: Rutgers University Press, 1987.
Camp, Helen C. *Iron in Her Soul: Elizabeth Gurley Flynn and the American Left.* Pullman: Washington State University Press, 1995.
Flynn, Elizabeth Gurley. *The Rebel Girl, an Autobiography: My First Life (1906–1926).* Rev. ed. New York: International Publishers, 1973.

Mary Anne Trasciatti

FOOD AND DIET

If one had to sum up the history of Americans and their food in a word, that word could be "abundance." Although the first English settlers suffered difficult times, most were soon much better fed than their counterparts across the Atlantic. Thanks mainly to better diets, George Washington's Revolutionary War troops were, on average, much taller than the British soldiers facing them. Citizens of the new republic prided themselves on what a Philadelphia physician called their "superabundance" of food. For most of the free population, this meant lots of meat, accompanied by breads made from corn, rye, and, increasingly, wheat. Fruits and vegetables were abundant in season, while wild animals inland and plentiful fish and seafood along the coasts provided additional sources of protein. The winter and early spring diet comprised preserved pork, bread, beans, and root vegetables—filling, if monotonous.

By the 1830s new roads, canals, and steamboats brought vast new areas of farmland into the market economy, making a wider variety of foodstuffs available for longer durations. Food reformers now cautioned against excessive indulgence. The minister and temperance advocate Sylvester Graham, warning that meat, alcohol, and spicy foods sapped the body's vital force, condemned such foods as processed white flour that had been altered from their God-given natural state.

America's slave population, totaling nearly 4 million by 1860, experienced a very different dietary environment. Slave families typically received a scant weekly ration of cornmeal and fatty pork. Some supplemented this unbalanced fare with fish, small game, eggs, and vegetables that they provided for themselves.

After midcentury, the expanding railroads transported affordable supplies of wheat, pork, and beef to the growing cities, market gardening and dairy farms proliferated around the railroads, and steamships brought exotic foods from abroad. By 1900, skilled chefs were turning out elaborate multicourse meals in the style of French haute cuisine for the wealthy. The growing middle and upper-middle classes could readily purchase the abundant foods but could not afford the servants to prepare and serve them in this style, and thus they were amenable to calls by a new generation of food reformers for dietary restraint.

The New Nutrition. The scientific basis for the reformers' crusade was the so-called New Nutrition: the discovery by chemists of proteins, carbohydrates, and fats, each with its unique physiological function. Proper nutrition now meant consuming as much of these as necessary: any less was unhealthful; any more, wasteful. Urging immigrant workers to economize, the reformers insisted that the proteins in beans were fully as nutritious as those in beefsteak. The middle classes, heeding the call to choose foods on the basis of their "physiological economy" rather than on the basis of their taste, made culture heroes out of dietary faddists like John Harvey Kellogg, who amplified Graham's theories with purgative nostrums based on recent scientific discoveries that the colon harbored large amounts of bacteria. The "scientific cooking" advocate Fannie Farmer offered simple menus and exact recipes in her *Boston Cooking-School Cook Book* (1896). Women in the new profession of home economics, teaching in the schools about food and health, similarly insisted that science rather than taste should guide one's food choices.

For the urban immigrant poor, meanwhile, providing even subsistence nutrition for their families proved difficult. In hard times, such as the Depression of the 1890s, it was more difficult still. Impure water, tainted milk, and spoiled meat contributed to illness, infant mortality, and periodic epidemics in the slums. Tougher public-health measures such as the 1906 Pure Food and Drug Act and milk pasteurization gradually ameliorated the worst of these dietary hazards, but ultimately the health of the poor improved mainly because of more ample and varied diets.

During World War I, the federal Food Administration used the New Nutrition to persuade Americans to substitute beans, whole grains, and fresh vegetables for the meat and wheat being shipped to Europe. Meanwhile, the discovery of vitamins in the early twentieth century gave rise to a new nutritional paradigm. Its dissemination was encouraged by the transformation of food production by mass-production industries characterized by large capital investments, mechanization, complex distribution networks, and large promotion and advertising budgets. Servants having disappeared almost entirely from middle-class homes, housewives were encouraged to buy labor-saving processed foods such as canned goods, as well as vitamin-rich citrus fruits and milk, which were said to be essential for children's health. Though still little understood, vitamins proved to be a food promoter's dream. Citrus growers, dairymen, the grain-milling industry, pickle producers—almost anyone could and did make extravagant claims. When synthesized vitamin pills became available in the late 1930s, food producers insisted that such supplements were unnecessary: a "balanced diet" would provide more than enough nutrients.

Neither the Depression of the 1930s nor World War II undermined confidence in America's abundant food supply. Indeed, the Depression-era agricultural crisis was defined as one of overproduction of food and maldistribution of income. And despite wartime rationing, many doubted that the shortages were real. Recurring rumors insisted that food supplies were more than adequate, but that government incompetence or crooked middlemen were keeping them off the market.

In the postwar baby-boom years, from 1946 to 1963, the long-term tendency of food preparation to move outside the home intensified as the food industries sold harried young mothers and homemakers on the "convenience" of their products. Frozen foods and other new kinds of processed, precooked, and packaged foods became popular. From 1949 to 1959, chemists developed more than four hundred additives to help food survive these new processes. Restaurants, especially the proliferating fast-food chains, welcomed this development: with food preparation reduced to defrosting, frying, or adding hot water, unskilled labor could replace expensive, often temperamental cooks.

Gastronomical considerations took a backseat in all of this, but few seemed to notice, since haute cuisine had long since fallen out of favor. In the 1920s, Prohibition had deprived expensive restaurants of the income from alcohol that had padded their profit margins. During World War II, a preoccupation with fine food had seemed unpatriotic. By the 1950s, food tastes were no longer an important mark of social distinction. Most Americans seemed satisfied by beefsteak, pizzas, fried chicken, canned-food casseroles, Jell-O molds, and frozen TV dinners. Regional differences, already undermined in the 1920s and 1930s, disappeared almost entirely under the onslaught of mass-produced foods aimed at supposedly homogeneous Middle American tastes. Government officials, educators, journalists, and the food industries insisted that Americans were the best-fed people on earth.

Negative Nutrition. The self-satisfaction eroded in the 1960s with the realization that, amid massive agricultural surpluses, millions of poor citizens could not afford an adequate diet. Programs were instituted to distribute surplus commodities and food stamps to the poor. As middle-class concerns over the healthfulness of their own diet increased, a new dietary paradigm—one that might be called "Negative Nutrition"—arose. Whereas earlier nutritional systems had emphasized consuming healthful foods, Negative Nutrition warned against eating certain foods, particularly those treated with potentially harmful pesticides and chemical fertilizers and those robbed of nutrients by overprocessing. Veterans of the New Left, meanwhile, redirected their critique of capitalism toward its effects on food and the environment. The giant corporations, they charged, used their immense advertising resources to brainwash Americans into eating overprocessed, denutrified, unhealthful, and environmentally hazardous products. They pointed out, for example, that the spread of cattle ranching in South America to meet U.S. demands for beef was contributing directly to the destruction of the rain forests. Both health and morality, they insisted, dictated a preference for "organic" and "natural" foods, preferably grown by small producers.

The food industry responded nimbly, reformulating and repackaging their products with labels such as "natural" and "nature's own." However, new findings in nutritional science reinforced another aspect of Negative Nutrition, as specific foods came to be identified as dangerous. Rising rates of heart disease were now blamed on high levels of cholesterol in many of America's favorite foods. Sugar, long linked to diabetes and now thought by some to be a factor in other diseases and psychological disorders, was called an addictive substance manipulated by food processors to "hook" children on nutritionally deficient products. Themes from the Graham and Kellogg eras resurfaced: vegetarianism, for instance, once the domain of cranks, became a serious option for many. Issues relating to obesity added a new twist to the nutrition debate. In the later nineteenth century a full figure had been a mark of beauty for women and a sign of health, wealth, and substance for men. Since the 1920s, however, evidence had accumulated of a relationship between excessive weight and higher mortality rates.

As in previous eras, food reformers mustered impressive scientific support. By the mid-1970s the federal government was supporting research on diet and health and was urging Americans to lose weight and reduce the animal fat, sugar, and sodium in their diets. Organizations such as the American Heart Association underscored the need for dietary change. "Low-fat," "lite," "no-cal," "cholesterol-free," and "sodium-free" products now lined supermarket shelves.

Paradoxes of Abundance. The result reflected the paradoxes of American abundance. Many took to frenetic diet-and-exercise regimens, yet the average weight of Americans continued to rise. Although consumption of full-fat dairy products and red meat fell, that of other fats soared, as did that of sugar and sodium. Dietary self-denial was undermined by the boom in foreign travel, which encouraged indulgence and helped to make food tastes once again a sign of social distinction. Consumers now had an unprecedented choice of foods and an unprecedented number of ways to consume them. As more women entered the workplace, the trend for food production to move outside the home accelerated. Take-home foods boomed, as did eating out, particularly at fast-food and other chain restaurants.

By the early twenty-first century, as obesity and associated medical problems loomed ever larger as a public-health issue, diet, nutrition, and weight loss became national obsessions. Parents protested the introduction of fast foods and sweetened soft drinks in public schools. Lawyers planned lawsuits against fast-food chains, analogous to the lawsuits against tobacco companies, for knowingly endangering their customers' health. Weight-loss programs proliferated, including the so-called Atkins diet, heavy on protein and low on carbohydrates, publicized by the cardiologist Dr. Robert C. Atkins in *Dr. Atkins' Diet Revolution: The High-Calorie Way to Stay Thin Forever*, first published in 1972. An extreme manifestation of the preoccupation with food and diet was the growing popularity of expensive gastric-bypass surgery, also known as stomach stapling, as a last-ditch means of cutting intake and losing weight.

Persisting moralism, in the form of guilty consciences, impeded indulging in the abundance of food choices, but the targets of the guilt constantly shifted, as experts regularly warned of new food dangers and absolved old ones. With the Negative Nutrition now superimposed on older nutritional ideas, many Americans simultaneously tried to eat more of those foods that were supposed to prevent or cure illness and promote general good health and less of those foods deemed unhealthy or likely to cause weight gain. Americans seemed doomed by their past both to celebrate their food abundance and to avoid enjoying it too much.

[*See also* **Advertising; Agriculture; Consumer Culture; Corporate Agriculture; Dairy Industry and Dairy Products; Factory Farming; Grain Processing; Grains; Livestock Industry; Marketing Cooperatives; Mass Marketing; Meatpacking and Meat-Processing Industry; Pure Food and Drug Act;** *and* **Sugarcane and Sugar Beets.**]

BIBLIOGRAPHY

Belasco, Warren J. *Appetite for Change: How the Counterculture Took On the Food Industry*. 2d updated ed. Ithaca, N.Y.: Cornell University Press, 2007.

Cummings, Richard Osborn. *The American and His Food: A History of Food Habits in the United States*. Chicago: University of Chicago Press, 1940.

Hooker, Richard J. *Food and Drink in America: A History*. Indianapolis, Ind.: Bobbs–Merrill, 1981.

Levenstein, Harvey. *Paradox of Plenty: A Social History of Eating in Modern America*. Rev. ed. Berkeley: University of California Press, 2003.

Levenstein, Harvey. *Revolution at the Table: The Transformation of the American Diet*. New York: Oxford University Press, 1988.

Nissenbaum, Stephen. *Sex, Diet, and Debility in Jacksonian America: Sylvester Graham and Health Reform*. Westport, Conn.: Greenwood Press, 1980.

Root, Waverley, and Richard de Rochemont. *Eating in America: A History*. New York: Morrow, 1976.

Stearns, Peter N. *Fat History: Bodies and Beauty in the Modern West*. New York: New York University Press, 1997.

Whorton, James C. *Crusaders for Fitness: The History of American Health Reformers*. Princeton, N.J.: Princeton University Press, 1982.

Harvey Levenstein

FORD, HENRY, AND FORDISM

Born on a farm near Dearborn, Michigan, the automobile manufacturer Henry Ford (1863–1947) held various jobs as a young man in Detroit, including machine-shop apprentice, traction-car operator, and engineer for the Edison Illuminating Company. He designed and built his first prototype automobile in 1896. In 1903 he formed the Ford Motor Company and began small-scale commercial production. In the turbulent world of early automobile manufacturing, Ford initially gained prominence for race cars and for his long, ultimately successful battle with George B. Selden, who tried to gain a monopoly over automobile manufacturing by taking out a series of patents in 1895.

1908 to 1914, Years of Genius. By 1914, three achievements—the 1908 Model T, the moving assembly line, and the Five-Dollar Day—coalesced to create Ford's worldwide reputation and place in the pantheon of U.S.

heroes. The Model T thrived in an America where, away from urban and long-haul rail systems, terrible roads punished flimsy cars and their passengers at every turn, and nearly nonexistent repair facilities left them to their own mechanical wits. The T offered an exceptionally strong steel frame, high wheel clearance, and fix-it-yourself simplicity. Surging demand forced the Ford team to a series of production breakthroughs between 1908 and 1914 that came to be known collectively as the "assembly line," one key element in what also came to be known as "Fordism" ("Fordismus" in Europe). "Fordism" embedded "Mr. Ford" within a manufacturing concept understood to be revolutionary: mass production aimed at a low profit margin and high volume, specialized machine tools and single-skill workers, and just-in-time materials handling. Fordism was also understood to mean superb wages for immigrant factory workers, together with an Americanization program including home inspections and English-language schools. The company's January 1914 announcement of the Five-Dollar Day, backed by technological achievement at the highest level, put Ford's image as a beneficent hero in newspapers all over the world.

Fordism was endlessly analyzed in business and engineering journals during the Model T's astonishing production run: the ugly indestructible little cars defined automobility from its inception in 1908 until Ford's design rigidity in the early 1920s allowed General Motors to establish itself as the new dominant standard for automotive production and marketing. In the public mind, however, "Mr. Ford" gave soul and identity to mass production's complexities. A dapper, articulate team leader marked by one innovative miracle after another, he also understood the workingman's life and needs. Doubling the daily wage, cutting the work shift from nine to eight hours, and teaching unlettered immigrants the subtleties of American life, he remained until his death in 1947 the plainspoken

workingman's friend for millions of Americans. Convincing evidence suggests that this image credibly reflects the agile leader of the innovation team that secretly designed the T at the Piquette Street plant and then responded to a whirlwind of market demand by transforming the industrial world's manufacturing practice. Ford's feel for workers shows in the early years at Piquette Street; Henry walked across the street from his home, up the stairs, and through a machine shop into his second-floor office, one of the men. It can also be argued, however, that the company's exponential growth transformed Ford: from his former supple leadership to an increasingly rigid addiction to control, and from plainspoken kinship with workers to a reclusive obsession with privacy.

Obsession with Control. As early as 1912, the run-up to a fully integrated assembly line led to a drastic increase in the number of supervisors—from 2 percent to 14.5 percent of the workforce—and a deskilling of most workers. This, along with the relentless pace of the line, resulted in extreme worker turnover: about 380 percent in 1913. From this perspective the Five-Dollar Day marks the first move in Ford's lifelong battle to control his workforce and his company. Doubling the daily wage came with house inspections aimed at separating workers from their cultures of origin. Soon, home inspectors were replaced with a network of in-factory spies and, by the mid-1920s, brutal enforcers. In 1919, Ford bought out all stockholders and forced out independent-thinking senior managers. During General Motors' rise to market dominance—a rise spurred by annual model updates, multiple models and colors, and attractive advertisements—Ford refused to consider changing the T's core concept until 1926's catastrophic market-share loss forced him to shut down production for half a year before releasing the beautifully engineered Model A. But neither the A nor the innovative V-8 engine, introduced in 1932, brought the company back to its earlier market dominance.

For Ford himself, fame took its toll, as his eccentricities and prejudices became increasingly evident. In an abortive effort to end World War I through arbitration, he chartered what was dubbed a "peace ship" in December 1915 and sailed to Europe. His awkward and unschooled responses during the 1919 *Chicago Tribune* libel trial invited ridicule and pity. Ford's newspaper, the *Dearborn Independent*, distributed in the 1920s through Ford dealers, disseminated virulent anti-Semitism. To settle a libel suit, Ford issued a retraction and halted publication in 1927. His bitter antiunionism led to outbreaks of bloody violence at Ford plants during the Great Depression, most notably in 1932 and 1937. Only in 1941 did Ford sign a contract with the United Auto Workers, forced, it is said, by his wife Clara. Adolf Hitler quoted Ford with approval in his 1925–1926 manifesto *Mein Kampf*, and in 1938 the Third Reich awarded Ford the Grand Cross of the German Eagle.

Henry and Edsel.

In later life Ford increasingly withdrew from day-to-day corporate operations and retreated to Fair Lane, his estate of about thirteen hundred acres, and the nearby historical museum and Greenfield Village. The stark contrast between Henry and his only son Edsel shows most vividly in the location of their homes. Henry's estate straddled the Rouge River in working-class Dearborn, one mile upstream from the big plant. Edsel's mansion, Gaukler Point, occupies eighty-seven acres of prime shoreline in Grosse Pointe Shores, then the heartland of Detroit's elite. Henry shunned public events, while Edsel's civic commitments remain memorialized in Diego Rivera's portrayal of Edsel and William Valentiner, director of the Detroit Institute of Arts (DIA), in the bottom right corner of the south panel of Rivera's *Detroit Industry* murals at the DIA. Edsel's

and his wife Eleanor's patronage of the arts helps explain why the DIA remains one of America's great encyclopedic museums.

The Ford Foundation, established by Henry Ford and his son Edsel in 1936, ultimately received many millions in nonvoting Ford Motor Company stock, making it one of America's wealthiest foundations. It operated with a board and a worldview independent of its primary benefactor, and after Henry's death it more and more often funded individuals and programs that might have displeased its benefactor.

Oral-history reminiscences suggest that Henry's grandchildren blamed him for Edsel's early death from stomach cancer—caused, it was said, by Henry's ceaseless and capricious interventions in corporate practice even as he retreated into the private world of the estate, the museum, and the village.

The Museum, Greenfield Village, and Fair Lane.

Beginning in the early 1920s, Ford's agents scoured New England, the Midwest, and Great Britain for artifacts relating to the history of technology and domestic life. In October 1929 the unfinished complex opened to a who's who of America's industrial elite. Over a national radio hookup, Thomas Edison switched on a replica of his first incandescent light for its fiftieth anniversary. Work on the museum and village continued for more than a decade, with Henry continually issuing sometimes minuscule design-change orders. The village took shape as a nostalgic re-creation of eighteenth- and nineteenth-century America, dotted with shrines to Henry's heroes, such as Thomas Edison, the Wright brothers, and the *McGuffey Reader*, and a one-room schoolhouse. By contrast, the museum's eight-acre main floor exhibited some of the world's finest collections of machines—steam engines, machine tools, farm equipment, locomotives, automobiles, airplanes—each laid out in a triumphantly self-confident display of linear progress.

Nowhere was this concept more elegantly achieved than in the design, completed by 1940, of the entrance as coordinated with the vast hall's central aisle. A visitor entered a replica of Philadelphia's Independence Hall, home for the Declaration of Independence and the U.S. Constitution, and proceeded into the main hall's central aisle, which was framed by two facing lines of bulky nineteenth-century steam tractors, themselves framing an enormous dynamo taken from the 1910 Highland Park plant. Ford intended a three-century celebration of progress: from eighteenth-century civics to nineteenth-century steam to twentieth-century electricity. The complex also housed a fully accredited school for kindergarten through grade twelve, where students could study amid physical reminders of technological progress.

An elusive figure, Ford shunned visitors but often roamed the grounds of the village alone at night. Oral histories of house servants at Fair Lane also tell of a secluded life with few visitors. After dinner, Clara ordinarily retired to the solarium and listened to the radio, while Henry spent time in his powerhouse and workshop, where first-name familiarity with the small technical crew provided a semblance of the early Piquette Street innovation team. Few guests were welcome, most notably Edison and Charles Lindbergh.

Henry, Diego Rivera, and Charles Sheeler.
Improbably, Diego Rivera was invited by Henry to lunch soon after he arrived in Detroit in 1932 to paint the now world-famous industrial murals at the heart of the DIA; the murals were completed in 1933. In Dearborn, the historical museum was not yet open to the public, but Ford invited Rivera to spend a day there alone, contemplating the collections. Rivera spent a month in the Rouge sketching for the murals. Rivera, the flamboyant Marxist, was commissioned and later defended from public outrage by Edsel Ford, but his cordial relationship with Henry continues to surprise. The improbable warmth between these two men reveals another facet of Ford's complex character. Despite his increasingly eccentric and often brutal obsession with privacy and control, he never lost a refined sense of the well-designed machine as beautiful. In this he shared soul space not only with Rivera but also with Charles Sheeler, who was commissioned in 1927 to photograph the Rouge and whose portraits of the industrial landscape stand with the Rivera murals as contrasting contemplations of industrial beauty on a massive scale—Rivera's murals pulsing with humanity, Sheeler's nearly devoid of any signs of unengineered nature or of human beings.

Ambivalent Common Man.
Ford's obsession with control, coupled with an enduring sense of beauty in the machine, together reveal a man caught in the classic ambivalence of the modernist technological aesthetic. It has been argued that his near-psychotic obsessions were allowed only because of the public relations protection of the Ford Motor Company. Another reading, favored here, suggests that Ford was an ordinary adult of his time, caught between exultant awe at transformative inventive forces and deep insecurity about any one person's place as a single tiny individual set against forces so vast. Sheeler's tiny running man, barely visible against a vast factoryscape in *American Landscape* (1930), could be imagined as Mr. Ford, wandering alone in his private nocturnal world of nostalgic shrines and gleaming machines. In this reading, Ford's fortune did less to protect him from the consequences of near-psychotic tendencies than to supply him with resources to act out the neurotic impulses of an American society suspended between confidence and anxiety. Most of his fellow citizens could not afford the luxury of such excesses and had to go back to work the next day.

[*See also* American System of Manufacturing and Interchangeable Parts; Automotive Industry; Battle of the Overpass (1937); Congress of Industrial Organizations; Deskilling; Five-Dollar Day; Industrialization and Deindustrialization; Labor Spies and Pinkertons; Mass Production; Reuther, Walter; Scientific Management; United Auto Workers; *and* Welfare Capitalism.]

BIBLIOGRAPHY

Davis, Donald Finlay. *Conspicuous Production: Automobiles and Elites in Detroit, 1899–1933.* Philadelphia: Temple University Press, 1988.

Lacey, Robert. *Ford: The Men and the Machine.* Boston: Little, Brown, 1986.

Lewis, David L. *The Public Image of Henry Ford: An American Folk Hero and His Company.* Detroit, Mich.: Wayne State University Press, 1976.

Jardim, Anne. *The First Henry Ford: A Study in Personality and Business Leadership.* Cambridge, Mass.: MIT Press, 1970.

Meyer, Stephen, III. *The Five Dollar Day: Labor, Management, and Social Control in the Ford Motor Company, 1908–1921.* Albany: State University of New York Press, 1981.

Nevins, Allan, with Frank Ernest Hill. *Ford.* 3 vols. New York: Scribner, 1954–1963.

Staudenmaier, John M. "Henry Ford's Relationship to 'Fordism': Ambiguity as a Modality of Technological Resistance." In *Resistance to New Technology: Nuclear Power, Information Technology, and Biotechnology*, edited by Martin Bauer, pp. 147–164. Cambridge, U.K.: Cambridge University Press, 1995.

John M. Staudenmaier, S.J.

FOREIGN TRADE

Trade and commerce have had a formative influence on America from the Colonial Era onward. The British colonial system embraced the doctrines of mercantilism, with its closely regulated trade, restricted economic development, and unfavorable balance of payments for the American colonists. After independence, Americans melded the free-trade doctrines of Adam Smith's *Wealth of Nations* (1776) with their revolutionary cause.

From the Early Republic to World War I.

The U.S. Constitution eliminated interstate trade barriers and provided for the consolidation of trade policy. Incorporating commercial values with national interest, Americans assumed that the territorial and commercial wars of the past would yield to a peaceful era of free economic exchange among nations. Foreign trade's relative importance declined in the nineteenth century, however, as internal development intensified. Exports fell to about 6 percent of gross domestic product (GDP), while exports and imports combined constituted an average 12 percent. The South's cotton economy remained export-led; economic growth overall was not.

Following the Napoleonic wars (1803–1815), Great Britain adopted free-trade policies, stimulating phenomenal growth in world trade per capita between 1800 and 1910. After 1850, international economic relationships strengthened so that the national economies of the Atlantic region showed common features of specialization, urbanization, trade cycles, and movements of capital and labor. In this same period, the United States moved steadily from the periphery of this system to the center, the core of the international economy.

Through the nineteenth century, American exports were largely raw materials. Primary products, including raw and processed foodstuffs, forest products, and minerals, constituted 80 percent of American exports. Manufactured and semimanufactured goods comprised about two thirds of imports. As the trans-Mississippi West came into production after the Civil War, half of the increase in wheat production was exported. But the expansion of manufacturing counted most in the accelerating *rate* of economic productivity. In 1860, manufactured goods accounted for 20 percent of U.S. exports; by World War I, the figure had climbed to 50 percent. Overall, until 1895, Americans bought more abroad than they sold, setting the deficit account by borrowing from abroad or paying in the internationally recognized exchange of gold.

Since tariff receipts were the largest source of federal revenue until 1913, when they were overtaken by tax revenues, tariff duties could only selectively restrict, not wholly prohibit, imports. American competitive advantage took the form of innovations in mass production and mass marketing of foodstuffs and retail goods, made possible by the large and comparatively affluent domestic market. The efficiency of these techniques, rather than the protective effects of the tariffs, enabled U.S. manufactures to compete effectively and generate a surplus trade account for most of the twentieth century.

From World War I through the 1960s.

The combined strength of agricultural and manufactured exports after World War I led to an anomalous situation in which the United States captured 27 percent of world trade, while its exports constituted only 6 percent of the total U.S. GDP. Since tariff disputes in Congress originated mostly among specific business interests, economic groups, and regions, the U.S. government did not sufficiently recognize the profound implications of the lopsided trade and credit balance. Corrective action required that the United States reduce its tariffs and encourage private lending abroad. Instead, a business–labor alliance embraced more highly protective tariffs, to offset alleged differences between foreign and domestic production costs occasioned by higher wages in the United States. This outlook pro-

duced the high Fordney–McCumber Tariff (1922) and the even higher Smoot–Hawley Tariff (1930).

Tight credit policies further contributed to a world credit collapse in 1929, from which industrial nations sought relief in regional trade blocs. These encouraged import substitution, or domestic production of what could be more cheaply produced and purchased abroad. The value of U.S. exports fell by half from 1929 to 1933, while the trade balance fell into a deficit position that lasted until 1940.

The economic and political crises precipitated by World War II produced a trade agreement among the industrial nations, at the 1944 Bretton Woods Conference in New Hampshire, to end trading blocs and import substitution. New international bodies, notably the General Agreement on Tariffs and Trade (GATT) and the International Monetary Fund (IMF), were established to negotiate tariff reduction and address precipitate currency fluctuations that jeopardized the free exchange of goods. Ostensibly multilateral (i.e., among all nations), tariff reduction as originated by the U.S. secretary of state Cordell Hull actually proceeded through bilateral, or reciprocal, negotiations. At the GATT's Geneva Conference in 1947, such negotiations reduced tariff barriers by an average of 50 percent. Most of the industrial economies, however, war-torn and plagued by competitive disadvantages, used nontariff barriers such as quotas and subsidies to protect recovering industry and agriculture and inadequate reserves of foreign currency.

Overall, the GATT arrangement did reconstruct a multinational trading system. By 1953, Japan and the European Common Market, enjoying U.S. economic assistance and protected home markets, experienced economic growth at rates double that of the United States. From 1948 to 1957, world trade increased 77 percent, playing a crucial role in the recovery of the industrialized nations and the emergence of the export-led industrial economies of Southeast Asia. Fearing the exclusion of American products, particularly agricultural ones, from the emerging European Common Market, Congress in 1964 passed the Trade Expansion Act, which granted the president sweeping (multilateral) authority to place entire categories of products on the bargaining table.

1970 and Beyond. In 1972, owing in part to the rising imports of high-priced foreign oil, the United States recorded its first postwar trade deficit on the merchandise account. Blue-collar jobs, especially those in steel, automobiles, and other heavy metallurgical industries, suffered from foreign competition. By 1985, Japan held 30 percent of the U.S. automobile market. American agricultural exports, which had doubled in the 1970s, fell as world agricultural trade declined in response to rising production and protectionism. China, meanwhile, began its meteoric rise to third place among suppliers to the U.S. consumer nondurables market.

The exports of American multinational corporations—which had proliferated as U.S. corporations invested abroad in the 1960s and 1970s—especially in chemicals, machinery, and transportation equipment, helped ease the U.S. trade deficit. Moreover, 40 percent of U.S. imports originated from the foreign affiliates of American multinationals. Although America's merchandise trade balance shifted decisively into the red (i.e., by the importation of far more goods than it exported), the often-criticized investment abroad partially countered the deficit by generating $100 billion more in exports to foreign affiliates than foreign firms gained from their investments in the United States.

Downward pressure on U.S. wage rates, popularly associated with the trade deficit, stimulated proposals to improve American "competitiveness" by retaliating against "unfair" trade barriers. These trading partners decried such actions, pointing to the excessive consumption indicated by historically low U.S. savings rates. When increased net borrowing in the 1990s erased the positive balance of foreign earnings (i.e., income on U.S. investment abroad), increasing the deficit, congressional trade restrictionists attacked U.S. capital exports, which had reached 25 percent of the world's total. These attacks proved ineffectual, but the restrictionists did have some success in extending trade controls.

Aware of the protectionist drift in Congress, Canada consolidated its premier position as the United States' largest trading partner by concluding a free-trade agreement in 1988 that progressively eliminated tariffs over a ten-year period, while making Canadian oil and gas more accessible to the U.S. market. The Mexican government, meanwhile, in pursuit of market-oriented reforms, sought closer economic ties with the United States. The resulting North American Free Trade Agreement (NAFTA) passed Congress over bitter restrictionist opposition and came into force in January 1994. As Canadian and Mexican exports to the United States shot upward, most analysts anticipated greater efficiencies, lower prices, and an increase in high-tech jobs in the United States to compensate for the expected loss of blue-collar jobs to Mexico.

In 1999 the U.S. trade deficit reached about $200 billion, an increase to 2.5 percent of the 1998 GDP from 1.7 percent in 1989. Some argued that the corresponding trade surpluses of foreign economies, much of which was reinvested in the United States, constituted an undependable component of U.S. financial markets (i.e., if withdrawn). Others emphasized that substantial rates of increase in government and business savings—represented, respectively, by an apparent end to federal budget deficits and by the phenomenally increased value of common stocks—showed that the nation had done well despite the trade deficit. Though the trade deficit reduced the GDP by

1.5 percent in 1998, they noted, the U.S. economy still grew at a rate of nearly 4 percent.

As the boom of the 1990s ended in a recession marked by serious job losses, particularly in manufacturing, the nation's commitment to free trade was put to the test. The trade deficit remained high as Americans continued to import far more than they exported. U.S. trade negotiators pressured China and other nations to open their markets to imported goods and to halt the pirating of compact discs and movie DVDs. President George W. Bush, like his recent predecessors, insisted that America's economic future lay with the global economy, but early in 2002 political calculations led him to slap import duties on cheap foreign steel. (Late in 2003, facing retaliation against U.S. exports and sanctions by the World Trade Organization—the successor to the GATT—Bush withdrew the tariffs.) The 2004 Democratic presidential candidate John Kerry denounced "Benedict Arnold" corporations that exported jobs to low-wage foreign countries and called for measures to penalize such firms.

While the long-term movement toward freer trade in a globalizing economy continued, the economic crisis of 2008–2010 raised further doubts about the impact of globalization on the domestic economy and its workers. The labor movement remained resistant to further free-trade pacts negotiated with various nations, as did members of Congress from areas affected detrimentally by imported goods. Resistance grew especially strong against China, which had become dominant in the market for cheaper mass-produced goods and with which the United States ran a large balance-of-trade deficit. Critics charged that China intentionally undervalued its currency and, when necessary, dumped its products on the world market at below cost. Others feared that China might use its multibillions of dollars in holdings of U.S. Treasury bonds to wage economic war against the United States. Still, the administration of

Barack Obama and congressional majorities favored and pursued more liberal trade policies despite the nation's ongoing balance-of-trade deficit and its deepening federal deficit. For the future, the United States will certainly remain a major player in world trade and its liberalization, but it will likely never again be as dominant as it was from 1945 to 1973.

[*See also* **Bretton Woods Conference; GATT and WTO; Globalization; Gold Standard; Tariffs;** *and* **Trade Policy, Federal.**]

BIBLIOGRAPHY

Brownlee, W. Elliot. *Dynamics of Ascent: A History of the American Economy.* 2d ed. New York: Alfred A. Knopf, 1979.
Dethloff, Henry C. *The United States and the Global Economy since 1945.* Fort Worth, Tex.: Harcourt Brace College, 1997.
Feldstein, Martin, ed. *The United States in the World Economy.* Chicago: University of Chicago Press, 1988.
Fishlow, Albert, and Stephan Haggard. *The United States and the Regionalisation of the World Economy.* Paris: Organisation of Economic Co-operation and Development, 1992.
Kester, Anne Y., ed. *Behind the Numbers: U.S. Trade in the World Economy.* Washington, D.C.: National Academy Press, 1992.

Paul P. Abrahams; updated by
Paul S. Boyer

FORESTS AND FORESTRY

In 1873, as the clearing of forests for agriculture, lumber, and fuel wood threatened the nation's future timber supply, the American Association for the Advancement of Science petitioned Congress and state legislatures to recognize the importance of timber cultivation and forest preservation. The resulting *Report on Forestry*

(1884), funded by Congress and compiled by Franklin B. Hough and Nathaniel H. Egleston, became the foundational document of American forestry. The establishment of the American Forestry Association in 1878 and of the Division of Forestry in the Department of Agriculture further signaled forestry's growing role. Hough, Egleston, and then Bernhard Fernow, a German-born forester, became the first chiefs of the division. Fernow was succeeded in 1898 by Gifford Pinchot in a revamped Bureau of Forestry, renamed the U.S. Forest Service in 1905. Pinchot, a confidant of Theodore Roosevelt, transferred federal forests held by the Interior Department to his own bureau, established the system of national forests, and promoted conservation measures. He also helped to form the American Society of Foresters and establish at Yale the first graduate forestry program in 1900.

The period 1900–1960 saw frequent clashes between the Forest Service and private lumbering interests over access to timber stands, as well as disputes with the National Park Service and the Fish and Wildlife Service, both of which sought to appropriate forest lands for their own purposes. After World War II, however, forestry's earlier exclusive emphasis on lumber production gradually expanded to incorporate recreation and environmental protection. The Multiple Use–Sustained Yield Act of 1960 decreed that timber, wildlife, range land, water, and recreation were all legitimate national-forest concerns. From 1970 on, environmentalists' attention to clear-cutting practices and endangered-species protection grew steadily. By the turn of the twenty-first century, the Forest Service and foresters, though still the guardians of the nation's arboreal heritage, increasingly shared that role with an informed and articulate public. Global warming had become a threat to the national forests as warmer temperatures in high altitudes fostered the growth and spread of destructive insect infestations and various arboreal diseases.

[*See also* Civilian Conservation Corps; Environmental Regulations; *and* Renewable Energy and Climate Change.]

BIBLIOGRAPHY

Davis, Richard C., ed. *Encyclopedia of American Forest and Conservation History.* 2 vols. New York: Macmillan, 1983.

Williams, Michael. *Americans and Their Forests: A Historical Geography.* Cambridge, U.K.: Cambridge University Press, 1989.

Michael Williams

FOSTER, WILLIAM Z.

(1881–1961), labor radical. Foster's life encapsulated the rise and fall of twentieth-century labor radicalism. Raised in Philadelphia's slums, he roamed widely. He joined the Socialist Party in 1901 and the Industrial Workers of the World (IWW) in 1909 before founding his own organization, the Syndicalist League of North America, in 1912. Foster came to national attention in 1918 with a spectacular union drive in the steel industry. His organizers had swept one hundred thousand workers into unions, and an unsuccessful strike launched in 1919 became the largest industrial conflict in U.S. history.

In early 1920, Foster organized the Trade Union Educational League, an influential opposition group within the mainstream unions. In 1921 he joined the new Workers (Communist) Party, directing much of its labor work throughout the 1920s. Foster ran for president on the Communist ticket in 1924, 1928, and 1932. During the 1932 campaign, following a beating and jailing, he suffered a breakdown that weakened him permanently. Marginalized by the Communist Party leader Earl Browder during the Popular Front years, Foster regained leadership only with a return to orthodox Stalinism in the wake of World War II. In the following decade, he led the party through its sharp decline—caused by both government repression and its own sectarianism. The distance between Foster's deathbed in Moscow and his grave near Chicago represents the tension between the two great influences in his life. A product of industrial America and a master organizer, he became a loyal soldier of the international Communist movement. These loyalties sustained, but they proved to be at odds.

[*See also* **Industrial Workers of the World; International Unionism and International Solidarity; Labor Leaders; Radicalism and Workers; Steel Strike of 1919;** *and* **Trade Union Educational League and Trade Union Unity League.**]

BIBLIOGRAPHY

Barrett, James R. *William Z. Foster and the Tragedy of American Radicalism.* Urbana: University of Illinois Press, 1999.

Johanningsmeier, Edward P. *Forging American Communism: The Life of William Z. Foster.* Princeton, N.J.: Princeton University Press, 1994.

James R. Barrett

FREED LABORERS

The Civil War transformed American society. No change was greater, perhaps, than the sudden alteration in status of millions of blacks in the South freed from the bonds of slavery. With this abrupt change, the freedpeople became a battleground for varying ideologies of labor, race, and economics. The former slaves' own actions and ideas, however, often confounded the expectations of white northerners and southerners alike as freedpeople carved out their own path in the postwar world.

Becoming Free.   The first freedpeople were those slaves freed by Federal troops even before the Emancipation Proclamation (1 January 1863). Federal troops early on found it difficult to acquire and maintain control of broad swaths of Southern territory, but they were able to acquire and hold a number of footholds, especially in the islands along the Atlantic coast. Establishing bases to help maintain the Federal blockade of the Southern coast, the U.S. military found that it needed a significant number of laborers for logistical support. Not surprisingly, slaves flocked to these Federal footholds, many of them finding employment—and, often, later enlisting—with the Federal army. Entire communities of freedpeople attached themselves to the Federal camps. Some Union generals, first and most famously the Radical Republican Benjamin F. Butler, acted on their own to end slavery where they governed, and communities of freedpeople tended to spring up in these areas as well.

Yet these first communities of freedpeople were not places of perfect cooperation between white northerners and former slaves. Julie Saville argues that, in a way that presaged postwar conflicts, freedpeople attached to Union camps on the coast of South Carolina often preferred cooperative work based on traditional familial and social hierarchies to the prospect of working for wages, as Northern officers expected of them. This, perhaps, was the first indication that the North's ideology of "free labor" did not correspond exactly to the concept of freedom that newly freed blacks preferred.

The most important developments for freedpeople, of course, came after the surrender of the Confederacy in 1865. The South was devastated both demographically and economically. The postwar period involved not only rebuilding southern society along more egalitarian racial norms, but also reconstructing an economy that was both derelict and based on a social order that no longer existed. The end of slavery, as Eric Foner frames it, broke down the paternalistic social system that had sustained southern plantation life, not only freeing slaves from their bondage, but also freeing owners from their obligations to slaves. There was also a severe shortage of labor, both because hundreds of thousands of white southerners had been killed or wounded during the war and because the end of slavery meant that black men labored fewer hours, while protecting their women, children, and elderly members from coerced work.

The northerners who attempted to reconstruct the South brought with them an ideology of free labor based on assumptions that the free man would choose voluntarily to work for wages to sustain himself and his family, and they attempted to introduce to the South a system of free wage labor. But both blacks and whites resisted the free-labor system. White southerners, still in the thrall of a long tradition that saw blacks as lesser humans with meager mental faculties, insisted that blacks lacked the work ethic required of a free laborer and that thus a free-labor economy could never be sustained in the South. Rather than rely on the individualism that the free-labor ideology glorified, blacks often preferred to work through familial structures and social hierarchies that had been established in slave communities. What was clear, then, was that the matter of constructing the postwar economy was complicated. A direct transplantation of a system based on free labor was rejected by southern laborers and their employers.

Emergence of a Hybrid System.

In the absence of consensus among the various parties in the postwar society as to the structure of the economy and labor relations, a hybrid system emerged. Though during the war, Federal officials had experimented with seizing and redistributing land belonging to white plantation masters, political pressure put an end to that practice soon after the war, leading to a series of conflicts between Federal officials and free blacks who had been settled on land that was now being returned to former owners. With little land available to them, freedpeople of necessity labored on lands that they had worked as slaves. Plantation owners often cajoled, coerced, or otherwise pressured freedmen to sign contracts binding them to work, often for long periods of time and under repressive, onerous conditions. Federal officials, confused and frustrated by the freedpeoples' resistance to a free-labor system, often refused to guarantee rights for blacks other than the right not to be bought and sold and (usually) the right not to be subject to corporal punishment. It was a system ripe for abuse and corruption. As Reconstruction proceeded and black political power waxed and waned in the South, contract labor—often paid not in money but in shares of crops—mutated into a sharecropping system that persisted into the twentieth century, whereby families of freedpeople cultivated land belonging to large landowners in return for a fixed percentage of the crop. It was a system that followed no one's ideals.

Insofar as the federal government attempted to shape the labor markets in the postwar South, that task fell to the Freedmen's Bureau, headed by a one-armed former general, Oliver Otis Howard. The Freedmen's Bureau, created in March 1865, incorporated several distinctly northern ideologies, including that of free labor. Many agents of the bureau sought to introduce the kind of personal discipline and work ethic that was assumed to be fundamental to a laborer in a free-market society. But, again, the bureau's assumptions about free labor and rational markets did not fit the situation in the postwar South. Agents of the bureau, Eric Foner explains, held a variety of beliefs about their ultimate mission: some sought simply to improve the living conditions of the plantation labor force, some wanted to allow blacks the same social mobility that supposedly characterized northern free laborers, and some followed the congressional mandate to settle freedpeople on homesteads of their own. In the relative chaos of the postwar South, and given the refusal of southerners to subscribe to the ideas of the free market, the bureau soon promoted the system of contract labor that tied freedpeople to the land and often to their former owners.

The freedpeople, too, sought to create institutions and to define their newfound freedom. As Julie Saville documents in the *Work of Reconstruction*, many of the collective actions that freedpeople took in the economic realm were rooted in structures that had developed under the repression of slavery. Many of the family and social structures that had originated on the plantation became centers of activism during Reconstruction. Family members assumed primary responsibility for defending themselves against the corporal punishment that they generally regarded as an egregious violation of their freedom. "Freedpeople [also] customarily tapped their kinship to other ex-slaves in order to forge resistance to postwar work arrangements, reaching for a shield that had once held somewhat at bay the intrusive intimacy of daily contact with a resident master." Some of the first such collective actions featured gatherings among freedpeople to protest the return of confiscated lands to the planters; later, blacks organized collective actions to preserve their control over the production of crops and over supplemental plots that they cultivated outside the formal sharecropping structure. Freedpeople adopted some elements of the free-labor structure while rejecting others. They exercised a kind of freedom that the northern carriers of the free-labor ideology failed to understand.

[*See also* **Freedom of Contract; Free-Labor Ideology; Sharecropping and Tenancy;** *and* **Slavery.**]

BIBLIOGRAPHY

Cimbala, Paul A., and Randall M. Miller, eds. *The Freedmen's Bureau and Reconstruction: Reconsiderations*. New York: Fordham University Press, 1999.

Donald, Henderson H. *The Negro Freedman: Life Conditions of the American Negro in the Early Years after Emancipation*. New York: Schuman, 1952.

Foner, Eric. *A Short History of Reconstruction, 1863–1877*. New York: Harper & Row, 1990.

Litwack, Leon F. *Been in the Storm so Long: The Aftermath of Slavery*. New York: Alfred A. Knopf, 1979.

Saville, Julie. *The Work of Reconstruction: From Slave to Wage Laborer in South Carolina, 1860–1870*. Cambridge, U.K.: Cambridge University Press, 1994.

Sandy Johnston

FREEDOM OF CONTRACT

During the eighteenth century the view that individuals should be free to make contracts, which courts would enforce, steadily gained ascendancy in colonial and revolutionary America. Such private bargaining was the key to the emerging free-market economy. American law generally left parties at liberty to protect their own interests through contract. Absent evidence of fraud, courts would not second-guess the economic wisdom of agreements. Belief in the sanctity of contracts, as well as in the need to protect voluntary arrangements from legislative interference, found expression in the contract clause of the Constitution. This clause provided that "No state . . . shall pass any law impairing the Obligation of Contracts." But the contract clause was directed against only the retroactive abridgment of existing contracts; it did not protect the right to enter contracts in the future.

After the Civil War, state and federal courts began to discover a constitutional justification of the private-law right to make contracts. Although the emerging notion of freedom of contract bore some relationship to the concerns behind the adoption of the contract clause, it was a distinct and further-reaching doctrine.

Sources of the Doctrine.

Freedom of contract as a constitutional principle can be traced to several sources. Some saw the right to make agreements as an element of natural law. Appeal to natural law was strengthened by the antislavery ideology, with its emphasis upon free labor. Congress pictured the right to make contracts as essential to the ability of former slaves to participate in the market economy. The Civil Rights Act of 1866 specifically included the right "to make and enforce contracts" among the liberties guaranteed to freedpersons. The Supreme Court justice Stephen J. Field, the most influential jurist of the Gilded Age, was instrumental in establishing due process protection for freedom of contract. In a series of famous dissenting opinions, Field blended natural-rights precepts with free-labor thought to fashion an argument that there was a constitutional right to follow lawful callings without unreasonable governmental interference. This right to pursue lawful trades morphed into a constitutional right to make contracts as a component of liberty safeguarded by the due process norm.

State courts led in developing the principle of liberty of contract. Starting in the 1880s, state courts began to strike down regulatory legislation as an interference with the right of individuals to make contracts. In 1895 the Supreme Court of Illinois invalidated a statute restricting the hours of work for women in factories, declaring that the "privilege of contract-ing is both a liberty and property right." Hence, contractual freedom was widely accepted as a part of state constitutional law even before the U.S. Supreme Court addressed the issue.

In *Allgeyer v. Louisiana* (1897), Justice Rufus W. Peckham, speaking for a unanimous Supreme Court, gave a broad reading to the notion of liberty safeguarded by the due process clause of the Fourteenth Amendment and adopted freedom of contract as a constitutional norm. The Court struck down a Louisiana law that prohibited individuals within the state from contracting for an insurance policy with an out-of-state company not qualified to do business in Louisiana. Yet the Supreme Court was hesitant to invoke consistently the principle of contractual freedom as a basis to overturn state regulations. For example, in *Holden v. Hardy* (1898) it rejected a liberty-of-contract challenge to a state law limiting the hours of work in underground mines.

Lochner and After.

The Supreme Court seemingly put new life into freedom of contract with its famous and much-contested decision in *Lochner v. New York* (1905). Writing for a 5-to-4 majority, Justice Peckham invalidated a state law that limited work in bakeries to ten hours a day or sixty hours a week as an infringement of contractual freedom. He declared that the "general right to make a contract in relation to his business is part of the liberty of the individual protected by the Fourteenth Amendment of the Federal Constitution." It is important to note that eight justices in *Lochner* agreed that there was a constitutional right to enter contracts: they differed only over the application of the doctrine to the facts of the case. Justice Oliver Wendell Holmes Jr. alone rejected the notion that contractual freedom was protected by the due process clause.

Notwithstanding *Lochner*, the Supreme Court rarely invoked the freedom-of-contract principle and upheld most challenged regulations. The

Court was far from a consistent champion of contractual freedom. Thus in *Muller v. Oregon* (1908) the Court brushed aside a liberty-of-contract argument and sustained a state law restricting the number of working hours for women in factories and laundries. Still, the doctrine was applied on occasion when the Court found no health or safety justification for restricting contractual freedom. In *Adkins v. Children's Hospital* (1923), Justice George Sutherland famously insisted that "freedom of contract is . . . the general rule and restraint the exception, and the exercise of legislative authority to abridge it can be justified only by the existence of exceptional circumstances." Although contractual freedom was not unlimited, the state was in effect required to show a necessity for restrictions on such freedom.

During the early decades of the twentieth century, scholars associated with the Progressive movement questioned the basis for the doctrine of freedom of contract, arguing that inequality of bargaining power meant that as a practical matter one party was often in a position to dictate the terms of contracts. This argument eventually bore fruit when the idea of contractual freedom as a constitutional right protected by the due process norm came to an abrupt end in *West Coast Hotel v. Parrish* (1937). The Supreme Court now took the position that legislators had power under the Constitution to limit freedom of contract to advance community welfare. Although some state courts persisted in treating freedom of contract as a constitutional right, the Supreme Court never again invoked the doctrine.

Yet freedom of contract remains a powerful norm in the private law governing contracts. Despite legislative regulation of such fields as consumer and insurance contracts, a good deal of room remains for bargaining by the parties. Courts generally enforce private agreements and do not police the substance of bargains.

[*See also Adkins v. Children's Hospital*; Contract, Sanctity of; Employment-at-Will; Free-Labor Ideology; *Lochner v. New York*; *Muller v. Oregon*; and *West Coast Hotel v. Parrish*.]

BIBLIOGRAPHY

Bernstein, David E. *Rehabilitating Lochner: Defending Individual Rights against Progressive Reform.* Chicago: University of Chicago Press, 2011.

Ely, James W., Jr. "The Protection of Contractual Rights: A Tale of Two Constitutional Provisions." *NYU Journal of Law and Liberty* 1 (2005): 370–403.

Mayer, David N. *Liberty of Contract: Rediscovering a Lost Constitutional Right.* Washington, D.C.: Cato Institute, 2011.

Scheiber, Harry N., ed. *The State and Freedom of Contract.* Stanford, Calif.: Stanford University Press, 1998.

James W. Ely Jr.

FREE-LABOR IDEOLOGY

Free-labor ideology emerged in the early nineteenth century as a peculiarly American, and distinctively northern, version of liberal contract theory. Northerners maintained that free labor—the ability of workers to form employment contracts and eventually to become property owners themselves—made for a more harmonious society and vigorous economy than the slave labor of the South did.

By the 1830s, America already had a centuries-old reputation as a place where, as John Smith originally put it, "every man may be master and owner of his owne labour and land." The decline of indentured servitude and apprenticeships after the Revolution sharpened the contrast between free and slave labor, and abolition in the North made that division a geographic one. Even as the population grew, individual property ownership remained a real possibility, owing to vast tracts of relatively inexpensive and arable land available in the West. But the ranks of dependent wageworkers also increased substantially: in 1850 the number of wage earners exceeded the number of slaves for the first time, and by 1860 America had more wage earners than self-employed artisans and farmers.

Partly in response to southern critiques of northern "wage slavery," defenders of free labor countered that, unlike slaves, workers could save money, buy land, and become independent property holders. A system of free labor increased productivity, they argued, because workers received the fruits of their labor, and it resulted in social harmony, because social and economic mobility created a classless society in which workers and employers shared common interests.

Before the Civil War, when most northerners worked for themselves or in a small shop, ideas of free labor accurately reflected life in the nonslave states. Paradoxically, however, the war that was fought to extend free labor across the country accelerated its decline. The war sped industrialization in the North and freed 4 million slaves in the South, and afterward millions of European immigrants began to arrive in northern ports.

For nearly a decade after the Civil War, most northerners tried to maintain the ideal of free labor, with voluntarily negotiated contracts enshrined as the essence of freedom. Congress created the Freedmen's Bureau in 1865 to oversee the transition to free labor in the South and passed the Civil Rights Act of 1866, which said that no state could deprive a citizen of the right to contract. The focus on contracts, however, cloaked the actual conditions of workers. Industrialization increased the economic gap between workers and employers and made it less likely that workers could ever own property. The influx of black and foreign workers brought racism into the labor market. It became difficult to claim that workers and employers still shared the same interests or that they negotiated contracts on an equal basis.

The shift from free labor to a world of dependent wageworkers was crystallized in 1873. That year's economic panic sharpened the class divide in the North and led Republicans in charge of Reconstruction to desist from enforcing free labor in the South. In the so-called Slaughterhouse Cases, the Supreme Court ruled that the meaning of the Fourteenth Amendment was limited to providing the freedom to contract, rather than to providing to citizens other "privileges and immunities." The classless vision of the ideal of free labor was over; the Gilded Age of capitalism had begun.

[*See also* **Artisanal Labor; Contract, Sanctity of; Freed Laborers; Freedom of Contract; Industrialization and Deindustrialization; Slaughterhouse Cases;** *and* **Slavery.**]

BIBLIOGRAPHY

Foner, Eric. *Free Soil, Free Labor, Free Men: The Ideology of the Republican Party before the Civil War.* New York: Oxford University Press, 1970.

Stanley, Amy Dru. *From Bondage to Contract: Wage Labor, Marriage, and the Market in the Age of Slave Emancipation.* New York: Cambridge University Press, 1998.

Scott Spillman

FREE SILVER AND BIMETALLISM

Traditionally the United States had a bimetallic monetary system in which sixteen ounces of silver equaled one ounce of gold. As the world supply of silver became scarce by the 1850s, the value of silver rose, and it was rarely used to coin money. In the 1860s, western miners discovered new supplies of silver, which decreased the commodity's value. By then more nations were adopting the gold standard. To maintain a stable currency, Congress passed a law, the Coinage Act (1873), that demonetized silver. At first there was little reaction, but as the price of silver fell, demands for the free and unlimited coinage of silver increased. To pacify the silver forces, Congress passed the Bland–Allison Act (1878), which authorized the Treasury to coin $2 million to $4 million in silver each month, and the Sherman Silver Purchase Act (1890), which provided for the monthly coinage of 4.5 million ounces of silver.

To this point, the silver issue had not been deeply divisive. In 1893, however, in response to the economic depression of 1893–1896, President Grover Cleveland persuaded Congress to repeal the Sherman Silver Purchase Act, thereby again demonetizing silver. Many people then exchanged silver money for gold, and the Treasury's gold reserve became seriously depleted. To bolster the reserve, the Cleveland administration sold bonds to New York bankers in return for gold bullion.

These developments revitalized the free-silver movement. Within the Democratic Party, William Jennings Bryan assumed leadership of the silver forces, and in 1896 the Democrats nominated Bryan for president on a free-silver platform, as did the Populist Party. The Republican Party, rallying behind William McKinley, endorsed the gold standard. In the ensuing campaign, the two sides offered competing visions. Silverites argued that instead of rigidly adhering to the gold standard, the government should devise a more flexible monetary system; Republicans insisted that gold be the sole basis for money. Silverites desired price inflation to combat depression; Republicans feared that inflation would worsen the economy. Silverites charged that eastern bankers used the gold standard to exploit farmers and the working class; Republicans responded that only the gold standard could ensure prosperity for all.

McKinley won the election, and the silver issue soon faded. Free silver appealed mostly to indebted farmers and mine owners, and the movement failed to bridge the division separating agriculturists and wage laborers. After 1897, however, new discoveries of gold enabled the nation to enjoy economic expansion and moderate inflation while maintaining the gold standard.

[*See also* **Depressions, Economic; Gold Standard; Greenbackism; Inflation and Deflation;** *and* **Monetary Policy, Federal.**]

BIBLIOGRAPHY

Nugent, Walter T. K. *The Money Question during Reconstruction.* New York: W. W. Norton and Company, 1967.
Ritter, Gretchen. *Goldbugs and Greenbacks: The Antimonopoly Tradition and the Politics of Finance in America.* Cambridge, U.K.: Cambridge University Press, 1997.

William F. Holmes

FRIEDMAN, MILTON, AND THE CHICAGO SCHOOL OF ECONOMICS

"Chicago school of economics" refers to the intellectual tradition that emerged out of the economics department of the University of Chicago in the years after World War II. The economists at the University of Chicago sought to counter the Keynesian economics that dominated the discipline during the postwar years. Their school of thought argued that the appropriate subject of analysis of economics was the behavior of individual consumers and firms, who tended, most of the time, to behave "rationally"—that is, to maximize utility. Focusing on individual maximization, Chicago economists claimed that in most circumstances, the free market will perform better than the state or other social groups in organizing economic life. Finally, the economists argued that the discipline of economics itself should be a science that makes predictions about individual behavior, rather than a descriptive, humanistic field of inquiry that studies the economy as rooted in historical and sociological institutions. The goal, for Chicago economists, was to develop universal models of human behavior to guide economic policy. By the late 1970s these assumptions about economics had come to dominate the discipline, and the methodological approach of the Chicago school, with its emphasis on individual choice, utility maximization, and the creation of mathematical models, has been applied to many other areas of social life—for example, law, political science, and sociology.

There are many important figures in the Chicago tradition, including Frank Knight, Aaron Director, George Stigler, Gary Becker, and Robert Lucas. (Friedrich von Hayek also taught at the University of Chicago in the postwar years, but he was never part of the Chicago economics department.) For most of the postwar period, though, the leading public voice of Chicago economics was Milton Friedman. Born in 1912 in Brooklyn—although his family soon relocated to New Jersey, where was raised—Friedman was educated at Rutgers, the University of Chicago, and Columbia. During the Great Depression, Friedman briefly worked for the National Bureau of Economic Research, and then during World War II he worked at the U.S. Treasury. In 1946 he was hired at the University of Chicago, where he taught until his retirement thirty years later. He served on the Economic Policy Advisory Board under Ronald Reagan in the 1980s and was affiliated with the Hoover Institution at Stanford University. He died in 2006.

As an academic economist, Friedman focused on consumption over the life cycle and on monetary policy. He is best known as a proponent of monetarism, which suggests that governments should restrict their macroeconomic policy to maintaining a tight control over the money supply to control inflation. In many ways, though, Friedman was best known for his deep engagement with politics and his active participation in the postwar debates over the appropriate scope of government. His 1962 book *Capitalism and Freedom* made a powerful case for the free market as a counter against state power. He did this not by posing an abstract philosophical case—as had earlier defenders of the market, such as Hayek—but by presenting a series of arguments tightly focused on the alleged inefficiencies of various government policies and by arguing that the free market could do better than the state could in several different areas, including drug policy, education, and the creation of parks. He worked on Barry Goldwater's presidential campaign in 1964. Taking his case to television, Friedman made a series for PBS in 1980 called *Free to Choose*. Through this political activism, as well as through his *Newsweek* column (which ran weekly throughout the 1970s), Friedman brought the ideals of the Chicago school into the mainstream of political conversation in America. As such, Friedman helped to legitimate the antigovernment agenda of conservative activists and politicians in the late years of the twentieth century.

Despite its importance in the intellectual life of the twentieth century, the Chicago school has received little attention from historians. Scholarly work since around the turn of the twenty-first century has explored the institutional history of Chicago economics, the surprising skepticism toward corporate power of thinkers such as Frank Knight (who taught in the 1930s and 1940s), and the diversity of approaches that characterized the work of the Chicago department in the immediate postwar period. There has also been some research on the role of Chicago economists in Latin America, especially in the dictatorship of Augusto Pinochet in Chile. The rise of Chicago methods within the academy has paralleled the growing prominence and prestige of economics in cultural and popular intellectual life, in particular the way that the discipline claims to dissect areas that are usually shrouded in sentiment and emotion and to show the operation of cold rationality underneath the surface in ways that run contrary to expectations. This has been accompanied by a deepening skepticism about the potential for collective action and the ability of the state to play a positive role in society. Even Chicago economists less politically active than Friedman have helped to reshape American politics and to shift the public to the right and away from public regulation of markets. Further research may help to illuminate the role of Chicago economics in changing not only the landscape of academic economics and its impact on policy, but also the broader political culture of the United States.

[*See also* **Deregulation, Financial; Economic Theories and Thought; Keynesian Economics;** *and* **Monetarism.**]

BIBLIOGRAPHY

Burgin, Angus. "The Radical Conservatism of Frank H. Knight." *Modern Intellectual History* 6, no. 3 (November 2009): 513–538.

Ebenstein, Lanny. *Milton Friedman: An Economist.* New York: Palgrave Macmillan, 2007.

Friedman, Milton. *Capitalism and Freedom.* Chicago: University of Chicago Press, 1962.

Friedman, Milton. *Essays in Positive Economics.* Chicago: University of Chicago Press, 1953.

Friedman, Milton, and Rose Friedman. *Free to Choose: A Personal Statement.* New York: Harcourt Brace Jovanovich, 1980.

Friedman, Milton, and Anna Schwartz. *A Monetary History of the United States, 1867–1960.* Princeton, N.J.: Princeton University Press, 1963.

Krugman, Paul. "Who Was Milton Friedman?" *New York Review of Books,* 15 February 2007.

Valdés, Juan Gabriel. *Pinochet's Economists: The Chicago School in Chile.* New York: Cambridge University Press, 1995.

Van Horn, Robert, Philip Mirowski, and Thomas Stapleford. *Building Chicago Economics: New Perspectives on the History of America's Most Powerful Economics Program.* New York: University of Cambridge Press, 2011.

Van Overtveldt, Johan. *The Chicago School: How the University of Chicago Assembled the Thinkers Who Revolutionized Economics and Business.* Chicago: Agate, 2007.

Kim Phillips-Fein

FUR TRADE

Animal pelts have probably been exchanged in North America since the beginning of human habitation, but large-scale fur trading began only after the arrival of Europeans. As the Eastern Hemisphere's fur stocks dwindled, Europeans regarded North America as a fur reservoir and created flourishing trade systems in New York, the lower Mississippi River valley, and the Pacific Northwest. The principal fur-trading arena stretched from the Great Lakes and the Ohio valley to the northern Great Plains and the Rocky Mountains. In the eighteenth and early nineteenth centuries, this region saw fierce rivalries among several American and Canadian enterprises that maintained hundreds of trading posts: at these, Native American trappers and processors bartered their deerskins and beaver, raccoon, and muskrat pelts for alcohol, firearms, metal tools, and other manufactured goods. The most powerful of these enterprises, John Jacob Astor's New York–based American Fur Company (1808–1865), featured several regional divisions and field offices and an elaborate international marketing system. Small, high-value fur-bearers dominated the American fur trade until the 1830s when declining beaver populations, replacement of beaver hats by silk ones, and the introduction of steamboat transportation shifted the emphasis to bison-robe production. The robe trade thrived until the 1870s when the destruction of bison herds on the Great Plains ended the traditional fur trade. By the late twentieth century the fur trade involved extensive importation, as well as limited domestic production of mink, fox, and muskrat coats and accessories; such production employed numerous individual trappers, hunters, fur breeders, and furriers.

Even during its peak, the fur industry amounted to only about 1 percent of the U.S. gross national product, and in many areas it formed only a transient phase that soon yielded to mining, lumbering, and agriculture. Yet the fur trade integrated peripheral areas into the national economy by stimulating exploration and investment and by boosting into prominence such distribution depots as Saint Louis, Missouri. The industry also wrought massive ecological changes. So-called mountain men virtually stripped the beaver from the central and northern Rocky Mountains in the 1820s and 1830s, and a three-way battle among Russian, British, and American traders on the Pacific coast threatened the sea otter with extinction by the 1850s. For the Indians, who formed the bulk of the industry's workforce, the fur trade proved a decidedly mixed blessing. Although it gave them new technologies, it also spread European diseases and tied their societies to a global economy over which they had little control.

[*See also* **Native Americans, Economic Aspects of U.S. Relations with.**]

BIBLIOGRAPHY

Phillips, Paul C. *The Fur Trade.* 2 vols. Norman: University of Oklahoma Press, 1961.

Wishart, David J. *The Fur Trade of the American West, 1807–1840: A Geographical Synthesis.* Lincoln: University of Nebraska Press, 1979.

Pekka Hämäläinen

G

GALBRAITH, JOHN KENNETH

(1908–2006), the leading advocate of left-wing Keynesianism in twentieth-century America. Born into a Canadian farming family that worked three hundred acres of land, John Kenneth Galbraith began his academic career studying animal husbandry in his home province of Ontario. In 1931 the University of California at Berkeley offered him a stipend to study agricultural economics; he earned a PhD in the subject in 1934. Shortly after arriving, however, he began to lose interest in agricultural studies. His professors facilitated the process by exposing him to the ideas of progressive economists. Galbraith took a particular liking to Thorstein Veblen, whose sardonic wit and disdain for quantitative analysis are evident in Galbraith's own work.

In 1938, Galbraith coauthored *Modern Competition and Business Policy*, which argued that monopolization had ended classic market competition. To restore a healthy economy, a wide array of reforms, loosely associated with the New Deal, were required. Galbraith later disavowed the book because it failed to reflect his growing interest in Keynesianism. In 1952, Galbraith published his first wildly successful book, *American Capitalism: The Concept of Countervailing Power*. In it, he contended that economic concentration had eliminated competition in industry, but the need for competition had been obviated by the "countervailing power" of labor unions and large retailers. Though popular, the book offended not only many conservatives, because of its assertion that competition was irrelevant, but also some liberals, because it sanctioned the unfettered expansion of large corporations.

Galbraith published prolifically after *American Capitalism*, but two books were particularly influential. Both of them shared the premise that left-wing Keynesianism ought to fill the void left by the disappearance of market capitalism. Left-wing Keynesians called for higher social spending and broad market manipulation, whereas more conservative Keynesians advocated deficit spending through tax cuts and military expenditures. In the first of these books, *The Affluent Society* (1958), Galbraith claimed that poverty had disappeared only to be replaced by the squandering of resources for false wants, manufactured by large corporations. The popular appeal of discretionary forms of consumption meant that public goods like education and mass transit had been neglected. In response, Galbraith recommended higher sales taxes and government spending to ease the imbalance of "private opulence and public squalor." The last of Galbraith's canonical works, the 1967 best seller *The New Industrial State*, portrayed an emerging knowledge-based economy. Galbraith argued that a "technostructure" of corporate managers had usurped traditional capitalists. The technostructure preferred stable economic growth to short-term profits and used the political and economic power of large corporations to manage growth. The new planned economy often neglected the interest of societies' weaker members, but another group, "the educational and scientific estate," could push planning in a more egalitarian direction.

Galbraith remains best known as a popular writer. Though he spent much of his life as a professor at Harvard, his reputation among academics was always mixed. He also served as a public official. During World War II he was employed by the Office of Price Administration (OPA). He later worked as speechwriter for both John F. Kennedy and Adlai Stevenson.

Kennedy, to whom he was particularly close, appointed him ambassador to India.

[*See also* **Economic Theories and Thought** and **Keynesian Economics**.]

BIBLIOGRAPHY

Parker, Richard. *John Kenneth Galbraith: His Life, His Politics, His Economics*. New York: Farrar, Straus and Giroux, 2005.

Reisman, David. *Galbraith and Market Capitalism*. New York: New York University Press, 1980.

Christopher England

GALLATIN, ALBERT, AND ECONOMIC DEVELOPMENT

Albert Gallatin (1761–1849), born in Geneva, Switzerland, played an important role in the original fiscal management of the United States and gave vigor to a Jeffersonian vision of political economy that greatly colored nineteenth-century debates of the proper relationship among taxes, debt, and internal improvements. Gallatin served Pennsylvania in the U.S. Senate and House of Representatives from 1793 to 1801, and he served as the secretary of the treasury from 1801 to 1813, the longest tenure of any man in that post.

Upon his election to Congress, Gallatin became one of the most vocal and influential leaders of the emerging Republican opposition to Federalist policies, particularly those that enlarged the federal debt and that seemed designed to ally American national trade policy too closely with Great Britain. He helped create what became the Ways and Means Committee in the House of Representatives to investigate and manage public expenditures, always attacking the lack of specificity and oversight of congressional requisitions. In 1796 he published a critique of Hamiltonian finance, *A Sketch of the Finances of the United States*, which attacked the lack of transparency and oversight in the Treasury Department's procedures, showed that the national debt had increased by nearly $1 million per year during the tenure of Secretary of the Treasury Alexander Hamilton, expressed a vision of economy in government expenditures, and called for the national debt to be rapidly extinguished.

As the leading Republican expert in matters of finance, Gallatin was the natural choice of President Thomas Jefferson for secretary of the treasury, and he remained in that position until 1813 when he was sent to Europe by President James Madison to help negotiate an end to the War of 1812. At the Department of the Treasury he stood for a clear fiscal mission: reduce expenditures on the military to the bare minimum, pay off the national debt as rapidly as possible, create transparency in the management of fiscal affairs, sell western lands in small portions to discourage speculators, and empower citizen-farmers. He rejected the overtly mercantilistic views of the Federalists with a more measured enthusiasm for road and canal building, and he believed that the rapid growth of the American population would create internal demand for the natural increase of American manufactures, aided by capital lent by the United States. Gallatin's vision, which was shared to some extent by Jefferson, anticipated the more robust American System of Henry Clay, which encouraged internal improvement, protective tariffs, and internal markets for home manufactures.

As secretary of the treasury, Gallatin sometimes found himself at odds with the political choices of both Jefferson and Madison. Because of the costs, he opposed sending fleets to deal with the Barbary pirates, the embargo, and the War of 1812, but he desired the rechartering of the Bank of the United States, considering it essential for lowest-cost government borrowing

and for paying off the debt. Yet even when policies that he rejected ultimately prevailed, he supported their execution with the rigor of his office. And despite the repeal of internal taxes, the purchase of Louisiana, the Barbary Wars, and the Non-importation and Embargo Acts, during his tenure as secretary the national debt shrank from more than $82 million to $45 million. In many respects it was Gallatin, and not Hamilton, who had the most sustained impact on the goals of American public finance in the first half of the nineteenth century.

[*See also* Bank of the United States, First and Second; Business Growth and Decline; Economic Development; Economic Theories and Thought; Hamilton, Alexander, and Economic Development; Industrial Policy, Theory and Practice of; *and* Taxation.]

BIBLIOGRAPHY

Aitken, Thomas. *Albert Gallatin: Early America's Swiss-Born Statesmen*. New York: Vantage Press, 1985.

Balinky, Alexander. *Albert Gallatin: Fiscal Theories and Policies*. New Brunswick, N.J.: Rutgers University Press, 1958.

Dungan, Nicholas. *Gallatin: America's Swiss Founding Father*. New York: New York University Press, 2010.

Walters, Raymond, Jr. *Albert Gallatin: Jeffersonian Financier and Diplomat*. New York: Macmillan, 1957.

Doug Bradburn

GARMENT INDUSTRY

Most American garment production in the late eighteenth and early nineteenth centuries was centered in the home for family consumption. The development of the American textile industry, transportation improvements, and protective tariffs spurred the growth of the men's readymade clothing industry in the 1820s. The introduction and improvements of the sewing machine by midcentury, along with the demand for uniforms during the Civil War, drove production and expanded the industry to include women's readymade clothing. Hundreds of thousands of immigrants from eastern and southern Europe in the late nineteenth century provided cheap labor for the growing concentration in New York City of tenement sweatshops, supplying products for the bourgeoning department-store sector. Manufacturers created a contracting system in which stages of production were subdivided and farmed out to other shops, creating cutthroat competition among thousands of small shops and driving down wages, all amid deplorable work conditions.

In the 1890s, skilled workmen centered in the men's garment industry formed the United Garment Workers (UGW). At the same time, mostly Jewish men in the women's garment industry organized unions in several East Coast cities; in 1900 they came together to form the International Ladies' Garment Workers' Union (ILGWU). Modern factories began to replace the tenement sweatshops, and in 1909, in what is known as the Uprising of 20,000, that number or more young Jewish and Italian women, who occupied the lower-skilled and less-well-paid jobs in the industry, went on strike in New York City to demand that the ILGWU take them seriously and that manufacturers accept the union. Their success inspired male cloak-makers to strike the following year, helping make the union the third largest in the American Federation of Labor by World War I. The ILGWU negotiated the so-called Protocols of Peace agreements with manufacturers in the 1910s, establishing a model of labor–management–government cooperation that inspired the creation of the federal labor laws in the 1930s. In 1914, militant members of the UGW left the

union to form the Amalgamated Clothing Workers of America (ACWA), which came to dominate the men's garment trades.

During the 1920s, garment manufacturers took advantage of rancorous divisions in the radical left following the 1917 Russian revolution and government repression of trade union radicals to go on the offensive to break the garment unions. The increasing availability of automobiles and good roads allowed shops in New York and other cities to escape from unions by moving to states and localities where there were fewer unions, or none. Shops that stayed began to hire black and Hispanic workers in an effort to divide the workforce. Despite the ravages of the Great Depression, and facing bankruptcy, the ILGWU recovered in the mid-1930s in part by embracing workers' ethnic and cultural differences. Together with the ACWA and the United Mine Workers of America, the ILGWU helped to found the Congress of Industrial Organizations.

After World War II, garment unions continued to grow, even after the 1947 Taft–Hartley Act made it more difficult to organize in the states of the South and other regions. By the 1960s the ILGWU reached its peak membership of 450,000, just as new technologies and production processes accelerated the deskilling of labor, manufacturers began to seek cheaper labor overseas, and a new wave of Chinese and Latin American immigrants entered the workforce. In decline, in 1976 the ACWA and the Textile Workers Union of America merged to form the Amalgamated Clothing and Textile Workers Union (ACTWU). Increasingly, the U.S. government was reluctant to protect the domestic garment trades from apparel-exporting countries that were allies in the Cold War. By the 1980s, competition from foreign imports drove down the costs of garments and wages, and Manhattan's Chinatown became a new haven for sweatshop production of women's garments. In 1982, twenty thousand

Chinese, mostly women workers, struck there and reestablished the ILGWU in the industry. But manufacturing continued to move overseas—encouraged by tax codes first put into place in the early 1960s, then facilitated further by the North American Free Trade Agreement in the mid-1990s—and domestic sweatshops proliferated. American companies producing in foreign markets began to lose their edge, however, when big-box American retailers restructured the entire global supply chain in the 1990s and 2000s. Drawing up contracts with producers in China and elsewhere, Target and Wal-Mart drove prices and wages down further than at any time since the 1930s, often bypassing American producers altogether. Clothing designers, especially for higher-priced fashions, may still do their work in the United States and in New York City showrooms, but garment manufacturing has with few exceptions fled overseas.

[*See also* **Congress of Industrial Organizations; Department Stores; Homework; International Ladies' Garment Workers' Union and Amalgamated Clothing Workers of America; Jewish American Labor Movement; Textile Industry; Triangle Shirtwaist Company Fire; Uprising of 20,000;** *and* **Women Workers.**]

BIBLIOGRAPHY

Bao, Xiaolan. *Holding Up More Than Half the Sky: Chinese Women Garment Workers in New York City, 1948–92.* Urbana and Chicago: University of Illinois Press, 2001.

Green, Nancy L. *Ready-to-Wear and Ready-to-Work: A Century of Industry and Immigrants in Paris and New York.* Durham, N.C.: Duke University Press, 1997.

Katz, Daniel. *All Together Different: Yiddish Socialists, Garment Workers, and the Labor Roots of Multiculturalism.* New York: New York University Press, 2011.

Lichtenstein, Nelson. *The Retail Revolution: How Wal-Mart Created a Brave New World of Business.* New York: Metropolitan Books, 2009.

Rothstein, Richard. *Keeping Jobs in Fashion: Alternatives to the Euthanasia of the U.S. Apparel Industry.* Washington, D.C.: Economic Policy Institute, 1989.

Daniel Katz

GASTONIA STRIKE (1929)

On 1 April 1929 the management of the Loray Mill in Gastonia, North Carolina, began firing textile workers who had attended a union-organizing rally two days earlier. Within hours, one of the most infamous strikes in southern labor history was underway.

Owned by the Manville–Jenckes Company of Rhode Island, the Loray Mill produced tire-cord fabric for the automobile industry. In the two years prior to the strike, Manville–Jenckes had initiated a series of efficiency changes designed to increase profits. Known as the "stretch-out" by southern textile workers, these changes reduced by a third the number of millworkers, increased individual workloads, and reduced earnings. As a result, worker dissatisfaction rose.

On Saturday, 30 March 1929, several hundred Loray workers attended the union's first public meeting, a rally led by the Communist labor activists Fred Beal and Ellen Dawson. Beal was a seasoned textile worker in his early thirties. He had participated in several New England strikes, including the famous 1912 "Bread and Roses" strike in Lawrence, Massachusetts. Dawson, a twenty-eight-year-old Scottish immigrant, had been a textile worker and leader in the 1926 textile strike in Passaic, New Jersey. She came to Gastonia from Massachusetts, where she and Beal played prominent roles in a 1928 strike in New Bedford.

During the first week of the Gastonia strike, National Guard troops arrived to protect the peace. Their effectiveness proved questionable. During the predawn hours of 18 April, as guardsmen slept, more than seventy-five masked men attacked the union headquarters and completely demolished the building.

On 7 June 1929, Orville Aderholt, the Gastonia police chief, was killed during a police raid on the strikers' tent city. Even in the twenty-first century, the debate over who killed Aderholt still rages, with no concrete evidence tying the murder to any of the striking workers or the union leaders. In response to Aderholt's death, local prosecutors charged fourteen labor activists with his murder. The ensuing murder trial drew international attention and was compared at the time to the trial of the anarchists Nicola Sacco and Bartolomeo Vanzetti. A mistrial was declared when the prosecution, borrowing an idea from a contemporary movie, produced in the courtroom a life-size wax model of the dead Aderholt.

During the chaotic week that followed the mistrial, Ella May Wiggins, a single mother and striking worker, traveling to a union rally with a group of workers, was shot and killed. Wiggins is remembered for her poetry, including "Mill Mother's Lament." No one was ever convicted of her murder.

At the second Aderholt murder trial, prosecutors limited the number of defendants to seven and reduced the charge to second-degree murder. The jury convicted the defendants, and the judge sentenced them to terms of from five to twenty years. While out on bail, most of the defendants escaped to the Soviet Union. Beal returned to the United States in 1939 and surrendered to North Carolina officials, who pardoned him in 1942. He then wrote a memoir in which he repudiated Communism and implied that Communist leadership had been partly responsible for the failure of the strike and lost jobs for the millworkers. The tragic events in Gastonia were among the most dramatic in a wave of industrial conflict that spread across the South's Piedmont from 1928 to 1934.

[*See also* **Repression of Unions; Stretch-Out, Worker Resistance to; Strikes;** *and* **Textile Industry.**]

BIBLIOGRAPHY

Beal, Fred E. *Proletarian Journey: New England, Gastonia, Moscow.* New York: Hillman–Curl, 1937.

McMullen, David Lee. *Strike! The Radical Insurrections of Ellen Dawson.* Gainesville: University Press of Florida, 2010.

Salmond, John A. *Gastonia 1929: The Story of the Loray Mill Strike.* Chapel Hill: University of North Carolina Press, 1995.

David Lee McMullen

GATES, BILL

(1955–), developer of computer software, businessman, and philanthropist. Born in Seattle, Washington, William H. "Bill" Gates III attended one of the few secondary schools in America that had access to computers at the time. He later attended Harvard College but left before graduating. Gates and his friend Paul Allen learned of the invention of the Altair personal computer (PC) in 1975. Recognizing the potential market for PC software, they developed the BASIC program for the Altair. Moving to Albuquerque, New Mexico, where the Altair was produced, they incorporated their firm, Microsoft. In 1979 they moved the company to Seattle. Gates married Melinda French in 1994.

Challenging the amateur tradition of software development, Gates argued that unless software authors could recover their costs, they would have no incentive to provide high-quality software. In 1980, Microsoft won the contract to develop the operating system for the new International Business Machines (IBM) PC. Because IBM, unlike other PC manufacturers, used an open architecture in its machine, and because a number of other firms copied the IBM machine and used its operating system, this arrangement gave Microsoft a vast and elastic market. By 1990, as the dominant firm in the PC operating-systems market, Microsoft was expanding its product line by developing or acquiring applications software. Because of its market dominance, it also influenced the design of applications packages developed by other vendors. In 1998 the U.S. Justice Department brought an antitrust suit against Microsoft for allegedly using its control of the operating-systems market to promote its own Internet Web browser and to prevent other companies from entering the market. In June 2000 the federal district judge Penfield Jackson ruled that Microsoft had violated the antitrust laws and should be divided into two companies. Microsoft appealed, and the D.C. Court of Appeals eventually overturned Jackson's rulings. The Department of Justice and Microsoft reached a settlement in 2001 that was to last until 2007 but was later extended by two years.

Even while the Justice Department sought to convict Microsoft for antitrust violations, Apple Computers began to cut into Microsoft's market dominance by manufacturing machines that many considered better designed, easier to use, and more attractive. Apple also pioneered and came to dominate the market for smartphones and tablets, a form of miniature, handheld computers, innovations in which Microsoft lagged. Even in computer software, in which Microsoft had long dominated the market, Apple competed successfully by designing its own proprietary software products and, more important, developing software or applications for smartphones and tablets. By the end of the first decade of the twenty-first century, Apple had become a more profitable enterprise than Microsoft.

Nevertheless, by the end of the twentieth century, Gates, a billionaire many times over, had become the richest person in the world. Though he has remained the nonexecutive chairman of Microsoft, Gates did step down as the chief executive officer in 2000. He turned his attention toward the Bill and Melinda Gates Foundation, established in 1994 with an initial gift of $94 million. Initially the foundation focused on promoting computer and Internet access, global health, children's issues, and projects concerning the Pacific Northwest, but it has since expanded to promote programs related to HIV/AIDS, education initiatives, and global poverty and development. By September 2011 the foundation had given approximately $26.1 billion in grants.

[*See also* **Antitrust Legislation** *and* **Technology.**]

BIBLIOGRAPHY

Gates, Bill, with Nathan Myhrvold and Peter Rinearson. *The Road Ahead.* New York: Viking, 1995.

Manes, Stephen, and Paul Andrews. *Gates: How Microsoft's Mogul Reinvented an Industry—And Made Himself the Richest Man in America.* New York: Doubleday, 1993.

Robert W. Seidel

GATT AND WTO

The General Agreement on Tariffs and Trade (GATT) was a multilateral trade agreement designed to lower tariffs and other barriers to free trade and to create a nondiscriminatory trade regime. The agreement ultimately encompassed relationships among 128 countries; its successor, the World Trade Organization (WTO), had 153 members in 2011. The idea for an international organization that would help liberalize world trade was floated as part of the same post–World War II planning by the Allies that produced the International Monetary Fund and the World Bank, but the proposed International Trade Organization never came to pass. In its place, GATT emerged in 1947 as an agreement among twenty-three nations based on an earlier, temporary trade agreement. After its creation, GATT was broadened and revised several times at subsequent rounds of negotiation—in 1949, 1951, 1955–1956, 1960–1962, 1964–1967, 1973–1979, 1986–1994, and 2001. During the Uruguay Round (1986–1994) of GATT, negotiators designed the WTO as an institution to implement and to enforce trade agreements, as well as to resolve trade disputes among member nations. GATT was supplanted by the WTO in 1995.

Since the WTO's creation, critics have charged the WTO with favoring free trade at the expense of environmental, consumer, and worker protections in many nations, charges that the WTO denies. By the late 1990s, rising dissatisfaction with the WTO led to massive popular protests. The biggest and most famous of these protests occurred in Seattle, Washington, in November 1999 when thousands of protestors disrupted the WTO's ministerial conference.

[*See also* **Bretton Woods Conference; Foreign Trade; Globalization; Trade Policy, Federal;** *and* **World Bank.**]

BIBLIOGRAPHY

Barton, John H., et al. *The Evolution of the Trade Regime: Politics, Law, and Economics of the GATT and the WTO.* Princeton, N.J.: Princeton University Press, 2006.

Kim, Soo Yeon. *Power and the Governance of Global Trade: From the GATT to the WTO.* Ithaca, N.Y.: Cornell University Press, 2010.

Paul Gibson

GENDER AND WORK

As elucidated by feminist theory, "gender" refers to socially constructed differences between the biological sexes. Through the sexual division of labor, the organization of work plays a key part in the production and reproduction of gender. Work, both paid and unpaid, is divided between the sexes, into "men's work" and "women's work." Assigned to the work thought proper to their sex, people are transformed into men or women, into masculine or feminine beings. Historically, women have been predominantly assigned to "intrafamilial" or private work—work within their family—while men have been assigned to "interfamilial" or public work. The complementarity between women's and men's work compels marriage.

At the same time, gender, along with race and class, affects the construction of work. The masculine/feminine contrasting pair has been associated with the contrasting pairs dominant/subordinate, paid/unpaid, competitive/cooperative, mind/body, and intellect/emotion, and these have been built into the tasks that constitute "men's work" and "women's work."

History of the Gendered Organization of Work.
In U.S. economic history, both gender and work have been transformed in connected ways. Among free whites in the colonial economy, small family businesses, shops, or farms predominated. In this so-called family economy, husbands were the household heads, property owners, and heads of the family businesses; wives centered their work on caring for family members, including assisting with the family business as needed. On family farms, men focused on the production of cash crops and supervised any hired hands, while women had kitchen gardens, made and maintained

clothing, and prepared and cooked food for the family and any additional workers. In some instances, women earned income directly—what was called their "butter and egg money." If her husband died without an adult son to take his place, it became his widow's job to take over the business. Among enslaved African Americans, predominantly employed on plantations, a sexual division of labor did exist, both in private household work (women sewed, cooked, and cleaned; men hunted) and in their work for their owners (women mostly did domestic work; women and men worked in sex-typed tasks in the fields). Sometimes, however, the needs of slave owners trumped gender; for example, if male slaves were unavailable, then women were assigned to the masculine task of plowing. Native American nations were very diverse, but they all had sexual divisions of labor that focused women more on intrahousehold work and men more on hunting and war.

The capitalist economy that emerged in the course of the nineteenth century was built on gender. That is, it developed with two distinct, opposite, and complementary arenas: a masculine sphere, characterized by individualism and competition, and a feminine sphere, "the home," where caring and sharing predominated. In the former, work was paid; in the latter, it was not, unless done by domestic servants. In the ideal white, middle-class family, the husband was a full-time breadwinner who earned a family wage, enough to support a full-time homemaker wife and their children. Most employed women were single, and they left their jobs at marriage. Jobs were sex- and race-typed, and women, especially women of color, were restricted to lower-paid, lower-status jobs, many of them, like domestic service, being paid forms of women's homemaking work. That men with lower earnings—who were disproportionately men of color—found it more difficult to keep their wives out of the paid labor force only reinforced racist and classist notions of white, middle-class superiority. Educated women could work in a small number of paid professions, such as teaching, social work, or nursing—but only if they were single, since homemaking was viewed a full-time job. Meanwhile, with the extension of markets, men, especially white, middle-class men, experienced a new freedom to move themselves up the economic hierarchy through hard work or entrepreneurship, and the concept of the self-made man was born. This organization of men's paid work as "breadwinning" built a focus on self-advancement, rather than on caring for others, into private enterprise, the firm, and the corporation.

Breakdown of the Gendered Organization of Work, and Its Persistence.

As natural and solid as this gender/class/race organization of work appeared, it began to break down in the twentieth century, especially after World War II. A growing share of women began to participate in paid work and in traditionally masculine jobs. A number of factors contributed to this sea change. The transformation of consumption into competitive consumerism, along with the commodification of much household work, meant that women began to feel that they best served their families by contributing directly to family income. Educated women asserted their right to combine marriage and career, and the married (middle-class) career woman replaced the full-time homemaker as the feminine ideal. A growing demand for clerical workers and labor shortages during the two world wars also drew women into paid work. And the Second Wave feminist movement, which crystallized in the early 1970s, successfully recast the sex typing of jobs as discrimination, pointed out the limitations and risks of full-time homemaking, and encouraged women to enter men's jobs.

Together these factors broke down the historical absence of women, especially married women, from paid work and from men's jobs. In 2005, 68 percent of married mothers were employed, compared to only 17 percent in 1948. Jobs that had been done exclusively by men, such as lawyer, doctor, and manager, became more commonly performed by women.

Still, gender differences and inequalities persist. Women experience sexual harassment, wage discrimination, and a glass ceiling when they work at so-called men's jobs, and they continue be concentrated in lower-paid, women's jobs such as clerical and service work. Employed mothers still do most household work, facing a taxing double day. Since most high-paying jobs were constructed for married men supported by full-time homemakers, women, especially mothers, have difficulty advancing in the labor market. Women have been pressured to reduce the time that they spend on parenting and household tasks and to take on the masculine qualities associated with men's jobs. These factors have brought new problems: a devaluation of all that is feminine and a reduction in unpaid work caring for others. Feminist theorists view the revaluation of caring labor—for instance, by paid parental leaves—and the elimination of discrimination against parents as key next steps. Some also foresee the injection of feminine, caring, cooperative qualities into the current overindividualistic, corrupt, and crisis-ridden economy as providing a possible path forward.

[*See also* Clerical Workers; Domestic Labor; Household Technology and Domestic Labor; Labor Markets; Racism; *and* Women Workers.]

BIBLIOGRAPHY

Amott, Teresa, and Julie A. Matthaei. *Race, Gender, and Work: A Multicultural Economic History of Women in the United States.* Boston: South End, 1991.

Folbre, Nancy. *Invisible Heart: Economics and Family Values.* New York: New Press, 2001.

Friedan, Betty. *The Feminine Mystique.* New York: W. W. Norton and Company, 1963.

Goldin, Claudia. *Understanding the Gender Gap: An Economic History of American Women.* New York: Oxford University Press, 1990.

Matthaei, Julie A. *An Economic History of Women in America: Women's Work, the Sexual Division of Labor, and the Development of Capitalism.* New York: Schocken Books, 1982.

Julie A. Matthaei

GENERAL AGREEMENT ON TARIFFS AND TRADE (GATT)

See GATT and WTO.

GENERAL ELECTRIC

Incorporated in 1892 as a manufacturer of lighting and power-generation equipment, General Electric (GE) has become one of the largest, most successful, and most highly diversified corporations in the world. Since the later twentieth century it has consistently made it to *Forbes* magazine's top-four listing of the largest global corporations. By the early twenty-first century the company, based in Fairfield, Connecticut, operated in 160 countries and employed more than 300,000 blue- and white-collar workers.

Beginning and Early Growth. GE was the offspring of a merger, engineered by J. P. Morgan and Boston financiers, that brought together Edison General Electric of Schenectady, New York, and the Thomson–Houston Electric Company of Lynn, Massachusetts. From the 1890s through the 1920s, General Electric concentrated on two product areas: lighting appliances (lamp manufacturing) and power generation. The firm was a major force in the electrification revolution that was sweeping both the nation and the world; it manufactured generators and turbines for central-city power stations, electric motors for trolleys, lamps for home and street lighting, and steam turbines for locomotives. Soon after its creation, GE began actively to forge an international presence and reputation, and by the 1930s it had become one of the most powerful forces in electrical-products manufacturing and marketing worldwide, with operations in Germany, England, France, Japan, Mexico, South America, Cuba, South Africa, northern Africa, and the Arabian Peninsula.

Under the leadership of Gerard Swope and Owen D. Young—together they led the firm from 1922 until 1939, with Swope as president and Young as chairman of the board—the firm began to modify its labor-management practices and its manufacturing trajectory. Swope had been a Hull House volunteer, and Young was a strong advocate of liberal corporatism. Their vision of liberal corporatism led to the firm's adoption and expansion of employee welfare practices: recreational programs, employment compensation enhancements, paid vacations, pensions, improvements in job security, and employee representation. It also led to their subsequent acquiescence to the unionization of a large part of GE's labor force.

Under Swope and Young's leadership, GE vastly expanded its product lines by moving rapidly into the business of consumer appliances, establishing plants for manufacturing electric ranges, refrigerators, irons, radios, washers, sewing machines, clocks, and more. The firm was also a pioneer in the development of early radio (and later television), holding a controlling interest in the Radio Corporation of America (RCA) and experimenting with commercial radio broadcasting at its WGY studios in Schenectady. It perfected the effective use of media as a marketing tool, hiring the advertising executive Bruce Barton and beginning a vigorous print and radio campaign to promote its new electrical appliances. GE has continued to be known for its original, creative, and highly effective advertising.

General Electric's successful expansion into consumer products led to the firm's dramatic growth in the 1920s. By the end of the decade, it had major manufacturing facilities in more than four dozen communities in the United States. Though the Great Depression slowed corporate growth, World War II, postwar consumerism, and the Cold War greatly stimulated production of both consumer and military goods. Emerging lucrative markets in the South and West, the appeal of advantageous tax opportunities and low-cost facilities in these regions, and a desire to flee heavily unionized plants in the Northeast all motivated GE managers to pursue expansion and decentralization of their manufacturing facilities. By 1961, General Electric had 170 plants operating in the United States, located in dozens of states, including New Mexico, Oregon, California, Georgia, and Texas.

Throughout the twentieth century, GE stood out not merely for its growing and highly profitable manufacturing ventures, but also for its pioneering role in corporate research. Within a decade of GE's incorporation, in 1900 two of the firm's most prominent scientists, the German-born consulting engineer Charles P. Steinmetz and Willis R. Whitney, a chemist recruited from MIT, established the first corporate research laboratory in the United States. The laboratory became and remains world renowned, and—like its parent firm—it has globalized. Research centers are spread across four continents, with major facilities located in Niskayuna, New York (the headquarters of GE Global Research), as well as Shanghai (China), Bangalore (India), Munich (Germany), and Rio de Janeiro (Brazil).

Late Twentieth-Century Shift. Since the 1970s—under the leadership of Reginald H. Jones (1972–1981), John "Jack" F. Welch Jr. (1981–2001), and Jeffrey Immelt (since 2001)—General Electric has undergone the most dramatic corporate sea change in its history. Its economic activities have radically shifted from the manufacturing of lighting, turbines, and consumer electrical products to services and research. Though it still possesses a strong manufacturing base—particularly in aircraft engines, turbines, medical hardware, and alternative energy and lighting products—a substantial percentage of the company's profits comes from service functions such as personal and corporate financing, aircraft leasing, media and entertainment, and real estate.

GE has also been transformed into a truly global corporation, dramatically enlarging its previous international footprint. By the twenty-first century it ran greatly expanded operations in South America, Europe, Asia, and Africa, drawing its managerial personnel from those regions. General Electric has become truly the quintessential global corporation, no longer tied to any region, state, or nation. Only time will tell what the long-term social and geopolitical implications of GE's new international status will be. Will the triumphalist celebration and prediction of a "boundaryless" corporation—to borrow Jack Welch's term—one that spreads its technical, managerial, and financial capital and raises living standards throughout the world, be affirmed? Or, instead, will the dire warnings of GE's detractors, envisaging the spread of global misery from an aggressively expansive and nationally unrooted corporation, be affirmed?

[*See also* **Advertising; Aviation Industry; Corporatism; Electricity and Electrification; Industrial Research Laboratories; Radio;** *and* **Welfare Capitalism.**]

BIBLIOGRAPHY

Gorowitz, Bernard, ed. *The General Electric Story: A Heritage of Innovation, 1876–1999.* Schenectady, N.Y.: Schenectady Museum, 1999.

Hammond, John Winthrop. *Men and Volts: The Story of General Electric.* New York: J. B. Lippincott, 1941.

O'Boyle, Thomas F. *At Any Cost: Jack Welch, General Electric, and the Pursuit of Profit.* New York: Alfred A. Knopf, 1998.

Schatz, Ronald W. *The Electrical Workers: A History of Labor at General Electric and Westinghouse, 1923–60.*

Gerald Zahavi

GENERAL MOTORS

See **Automotive Industry.**

GENERAL MOTORS STRIKE (1945)

The General Motors (GM) strike of 1945 was a watershed moment in the history of the American labor movement. The result of the 113-day work stoppage held implications for the future of collective bargaining, industrial relations, and social welfare. In the aftermath of the strike, however, organized labor focused on gaining middle-class status for American workers—as opposed to the more visionary goals that characterized industrial unions of the Congress of Industrial Organizations in the late 1930s and early 1940s.

The origins of the strike were rooted in the wartime economy, which froze workers' wages and ensured that the nation's defense industries, including GM, would have uninterrupted production. By April 1945, however, GM was poised to post multimillion-dollar profits. Walter Reuther, the vice president of the United

Auto Workers and a rising star within the union, was convinced that the only way for the country to maintain postwar economic stability and not slide back into depression was for workers' purchasing power to be increased. In the spring of 1945, Reuther spearheaded a campaign that demanded that GM raise workers' wages by 30 percent without increasing the prices of GM vehicles.

On 21 November 1945 the UAW officially went on strike at GM. To demonstrate GM's ability to pay, the UAW sponsored a public relations campaign. The union asserted that because GM's earnings were projected to rise by 50 percent, the company could afford to increase the wages of its workers by 30 percent and hold the prices of its new cars stable—all while still earning high profits. The company disputed the union's findings and insisted that the UAW's demands infringed upon the corporation's right to manage its business.

UAW critics of Reuther—mostly radicals, many of whom were Communists—charged him with waging a bureaucratic strike that occurred primarily in corporate boardrooms. UAW radicals believed that Reuther's strike tactics marginalized militant workers and made the labor movement less receptive to issues involving social justice.

For better or worse, the GM strike was settled on 13 March 1946. The union secured an hourly raise of 18.5 cents (just shy of the 30 percent goal), vacation pay, improved overtime rates, and equal pay for female employees. The UAW was forbidden, however, from punishing workers who left the union, thus opening the door for GM to build a nonunion coalition within its shops. GM retained the right to manage its business operations, including pricing its products.

The resolution of the GM strike was a bittersweet moment in labor history. On the one hand, it laid the foundation for what historians have termed the "Treaty of Detroit." Under this accord, which had national implications, workers would be guaranteed a livable wage, fringe benefits, and continued union recognition, thus enabling millions of industrial workers to join a society of middle-class consumers. Critics of Reuther argued that the settlement would prove impermanent because corporations, including GM, viewed the settlement as a temporary truce. Reuther's style of union leadership, they suggested, limited labor's future ability to mobilize grassroots efforts to address such issues as the so-called urban crisis, deindustrialization, and globalization—issues that did indeed weaken unionism in the latter half of the twentieth century.

[*See also* **Automotive Industry; Flint General Motors Strike; Industrial Relations; Reuther, Walter; Treaty of Detroit and Postwar Labor Accord;** *and* **United Auto Workers.**]

BIBLIOGRAPHY

Halpern, Martin. *UAW Politics in the Cold War Era.* Albany: State University of New York Press, 1988.

Keeran, Roger. *The Communist Party and the Auto Workers Unions.* Bloomington: Indiana University Press, 1980.

Lichtenstein, Nelson. *The Most Dangerous Man in Detroit: Walter Reuther and the Fate of American Labor.* New York: Basic Books, 1995.

Ryan S. Pettengill

GEORGE, HENRY

(1839–1897), philosopher and reformer. Henry George won international repute with his book *Progress and Poverty* (1879), in which he argued that a single tax on land would alleviate poverty and stabilize republican government.

George, the son of a middle-class bookseller, was born on 2 September 1839 in Philadelphia. Largely self-educated, he left school before turning fourteen. After moving to San Francisco he rose up the ranks of the newspaper business to become, by the age of twenty-eight, a managing editor and an important spokesman for land reform, the Democratic Party, and Chinese exclusion.

In 1879, Henry George published his first book, *Progress and Poverty*, the best-selling economic treatise of the nineteenth century. It argues that increases in land value that do not come through direct improvements on the land should be confiscated. Increases in the value of unimproved land, George theorizes, result from social progress; thus, what society created—far more valuable real estate—should be taxed to benefit the entire community. Land and other natural monopolies stand in the way of a competitive market, but by socializing their proceeds, the tax burden can be lifted from productive industry. In 1887, Thomas Shearman rebranded this idea as the "single tax."

Irish nationalists, upset with English landlordism, were early converts to George's ideas. With Irish immigrants' support, George ran for mayor of New York City in 1886 on a labor party platform. He placed second, after the Democrat Abram Hewitt, but ahead of the Republican, Theodore Roosevelt. In 1897, George ran for mayor again, but he died just before Election Day. Several Progressive Era reformers, including Tom Johnson, Samuel Jones, and Newton Baker, were followers of George. In England his influence culminated in David Lloyd George's 1909 campaign to pass a land tax.

[*See also* **Single-Tax Movement** *and* **Taxation**.]

BIBLIOGRAPHY

Barker, Charles Albro. *Henry George*. New York: Oxford University Press, 1955.

Johnston, Robert D. *The Radical Middle Class: Populist Democracy and the Question of Capitalism in Progressive Era Portland, Oregon*. Princeton, N.J.: Princeton University Press, 2003.

Thomas, John L. *Alternative America: Henry George, Edward Bellamy, and Henry Demarest Lloyd and the Adversary Tradition*. Cambridge, Mass: Belknap Press, 1983.

Christopher England

GIBBONS v. OGDEN

In 1798, New York State gave Robert Livingston an exclusive fourteen-year franchise to operate a steamboat "within the state." In 1808 the legislature extended this monopoly, now shared with Robert Fulton, until 1838. Chief Justice James Kent, speaking for New York's highest court in 1812, approved the monopoly. In 1815, Livingston and Fulton sold part of their franchise rights to Aaron Ogden of New Jersey, who began operating a steamboat between New Jersey and New York City. In 1819, Ogden's former partner Thomas Gibbons began operating his own boat between New Jersey and New York. Ogden sued Gibbons, and in 1820 the New York court again upheld the steamboat monopoly. Gibbons appealed to the U.S. Supreme Court, which decided the case, *Gibbons v. Ogden*, in 1824. Daniel Webster, representing Gibbons, argued that his client had the right under federal law to "navigate freely" in all of the waters of the United States.

In one of his most important opinions, Chief Justice John Marshall struck down the monopoly as it applied to interstate commerce. The authority that the Constitution granted to the federal government to regulate interstate commerce, Marshall asserted, was a linchpin of the national government's power. Commerce, he declared, "is traffic, but it is something more; it is the commercial intercourse between nations and parts of nations, in all its branches." The Constitution, Marshall ruled, vested in Congress alone the complete power to regulate all commerce "among the states." The states could regulate "completely internal commerce," Marshall conceded, but all commerce that began in one state and entered into a second state fell exclusively within the federal government's regulatory power. In striking down an unpopular monopoly, Marshall also skillfully interpreted the Constitution's commerce clause to expand the power of the federal government. His decision was widely applauded by nationalists and by advocates of states' rights alike.

[*See also* **State Regulatory Laws.**]

BIBLIOGRAPHY

Baxter, Maurice G. *The Steamboat Monopoly: "Gibbons v. Ogden," 1824*. New York: Alfred A. Knopf, 1972.
White, G. Edward. *The Marshall Court and Cultural Change, 1815–35*. New York: Macmillan, 1988.

Paul Finkelman

GI BILL

Officially known as the Servicemen's Readjustment Act, the GI Bill was signed into law by President Franklin D. Roosevelt on 22 June 1944. Passed by the U.S. Congress as American soldiers stormed the beaches of Normandy in the epic D-day invasion, the bill was intended to facilitate the readjustment of World War II soldiers, two thirds of whom were drafted, back to civilian life. Different benefits—education tuition and expenses, hospitalization rights, unemployment compensation, and government-insured housing or business loans—were divided into different titles in the bill. Its progressive and generous benefits, as well as Roosevelt's signature on it, have led many schol-

ars to view the GI Bill as the last great act of the New Deal. Others detect conservative influences in the bill, most noticeably in its restrictions on federal power and the manner in which it was administered by state and local authorities in order to deny benefits to many veterans. Scholars also disagree about the bill's immediate and ultimate impact on society and the economy. American political culture routinely pays homage to the GI Bill as the progenitor of the modern American middle class, but scholars generally offer more circumscribed claims.

The GI Bill, as implemented by the Veterans Administration and available to World War II soldiers discharged between 1944 and 1954 on terms other than dishonorable, marked the first time the federal government assumed an entitlement obligation toward able-bodied veterans. It was one of the most expensive and expansive social policies undertaken by the U.S. government in the twentieth century, and its enduring political popularity suggests that it was also one of the most successful. Certainly, as measured by the relative ease of the readjustment of the 16 million World War II soldiers to civilian life, the GI Bill proved a tremendous achievement.

[*See also* **New Deal and Institutional Economics** *and* **Pensions, Civil War.**]

BIBLIOGRAPHY

Altschuler, Glenn C., and Stuart M. Blumin. *The GI Bill: A New Deal for Veterans*. New York: Oxford University Press, 2009.
Frydl, Kathleen J. *The GI Bill*. New York: Cambridge University Press, 2009.
Mettler, Suzanne. *Soldiers to Citizens: The GI Bill and the Making of the Greatest Generation*. New York: Oxford University Press, 2005.
Ortiz, Stephen R. *Beyond the Bonus March and GI Bill: How Veteran Politics Shaped the New Deal Era*. New York: New York University Press, 2010.

Kathleen J. Frydl

GLASS–STEAGALL, REPEAL OF

In 1999, President Bill Clinton signed into law the Financial Services Modernization Act, also known as the Gramm–Leach–Bliley Act after its Republican authors, Senator Phil Gramm of Texas and Representatives Thomas J. Bliley of Virginia and Jim Leach of Iowa. The act not only removed the legal division between commercial and investment banks that had been established by the Glass–Steagall Act of 1933, but also allowed for the consolidation of such institutions with securities firms and insurance companies.

For several decades there had been increasing pressure for the deregulation of the financial services sector. The United States stood almost alone internationally in maintaining its Depression-era separation of commercial and investment banking. By the 1990s Glass–Steagall had already diminished in its effectiveness in regulating new innovations and technologies, yet it represented a final obstacle that limited the range of financial services that American banks could offer to consumers.

The advocates of Gramm–Leach–Bliley argued that it would increase competition in the financial services industry by removing burdensome regulatory barriers and providing a framework for the affiliation of banks, securities firms, and insurance companies. Though many of the larger banks supported deregulation, there was some resistance on the part of smaller independent banks, who feared that it would lead to increased industry consolidation.

In the wake of the financial crisis of 2008, the repeal of Glass–Steagall faced criticism from some economists. They charged that commercial banks had adopted a "high-risk gambling mentality" that had previously been characteristic of investment banking and that Gramm–Leach–Bliley had contributed to several companies' becoming "too big to fail."

[*See also* Deregulation, Financial; Financial and Banking Promotion and Regulation; Great Recession of 2008 and After; New Deal Banking Regulation; *and* Shadow Banking System.]

BIBLIOGRAPHY

Barth, James R., R. Dan Brumbaugh Jr., and James A. Wilcox. *The Repeal of Glass–Steagall and the Advent of Broad Banking*. Washington, D.C.: U.S. Office of the Comptroller of the Currency, 2000.

Busch, Andreas. *Banking Regulation and Globalization*. Oxford and New York: Oxford University Press, 2009.

Singh, Dalvinder. *Banking Regulation of U.K. and U.S. Financial Markets*. Aldershot, U.K.: Ashgate, 2007.

Patrick M. Dixon

GLOBALIZATION

The term "globalization" refers to increasingly interconnected economic, social, and political interactions among nations, peoples, and cultures. Though the term entered popular parlance only in the late twentieth century, the transnational relationships that it describes have existed for centuries. Certain aspects distinguish twenty-first-century globalization: its vast scope, the speed at which it has proceeded, and its pervasive and often destructive impact on both America's economy and its working class. Global production, services, and trade have eclipsed largely national commercial networks, resulting in the systemic relocation of capital and high-wage jobs, the erosion of American workers' standard of living, the decline of many core industries and the unions within them, and, in labor relations, a dramatic power shift toward businesses.

Large and powerful corporations dominate the global economy of the twenty-first century. In central economic sectors such as banking, finance, steel, automobiles, oil, earthmoving equipment, and textiles, major enterprises have developed highly integrated production and supply chains, drawing and shifting raw materials, workers, money, and jobs from around the globe. The overarching goals of high profit rates, securing cheap and unregulated labor, and market dominance guide such corporations. Labor interests, meanwhile, face the daunting task of ensuring workers' rights, health, and safety, providing decent standards of living, enacting environmental and consumer protections, and regulating corporate power.

Growth of Corporate Power. Significant developments in American society, as well as managerial behavior and structure, had by the early twentieth century fundamentally augmented corporate power. Tens of millions of immigrants from Europe, Asia, and Mexico populated America and its factories with abundant, inexpensive labor. Businesses created personnel departments to maximize "efficiency" and forestall unionization through scientific management, or Taylorism, subdividing skilled jobs into basic, repetitious, less-skilled tasks, closely supervising workers and production, and linking wages to production. Mass-production and assembly-line techniques honed in this period fueled a more consumer-oriented economy, with food, autos, and other goods produced less expensively and sold at affordable prices. Although during World War I, workers formed unions to achieve higher wages and shorter working hours, the absence of legislative protection enabled businesses' postwar open-shop drives that eliminated many unions. To try to minimize labor strife, businesses implemented so-called corporate welfare plans that offered pensions, health insurance, and profit sharing.

The Great Depression saw the failure of corporate welfare plans and a return to widespread and often violent labor battles.

Abetted by the National Labor Relations (Wagner) Act of 1935 that protected unions' rights to organize, bargain collectively, and strike, trade unions in the Congress of Industrial Organizations and the American Federation of Labor grew rapidly in numbers, power at work, and political influence within the Democratic Party. Dominating many major industries such as mining, automobiles, steel, oil, meatpacking, earthmoving, electrical manufacturing, and textile manufacturing, unions represented 35.7 percent of private-sector workers by 1953. They extracted from employers consistent wage increases, cost-of-living allowances to match inflation, benefits such as pensions and health-insurance coverage, and job and safety protections. For America's working class, this yielded an unprecedented standard of living, access to higher education, and purchasing power.

Growth of Globalization. Yet the post–World War II period also represented an intensified phase of globalization, spurred by that very strength of organized labor, the growth of transnational corporations (TNCs), and technological innovations that integrated business operations. Many U.S.-based corporations that dominated key economic sectors such as finance, banking, and manufacturing operated on a far wider, global scale than before. To avoid protective tariffs on U.S.-made goods and save on labor costs, firms established operations abroad—particularly in Europe, where the largest, most lucrative markets existed. Yet by the mid-1960s, as developing nations adopted export-related industrialization strategies, TNCs shifted capital and, later, jobs to Asia, Latin America, and parts of Africa.

Cold War economic policies to rebuild war-ravaged industrial economies established the

United States as the world's buyer of last resort for imported goods. However, particularly in Japan and Germany, state industrial planning, export strategies, and technological advances put these countries' automobile and steel industries at an advantage against American competitors. Global competition in these and other industries, coupled with antiunion policies and more favorable corporate tax rates under the administration of Ronald Reagan, intensified pressure upon workers and unions to accept concessions in wages, benefits, and work rules, resulting in earnings that were stagnant relative to those of wealthier Americans. Borrowing from Japanese firms, from the late 1970s onward American companies implemented lean production strategies, combining just-in-time supply chains, quality teams, and joint labor-management strategies to circumvent union power, accelerate production, and eliminate jobs through outsourcing and automation.

Trade agreements became more prevalent near the end of the twentieth century, creating business-friendly climates with fewer protections for workers, communities, or the environment. Often crafted in secret, trade agreements such as the North American Free Trade Agreement (NAFTA), in force since 1994, have hastened the exodus of capital and manufacturing jobs from the United States, especially to Mexico. Despite advocates' promises of job growth through the agreement, roughly 900,000 U.S. jobs were lost under NAFTA from 1993 to 2003. Employer antiunionism, outsourcing, global competition, and automation have devastated American industrial unions. Private-sector union density plummeted to 7.4 percent in 2006, resulting in fewer than fifty strikes of more than a thousand workers each year since 1987.

Some unions have tried to foster international ties and develop strategies with foreign unions. The United Auto Workers formed World Company Councils in 1966 with unions around the world to research and attempt to bargain collectively with TNCs. Later in the century, unions such as the United Steelworkers of America and the Service Employees International Union formed cross-border alliances and solidarity networks with Mexican unions, especially in the maquiladoras near the border between the United States and Mexico. Some corporate campaigns, such as that by the United Steelworkers against the aluminum manufacturer Ravenswood in 1990, illustrated that unions can successfully pressure companies through innovative international campaigns. These efforts, however, proved largely unsuccessful in opposing the diffusion of capital, production, and employment. Several factors have historically hampered effective solidarity among workers worldwide, such as insufficient research on transnational corporations, disparate legal and labor-relations systems, inadequate resources, and nationalistic resentment from workers who have lost well-paying, previously secure jobs. Into the twenty-first century, workers and unions have remained hamstrung in their efforts to confront globalization and corporate power.

[*See also* **American Federation of Labor and Congress of Industrial Organizations; Foreign Trade; Industrial Policy, Theory and Practice of; International Unionism and International Solidarity; Labor Movement, Decline of the; Rust Belt and Deindustrialization; Tariffs;** *and* **Trade Policy, Federal.**]

BIBLIOGRAPHY

Barnet, Richard J., and Ronald E. Müller. *Global Reach: The Power of the Multinational Corporation.* New York: Simon and Schuster, 1974.
Bronfenbrenner, Kate, ed. *Global Unions: Challenging Transnational Capital through Cross-Border Campaigns.* Ithaca, N.Y.: ILR Press, 2007.

Cowie, Jefferson. *Capital Moves: RCA's Seventy-Year Quest for Cheap Labor.* Ithaca, N.Y.: Cornell University Press, 1999.

Dicken, Peter. *Global Shift: Mapping the Changing Contours of the World Economy.* 6th ed. New York: Guilford Press, 2011.

Mittelman, James H. *The Globalization Syndrome: Transformation and Resistance.* Princeton, N.J.: Princeton University Press, 2000.

Moody, Kim. *Workers in a Lean World: Unions in the International Economy.* London: Verso, 1997.

Jason C. Kozlowski

GODCHARLES v. WIGEMAN

In *Godcharles v. Wigeman*, the Supreme Court of Pennsylvania nullified a statute prohibiting employers from paying wages in company-issued "scrip" that workers could use only in company-owned stores. Relying upon its general powers of equity rather than upon any specific provision of the state or federal constitutions, the court held that the statute interfered with the right of both employers and employees to make "their own contracts."

The Pennsylvania legislature enacted the statute in 1881 despite considerable opposition from mining and manufacturing companies, which complained that the law violated the state constitution's prohibition against "class legislation" insofar as it singled out certain kinds of employees for special protection and that it interfered with the principles of free-labor rights and subjected workers to paternalism. Employers also contended that their paying wages in scrip benefited working-class families because it prevented men from squandering wages on alcohol or gambling.

Advocates of the statute believed that it constituted a proper exercise of the state's "police power" because it promoted the welfare of the workers, who paid inflated prices at company stores and whose lack of cash restricted their ability to seek or accept alternative employment. Payment in scrip, they argued, reduced workers to "wage slaves." Some proponents of the legislation contended that it would reduce labor unrest and retard efforts to organize labor unions. Advocates of the anti-scrip legislation denied that workers freely entered into contracts for payment in scrip. They contended that workers lacked bargaining power to refuse such contractual terms: often they were in urgent need of jobs and lacked the ability to seek alternative employment. Thus proponents of the statute argued that the legislation promoted rather than constricted the liberty and autonomy of workers.

Although several other states had upheld similar legislation, the court in *Godcharles* denounced Pennsylvania's anti-scrip law as "an insulting attempt to place the laborer under a legislative tutelage, which is not only degrading to his manhood, but subversive of his rights as a citizen of the United States." According to the court, a worker "may sell his labor for what he thinks best, whether money or goods, just as his employer may sell his iron or coal, and any and every law that proposes to prevent him from doing so is an infringement of his constitutional privileges, and consequently vicious and void."

Although the court did not invoke specific constitutional authority, the decision presaged the later rise of the doctrine of substantive due process, under which state and federal courts sometimes invalidated economic regulatory legislation as a denial of "liberty" or a taking of "property" in violation of the due process clauses of the Fifth and Fourteenth Amendments of the U.S. Constitution. State and federal courts continued to invoke substantive due process to evaluate the constitutionality of economic legislation until 1937.

[*See also* **Employment-at-Will** *and* **Freedom of Contract.**]

BIBLIOGRAPHY

Forbath, William E. "The Ambiguities of Free Labor: Labor and the Law in the Gilded Age." *Wisconsin Law Review* 4 (1985): 767–817.

Stanley, Amy Dru. *From Bondage to Contract: Wage Labor, Marriage, and the Market in the Age of Slave Emancipation.* New York: Cambridge University Press, 1998.

William G. Ross

GOLDMAN, EMMA

(1869–1940), anarchist, social activist, free-speech advocate, and spokesperson for women's freedom. Born in a Jewish ghetto in present-day Lithuania, Emma Goldman moved with her family to Prussia and in 1881 to Saint Petersburg, Russia. Fleeing provincialism and anti-Semitism, she migrated to the United States in 1885 with a half sister and settled in Rochester, New York, where she worked in a clothing factory. Her marriage to Jacob Kersner in 1887 ended in divorce. The Haymarket affair (1886), coupled with harsh industrial conditions and violence against striking workers by government and business, propelled her toward anarchism and support of the movement for the eight-hour day. Moving to New York City in 1889, she encountered such émigré radicals as Johann Most and Alexander Berkman. Goldman's involvement with Berkman's attempted assassination of the industrialist Henry Clay Frick and her alleged link to the 1901 assassination of President William McKinley—by an anarchist who claimed to have been inspired by her speeches—resulted in her public demonization by the press.

Goldman reclaimed her voice in 1906 by founding a literary and political magazine, *Mother Earth*, and through her lively cross-country tours lecturing on anarchism, feminism, sexual radicalism, birth control, and new literary trends, especially modern drama. Liberals and radicals formed free-speech clubs to protest the suppression of Goldman's talks, and Roger Baldwin attributed his founding of the American Civil Liberties Union to Goldman. Goldman had been a mentor to Margaret Sanger and in 1916 was arrested for advocating birth control. Along with Berkman, she was tried, convicted, and imprisoned in 1917 for protesting wartime conscription, and in 1919, amid the post–World War I Red Scare, she and Berkman were deported with several hundred other alien radicals to Russia. In *My Disillusionment in Russia* (1923, full text 1925), she exposed the hypocrisy of Russia's Bolshevik regime and protested its suppression of dissent. Criticized and isolated by both the left and the right, Goldman found refuge in southern France, while frequently visiting England and Canada. Her compelling biography, *My Life* (1931), precipitated a final visit to the United States in 1934. Bereaved by the suicide of Berkman, her longtime comrade, in 1936, Goldman plunged into propaganda work for the Spanish anarchists during the Spanish civil war, basing herself in London and Barcelona (1936–1938). She died in Canada, championing the cause of Spanish refugees and maintaining her lifelong commitment to free expression.

[*See also* **Anarchism and Labor** *and* **Radicalism and Workers.**]

BIBLIOGRAPHY

Falk, Candace, et al., eds. *Emma Goldman: A Guide to Her Life and Documentary Sources.* Alexandria, Va.: Chadwyck–Healey, 1995.

Falk, Candace, et al., eds. *The Emma Goldman Papers: A Microfilm Edition.* 69 reels. 1991.

Wexler, Alice. *Emma Goldman in America.* Boston: Beacon Press, 1984.

Candace Falk

GOLDMAN SACHS

The investment banking company Goldman Sachs was founded by Marcus Goldman immediately after the Civil War. Twenty years later he opened a small finance house near Wall Street and began trading in commercial bills, which later became known as "commercial paper." Before World War I the firm entered into an agreement with Lehman Brothers that allowed the two firms to share underwritings for new stock issues. Over the next twenty years the two shared more than a hundred underwritings, many for retailers. In the 1920s, in the years prior to the stock market crash of 1929, the firm embarked upon marketing its own investment trusts. The trusts did not fare well in the aftermath of the crash and tarnished the firm's reputation.

Goldman's most notable success in the years following World War II was the initial public offering of Ford Motor Company. The deal secured the firm's position as one of Wall Street's leading equity houses. Commercial paper continued to be one of its specialties. In the 1970s and 1980s the firm began to expand internationally but still operated as a partnership. Many of its senior members also served Democratic and Republican administrations in Washington, D.C., in diverse capacities, ranging from economic advisers to treasury secretary. Persistent pressures to expand and several poor financial years led the firm's partners to consider a public offering. In 1999 the firm finally marketed stock shares, making Goldman the last major Wall Street investment bank to go public.

In the 2000s Goldman emerged as the preeminent investment bank on Wall Street in underwriting, mergers and acquisitions, and trading. Its activities in the market for mortgage-related securities, one of the precipitants for the financial crisis of 2008–2009, brought a fine of $550 million by the Securities and Exchange Commission (SEC) in 2010—the largest fine in SEC history.

[*See also* **Financial and Banking Promotion and Regulation; Financial Crises, 1980s– 2010; Lehman Brothers;** *and* **Shadow Banking System.**]

BIBLIOGRAPHY

Cohan, William D. *House of Cards: A Tale of Hubris and Wretched Excess on Wall Street.* New York: Doubleday, 2009.
Ellis, Charles D. *The Partnership: The Making of Goldman Sachs.* New York: Penguin, 2008.

Charles Geisst

GOLD RUSHES

The nineteenth century was the great era of North American gold rushes. Beginning in North Carolina in 1799, gold rushes were initially a southern phenomenon, centered along the eastern piedmont of the Appalachians. A rush in the lands of the Cherokee nation contributed to the forced removal of Cherokees in the 1830s.

The western rushes began in 1848—just as the United States acquired California from Mexico—with a gold discovery in the foothills of the Sierra Nevada, and they shared characteristics with those in the South. They dispossessed native peoples, focused on placers (surface gold deposits), and attracted disproportionately male and stunningly diverse populations. California's was the most male of the rushes, though native women were present in the diggings, and Miwok women, for example, took up mining in order to supplement older subsistence strategies. The rush drew gold seekers from around the world, especially from Mexico, Chile, the United States,

China, and several European nations. California also set a pattern for future rushes in that Anglo-Americans, sometimes aided by the state, fought to control the placers. As Anglo women began to arrive, they, too, inaugurated a pattern common in later rushes by campaigning against such public amusements as dance halls and brothels, which often employed Mexican, Chilean, French, and Chinese women.

These patterns were repeated during gold rushes in Nevada and Colorado in the late 1850s; in Montana, Idaho, and Arizona in the 1860s; and in Dakota Territory in the 1870s. By the 1880s the emphasis in western mining was shifting to the underground, hard-rock mining of gold, silver, and copper, which required heavy capital investment, industrial processes, and large numbers of wageworkers. Not until the 1890s, however, did hard-rock miners outnumber placer miners in the West. And the 1890s saw new placer rushes following a series of discoveries in Alaska Territory and Canada's Yukon Territory.

The western rushes coincided with industrialization and class formation in the United States and with an era of North Atlantic global economic dominance. For many in industrializing nations and in countries ruled by colonial powers, the rushes seemed to provide opportunities outside the economic and geopolitical bounds that circumscribed their lives. That so many people from so many different places descended on the placers and contended with one another over access to gold, and that Anglo-American men often succeeded in limiting access for so many others, demonstrates that gold rushes were no sideshow: they were part of the main event of nineteenth-century history. Even Anglo men, however, try as they might to impose themselves as the rightful claimants of North American gold, could not extract from the hills the promise they sought: at most, a fortune; at least, an escape from a lifetime of wage labor. For most participants, gold rushes never lived up to the hopes they inspired.

[*See also* **Mining Industry.**]

BIBLIOGRAPHY

Blodgett, Peter J. *Land of Golden Dreams: California in the Gold Rush Decade, 1848–1858.* San Marino, Calif.: Huntington Library, 1999.

Paul, Rodman Wilson, and Elliott West. *Mining Frontiers of the Far West, 1848–1880.* Rev. ed. Albuquerque: University of New Mexico Press, 2001.

Williams, David. *The Georgia Gold Rush: Twenty-Niners, Cherokees, and Gold Fever.* Columbia: University of South Carolina Press, 1992.

Susan Lee Johnson

GOLD STANDARD

The gold standard was characterized by the free flow of gold between individuals and countries, the maintenance of fixed values of national currencies in terms of gold and therefore each other, and the absence of an international coordinating organization. Together these arrangements implied that there was an asymmetry between countries experiencing balance-of-payments deficits and surpluses. There was a penalty for running out of reserves—and thus being unable to maintain the fixed value of the currency—but no penalty (aside from foregone interest) for accumulating gold. The adjustment mechanism for deficit countries was deflation rather than devaluation, that is, a change in domestic prices instead of a change in the exchange rate.

This last point—the choice of deflation over devaluation—can be seen clearly in contemporary views at the nadir of the Great Depression. The British economist Lionel Robbins argued that a greater flexibility of wage rates would reduce unemployment and applied this view to the Depression: "If it had not been for the prevalence of the view that wage rates must at all costs be maintained in order to maintain the purchasing power of the consumer, the violence of the present depression and the magnitude of the unemployment which has accompanied it would have been considerably less" (Lionel Robbins, *The Great Depression* [London: Macmillan, 1934], p. 186). Robbins had the wit to acknowledge that this was a hard saying and to insist that all prices, not just wages, needed to be flexible. But these caveats did not moderate his prescription; they simply exposed the depth of his conviction that internal deflation was the only way to deal with a fall in demand. (He later regarded this view as a fundamental misconception.)

The gold standard spread in the late nineteenth century as more and more industrializing countries fixed the value of their currencies in gold. In order to maintain the policy of buying and selling gold at a fixed price, governments had to conduct their affairs within certain bounds. This discipline in turn promoted economic stability in the countries that adhered to the system, and the ability of governments to maintain this discipline was taken as a marker of the extent of the civilized world. The struggling countries of Latin America and eastern Europe kept trying and failing to adopt the gold standard, making adherence a hallmark of a developed economy. Asian and African societies out of the orbit of European and American industry made no effort to join this club.

World War I was a great shock to this international order, and financial leaders considered the reconstruction of the gold standard to be a key component of postwar stability. But in fact the interwar gold exchange standard, as it is sometimes called to distinguish it from the earlier gold standard, produced great instability until its demise in the 1930s. Most European countries had inflated during the war, and they had to deflate in order to resume buying gold at prewar prices. Prices were no longer fully flexible, as Robbins noted, and the attempt to reduce them led to the Fascist takeoff in Italy, a general strike in Britain, and political paralysis in France.

[*See also* **Inflation and Deflation; Trade Policy, Federal;** *and* **Wages, Real and Nominal.**]

BIBLIOGRAPHY

Eichengreen, Barry. *Golden Fetters: The Gold Standard and the Great Depression, 1919–1939.* New York: Oxford University Press, 1992.
Eichengreen, Barry, and Peter Temin. "The Gold Standard and the Great Depression." *Contemporary European History* 9, no. 2 (2000): 183–207.

Peter Temin

GOMPERS, SAMUEL

(1850–1924), labor leader and president of the American Federation of Labor (AFL). Born into a poor family of Dutch Jewish cigar makers in London's East End, Gompers immigrated to New York City in 1863. The oldest of six children, he learned his father's trade and became a union member in his early teens. Working in the cigar shops of New York City, Gompers absorbed the culture of reform and self-improvement in the German-dominated cigar trade. By the early 1880s he had reshaped the conservative Cigar Makers' International Union into a dynamic workers' organization modeled after both British craft unions and German political labor organizations. As the representative of the cigar makers, he was a founding member of the Federation of Organized Trades and Labor

Unions in 1881, and it was largely his energetic pursuit of a unified labor movement that led to the founding of the American Federation of Labor in 1886, with Gompers the first president. By then he had become well known not only as a union leader and organizer of the 1886 eight-hour-day movement, but also as a proponent of "pure and simple" trade unionism, which concentrated on higher wages and better working conditions and denigrated ethnic or party politics.

Gompers's hostility to the Marxist-led Socialist Labor Party cost him the AFL presidency for one year in 1895. Once reinstated in the office, which he held until his death, he presided over a growing AFL, continuing his aggressive defense of workers' rights to organize, strike, and boycott. Working skillfully within the federal structure of the organization, Gompers at first tried to broaden the membership of its affiliated unions beyond skilled white workers but later largely abandoned this quest in favor of a dominant craft unionism. In 1901 he joined the National Civic Federation, a group of employers, union representatives, and public figures who sought to mediate industrial disputes. Gompers refrained from supporting political parties and party programs but did selectively endorse candidates and legislative initiatives in the name of the labor movement. A supporter of President Woodrow Wilson, Gompers served on the Advisory Committee of the Council of National Defense during World War I, traveled to the European battlefronts, and participated in the Versailles peace negotiations. After the war, however, he could do little to prevent the erosion of organized labor. At his death, Gompers had come to symbolize the tremendous potential power of American labor, which seemed forever thwarted by its own internal divisions, the hostility of employers, and a mostly unsympathetic state.

[*See also* **American Federation of Labor; Corporatism; Eight-Hour Day; Federation of Organized Trades and Labor Unions; Labor Leaders; Labor Movements;** *and* **Labor's Role in Politics.**]

BIBLIOGRAPHY

Kaufman, Stuart B. *Samuel Gompers and the Origins of the American Federation of Labor, 1848–1896.* Westport, Conn.: Greenwood, 1973.

Laslett, John H. M. "Samuel Gompers." In *Labor Leaders in America*, edited by Melvyn Dubofsky and Warren Van Tine, pp. 62–88. Urbana: University of Illinois Press, 1987.

Dorothee Schneider

GOVERNMENT REGULATION AND PROMOTION

See **Economic Regulation.**

GRAIN PROCESSING

An ancient industry, grain processing in America can be traced from the simple mortar and pestle used by Native Americans and colonists alike to complex modern processing centers and multinational enterprises. The industry's rise paralleled the broader economic, agricultural, and technological developments that made the United States the world's leading food exporter.

Gristmills, such as the one at Jamestown in 1621, ground corn and wheat for meal and flour, helping to feed the colonists and making the millers key local figures. The earliest mills, and the vast majority up to about 1800, operated as custom mills that ground the farmer's grain for a toll in flour paid to the miller. The essential role of milling in local agricultural markets is evident in that public authorities offered development incentives and regulated the mills closely. Distant and foreign markets soon became important as well. As more farmers grew surplus wheat, many millers were acting more like merchants, buying and processing wheat for sale as flour. By 1792, these mills near the major seaports exported 824,000 barrels of flour to the West Indies and southern Europe. From 1815 to 1827, Baltimore was the leading U.S. flour market, with Rochester and Buffalo growing in stature after completion of the Erie Canal.

As late as the 1780s, the milling process—sieving, cleaning, winnowing, and grinding the grain by millstones—involved strenuous human labor. The industry's subsequent history is linked to improvements in power sources and technological innovations, from human and animal labor (horses, mules, oxen) to wind, water, steam, and electrical power. In 1782, Oliver Evans, a Delaware-born inventor, developed an automated process that used a water-wheel to turn the millstone, reducing by half the labor force needed in larger mills, eliminating much of the hard physical labor, and increasing the amount of flour extracted from wheat.

Grain processing mirrored the increasing corporatizing of the economy. The rise of Saint Louis, Missouri, as an important milling center by 1870, for example, reflected not only its proximity to the prime areas for growing winter wheat, but also its access to river navigation and its ability to negotiate favorable railroad rates.

In 1871, Edmond LaCroix built a new type of grinding machine that overcame Minnesota's hardy spring wheat, which was difficult to grind and produced a poorer quality of flour. This "new process" gave spring-wheat flour, and Minneapolis, market dominance. Compact and efficient metal roller grinders that increased production and lowered costs, introduced from Hungary in 1873, marked another key technological advance. After 1900, bleaching processes improved quality and ended the adulteration of flour with alum or chalk.

Minneapolis's preeminence also reflected new modes of business operation, mass production, aggressive marketing strategies, trade associations, strong local financial institutions, railroad expansion into new wheat areas—and the business acumen of Charles A. Pillsbury (1842–1899), whose Pillsbury Company led all others by 1880. By the 1890s, facing competition from the expanding Kansas City Turkey Red wheat market, as well as a shift in consumption patterns from home-baked to store-bought bread, Minneapolis milling companies sought new locations, such as Buffalo, closer to urban markets in the East. Mergers in the 1920s consolidated milling and baking companies into such conglomerates as the General Mills Corporation. From the local mills of early America, the U.S. grain-processing industry by the late twentieth century had evolved into vast corporate enterprises with a global reach.

[*See also* **Agriculture; Farm Machinery; Food and Diet; Technology;** *and* **Transportation Revolution.**]

BIBLIOGRAPHY

Kuhlmann, Charles Bryon. *The Development of the Flour-Milling Industry in the United States, with Special Reference to the Industry in Minneapolis.* Boston: Houghton Mifflin, 1929.

Sharrer, George Terry. "Flour Milling and the Growth of Baltimore, 1783–1830." PhD diss., University of Maryland, 1975.

Steen, Herman. *Flour Milling in America.* Minneapolis, Minn.: T. S. Denison, 1963.

Ginette Aley

GRAINS

Grains, or cereals, are cultivated grasses with edible seeds. Examples of grains include wheat, rice, corn (maize), oats, barley, sorghum, rye, and millet. As the world's most significant staple crops, just three grains—rice, wheat, and corn—are the most widely grown and eaten crops in the world, and they are sources of carbohydrate, protein, and fat, the three essential human macronutrients. The commonly held view regarding the origin of these crops is that each was domesticated separately between eight thousand and twelve thousand years ago in the Fertile Crescent (wheat), the Yangtze River valley (rice), and central Mexico (corn). By the twenty-first century, varieties of the three major grains were grown on all six inhabited continents. Prices of all three crops spiked during 2007–2008 and again during 2011 (except for rice), causing economic and political turmoil worldwide.

Rice is the primary staple crop for more than half the world's population, especially in Asia and Africa. Because rice requires special conditions to grow, including high temperatures and large amounts of water, its production in the United States is limited to four regions: Arkansas, the Mississippi delta, the Gulf coast, and the Sacramento valley. Rice farming in the United States has high costs and is dependent on irrigation. Rice farmers receive a variety of government payments, including price and income supports and export assistance.

Wheat ranks third among U.S. field crops—behind corn and soybeans—for planted acreage and gross farm receipts. The prairie states constitute the wheat belt, including the primary wheat-producing states of Montana, North Dakota, South Dakota, Kansas, Oklahoma, and Texas. About half of the wheat crop is exported, and the other half is used for food. Like rice farmers, wheat farmers also enjoy support from a variety of government farm programs. The wheat area harvested has declined since the later twentieth century, in part because of the increased preference for low-carbohydrate diets, but also because of a shift in acreage to other crops, including corn.

The United States is the world's largest corn producer, accounting for about 40 percent of world production. The corn belt stretches across the heartland region, including the top producers Illinois and Iowa, as well as Indiana and portions of neighboring states. Corn is a key ingredient in the food supply in the United States, entering (somewhat) directly by means of processed foods and indirectly by means of livestock feed. The majority of the corn crop has historically been used to feed livestock, including cattle, hogs, chickens, and even fish. In the twenty-first century, government policy has increased the proportion of the corn crop diverted to ethanol production. These measures, on top of corn programs already in place, have drawn much criticism. In 2011, about 38 percent of corn production was used for feed and alcohol each, compared to 54 percent for feed and 14 percent for alcohol in 2005–2006. Exports accounted for about 14 percent of use, and food, seed, and industrial uses accounted for the remaining 10 percent. Corn is a key ingredient in processed foods and industrial products in the form of starch, sweetener—including high-fructose corn syrup—oil, and alcohol.

[*See also* **Agriculture; Grain Processing; Renewable Energy and Climate Change; Subsidies, Agricultural;** *and* **Trade Policy, Federal.**]

BIBLIOGRAPHY

Corn Briefing Room. United States Department of Agriculture Economic Research Service. http://www.ers.usda.gov/Briefing/Corn.
Rice Briefing Room. United States Department of Agriculture Economic Research Service. http://www.ers.usda.gov/Briefing/Rice.
Wheat Briefing Room. United States Department of Agriculture Economic Research Service. http://www.ers.usda.gov/Briefing/Wheat.

Elizabeth A. Ramey

GRANGER MOVEMENT AND LAWS

A major goal of the Granger movement of the early 1870s was to bring about public regulation of railroads. Western farmers, who had applauded the rapid expansion of the rail system, now believed that rates were unreasonably high and fluctuated suspiciously, especially at non-competitive points. These activist farmers also claimed that rail carriers discriminated between places and persons, formed illegal business combinations, and gave free passes to politicians and others who could serve the railroads' interests.

As the political power of organized farmers grew in the 1870s, agrarian representatives in the state legislatures, aided by spokesmen for certain business interests, pushed through legislation in Illinois, Iowa, Wisconsin, and Minnesota that collectively were known as the Granger laws. These laws varied from state to state, but generally they sought to outlaw the widespread abuses by railroads, establish maximum rates in some instances, and create regulatory agencies to administer and enforce the laws. Beyond their immediate importance, the Granger laws mark an early attempt by a previously rural nation to adjust to the conditions and challenges of an increasingly urban and industrial society.

The railroad corporations either ignored the Granger laws or fought them in the courts. In due course, a case arising in Illinois found its way to the U.S. Supreme Court. In *Munn v. Illinois* (1877), the Court upheld the constitutionality of the Granger laws. Rejecting the contention of a warehouse operator that the regulatory actions of the Illinois Railroad and Warehouse Commission—the agency established to administer the Granger law in that state—deprived the company of property and thus violated the Fourteenth Amendment of the U.S. Constitution, the Court ruled instead that enterprises such as railroads and warehouses that substan-

tially affected the public interest had to submit to some degree of public control. This, in turn, opened the way for state regulation of a variety of businesses.

In 1886 the issue of state regulation of railroads again came before the courts. The Wabash railroad, an interstate carrier in the Middle West, appealed a decision of the Illinois courts to the Supreme Court. In *Wabash, St. Louis & Pacific Railway v. Illinois* (1886), the Court found for the railroad, ruling that a state could not regulate interstate commerce, since the Constitution granted that power solely to the federal government. This decision led Congress to enact the Interstate Commerce Act in 1887. That measure assigned the task of regulating railroads to the newly created Interstate Commerce Commission, the nation's first independent regulatory agency.

[*See also* **Agricultural Workers; Federal Regulatory Agencies; Railroads;** *and* **State Regulatory Laws.**]

BIBLIOGRAPHY

Buck, Solon J. *The Granger Movement: A Study of Agricultural Organization and Its Political, Economic, and Social Manifestations, 1870–1880.* Cambridge, Mass.: Harvard University Press, 1913.
Miller, George H. *Railroads and the Granger Laws.* Madison: University of Wisconsin Press, 1971.
                                                    Roy V. Scott

GREAT DEPRESSION (1929–1939)

The world depression of the 1930s was the greatest peacetime economic catastrophe in history. There had been hard times before, but never without war, natural disaster, or pestilence. The massive and long-lasting unemployment and hardship of the 1930s was a pathology of industrial society, caused by a malfunctioning of the economic system.

Industrial production fell by almost half in the United States and Germany. Because services did not contract as much, national income did not fall as far as industrial production did, but it also fell; real per capita gross national product (GNP) in the United States fell by one third, for example. National experiences in the Great Depression varied greatly, but few escaped the economic hardship of the 1930s. Prices fell at the same time as production, and unemployment grew dramatically in almost all countries. Only in the United Kingdom were unemployment rates even approximately as high in the 1920s as in the 1930s, owing to depressed conditions in Britain during the 1920s.

All these countries had negative demand shocks at the same time because they adopted deflationary policies according to the dictates of the gold standard. The gold standard was characterized by the free flow of gold between individuals and countries, the maintenance of fixed values of national currencies in terms of gold and therefore in terms of each other, and the absence of an international coordinating or lending organization like the International Monetary Fund. Under these conditions, the adjustment mechanism for a deficit country was deflation rather than devaluation—that is, a change in domestic prices instead of a change in the exchange rate. Lowering prices and possibly production, too, would reduce imports and increase exports, improving the balance of trade and attracting gold or foreign exchange. (This is the price-specie-flow mechanism first outlined by David Hume in 1752.)

Even for the United States, with its vast economic resources and gold reserves, going off gold was a necessary prerequisite to economic expansion. Great Britain avoided the worst of the Great Depression by going off gold in 1931. Spain avoided the Depression by never being on the gold standard; Japan avoided it by a massive devaluation in 1932. At the other extreme,

the members of the gold bloc, led by France, endured contractions that lasted into 1935 and 1936. The single best predictor of how severe the Depression was in different countries was how long the country stayed on gold.

The Federal Reserve raised the discount rate from 1.5 percent to 3.5 percent in October 1931 to preserve the gold value of the dollar—even though American gold reserves were high. This action cured the disease but killed the patient; the American economy continued to contract until President Franklin D. Roosevelt took office in March 1933. He introduced a new policy regime of abandoning the gold standard, tolerating budget deficits, and expanding government spending and regulation. The American economy enjoyed four years of rapid growth as a result. Belief that the Depression had ended led to contractionary policies in 1937 that produced a recession and left unemployment high at the start of World War II.

[*See also* **Gold Standard; Inflation and Deflation; Keynesian Economics;** *and* **Monetary Policy, Federal.**]

BIBLIOGRAPHY

Feinstein, Charles H., Peter Temin, and Gianni Toniolo, *The World Economy between the World Wars.* New York: Oxford University Press, 2008).

Keynes, John Maynard. *The Economic Consequences of the Peace.* London: Macmillan and Co., 1919.

Kindleberger, Charles P. *The World in Depression.* Berkeley: University of California Press, 1986.

Peter Temin

GREAT RECESSION OF 2008 AND AFTER

The National Bureau of Economic Research, the official arbiter of business cycles in the

United States, defines a "recession" as a period in which "a significant decline in economic activity spreads across the economy... [that] can last from a few months to more than a year" (www.nber.org/cycles/general_statement. html). The bureau determines whether a recession has occurred by inspecting a variety of indicators, including gross domestic product (GDP), employment, income, sales, and industrial production. The American economy has undergone business cycles, with alternating expansions and recessions, since the capitalist economic system emerged in the United States in the early nineteenth century. For more than a century economists have debated the causes of business-cycle recessions under capitalism but they have never reached any agreement, although the existence of this phenomenon is not in doubt.

The recession that began in the United States in 2008, following the business-cycle peak of December 2007 and continuing until June 2009, is often referred to as the "Great Recession." The term suggests that this recession is reminiscent of the Great Depression of the 1930s, during which output fell by about 30 percent in the United States in a recession lasting from 1929 to 1933. Since World War II, recessions had been far milder—as measured by the duration and extent of economic decline—than the Great Depression. The Great Recession of 2008 broke the postwar pattern, thus earning its popular name.

Characteristics and Severity.

The Great Recession was, by every measure, more severe than earlier post–World War II recessions. There have been eleven recessions in the United States since 1948, a business-cycle peak year that marks the end of the postwar economic readjustment (and the beginning of official quarterly data on the GDP). The Great Recession was more severe and lasted longer than did the previous ten post-1948 recessions. In 2008–2009, GDP fell by 4.0 percent, compared to the average 1.7 percent decline for the preceding ten recessions and 3.2 percent for the next-largest decline, that of 1973–1975. The unemployment rate rose by 5.8 percentage points in the Great Recession, compared to an average rise of 3.2 percentage points in the previous ten recessions and a previous maximum rise of 4.5 percentage points in 1948–1949. The Great Recession lasted 18 months, compared to an average of 10.4 months for the previous ten and a previous maximum of 16 months in 1973–1975 and 1981–1982. The unemployment rate hit a high of 10.2 percent in October 2009, and the rate of utilization of industrial capacity hit a low of 68.2 percent in June 2009.

Although the Great Recession exceeded by every measure the previous ten recessions, it must be admitted that the amount by which it topped the largest previous decline by the various measures is not enormous. Several factors, however, explain the near-universal view that the 2008–2009 recession earned its nickname of "Great Recession." First, the recession listed in second place varies depending on the measure of decline, which means that no earlier recession stands out as does this one. Second, in February 2009 the federal government enacted a $787 billion antirecession stimulus program of spending increases and tax cuts. A stimulus program on such a scale was never undertaken in past postwar recessions. The stimulus, which was spread over two years, equaled 2.8 percent of GDP per year at the time it was enacted, which is significant compared to the actual 4.0 percent decline in GDP during the recession. Most economists believe that, without the large stimulus measure, the recession would have been significantly more severe. Still another reason for considering this recession as unique in the postwar period is the rapid global spread of the recession to almost every country in the world.

The previous two economic downturns, in 1990–1991 and 2000–2001, had been mild and short, and each was preceded by a long expansion, of 92 months in 1982–1990 and of 120 months in 1991–2000. This led many economists to believe that severe recessions had been confined to the past. In 2007, Christina D. Romer, a professor at the University of California, Berkeley, and the chair of the President's Council of Economic Advisers in 2009–2010, referred in a paper presentation to "the virtual disappearance of the business cycle in the last 25 years," attributing its elimination to wise government policies followed since the early 1980s—policies that, she asserted, meant that "the future of stabilization looks bright" ("Macroeconomic Policy in the 1960s," pp. 2 and 20, available at http://elsa.berkeley.edu/~cromer/MacroPolicy.pdf). Against this widespread confident view of recent history, the sharp recession of 2008–2009 came as a big shock.

The historically sluggish recovery from the 2008–2009 recession in the United States reinforced the view that it deserves its appellation. During the eighteen months following the low point of GDP in the second quarter of 2009, the annual GDP growth rate was only 2.9 percent. In the previous deeper recessions in the postwar period, GDP recovered rapidly in the succeeding eighteen months, growing at 5 percent per year or higher, as would be expected with an initially high level of unemployment and a low rate of utilization of productive capacity. In May 2011 the unemployment rate remained at the historically very high rate of 9.1 percent.

Explanations. One explanation for the severity of the Great Recession is that it occurred alongside a financial crisis. In the fall of 2008 a major financial panic occurred, centered in the United States but spreading to much of the global financial system. A widely cited study by Carmen M. Reinhart and Kenneth S. Rogoff found that recessions associated with a financial crisis tend to be relatively severe. A financial crisis can produce a severe recession by restricting credit to the business sector or by creating uncertainty or outright fear about future economic prospects, either of which can cause a large drop in business investment—which did indeed occur in the Great Recession.

A second explanation points to the bursting of the huge housing bubble that developed in the United States during the early 2000s. The ratio of the house price index to the homeowner's equivalent rent (the latter a measure of the economic value of owning a home) rose from 108.9 in 1995 to 157.1 in 2005, and as home prices kept rising month after month, a large amount of consumer spending came to be financed by homeowners' taking out second mortgages against their rising home value. Consumer spending rose from 91.4 percent of after-tax income in 1995 to 95.1 percent in 2005, its highest level since 1938. Once the housing bubble began to deflate in 2006–2007, households could no longer finance their spending through borrowing, and from 2007 to 2009, consumer spending fell from 94.1 percent to 90.6 percent of after-tax income. Since consumer spending was about 70 percent of GDP in this period, its decline—which started in the first quarter of 2008 and continued through the second quarter of 2009—might account for the severity of the recession, particularly given that a decline in consumer spending leads to rapidly falling business investment.

Either of the above explanations for the severity of the Great Recession of 2008 could also account for the sluggishness of the recovery following the recession. Another view is that the combined financial and real-sector crisis starting in 2008 marked the beginning of a deeper economic problem than just a particularly severe recession. According to this view, in 2008 the American economy entered a period of structural economic crisis resulting from the end of the potential for the neoliberal form of capitalism to promote vigorous economic expansion. This explanation holds that the economy will remain relatively stagnant unless or until a new, effective form of capitalism is constructed, as happened following previous structural crises such as those of the 1930s and 1970s.

[*See also* **Business Cycles; Depressions, Economic; Financial Crises, 1980s–2010;** *and* **Neoliberalism.**]

BIBLIOGRAPHY

Kotz, David M. "The Financial and Economic Crisis of 2008: A Systemic Crisis of Neoliberal Capitalism." *Review of Radical Political Economics* 41 (2009): 305–317.

Krugman, Paul. "How Did Economists Get It So Wrong?" *New York Times Magazine*, 2 September 2009.

Reinhart, Carmen M., and Kenneth S. Rogoff. "The Aftermath of Financial Crises." National Bureau of Economic Research, Working Paper 14656, January 2009. Available at http://www.nber.org/papers/w14656.

Stiglitz, Joseph E. *Freefall: America, Free Markets, and the Sinking of the World Economy*. New York and London: W. W. Norton and Company, 2010.

David M. Kotz

GREAT SOCIETY

In 1964, President Lyndon B. Johnson challenged the citizens of the United States to build a "great society." In his State of the Union address that year, he declared an "unconditional war on poverty" to assist one fifth of the nation's families "escape from squalor and misery and unemployment rolls where other citizens help to carry them." Subsequent legislative victories included both procedural and material programs. The Civil Rights Act of 1964 and the Voting Rights Act of 1965 were strictly procedural, providing no material resources. Medicare and Medicaid, passed in 1965, were substantive programs that gave millions of Americans over the age of sixty-five, as well as the poor, access to hospital and medical care. The Economic Opportunity Act of 1964 created programs that initially appeared substantive but by and large failed to meet their goals.

Programs and Effects. The Economic Opportunity Act created the Office of Economic Opportunity, which administered services to provide the poor with marketable skills, as well as having a community-action component to develop support for political and social change. The Community Action Program handled organizing activities, while also managing numerous direct services such as the Job Corps, Volunteers in Service to America (VISTA), Upward Bound, Foster Grandparents, Head Start, Community Health Centers, the Migrants Program, and Health Service Centers. After the Office of Economic Opportunity was terminated in 1981, its programs were reassigned to other federal departments, including the Department of Labor, the Office of Education, the Welfare Administration, the Farmers Home Administration of the U.S. Department of Agriculture, and the U.S. Small Business Administration.

Although the antipoverty reforms of the Great Society derived from the nation's most concerted effort to address poverty, the reforms failed to achieve substantial reductions in poverty. The decline in the nation's poverty rate from 22.4 percent in 1959 to 11.1 percent in 1973 was probably the result of the great increase in the nation's gross domestic product, which nearly doubled between 1960 and 1970. The War on Poverty failed to develop an aggressive but necessarily expensive strategy to eliminate the structural causes of poverty; instead it created programs based on the assumption that the character and skills of the poor prevented their economic rise. That is, the War on Poverty was more about "moral reform" than economic and social change.

Although the Great Society antipoverty programs likely had little effect on poverty, Charles Murray, a prominent conservative, argued that those programs—in particular, cash welfare, then called Aid to Families with Dependent Children—actually created poverty and dependency by providing incentives to avoid work. Murray drew a vigorous response from critics such as James T. Patterson and Robert H. Haveman, who disputed his evidence, logic, and goals. For conservatives such as Murray, poverty grew because the poor depended on relief, and thus the elimination of easily accessible welfare was the solution; for liberals, poverty itself was the problem, and the solution would consist of government programs to eliminate the structural barriers that caused impoverishment.

Interpretations for the Programs' Failure.

One interpretation for the failure, despite the nation's great wealth, of both the War on Poverty and subsequent antipoverty legislation in the United States lies in the nation's bifurcated welfare provisions. The distinction between social insurance (old-age benefits and health care for the elderly) and public assistance programs (welfare) expressed the belief held by many citizens that the attainment of a decent standard of living was a personal, as opposed to a social, responsibility. As William M. Epstein argued, providing the poor with only minimal material support paid tribute to "heroic individualism," the belief that people need to overcome their own problems. Linda Gordon has suggested that gender best explains the distinction between social insurance and welfare: social insurance originated in the concept that the primary male wage-earner earned his benefits, while the nonworking single mothers who

received discretionary welfare required "maternal" supervision. In this sense the War on Poverty flowed from the nation's conservative perspective.

A second interpretation, put forth by Frances Fox Piven and Richard A. Cloward in 1971, maintained that elites are to blame for inadequate social-welfare programs whose goal is the regulation of the poor rather than their material betterment. Piven and Cloward argued that social-welfare spending rose and fell in response to threats by the poor to political and social stability. However, David Dodenhoff later exposed faults in Piven and Cloward's argument: civil unrest, Dodenhoff concluded, was only one of many factors that affected the making of social policy, and welfare spending had failed to behave as Piven and Cloward had predicted, rising in response to insurrection and falling during calmer times. For example, violent protests peaked in 1968 then declined in 1970 and after, whereas spending on nonentitlement antipoverty programs grew exponentially until 1978.

Perhaps the idea of building a "great society" was problematic from its inception. Johnson's vision of a great society involved the provision of many different services to pull citizens out of poverty. Yet the programs proved superficial and failed to ameliorate poverty or even to achieve more limited goals. The Great Society's failures both expressed and reinforced the popularity of attributing economic failure to the character deficiencies of the poor. Considering the nation's great wealth, the antipoverty programs of the Great Society could have been more generous and could have attacked the structural causes of poverty with more generous income support, improved job training, and, as a last recourse, the creation of publicly funded jobs for the unemployed. Instead, the Great Society chose the far less costly option of reforming, as Linda Gordon put it, the "internal, moral, or psychological" characteristics of the poor. Its implementation suggests that policy minimalism is a broadly shared American value.

[*See also* **Poverty.**]

BIBLIOGRAPHY

Dodenhoff, David. "Is Welfare Really about Social Control?" *Social Service Review* 72, no. 3 (1998): 310–336.

Epstein, William M. *Democracy without Decency: Good Citizenship and the War on Poverty.* University Park: Pennsylvania State University Press, 2010.

Gordon, Linda. "Social Insurance and Public Assistance: The Influence of Gender in Welfare Thought in the United States, 1890–1935." *American Historical Review* 97, no. 1 (1992): 19–54.

Haveman, Robert H. *A Decade of Federal Antipoverty Programs: Achievements, Failures, and Lessons.* New York: Academic Press, 1977.

Murray, Charles. *Losing Ground: American Social Policy, 1950–1980.* New York: Basic Books, 1984.

Patterson, James T. *America's Struggle against Poverty in the Twentieth Century.* Cambridge, Mass.: Harvard University Press, 2000.

Piven, Francis Fox, and Richard A. Cloward. *Regulating the Poor: The Functions of Public Welfare.* New York: Pantheon Books, 1971.

Salina Offergeld

GREAT UPHEAVAL OF 1886

The "Great Upheaval" is a term used by historians to describe a massive series of strikes that rolled across industrial America in the spring of 1886, culminating on 1 May in a coordinated general strike for the eight-hour day. Since the 1830s, American workers had been attempting to shorten the workday—first to ten, then to eight hours—through state and federal legislation, but in 1884 the national Federation of Organized Trades and Labor Unions, a forerunner of the American Federation of Labor, met in Chicago and adopted a resolution calling for the adoption of the "eight-hour system" on 1 May 1886. If employers refused to accept, then workers would refuse to work. Although the Knights of Labor opposed the 1 May strike, thousands of its members joined trade unionists and unorganized workers in a mammoth general strike that affected at least 200,000, and perhaps as many as 350,000, workers in many cities and towns. Not only did many Knights join the eight-hour movement, but their organization swelled in membership in 1886: this was another facet of the Great Upheaval, one that led newspapers to warn about organized labor's dictatorial powers and caused employers to engage in an aggressive antiunion campaign.

The strike was the most significant demonstration of solidarity and workers' power that had been seen in any industrial nation up to that time. In Chicago, where a potent anarchist group mobilized thousands of German workers, at least forty thousand strikers took to the streets. Some employers conceded to the eight-hour demand, and others offered a nine-hour day as a compromise. The strike movement collapsed in the aftermath of the Haymarket bombing in Chicago on 4 May, a tragic event that deflated the eight-hour movement and created the nation's first Red Scare when the police and the press created public hysteria over the threat of anarchy in America.

The Great Upheaval of May 1886 led to a permanent reduction in hours for most skilled workers, as well as for many unskilled workers. The upheaval was significant because it was the first giant step that workers took toward the eventual establishment of the eight-hour workday as a national norm. The upheaval was also significant because the great strike became associated with the creation of 1 May, May Day, as the international workers' holiday.

[*See also* **Anarchism and Labor; Eight-Hour Day; Factory and Hours Laws; Haymarket Affair; Knights of Labor; Labor Movements; Radicalism and Workers;** *and* **Strikes.**]

BIBLIOGRAPHY

Green, James. *Death in the Haymarket: A Story of Chicago, the First Labor Movement, and the Bombing That Divided Gilded Age America.* New York: Pantheon, 2006.

James Green

GREEN, WILLIAM

(1873–1952), labor leader. William Green served as the president of the American Federation of Labor (AFL) for twenty-eight tumultuous years from 1924 to his death in 1952. Born in Coshocton, Ohio, he was the son of Welsh immigrants. He aspired to the Baptist ministry, but as a young man he followed his father into the coal mines and ultimately union activism. He joined the Progressive Miners Union, a forerunner of the United Mine Workers of America (UMWA). Then after the turn of the century he rose through the ranks of leadership in the UMWA's Ohio district. He ran unsuccessfully for national offices in the UMWA in 1909 and 1910 before finally winning election as secretary-treasurer in 1913. John L. Lewis subsequently outmaneuvered Green to win the presidency of the UMWA, succeeding John White. But after the death of Samuel Gompers in December 1924, Green won the presidency of the American Federation of Labor after Lewis and Matthew Woll were deadlocked in a bitter contest for the post.

Green led the AFL though its most difficult years, as first open-shop campaigns and later the Great Depression undermined union organization. Green's relationship with Lewis soured when Lewis laid plans to push the AFL into chartering industrial unions; Lewis was responding to both the crisis of the 1930s and the opportunities created by the National Labor Relations (Wagner) Act of 1935. Green blocked his old rival from achieving his plans, which led Lewis to leave the AFL and form the Congress of Industrial Organizations (CIO). A staunch anti-Communist, Green disdained the openness to Communist activists of the Lewis-led CIO. He led the AFL in a bitter struggle with the rival federation, a struggle that moderated with the onset of World War II. In his later years, Green gradually ceded power to the AFL's secretary-treasurer George Meany, who ultimately succeeded him as president and who reunited the rival federations in 1955.

[*See also* **American Federation of Labor; Labor Leaders; Lewis, John L.;** *and* **United Mine Workers.**]

BIBLIOGRAPHY

Phelan, Craig. *William Green: Biography of a Labor Leader.* Albany: State University of New York Press, 1989.

Joseph A. McCartin

GREENBACKISM

Greenbacks were a paper currency first issued by the federal government to help finance the Civil War. They remained in circulation after the war, but in 1873 Congress enacted a specie resumption law that demonetized silver and called for the nation by 1878 to redeem greenbacks in gold. The decision to return to a gold-backed currency coincided with a protracted period of price deflation that lasted from the depression of the 1870s through the depression of the 1890s. Congress's decision to restrict the money supply adversely affected debtors and those who needed loans to start new enterprises. Farmers were, perhaps, the greatest victims of deflation and tight money. They had to borrow to develop their farms, to plant their crops, and to harvest their crops. Tight money and deflation made it harder for them to pay off their debts as crop prices steadily fell. Many farmers were unable to pay off mortgages on their land or the loans undertaken to plant and harvest crops. Deflation and periodic depressions partly explained the rise of farm tenancy. Farmers and those who were unable to obtain loans blamed bankers and monopolists for their plight.

Farmers remained the largest single voting bloc in the late nineteenth century, and the so-called money question and antimonopolism generated heated political conflict. Indebted farmers sought "loose money" as the solution to their plight. For a short time between 1874 and 1880, farmers allied with workers in the Greenback Labor Party, whose chief demand was for a government-issued paper currency. For most workers, however, inflation posed a greater threat than soft money did. When prices rose, wages typically lagged. Thus labor groups drifted away from Greenbackers. Agriculturists continued their interest in greenbacks until the 1890s when a demand for the free and unlimited coinage of silver became their preferred means to obtain cheaper credit and higher prices.

[*See also* **Free Silver and Bimetallism; Inflation and Deflation;** *and* **Monetary Policy, Federal.**]

BIBLIOGRAPHY

Nugent, Walter T. K. *Money and American Society, 1865–1880.* New York: Free Press, 1968.
Unger, Irwin. *The Greenback Era: A Social and Political History of American Finance, 1865–1879.* Princeton, N.J.: Princeton University Press, 1964.

Weinstein, Allen. *Prelude to Populism: Origins of the Silver Issue, 1867–1878.* New Haven, Conn.: Yale University Press, 1970.

Melvyn Dubofsky

GREENBACK LABOR PARTY

The Greenback Labor Party represented a brief but potent Gilded Age expression of working-class antimonopoly sentiment. In the aftermath of the depression of 1873, the formation of the agrarian-based Greenback Party in 1874–1875, the railroad strikes of 1877, and the electoral success of local workingmen's parties in industrial states in 1877, 150 delegates assembled in Toledo, Ohio, in February 1878 to organize the National Party, also known as the Greenback Labor Party. Its labor-oriented platform called for shorter working hours, a ban on contract prison labor, immigration restriction, and government bureaus of labor statistics. The party attracted a million votes in the 1878 midterm election and elected fifteen congressmen across the East, South, and Middle West. In some localities it took on a distinctly radical character; in the coal districts of Alabama, black Greenback-Laborites exercised leadership among both black and white miners.

The party's 1880 platform included farmer-labor planks that foreshadowed the Populist Party's 1892 Omaha Platform, calling for government control of transportation and communications, a graduated federal income tax, opposition to a standing army, and the lifting of all restrictions on suffrage. Despite the party's impressive start, however, its 1880 presidential candidate, the Civil War general James Weaver of Iowa, attracted only 3 percent of the vote, mostly in agricultural districts. For most workers, inflation posed a greater threat than soft money did. When prices rose, wages typically lagged. Thus labor had no great love for

Greenbacks. The end of the depression in 1878 and the government's resumption of specie payments (the gold standard) in 1879 had sapped the party's fortunes. Nevertheless, hopes for an independent labor party revived with the rise to prominence of the Knights of Labor after another wave of national strikes in the 1880s.

[*See also* **Agriculture; Gold Standard; Greenbackism; Immigration-Restriction Laws; Inflation and Deflation; Knights of Labor; Labor's Role in Politics;** *and* **Monetary Policy, Federal.**]

BIBLIOGRAPHY

Ritter, Gretchen. *Goldbugs and Greenbacks: The Antimonopoly Tradition and the Politics of Finance in America.* Cambridge, U.K.: Cambridge University Press, 1997.
Sanders, Elizabeth. *Roots of Reform: Farmers, Workers, and the American State, 1877–1917.* Chicago: University of Chicago Press, 1999.

Shelton Stromquist

GROUP OF EIGHT (TWENTY)

Beginning in November 1975 at Rambouillet, France, the annual Group of Seven (G7)—later Group of Eight (G8)—held informal conferences that brought together senior officials from the United States, Germany, France, Japan, Italy, Great Britain, and Canada to coordinate policies. The gatherings began after the collapse of the post–World War II Bretton Woods monetary system and the delinking of the U.S. dollar from gold; U.S. policy makers sought new ways to coordinate international economic policies with their counterparts elsewhere. Participants also discussed arms control and such global issues as the environment, illicit drugs, money laundering, and the Inter-

net. Each nation's delegation typically included the head of state or government, the foreign minister, the finance minister, and his or her leading economic advisers. Among the most important of the early conferences was that of September 1985, which set up the managed floating of exchange rates. In addition to the regular summits, special meetings in 1985 and 1996 inaugurated Russian participation, which became formal in 1999, thus creating the Group of Eight.

Although the G7/G8 system evolved significantly over its first twenty-five years, it lagged behind global economic and political changes. For example, the conferences neglected globalization's effects on national culture and law. Such important nations as China, India, Mexico, and Brazil remained outside, and international organizations such as the International Monetary Fund, the World Trade Organization, the United Nations, and the World Bank were not regular participants. Nevertheless, the G7/G8 system did illustrate the ability of the United States and other nations to create informal political structures to coordinate international policies.

As economic globalization spread and other nations developed prosperous and productive economies, the G8 appeared less representative. By the midpoint of the first decade of the twenty-first century, the so-called BRIC nations—Brazil, Russia, India, and China—appeared to be the world's most dynamic economies, and many other Asian and Latin American nations sought a place in the world economy. To deal with an altered economic reality, the G8 nations assisted in the creation of the Group of Twenty, which included all the G8 members plus a representative for each of the European Community, Brazil, China, India, South Africa, and seven other nations. Like the G8, the G20 convened for informal conferences attended by heads of state and other conferences attended by finance ministers and central-bank governors. At their start in 1999 such conferences were held biannually, but the global economic crisis that erupted in 2008 ensured a more important role for the G20 and led to the holding of annual conferences. Although both the G8 and the G20 sought to coordinate a response to the post-2007 economic crisis together with the International Monetary Fund and the World Bank, the members failed to devise effective policies. In the twenty-first century the conferences of the G8 and the G20 also became the sites of mass, disruptive demonstrations by critics and victims of globalization in its neoliberal capitalist form.

[*See also* **Bretton Woods Conference; Globalization;** *and* **Trade Policy, Federal.**]

BIBLIOGRAPHY

Bergsten, C. Fred, and C. Randall Henning. *Global Economic Leadership and the Group of Seven.* Washington, D.C.: Institute for International Economics, 1996.

Hajnal, Peter I. *The G7/G8 System: Evolution, Role, and Documentation.* Aldershot, U.K.: Ashgate, 1999.

Hajnal, Peter I. *The G8 System and the G20: Evolution, Role, and Documentation.* Aldershot, U.K.: Ashgate, 2007.

Susan Ariel Aaronson

H

HAMILTON, ALEXANDER, AND ECONOMIC DEVELOPMENT

Alexander Hamilton (1755–1804) served as the first secretary of the treasury of the United States, from 1789 to 1795. Although he played only a small role in the 1787 constitutional convention, Hamilton was involved in the campaign to ratify the Constitution, most famously as one of the authors of the *Federalist* essays. Involved in New York politics, Hamilton was encouraged to take a seat in Congress as a representative or a senator, but he preferred a role in the new executive branch. He had a close relationship with George Washington, whose aide he had been for much of the War of Independence, and Hamilton desired to use the Department of the Treasury to strengthen the national government.

Dealing with Debt. When Hamilton took office, the finances of the country were in great chaos. Without an ability to borrow and refinance its debt, the United States remained solvent only at the pleasure of European states and lenders. Congress asked the new secretary of the treasury to outline a plan for the public credit of the country—to determine the proper measures that the government should take to ameliorate the problems of America's labyrinth of debt. Hamilton responded with what became a famous series of reports, released gradually to Congress and intended to put into place his vision for the future of the American nation. His plans never were simply fiscal policy but reflected his vision of how the citizenry could be taught to love their new government, how the influence of the states could be weakened, and how the Constitution could be interpreted broadly to become the fundamental law of a strong, wealthy, and powerful national-state. At root his policies were based upon an enthusiasm to establish a system of finance and administration that emulated the success and stability of Great Britain in the eighteenth century.

His first plan, the *Report on the Public Credit*, was the cornerstone of his new financial system. He advocated for the creation of a permanent national debt from a consolidation of state debts, foreign loans, and outstanding Continental obligations; the debt would be administered and funded through tax revenues. He intended the debt to be a permanent engine of government and to provide a steady flow of investment capital to the holders of the debt. Opponents of the plan tended to represent states—such as Virginia and North Carolina—that had little debt left and would therefore be paying off other states' obligations to little noticeable benefit to their own economies. The holders of the debt tended to be clustered in mercantile states such as New York and Pennsylvania and, because of the port of Charleston, South Carolina. Other states, such as Massachusetts, still struggled with the financial burden of their own obligations from the war and so supported the program of debt assumption. Some opponents also believed that the outstanding obligations of the government should not be funded at par, because many original loan office certificates intended to compensate soldiers were held by speculators who had bought them for well below face value.

One of the more remarkable, and popular, features of the changes wrought by the assumption of state debts and the institution of Hamilton's plan was a rapid decrease in direct taxes paid by farmers throughout the country. States attempting to service their wartime obligations created a series of direct taxes that burdened farmers and the owners of property. High taxes had helped excite defiance in numerous states, including open insurrection in Massachusetts. But

after the assumption of state debts, state burdens decreased substantially, and local taxation became much less onerous. With the return of public credit to the United States, foreign capital and investment returned. Even states that attacked the assumption of state debts as unconstitutional subsequently lowered their internal taxes. The resulting prosperity throughout many regions of the country encouraged greater speculation, a rapid expansion of credit, and the increased incorporation of banking, turnpike, and manufacturing companies. Though at various times in the 1790s attempts at increased federal taxation were employed—in excise taxes, as well as in a direct tax—for the most part, for the first few generations of its existence the federal government generated the bulk of its revenue through customs duties, and direct taxation on farmers, laborers, and consumers remained low. Population growth was the real strength of the American financial model.

National Bank and Manufactures.

With his second plan Hamilton called for the organization of a national bank, a private corporation that would be partially owned by the United States. Hamilton modeled his bank on the Bank of England and intended the American version to provide an institution that would serve as an administrative aid and banking resource for the government. In theory, it would function as a central bank. Although his proposed bank passed Congress by the narrowest of margins, it led to the creation of an opposition party against his system, which many people believed too closely followed an English model that would lead to the corruption of representative government. Thomas Jefferson and James Madison's failure to convince George Washington to veto the bank bill was what spurred them to organize an opposition newspaper.

Hamilton's final plan, the *Report on Manufactures*, presented an ambitious design for the encouragement of industrial manufacturing, commercial agriculture, internal trade, and internal improvement throughout the United States through the implementation of a series of protective tariffs and government bounties and the creation of a state board for the promotion of arts, agriculture, manufactures, and commerce. Rejecting Adam Smith's belief that the United States would never be suitable for manufacturing until its vast lands had been filled with laborers and the natural advantages of agriculture had therefore diminished, Hamilton argued that the United States would never be strong and safe without the productive capacity and wealth necessary to defend its interests in the world and that it would never be united in support of a national policy without an integrated national economy. With the exception of a few subsidies for the fisheries, Hamilton failed to achieve much from his vision.

Neither Hamilton's view of the Constitution nor his view of the proper direction of American economic policy achieved ascendancy until long after he died. The Bank of the United States was not renewed in 1811, was reconstituted after the War of 1812, and—amid great political controversy—was not renewed in 1832. State competitors often competed directly with the national bank, so it had never really served the role of a central bank. Hamilton's plan for a permanent national debt, which would transfer money from taxes into investment capital, was rejected for a policy of paying off the debt as rapidly as possible. And his plan for the government promotion of manufactures never became policy in his lifetime. America developed an industrial economy, but it did so with a much less robust presence of the federal government than Hamilton had envisioned. In many compelling ways, however, the state capitalist model of the United States in the twentieth century reproduced a part of Hamilton's vision for the relationship between national economic growth and the national government.

[*See also* **Bank of the United States, First and Second; Business Growth and Decline; Economic Development; Economic Theories and Thought; Gallatin, Albert, and Economic Development; Industrial Policy, Theory and Practice of; Mercantilism;** *Report on Manufactures;* **Tariffs;** *and* **Taxation.**]

BIBLIOGRAPHY

Bradburn, Douglas. *The Citizenship Revolution: Politics and the Creation of the American Union, 1774–1804.* Charlottesville: University of Virginia Press, 2009.

Chernow, Ron. *Alexander Hamilton.* New York: Penguin, 2004.

Ferguson, E. James. *The Power of the Purse: A History of American Public Finance, 1776–1790.* Chapel Hill: University of North Carolina Press for the Institute of Early American History and Culture at Williamsburg, Va., 1961.

McDonald, Forrest. *Alexander Hamilton: A Biography.* New York: W. W. Norton and Company, 1979.

Miller, John C. *Alexander Hamilton: Portrait in Paradox.* New York: Harper & Row, 1959.

Stourzh, Gerald. *Alexander Hamilton and the Idea of Republican Government.* Stanford, Calif.: Stanford University Press, 1970.

Swanson, Donald F., and Andrew P. Trout. "Alexander Hamilton, 'the Celebrated Mr. Neckar,' and Public Credit." *William and Mary Quarterly* 3d ser., 47, no. 3 (July 1990): 422–430.

Doug Bradburn

HANNA, MARK

(1837–1904), central figure in the politics of the 1890s and early 1900s. Based in Cleveland, Ohio, Marcus Alonzo Hanna became rich as a shipper and broker serving the coal and iron industries, which developed as a result of Cleveland's strategic location. One of the few industrialists fascinated less by profits than by the machinations of politics, Hanna served as a key adviser for the

Ohio Republican governor William McKinley, who established himself as the outstanding Republican spokesman for high tariffs, high wages, and renewed prosperity in the face of the depression of the 1890s. Hanna helped to secure McKinley's presidential nomination in 1896 and to defeat William Jennings Bryan's free-silver movement. Hanna nationalized the GOP campaign, raising $3.5 million, mostly from corporations fearful of Bryan's policies. Hanna's campaign reached millions of voters with a firm, insistent message of sound money, prosperity, and cultural pluralism. The Democrats caricatured him as an archvillain who put corporate interests ahead of the national interest. Serving as a U.S. senator (1900–1904), he emerged as a Republican leader in his own right. Hanna also worked with the National Civic Federation to conciliate labor strife. He sought to bring unions into the Republican fold and to avert major strikes that would be economically damaging, as well as politically and socially divisive. Hanna's death at the peak of his power in 1904 ended a struggle with Theodore Roosevelt for control of the Republican Party.

[*See also* Free Silver and Bimetallism.]

BIBLIOGRAPHY

Croly, Herbert. *Marcus Alonzo Hanna: His Life and Work*. New York: Macmillan, 1912.
Marcus, Robert D. *Grand Old Party: Political Structure in the Gilded Age*. New York: Oxford University Press, 1971.

Richard Jensen

HARRIMAN, E. H.

(1848–1909), railroad financier. Born in Hempstead, New York, Edward Henry Harriman began his business career as a Wall Street stockbroker but soon became a railroad financier by acquiring the all-important Illinois Central Railroad. His biggest coup was gaining control of the Southern Pacific and Union Pacific railroads. Joining with J. P. Morgan, James J. Hill, and others, he created the Northern Securities Company, a holding company that integrated the ownership of the Union Pacific, Northern Pacific, Great Northern, and Burlington railroads. In the Northern Securities Case of 1904, the Supreme Court found this company an illegal combination in restraint of interstate commerce and ordered it dissolved. Harriman also earned notoriety following accusations of stock manipulation. Having purchased the Chicago and Alton Railroad in 1899, he issued stock that increased his personal profit with no benefit to the line. A classic example of the practice of "watering" stock, this action was investigated by the Interstate Commerce Commission (ICC) in 1906–1907. Some have seen the investigation as politically motivated, arising from personal animosity between Harriman and President Theodore Roosevelt, but the ICC did find Harriman's corporate empire and business practices to be "contrary to public policy."

Harriman also engaged in philanthropy, funding the Tompkins Square Boys Club in New York City and a scientific expedition to Alaska—Harriman Fjord in Prince William Sound is named for him—and donating forest land to New York State that became Harriman State Park. It is, however, as the quintessential Gilded Age robber baron that he is remembered by history.

[*See also* Antitrust Legislation; Brown Brothers Harriman & Company; Hill, James J.; Morgan, J. P.; Northern Securities Case; *and* Railroads.]

BIBLIOGRAPHY

Mercer, Lloyd J. *E. H. Harriman: Master Railroader*. Boston: Twayne, 1985.

Ripley, William Z. *Railroads: Finance and Organization.* New York: Longmans, Green, 1915.

Colin J. Davis

HAYMARKET AFFAIR

On 1 May 1886, workers throughout the United States struck to win the eight-hour day. On 4 May in Chicago, the strike's center, workers gathered in Haymarket Square to protest a police attack on strikers the previous day that had left at least two dead. The meeting was called by anarchists affiliated with the revolutionary International Working People's Association. The rally was ending when a police squad under Inspector John Bonfield commanded the crowd to disperse. Suddenly someone threw a dynamite bomb into the ranks of the police. One officer died instantly and seven later succumbed, most as a result of bullets fired by panicked policemen.

Many Americans, including preeminent ministers, journalists, and conservative politicians, saw the bombing as part of a conspiracy designed by anarchist-inspired immigrants to overthrow the republic. Responding to public hysteria, Chicago officials banned public meetings and processions. Eight anarchist leaders stood trial for conspiracy to commit murder. Although the identity of the bomb thrower remained unknown, a court convicted the anarchists of murder. On 11 November 1887, August Spies, Albert Parsons, George Engel, and Adolph Fischer were hanged; Louis Lingg had earlier committed suicide. The Illinois governor John P. Altgeld commuted the sentences of the other three in 1893. The novelist William Dean Howells was one of the few prominent figures to protest the executions.

The Haymarket tragedy was part of a reaction by business leaders and public officials to labor's so-called Great Upheaval of the mid-1880s, including the rapid growth of the Knights of Labor. Despite repression, skilled workers made significant progress in organizing unions and winning trade agreements after Haymarket. The American Federation of Labor sponsored another nationwide eight-hour strike on 1 May 1890, and in Paris the Socialist Second International adopted 1 May as an international labor day. Revolutionary anarchism, meanwhile, evolved into the syndicalism that flourished at the margins of the labor movement in the early twentieth century.

[*See also* **Altgeld, John P.; Anarchism and Labor; Eight-Hour Day; Great Upheaval of 1886; Knights of Labor; Labor Spies and Pinkertons; Parsons, Albert; Radicalism and Workers;** *and* **Strikes.**]

BIBLIOGRAPHY

Avrich, Paul. *The Haymarket Tragedy.* Princeton, N.J.: Princeton University Press, 1984.
Schneirov, Richard. *Labor and Urban Politics: Class Conflict and the Origins of Modern Liberalism in Chicago, 1864–97.* Urbana: University of Illinois Press, 1998.

Richard Schneirov

HAYWOOD, WILLIAM D.

(1869–1928), labor leader. Born Salt Lake City, Utah Territory, and dead at age fifty-nine in Moscow, Soviet Union, William Dudley "Big Bill" Haywood was internationally known as a dynamic official of the Western Federation of Miners (WFM) and was the most famous leader of the Industrial Workers of the World (IWW). For a time he also served on the national executive committee of the Socialist Party of America, a position from which he was ousted because he refused to renounce violence as a means to defend workers. As a young hard-rock miner in Idaho, Haywood first became affiliated with the WFM in 1896. Thereafter he devoted himself to improving working conditions for all industrial workers. He served as the WFM's secretary-treasurer from 1901 to 1906, leading it through the violent Colorado labor wars of 1903–1904 and editing its *Miners' Magazine*. Accused as an accomplice in the assassination of the former Idaho governor Frank Steunenberg— who had used state power to break a strike led by the WFM in 1899—Haywood was tried and acquitted in 1907. The trial featured a memorable closing argument by the legendary defense attorney Clarence Darrow, who pled for Haywood's life as a workingman's hero. Haywood believed that all workers of an entire industry should organize together, that division in the ranks of labor led to failure, and that "one big union" for the working class would end capitalism. As the IWW's general secretary, he played key roles organizing eastern textile and western agricultural workers. Convicted along with a hundred other IWW leaders of violating the Espionage Act of 1917 during World War I, he was sentenced to a long term in the federal penitentiary in Leavenworth, Kansas. In 1921, while his attorneys appealed the conviction and Haywood remained at liberty, he jumped bail and fled to Soviet Russia. There, like the American Socialist John Reed, Haywood at first was lionized as a proletarian hero. Never truly at home in an alien culture, Haywood lost stature in the Soviet Union and was forgotten in his homeland. Too many years of alcoholism and neglect for his health resulted in an untimely death. His ashes were split: half were interred under Moscow's Kremlin wall (near Reed's) and half in Chicago's Waldheim Cemetery, the burial site for the Haymarket riot martyrs that had become a mecca for many American radicals.

[*See also* Colorado Labor Wars (1903–1905); Industrial Workers of the World; Mining Industry; Radicalism and Workers; *and* Western Federation of Miners.]

BIBLIOGRAPHY

Carlson, Peter. *Roughneck: The Life and Times of Big Bill Haywood*. New York: W. W. Norton and Company, 1983.

Haywood, William D. *Bill Haywood's Book: The Autobiography of William D. Haywood*. New York: International Publishers, 1929.

Lukas, J. Anthony. *Big Trouble: A Murder in a Small Western Town Sets Off a Struggle for the Soul of America*. New York: Simon and Schuster, 1997.

Katherine Scott Sturdevant

HEPBURN ACT

The 1906 Hepburn Act, along with the Elkins Act of 1903 and the Mann–Elkins Act of 1910, strengthened federal authority to regulate the nation's railroads under the 1887 Interstate Commerce Act. Named for the Republican congressman William Hepburn of Iowa, the law empowered the Interstate Commerce Commission (ICC) to set maximum railroad rates. Democratic congressmen and Progressive Republicans like Theodore Roosevelt played key roles in crafting the Hepburn Act. Its passage signaled Congress's commitment to an administrative form of railroad regulation that aimed to limit economic discrimination against rural and low-volume shippers without undermining corporate power.

The Hepburn Act originated in the Interstate Commerce Commission's failure to set "reasonable and just" railroad rates or to prohibit rate discrimination. Congress established the ICC to monitor railroad practices and enforce the law. The ICC's powers were substantially weakened, however, by the Supreme Court: in 1897 the Court denied the ICC the authority to set reasonable rates. Without additional legislation, the ICC had little influence over rates.

Congressional Democrats, federal administrators, and President Roosevelt called for rate regulation. By 1900 such financiers as J. P. Morgan had assisted railroad owners and managers in creating several giant, nationwide railroad combinations. With reduced competition, rates rose—and so, too, did public support for regulation. The Democratic Party made railroad regulation a key part of its platforms in 1896, 1900, and 1904. Members of the ICC urged Congress to grant the commission power to set rates "in view of the rapid disappearance of railway competition and the maintenance of rates established by combination" (quoted in Sanders, 1999, p. 198). President Roosevelt made railroad regulation part of his 1904 campaign pledge to give Americans a "square deal."

Roosevelt sought to mollify anti-railroad congressional Democrats without alienating conservative Republicans. He supported Hepburn's bill, which granted the ICC power to establish maximum rates and oversee railroad bookkeeping practices and expanded its jurisdiction to private cars. The bill passed the House. In the Senate, Democrats campaigned to grant even greater powers to the ICC, but conservative Republicans, supported by Roosevelt, defeated those efforts. The Senate nonetheless strengthened the Hepburn Act by expanding ICC jurisdiction over oil pipelines and ancillary railroad facilities, by eliminating a requirement that railroad rates be "fairly remunerative," and by augmenting the ICC's power to solicit information from the railroads.

The Hepburn Act passed with the support of Democrats and moderate Republicans. Some conservative Republicans acquiesced to the bill, reasoning that the Supreme Court might strip the ICC of its rate-setting authority. But that did not happen. In 1910 the Court ruled that it could not "usurp merely administrative functions [of government] by setting aside a lawful administrative order" (quoted in Ripley, 1912, p. 541). Thus Congress had ensured that an expert commission, not a democratic assembly, would regulate the nation's railroads.

[*See also* **Railroads.**]

BIBLIOGRAPHY

Martin, Albro. *Enterprise Denied: Origins of the Decline of American Railroads, 1897–1917.* New York: Columbia University Press, 1971.

Ripley, William Z. *Railroads: Rates and Regulation.* New York: Longmans, Green, 1912.

Sanders, Elizabeth. *Roots of Reform: Farmers, Workers, and the American State, 1877–1917.* Chicago: University of Chicago Press, 1999.

Joshua Salzmann

HERRIN MASSACRE (1922)

The Southern Illinois Coal Company operated a strip mine near Herrin, Illinois, that was closed as a result of a general strike called by the United Mine Workers of America (UMWA) on 1 April 1922. The UMWA allowed the mine owner William Lester to continue mine operations during the strike, however, so long as he used union workers and no coal would be loaded or shipped.

As the strike persisted, Lester decided to begin shipping coal and dismissed UMWA workers on 13 June 1922. Replacement workers were recruited from Chicago, and the mine resumed full operation. Lester further antagonized the local population when he deployed armed guards and closed public highways that passed through the mine's property. A witness later claimed that Lester bragged, "I've broken strikes before and I'll break this one."

On 19 June 1922 the UMWA president John L. Lewis telegraphed the union local, suggesting that the striking miners were "justified in treating this crowd as an outlaw organization and in viewing its members in the same light as they do any other common strikebreaker." The Illinois adjutant general's office offered troops repeatedly to Williamson County officials, but the Williamson County sheriff, Melvin Thaxton, a UMWA member and candidate for local office, declined each time. State law, however, did not require the consent of local authorities before state officials intervened.

On 21 June, Lester and the UMWA agreed to a truce that would close the mine and allow the strikebreakers to leave. Unfortunately, government and union officials failed to relay the terms of the truce to the workers at the mine. That afternoon an armed mob of striking miners held the mine under siege. An airplane circled the mine property, dropping dynamite on the heavy equipment, and two UMWA members suffered gunshot wounds. The mine manager, guards, and scab workers all clung to cover under the frequent exchange of gunfire.

The following day, 22 June, with ammunition and provisions dwindling, guards and replacement workers surrendered on the condition that they be safely escorted out of the county. A mob of union members and their local sympathizers, however, shot and battered the departing guards and workers as they trekked toward Herrin. In all, twenty-three people were killed, and more were wounded.

The incident inspired national condemnation from the news media, Congress, and even President Warren G. Harding, who referred to the massacre as "butchery . . . wrought in madness." However, a Williamson County coroner's jury found "that the deaths of the decedents were due to the acts direct and indirect of the officials of the Southern Illinois Coal Company," recommending that an investigation of its officers be undertaken. Newspapers and the National Coal Association demanded that the perpetrators be punished, and organized labor

replied that the violence in Herrin had created "a Roman holiday for union haters." At its 1922 state convention the UMWA levied a 1 percent assessment on members to provide for the legal defense of union miners.

In the course of two trials, six men were prosecuted, although all were acquitted by Williamson County juries. After the acquittals, State's Attorney Delos Duty announced that there would be no more trials, adding, "it's a hopeless proposition."

[*See also* **Mining Industry; Strikes;** *and* **United Mine Workers.**]

BIBLIOGRAPHY

Angle, Paul M. *Bloody Williamson: A Chapter in American Lawlessness.* New York: Alfred A. Knopf, 1952.
Everett, Woodrow W., Jr. *A Caterwaul from Egypt: Anatomy of the 1922 Herrin Massacre.* New York: Vantage Press, 1970.

Greg Boozell

HIGHWAYS AND INTERSTATES

The American highway system is a twentieth-century creation. Before 1916, roads remained a local responsibility. Bicyclists and railroad executives lobbied for better roads in the 1890s, and by 1910 the automotive industry echoed those demands. Reflecting many elements of the Progressive Era reform movement—especially central administration by technical experts—the Federal-Aid Road Act of 1916 created the first national road system, funded by $50 million over five years for construction of rural roads for mail deliveries. Consistent with federalism, the bill mandated cooperation between state highway departments and the Bureau of Public Roads (BPR, later the Federal Highway

Administration). Thus states designed, built, and maintained the roads, while federal engineers inspected and approved plans, specifications, and construction. Initially costs were shared equally, although because of their superior technical expertise, BPR engineers always exercised greater influence than this fifty–fifty balance would suggest.

In 1921, Congress shifted federal emphasis from rural mail delivery to a national network of primary and secondary roads between cities. As first mapped in 1923, this federal-aid highway system totaled 169,000 miles, or 7 percent of the nation's highway mileage. Under a numbering scheme adopted in 1925, odd-numbered roads ran north to south, with the numbering starting at the Atlantic coast, while even-numbered roads ran east to west, with the numbering starting at the Canadian border. Federal appropriations averaged about $75 million annually during the 1920s, increased during the Depression, but really jumped after 1945. Gasoline taxes, first introduced in Oregon in 1919, rapidly became the primary source of state funds. System additions included extensions into urban areas (1938), additional secondary roads (1940), and the interstate system, authorized in 1944. The states and the BPR first designated interstate routes in 1947, although special funding began only in 1954. Massive appropriations for the 42,500 miles of the National System of Interstate and Defense Highways came in 1956, with the federal government assuming 90 percent of the original estimated cost of $25 billion. When the last section opened in 1991, the total cost had climbed to $114 billion (adjusted for inflation), and the system had expanded to 46,720 miles.

This highway network altered many facets of American life, facilitating the development of a mobile culture and the rise of standardized national fast-food and motel franchises. Long-distance family summer vacations spent in campgrounds or motels became common, and long-haul trucking replaced railroads as primary freight haulers. The decline of central-city business districts, the "malling" of America, rapid postwar suburbanization, and new patterns of land use all resulted from easy access to express highways after 1950.

At the same time, the scale of interstate highway construction inside cities engendered significant resistance from neighborhood groups and environmentalists. After 1960 a so-called freeway revolt made headlines, and its partisans won numerous court cases, halting interstate construction projects in such cities as San Francisco, Boston, New Orleans, and Philadelphia. Although several disputed freeways were eventually completed in the late 1980s, the momentum for road construction was lost. Even so, by 2006 the federal-aid system encompassed 985,128 miles out of the national total of more than 4 million miles of roads and highways. Annual federal appropriations for this system alone increased from $5 million in 1916 to $585 million in 1954 to more than $38 billion in 2006, when total highway spending surpassed $161 billion.

[*See also* **Automotive Industry; International Brotherhood of Teamsters; Shopping Centers and Malls; Transportation Revolution;** *and* **Turnpikes and Early Roads.**]

BIBLIOGRAPHY

Rose, Mark H. *Interstate: Express Highway Politics, 1939–1989.* Rev. ed. Knoxville: University of Tennessee Press, 1990.

Seely, Bruce E. *Building the American Highway System: Engineers as Policy Makers.* Philadelphia: Temple University Press, 1987.

U.S. Department of Transportation, Federal Highway Administration. *America's Highways, 1776–1976: A History of the Federal-Aid Program.* Washington, D.C.: Government Printing Office, 1977.

Bruce E. Seely

HILL, JAMES J.

(1838–1916), businessman and railroad promoter. As the creator of the railroad network that dominated the late nineteenth-century economic expansion in the Northwest, from the prairies of western Minnesota to Seattle, Washington, James J. Hill embodied the canny foresight, organizational brilliance, and ruthless drive that characterized his generation of capitalist leaders.

Born in Ontario, Canada, Hill moved to Minneapolis, Minnesota, two decades later and worked as a shipping clerk for a steamship line. In 1867, using his extensive knowledge of freight rates, he formed his own shipping company and contracted to furnish the Saint Paul and Pacific Railroad with fuel. When the railroad fell into receivership in the 1870s, Hill and Canadian financier friends bought it and extended it first to Manitoba, then westward through the Dakotas and Montana to Great Falls (1887), and finally over the Cascades to the Pacific in 1893. In 1890 he consolidated separate lines into the Great Northern Railroad.

Mastering every detail of the railroad's organization and operation while retaining a vision of long-term goals, Hill drove his workers hard, fired anyone he disliked, and fought off hostile acquisition attempts. His personal fortune swelled as he invested in iron and copper mines, and he built an imposing mansion in Saint Paul. His 1901 attempt to control his empire through the Northern Securities holding company was struck down by the Supreme Court in 1904, but until his death Hill retained a reputation as the empire builder of the Northwest.

[*See also* **Northern Securities Case** *and* **Railroads.**]

BIBLIOGRAPHY

Malone, Michael P. *James J. Hill: Empire Builder of the Northwest.* Norman: University of Oklahoma Press, 1996.

Martin, Albro. *James J. Hill and the Opening of the Northwest.* New York: Oxford University Press, 1976.

Clifford E. Clark Jr.

HILL, JOE

(1879–1915), labor activist and songwriter. When Joe Hill arrived in the United States in 1902 under the name Joel Emmanuel Hägglund, little distinguished him from the other immigrants who arrived every year. By 1915, when a Utah firing squad executed Hill, he had become the poet laureate of the labor movement, his songs sung by workers across the globe.

Born in Sweden in 1879, Hill had devout parents who taught him to sing hymns and play several instruments. When his mother died, Joe and a brother left for New York, and Joe worked his way westward, laboring on farms, docks, and mines. Around 1910 in California he joined the radical labor union the Industrial Workers of the World (IWW) and began to pen songs that championed the working class, publishing the first of many, "The Preacher and the Slave," in the union's *Little Red Songbook* in 1911. Hill appropriated its melody from a well-known popular song, "In the Sweet Bye and Bye," parodying the original lyrics' promise of heavenly salvation with the famous line, "You'll get pie in the sky when you die, by and by."

In Salt Lake City, Utah, in January 1914, Hill was shot in what he vaguely explained as a disagreement over a woman, the same night that a local grocer and his son were gunned down in an apparent robbery. Authorities ultimately charged Hill with the murders. Hill maintained his innocence, but he refused to divulge any details about the circumstances leading to his wound. He was found guilty and sentenced to die; given the choice of the gallows or a firing squad, he chose the latter. In spite of scores of appeals for clemency, even from President Woodrow Wilson and international figures, Utah executed Joe Hill on 19 November 1915. In his putative last will and testament, Hill admonished the world's workers: "Don't waste any time in mourning: Organize!"

[*See also* **Industrial Workers of the World** and **Little Red Songbook**.]

BIBLIOGRAPHY

Rosemont, Franklin. *Joe Hill: The IWW and the Making of a Revolutionary Workingclass Counterculture*. Chicago: Charles H. Kerr, 2002.
Smith, Gibbs M. *Joe Hill*. Salt Lake City: University of Utah Press, 1969.

Gerald Ronning

HILLMAN, SIDNEY

(1887–1946), one of the most important American labor leaders of the twentieth century. As president of the Amalgamated Clothing Workers of America (ACW), Sidney Hillman pioneered the so-called new unionism of the Progressive Era, cofounded the Congress of Industrial Organizations (CIO), served as labor's key liaison to Franklin Delano Roosevelt's Democratic Party, and masterminded the nation's first political action committee, CIO-PAC.

Born in Zagare, Lithuania, a part of the tsarist Russian empire, Hillman was the grandson of a learned rabbi. His family planned for him to become a rabbi, too, but his studies led him instead to dedicate himself to work among Jewish workers in Russia—to advance their interests through unionism and socialism. He became involved in the Yiddish labor movement and the Yiddish-language Bund. His Bundist activities, which culminated in his participation in the Russian revolution of 1905, caused him to emigrate to the United States to

escape the government's repression of radicals. Settling in Chicago, he became a skilled cutter in the men's-clothing industry and a union activist. As one of the leaders of a successful strike in 1910, Hillman rose rapidly in the Jewish American labor movement. In 1914 the International Ladies' Garment Workers' Union (ILGWU) invited him to New York to serve as that union's primary representative in administering its bargaining relationship with garment manufacturers. A year later when immigrant men's-clothing workers rebelled against the leadership of what was then their union, the craft-oriented United Garment Workers, and formed a new industrial union, the ACW, the rebels chose Hillman as their president. As union president, Hillman espoused socialism but allied with American Progressives such as Jane Addams. The unionism of Hillman's ACW wed American Progressivism to Bund socialism, rank-and-file militancy to scientific management, and millennial rhetoric to bread-and-butter objectives, all under the rubric of "industrial democracy."

The ACW placed the demand for industrial democracy on the national agenda during World War I. Postwar reaction convinced Hillman that labor needed political power and influential allies to keep industrial democracy alive. He also realized that only a reformed political economy could better the lives of workers and increase the power of their unions. Thus Hillman allied with Progressive labor economists, more-liberal mass-market-oriented producers, retailers, and financiers, and the Harvard law professor Felix Frankfurter to outline what later became the demand-side economics policy of the New Deal, a policy that assumed that a thriving economy necessitated government spending, economic regulation, and union power.

Hillman played a key role during the New Deal, influencing the National Industrial Recovery Act of 1933, staffing federal agencies with labor's allies, and building coalitions with

New Deal Democrats. In 1935, Hillman joined with John L. Lewis, David Dubinsky, and some seven other labor leaders to launch the Committee for Industrial Organization in an effort to organize mass-production workers.

Equally attentive to politics, Hillman built a labor–Democratic alliance. In 1936 he promoted Labor's Non-Partisan League to urge Roosevelt's reelection. In 1944 he launched the CIO's political action committee, CIO-PAC, which became the Democratic Party's most muscular electoral arm. Hillman's political activities in support of Roosevelt led to his wartime appointments as associate director of the Office of Production Management and subsequently head of the labor division of the War Production Board.

Hillman died before he could observe the new role that he—more than any other labor leader—had built for labor in the postwar world. Union rivals and later historians criticized him for sacrificing labor's political independence by having too much faith in Democratic allies, but even his critics acknowledged his impact.

[*See also* **Congress of Industrial Organizations; Industrial Democracy; International Ladies' Garment Workers' Union and Amalgamated Clothing Workers of America; Jewish American Labor Movement; Labor Leaders; Labor Movements;** *and* **Labor's Role in Politics.**]

BIBLIOGRAPHY

Fraser, Steven. *Labor Will Rule: Sidney Hillman and the Rise of American Labor.* New York: Free Press, 1991.

Josephson, Matthew. *Sidney Hillman, Statesman of American Labor.* Garden City, N.Y.: Doubleday, 1952.

Soule, George Henry. *Sidney Hillman, Labor Statesman.* New York: Macmillan, 1939.

Joseph A. McCartin

HOFFA, JAMES R.

(1913–1975?), labor leader. A controversial figure in U.S. labor history, James Riddle "Jimmy" Hoffa was born on 14 February 1913 in Brazil, Indiana, the son of a coal miner. Hoffa was president of the International Brotherhood of Teamsters (IBT) from 1957 to 1971. The controversy surrounding Hoffa stemmed partly from his apparent willingness to work with organized-crime figures and to abet the worst cases of local union corruption within the Teamsters. But it also reflected Hoffa's aggressive tactics as a union organizer and his innovative changes in the structure of the IBT's bargaining unit that allowed the Teamsters to achieve strategic organizing breakthroughs and ultimately become the nation's largest and most powerful union. Congressional hearings held by the McClellan Committee (1957–1959) helped bring both these issues into the national spotlight and transformed Hoffa into a notorious figure. In 1964 he was convicted on charges of mail fraud and witness tampering, and he began serving a thirteen-year prison sentence in 1967.

Despite controversy and Hoffa's criminal convictions, he continued serving as president of the IBT until he resigned in 1971. His hold on power highlighted the difficulties facing union insurgencies, but it also stemmed from the important gains won by the Teamsters under his leadership. As president of the IBT he signed the first-ever National Master Freight Agreement (NMFA) in 1964, which created a nationwide contract for members involved in the trucking and warehouse industries. Freight-industry workers enjoyed significant gains in wages and benefits during Hoffa's tenure. Granted an early release from prison in 1971, he disappeared in 1975, apparently murdered by organized-crime figures who found it easier to work with his successor.

[*See also* **International Brotherhood of Teamsters; Labor Leaders;** *and* **Union Corruption.**]

BIBLIOGRAPHY

Russell, Thaddeus. *Out of the Jungle: Jimmy Hoffa and the Remaking of the American Working Class.* New York: Alfred A. Knopf, 2001. The best-researched biography of Hoffa.

Witwer, David. *Corruption and Reform in the Teamsters Union.* Urbana: University of Illinois Press, 2003. Places Hoffa's career in the larger context of the Teamsters' history.

David Witwer

HOME OWNERS' LOAN CORPORATION

The Home Owners' Loan Corporation (HOLC) was created in 1933 as part of President Franklin D. Roosevelt's New Deal. During the Great Depression, the nation suffered both a banking and a housing crisis. The HOLC aimed to protect homeowners from foreclosure and to assist banks that held mortgages on those homes. The parent organization for the HOLC was the Federal Home Loan Bank Board, created in 1932.

HOLC loans were available only for mortgages that were in default or that were held by troubled financial institutions. Only nonfarm, owner-occupied structures consisting of no more than four units and worth less than $20,000 were eligible. The HOLC loan could be no more than 80 percent of the appraised value of the property. Between 1933 and 1935 the HOLC received more than 1.8 million applications for aid. Not everyone who applied received a loan. The HOLC provided more than a million loans, totaling $3.1 million. Its loans covered 10 percent of all nonfarm, owner-occupied homes and 20 percent of all mortgaged homes. The HOLC also provided loans to homeowners to cover property taxes and home insurance.

Despite the mortgage assistance—and lenient terms—provided by the HOLC, around nearly 20 percent of participating homeowners still lost their homes. That meant that the HOLC acquired some 200,000 homes during its lifetime. Although the HOLC stopped accepting new applications in 1935, it remained in operation until 1951 as it serviced borrowers and worked to manage and eventually sell its inventory of foreclosed homes. According to one estimate, the HOLC closed its books in 1951 with a small profit.

The HOLC not only made it possible for many people to keep their homes during the Depression, but also changed the way in which homes would be purchased in the future. Together with the Federal Housing Administration (FHA), the HOLC ushered in the use of long-term, self-amortizing mortgages, which quickly also became standard practice among private lenders. Prior to the 1930s, home mortgages were generally for shorter periods—around five years—and mortgagees rarely paid in full at the end of the loan period. Self-amortizing, long-term mortgages stimulated the postwar housing boom.

The HOLC also worked to standardize real estate appraisals. Not only was it important to analyze the credit-worthiness of borrowers, but also lenders needed better tools for calculating the future value of the properties they might finance. Therefore, HOLC appraisers applied a uniform set of standards that divided cities into distinct neighborhoods, based on income, housing age and quality, property values, and such demographic factors as the race and ethnicity of the population. The HOLC provided appraisers with intensive training in its methods.

These appraisals divided urban neighborhoods into four different "grades"—rated A, B, C, and D—with corresponding color codes of green, blue, yellow, and red, respectively. Neighborhoods given an "A" rating were deemed "best," whereas "D"-rated neighborhoods were considered "hazardous." These appraisals were recorded onto color-coded "residential security maps." Neighborhoods receiving higher grades tended to be largely residential areas that were farther from the central city and were populated by middle-class native-born whites. Neighborhoods receiving lower grades clustered closer to the central city, were more densely populated, and contained mostly older housing stock and poorer residents, especially recent immigrants and their children and racial minorities.

Some scholars maintain that the appraisal maps institutionalized a process known as "redlining," which made it difficult for residents of low-income, inner-city neighborhoods to obtain bank loans. They hypothesize that such policies hardened racial segregation and accelerated the decline of inner-city neighborhoods in favor of suburban development. They also argue that the HOLC maps influenced the FHA in setting its own housing policies.

More recent scholarship, however, has cast some doubt on these theories. The lending patterns of the HOLC evinced few discriminatory patterns; it provided loans to homeowners at all appraisal grades. It is also not demonstrable that the FHA subsequently used the HOLC maps. The HOLC maps instead seem to have mirrored already-existing ideas and prejudices regarding urban lending. Although there is no doubt that banks were much less likely to provide loans to poor, inner-city neighborhoods in the postwar years, the indictment charging government programs such as the HOLC with discriminatory intent remains debatable.

[*See also* **Federal Housing Administration; New Deal Banking Regulation;** *and* **Racism.**]

BIBLIOGRAPHY

Harriss, C. Lowell. *History and Policies of the Home Owners' Loan Corporation.* New York: National Bureau of Economic Research, 1951.

Jackson, Kenneth T. *Crabgrass Frontier: The Suburbanization of the United States.* New York: Oxford University Press, 1985.

Vincent J. Cannato

HOMESTEAD ACT

The Homestead Act was an attempt to transform the settlement of the public domain in the West. Passed by Congress in 1862 and put into operation on 1 January 1863, it offered actual settlers free title to 160 acres (a quarter section) after they had established residence and improved the land for five years. The act also sought to bind the West to the North during the Civil War. It altered the historic policy—since the Land Ordinance of 1785—of cash sale of the public domain. Potential settlers saw the Homestead Act as a great boon, but much of the available land was in regions of insufficient rainfall such as the midcontinent High Plains. In fact, farmers west of the ninety-eighth meridian—which passes through central Kansas, Nebraska, and the Dakotas—needed four to eight times the allotted acres for successful settlement. In the 1870s, of some 1.3 million new farms carved out of the public domain, only around 320,000 were actual homestead entries. In some areas, fewer than a quarter of the original entries actually completed the process and established homesteads. Farm families that did persevere described the initial five years as their "period of starvation." Homesteading was abused by fraudulent surveys and deceptive multiple claims by ranchers, lumbering interests, and other speculators. A series of legislative efforts between 1873 and 1916 to correct some of the problems resolved neither the climate realities nor the fraud. Dryland farming techniques, however, stabilized some High Plains settlement. Between 1863 and 1904, some 720,000 farms, totaling nearly 100 million acres, had been established under the Homestead Act. Homesteading of at least 3 million acres a year continued until the 1930s Depression.

[*See also* **Agriculture** *and* **Public Land Policy.**]

BIBLIOGRAPHY

Gates, Paul W. *History of Public Land Law Development.* Washington, D.C.: Government Printing Office, 1968.
Opie, John. *The Law of the Land: Two Hundred Years of American Farmland Policy.* Lincoln: University of Nebraska Press, 1987.

John Opie

HOMESTEAD STRIKE (1892)

Arguably the most infamous confrontation between workers and employers in the nineteenth century, the Homestead strike began on 1 July 1892 when Henry Clay Frick, the coal magnate who managed Andrew Carnegie's steelmaking company, closed down the immense Homestead Steel Works near Pittsburgh, Pennsylvania, rather than bargain with the Amalgamated Association of Iron, Steel, and Tin Workers. Frick announced that the Carnegie company would no longer recognize any union and that all thirty-eight hundred employees would have to sign individual contracts. Homestead's workers knew that Frick had constructed fortified barriers around the mill as a defense for strikebreakers, who would also be protected by the Pinkerton National Detective Agency, a private police force that the company had used earlier to suppress trade unionism.

The workers responded by mobilizing virtually all twelve thousand residents of the town of Homestead, whose government was dominated by committed trade unionists. The workers also blocked all access to the mill. An uneasy calm prevailed until 6 July when three hundred Pinkertons arrived by river barge at the mill and engaged the workers in a pitched battle. Three Pinkerton agents and seven workers were killed; after surrendering, the Pinkertons were forced to run a gauntlet of thousands of enraged men, women, and children.

The workers' victory proved short-lived. At Frick's request, the Pennsylvania governor Robert E. Pattison sent in eight thousand state militiamen. Homestead was placed under martial law, and the company reclaimed the mill. Soon strikebreakers were at work, union leaders had been arrested on charges ranging from murder to treason, and the workers were defeated. The strikers were convinced that labor had a fundamental right to employment and that Frick and Carnegie, by abrogating this right, had violated the most basic tenets of justice. Frick and Carnegie, however, believed that they enjoyed the right to dispose of their property as they saw fit and therefore to hire whomever they chose. Thus, in fundamental ways, the dispute at Homestead arose from conflicting concepts of right and property.

The victory of Frick and Carnegie decimated the Amalgamated Association and signaled an industrywide collapse of unionism that would not be reversed until the 1930s. The lockout also proved to many Americans that in a showdown, private industry could summon the power of the state to defeat unions.

[*See also* **Amalgamated Association of Iron, Steel, and Tin Workers; Carnegie, Andrew; Iron and Steel Industry; Labor Spies and Pinkertons; Repression of Unions;** *and* **Strikes.**]

BIBLIOGRAPHY

Burgoyne, Arthur G. *The Homestead Strike of 1892* (1893). Pittsburgh, Pa.: University of Pittsburgh Press, 1979.

Krause, Paul. *The Battle for Homestead, 1880–1892: Politics, Culture, and Steel.* Pittsburgh, Pa.: University of Pittsburgh Press, 1992.

Paul Krause

HOMEWORK

Homework, or manufacturing in family residences, first became common in the shoe and textile industries. It characterized garment production in the nineteenth and early twentieth centuries and reemerged in the late twentieth to include telecommuting and business services, as well as high-fashion and cheap-apparel production. Concentrated in urban tenements and immigrant neighborhoods, from New York City's Lower East Side to San Francisco's Chinatown, homework reached into southern mill towns, Appalachian farms, Pennsylvania villages, and East Coast suburbs. Relying on a chain of contractors, manufacturers lessened expenses by paying a temporary workforce by the piece and requiring the worker to use his or her own tools and workplace. Employers took advantage of the gender division of labor within the household and between the household and the larger society to hire married women who had small children, whose husbands earned inadequate wages, or whose cultural traditions or family responsibilities kept them homebound. The homework labor force also included the elderly, the disabled, children, and, in rural regions, older daughters— people who lacked other employment options.

Homework undercut the labor standards of factory workers, weakening unionization and threatening their ability to win higher wages. Reformers condemned it for spreading disease and disorder, for turning homes into factories, and for perverting motherhood and childhood. Beginning in the 1890s, because courts blocked outright bans of homework as violations of the rights of privacy and contract, states regulated health and sanitary conditions for homeworkers. The federal government prohibited homework on army uniforms during World War I, but only in the New Deal era, initially through National Recovery Administration codes, did the government impose more general restrictions on homework. In the early 1940s, the administrator of the Fair Labor Standards Act (1938) banned homework in seven garment industries to protect the standards won by factory workers. In the 1980s, however, the administration of Ronald Reagan removed all bans except those related to ladies' garments. By the end of the twentieth century the notion that homeworkers might combine earnings with family care threatened a return to sweatshop conditions; with the offshoring of garment production, the fight against exploitative homework became a global struggle.

[*See also* **Artisanal Labor; Domestic Labor; Garment Industry; Gender and Work; Shoe Industry; Textile Industry;** *and* **Women Workers.**]

BIBLIOGRAPHY

Boris, Eileen. *Home to Work: Motherhood and the Politics of Industrial Homework in the United States.* Cambridge, U.K.: Cambridge University Press, 1994.

Boris, Eileen, and Cynthia R. Daniels, eds. *Homework: Historical and Contemporary Perspectives on Paid Labor at Home.* Urbana: University of Illinois Press, 1989.

Eileen Boris

HORMEL P-9 STRIKE (1985)

When on 17 August 1985 meatpackers at the George A. Hormel & Company plant in Austin,

Minnesota, went on strike, they began one of the most bitter labor conflicts of the 1980s. The Hormel workers of Austin were members of Local P-9 of the United Food and Commercial Workers (UFCW) union. Their strike was prompted by the plant's effort to cut wages from $10.69 an hour to $8.25 at a time when Hormel earned significant profits. Hormel argued that unless the union made concessions, the company would be unable to compete with the sudden rise of low-wage, nonunion producers such as the Iowa Beef Processors (IBP). Although workers in other Hormel plants signed concessionary contracts with support from the UFCW, which sought to preserve the union's foothold in the fast-changing industry, Local P-9, led by its president Jim Guyette, struck on its own.

Like many other employers in the 1980s, the company soon hired replacement workers. Guyette sought assistance from the consultant Ray Rogers of Corporate Campaign, Inc., who helped initiate a "Cram Your Spam" boycott that targeted the Austin plant's signature meat product. However, divisions between P-9 and the UFCW president William Wynn deepened as the strike progressed. In June 1986 the UFCW placed Local P-9 in trusteeship and ousted Guyette, and three months later it settled the strike.

Though Hormel's wages at the Austin plant returned to previous levels, the company rented part of the plant to a low-wage producer, and some strikers were unable to regain their old jobs. Controversy followed. Many union militants blamed the UFCW for undercutting P-9, while those who sympathized with the UFCW's dilemma in an industry pressured by nonunion employers like IBP blamed Guyette for launching an ill-advised strike without the support of other Hormel locals. The strike came to symbolize growing weakness, division, and disenchantment within the labor movement.

[*See also* Labor Movement, Decline of the; Meatpacking and Meat-Processing Industry; *and* Strikes.]

BIBLIOGRAPHY

Green, Hardy. *On Strike at Hormel: The Struggle for a Democratic Labor Movement.* Philadelphia: Temple University Press, 1990.
Rachleff, Peter. *Hard-Pressed in the Heartland: The Hormel Strike and the Future of the Labor Movement.* Boston: South End Press, 1993.

Joseph A. McCartin

HOUSEHOLD TECHNOLOGY AND DOMESTIC LABOR

Industrialization transformed American society, permanently altering the tools and work processes of preindustrial America. New technologies helped change how households fed, clothed, cleaned, and cared for their members, though these technologies affected men, women, and children differently. In addition, the rich and the urban tended to gain access to new technologies before the poor and the rural did. Despite the unevenness and inequities of these changes, developments in household technology played an important role in elevating the American standard of living through the nineteenth and twentieth centuries.

In the Colonial Era, most households used simple tools to maintain their living standards, which for all but the very rich consisted of simple diets, limited wardrobes, and low standards of cleanliness. Open, wood-burning hearths provided heat and a place to cook, while candles gave light. Women prepared and preserved food, made medicines, and used spinning wheels, looms, and needles to turn wool and flax into clothing. Men farmed, cut and hauled wood, whittled, and sewed leather items.

Metalware such as kettles, pots, axes, and knives eased food preparation, wood gathering, and agricultural labor. Servants, slaves, and children, as well as male and female heads of house, provided household labor. Occasional reliance on people outside the household who produced and repaired metalware and sold staples such as salt and lime linked relatively self-sufficient households to the developing market economy.

Through the nineteenth century, the mass production of goods by new industries removed many traditionally male tasks from homes and placed most household technology in the hands of women and servants. Beginning in the 1830s, versions of Benjamin Franklin's 1740s cast-iron stove, modified to include ovens and stove-top hot plates, began replacing open hearths and altering cooking practices. By 1850, many households were purchasing coal and commercially ground flour, eliminating traditional male tasks such as gathering wood, shelling corn, pounding grain, and, increasingly, farming itself. New technology diversified women's housework as well, removing some jobs and adding others. Kerosene eliminated the job of making candles. Purchasing textiles reduced long hours spent spinning and weaving, and after the Civil War, Isaac Singer's manufacture of a practical, treadle-operated sewing machine allowed women to sew family clothes without hiring seamstresses. The shift from leather and woolen clothing to cotton garments boosted standards of cleanliness but added the arduous weekly task of hand-cleaning laundry. As culinary standards advanced, women invested more time preparing more varied meals.

Between 1880 and 1920, private industries began providing even more of the goods and services that households had traditionally produced. As increasing numbers of Americans moved from rural to urban areas, for example, many families began purchasing goods and services that they had previously provided them-

selves: foodstuffs from grocery stores, health care from physicians and hospitals, and ready-made clothing from department stores. As municipalities developed water systems, many homes acquired running water, water heaters, sanitary fixtures, and indoor bathrooms. Following Thomas Edison's invention of electric lights in 1879 and the first electric power station in 1882, many urban families gradually switched from kerosene lamps to electric light bulbs. By 1910, after the Westinghouse Corporation introduced alternating current (AC) motors, industries mass-produced electric fans, sewing machines, washing machines, and vacuum cleaners for a national market. By 1920 when 35 percent of American homes had electricity, devices using resistance-coil heaters, such as irons and toasters, were widely available. A small but growing number of families also owned telephones and automobiles.

The national standard of living rose through the 1920s, fell in the 1930s, and rose steadily again after World War II as household technologies spread. General Electric began the assembly-line production of home refrigerators in 1926, enhancing the ability to preserve food and enabling the Birds Eye Corporation to make frozen food widely available by the 1930s. Owners of electric dishwashers and other new kitchen appliances found cooking and cleaning easier, if still time-consuming. Radio, the phonograph, and then television brought free entertainment into homes around the nation. Businesses cut back on home-delivery services in response to the spread of automobiles. The Great Depression of the 1930s reduced the number of households that could afford servants, but labor-saving technologies such as automatic washing machines made it easier and more acceptable for housewives—still the primary operators of household technologies—to perform domestic work without hired help. New products ceaselessly altered household tasks and responsibilities. By the 1980s microwave ovens speeded and eased meal preparation, while personal computers brought new sources of information and entertainment into the home. By the early twenty-first century, wireless Internet, smartphones, and multiplatform tablets made their appearance and facilitated the easier organization of a multitude of tasks. Even more remarkable than the range of new technologies was the speed and extent to which citizens of all regions and social levels gained access to them.

[*See also* Domestic Labor; Electricity and Electrification; Farm Machinery; Food and Diet; Technology; *and* Women Workers.]

BIBLIOGRAPHY

Bushman, Richard L. *The Refinement of America: Persons, Houses, Cities.* New York: Alfred A. Knopf, 1992.

Cowan, Ruth Schwartz. *More Work for Mother: The Ironies of Household Technology from the Open Hearth to the Microwave.* New York: Basic Books, 1983.

Larkin, Jack. *The Reshaping of Everyday Life, 1790–1840.* New York: Harper & Row, 1988.

McGaw, Judith A., ed. *Early American Technology: Making and Doing Things from the Colonial Era to 1850.* Chapel Hill: University of North Carolina Press for the Institute of Early American History and Culture, Williamsburg, Va., 1994.

Strasser, Susan. *Never Done: A History of American Housework.* New York: Pantheon Books, 1982.

Christopher W. Wells

HULL HOUSE

The shift from agriculture, trade, and the artisanal workshop to monopoly capital, consumerism, and factory production nearly rent the social fabric of the modernizing United States. Though the new mode of production brought the excitement and promise of an economic frontier, it also ushered in severe problems: urban overcrowding; lack of safety and hygiene in factories, in workers' housing, and on city streets; poverty and social inequality; the degradation of work and the growth of an underclass of unskilled workers; the mystification of the manufacturing process; social antagonism and political violence; alienation and despair. As the so-called new immigrants, largely from eastern Europe, poured into the United States in the late nineteenth and early twentieth centuries, reformers worried about the potentially dire consequences of the Industrial Revolution for the well-being of both immigrants and also the new nation, with its aspirations for a democratic collective life.

Jane Addams, from an abolitionist family and among the first generation of female college graduates, founded Hull House with her close friend Ellen Gates Starr in Chicago in 1889. Inspired by London's Toynbee Hall, which was run by Oxford University men to help workingmen, Addams's Chicago settlement house was staffed largely by middle-class female college-student "residents" living in the midst of their impoverished "neighbors." Operating out of a rundown Italianate mansion on the corner of Polk and Halstead in Chicago's Near West Side, Hull House at first concentrated on cultural activities but, attuned to the needs of the surrounding neighborhood and committed to a unique marriage of delivery of services and far-reaching social betterment, was soon at the forefront of progressive reform. It offered lectures and classes, child care and instruction, a gym, a public bathhouse, a playground, a dispensary of food, and many other forms of assistance and edification. From all accounts, it was a vibrant intellectual salon of sorts, as well as a community center—a place that had many practical day-to-day rewards for residents, too, just as much as for their neighbors.

Addams's intellectual influences ranged from abolitionism to Auguste Comte, John Ruskin, Leo Tolstoy, and John Dewey, who worked at Hull House for a time. She shared the Arts and Crafts movement's belief in the ethical role of the arts and the dignity of handicraft work. Following Addams's doctrine of "immigrant gifts," Hull House offered exhibitions and plays to celebrate the culture riches of the newcomers, but it also gathered information about everything from dangerous living and working conditions to child labor, using sociological observation as a springboard for legal and political change. On the National Register of Historic Places since the 1960s, by the twenty-first century Hull House had become home to the Jane Addams Hull-House Museum, and a Hull House offshoot, along the lines of a modern nonprofit, delivers services under the guise of the Jane Addams Hull House Association.

Though Hull House, and the American social-settlement movement that it led, could not possibly single-handedly end the ravages of the new industrial system, its influence extended far and wide as an oasis to the thousands who walked through its doors and as a voice for sanity in the dehumanizing madness of industrialization. Among its residents were Alice Hamilton, Florence Kelley, Julia Lathrop, and Frances Perkins; among its visitors were Sidney and Beatrice Webb; and among its "graduates" was Benny Goodman. Its mission: to keep the whole human being alive in the age of the machine.

[*See also* Immigration.]

BIBLIOGRAPHY

Addams, Jane. *Twenty Years at Hull-House, with Autobiographical Notes.* New York: Macmillan, 1910.

Elshtain, Jean Bethke. *Jane Addams and the Dream of American Democracy: A Life.* New York: Basic Books, 2002.

Elshtain, Jean Bethke, ed. *The Jane Addams Reader.* New York: Basic Books, 2002.

Jane Addams Hull House Association. http://www.hullhouse.org.

Jane Addams Hull-House Museum. http://www.uic.edu/jaddams/hull/hull_house.html.

Scott, Anne Firor. "Jane Addams." In *Notable American Women, 1607–1950*, edited by Edward T. James, vol. 1, pp. 16–21. Cambridge, Mass.: Belknap Press of Harvard University Press, 1971.

Elisabeth Lasch-Quinn

HUNTINGTON, COLLIS P.

(1821–1900), railroad entrepreneur. Born in Connecticut, Collis P. Huntington, after an early business career in New York City, moved to Sacramento, California, during the 1849 gold rush and started a merchandise business with Mark Hopkins. In 1861 he joined with Hopkins, Leland Stanford, and Charles Crocker—the "Big Four," as they became known—to create the Central Pacific Railroad. Using Chinese labor and relying on government loans and subsidies, the Central Pacific built nearly seven hundred miles of the transcontinental railroad that in 1869 linked with the Union Pacific at Promontory Point, Utah. Huntington and his partners reaped huge profits from the venture.

In 1865, Huntington and his partners started the Southern Pacific Railroad. To maintain the railroad's dominance over competitors in California and the Southwest, as well as to avoid government regulation, Huntington lobbied in Washington, dominated the California legislature, and showered bribes on corrupt politicians. His candid private letters, some of which became public in 1883, revealed his cynical calculations about who could be bought to achieve his purposes. During the 1870s and 1880s, the period of his greatest economic and political power, Huntington was controversial and hated, personifying as he did the acquisitive business practices of the Gilded Age. His excesses helped spark a movement within the California Democratic Party in the 1880s and 1890s to curb the power of the Southern Pacific. The estate of his nephew and business partner Henry E. Huntington in San Marino, California, became the site of the Huntington Library, Art Collections, and Botanical Gardens, a major cultural center near Pasadena.

[*See also* **Crédit Mobilier; Railroad Land Grants;** *and* **Railroads.**]

BIBLIOGRAPHY

Lavender, David. *The Great Persuader*. Garden City, N.Y.: Doubleday, 1970.

Williams, R. Hal. *The Democratic Party and California Politics, 1880–1896*. Stanford, Calif.: Stanford University Press, 1973.

Lewis L. Gould

HUTCHESON, WILLIAM

(1874–1953), labor leader. William L. Hutcheson led the United Brotherhood of Carpenters and Joiners (UBCJA) for thirty-seven years, from 1915 until his retirement in 1952. Like P. J. McGuire, the union's first leader, Hutcheson led an aggressive campaign of jurisdictional strikes against both the labor organizations that claimed work that carpenters traditionally did and the employers that hired them. Unlike the radical McGuire, Hutcheson was a Republican and a conservative. Through two world wars, the Great Depression, and the New Deal, he fought both the growth of government power and the rise of industrial unionism. Hutcheson's commitment to business unionism included a dedication to free enterprise, the American political process, anti-Communism, and the dominance of craft unions.

Born in Saginaw, Michigan, Hutcheson began work as a carpenter while still a teenager. He joined the UBCJA in 1902 and was a business agent for a UBCJA local by 1906. In 1912 he became a national vice president of the union, and in 1915 he was elected president. Immediately, Hutcheson set about consolidating power in the organization's national headquarters. Within a few months of taking office, he had suspended scores of New York City locals that refused to follow his orders. For the next three and half decades, Hutcheson ran the union as he saw fit, suspending locals and revoking charters, withdrawing from and then rejoining the American Federation of Labor (AFL), and defying directives from the local, state, and federal government whenever he believed that the interests of the trade, or his own power, were threatened.

Hutcheson firmly believed that only skilled craftsmen could be relied upon to be both union members and responsible citizens. He fought to keep unskilled industrial workers and their organizations out of the AFL, and he refused to accept machine woodworkers into the UBCJA as full members. At the 1935 AFL convention, Hutcheson argued against John L. Lewis, the president of the United Mine Workers and an advocate for the organization of mass-production workers and other unskilled laborers. In one of the most famous incidents in labor history, Lewis punched Hutcheson during a climactic moment at the convention, highlighting the emerging rift within the AFL that gave rise to the Congress of Industrial Organizations.

Throughout his career, Hutcheson fought to defend the carpenters' work jurisdiction. He clashed with machinists about the installation of machines at building sites, with sheet-metal workers over the framing of windows and doors, and with the woodworkers' union over employees in lumber and shingle mills. A fervent critic of most Democratic politicians, Hutcheson despised Franklin D. Roosevelt and regularly criticized New Deal policies, opposing both unemployment insurance and government domination of the economy. He also opposed Truman's Fair Deal.

Hutcheson resigned as president of the UBCJA in 1952, and like a ruling monarch he handed over the office to his son, Maurice. He died the following year.

[*See also* **American Federation of Labor; Labor Leaders; Lewis, John L.; McGuire, P. J.;** *and* **United Brotherhood of Carpenters and Joiners.**]

BIBLIOGRAPHY

Christie, Robert A. *Empire in Wood: A History of the Carpenters' Union.* Ithaca, N.Y.: Cornell University Press, 1956.

Cummins, E. E. "Jurisdictional Disputes of the Carpenters' Union." *Quarterly Journal of Economics* 40, no. 3 (May 1926): 463–494.

Galenson, Walter. *The United Brotherhood of Carpenters: The First Hundred Years.* Cambridge, Mass.: Harvard University Press, 1983.

Timothy J. Houlihan

HYDROELECTRIC POWER

Electricity generated through the use of waterwheels or hydraulic turbines is known as hydroelectric power. In the early 1880s, small water-powered mills were utilized to produce direct current (DC) electricity. However, the full potential of hydroelectric power was not realized until the proliferation of alternating current (AC) power systems in the 1890s. In contrast to direct current, which could not be transmitted efficiently more than about ten miles, polyphase AC systems proved capable of transmitting power hundreds of miles. As a result, AC systems allowed the development of large waterpower sites in remote locations far removed from urban markets.

America's first polyphase AC hydroelectric power system came online in 1893 near San Bernardino, California. California subsequently led the nation in long-distance hydroelectric-power development; Fresno received power over a 35-mile transmission line in 1896, and by 1901 San Francisco was connected to generating plants in the Sierra Nevada mountains, more than 140 miles away. In the eastern United States, Niagara Falls became the focus of hydroelectric-power development; in 1896, AC power was first transmitted over a 22-mile line connecting Niagara Falls to Buffalo, New York.

In the early twentieth century, the conservationist Gifford Pinchot championed a movement advocating government regulation of hydroelectric-power systems built by privately owned utilities. In the 1920s the struggle between public and private interests over control of the electric-power industry focused on the Muscle Shoals (or Wilson) Dam on the Tennessee River in northern Alabama. The government had started the Muscle Shoals project during World War I to manufacture nitrates used in explosives. After the war, Henry Ford proposed buying the dam for general industrial purposes. However, public-power supporters in Congress blocked the transfer of control into private hands. In 1933, President Franklin Delano Roosevelt successfully incorporated Wilson Dam—and several other proposed dams—into the newly created and publicly administered Tennessee Valley Authority (TVA).

In the West, hydroelectric power constituted a key component of the Boulder Canyon Project. Authorized in 1928 by President Calvin Coolidge, this project included federal financing of the Hoover Dam across the Colorado River near Las Vegas, Nevada. During

Roosevelt's New Deal, many other large-scale hydroelectric-power dams were built in the West by the federal government. These included Grand Coulee Dam in Washington State, Shasta Dam in California, and Marshall Ford Dam in Texas.

After World War II, still more hydropower dams were built, including Glen Canyon Dam in northern Arizona, but the economic importance of hydroelectricity waned as fossil-fuel and nuclear generating plants grew in size and numbers. By the end of the twentieth century, hydroelectric power accounted for about 10 percent of electricity used in the United States; at the same time, public concern over environmental costs associated with reservoir construction prompted a movement to remove hydroelectric dams in order to restore river valleys to a more natural state.

[*See also* **Electricity and Electrification; Public Works Administration; Renewable Energy and Climate Change; Tennessee Valley Authority; Water and Irrigation;** *and* **Works Progress Administration.**]

BIBLIOGRAPHY

Hubbard, Preston J. *Origins of the TVA: The Muscle Shoals Controversy, 1920–1932.* Nashville, Tenn.: Vanderbilt University Press, 1961.

Hughes, Thomas P. *Networks of Power: Electrification in Western Society, 1880–1930.* Baltimore: Johns Hopkins University Press, 1983.

Donald C. Jackson

IMMIGRATION

International migration, as an aspect of the process of globalization, has been taking place on a large scale since 1500. For the European powers, North America, as well as Asia, Africa, Australasia, and South America, became a site of competing imperial ambition and capitalist enterprise. Imperialism required the voluntary and involuntary migrations of labor to exploit resources, build markets, transportation networks and other infrastructures, and operate agricultural, commercial, and industrial establishments. Human migration has never been solely an economic phenomenon, however; persecution, genocide, war, and famine have also stimulated it. Similarly, the familiar dichotomy of slave and free migrations is too simple.

In the coerced category, one can distinguish among slaves, exiles, deported convicts, and refugees, while the voluntary category includes colonists, labor migrants, sojourners, adventurers, and entrepreneurs. America has received all of these.

Colonial Era. Although the earliest migrations, perhaps as many as forty thousand years ago across the land bridge from Asia, brought the ancestors of the indigenous inhabitants of the Americas (denoted "Indians" by Europeans), this article focuses on the post-1500 migrants who crossed national borders from both adjacent and transoceanic countries. The Spanish planted Saint Augustine, Florida, in 1565 and established early settlements in the Southwest several decades before the English arrived at Jamestown in 1607. Unlike the Southwest, where the impact of the Spanish culture continued for years, Florida lost its Spanish influence early. French, Dutch, Swedish and Finnish, and Russian colonizers were eventually incorporated into the British colonies (and then the United States)—again by means of warfare, the conquest of territories from the natives, treaty agreements, or purchase. Meanwhile, of the 12 million Africans brought in chains to the New World, some 450,000 landed after 1619 in the British mainland colonies (and then the United States), most of them before the American Revolution.

Because of differing policies regarding proprietors and joint-stock companies, natural resources, and land-distribution systems, other British colonies attracted different mixes of immigrants. Organized migrations of coreligionists established the New England colonies, homogeneous communities with a strong Puritan character. By contrast, the middle colonies attracted a polyglot, religiously diverse population, sometimes including even Roman Catholics and Jews. Land-hungry German Lutherans and Pietists and Scotch-Irish Presbyterians, driven by a bleak economy, flocked to Pennsylvania, settling the backcountry as far south as Georgia. Although religious motives impelled a minority, most colonists aspired to improve their material conditions. The southern colonies, growing staple crops such as tobacco and indigo, initially recruited British indentured servants or imported convicts, but by the eighteenth century, African slaves, first introduced in Virginia in 1619, had become the major source of labor. Bonded Europeans continued to arrive in the North, but during the American Revolutionary era and after, free labor replaced indentured servitude. Colonial immigration thus determined long-lasting regional racial, ethnic, and social patterns within the original states and beyond.

Far from being a homogeneous Anglo-American population, colonial America was very diverse in culture, language, religion, and race. Of the 3.9 million persons enumerated in the first federal census in 1790 (Indians were not counted), those of English stock constituted only 48 percent; 19 percent were of African ancestry; and another 12 percent were Scots and Scotch-Irish. Germans accounted for 10 percent, with smaller numbers of French, Irish, Welsh, Dutch, Jews, and Swedes.

1776–1840. Reflecting this heterogeneity, the Revolutionary War was, in a sense, a civil war pitting certain groups against others, often along ethnic and religious lines. After the war, in the first of a number of emigrations, some eighty thousand loyalists left for Canada and Britain. A few went to the British West Indies and took their slaves with them.

Having achieved independence, the leaders of the new republic faced the task of nation building. Lacking deep roots in the soil and ancient ties of blood, they fashioned an American identity from the Enlightenment's doctrine of natural rights; a person became an American by assent, not by descent. Such a conception of nationhood suited well a "nation of immigrants." The Constitution alluded to immigration only indirectly: it provided that slave importation would not be prohibited prior to 1808, it gave Congress the power to regulate foreign commerce, and it authorized the judicial doctrine granting the federal government exclusive jurisdiction over naturalization. Authorized by the Constitution to establish a "uniform rule of naturalization," Congress in 1790 defined the criteria for naturalization as two years' residence (subsequently changed to five years), good character, an oath to support the Constitution, and the renunciation of all foreign allegiances. These liberal requirements enabled millions of immigrants to become American citizens. Equally important, the United States adopted the principle that place of birth, not blood, determined nationality; native-born children of foreign parents were citizens by birthright. The 1790 law, however, also restricted naturalization to "free white person[s]," thus making the racial test of "whiteness" essential to American citizenship. In 1870, during Reconstruction, Congress extended the privilege of naturalization to "aliens of African nativity and to persons of African descent." Only the Immigration and Nationality Act of 1952 finally removed all racial bars to citizenship.

Between 1790 and 1820, as war interrupted transatlantic commerce, only a few hundred thousand immigrants arrived. Immigration grew slowly thereafter, surpassing a million in the decade of the 1840s as canal and railroad projects, mining and lumbering, urban construction, and western land settlement created an insatiable demand for labor. Meanwhile, a more than doubling of Europe's population in the nineteenth century and the disruption of traditional livelihoods by the Industrial Revolution or a shortage of desirable land displaced millions of peasants and artisans. Not a desire for change, but rather a need to escape radical social and economic transformations, impelled many immigrants. They hoped in America to conserve their customary ways of life, but with an improved standard of living. Meanwhile burgeoning transoceanic commerce, resulting in regular and improved shipping (steamships were introduced by the 1840s), facilitated the migration process. Immigration became an integral part of an Atlantic economy involving the exchange of capital, commodities, and labor.

From the 1840s on, recurring waves of immigration brought some 60 million persons to America. But the volume of immigration has varied, with peaks and valleys reflecting economic and political conditions in both the United States and the sending countries. Business cycles, famines, persecutions, wars, and migration policies on both ends of the migration process affected the volume and direction of migrations. Usually voluntary immigrants

and mostly men, the newcomers chose when to leave, how to travel, and where to go. Individual migrants were atypical; families and even communities often made collective decisions and departed together. Once established, the immigrants called on relatives and friends to join them. Thus international networks linked specific villages in Europe with settlements in the United States. The lure of America was exerted not only by the advertising of shipping companies, land speculators, and state agencies, but even more by the "America letters" from those who had already come.

So, too, did remittances flow to Europe from immigrants in America, along with prepaid tickets. Transportation (steamships and railroads), the international cable, Western Union, and the many banks in immigrant neighborhoods that were developed in this era made the connections between the United States and Europe quicker and much cheaper. The fact that many immigrants who came to America worked for a period of some months and returned and then immigrated again was made possible by cheaper, safer, and more comfortable journeys. This global economy and its mobility of capital, goods, and labor contracted in the 1920s and 1930s, only to reemerge on a grander scale after 1945.

1840–1890. The history of American mass immigration after 1840 falls into four periods. During the first, 1840–1890, almost 15 million newcomers arrived, including more than 4 million Germans, 3 million Irish, another 3 million British, and a million Scandinavians. The second period, 1891–1920, brought an additional 18-plus million, including almost 4 million from Italy, 3.6 million from Austria-Hungary, and 3 million from Russia. This period saw the emergence of a global or transnational world. In the third period, 1920–1960, only 7.5 million immigrants—including many Mexicans from the Western Hemisphere—arrived.

But also, in the 1930s, local, state, and federal governments deported several hundred thousand Mexican immigrants—often with their children who were American citizens by birth—rather than allow them to participate in whatever welfare programs existed. Economic depressions and wars hot and cold all influenced various peoples to leave their homeland. The ongoing fourth period, which began in the 1960s, accounted for approximately 30 million legal immigrants by 2010, of whom nearly one third were from Mexico, another 24 percent from Central and South America and the Caribbean, and 35 percent from Asia. Whereas almost 90 percent of immigrants of the first three periods originated in Europe, only 15 percent of those of the fourth period did. During the post-1965 period, the United States admittedly opened the so-called golden door a bit by permitting not only Europeans but also Asians to head for the United States. Congress did try to cut immigration for Hispanics when it passed the Immigration and Nationality (Hart–Celler) Act of 1965, but the legislators quickly changed the law, making it possible for people from the Western Hemisphere to increase their numbers after 1980. However, many more people wanted to immigrate to the United States, and as a result, long waiting periods developed after 1965, especially for Mexicans, Filipinos, Chinese, and Indians. As might be predicted, rather than waiting for five years or longer, immigrants joined the move to America as illegal immigrants; they numbered nearly 11 million by 2010.

During the 1840–1890 period, British immigrants, English-speaking and Protestant, were readily absorbed. Though the Welsh, Scots, and Scotch-Irish immigrants initially organized their own settlements, societies, and churches, they gradually merged into a British American ethnicity, strengthening the emerging definition of the American nationality as white, Anglo-Saxon, English-speaking, and Protestant. Although some British immigrants established agricultural and utopian colonies, tradesmen and industrial workers among them tended to settle in the urban centers of the East. The British often occupied managerial and skilled-labor positions in such emerging industries as mining, steelmaking, and textiles. Experienced in trade unionism, they provided leadership for the emerging American labor movement.

Although Irish Catholic emigration began well before and continued long after the famine years of the 1840s, it was the more than a million fugitives from the so-called Great Hunger who established the negative stereotype of the Irish immigrant as pauperized and disease-ridden. Few of the Irish chose to become farmers, preferring the cities and towns of the East and Middle West. Some were craftsmen, but most held low-paid, dirty, and often dangerous jobs as railroad and construction laborers, miners, and factory hands. The Erie Canal owes much to the Irish immigrants who preformed the difficult labor in digging the canal in an age before machines could do the job. From the 1860s, females, often single young women, predominated among the Irish immigrants. Many worked as domestic servants, textile hands, and seamstresses, sending money back to their families or to bring relatives to America. The Irish of all the immigrant groups before World War II were the only one to have a female majority among the immigrants.

Like the British, the Irish figured prominently in establishing trade unions. They also brought modes of resistance that had been used against landlords in Ireland: sabotage and assassination. In the 1870s a group known as the Molly Maguires conducted a campaign of violence against the mining companies in Pennsylvania's anthracite region. The Irish quickly demonstrated talent for American politics; the saloonkeeper became an important agent for mobilizing Irish voters. By 1900, many mayors of northern cities and the majority of their policemen and firemen were of Irish origin. The Irish ability to speak English gave them an advantage other than in politics. In the early days of the subways in New York City, the ticket sellers had to know English. When the Transport Workers Union emerged in the early 1930s, the Irish dominated the leadership well into the 1940s.

The Irish also organized savings banks for immigrants, a practice followed by many other immigrants around the turn of the twentieth century. Federal investigators found thousands of these small, and sometimes unstable, banks in the first decade of the twentieth century.

Irish immigration made Roman Catholicism a major force in America. Among the Irish themselves, the church exerted both political and spiritual leadership. The parish became synonymous with the community and the priest the acknowledged authority. Irish immigrants had suffered religious as well as economic persecution at the hands of the British, and Catholicism became inextricably intertwined with Irish American ethnicity.

Their Catholicism also subjected the Irish to fierce religious prejudice. The nativist movement that culminated in the Know-Nothing Party of the 1850s sought to exclude the Irish from political life and even from the country, although in the nineteenth century the nativists never were able to persuade Congress to restrict Catholic immigrants. The Irish suffered both verbal abuse in Protestant churches and the U.S. Congress and also physical violence on city streets. Anti-Catholicism remained a major theme of American nativism well into the twentieth century and was a factor when Congress enacted rigid numerical controls on European immigration.

Objects of bigotry, Irish Americans, ironically, became major antagonists of other racial groups. Competing with urban blacks for jobs, the Irish sought to achieve the privileges of whiteness by venting their hostility toward African Americans. Irish workers also figured prominently in the anti-Chinese movement in California and displayed hostility toward later immigrants from southern and eastern Europe. Nurturing memories of colonial oppression, Irish Americans reserved their deepest hatred for the British. Their support of Irish liberation movements extended from the 1850s to the 1990s. Irish American ethnic nationalism, symbolized by the celebration of Saint Patrick's Day, fused Catholicism, nostalgia for the "auld sod," and bitterness for injuries inflicted by Anglo-Americans.

Ethnic Germans—often espousing provincial identities as Bavarians, Pomeranians, and so forth—constituted the largest group of European immigrants, eventually totaling more than 7 million. Unlike the Irish, religion was not so unifying a force for German immigrants, who included Roman Catholics, Protestants (Lutheran and Reformed), Jews, and freethinkers. German American ethnicity was thus largely invented in the United States, in particular following the creation of the modern country of Germany in 1870. More than most immigrant groups, German immigrants came from various ranks of society, with merchants, professionals, artisans, skilled workers, and farmers well represented, along with a cultural elite of intellectuals and artists. Within "Little Germany" neighborhoods in Cincinnati, Saint Louis, Milwaukee, Chicago, and other cities, Germans established clubs, churches, schools, and beer gardens, as well as newspapers, symphony orchestras, choral societies, and literary circles. Unlike members of other immigrant groups, German immigrants were not intimidated by American culture; indeed, many viewed their culture and language as superior to those of the uncouth Americans. Their attitude, plus beer drinking and boisterous singing, particularly on Sundays, antagonized Anglo-Americans. Conflicts over cultural issues such as Sabbatarianism, temperance, and German-language schools long plagued relationships between German Americans and Anglo-Americans.

German immigrants were also denounced as dangerous radicals. Many so-called 48ers—veterans of the 1848 revolutions in Europe—and their turnvereins (cultural and athletic clubs) did indeed profess radical republicanism and atheism. Some espoused Marxist socialism and anarchism. German immigrants established strong labor unions and socialist organizations modeled after those in Germany. The 1886 Haymarket affair in Chicago resulted in the suppression of the German-led anarchist movement and fixed in the minds of many Americans the image of the immigrant radical as a wild-eyed bomb thrower. Recurring "Red Scares" based on such fears became yet another theme of American nativism.

Many German and Scandinavian immigrants shunned urban industrial areas for the rich and affordable farmlands of the Middle West. Arriving in family groups, often coming from the same localities, they settled large contiguous areas. Ethnic maps of rural America resembled patchwork quilts. While they adjusted to new crops, farming methods, agricultural markets, and environmental conditions, their relative isolation enabled them to maintain their cultures and languages over several generations. The church, whether Catholic or Lutheran, played a central role both as community center and as place of worship. But the lure of city lights attracted the youth, and urban migration gradually eroded the demographic base of these German and Scandinavian settlements.

Two other sources of immigration figured significantly in this first period: China and Canada. Although Chinese immigrants numbered only some 200,000—90 percent of whom were men—the reaction they elicited influenced U.S. immigration policy for a century. Initially drawn by the gold rush of 1849, Chinese workers in the West provided an important labor supply for building the transcontinental railroad, mining, and agriculture. Sojourners like many Europeans, these predominantly male immigrants came to make money and return home. The objects of vicious stereotypes that depicted them as morally degenerate pagans, they were subjected to riots, lynching, and legal restrictions. Supported by many European immigrants and labor unions, the anti-Chinese movement gained national dimensions, and it culminated in the Chinese Exclusion Act of 1882. Erecting a racial barrier to immigration by excluding Chinese laborers, this precedent-setting law was subsequently extended by other laws and judicial decisions to Asians generally.

Migration from Canada, often slighted in accounts of U.S. immigration history, has been highly important, especially in New England, where it totaled more than 1 million from 1840 to 1890. Eventually over 3 million Canadians came to America. Of these, some two thirds were Anglo-Canadians who quickly blended into the larger American population. However, the other third, the French Canadians, had a distinctive history and influence. In the province of Quebec, a peasantry with large families and few resources increasingly migrated to the mill towns of New England. Because the textile industry employed women and children, this was a family migration. Strong kinship ties, proximity to places of origin, and the French language made the Quebecois resistant to assimilation. The Catholic Church's structure of parishes, parochial schools, and benefit societies represented another powerful cohesive force. For this colonized group subject to Anglo-Protestant domination, Catholicism became, as it did for Irish Catholics, a core element of Franco-American ethnicity.

1891–1930. The period from 1891 to 1930 witnessed a level of immigration not surpassed until 1980–2010. In several years the annual total exceeded a million. In 1900, almost 14 percent of the U.S. population was foreign-born; with their American-born children, immigrant families accounted for more than a third of the total population. In the succeeding decades the so-called foreign element grew ever larger and more diverse. Before the 1890s most immigrants came from northern and western Europe; thereafter, eastern and southern Europeans predominated: Italians, eastern European Jews, and Slavs. This shift reflected the movement eastward of European railroads and the rise of industrial and agricultural capitalism. Finns, Slovaks, and Greeks now migrated for reasons similar to those that had earlier uprooted Norwegians, Irish, and Germans: modernization was undermining time-honored forms of work and life. However, owing to improved transportation and differing aspirations, the post-1890s immigrants were much more likely than their predecessors to be temporary sojourners. Like the Chinese, they wanted to earn money and then return home to buy land. For this reason the southern and eastern European immigration was also overwhelmingly male (the Finns were an exception). If they decided to remain, as many did, they sent for wives, brides, and children. In the emerging global economy, the rate of return varied by nationality, but often it was more than 50 percent. Many immigrants made multiple trips back and forth across the Atlantic. Even more remarkable, Chinese laborers—who had arrived before the exclusion acts—went home for visits and sent money to China. The exceptions were Jews and Armenians fleeing religious and ethnic persecution. The major movement of Europeans was echoed by migration from Asia. After the Chinese were excluded, Japanese headed first for Hawai'i to work on plantations and then for the West Coast, until they, too, faced immigration restrictions.

This vast immigration also reflected the labor demands of an expansive, if volatile, American economy. Industrialization and urbanization required workers, skilled and unskilled. Few of the post-1890s immigrants became farmers; they sought out the cities, factory towns, and mining and lumber camps offering immediate wages. With few exceptions, these immigrants bypassed the still largely agrarian South.

Southern states did attempt to recruit immigrant Chinese as plantation workers, but they were not successful and eventually turned against the influx of large numbers of immigrants. Southern and eastern European immigrants for the most part entered the labor force as common laborers. Not only did employers consider them less desirable, but the Germans, Irish, and British who had preceded them—as well as old-stock Americans—resisted their entry into the skilled trades and trade unions Though partly motivated by fear of labor competition, such discrimination also expressed prejudice against southern and eastern European "races" that were not truly "white men" but "black labor."

Although denounced as strikebreakers and wage cutters (which on occasion they were), the southern and eastern Europeans generally proved amenable to labor organization. In their home countries, in fact, many had been involved in socialist and anarchist movements and had participated in strikes and protests. When admitted into unions such as the United Mine Workers or the United Packinghouse Workers, Slavs, Lithuanians, and Hungarians demonstrated strong solidarity. Jews and Italians, excluded from craft unions, formed industrial unions in the clothing and textile industries. Eastern and southern European immigrants were in the forefront of early twentieth-century labor struggles, and they and their children formed the backbone of what became the Congress of Industrial Organizations (CIO) in the 1930s.

Some eastern European Jews and Italians dispersed throughout the country—the Jews often as peddlers and merchants, the Italians as miners and in agriculture. Most, however, initially concentrated in Manhattan, with the Jews on the Lower East Side and the Italians to the immediate west of the Jews and also in East Harlem. Migrants from the shtetls of Poland, Lithuania, and Russia and from the *paesi* of Sicily, Calabria, and Campania, they clustered in tenements with their townspeople. Orthodox Jews eager to observe their religion formed shuls and landsmanshaften and patronized kosher butchers and grocers. A large and important segment of Jewish immigrants, however, was secular and socialist. Active in politics and labor organizations, they sponsored bunds, theaters, newspapers, and discussions clubs. Many men and women were tailors and seamstresses, peddlers and small shopkeepers. Entrepreneurial and thirsty for education, the second generation tended to move into business or the professions. These Yiddish-speaking Jews had a difficult relationship with the more established German Jews, who feared a growth of anti-Semitism because of the newcomers' exotic appearance and behavior. Religious, cultural, and political differences, including Zionism, divided Jewish immigrants, old and new, into numerous conflicting camps.

Internal divisions based on regional and local origins plagued the Italians even more. Membership in mutual-benefit societies was often limited to those from the same place in Italy. Family loyalties were so intense and exclusive that the Italians created few other institutions. Although they were nominally Roman Catholics, even their religious piety focused upon the local patron saint, whose annual *festa* was the year's high point. Their alleged religious indifference attracted Protestant proselytizers and the disdain of ardent Irish Catholics. Like the Jews, many Italians were radicals (particularly syndicalists and anarchists) and

freethinkers. They were militant, they were active in the Industrial Workers of the World, and some anarchists resorted to violence. Most Italian immigrants remained unmoved by Italian nationalism. However, patriotic passions aroused by World War I evolved into a pro-Fascism that, despite the opposition of an anti-Fascist minority, dominated Italian American communities into the 1930s.

Beginning as unskilled laborers on the railroads and in mines and factories, Italian Americans rarely rose to the level of skilled workers. Exceptions were those with trades such as stonecutters, tailors, and barbers. Others engaged in petty commerce, providing goods and services in the Little Italy neighborhoods. The children normally left school at an early age. The second generation remained largely proletarian, although many moved into the ranks of skilled blue-collar workers. For Italian Americans, the breakthrough into the middle class was largely a post–World War II phenomenon.

Among the millions of Slavic immigrants from the German, Russian, and Austro-Hungarian empires, Poles were the most numerous. Largely unschooled peasants, they, too, entered the ranks of unskilled labor. Valued by employers for their brawn and reliability, Poles were largely employed in heavy industry: coal mining, meatpacking, steelmaking, and automobile manufacturing. Unlike the Italian and Jewish women who worked in sweatshops and tenements, Polish women more often were employed as domestics and factory hands. Densely populated "Poletowns," dotting the industrial heartland from Cleveland to Chicago and south to Pittsburgh, provided an environment in which Polishness prevailed. Dominated by Germans or Russians since Poland's partition in the eighteenth century, Polish immigrants shared the Irish sense of being a colonial people and similarly found a source of identity and resistance in the Catholic Church. Community and parish were congruent, and within both the priest acted as the accepted leader.

The immigrants' Polish and Catholic identities sometimes clashed, however—resulting, for example, in the formation of rival fraternal organizations, one nationalist, the other religious. Opposition to control by an Irish American Catholic hierarchy gave rise to bitter conflicts and even a schismatic church, the Polish National Catholic Church. World War I catalyzed Polish American nationalism and contributed greatly to Poland's reunification.

Though fewer in number than the Poles, Slovaks shared a common experience. They, too, began work at the bottom of the economic ladder, often in steel factories such as those in Pittsburgh. Life could be dangerous in such occupations. They developed fraternal orders to help pay for injury or death on the job. These payments were rather modest, however. Their churches, whether Lutheran or Catholic, offered spiritual help, but most immigrants found themselves in a land where the state did not support churches. Thus they had to contribute to build churches and their charities. One way for immigrants to make extra money was to take in boarders, a common practice among immigrants. Boarders were often male relatives, but complete strangers were welcome during hard times. For the women keeping the boarders, life could be exceedingly difficult. Slavic immigrant widows faced limited prospects for making a living in their new land, so operating a boardinghouse was perhaps their best alternative.

This era also marked the first wave of immigrants from the Middle East, including Armenians. American Protestant missionaries, of whom there were many in the Middle East in the late nineteenth century, often encouraged people to seek a better life in America. Armenians in particular clung to their churches in America, but many of the Syrian-Lebanese blended with other Christians and often converted to Catholicism. Because the Syrian-Lebanese peddled goods throughout the United States, they formed communities in many areas, not necessarily in the large urban centers of so many immigrants.

The tide of new immigrants evoked anxieties among Anglo-Americans and calls for greater immigration restriction. To the fears of Roman Catholicism and immigrant radicalism was now added the menace of biological pollution. In the late nineteenth century, "scientific" racialism based on eugenics and an assumed hierarchy of races (Nordics, those from northern Europe, being the superior race) became a major tenet of Anglo-American nationalism, justifying imperialism abroad and immigration restriction at home. The influx of southern and eastern Europeans and Asians—people of supposedly inferior racial stock—triggered a nativist campaign against what were called "undesirable and dangerous immigrants."

Already in the 1880s, along with entrance requirements—the Chinese Exclusion Act, passed in 1882 and made permanent in 1902—a second law had established health and moral standards for admission. In 1892, Upper New York Bay's Ellis Island became the main federal immigrant-receiving station to screen immigrants arriving in steerage. For Asians, from 1910 onward Angel Island in San Francisco Bay was the place for screening. The Immigration Restriction League, founded in Boston in 1894, and the American Federation of Labor demanded even stricter immigration laws.

World War I intensified the anti-immigrant climate, with demands for "one hundred percent Americanism" and attacks upon "hyphenated Americans." Although this patriotic hysteria focused on German Americans, no foreigners were excluded. Germans, who had been admired for their contributions to science and medicine, became suspect. Linguistic and other aspects of ethnicity were suppressed or monitored by authorities and vigilante organizations.

In this atmosphere, the nativist agenda prevailed. Wartime laws against "seditious" organizations, publications, and expressions were aimed particularly at immigrant radicals who opposed the war. Domestic labor strife and Bolshevism abroad further fueled the 1919–1920 Red Scare, leading to the imprisonment of thousands of immigrants and the deportation of hundreds. The eugenic argument loomed especially large in public discussions and congressional debates. The immigration law of 1921 and the 1924 National Origins Act allocated quotas according to the criteria of allegedly superior and inferior races, favoring "Nordics" over "Alpines" and "Mediterraneans" and excluding almost all Asians. The Filipinos—90 percent of whom were young men—were not included in the laws of the 1920s, but in 1934 they were granted a quota of only fifty a year. These laws sought to protect the genetic character of the American people from foreign contamination.

The debate over immigration involved no less than the issue of what America as a nation was to become. Americans differed on the issue. Countering the xenophobia of the restrictionists, proponents of a liberal immigration policy cited Christian and democratic ideals of universal brotherhood and quoted Emma Lazarus's 1883 sonnet "The New Colossus," engraved on the Statue of Liberty, portraying the United States as an asylum for the oppressed. During much of the nineteenth century, Americans had generally believed that by some alchemy immigrants would be melded into a common national identity. Israel Zangwill's play *The Melting Pot* (1909) provided the metaphor for this assimilationist ideology. However, World War I and its aftermath caused many to question whether the world's "wretched refuse" could be transformed into worthy citizens. Others, including Horace Kallen and Randolph Bourne, had an antithetical vision, espousing what was called "cultural pluralism." But during

the 1920s, hard-line Americanizers held the upper hand, and coercive Americanization programs demanded total Anglo conformity.

1930–1960. During the 1930s, 1940s, and 1950s, only 4 million immigrants arrived, most after 1945. World War I, by interrupting transatlantic migration and creating an urgent demand for labor, had stimulated two alternative intracontinental migrations: African Americans from the rural South to the industrial North and Mexicans from south of the border. The National Origins Act did not apply to the Western Hemisphere because railroad and agricultural entrepreneurs convinced Congress that labor from south of the border was vital. Mexicans had long found employment in the agricultural fields and mines of the Southwest, but they now moved farther afield, to work on the railroads and in the packinghouses, steel mills, and automobile plants of the Midwest, establishing barrios in cities along the paths of migration. It was relatively easy for Mexicans to enter, even without immigration documents; there was no border patrol until 1924, and even then the border wardens were more interested in keeping out alcohol than in keeping out Mexican laborers. During the 1920s, as many Mexicans came illegally as came legally, that is, with documents. With the onset of the Depression of the 1930s, however, the government instituted a program of forced repatriation, sending hundreds of thousands, including native-born citizens, "home" to Mexico. Yet Mexico continued to supply a "reserve army of labor" for American industry and agriculture. Federal agencies encouraged Mexican workers with the World War II bracero program and then in the 1950s reinstituted mass deportations for those unable to become braceros. In its peak year, 1956, more than 450,000 braceros were recorded. The program ended in 1964. By then nearly 5 million braceros had worked in the United States. This figure did not mean 5 million different persons came north, as many braceros signed on for more than one work period. Officials estimated that 2.5 million actual persons had become braceros during the program's operation.

The Depression ended a century of increasing, if fluctuating, immigration. In some years during the 1930s, thanks to both widespread unemployment and strict enforcement of the quota system, more people left than entered the country. Even Jewish and other refugees desperately seeking asylum from fascist regimes were denied admission, partly because of virulent anti-Semitism.

The 1930s brought both heightened ethnic and racial conflict, as organized hate groups mimicked Europe's fascists, and also a blooming of cultural democracy. In literature, the arts, and popular culture, intellectuals and New Deal agencies celebrated American diversity. In *The Native's Return* (1934) and other writings, the Austrian immigrant Louis Adamic popularized the idea that immigrants were as fully American as those whose ancestors had arrived at Plymouth Rock.

The outbreak of World War II further limited traditional sources of immigration and led to a campaign of national unity under the slogan "Americans All." With few exceptions, immigrants and their descendants, along with African Americans, supported the war effort through military service and work in defense industries. Compared to World War I, this war saw less persecution of suspected "enemy aliens"—with one major exception: the confinement of some 112,000 Japanese Americans, including the American-born, in concentration camps, a policy clearly based on racial prejudice. A few German and Italian immigrants were also interned as enemy aliens.

With the end of World War II came the Cold War between the United States and the Soviet Union and an upsurge of anti-Communism that influenced American immigration policy

for half a century. Some post-1945 efforts were made to resettle millions of European refugees, but Congress belatedly admitted only a modest number of these displaced persons. It became a principle of America's Cold War immigration policy to admit persons fleeing Communist regimes, while excluding those escaping from sometimes brutal right-wing dictatorships. Thus Hungarians, Czechs, Cubans after Fidel Castro's rise to power, and Jews from the Soviet Union received preferential treatment. Cold War immigration policy also concentrated on deporting, denying visas to, or seizing the passports of persons who allegedly had "subversive" ideas or associations. Paul Robeson, W. E. B. Du Bois, Charlie Chaplin, Bertrand Russell, and many others fell afoul of these policies.

The Immigration and Nationality (McCarran–Walter) Act of 1952 embodied this anti-Communist bias. Although it eliminated the racialist constraints on Asian immigration and naturalization, the law perpetuated the national-origins system. Yet there were some indications that the restrictions of the 1920s were coming to an end. The acts related to refugees and displaced persons admitted more than 600,000 persons in excess of the national-origins quotas. Still others from war-ravaged nations with large quotas looked west for opportunity. The British establishment grew alarmed because so many well-educated English were heading west; these English constituted the first wave of the "brain drain," which subsequently alarmed some Asian nations.

Moreover, the 1952 law offered Asians the right to immigrate and to become citizens, but it set a ceiling of only two thousand visas for all Asian nations. Asians who married American servicemen were exempt from the limit, as were refugees. The process of exemption began for Chinese women when Congress passed the War Brides Act in 1945 and then amended it to include Chinese women. In 1965 when Congress passed the Hart–Celler Act that scrapped the national-origins system, the number of Asians admitted was twenty thousand, ten times the number set by the McCarran–Walter Act. The 1952 law also included special provisions for screening out "subversives" and deporting immigrants—even those who became U.S. citizens—who belonged to suspected Communist organizations.

1960 Onward. Thus, in spite of the tight restrictions enacted after 1945, U.S. policy drifted toward a more liberal immigration system. The 1960s brought many changes in American society, including rejection of the "melting pot" ideal and the affirmation of particularistic identities, initially by African Americans and then by other racial and ethnic groups. This process of ethnicization, a revolt against Anglo-American conformity and dominance, affirmed the survival, despite assimilationist pressures, of cultural memories, forms, and communities stemming from the great migrations of the past. Native Americans, Chicanos, Asian Americans, and groups of people of European descent (labeled "white ethnics") celebrated their distinctive heritages and mobilized politically. Such manifestations of ethnicity among second- and third-generation European Americans, people thought to have been thoroughly assimilated, surprised scholars and policy makers.

After the 1970s the ideology of multiculturalism, celebrating racial and ethnic differences, proved profoundly influential, but it also encountered vigorous opposition from political and religious champions of "traditional values." The resulting culture wars were exacerbated by an explosive growth in immigration in the wake of the 1965 immigration act, which had substantially altered the rules for entry. This law eliminated the national-origins quota system and established preferences favoring relatives of U.S. citizens or of resident aliens, persons with particular skills and talents, and refugees

from Communist countries or the Middle East. The law's annual caps on immigration were soon exceeded because of the principle of family reunification and special provisions for refugees. To win eradication of national origins, lawmakers were forced to place a limit of 120,000 for the Western Hemisphere. A little-debated provision of the act was for immediate family members of U.S. citizens to enter above the quotas. These exceptions were expected to total only 40,000 to 50,000 a year but were running well over 400,000 a year in the 2000s. In that decade, immediate family members (defined as spouses, minor children, and parents of adult U.S. citizens) accounted for nearly one half of all immigrants.

The limits on the Western Hemisphere, largely directed at growing Hispanic immigration to America, quickly broke down. A special act for Cubans in 1966, an amnesty for nearly 3 million illegal immigrants in 1986, and further increases in immigration in the Immigration Act of 1990 opened the golden door wider. Yet even as legal immigration surged, exceeding 1 million a year by the 1990s, also every year an estimated several hundred thousand undocumented immigrants filtered through the country's porous borders. The 1986 law for an amnesty was coupled with provisions against hiring undocumented immigrants, but the outlawing of illegal immigrants in the workplace was not tightly enforced. Moreover, the federal government gave states money to help the illegal immigrants obtain amnesty. As a result of federally subsidized language and educational programs, one third of those receiving the amnesty became citizens by 2000, and as citizens, they could in turn bring their immediate families to join them in the United States. Not since early in the century had immigrants arrived in such numbers, totaling as many as 30 million from 1970 to 2010. The decade from 2000 to 2010 was a record one for immigration: more than 10 million newcomers arrived then, more than had arrived in any other decade in American history. By opening America's doors to southern and eastern Europeans, Asians, and Africans, the 1965 act permitted thousands of Portuguese, Greeks, and Italians to immigrate to the United States, but within a few years the historical pattern of a predominantly European immigration was reversed. The great majority of post-1965 immigrants—more than 80 percent of the total—arrived from Asia and Latin America, with Mexicans, Chinese, Filipinos, and Koreans among the largest contingents. Increasing numbers also arrived from Central America, the Caribbean, the Middle East, and Africa.

Like so many in the past, most immigrants to the United States wanted to better their economic position. Yet many fled in terror. Many Central Americans had lived with daily violence, and so they were willing to take their chances even if they lacked immigration papers. Other immigrant refugees entered under government-sponsored refugee programs. The most numerous were South Asian refugees from the violent Vietnam War that ended in a Communist victory in 1975. Others came as refugees from Africa or eastern Europe before the collapse of Communism in 1989.

But the bulk of refugees, like those entering under the family-unification provisions of the law, looked for better opportunities in America. The post-1965 immigrants were as diverse socially and economically as they were ethnically and racially.

Included among their elite were Asian Indians (often doctors), Pakistanis, Europeans, Chinese, Filipinos, and, in later years, Africans. These newcomers were often connected to American medicine, high-tech firms, and businesses. The Koreans, for example, included a number of college graduates who went into businesses in the United States, running green-groceries, dry cleaners, and nail salons. On the whole they did well economically, and the Indian doctors fared even better. Scarcely any

hospital in a major American city did not have some Indians and Pakistanis on the staff. The highly skilled and highly paid newcomers integrated smoothly into upper- and middle-class American life, residing in ethnically diverse suburbs with good schools. But by no means did all Asians fare well. South Asian refugees often had a difficult time finding employment in the American economy; many South Asian women replaced Korean women in nail salons, which paid low wages. Among Chinese women, the primary employment for those who lacked English was in the garment industry, where sweatshops beckoned. Many other Asians, speaking English poorly, could find employment only in Chinese and other Asian restaurants that dotted the landscape. In one way the latest immigrants from Asia differed from their predecessors: they were willing to settle in areas where few had gone before. By 1990, 20 percent of Asian immigrants were settling in the South.

Also at the bottom of the economic ladder were Hispanics, many of whom worked in construction or as farmworkers, landscapers, and day laborers. The women cleaned motels, hotels, and homes. If the immigrants lacked education and English-language skills, only low-paying jobs in the growing service economy offered employment.

The movement of Hispanics out of the Southwest, especially California and Texas, accelerated. New York City claimed few Mexican citizens in 1980, but by 2010 the figure approached 300,000. States such as Nevada, North Carolina, Iowa, and Georgia had only small pockets of Hispanics before the 1970s, but by the early 2000s their Hispanic populations exploded, with Hispanics increasingly finding work in the states' meatpacking and chicken-processing plants.

Yet immigrants were hardly bipolar, either elite or poor. A rising middle class found employment in small businesses or in the white-collar service sectors. West Indians, for example, were particularly prominent in health care, filling the ranks of big-city nurses.

An important part of the immigrant experience, whether of the high-skilled or the low-skilled, remained the sending of remittances back home to aid friends and families. The World Bank estimated in 2010 that more than $300 billion was sent across borders in that year. From the United States to Mexico alone, remittances totaled more than $20 billion. These figures were underestimates. In the modern global economy, immigrants were able to travel cheaply by air and to use modern communication to keep in touch with events at home. Often they returned with money.

The post-1965 immigration shook the American kaleidoscope, producing a dramatic reconfiguration of ethnicities. The range of skin hues expanded (some called it the "browning of America"); the country's linguistic, musical, and culinary repertoire grew; and new forms of worship enriched the religious spectrum. The umbrella labels "Hispanic" and "Asian" obscured an extraordinary diversity: Spanish-speaking immigrants included several million each of Puerto Ricans (who are U.S. citizens), Mexicans, and Caribbean islanders, while Chinese, Filipino, Korean, Asian Indian, and Southeast Asian (Vietnamese, Cambodians, Hmong, and Laotians) immigrant groups each totaled a million or more. A less noted influx brought several million Arabic, Persian, and African speakers from Lebanon, Jordan, Syria, Iran, Nigeria, Somalia, and Ethiopia. With perhaps 3 million Muslims and five hundred thousand each of Buddhists and Hindus, the familiar Protestant–Catholic–Jewish triad no longer adequately described the American religious scene.

Many Americans viewed the changes with alarm. But proposals to reduce legal immigration failed. By the mid-1990s the debate centered on illegal immigration. After the terrorist attacks of 11 September 2001, Congress provided the newly created Department of Homeland Security with funds to increase the border patrol and to build fences along the border with Mexico. But these measures were costly and not entirely effective. Adding to the woes of the border patrol were the 3 million Mexicans who held Border Crossing Cards that enabled them to visit the United States for three days to visit family and friends and to shop: many likely worked during those three days. The border patrol also had to examine persons who held American green cards and citizenship who were allowed to live in Mexico and cross daily to their jobs in the United States. In all, the human traffic—to say nothing of trucks carrying goods—amounted to more than 200 million crossings each year. Moreover, 40 million persons—as students, temporary workers, businessmen and businesswomen, and tourists—entered the United States in 2010, and the immigration system did not know how many actually left and how many stayed beyond the date of their visa. Internally, the immigration authorities were active in deporting those persons who lacked immigration papers or were legal immigrants who had run afoul of the law. Deportations steadily increased; they numbered roughly 400,000 in 2010. Many state and local governments cooperated with the federal authorities in identifying persons who broke the law, but others did not. Of course, the American economy also played a role; during the recession of the late 2000s, persons wanting to enter illegally found their employment prospects dismal.

In sum, the foreign-born had grown conspicuously present at all levels. But immigrants of rural or working-class backgrounds experienced greater adjustment difficulties and sought security among their own kind. At the bottom of the ethnic-class hierarchy, they competed with disadvantaged native-born Americans for jobs, housing, and welfare benefits. In fact, the availability of cheap Asian and Hispanic labor resulted in a revival of sweatshops in manufacturing. Since the economy no longer needed armies of workers to build railroads, mine coal, and tend machines, new arrivals often found traditional entry-level jobs unavailable and instead took work in agriculture, construction, and low-wage service positions at hotels and restaurants. In many respects their experience mirrored that of the Europeans who had preceded them. Families and clans settled in particular locations, creating new ethnic neighborhoods with specialty food shops, churches, temples, mosques, cultural centers, and publications. Constructing new ethnic identities, they created self-help and political organizations. And as before, ethnic animosities and generational conflicts often made the process of adjustment painful. Hispanics were particularly noticeable in Catholic churches, where they accounted for roughly 40 percent of the membership in a church that lacked Spanish-speaking priests. Where Koreans settled, there was sure to be a Protestant church. Just as striking were the growing religious affiliations of Hindus, Buddhists, and especially Muslims, groups that had only tiny memberships before World War II.

Although the cumulative impact of 39 million new immigrants had profound implications for the nation's future, grim forebodings about an "unprecedented immigrant invasion" seemed exaggerated. The *rate* of immigration—the number of immigrants as a percentage of the total population—was 10 per thousand in the 1900s but only 3.5 per thousand in the 1980s. And although the number of foreign-born people reached an all-time high by 2010, they accounted for slightly less than 13 percent of the population, as compared with 14.7 percent in 1910. Yet in 1970 the foreign-born had accounted for less than 5 percent of the American people; by the turn of the twenty-first century, clearly the trend was toward immigrants playing an increasing role in American society.

All these different peoples—their different languages and cultures, as well as their numbers—spawned a neo-nativist reaction. Those wanting immigration restrictions insisted that the high birthrates of the newcomers, along with their accounting for much more than 12 or 13 percent of people under the age of twenty-one, indicated a perilous future. Though eschewing explicit racialism, advocates of immigration restriction expressed anxiety that the immigrants posed a threat to the homogeneity of the United States. Projecting immigration and birthrates forward, some demographers predicted that the people called "minorities"—persons of American Indian, African, Asian, and Hispanic ancestry—would make up more than half of the American population by 2050 and that the United States would thus cease to be a predominantly white society. But because intermarriage rates are so high, and the economy is as difficult to predict as congressional laws are, what this means cannot be ascertained precisely.

The 1990 U.S. Census underscored the reality of ethnic diversity in America. The 90 percent who responded to a question about ancestry or ethnic origin were classified into 215 ancestry groups. The largest was German, followed by Irish, English, and African American; next came Italian, Mexican, French, Polish, American Indian, Dutch, and Scotch-Irish. Another twenty-one groups accounted for more than a million each, and even many smaller groups had sizable representations: Maltese, Basque, Rom, Wendish, Paraguayan, Belizean, Guyanese, Yemini, Khmer, and Micronesian, among others. Like glacial terminal moraines, these population groups represented deposits resulting from four centuries of immigration. The 2000 census allowed a place for multiracialism, but its estimate of 3 percent was obviously much too low.

Bilingualism became a lightning rod for nativist anxieties in the 1990s. Some groups, deploring schools' bilingual programs and the use of foreign languages in official documents as threats to the nation's cultural and political integrity, lobbied for a constitutional amendment making English America's official language. Innocent of the country's linguistic history, proponents of this reform asserted that earlier immigrants had speedily and gladly learned and used English and that new immigrants must do likewise. Proponents of bilingualism responded that coerced linguistic conformity violated the rights of non-English speakers and was in any case unnecessary, given the overwhelming dominance of English. The struggle over language, symptomatic of broader ideological and political conflict, seemed sure to continue.

Despite the neo-nativism, the newcomers generally received a more cordial welcome than Japanese or Greeks did at the turn of the twentieth century. In contrast to earlier eras' laissez-faire attitude, public programs and voluntary agencies provided assistance and social services to newcomers. Further, federal policies and Supreme Court decisions regarding bilingualism, voting rights, and affirmative action legitimized ethnic pluralism. Multiculturalism, a loosely defined movement to make American culture and institutions fully representative of the country's increasing diversity, influenced popular consciousness. Although racism and xenophobia persisted, Americans in the twenty-first century appeared more accepting and even appreciative of racial and ethnic differences. What would happen if massive immigration continued and the economy remained weak, or if fears of biological or ideological contamination revived, remained to be seen.

[*See also* **Braceros; Capitalism and Immigration; Immigration-Restriction Laws; Indentured Labor; Racism;** *and* **Trade Policy, Federal.**]

BIBLIOGRAPHY

Barkan, Elliott Robert. *From All Points: America's Immigrant West, 1870s–1952.* Bloomington: Indiana University Press, 2007.

Daniels, Roger. *Coming to America: A History of Immigration and Ethnicity in American Life.* 2d ed. New York: Perennial, 2002.

Foner, Nancy. *From Ellis Island to JFK: New York's Two Waves of Immigration.* New Haven, Conn.: Yale University Press, 2000.

Gleason, Philip. *Speaking of Diversity: Language and Ethnicity in Twentieth-Century America.* Baltimore: Johns Hopkins University Press, 1992.

Hatton, Timothy J., and Jeffrey G. Williamson. *Global Migration and the World Economy: Two Centuries of Policy and Performance.* Cambridge, Mass.: MIT Press, 2005.

Higham, John. *Strangers in the Land: Patterns of American Nativism, 1860–1925.* 2d ed. New Brunswick, N.J.: Rutgers University Press, 1992.

Jacobson, Matthew Frye. *Whiteness of a Different Color: European Immigrants and the Alchemy of Race.* Cambridge, Mass.: Harvard University Press, 1998.

Martin, Susan F. *A Nation of Immigrants.* Cambridge, U.K.: Cambridge University Press, 2011.

Reimers, David M. *Other Immigrants: The Global Origins of the American People.* New York: New York University Press, 2005.

Roediger, David R. *How America's Immigrants Became White: The Strange Journey from Ellis Island to the Suburbs.* New York: Basic Books, 2005.

Takaki, Ronald. *Strangers from a Different Shore: A History of Asian Americans.* Boston: Little, Brown, 1989.

Vecoli, Rudolph J., and Suzanne M. Sinke, eds. *A Century of European Migrations, 1830–1930.* Urbana: University of Illinois Press, 1991.

Waters, Mary C., and Reed Ueda, eds. *The New Americans: A Guide to Immigration since 1965.* Cambridge, Mass.: Harvard University Press, 2007.

Zolberg, Aristide R. *A Nation by Design: Immigration Policy in the Fashioning of America.* New York: Russell Sage Foundation, 2006.

David M. Reimers

IMMIGRATION-RESTRICTION LAWS

Prior to 1875, the United States did not restrict immigration on the basis of nationality or race; however, in response to an increase in Chinese migration to America, a rising demand for laborers to work in growing industries after the Civil War, and concerns of unfair job competition between white workers and Asian immigrants, the United States began to prohibit Asian migration beginning in 1882 with the first Chinese Exclusion Act. Although the U.S. Congress passed several laws that restricted or prohibited migration for a wide variety of groups during the years between the end of the Civil War and World War II, such legislation especially targeted Asian immigrants, particularly Chinese and Japanese laborers.

The Chinese. Asian migration to the United States rose sharply during the nineteenth century, with many immigrants from China arriving in California to work in mining fields during the gold rush (1848–1855). Though at first California welcomed the Chinese miners as a source of tax revenue, hospitality turned to hostility when opportunities for mining diminished. Then between 1864 and 1869, as entrepreneurs sought to build the federally subsidized transcontinental railroad, the Chinese sought employment in railroad construction. Fearing job competition from Chinese workers and lowered wages, white American laborers on the West Coast criticized employers who hired Asian immigrants, used violence and intimidation against the Chinese, and ultimately called on senators, representatives, and governors to prohibit the flow of Chinese immigrants to the United States. Although the Page Act of 1875 already denied entrance both to Asian women suspected of prostitution and to any Asian migrant suspected of being a

contract or "coolie" laborer, the push from white laborers for complete exclusion created an increased demand for stronger federal action in restricting Chinese migration. Denis Kearney, leader of the Workingman's Party—a labor organization that Kearney formed in the 1870s to protest the Central Pacific Railroad's hiring of Chinese immigrants—used the anti-Chinese sentiment of the white workers to urge California and national politicians to end Chinese migration to the United States.

The result of Kearney's and the white laborers' protests was the Chinese Exclusion Act of 1882, which prohibited all Chinese laborers from entering the United States and was to remain in force for ten years; Congress renewed the act in both 1892 and 1902 and ultimately did not repeal Chinese exclusion until 1943. The act had lasting effects on both the Chinese population in the United States and labor. Riots and violence against the Chinese and particularly against Chinese laborers continued after Congress passed the act, and as a result many Chinese, fleeing the anti-Asian sentiment of white workers in rural areas, moved to urban Chinatowns. As demand for agricultural and industrial labor remained strong on the West Coast and law made Chinese workers less available, employers turned to a new labor pool: the Japanese.

The Japanese. During the late nineteenth century, Japanese immigrants migrated to Hawai'i, California, and other West Coast areas in larger numbers to work primarily as agricultural laborers, and many came to rent or to purchase their own farmland. Soon anti-Japanese violence and discrimination broke out among white workers on the West Coast. The United States and Japan attempted to negotiate immigration restrictions, most notably with the gentlemen's agreement of 1907, in which Japan agreed to prohibit Japanese workers from migrating to the United States in return for equal and fair treatment of Japanese citizens in America. But nevertheless Congress responded to anti-Japanese and anti-Asian violence and discrimination on the West Coast with the Immigration Act of 1917.

Also known as the Asiatic Barred Zone Act, the Immigration Act of 1917 prevented any person from an Asian nation—excluding Filipinos, who were technically American colonial subjects at the time, and Japanese wives and children, who were protected by the gentlemen's agreement—from settling in America. (The act also denied entrance to the mentally and physically ill, criminals, and the illiterate.) With practically all other Asian groups excluded from the United States, employers used the Japanese and Filipinos as cheap sources of labor and a means to prevent solidarity and unionizing among white workers. Ethnic tensions between the Japanese and Filipinos also led to competition between the two groups in the workforce.

Following the 1917 Immigration Act, pressure from citizens, politicians, and anti-immigrant groups prompted Congress to pass the 1921 Immigration Act, also known as the Emergency Quota Act. Using data from the 1910 U.S. Census, this act established that the number of people admitted from each sending country could be equal to just 3 percent of the number of immigrants from that country already living in the United States. The 1924 Immigration Act, also known as the National Origins Act or the Asian Exclusion Act, lowered the quota cap to 2 percent and completely excluded immigrants from all Asian nations, including Japan.

Filipinos. Although immigrants from Japan were barred, because the Philippine Islands remained a territory of the United States and therefore technically not an Asian country, the United States still allowed Filipinos to enter the United States. By the 1920s, thousands of Filipino men migrated to the United States in search of work. Demand for workers in the salmon-canning industries of Alaska and the state of Washington, as well as in migratory field labor in California, provided opportunities for Filipinos. Employers hired Filipinos as strikebreakers during labor disputes and to incite ethnic tensions among white and Mexican workers.

Though the Immigration Act of 1924 remained in effect during the 1920s and 1930s, Congress began to repeal the Asian exclusion acts during and following World War II. By the mid-1960s, Congress lifted the ban on immigration from the Asiatic Barred Zone and removed nationality quotas with the Immigration and Nationality Act of 1965.

[*See also* **Braceros; Capitalism and Immigration; Immigration; Migratory Labor and Migrant Workers; Racism;** *and* **Sandlot Riots and Anti-Chinese Movement.**]

BIBLIOGRAPHY

Higham, John. *Strangers in the Land: Patterns of American Nativism, 1860–1925.* 2d ed. New Brunswick, N.J.: Rutgers University Press, 1992.

Lee, Erika. *At America's Gates: Chinese Immigration during the Exclusion Era, 1882–1943.* Chapel Hill: University of North Carolina Press, 2003.

Ngai, Mae M. *Impossible Subjects: Illegal Aliens and the Making of Modern America.* Princeton, N.J.: Princeton University Press, 2004.

Takaki, Ronald. *Strangers from a Different Shore: A History of Asian Americans.* Rev. ed. New York: Little, Brown, 1998.

Stephanie Hinnershitz

INDENTURED LABOR

Indentured labor or servitude, which had appeared in colonial America by 1620, was developed by the Virginia Company as a means to connect the English labor supply to colonial demand. Most hired labor in preindustrial England was performed by servants in husbandry— youths who lived and worked in the households of their masters on annual contracts. Since passage fares to America were high relative to the earnings of these servants, few could afford the voyage. The Virginia Company's solution was to pay the passage of prospective laborers who contracted to repay this debt from their earnings in America.

This arrangement was soon adopted by merchants in England's ports, as migrants signed indentures that the merchants sold to colonial planters upon the servants' arrival in America. Servitude became a central labor institution in early English America: between one half and two thirds of all white immigrants to the British colonies arrived under indenture. Indentured servitude therefore enabled between 300,000 to 400,000 Europeans to migrate to the New World. Unmarried men predominated among the servants throughout the Colonial Era. Most were in their late teens or early twenties—the same ages that were prevalent among servants in husbandry in England.

Indentured servants were most important in the early history of those regions that produced staple crops for export, particularly the sugar islands of the West Indies and the tobacco colonies on the Chesapeake Bay. Over time, as colonial conditions for servants deteriorated and economic conditions improved in England, attracting indentured workers to these colonies became more difficult. Planters increasingly found African slaves a less expensive source of labor and responded by substituting slaves for servants.

Some historians have characterized the indenture system as debased and the servants who participated in it as disreputable. Yet indentured workers were governed by the same basic legal conditions that English farm servants were, and studies of emigration lists have

shown that the servants were drawn, not from England's poorest or least-skilled workers, but rather from a broad cross section of English society. Historians have also argued that servants were exploited economically by English merchants. Yet the servants' long terms did not imply exploitation, for the large debt for passage meant that repayment would necessarily take longer than the standard single year worked by farm servants in England. Analysis of collections of contracts has further revealed that more-productive servants received shorter terms, evidently because they could repay their debts more quickly. Servants bound for colonial destinations that were less desirable also received shorter terms. Competition among merchants thus protected servants from economic exploitation.

[*See also* **Agricultural Workers; Alien Contract Labor Law; Apprenticeship Systems; Capitalism and Immigration; Immigration; Labor Markets; Master and Servant Law;** *and* **Slavery.**]

BIBLIOGRAPHY

Galenson, David W. *White Servitude in Colonial America: An Economic Analysis,* Cambridge, U.K.: Cambridge University Press, 1981.

Smith, Abbot Emerson. *Colonists in Bondage: White Servitude and Convict Labor in America, 1607–1776.* Chapel Hill: University of North Carolina Press for the Institute of Early American History and Culture, Williamsburg, Va., 1947.

David W. Galenson

INDUSTRIAL DEMOCRACY

Industrial democracy offers the promise for workers of greater control over their working lives. Employers have also supported forms of industrial democracy to improve worker morale and productivity. Industrial democracy can have a variety of implications for capitalism. Workers' control through workers' cooperatives, in which workers owned the business, challenged the traditional notion of the capitalist firm and could ultimately supplant it. Other forms of industrial democracy are less challenging for capitalism. Representative or indirect forms of industrial democracy include works councils and joint consultation, during which representatives of workers and managers sit and discuss problems. These can be nonunion, as with the employee representation plan (ERP), or have union involvement. In the United States the term "industrial democracy" also refers to collective bargaining, in which employers recognize unions and negotiate a collective agreement that covers wages and working conditions. Direct forms of industrial democracy focus on the way work is organized at the workplace level: these can include team-focused work and semiautonomous work groups. Financial forms of industrial democracy focus on the way financial rewards are distributed through employee stock ownership and profit sharing. The terms "employee democracy," "employee involvement," and "employee consultation" are used interchangeably with "industrial democracy."

Early Initiatives. Within the U.S. trade union movement and among socialists in the last half of the nineteenth century, there were diverging views of the meaning of industrial democracy, and the term only rarely appeared in print before the 1890s. Whereas socialists and syndicalists favored producer cooperatives, Samuel Gompers, the president of the American Federation of Labor (AFL), and craft unions generally rejected the radicals' arguments and claimed that workers could obtain a voice in the workplace, achieve industrial democracy, and ameliorate the worst conditions of capitalism through organizing into trade unions and bargaining collectively.

Though U.S. employers generally believed that they had the right to run their own business as they saw fit, there were some who advocated approaches to industrial democracy to improve industrial life. In 1878, Abram Hewitt, a New York iron manufacturer, advocated "joint ownership" with workers through employee stock ownership and profit sharing. He was sympathetic to craft unionism, and in the wake of the Great Railroad Strike of 1877, he believed that industrial conflict could be minimized and even avoided through a recognition of the mutual interests of labor and business. Over the next few decades, employers showed a growing interest in profit sharing: the Association for the Promotion of Profit Sharing, for instance, was formed in 1892.

ERPs versus Union-Management Cooperation. From 1914 until 1935, there were two main approaches to industrial democracy: the ERP and union-management cooperation. Funded by the employer, ERPs were joint committees made up of representatives of employees and management that discussed a range of issues including wages and conditions, safety and accidents, and company housing. Workers could appeal to various levels of company management, and there was even a provision in some ERPs for appeal to an external court if mediation failed. The company paid for all costs associated with the plan, including reimbursement for the loss of work time by employee representatives. The promoters of ERPs viewed them as alternatives to both individual contracts and independent trade unions. John D. Rockefeller Jr. initially championed ERPs as a solution to labor problems at Colorado Fuel and Iron Company following the Ludlow massacre in Colorado in 1914.

The ERPs spread beyond Colorado Fuel and Iron to a range of industries in the United States.

The U.S. entry into World War I in April 1917 assisted the spread of ERPs. War production and a decline in net immigration led to labor shortages. There was labor unrest owing to inflation and a deterioration of shop-floor conditions. Labor turnover doubled, and the number of strikes dramatically increased. Management wanted to obtain employee goodwill and minimize the intervention of the state and trade unions. The wartime sentiment that favored making the world "safe for democracy" led to an increase in public favor for industrial democracy at home. Business also feared the growing appeal to workers of radical alternatives such as socialism and the Industrial Workers of the World. Of the 225 ERPs surveyed in 1919 by the National Industrial Conference Board, 120 arose through the intervention of the federal government, and companies voluntarily introduced 105. Employers saw employee representation as a welcome substitute for bargaining collectively with unions.

Although the number of companies with plans or a company union declined in the late 1920s, the number of employees covered by the plans continued to increase: the plans covered almost 1.6 million workers in 1928. Although state intervention in U.S. industrial relations declined and the trade union challenge diminished with an economic downturn in 1920–1921, employers continued to see ERPs as a valuable device for avoiding unions. Alongside this, there was a greater interest in more sophisticated personnel management practices to improve worker commitment, morale, and productivity. The founders of the personnel management movement called for a recognition of the "human factor" and a more systematic approach to labor management. Some large companies, such as U.S. Steel, rejected ERPs and favored stock ownership, believing that representation of any kind would ultimately lead to a union or closed shop. Judge Elbert Gary of U.S. Steel also argued that ERPs failed to prevent labor unrest—as highlighted by the employee walkout at the Pueblo steel plant of Colorado Fuel and Iron during the 1919 steel strike.

Ongoing debate occurred within the labor movement concerning alternatives to the ERPs. Groups such as the Industrial Workers of the World called for shop committees and works councils, in which workers rather than managers took the initiative in increasing production and even ultimately transformed capitalism into socialism. The Plumb plan, conceived by Glenn Plumb, an Illinois attorney who represented the railway unions at the end of World War I, would have nationalized the railways and administered them through a tripartite commission made up of representatives of the public, railway management, and employees. The advocates of the Plumb plan, who believed that the idea was applicable to all industry, drew links to guild socialism.

The AFL supported the moderate alternative of union–management cooperative committees. In organized workplaces with collective agreements, union representatives and managers met together on committees to discuss a range of issues that could eliminate waste, improve productivity, and enhance safety. Wages and working conditions were part of the collective-bargaining process between management and labor. Management under this scheme accepted trade unions as necessary and constructive in the running of their enterprise, while unions agreed to assist the companies in the marketing of their services and the winning of government contracts. Other objectives included the stabilization of employment and sharing the gains of cooperative management. Unlike in the ERPs, employees did not generally elect the representatives. Current union workplace representatives were the employee representatives on the cooperative committees. The unions' version of the cooperative plan contrasts with versions of the ERP set out by nonunion and indeed antiunion employers.

Though there were earlier examples of union–management cooperation, civil servants such as Otto Beyer and others who were serving in such agencies as the military arsenals and the United States Railroad Administration during and immediately after World War I promoted the concept. Beyer was strongly influenced by Whitleyism, a system devised by a wartime committee appointed by the British government to examine the improvement of labor relations. Whitleyism focused on industries in which labor was well organized and proposed industrial councils composed of employer and employee representatives. Similar committees at a local and workshop level would supplement the industrial council's activities. The industrial council could deal with or allocate to ancillary committees questions such as methods of fixing and adjusting earnings, technical education and training, and proposed legislation affecting industry.

The Beyer plan stalled during the economic downturn that followed World War I, but nevertheless Beyer gained support from William Johnston, the president of the International Association of Machinists (IAM), and Daniel Willard, the president of the Baltimore & Ohio Railroad (B&O). The B&O introduced workshop cooperative committees in February 1923. Cooperative management spread beyond the B&O but never achieved anything like the success of the ERP movement. Three other major U.S. railways adopted cooperative management and had varying degrees of success; the management of the Chesapeake & Ohio Railway, for example, introduced it into its workshops in Richmond, Virginia, in July 1924 but quickly lost interest. Outside the railway companies, a small but notable example was the Chicago firm of Yeomans Brothers, which adopted union–management cooperation in July 1930. The firm sold electric pumps for use in water supply and sewerage and was the only union shop in its industry at the time.

The fledgling movement built around cooperative management faced a number of barriers. One was opposition by rank-and-file union members. The idea was introduced in a top-down manner and was linked in some cases to wage cuts, layoffs, and work intensification. Union members faced restricted participation at the B&O: their participation was limited to the dissemination of the minutes of meetings. The Communist Trade Union Educational League, through factions in key unions such as the IAM, encouraged opposition. The 1930s Depression generally weakened cooperative management. It survived at the B&O but disappeared at other railways. The Chicago & North Western Railroad dropped the scheme in February 1932, later claiming that the reduction of the workforce and the curtailment of repair work meant that the scheme was no longer needed.

The Impact of the New Deal and Collective Bargaining.

Both the ERPs and union–management cooperation were challenged during the 1930s. Section 7(a) of President Franklin D. Roosevelt's National Industrial Recovery Act of June 1933 recognized that workers had the right to bargain and organize collectively through their own representatives without employer interference. Unionism took off, and employers rushed to set up ERPs to stop unions from organizing in their workplaces. Critics condemned these ERPs, as well as company unions generally, as sham organizations that impeded economic recovery, and they were outlawed in the National Labor Relations (Wagner) Act of 1935. A small number of ERPs evolved into independent local unions. The National Labor Relations Act not only eliminated ERPs, but also weakened unions' enthusiasm for cooperative management. Unions feared that the cooperative committees might weaken the trade union movement, and the legitimation of collective bargaining had made the committees redundant. Yet cooperative management continued at the B&O until 1962.

Though collective bargaining became the mainstream ideal of industrial democracy for the U.S. labor movement after the passage of the National Labor Relations Act, there still was some interest in pushing it beyond its traditional boundaries. In 1940, Philip Murray, then head of the Steel Workers Organizing Committee, and Morris Cooke, a consulting engineer and advocate of scientific management, proposed a form of industrial democracy that included the full sharing of business and industrial information and the seating of union officials on company boards of directors. Their proposal, which also called for close cooperation among labor, management, and government at the national level, was largely ignored. During World War II, approximately five thousand joint management–labor production committees were set up under federal government sponsorship to improve wartime morale and productivity. Only a few hundred had any impact, and virtually all of them disappeared at the end of the war.

During the late 1950s and 1960s, unions and management in such key industries as meatpacking, longshoring, and steel set up discussion committees to deal with issues such as technological changes. Management experimented with ideas such as rotating committees, which rotated membership and discussed workplace issues. These alternative forms of participation allowed for employee representation but inhibited wage bargaining and reduced the possibility of influence by national unions. However, the Supreme Court in the *Labor Board v. Cabot Carbon Co.* in 1959 ruled that an employee committee was a labor organization dominated by an employer and thus was in breach of the National Labor Relations Act. Most employers abandoned these committees and focused on team building and communication programs that were more individualized and based on the social sciences.

Developments since the 1980s. The decline of union membership and collective bargaining in the United States since the last decades of the twentieth century has led management to experiment with direct forms of industrial democracy. Though management has evinced interest in high-involvement and high-performance workplaces, the impact of management's experiments has been minimal and piecemeal. Some discussion has examined job redesign, which changes the nature of work organization and enables workers or groups of workers to exercise greater discretion in the way they conduct their work activities. A well-known example of this is New United Motor Manufacturing, Inc. (NUMMI), a joint venture between General Motors and Toyota, begun in 1984 and located at Fremont, California. With UAW participation, management set up a work system whereby workers were hired to work in teams that were responsible for planning and conducting work on a "continuous improvement" basis. Joint management–union committees chose the team leaders. Critics described the NUMMI scheme as "humanized Taylorism" because it failed to alter assembly-line work. There has also been a resurgence of interest in the long-standing idea of employee stock-ownership schemes. Support for employee stock-ownership plans (ESOPs) grew in the 1980s, and by the early twenty-first century they covered more than 11 million employees. As in the past, unions have criticized these schemes for creating an illusion of ownership—an illusion because they fail to give workers any greater control over the production process.

The calls for a greater use of direct-participation industrial democracy in the United States led to a movement to weaken the special role given to unions in the National Labor Relations

Act. An argument developed in the 1990s that legislation should allow industrial democracy to thrive particularly in the nonunion sector, because without unions, many workers no longer had a voice in the workplace. The Commission on the Future of Worker–Management Relations, established by the administration of Bill Clinton in March 1993, recommended the retention of the ban on company unions, but it called for the legalization of nonunion employee-participation programs. A minority report by labor representatives on the commission argued that "real industrial democracy" is not possible without an independent trade union movement and collective bargaining. Though the Clinton administration did not act upon the recommendations, a coalition of Republicans and conservative Democrats introduced legislation known as the Teamwork for Employees and Managers (TEAM) Act, which significantly weakened the relevant section of the National Labor Relations Act by allowing employees in nonunion firms to meet with management to discuss issues of mutual interest. The bill passed both houses of Congress in 1996, but President Clinton vetoed it.

[*See also* **Collective Bargaining; Company Unions; Cooperatives; Cooperatives and Worker Management; Employee Representation Plans; Industrial Relations; Labor Movements; National Labor Relations (Wagner) Act; Resistance to Management; Rockefeller Plan, The; Scientific Management; Welfare Capitalism;** *and* **Workers' Self-Management.**]

BIBLIOGRAPHY

Blasi, Joseph R., and Douglas L. Kruse. "The Political Economy of Employee Ownership in the United States: From Economic Democracy to Industrial Democracy?" *International Review of Sociology* 16 (2006): 127–147.

Derber, Milton. *The American Idea of Industrial Democracy, 1865–1965.* Urbana: University of Illinois Press, 1970.

Jacoby, Sanford M. "Current Prospects for Employee Representation in the U.S.: Old Wine in New Bottles?" *Journal of Labor Research* 16 (1995): 387–398.

Jacoby, Sanford M. "Union-Management Cooperation in the United States: Lessons from the 1920s." *Industrial and Labor Relations Review* 37 (1983): 18–33.

Lansbury, Russell D., and Nick Wailes. "Employee Involvement and Direct Participation." In *The SAGE Handbook of Industrial Relations*, edited by Paul Blyton, Nick Bacon, Jack Fiorito, and Edmund Heery, pp. 434–446. London: Sage, 2008.

Lichtenstein, Nelson, and Howell John Harris, eds. *Industrial Democracy in America: The Ambiguous Promise.* Cambridge, U.K.: Cambridge University Press, 1993.

Patmore, Greg. "Employee Representation Plans in the United States, Canada, and Australia." *Labor* 3 (2006): 41–65.

Vrooman, David M. *Daniel Willard and Progressive Management on the Baltimore & Ohio Railroad.* Columbus: Ohio State University Press, 1991.

Greg Patmore

INDUSTRIAL DESIGN

As industrialization accelerated and consumer goods proliferated after 1865, competition forced manufacturers to focus on product appearance. Ordinary citizens aspired to comfort, even luxury: patent furniture, lush domestic interiors, eclectic mail-order goods. New materials like celluloid simulated expensive ivory and tortoiseshell. Although an industrial-design profession did not exist in the late nineteenth century, the architect Frank Lloyd Wright articulated the principles of industrial design in 1901 by advising artists to abandon craft production and create prototypes for factory reproduction.

After 1900, manufacturers struggled to give form to electrical appliances, automobiles, and other new technologies. Consumers often demanded the future in the guise of the past. The "horseless carriage" was just one novelty whose acceptance depended in part on traditional associations. Engineers planning new products were uncertain how to proceed. Art schools trained applied artists to create commercial art and decorative furnishings but offered no training in new technologies. In the 1920s, some decorators adopted French "modernistic" styling to express the tempo of the machine age. Promoted by architects and museum curators, Art Deco reached industry in the later 1920s.

Industrial design emerged as a business response to the Great Depression, an application of the principles formulated by the efficiency expert Frederick W. Taylor. Commercial artists and stage designers turned to product design and employed streamlining as a comprehensive style for the machine age. Borrowed from aerodynamics, streamlining transformed automobiles, washing machines, and radios. For manufacturers it lubricated the flow of goods to consumers; for consumers it promised a future of material abundance. Consultant industrial designers such as Henry Dreyfuss, Norman Bel Geddes, Raymond Loewy, and Walter Dorwin Teague became celebrities. General Electric, Sears, Roebuck, and other companies established in-house design departments. Some designers sought to transform society, as at the utopian New York World's Fair of 1939, but more commercial considerations inspired Egmont Arens to describe his profession as "consumer engineering." During World War II, designers boosted morale by visualizing postwar products in magazine advertisements: prefabricated housing, bubble-domed automobiles, and push-button telephones. The profession became institutionalized in the American Designers Institute, founded in 1938, and the Society of Industrial Designers, founded

in 1944; in 1965 the two consolidated to form the Industrial Designers Society of America.

Beginning in the 1930s, art, business, and government contributed to a so-called high modernism that lasted into the 1960s. The Museum of Modern Art in New York City promoted a succession of noncommercial design statements: an abstract "machine art," a warmer "organic design," and a reformist "good design." Refugees from Nazism like László Moholy-Nagy brought to America the advanced ideas associated with the Bauhaus, the German school of design founded by Walter Gropius in 1919. Influenced by this climate of opinion, Walter Paepcke, president of the Container Corporation of America, supported Chicago's Institute of Design and established the Aspen Design Conference for business leaders and policy makers. Eero Saarinen and Charles and Ray Eames designed organic furniture for institutional and corporate America. George Nelson publicized high modernism through the journal *Industrial Design* and such official consumerist celebrations as the U.S. pavilion at the Brussels World's Fair in Belgium in 1958 and the Moscow trade fair in the Soviet Union in 1959.

"Good design" principles rarely inhibited profit-driven corporate marketers, however, whose approach was epitomized by the chrome-laden chariots produced by the postwar American automotive industry. Abandoning 1930s idealism, J. Gordon Lippincott's *Design for Business* (1947) insisted that industrial design existed only to increase a client's profits. Although well-trained designers graduated from many educational programs in the 1950s, few became consultants. Most joined in-house departments that treated design as cosmetic styling that often became anonymous, dull, and repetitive. Harley Earl's styling division at General Motors, founded in the late 1920s to rationalize planned obsolescence, introduced flaring tailfins and two-tone paint jobs that influenced the appearance of gas pumps, coffee tables, sectional sofas, and even suburban carports. Amoeba and boomerang shapes of the "populuxe" era reflected faith in scientific progress and a cornucopia of essentially disposable products.

Reactions against postwar excess, mirroring countercultural disgust with American affluence, often targeted industrial design. Victor Papanek's *Design for the Real World* (1972) dismissed much design as worthless and admonished designers to address the needs of poorer nations, the disabled, and the aging. Beginning in 1968, Stewart Brand's series titled the *Whole Earth Catalog* promoted decentralized living with limited reliance on technological systems. Such views contributed to subsequent environmentally sensitive "green design" and "eco design" movements. A series of expensive product-liability lawsuits forced corporations to adopt design awareness for safety as well as for profits.

Just as the 1930s Great Depression challenged designers to create a cohesive style for the machine age, the global competition of the 1980s and 1990s compelled designers to give shape to the hardware and immaterial software of the information age. Prophets of quality urged executives to upgrade design from its status as a cosmetic afterthought and to expand the designer's responsibility to encompass corporate strategy. The result was a design revival reminiscent of the 1930s—with its utopianism now based not on the machine but on flowing streams of electrons.

[*See also* **Advertising; Consumer Culture;** *and* **Mass Marketing.**]

BIBLIOGRAPHY

Fiell, Charlotte, and Peter Fiell. *Design of the 20th Century*. Cologne, Germany: Taschen, 1999.
Meikle, Jeffrey L. *Design in the USA*. London and New York: Oxford University Press, 2005.
Sparke, Penny. *As Long as It's Pink: The Sexual Politics of Taste*. London: Pandora, 1995.

Jeffrey L. Meikle

INDUSTRIALIZATION AND DEINDUSTRIALIZATION

The concept of industrialization encompasses the growth of manufacturing, the increased adoption of mechanical means of production and natural-resource forms of energy, the spread of the wage-labor system, and the advent of factory enterprise. Although industrial development in the United States dates to the 1820s, the process unfolded unevenly in different trades and regions at different times and rates. In the late twentieth century, with plant closings and significant losses in manufacturing jobs, the United States experienced industrial decline.

Before 1800, many manufactured goods—for example, garments, shoes, furniture, and tools—were produced in the home for direct family consumption. European settlers in North America also relied on British imports. Urban artisans produced elite custom goods based on venerable craft traditions and practices. In theory, British mercantile policies and prohibitions on colonial manufacture may have constrained manufacturing—and sparked grievances among the colonists—but in practice, a limited market, natural obstacles to transportation, and cheap imports effectively dampened colonial industrial progress.

Beginnings in the Early National Era. Despite their new nation's underdeveloped industry, Americans of the early national period vigorously debated the benefits and pitfalls of industrialization. Advocates such as Alexander Hamilton and the Pennsylvania political economist Tench Coxe argued that industrialization would ensure America's fiscal integrity and economic autonomy and eliminate idle labor. In the early 1790s, Coxe and Hamilton even promoted a failed experiment to build an industrial city in what later became Paterson, New Jersey. Thomas Jefferson and his allies, on the contrary, feared that a large, permanent class of factory workers would threaten a democratic republic based on virtuous yeoman producers and citizens.

This debate shaped but did not thwart industrialization, especially in textile production. U.S. textile manufacturing, benefiting from a period of extraordinary invention of textile machinery in Great Britain, followed four distinct paths.

In 1789, Samuel Slater immigrated to America from Great Britain fresh from an apprenticeship in a cotton textile mill. He was only the first of a cohort of immigrant British mechanics who brought new technologies. Financed by the Brown family of Providence, Rhode Island, Slater established the nation's first successful cotton mill in Pawtucket, Rhode Island, in 1793, and then built similar mill villages throughout southeastern New England. The villages were characterized by water-powered spinning mills operated by women and children, handloom weaving by men in company-provided houses, and company-established schools, churches, and stores. Spreading across the Northeast and the South, the company-owned mill village based on family labor became a basic component of American industrialization.

Francis Cabot Lowell of Massachusetts had a grander vision. After observing the latest technological developments in Britain, Lowell secured financial support from other Boston merchants and constructed a fully integrated and mechanized textile factory in Waltham, Massachusetts, in 1814. When waterpower there limited expansion, Lowell and his associates planned a large industrial works at the falls

of the Merrimack River, thirty-five miles north of Boston. Lowell died before the industrial city bearing his name was built.

Textile production at the Lowell mills represented a revolution in business practices, including the corporate form of ownership and the large amount of capital amassed; the concentration of all stages of production under a single roof, from the cleaning, carding, and spinning of raw fibers to the weaving and finishing of cloth; the application of technology, including fully mechanized power looms; the large scale of employment (by the 1850s, more than thirteen thousand workers labored in the city's fifty-two mills); and the encouragement of mass consumption as bolts of inexpensive broadcloth flowed from the mills. Lowell also entailed a remarkable human story, as young New England farm women came to work in the factories and reside in company boarding-houses. In the 1830s and 1840s, protesting deteriorating working conditions, they participated in the nation's earliest strikes by industrial workers.

Along with Lowell- and Slater-like mill villages, a third kind of industrial system, this one characterized by diversity and specialization, emerged in the larger cities. Textile production in Philadelphia, for example, involved the manufacture of fancy cloth in separate spinning, weaving, and finishing establishments. A vast array of products—from garments to jewelry, machine parts, fine surgical instruments, pottery, and paints—flowed from homes, sweatshops, craft shops, mills with hand-powered machinery, and more mechanized factories in the nation's metropolitan centers. The typical nineteenth-century manufacturing firm in New York City or Philadelphia was small to medium in size, was family owned and operated, produced small batches of quality or seasonal wares, and often relied on skilled labor. Insufficient waterpower, the presence of niche markets and skilled workers, and the technological know-how and entrepreneurialism of British and German immigrants all figured in the creation of an urban industrial base characterized by variety and small-scale modes of production.

The American South added a fourth strand to early American industrialization: industrial slavery. Before the Civil War, leased and directly owned African American slaves worked in southern textile factories, ironworks, tobacco-processing plants, and lumber and grain mills. However, the profitability of cotton plantation agriculture, coupled with white southerners' fears of forming a concentrated urban workforce of slaves and their preference for northern and imported manufactured goods, limited industrialization in the antebellum South. Investment flowed more readily into the purchase of land, cottonseed, and slaves than into industrial facilities.

Factors Influencing Industrial Development.

In the North and the South, population growth, abundant natural resources, prosperous agriculture, and an expanding market stimulated industrial development. Government played a minimal role. Though the federal, state, and local governments subsidized the building of canals and railroads, public moneys were not advanced toward manufacture. Protective tariffs remained a politically contentious issue, and in only a few areas, such as the iron and steel industries, did tariff protection significantly help domestic industries. The nation's political and legal system, however, did affect economic development. The U.S. Constitution, for example, established patent procedures that encouraged invention and reserved to the states substantive powers that included authority to charter businesses. Thus during the 1840s, states enacted general incorporation laws that promoted the corporate form of enterprise. Judicial decisions also fostered industrial expansion.

One seeming obstacle to industrial development, a relative scarcity of labor, especially skilled labor, actually proved an asset, motivating entrepreneurs to mechanize and to substitute capital for labor. In Lowell, for example, lacking a preexisting labor base, textile manufacture could be conducted only in fully mechanized ways. (Conversely, in places where skilled hands abounded, such as Philadelphia, handwork production persisted.) Similarly, with few skilled assemblers of guns available, federal arsenals and private companies pioneered in the mass production of standardized interchangeable parts that could be assembled by relatively unskilled labor. British investigators, impressed by the progress achieved in U.S. mass-production techniques in gun manufacture, clock making, sewing-machine production, and other trades, dubbed what they saw the "American system of manufactures."

Still, the so-called American system was slow in developing. In the late nineteenth century, U.S. factories still needed skilled assemblers to file and fit in place components that were less than precision-tooled. Only with the twentieth-century advent of conveyor-belt mass assembly, first in the automotive industry, did the system of interchangeable-parts production become fully realized.

Except in Lowell, U.S. industrial development encompassed older forms of production alongside new techniques. In Lynn, Massachusetts, the center of shoe manufacture, for example, shoes were first produced in homes through an outwork system; later, the attachment of the upper leathers to the soles moved into centralized handwork shops. Mechanized factories emerged by the mid-nineteenth century, but older work settings persisted.

Labor conflict also marked early American industrialization. Journeymen protested both the dilution of craft practices in artisan shops and also their subordination as wage laborers. In the new factories, industrial workers protested the harsh conditions of work. Women in particular led and participated in notable strikes in Lowell and Lynn.

Extraordinary Industrial Growth after the Civil War.

By the Civil War, industrialization had made great strides. Though the war was affected by industrialization—the accuracy of machine-tooled rifles increased casualties and altered military strategies—it did not modify the established path of economic growth. The post–Civil War era, however, saw extraordinary manufacturing growth, with a fivefold increase in output between 1870 and 1900, by which time 35 percent of the world's production of manufactured goods was pouring from U.S. factories, more than the combined output of Great Britain, Germany, and France.

This industrial growth was based primarily on more workers in more factories producing more goods, rather than on technological innovation or gains in productivity. The geographic expansion of industry in the late nineteenth century abetted the nation's rise to industrial supremacy. During this period, a wide manufacturing belt stretched from the Northeast to Chicago, extending southward to Ohio and Pittsburgh, Pennsylvania, the world's center for iron and steel production. Chicago, with its mechanized meatpacking and meat-processing plants, steel mills, and farm-machinery works, attracted the greatest attention, yet diversified industry flourished throughout the new industrial heartland. Philadelphia and New York City, with their shops, mills, and factories, remained major manufacturing centers, and textile production spread across New England. Wilmington, Delaware, became famous for gunpowder, leather tanning, and—somewhat later—chemicals; Trenton, New Jersey, for ceramic wares and wire cable; Paterson for silk cloth; Providence for machinery and jewelry; Troy, New York, for iron stoves; Rochester, New York, for photographic materials and equipment; Buffalo, New York, and Cleveland, Ohio, for steel; Cincinnati, Ohio, for soap; and Grand Rapids, Michigan, for furniture.

Firms of small to medium size dominated this Northeast and Midwest industrial belt, but a new kind of manufacturing concern emerged in the late nineteenth century, eventually to dominate the economic landscape: the large-scale, corporately owned, bureaucratically managed industrial enterprise. Several factors contributed to the rise of big business. A transcontinental railroad system created a national marketplace that heightened competition and encouraged manufacturing concerns to grow vertically, from accessing raw materials to distributing final products. Intense competition also led to a wave of corporate mergers and consolidations, including J. P. Morgan's amalgamation of key steel producers into the giant U.S. Steel Corporation in 1901. Finance capitalists encouraged mergers, because these capitalists profited by underwriting, issuing, and exchanging corporate securities. Those consolidated firms that created profitable economies of scale and scope through professional managerial structures justified the emergence of mammoth enterprises.

Labor Conflict in the Industrial Age.

Intense labor conflict accompanied the geographic and corporate manufacturing expansions of the late nineteenth century. Between 1880 and 1900, an average of more than a thousand strikes involving 200,000 workers, and ranging from crippling nationwide walkouts to local job actions, occurred. Workers struck for more than higher wages and shorter hours. The economic and political threat that giant corporations posed to belief in equality and yeoman producership fueled grievances and produced community support for workers' demands. The capricious rule of foremen in large enterprises generated strike activity and calls for union recognition, as well as union-determined work rules to ensure fairness and security.

The power of skilled workers over production processes proved another source of labor tension. Business executives attempted in various ways to assert greater managerial control over their skilled employees: through technology, embedding the production process in machines and measuring devices; through the principles of scientific management, set out by Frederick Winslow Taylor and others; and through concerted antiunion efforts. Two dramatic late nineteenth-century labor battles involved skilled workers. In Chicago in May 1886, conflict between managers and craft unionists at the McCormick Reaper Company coincided with a nationwide labor protest for an eight-hour workday; the McCormick strike presaged the Haymarket Square bombing and police riot. In July 1892, a decision by the steel magnate Andrew Carnegie and his chief associate, Henry Clay Frick, to eliminate craft unionism in Carnegie's steelworks in Homestead, Pennsylvania, led to a pitched battle between strikers and Pinkerton agents.

Not every firm dealt with labor tension through repressive tactics. Some tried to win their employees' loyalty through positive means. George Pullman, the manufacturer of the famed Pullman railroad sleeping and dining cars, introduced a notable experiment in corporate benevolence by building a corporate town outside Chicago with housing and other amenities for his employees. Pullman's altruism, however, did not prevent his employees from striking in 1894. The Pullman strike and railroad boycott dampened such paternalistic initiatives but did not deter other corporate efforts to gain workers' loyalty through an elaboration of fringe benefits. In the early twentieth century, many large industrial firms introduced profit-sharing plans, social and sports activities, and medical, life, and retirement insurance plans.

The Assembly Line.

The rise of new corporate bureaucracies and of heavy industries such as steel and machine manufacture led scholars to characterize developments in the late nineteenth century as a second Industrial Revolution. Yet important continuities link the ante- and postbellum periods. Product diversity; uneven technological progress; varied work environments; the persistence of specialized, small-batch production; and control by skilled workers and foremen of work processes, even in large-scale enterprises, remained hallmarks of American industrialization into the early twentieth century. Manufacturing growth could still be characterized as more extensive than intensive.

A definite growth in productivity, however, occurred in the twentieth century. The most dramatic breakthrough came in automobile manufacturing, with the introduction of the moving assembly line. At first, cars were produced by teams of skilled assemblers who fit together crudely made components. Henry Ford, determined to produce an inexpensive car for the mass market, conceived of a different system. Ford first had to improve the production of standardized parts. Rather than relying on suppliers, Ford assumed direct control of components manufacture, overseeing innovations with new precision measuring devices and machinery. Having standardized parts fabrication, Ford in 1910 opened a revolutionary car-assembly plant in Highland Park, Michigan. Thousands of workers were stationed along a conveyor-belt-driven assembly line, each repetitiously adding parts to Ford's Model T car.

Ford's system did not work flawlessly. Until Ford introduced his innovative wage plan, the Five-Dollar Day, the company experienced high labor turnover. By the late 1920s, Ford's standardized-production methods also proved an impediment. General Motors (GM), a new conglomerate of firms, quickly surpassed Ford with a sales strategy that offered a different car for every income level and implemented a more flexible production system involving multipurpose machinery and relying more on skilled labor. Ford adjusted to the challenge only slowly.

Despite its difficulties, assembly-line production spread rapidly in the 1920s, from food processing to electric appliances. Indeed, the 1920s saw a flowering of American manufacture. Automobile production stimulated additional growth in the steel and rubber industries. Such new industries as petrochemicals, electronics, and aviation appeared. Following the lead of the DuPont chemical company and GM, large-scale firms diversified their product lines, decentralized production and management, and widened their productive capacities in order to tap new mass consumer markets. Industrial workers shared somewhat in the prosperity of the 1920s as the recipients of broader corporate fringe benefits.

Harbingers of Deindustrialization.

Below the surface, however, lay harbingers of economic crises to come—not just the collapse of the economy during the Great Depression of the 1930s, but long-term declines in industrial production and employment. Indeed, deindustrialization had its origins in the 1920s. New England textile mills closed in the face of low-wage competition, particularly from the South. Boarded-up factories appeared in America's earliest industrial sites. To reduce competition, national corporations bought out firms in older industrial centers such as Trenton, New Jersey, and rather than modernize antiquated facilities, they simply liquidated operations. In Philadelphia, older firms producing specialized goods failed as American consumers preferred cheaper mass-produced goods.

The depression-wracked 1930s witnessed a more general contraction in manufacture: industrial production fell by 35 percent. This was the worst of a series of depressions, including contractions in the 1830s, 1870s, and 1890s that severely tested America's economic development.

Industrial firms during the 1930s also faced a newly militant labor force. Unskilled and semiskilled workers in mass-production industries—largely first- and second-generation eastern and southern Europeans who remained outside the craft unions affiliated with the American Federation of Labor—successfully organized and gained union recognition and contracts through the Congress of Industrial Organizations. By the early 1940s the U.S. mass-production industries were heavily unionized.

The Depression of the 1930s did not end until World War II, when military production regenerated the economy. As in World War I, war production provided employment opportunities for women, African Americans, and other minorities who had been discriminated against in hiring for better manufacturing jobs.

High military production continued during America's Cold War arms race with the Soviet Union. For the first time, military manufacture constituted a critical element in the nation's industrial system. Military production also led to a geographic shift away from the older industrial heartland. Defense-related industries, including aerospace manufacture, clustered in southern California and the Pacific Northwest near Seattle, Washington, and in an arc stretching across the South from Columbia, South Carolina, through Huntsville, Alabama, to Houston, Texas.

Deindustrialization.

The end of the Cold War reduced defense spending and eliminated employment in areas that had prospered through military-goods production. These regions joined older industrial areas in experiencing decline. From a historic peak of nearly 20 million in 1979, around 5.2 million manufacturing jobs were lost in the following quarter of a century, to a level of 14.3 million by the start of 2004. Although worker productivity consistently improved, consumption did not follow at the same pace, as individual spending trended away from consumer goods in the direction of services. In 1991 the service sector displaced manufacturing as the single-largest area of employment in the United States. The following year, employment in the finance, insurance, and real estate sector likewise surpassed that in manufacturing.

During the late twentieth and early twenty-first centuries the effects of globalization increasingly reshaped the U.S. economy. Decade after decade, the value of American exports continued to increase, and manufactured goods for consumers became ever more affordable. However, the new leaders in manufacturing—computer and electronic products, aerospace and transportation equipment, chemicals and agricultural products—did not replace all the jobs lost to foreign manufacturers. The costs of domestic production of textiles, apparel, furniture, plastic products, paper, and metals could not match the reduced costs of production outside the United States, and thus these goods became cheaper to import. Expanding industries often favored climates warmer than that of the old industrial Midwest and located in expanding southwestern cities. Though some cities, including Pittsburgh and Denver, Colorado, reinvented themselves as sites of finance and telecommunications, abandoned and vandalized factory buildings and vacant lots in once proud industrial centers such as Youngstown and Cleveland in Ohio and Detroit in Michigan overshadowed a region that came to be called the "Rust Belt."

[See also **American System of Manufacturing and Interchangeable Parts; Automotive Industry; Business Growth and Decline; Consumer Culture; Deskilling; Economic Development; Factory System; Globalization; Hamilton, Alexander, and Economic Development; Hydroelectric Power; Industrial Policy, Theory and Practice of; Industrial Relations; Iron and Steel Industry; Labor Movements; Labor Productivity Growth; Mass Marketing; Mass Production; Occupational Diseases and Hazards; Productivity; Proletarianization;** *Report on Manufactures;* **Rust Belt and Deindustrialization; Scientific Management; Steam Power; Strikes; Technology; Textile Industry; Trade Policy, Federal;** *and* **Vertical Integration, Economies of Scale, and Firm Size.**]

BIBLIOGRAPHY

Bensel, Richard Franklin. *The Political Economy of American Industrialization, 1877–1900.* Cambridge, U.K.: Cambridge University Press, 2000.

Bluestone, Barry, and Bennett Harrison. *The Deindustrialization of America: Plant Closings, Community Abandonment, and the Dismantling of Basic Industry.* New York: Basic Books, 1982.

Chandler, Alfred D., Jr. *The Visible Hand: The Managerial Revolution in American Business.* Cambridge, Mass.: Belknap Press of Harvard University Press, 1977.

Cobb, James C. *Industrialization and Southern Society, 1877–1984.* Lexington: University Press of Kentucky, 1984.

Cumbler, John T. *A Social History of Economic Decline: Business, Politics, and Work in Trenton.* New Brunswick, N.J.: Rutgers University Press, 1989.

Hounshell, David A. *From the American System to Mass Production, 1800–1932: The Development of Manufacturing Technology in the United States.* Baltimore: Johns Hopkins University Press, 1984.

Jacoby, Sanford M. *Employing Bureaucracy: Managers, Unions, and the Transformation of Work in American Industry, 1900–1945.* New York: Columbia University Press, 1985.

Jeremy, David J. *Transatlantic Industrial Revolution: The Diffusion of Textile Technologies between Britain and America, 1790–1830s.* North Andover, Mass.: Merrimack Valley Textile Museum; Cambridge, Mass.: MIT Press, 1981.

Licht, Walter. *Industrializing America: The Nineteenth Century.* Baltimore: Johns Hopkins University Press, 1995.

Markusen, Ann, ed. *Rise of the Gunbelt: The Military Remapping of Industrial America.* New York: Oxford University Press, 1991.

Nelson, Daniel. *Managers and Workers: Origins of the New Factory System in the United States, 1880–1920.* Madison: University of Wisconsin Press, 1975.

Piore, Michael J., and Charles F. Sabel. *The Second Industrial Divide: Possibilities for Prosperity.* New York: Basic Books, 1984.

Scranton, Philip. *Endless Novelty: Specialty Production and American Industrialization, 1865–1925.* Princeton, N.J.: Princeton University Press, 1997.

Walter Licht; revised and updated
by Patrick M. Dixon

INDUSTRIAL POLICY, THEORY AND PRACTICE OF

Industrial policy involves a government's encouragement of selected types of economic activity. Governments pursue industrial policies because the favored production is a foundation for other parts of the economy, a key to national security, or politically influential. Actions associated with industrial policies include subsidies, loan guarantees, tax incentives, infrastructural improvements, marketing and technological advice, trade barriers to discourage foreign competition, and the negotiation of international regulations to prevent foreign governments from assisting producers of their own.

In Article I, Section 8, the Constitution empowers Congress to legislate in the areas that the federal government might employ to create industrial policy. Congress may set taxes, borrow money, regulate commerce among the states and with other countries, and provide for the common defense and welfare. Presidents interact with Congress and influence congressional actions, and under Article II, Section 2, they handle any international negotiations that are required. State governments also can implement industrial policies within their borders.

The explicit discussion of an American industrial policy began in the 1970s when some analysts called for the United States to adopt such an approach to counter the commercial advantages that Japan and other countries reaped by having industrial policies. Advocates of a U.S. industrial policy argued that government needed to support cutting-edge industries to guarantee future economic growth and U.S. international competitiveness. Those preferring decentralized free markets, including Ronald Reagan and most Republicans, claimed that governments are not suited for such a role and that political influence instead of economic considerations would determine which producers benefited from industrial policy. Opponents also argued that an industrial policy would inappropriately expand the size of the government and lead to wasteful spending if unprofitable businesses received too much support.

During the debate from the 1980s onward, opponents maintained the upper hand, and the United States never created a unified national industrial policy. An examination of policy past and present, however, reveals that the United States has had ad hoc industrial policies for two centuries that have affected many parts of the economy. Actions regarding transportation, trade, and energy policy provide examples.

Transportation Policy. The earliest U.S. industrial policies focused on transportation.

As Alexander Hamilton's 1791 *Report on Manufactures* noted, canal and road construction would be valuable for enhancing economic growth and protecting national security. Henry Clay's promotion of what he called the "American System" two decades later included similar arguments.

Among the earliest transportation projects were the National Road and the Erie Canal. The National Road (now U.S. Route 40) was constructed by the federal government between 1811 and 1837 to link the upper Potomac River to the Midwest and encouraged agricultural production west of the Appalachian Mountains. Completed in 1825, the Erie Canal was built by New York State at the behest of Governor DeWitt Clinton to link the Great Lakes to the Atlantic coast, thereby assisting growth in upstate counties and routing ever-greater volumes of goods through New York City's harbor, which soon became the largest U.S. port.

Additional transportation projects were the transcontinental railroad and the Interstate Highway System. Built between 1863 and 1869 and financed by government bonds and land grants to the Union Pacific and Central Pacific corporations, the transcontinental railroad linked the Midwest to the Pacific coast and helped increase agricultural production and mining in western states. As for the Interstate Highway System, President Dwight Eisenhower envisioned the system as a way to encourage economic activity throughout the United States and to ensure national defense. Initially financed by the Highway Act of 1956, the interstate system can be credited with spurring the growth of an array of businesses, ranging from tourism to auto production, long-haul trucking, and motels and service stations.

Trade Policy. Trade policy has contributed to industrial policy by protecting producers from foreign competition, opening markets to American goods, and setting international rules to prevent foreign governments from employing their own industrial policies. Between 1800 and 1930, the process that Congress used for setting tariffs—namely, calculating new rates for specific goods every few years—was an inherent form of industrial policy because it always favored selected producers, depending upon the role that the producers played in the economy and their political clout.

After World War II, international agreements lowered tariffs and left some American businesses vulnerable to imports, leading to calls for protection. The steel and auto industries are examples of producers that by 1970 faced growing foreign competition. Periodic energy crises also troubled the auto industry. Because steel and autos were regarded as essential to national security and as bedrocks for other industries, and because both had substantial political influence, both received assistance.

For steel, the aid included an initiative by the administration of Jimmy Carter that balanced low international steel prices with higher tariffs, the negotiation in the mid-1980s of an agreement that limited imports to 20 percent of the U.S. market, and the imposition by the administration of George W. Bush in 2002 of temporary tariffs to provide relief from a surge in steel imports. Auto assistance comprised 1979 loan guarantees to the Chrysler Corporation, a 1981 bargain that limited Japanese exports to the United States, and funding in 2009 to the bankrupt Chrysler and General Motors Corporations in exchange for partial government ownership.

Another trade-related industrial policy pertains to opening foreign markets. For instance, in 1985 the Reagan administration pursued the Market-Oriented Sector-Selective (MOSS) talks with Japan to promote American electronics, pharmaceuticals, and telecommunications exports. The following year saw an agreement calling for Japan to import American semiconductors. In his Framework Talks of 1993–1994 and Enhanced Initiative of 1997–1998, President Bill Clinton pursued similar deals with Japan regarding auto parts, medical technology, and insurance and telecommunications services.

U.S. bargaining over the World Trade Organization (WTO) Subsidies Agreement, in effect from 1 January 1995, illustrates the use of multilateral trade negotiations to stymie industrial policies in other countries. In these negotiations, the United States insisted upon a "specificity" rule to forbid government transfers of benefits to producers engaged in international commerce, thereby limiting foreign governments' use of one of the primary tools of industrial policy. The U.S. insistence upon "national treatment" in WTO rules pertaining to foreign investment, trade in services, intellectual property, and government procurement also was designed to prevent governments from favoring local producers over foreign corporations, thereby restricting another common tool of industrial policy.

Energy Policy.   Vital to most economic activity, the energy sector is a natural arena for industrial policy. Since 1900, because of its dominant role in meeting American energy needs, petroleum has been one focal point of U.S. policy. In dealing with the industry, the federal government promoted domestic production and price stability. For example, fearing shortages and high prices if one company dominated production and sales, in 1909 the Sherman Antitrust Act was invoked to force the dissolution of the Standard Oil Company. Other moves encouraging production were laws passed in 1916 and 1926 permitting tax deductions for the costs of new wells and an allowance to account for the depletion of oil reserves, as well as a 1959 quota system limiting oil imports. Price stability relied primarily on a system of production controls for crude oil that were first established in the 1930s and managed by the Interior Department.

Energy policy changed in the 1970s when an increased reliance on imported oil combined with crises in the Middle East to raise fuel prices amid uncertainty over supplies. One U.S. response stressed conservation and alternative fuels. Conservation moves included laws in 1975 setting fuel-efficiency regulations for new vehicles—known as Corporate Average Fuel Economy, or CAFE, standards—and in 1978 imposing a tax on gas-guzzling new cars and offering tax credits for the use of insulation and efficient equipment. Legislation in 1990, 1992, 1999, and 2004 extended parts of the 1978 law, and a 2007 law increased the CAFE standards. These moves fundamentally reshaped the affected industries.

U.S. industrial policy related to energy also promoted new industries by emphasizing alternative fuels and vehicles. Legislation in 1978 offered tax incentives to encourage the installation of solar, wind, and geothermal energy generating systems. These tax benefits were refined in 1992, 1999, 2004, and 2005, and the 2009 economic stimulus bill included loan programs relating to these power sources. Tax policy from 1978 onward, with revisions in 1992 and 2004, also promoted the use of ethanol–gasoline blends as motor fuels, and a 1980 ethanol tariff encouraged domestic production. Additionally, legislation in 1988 required federal agencies to purchase vehicles that use ethanol or natural gas, the 1990 Clean Air Act boosted ethanol–gasoline combinations to reduce carbon monoxide emissions, the 1992 Energy Policy Act pushed states and cities to buy alternative vehicles, and laws in 2005 and 2007 mandated yearly increases through 2022 in the use of ethanol as a motor fuel. Finally, legislation in 2005, 2008, and 2009 helped the electric car industry by allowing tax incentives for car purchases and conversions and for commercial and residential refueling equipment.

Critics of these energy policies argue that they have not reduced American dependence on foreign oil, that they encourage products that consumers do not want and that are not economically viable, and that they waste taxpayers' money. The bankruptcy in 2011 of the Solyndra Corporation, a maker of solar panels, after receiving large federal loans is seen by many as illustrating a basic problem with industrial policies.

[*See also* **Foreign Trade; Hamilton, Alexander, and Economic Development; Mercantilism; Railroad Land Grants; Renewable Energy and Climate Change;** *Report on Manufactures*; **Subsidies, Agricultural; Tariffs; Taxation;** *and* **Trade Policy, Federal.**]

BIBLIOGRAPHY

Bingham, Richard D. *Industrial Policy American Style: From Hamilton to HDTV*. Armonk, N.Y.: M. E. Sharpe, 1998.

Diebold, William, Jr. *Industrial Policy as an International Issue*. New York: McGraw–Hill, 1980.

Graham, Otis L., Jr. *Losing Time: The Industrial Policy Debate*. Cambridge, Mass.: Harvard University Press, 1992.

Johnson, Chalmers. *MITI and the Japanese Miracle: The Growth of Industrial Policy, 1925–1975*. Stanford, Calif.: Stanford University Press, 1982.

Nester, William R. *American Industrial Policy: Free or Managed Markets?* New York: St. Martin's Press, 1997.

Noland, Marcus, and Howard Pack. *Industrial Policy in an Era of Globalization: Lessons from Asia*. Washington, D.C.: Institute for International Economics, 2003.

John M. Rothgeb Jr.

INDUSTRIAL RELATIONS

"Industrial relations" is a term that signifies both an academic field of study and a functional area of business practice. The focus of industrial relations (IR) in both the academic and the business arenas is on the employer–employee relationship. In particular, IR specialists examine the causes of various kinds of employment problems and maladjustments and seek to discover and implement new ideas, institutions, policies, and practices that can resolve or ameliorate these problems. IR is thus a field of both study and practice, involving economic, political, legal, social, and psychological aspects of employment. Historically, IR specialists have emphasized applied problem-solving and concern for employee rights and interests.

Origins and Development through World War II. IR emerged at the beginning of the twentieth century with the widespread growth and development of a modern industry and a wage-earning labor force. First and foremost as a source of public concern was labor–management conflict, epitomized by violent strikes, riots, bombings, and destruction of property. Other labor problems also gained increasing attention. Several of these particularly affected employers, including high employee turnover, sporadic work effort, and wasteful production. Workers, meanwhile, suffered from poverty-level wages, long hours, and unsafe working conditions. Many of these problems also imposed large costs on society, as when children's health and education were stunted by long work hours in mills and mines. Public and business concern about labor–management problems coalesced during the World War I period, giving rise to IR as a field of study and practice.

In the 1920s a consensus emerged concerning three distinct approaches to solving labor problems and thus improving IR. The first, sometimes called the "workers' solution," relied on trade unionism and collective bargaining. The second, called the "community's solution," advocated protective labor legislation, such as laws on minimum wages and child labor, and social-insurance programs, such as unemployment compensation and old-age insurance. The third, called the "employers' solution," involved the practice of personnel management and human relations in the workplace. The post-1920 history of IR is a chronicle of the changing nature of labor problems in the workplace and of the attempts to redress them using one or more of these three approaches.

During the prosperous and politically conservative 1920s, employers held the upper hand and dealt with labor problems through new practices of personnel management. Progressive companies trained foremen in human relations, provided health insurance and paid vacations, codified employment policies, and promoted from within on the basis of internal job ladders. Companies also introduced employee representation plans, which they characterized as a form of industrial democracy or citizenship. Labor unions and government labor legislation, by contrast, lacked broad-based public, government, or business support between 1919 and 1929.

The Great Depression of the 1930s brought radical changes in IR. The Depression forced most firms to resort to repeated rounds of employee layoffs, wage cuts, and work speedups. By 1932–1933, mass unemployment and the collapse of welfare capitalism had created a growing sense of disillusionment, demoralization, and injustice among masses of workers. The New Deal labor policies of the administration of Franklin Delano Roosevelt, most particularly the National Labor Relations (Wagner) Act (NLRA) of 1935, stimulated the growth of unions across the economy, especially in the mass-production industries. The NLRA, a wave of militant strikes, the rejuvenation of the American Federation of Labor (AFL), and the birth of a new labor federation, the Congress of Industrial Organizations (CIO), all stimulated unionization.

Whereas less than 10 percent of the nonagricultural workforce was unionized in 1932, by 1940 that proportion had risen to 27 percent.

During World War II, union membership and coverage spread further, buoyed by a full-employment economy and government pressure on employers to avoid strikes and labor unrest. When the war ended in 1945, union membership had quadrupled over the 1932 level and encompassed more than one third of all nonagricultural employees.

Post–World War II Era. The Great Depression and World War II fundamentally changed the IR landscape as unions organized most employees in the mass-production industries. Whereas employers had pioneered innovative employment practices in the 1920s, now unions more often performed this role. Through collective bargaining, unions negotiated for cost-of-living adjustment clauses in their contracts, formal grievance systems, and extensive health and retirement benefit programs.

In the academic world, the rise of organized labor and the newfound importance of labor–management relations led to the establishment of several dozen IR centers and programs in major public and private universities. Although these programs recruited faculty and offered courses covering each of the three approaches to labor problems, most stressed trade unionism and collective bargaining as the preferred means to improve IR.

In the twentieth century's concluding decades, IR again underwent fundamental changes. As organized labor suffered a substantial long-term decline in membership and power, both human resource management—the new name for personnel management—and government legislation assumed more influence. Whereas most unions proved unable or unwilling to combat racial, gender, and other forms of discrimination in the workplace, for example, the federal government addressed these issues through legislation and regulations. Also, because unions now represented a much smaller proportion of the workforce, many workers lacked protection against such abuses as pension fraud and unsafe working conditions. Again the government stepped in to enact legislation to protect workers against these abuses. A third area of new legislation treated such social issues in the workplace as family and medical leave for employees.

Beginning in the late 1960s, employers also regained power and prestige in IR. The renaming of personnel management as "human resource management" (HRM) carried with it a stronger rhetorical emphasis on employees as valuable assets rather than as an expense to be minimized. Companies developed new HRM practices aimed at increasing organizational efficiency, enhancing workers' satisfaction, and reducing their desire for union representation. Managements instituted self-managed work teams, alternative methods of dispute resolution (for example, peer-review panels), profit-sharing plans, and programs for employee involvement.

By the mid-1990s, the union share of the workforce had fallen to 16 percent. Unions had substantially increased their representation among public-sector employees since the 1960s, but in the private sector union membership fell to only 10 percent—a level not seen since the early 1930s. By the end of the first decade of the twenty-first century, union power and membership had declined even further. Less than 7 percent of private employees belonged to a union, and public-employee union membership declined as the economic crisis of 2008–2010 resulted in reductions in public employment and a concerted attack on public-employee unionism by Republican state legislators and governors. A number of factors underlay this trend, primarily increased domestic and especially global competition, as well as sophisticated union-avoidance tactics by employers—tactics that found favor with many public officials and jurists.

A similar decline affected IR as an academic field. After 1960, the field of personnel or

human resource management gradually broke away from IR and established itself as a separate and competing area of study situated in university business schools. IR programs in academia thus became increasingly associated with the two remaining approaches to solving labor problems, government legislation and collective bargaining. But as labor unions' size and power declined, so did interest in IR, while the HRM side of the field grew commensurately. Even in such institutions as schools of industrial and labor relations, notably the one located at Cornell University, courses and the training of students in HRM came to replace or dominate those about IR.

Assessment.   Industrial relations as a topic of study and an area of business practice began as a Progressive Era reform-oriented movement to improve workplace efficiency, equity, and human well-being through some combination of improved management practices, collective bargaining, and legislation. The emphasis given to each solution changed markedly over the years in response to new events and ideas. Between 1933 and 1973, industrial relations became increasingly associated with trade unionism and collective bargaining. After 1973 the approach known as human resource management became more popular.

But whatever the name given to the field, or however it is subdivided, the study of the employment relationship, the problems that grow out of it, and the resolution of these problems remained high on the academic and social agendas in the twenty-first century. Moreover, in the absence of union representation, decades of wage stagnation or decline, high and protracted unemployment following the financial crisis of 2008, and the instability of employment for millions of workers, workplace practices and relations, whether under the rubric of IR or under the rubric of HRM, have remained crucial aspects of society and the economy.

[*See also* Collective Bargaining; Company Unions; Employee Representation Plans; Industrial Democracy; Labor Movement, Decline of the; Labor Movements; Rockefeller Plan, The; Scientific Management; Welfare Capitalism; *and* Workers' Self-Management.]

BIBLIOGRAPHY

Cohen, Lizabeth. *Making a New Deal: Industrial Workers in Chicago, 1919–1939*. 2d ed. Cambridge, U.K.: Cambridge University Press, 2008.

Dulebohn, James H., Gerald R. Ferris, and James T. Stodd. "The History and Evolution of Human Resource Management." In *Handbook of Human Resource Management*, edited by Gerald R. Ferris, Sherman D. Rosen, and Darold T. Barnum, pp. 18–41. Cambridge, Mass.: Blackwell, 1995.

Jacoby, Sanford M. *Employing Bureaucracy: Managers, Unions, and the Transformation of Work in American Industry, 1900–1945*. New York: Columbia University Press, 1985.

Kaufman, Bruce E. *The Origins and Evolution of the Field of Industrial Relations in the United States*. Ithaca, N.Y.: ILR Press, 1993.

Kaufman, Bruce E., ed. *Government Regulation of the Employment Relationship*. Madison, Wis.: Industrial Relations Research Association, 1997.

Kochan, Thomas A., Harry C. Katz, and Robert B. McKersie. *The Transformation of American Industrial Relations*. New York: Basic Books, 1986.

Lewin, David, Daniel Mitchell, and Mahmood Zaidi, eds. *Handbook of Human Resource Management*. Greenwich, Conn.: Jai Press, 1997.

Nelson, Daniel. *Shifting Fortunes: The Rise and Decline of American Labor, from the 1820s to the Present*. Chicago: Ivan R. Dee, 1997.

Bruce E. Kaufman

INDUSTRIAL RESEARCH LABORATORIES

Organized research on new products and processes began in large business organizations in the last decades of the nineteenth century. The pioneers were companies in the new fields of electricity, chemistry, and telecommunications, which faced stiff international competition and rapidly changing technology. Until Thomas Edison established his famous Menlo Park laboratory in New Jersey in 1876, industrial laboratories concentrated on product testing and improvement rather than on exploring new technology. Edison's innovative idea was that organized research could develop new products in a wide range of fields and that the process could be managed like any other industrial endeavor. His Menlo Park and West Orange laboratories proved his point by producing a steady flow of innovations, including the incandescent electric light, the phonograph, and the motion-picture camera.

The scope and scale of Edison's laboratories provided an example for others to follow. By 1900 his West Orange laboratory employed more than a hundred workers who experimented in areas as diverse as motion pictures and automobile storage batteries. Edison organized his laboratory to move into promising new areas. Companies such as General Electric and the American Telephone and Telegraph Company (AT&T) also sponsored industrial research but never matched the scale or the ambitions of Edison; their goals were to improve existing products and seek out new technologies to serve established businesses. The commercial rewards of new types of light bulbs and long-distance telephony convinced these companies that industrial research was not only a vital part of their core business but also the key to new and more profitable endeavors. In addition to maintaining its dominance in telephony, AT&T's Western Electric Laboratories opened up the fields of wireless communication and sound films for the parent company.

Though industrial research laboratories in the big companies involved extensive facilities at several sites staffed by large numbers of workers, many smaller businesses maintained modest laboratories employing only one or two experimenters. The independent research laboratory pioneered by Edison virtually died out in the twentieth century as the corporation became the primary source of new technology. In 1885 only 12 percent of patents were issued to corporations, but by 1950 this figure had risen to 75 percent. Industrial research had become an activity carried out by large, integrated companies that could afford the high cost of research.

Whereas Edison had hired both formally trained scientists and skilled craftsmen, industrial research laboratories tended to hire engineers and scientists with advanced degrees. The presence of well-known scientists such as Charles Steinmetz and William Coolidge at General Electric's laboratories gave that institution great prestige; Bell Laboratories could later claim several Nobel Prize laureates in its employ. Industrial research laboratories also helped business organizations increase their public visibility and sell products.

The union of business and academia in industrial research grew dramatically closer during times of war when the U.S. government took over the laboratories and accelerated the pace of technological development. Government involvement in research began during World War I and grew substantially during World War II, when industrial research was carried out on an unprecedented scale. The Manhattan Project to develop the atomic bomb used the same research principles established by Thomas Edison but employed an army of scientists and engineers at a cost of some $3 billion. After the war, government-sponsored industrial research remained at high levels and contributed to numerous important technologies such as space exploration and computers.

In the post–World War II economy, companies large and small carried out industrial research. As dramatic technological advances captured the American imagination, "new and improved" became something that every company wanted to claim for its products, even though it might not have employed industrial research. Industrial giants such as General Electric, the Radio Corporation of America (RCA), and DuPont used well-known research laboratories to differentiate their products from those of their competitors and to impress their customers. Slogans such as DuPont's "Better Living through Chemistry" became the foundation for advertising campaigns aimed at connecting industrial research with the benefits of new technology. The U.S. government used the same strategy to promote nuclear power and to justify massive federal expenditures on research and development. By the twenty-first century, industrial research had become a vital part of modern life, viewed as essential to a healthy economy. It served as a barometer of economic well-being and helped set the standards of scientific education.

[*See also* **Education and Human Capital; Military-Industrial Complex;** *and* **Technology.**]

BIBLIOGRAPHY

Kline, Ronald R. *Steinmetz: Engineer and Socialist.* Baltimore: Johns Hopkins University Press, 1992.

Millard, Andre. *Edison and the Business of Innovation.* Baltimore: Johns Hopkins University Press, 1990.

Noble, David. *America by Design: Science, Technology, and the Rise of Corporate Capitalism.* New York: Alfred A. Knopf, 1977.

Reich, Leonard S. *The Making of American Industrial Research: Science and Business at GE and Bell, 1876–1926.* Cambridge, U.K.: Cambridge University Press, 1985.

Wise, George. *Willis R. Whitney, General Electric, and the Origins of U.S. Industrial Research*. New York: Columbia University Press, 1985.

Andre Millard

INDUSTRIAL WORKERS OF THE WORLD

Founded in Chicago in 1905, the Industrial Workers of the World (IWW), or Wobblies, counted its membership only in the tens of thousands even at its peak. However, from 1906 until the early 1930s, its combination of revolutionary unionism, tactical experimentation, racial inclusiveness, and cultural creativity enabled the IWW to influence organized labor out of proportion to its numbers. Inspired by European theorists of anarcho-syndicalism and by the growth of low-wage, unskilled, and insecure jobs within American industry, the IWW differed from the more conservative American Federation of Labor by seeking to organize all workers into "One Big Union" across lines of skill, nationality, and gender—by seeking to create an amalgamation that would enable its members to end capitalism through a nationwide general strike.

Called "American syndicalism" by one of its first chroniclers, the IWW's ideological foundations represented a unique synthesis of New and Old World ideas tempered by the Wobblies' practical experience in the mines and on the shop floors of the nation. The radical priest Father Thomas Hagerty offered the first outline of the IWW's syndicalist plan at the union's founding, a utopian wheel-shaped chart that divided the administration of the nation's economy among the industrial branches of the One Big Union. Few Wobblies seemed to pay much attention to the details of what the world would look like after their revolutionary general strike; they seemed to presume that if that day ever came, then the union and its members would come to a consensus. Though many Wobblies' understandings of radicalism had been influenced by European ideas, most Wobblies eschewed the term "syndicalism," preferring "industrial unionism." In practice, the IWW's revolutionary industrial unionism disdained gradual gains and collective bargaining, seeking instead, as the preamble to the IWW's constitution states, the "abolition of the wage system."

The IWW enjoyed its greatest success in the extractive and textile industries. Affiliated briefly with the Western Federation of Miners, the Wobblies led mass strikes among miners at Goldfield, Nevada, in 1906–1907 and on the Mesabi iron range in Minnesota in 1916. Its activities in the forests of Louisiana and Texas resulted in fiercely contested strikes in 1912–1913. More successful organizing marked IWW campaigns among timber workers in the Pacific Northwest. Although it also recruited domestic servants, longshoremen, and cigar makers, the IWW's most stirring and publicized moments came in the textile strikes in Lawrence, Massachusetts, in 1912 and in Paterson, New Jersey, in 1913. The Wobblies' ability to maintain unity among highly diverse immigrant workers, to emphasize as strike goals not only wages but also dignity, and to dramatize the issues of child labor and industrial safety made these struggles significant.

The union's reach was also impressive, and among the union's more practical successes were the organization of agricultural workers in the West and the founding of the Agricultural Workers Organization (AWO) in 1915. The IWW sent "camp delegates" out with literature, enrollment books, union cards, and dues stamps to form virtual mobile union halls among migrant workers. The strategy paid off, bringing in tens of thousands of members by the close of the 1917 harvest season—and thus making real the IWW's call for an eight-hundred-mile picket line.

The early IWW, however, suffered severe repression. Between 1907 and 1917, the union waged many free-speech fights, as they were known, to exercise First Amendment rights. During and after World War I, IWW members were prosecuted under state laws against criminal syndicalism, and in Chicago in 1918, one hundred of the union's most effective leaders and organizers were sentenced to terms ranging from two to twenty-five years at the federal prison in Leavenworth, Kansas, for violating federal espionage statutes. Mob attacks on union halls and on individual Wobblies such as Frank Little and Wesley Everest, later revered as martyrs, further damaged the IWW. Even as federal prosecutions and the imprisonment of dozens of the union's most effective organizers hobbled the IWW, for a time it remained a surprisingly potent agent of change, especially among marine transport workers and Mexican and Mexican American workers in the West. The IWW-led strike against the Colorado Fuel and Iron Company that lasted from late 1927 through the first month of 1928 involved thousands of striking miners and demonstrated a surprising resilience. Nevertheless, internal conflicts and legal repression drained the IWW during the 1920s. By the 1930s the organization was a shadow of its former self.

The IWW's lasting contributions to the U.S. labor movement were indirect and largely cultural. The founders included such well-known radical leaders as Mary "Mother" Jones, Eugene V. Debs, and William "Big Bill" Haywood, a Utah-born miner who had joined the Western Federation of Miners in 1896. Its leading figures included the labor songwriter Joe Hill, the poet Covington Hall, and the humorist T-Bone Slim. The anthem of organized labor, "Solidarity Forever," was written by the Wobbly Ralph Chaplin. The IWW also pioneered mass civil disobedience to secure free speech, the use of sit-down strikes, and integration with African American–led labor organizations.

[*See also* **American Federation of Labor; Debs, Eugene V.; Haywood, William D.; Hill, Joe; Industrial Relations; Jones, Mary "Mother"; Lawrence "Bread and Roses" Strike (1912); Little, Frank;** *Little Red Songbook*; **Mesabi Range and Michigan Hard-Rock Miners' Strikes (1907–1916); Mining Industry; Paterson Strike and Pageant; Radicalism and Workers; Repression of Unions; Strikes; Textile Industry;** *and* **Western Federation of Miners.**]

BIBLIOGRAPHY

Dubofsky, Melvyn. *We Shall Be All: A History of the Industrial Workers of the World*. 2d ed. Urbana: University of Illinois Press, 1988.

Salerno, Salvatore. *Red November, Black November: Culture and Community in the Industrial Workers of the World*. Albany: State University of New York Press, 1989.

David R. Roediger; revised by
Gerald Ronning

INFLATION AND DEFLATION

Inflation and deflation indicate the increase or decrease in the overall price level and have been constant features of the U.S. economy. Both phenomena can have important economic effects, particularly for debtors, who gain from unanticipated inflation and suffer from unanticipated deflation. The default of debtors who are unable to service their debts has frequently aggravated the economic downturns associated with deflation; this type of "debt deflation" was a hallmark of the financial crises of the nineteenth and early twentieth centuries.

The nineteenth century was characterized by deflation: the consumer price index in 1900 was about two thirds of what it had been in 1800. Two notable exceptions to this deflationary tendency were associated with wars: prices rose by about one third during the years surrounding the War of 1812 (and the nearly contemporaneous demise of the First Bank of the United States) and doubled during the Civil War period. In both cases, prices eventually returned to their prewar levels, although the return was more rapid after the War of 1812, when the prewar price level was reached by 1820, than after the Civil War, when the prewar price level was not reached until the turn of the twentieth century. The deflation following the Civil War was most intense during the years between the financial crises of 1873 and 1893, a period that was called the "Great Depression" before that name was appropriated by the far more destructive downturn of the 1930s.

The first two decades of the twentieth century were characterized by inflation, which became pronounced from the beginning of World War I through 1920, when prices doubled. Prices fell during the postwar slump of the early 1920s, but the price level never dipped to pre–World War I levels—even after deflation caused prices to fall by more than 25 percent during 1930–1933.

During the four years of U.S. involvement in World War II, inflation was much more subdued—in part because of price controls—than during earlier war episodes, rising only about 20 percent. And unlike what happened during earlier war-related episodes, inflation persisted after World War II, with prices rising by about 30 percent during the four years following the war. Inflation again slowed during the Korean War, with the price level rising by only about half as much as during World War II.

The more than half a century since the end of the Korean War has been the longest sustained period of inflation rising prices in U.S. history. The inflation rate rose substantially during the 1960s and 1970s, fed by expansive social programs at home and by involvement in the Vietnam War, and reached double digits during 1979–1981. Beginning in October 1979 the Federal Reserve, under the chairmanship of

Paul Volcker, adopted a more contractionary monetary-policy regime, bringing the annual inflation rate down to about 3.5 percent by the end of Volcker's term in 1987. Inflation continued to decline after that, averaging about 3 percent per year during the 1990s and 2.3 percent during 2000–2010, reaching a low of approximately 0.2 percent in 2008, in the aftermath of the subprime financial crisis.

[*See also* **Depressions, Economic; Federal Reserve System; Monetary Policy, Federal; Stagflation; Volcker, Paul; Wages, Real and Nominal;** *and* **Wartime Economic Regulation.**]

BIBLIOGRAPHY

Hanes, Christopher, ed. "Prices and Price Indices." In *Historical Statistics of the United States*, edited by Susan Carter, Scott Sigmund Gartner, Michael R. Haines, Alan L. Olmstead, Richard Sutch, and Gavin Wright, chapter Cc. Millennial ed. Cambridge, U.K.: Cambridge University Press, 2006.

Richard S. Grossman

INSTITUTIONAL AND HISTORICAL ECONOMICS

Some Americans were never comfortable with classical English economics with its deductive reasoning and its universal prescription of laissez-faire. For the country's first century, this discomfort was not expressed in academic economics, which remained firmly within the English orthodoxy. Most college teaching before the 1880s was done by autodidacts, including ministers, who preached the moral virtues of laissez-faire and free trade. Public policy, however, was shaped by such figures as Alexander Hamilton, Henry Carey, and Friedrich List, who rejected both the method and the conclusions of economic orthodoxy. Instead they advocated tariffs and restrictions on imports to promote American industrialization; they argued for a so-called national economics whereby a nation could develop economically by promoting a diversity of industries and an expanded social division of labor.

Institutionalist ideas entered the American academy in the 1880s through American students who returned from graduate studies in Germany. Lacking opportunity for advanced study in economics in the United States, a generation of Americans learned a different economics while studying in Germany with scholars associated with the German historical school. Instead of deductive reasoning founded on universal principles, they learned methods of inductive reasoning, empirical analysis of the development of social institutions that took "account of time and place" (*The Past and the Present of Political Economy* [Baltimore: Johns Hopkins University, 1884], p. 233). They also learned from their German teachers how the new empirical and institutional economics could be joined to social reform, an alliance institutionalized in the Verein für Socialpolitik formed in Germany in 1873 to provide a forum for historical economists to meet together and with like-minded political activists.

Returning from their German studies, the young Americans with their new ideas and PhD degrees sought to transform and to revitalize academic economics in the United States. Led by Richard T. Ely, in 1885 they founded the American Economic Association (AEA) as an American version of the German Verein, an organization of empirical and institutional economists in service of social reform. Though the AEA quickly shed its sectarian and political mission to become a professional organization for all economists, Ely and his growing body of students and colleagues continued to urge an economics sensitive to time and place and committed to social reform. Institutionalist economists were active at many universities, including

the University of Michigan, the University of Pennsylvania, the University of California, and Amherst College. Institutionalism was strongest at America's two leading graduate schools, the University of Wisconsin at Madison and Columbia University. Wisconsin economists, including John R. Commons, were involved in drafting state labor reforms, including laws providing for workers' compensation and regulating industrial enterprises. Edwin Seligman at Columbia helped to draft the Sixteenth Amendment to the Constitution, which authorized the income tax.

The Great Depression of the 1930s and the subsequent New Deal gave institutionalist economists a chance to reshape the American economy. Columbia economists, notably Rexford Tugwell and Adolf Berle, were major figures in President Franklin Delano Roosevelt's brain trust. Other institutionalists active in New Deal Washington included Columbia's John Maurice Clark, Wesley Clair Mitchell, and Leon Keyserling, Wisconsin's William Leiserson and Edwin Witte, and Harvard's Gardiner Means and Alvin Hansen. The New Deal allowed them to shape a new era in economic and social policy. Institutional economists drafted much of the seminal legislation of the New Deal and administered many of its programs; Leiserson, for example, served on the National Labor Relations Board, and Keyserling was the first chair of the Council of Economic Advisers. During World War II, institutionalist economists administered the new agencies of the wartime economy, including John Kenneth Galbraith at the Office of Price Administration, Clark Kerr at the War Labor Board, and John Dunlop at the Office of Economic Stabilization.

In their 1932 book *The Modern Corporation and Private Property*, Berle and Means provided the intellectual grounding for New Deal–era institutionalism. They identified the key institution in modern society to be the business corporation, which they associated with the development of technology and economies of scale in production. They warned that the size, wealth, and market power of these behemoths enabled them to regulate prices and production levels, as well as to manipulate demand through advertising. Their immense size gave them power over their employees that they magnified by creating so-called internal labor markets. By balkanizing labor markets and locking workers into particular jobs, employers achieved monopsonistic power over their employees.

By promoting collective bargaining and government regulation of business, including minimum-wage laws, institutionalist economists inaugurated three decades of unprecedented prosperity and rising economic equality. Notwithstanding this success, orthodox economists remained suspicious of institutionalist reasoning that challenged their use of models of competitive markets and equilibrium pricing. Those opposed to the redistributive policies of the New Deal funded orthodox neoclassical economists and other opponents of institutionalist ideas, arranging conferences to spread orthodox ideas and subsidizing economists opposed to institutionalism. By the 1980s the intellectual challenge of the competitive model and the material challenge posed by affluent conservatives had virtually eliminated institutionalist thought in American economics.

[See also American Economic Association and the New Economics; Berle, Adolf, and Gardiner Means and the Modern Corporation; Clark, John Maurice; Economic Theories and Thought; Galbraith, John Kenneth; New Deal and Institutional Economics; and Technocracy.]

BIBLIOGRAPHY

Berle, Adolf A., and Gardiner C. Means. *The Modern Corporation and Private Property*. New York: Macmillan, 1932.

Ely, Richard T. *The Past and the Present of Political Economy*. Baltimore: N. Murray, publication agent, Johns Hopkins University, 1884.

Frege, Carola M. *Employment Research and State Traditions: A Comparative History of Britain, Germany, and the United States*. Oxford and New York: Oxford University Press, 2007.

Herbst, Jurgen. *The German Historical School in American Scholarship: A Study in the Transfer of Culture*. Ithaca, N.Y.: Cornell University Press, 1965.

Phillips-Fein, Kim. *Invisible Hands: The Making of the Conservative Movement from the New Deal to Reagan*. New York: W. W. Norton and Company, 2009.

Ross, Dorothy. *The Origins of American Social Science: Ideas in Context*. Cambridge, U.K.: Cambridge University Press, 1991.

Tugwell, Rexford G., ed. *The Trend of Economics*. New York: Alfred A. Knopf, 1924.

Yonay, Yuval P. *The Struggle over the Soul of Economics: Institutionalist and Neoclassical Economists in America between the Wars*. Princeton, N.J: Princeton University Press, 1998.

Gerald Friedman

INSULL, SAMUEL

(1859–1938), businessman and utilities-industry spokesman. Born near London, Samuel Insull learned stenography, immigrated to America, and landed a job in 1880 as the personal secretary of Thomas Edison. Learning the electric-lighting business from the ground up, Insull helped establish the manufacturing arm of what became the General Electric Company in Schenectady, New York. In 1892 he became president of the Chicago Edison Company, one of several electric companies in the city.

Over the following decade, he mastered the unique economics of the electric-utility business and emerged as a national leader of the industry. Proclaiming that "low rates may mean good business," Insull developed a business strategy that encouraged the use of electricity by all types of energy consumers. This approach made him an innovator in the use of novel technologies, financial instruments, rate structures, and promotional campaigns to create a mass market for electric light and power. Moreover, he mounted a successful effort to establish a monopoly of central-station service in Chicago for the renamed Commonwealth Edison Company. He also became a pioneer in building larger, regional networks of power and related holding-company devices to maintain control of his sprawling utilities empire.

During World War I, Insull was appointed chairman of the Illinois Council of Defense. In the 1920s he was regarded as one of the nation's leading businessmen. The Great Depression and the collapse of his utilities empire turned Insull into a target of popular anger. Arrested and tried for securities fraud, he was acquitted in 1934 but remained a broken man until his death.

[*See also* **Electricity and Electrification; General Electric;** *and* **Public Utility Holding Company Act.**]

BIBLIOGRAPHY

McDonald, Forrest. *Insull.* Chicago: University of Chicago Press, 1962.
Platt, Harold L. *The Electric City: Energy and the Growth of the Chicago Area, 1880–1930.* Chicago: University of Chicago Press, 1991.

Harold L. Platt

INSURANCE

The history of insurance in the United States involves two major themes: risk protection and capital accumulation. Colonial and early-national insurance companies adopted British insurance firms' practices in covering marine and fire hazards. Organized underwriters, usually merchants and real estate men, assessed risk, estimated profitable premium rates, and insured policyholders for lost cargoes and the destruction of buildings by fire. (Risk has since come to be calculated by professional actuaries using complex statistical models.)

The most significant nineteenth-century outgrowth of fire and marine insurance was life insurance. The nation's first successful life-insurance company was founded in Philadelphia in 1812. Most major life-insurance companies, founded in the 1830–1870 period, were mutually owned by policyholders, as were many fire-insurance companies. After the Civil War, these companies became fiduciary agents of middle-class—and eventually working-class—savings, as well as key investors in transportation, financial, and industrial corporations. By 1900, life-insurance companies rivaled banks in terms of financial power. In *Paul v. Virginia* (1869) the Supreme Court had ruled that insurance was not "commerce" and therefore was not subject to federal regulation. Insurance remains subject to state regulation. In 1871 state regulators formed the National Association of Insurance Commissioners to coordinate legislation, regulation, and other matters.

Social and economic changes of the twentieth century, coupled with the increasing sophistication of actuarial methods, helped insurance spread to broader aspects of property, finance, and society, including such diverse areas as automobile insurance, crop insurance, comprehensive homeowners' policies, product-liability coverage, malpractice insurance for physicians, and, in finance, bond insurance, also known as credit default swaps (CDS). The New Deal era saw the growth of various forms of social insurance, including bank-deposit insurance, workers' injury compensation, unemployment coverage, and Social Security. Health insurance expanded rapidly with the founding of Blue Cross in New York in 1934 and its spread to other states. The Medicare and Medicaid programs of the 1960s, coupled with many private systems for employees, extended health insurance still further.

In the late twentieth century the insurance industry grew in both scope and investment power. The United States has remained the largest market for insurance in the world. The Financial Services Modernization Act (1999) gave insurance companies and banks greater freedom to compete and collaborate in various financial services. American International Group (AIG), one of the largest insurers in the United States and the world, was at the center of the 2008 economic crisis when it became clear that AIG was unable to pay billions of dollars on unregulated CDSs to other financial firms. The company had received premiums but failed to accumulate reserves to cover potential claims. It received a federal bailout. In 2010 the nation's largest life-insurance carrier was MetLife, and the largest carrier of property and casualty insurance was Berkshire Hathaway. They represent an industry that by the early twenty-first century employed 2.3 million workers. With assets of some $6.8 trillion invested in banks, mortgages, and corporate and government securities, the insurance industry has become an important financial intermediary and savings institution.

[See also Deregulation, Financial; Federal Deposit Insurance Corporation; Financial and Banking Promotion and Regulation; and Financial Crises, 1980s–2010.]

BIBLIOGRAPHY

Graham, Loftin, and Xiaoying Xie. "The United States Insurance Market: Characteristics and Trends." In Handbook of International Insurance: Between Global Dynamics and Local Contingencies, edited by J. David Cummins and Bertrand Venard. New York: Springer, 2007.

Tom Mertes

INTERNAL IMPROVEMENTS

See Economic Development *and* Transportation Revolution.

INTERNAL LABOR MARKETS

The term "internal labor markets" refers to the way in which firms price and allocate labor within their operations. Starting in the late nineteenth century, some firms implemented formal rules and bureaucratic procedures for determining how they hire, promote, transfer, lay off, and pay their workers. This marked a shift from relying heavily on (external) labor markets and hiring workers each day at the factory gate. The particular rules and procedures adopted by a firm shape its internal labor market.

Many firms developed internal labor markets in the pursuit of profit. Firms can extract higher levels of effort from their workers by providing them with a range of rewards and punishments. Providing regular pay increases discourages workers from quitting to take jobs at rival firms, reducing the cost of turnover. By filling positions from within, firms retain the training and experience of their existing workforces. Firms that require workers with specific skills gain the most from developing substantial internal labor markets. Internal labor markets may be critical to the success of large, vertically integrated businesses.

Internal labor markets are essentially small-scale command economies, since they price and allocate labor following a set of rules instead of relying on the market. In his 1967 book *The New Industrial State*, John Kenneth Galbraith emphasizes that firms develop internal labor markets in both capitalist and state-socialist economies. When facing competitive product markets and labor markets, firms must develop rules and procedures that allow them to sell their output at a competitive price while maintaining an appropriate workforce. So although internal labor markets may be buffered from external market forces, they are not completely detached from the larger market.

Economic Theory. Neoclassical economists argue that it is often more efficient for firms to develop internal labor markets than it is for them to rely exclusively on the external labor market. External labor markets can be inefficient when inefficiencies rise in using the external labor market or when there are significant costs to training new workers. Although the Coase theorem, put forth by the Nobel Prize–winning economist Ronald Coase, states that in the absence of transaction costs, it would be efficient for firms to contract out all jobs to the lowest bidder in the labor market, in the real world it is often more efficient for firms to hire long-term employees and price and allocate labor following set rules and procedures.

Within neoclassical economics, personnel economics especially stresses the efficiency of internal labor markets. Personnel economics assumes that both firms and workers are rational, optimizing agents and that competition between firms leads all firms to develop optimal rules for pricing and allocating labor. Though this view is theoretically attractive, it is difficult for personnel economics to explain the full diversity of internal labor markets across firms, across countries, and over time.

Institutional economists tend to view internal labor markets as the product of conflict among key interest groups, particularly owners,

managers, workers, unions, and the state. Although institutional economists agree that competition can compel firms to abandon especially inefficient rules and procedures, they question the notion that persistent rules and procedures are necessarily efficient. Rather, they understand internal labor markets as political compromises between opposing interest groups. This view may be more realistic than the neoclassical view, but its complexity provides few testable hypotheses.

Marxist economists agree that firms shape their internal labor markets to maximize profits, but they contend that profitable structures are not necessarily efficient. Many Marxists argue that firms construct hierarchical internal labor markets to divide and control their workforces. Some work rules and procedures also effectively split workers along racial, ethnic, and gender lines. When workers compete to earn promotions or to avoid layoffs, their energy is diverted from their collective struggle against capital. Although internal labor markets may indeed undermine worker solidarity, the Marxist view may overstate the power of capitalists—and understate the power of workers—to shape firms' internal labor markets.

Historical Development. Throughout the nineteenth century, most industrial production was organized without sophisticated internal labor markets. Capitalists depended on fairly independent foremen to hire, manage, and lay off their workers, and many workers were hired on a daily basis at the factory gate. In this so-called traditional system, labor turnover was high. Some firms had annual turnover rates of more than 300 percent. In the early twentieth century, firms began to organize production more rationally to maintain high levels of throughput. This led many also to manage their workforces more systematically to reduce the cost of absenteeism, turnover, and training. By the 1940s, most large firms had established human resources departments to manage their internal labor markets.

The development of internal labor markets is intricately tied to the unionization of American industry, which occurred over about the same period. In some cases, firms established rules and procedures that workers deemed unfair, leading workers to organize unions. In other cases, firms established formal rules in an attempt to forestall unionization. In yet other cases, firms did not establish formal rules for dealing with their employees until unions forced them to do so. Unions' collective-bargaining agreements with management deal largely with the shape of firms' internal labor markets. These agreements state how management must hire, pay, promote, and lay off workers.

In the United States, the importance of internal labor markets may have peaked in the 1950s and 1960s. During this period, many firms offered workers lifelong careers with stable employment, health care, defined-benefit pensions, and opportunities for promotion. Most workers welcomed this new economic security. However, some observers worried that firms' offering lifelong careers would transform independent workers and citizens into "organization men." In 1958 the economist Arthur M. Ross lamented the decline in workers' quit rates as a path to "industrial feudalism."

Internal labor markets have eroded since the 1980s. The number of firms that offer long-term job security and opportunities for advancement has declined. Many firms have cut their workforces and instead outsource projects to contingent workers and contractors, shifting greater risk to workers. Even well-educated workers—who are best suited to this new labor market—are less likely to work their way up within a single firm and are more likely to change firms to earn promotions. Competing explanations have been offered for the diminishing importance of internal labor markets. The erosion of internal labor markets may reflect the fact that firms face greater international competition in the twenty-first century than they did in the mid-twentieth century. New information technologies may reduce the cost to firms of contracting work to the labor market, making internal labor markets less valuable. The shift away from internal labor markets has also tracked the precipitous decline in union density in the private sector from the 1980s onward.

Sanford M. Jacoby (2004) has cautioned that it is easy to exaggerate the "deconstruction" of internal labor markets since the 1980s. He contends that the proportions of American workers who have career-type jobs in the twenty-first century are about the same as the proportions of American workers who had career-type jobs in the mid-twentieth century. Certainly internal labor markets in the twenty-first century are much closer to those from 1960 than to those of 1900. It seems highly unlikely that most twenty-first-century firms and workers would revert to nineteenth-century forms of employment, since there are good economic reasons for maintaining some form of internal labor markets. Although the exact future of internal labor markets is unclear, they do have a future.

[*See also* **Economic Theories and Thought; Labor Markets; Labor Movements; Segmented Labor Markets, Primary and Secondary;** *and* **Vertical Integration, Economies of Scale, and Firm Size.**]

BIBLIOGRAPHY

Chandler, Alfred D., Jr. *The Visible Hand: The Managerial Revolution in American Business.* Cambridge, Mass.: Belknap Press of Harvard University Press, 1977.

Doeringer, Peter B., and Michael J. Piore. *Internal Labor Markets and Manpower Analysis.* Lexington, Mass.: Heath Lexington Books, 1971.

Edwards, Richard. *Contested Terrain: The Transformation of the Workplace in the Twentieth Century.* New York: Basic Books, 1979.

Jacoby, Sanford M. *Employing Bureaucracy: Managers, Unions, and the Transformation of Work in the 20th Century.* Rev. ed. Mahwah, N.J.: Lawrence Erlbaum, 2004.

Osterman, Paul. "Institutional Labor Economics, the New Personnel Economics, and Internal Labor Markets: A Reconsideration." *Industrial and Labor Relations Review* 64, no. 4 (July 2011): 635–651.

Ross, Arthur M. "Do We Have a New Industrial Feudalism?" *American Economic Review* 48, no. 5 (1958): 903–920.

Anders Fremstad

INTERNATIONAL ALLIANCE OF THEATRICAL STAGE EMPLOYEES

The International Alliance of Theatrical Stage Employees, Moving Picture Technicians, Artists, and Allied Crafts of the United States, Its Territories, and Canada (IATSE) was founded in 1893 by traveling stage mechanics, also known as stagehands, to unite a collection of local protective associations of stagehands that had developed in the 1880s in response to unfair treatment by many traveling stage-show producers. These shows included sets and props that were built by expert stagehands who typically worked out of New York City or Philadelphia. When the stagehands traveled with the show, they would set up the staging but were often replaced with lower-paid local workers during the run of the show. They were also left stranded in distant towns or cities when unscrupulous producers skipped town without paying them. The 1893 founding organization, chartered by the American Federation of Labor (AFL), was called the National Alliance of Theatrical Stage Employees, but when Canadian locals were added in 1903, "National" was replaced by "International." Most of the early local IATSE unions were located in eastern cities in the United States, but through the efforts of the traveling stage mechanics, the organization gradually spread to all major cities.

Just at the time that the IATSE formed, inventors in France and the United States were developing motion-picture cameras and projectors. At first in most cities films were only a minor part of larger live stage shows. But the films gradually became a stand-alone attraction that drew large audiences at a cost much lower than that of the live stage shows. The IATSE recognized this change in the entertainment industry and, by 1908, began to organize film projectionists' locals in major cities. By 1910, local stagehand unions in New York City had organized the workers in the burgeoning motion-picture production industry there. The IATSE, however, had less success in organizing the workers in the Los Angeles film studios. Los Angeles was a notorious open-shop city where employers in all fields simply refused to recognize unions. The film producers, recognizing this price advantage, soon moved most of their productions to Los Angeles.

After a series of struggles between 1912 and 1926 with film producers—who bargained as a group under the title Association of Motion Picture Producers—and other AFL unions competing for work in the studios, the IATSE finally managed to organize a large number of studio technicians in the largest studios. The IATSE shared jurisdiction in certain categories of workers with the International Brotherhood of Electrical Workers (IBEW). In essence, the IATSE by 1926 was an industrial union along the lines of the later mass-production unions of the Congress of Industrial Organizations (CIO) in which workers in a variety of crafts were organized on the basis of their common employment in the technical side of motion-picture production, motion-picture projection, or theatrical stage production.

The passage of the National Labor Relations (Wagner) Act in 1935 aided the IATSE in organizing the remainder of studio workers by 1938. Yet in this same period, the union fell under the control of organized crime. The Chicago gang originally fronted by Al Capone had taken control of the Chicago locals and quickly managed through intimidation and murder to gain control of the IATSE. George Browne and Willie Bioff became the union's leaders. These two men established various skimming and kickback schemes to generate money for the Chicago gang. By 1940 their extortion schemes had been exposed, and in the early 1940s both Browne and Bioff spent time in jail, while a reformed IATSE managed to hold on to a majority of the union jobs in the motion-picture industry.

During the period of corruption, various progressive union factions attempted to wrest control of the IATSE jurisdiction. These fratricidal struggles culminated in the massive studio strikes that occurred between 1945 and 1947. At the end of this period, union dissidents were driven out of the industry, and what remained was an entrenched IATSE in control of nearly all jobs in the studios. Since that tumultuous period the IATSE has maintained its position as the dominant union in the technical side of motion-picture, filmed network television, and theatrical production.

Even though union membership in the general workforce has been in decline since the later twentieth century, the IATSE's membership grew from 74,000 to 110,000. Of that number, 35,000 work in the motion-picture and television industries in Los Angeles. The IATSE maintains several health and welfare funds that are supported by mandatory employer contributions. The film production workers' fund alone has assets valued at greater than $5 billion.

Although the IATSE formerly organized only expensive productions, such as movies that had a budget of $8 million or more, since 1995 the union has negotiated for union jobs on lower-budget productions. The biggest challenges facing the union since the late twentieth century have been overseas productions of U.S.-backed films and TV programs and new technologies that either create whole new categories of work or eliminate jobs formerly held by union workers. The leaders of the IATSE have joined with the film and TV producers to fight digital piracy of films and TV programs. Despite these problems, every movie and TV program can be considered a handmade craft item that requires exceedingly specialized skills.

[*See also* **Film and Labor; Labor Movements; Theatrical Unions;** *and* **Union Corruption.**]

BIBLIOGRAPHY

International Alliance of Theatrical Stage Employees and Moving Picture Machine Operators of the United States and Canada. *IATSE, 1893–1993: 100 Years of Solidarity*. New York: IATSE, 1993.

Nielsen, Michael C., and Gene Mailes. *Hollywood's Other Blacklist: Union Struggles in the Studio System*. London: British Film Institute, 1995.

Michael Nielsen

INTERNATIONAL ASSOCIATION OF MACHINISTS

North America's largest union of workers in the metal trades traces its roots to a meeting of railroad mechanics held in Atlanta, Georgia, in 1888 that gave birth to the Order of United Machinists and Mechanical Engineers. At its first convention, in 1889, the organization adopted the name National Association of Machinists, and in 1894, after establishing its first local lodge in Canada, it rechristened itself as the International Association of Machinists (IAM). During these years, the IAM spread in railroad roundhouses and machine shops across the country. In 1895 it affiliated with the American Federation of Labor (AFL) and soon became the nation's most potent union in the metal trades.

The IAM's affiliation with the AFL was controversial because the union excluded African Americans, which violated AFL policies. In order to gain admission to the AFL, the IAM dropped references to the exclusion of blacks from its constitution and shifted the color bar to the ritual used to induct union members. This ruse allowed the AFL both to accept the IAM and to continue to claim that it did not sanction discrimination, even as the IAM continued to exclude blacks until 1948.

During the first half-century of its existence, the IAM's nemesis was the National Metal Trades Association (NTMA), an employers' group that fought the union. After a short-lived peace pact between the organizations—the Murray Hill Agreement of 1900–1901—collapsed, relations between the IAM and the NTMA deteriorated, and the NTMA waged a vigorous open-shop campaign, blacklisting union activists. Changes in technology that brought an increasing number of semiskilled workers into machine shops challenged the union's hold on metalworking.

These challenges pushed the IAM to open its ranks to semiskilled workers and to women, as well as to elect the Canadian-born socialist William H. Johnston as president in 1911. Under Johnston the union waged costly strikes against the Illinois Central and the Harriman lines, further straining its resources. But the advent of World War I created conditions for a turnaround. During the war, IAM membership ballooned as full employment and government policies fostered organization of munitions factories and railways. But the union suffered staggering losses in the 1920s, the worst resulting from the failed 1922 walkout of railroad shopmen.

The fortunes of the IAM remained closely tied to government policies. During the Great Depression the IAM revived as it recaptured members in the railroad roundhouses and won new members in the burgeoning airline industry, thanks to New Deal labor policies. World War II further raised IAM membership figures as defense workers joined the union. And in the postwar era, the IAM grew in the government-supported aerospace industry. So important did the aerospace industry become to the union that in 1964 it changed its name to the International Association of Machinists and Aerospace Workers (IAMAW). During the postwar era the union was able to flex its muscles effectively on behalf of its members, as during a 1966 strike that grounded five major airlines for forty-three days.

Since the 1960s the IAMAW has struggled with the same forces that have beset all unions, as well as with some that have hit it harder than most other unions: airline deregulation placed increasing pressure on unionized carriers, which led the companies to drive harder bargains with the union in the 1980s. Like other unions, the IAMAW broadened its reach to cope with threatening market forces, merging with the International Woodworkers of America in 1994 and the National Federation of Federal Employees in 1999. These moves helped keep it a formidable force in the early twenty-first century.

[*See also* **Airplanes and Air Transport; American Federation of Labor; Labor Movements;** *and* **Railroad Brotherhoods.**]

BIBLIOGRAPHY

Montgomery, David. *Workers' Control in America: Studies in the History of Work, Technology, and*

Labor Struggles. Cambridge, U.K.: Cambridge University Press, 1979.

Rodden, Robert G. *The Fighting Machinists: A Century of Struggle*. Washington, D.C.: Kelly Press, 1984.

Joseph A. McCartin

INTERNATIONAL BROTHERHOOD OF TEAMSTERS

The International Brotherhood of Teamsters (IBT) was formed in 1903. A union originally organized to represent the men who worked on the horse-drawn freight wagons in the cities of the turn of the twentieth century, the IBT evolved throughout the twentieth century in both its jurisdiction and its membership. As the motor-freight industry emerged, the union came to represent truck drivers, and then it expanded its jurisdiction to include those whose interests intersected with the drivers, including warehouse workers and employees in the food-processing and distribution industries. The dramatic growth of the trucking industry, combined with the broadening jurisdiction of the union, helped make the IBT the nation's largest union by 1941.

The organization's bureaucratic structure evolved in similarly dramatic fashion. In the early decades of the twentieth century, Teamster locals operated with a great deal of autonomy, organizing their own workers and negotiating contracts that were specific to the hauling industry in their particular city. As the intercity motor-freight industry grew in the 1930s, a new generation of Teamster leaders, including Dave Beck, Farrell Dobbs, and James R. Hoffa, promoted larger organizing and bargaining units within the Teamsters, including statewide and then regional conferences. These units allowed the Teamsters to use secondary boycotts and other similar tactics to leverage strength in one area into organizing victories in other areas. The Teamsters used such tactics to break into traditionally antiunion bastions in the West and the South. During Hoffa's presidency of the union from 1957 to 1971, this pattern culminated in 1964 when he signed the National Master Freight Agreement, a collective-bargaining agreement covering the employees in the trucking industry across the country. Such organizational changes were accompanied by significant gains in wages and benefits for members, but they came at the cost of eroding the independence of local union leaders and increasing the problems faced by internal union-reform efforts.

These costs became increasingly significant as the union developed serious problems with corruption at its national level of leadership. Pockets of corruption had long existed at the local level, often reflecting the collusive arrangements common in sectors of the local hauling industry. Daniel Tobin, who led the union from 1907 to 1952, initially had policed such corruption quite actively, but over time his efforts in this area subsided. By the 1930s the proliferation of local Teamster leaders engaged in corrupt activity or linked to organized-crime figures had led one text to label the union "the most racketeer-ridden union in the United States." Though such charges reflected actual criminal activity, they also stemmed from the fact that conservative antiunion forces labeled many legal but aggressive union tactics, such as secondary boycotts, as a kind of racketeering. The powerful Teamsters became a frequent target for this sort of political use of terms such as "corruption" and "racketeering." But it is also true that President Hoffa and several of his successors, including Frank Fitzsimmons, Roy Williams, and Jackie Presser, had ties to organized-crime figures and abetted corruption both at the local union level and within the union's pension and benefit funds.

[*See also* **Hoffa, James R.; Landrum–Griffin Act; Tobin, Dan; Union Corruption;** *and* **Union Reform Movements.**]

BIBLIOGRAPHY

Garnel, Donald. *The Rise of Teamster Power in the West*. Berkeley: University of California Press, 1972.

Leiter, Robert. *The Teamsters Union: A Study of Its Economic Impact*. New York: Bookman Associates, 1957.

Witwer, David. *Corruption and Reform in the Teamsters Union*. Urbana: University of Illinois Press, 2003.

David Witwer

INTERNATIONAL CONFEDERATION OF FREE TRADE UNIONS

The International Confederation of Free Trade Unions (ICFTU) emerged from the World Federation of Trade Unions (WFTU) in 1949 after a dispute erupted between members over implementation of the Marshall Plan. Specifically, the dispute was between the Western trade union federations, headed by the U.S. Congress of Industrial Organizations (CIO) and the British Trade Union Congress (TUC), which supported the plan, and the Communist-led trade union federations in the Soviet Union, central and eastern Europe, France, Italy, Latin America, and Asia, which opposed it. As a result of the dispute, the CIO and the TUC established the ICFTU.

At the ICFTU's founding conference in London on 28 November 1949, 261 delegates representing sixty-three national trade union centers drafted a constitution defining "free trade unions" as labor organizations that, autonomous of any outside control, serve as independent bargaining agents and obtain their power from their members. Affiliates were to achieve their goals primarily through collective bargaining and would pursue government help only when negotiation failed. Though many ICFTU affiliates were ostensibly socialist or social democratic, no official ties existed to the Socialist International.

The ICFTU opposed all totalitarian ideologies, including Communism, fascism, and militarism, and attempted to prevent labor organizations from being penetrated by political movements expressing such ideologies. Undoubtedly, the guiding theme in the ICFTU's early program was anti-Communism. Because of the ICFTU's connections to the North Atlantic Treaty Organization, the confederation was organically linked to the Western power bloc.

From 1955 to 1967 the ICFTU adopted a hard line concerning whether and how its affiliates should deal with WFTU members. Generally speaking, the ICFTU argued that the WFTU affiliates were interested only in promoting Soviet policy and had no desire to improve the international proletariat's lot. The confederation remained steadfast in this position, even though it had many concerns and positions in common with the WFTU throughout the 1950s and 1960s, such as the dangers caused by Cold War militarism, opposition to apartheid, and the wish to enlarge women workers' rights around the globe.

As détente bloomed in the 1970s, various national trade union centers that were affiliated with the ICFTU met with WFTU affiliates. The organization as a whole, however, refused to pursue relationships with any organizations whose programs the ICFTU believed conflicted with free and democratic trade union principles. Despite the confederation's official position, ICFTU affiliates established multilateral contact with WFTU members in 1974 at the Second European Conference of the International Labor Organization; there Western and Eastern European labor organizations met informally for the first time since the 1949 schism. Subsequent meetings between European affiliates of the ICFTU, WFTU, and the World Confederation of Labor (WCL) took place in 1975 and 1977; topics discussed included work environments, the use of hazardous material in industry, and trade union training and education.

Upon the Soviet Union's collapse at the end of 1991, confederation membership rose dramatically when trade union centers from the nations of the former Soviet bloc affiliated with the ICFTU. Immediately prior to its merger with the WCL on 1 November 2006 to form the International Trade Union Confederation, the ICFTU represented 157 million members across 148 nations and territories throughout the world.

[*See also* **International Unionism and International Solidarity; Labor and Anti-Communism;** *and* **World Federation of Trade Unions.**]

BIBLIOGRAPHY

Carew, Anthony, Michel Dreyfus, Geert van Goethum, Rebecca Gubrell-McCormick, and Marcel van der Linden, eds. *The International Confederation of Free Trade Unions*. Bern, Switzerland: P. Lang, 2000.

Windmuller, John P. "Realignment in the I.C.F.T.U.: The Impact of Détente." *British Journal of Industrial Relations* 14, no. 3 (1976): 247–260.

Victor G. Devinatz

INTERNATIONAL LABOR DEFENSE

The International Labor Defense (ILD) was a legal and political organization sponsored by, although nominally independent of, the Communist Party USA. Founded in 1925, the ILD in its early years attempted to aid and secure freedom for American radicals who had been imprisoned during the World War I era. In 1931 it came to the defense of the Scottsboro Boys, nine black teenagers charged with raping two white women and sentenced to die by an Alabama jury. The ILD won several new trials for the defendants, while building a national and international publicity and protest campaign that involved not only the boys' families but also one of their original accusers, who recanted. By 1937 four of the nine were released, although the others remained imprisoned for years thereafter.

In other cases in the South, the ILD drew attention to the exclusion of blacks from juries and the violation of free-speech rights exemplified by states' so-called anti-insurrection laws. By the mid-1930s the ILD began collaborating more closely with its former bitter rival, the National Association for the Advancement of Colored People, and other liberal organizations. Vito Marcantonio, a prominent New York leftist politician and congressman, became ILD president, and the organization changed its publication's name from *Labor Defender* to the more neutral *Equal Justice*.

During World War II the ILD forcefully and often effectively defended African American workers and soldiers, and its legal strategies influenced civil rights and civil liberties lawyers. The ILD disbanded in 1946, merging with other organizations to establish the Civil Rights Congress.

[*See also* **Racism; Sacco and Vanzetti Case;** *and* **Scottsboro Case.**]

BIBLIOGRAPHY

Carter, Dan T. *Scottsboro: A Tragedy of the American South*. Baton Rouge: Louisiana State University Press, 1969.

Martin, Charles H. *The Angelo Herndon Case and Southern Justice*. Baton Rouge: Louisiana State University Press, 1976.

Martin, Charles H. "The International Labor Defense and Black America." *Labor History* 26 (1985): 165–194.

Jonathan D. Bloom

INTERNATIONAL LADIES' GARMENT WORKERS' UNION AND AMALGAMATED CLOTHING WORKERS OF AMERICA

The apparel industry has long been a central battleground in labor history. Of the many unions that have attempted to organize apparel workers in the United States, the two most influential were the International Ladies' Garment Workers' Union (ILGWU) and the Amalgamated Clothing Workers of America (ACWA).

Founded in 1900 by a disparate group of small apparel unions, the ILGWU had its first major period of growth in 1909 with the so-called Uprising of 20,000, a series of strikes that arose from the grass roots and centered among immigrant women workers in New York City. Along with a 1910 cloak makers' strike, the uprising resulted in significant membership gains. By the end of World War I, the ILGWU was the largest and most successful union organizing less-skilled immigrant and women workers. After 1919, however, the union faltered, largely because of divisive internal fights over the role of Communists.

The ACWA emerged in 1914, forged out of similar struggles. A primary impetus for its creation lay with the frustration among clothing workers in New York City and Chicago with the leadership of the United Garment Workers (UGW), the men's clothing industry union affiliated with the American Federation of Labor (AFL). The ACWA from its founding until 1914 charted an independent course from the AFL and pioneered innovative thinking regarding labor–management relations.

Both the ILGWU and the ACWA fostered forms of social unionism that distinguished them from more conventional American unions. Their leaderships were firmly committed to organizing across ethnic and racial lines—even if their practice often fell short of their aspirations. Furthermore, the unions developed numerous social benefits for their members, most notably the construction of cooperative housing developments, union-funded health programs, a limited form of unemployment insurance, and in the case of the ACWA, a bank funded and administered by the union.

The 1920s proved difficult for the ILGWU and the ACWA, yet it was also then that the two most significant leaders in these unions' histories enhanced their reputations and influence: Sidney Hillman at the ACWA and David Dubinsky at the ILGWU. Both Jewish immigrants influenced by socialist ideas, Hillman and Dubinsky sustained their unions until New Deal labor policies facilitated reinvigorated organizing and growth. As unions that had long adopted an industrial (as opposed to a craft) model of organization, the ACWA and the ILGWU stood at the center of the battles over labor's future in the 1930s. Though both men participated in creating the Committee for Industrial Organization (CIO), Dubinsky and Hillman split when the CIO acted to create itself as an independent labor federation. Dubinsky insisted on keeping the ILGWU in the AFL, while Hillman served as the second most important leader of CIO.

At the end of World War II, textile workers in the South became a prime target for AFL and CIO organizing drives, but the failure to organize southern workers seriously limited U.S. labor's power. By the early 1970s the U.S. clothing industry's decline intensified as technological change, the increasing concentration of domestic manufacturing in the largely union-free South, and the rise of global competitors challenged the unions' power. This led the unions in the clothing and textile industries to a series of mergers that culminated in 1995 with the creation of a single unified organization, the Union of Needle Trades, Industrial, and Textile Employees (UNITE). Soon after, UNITE merged with the Hotel Employees and Restaurant Employees to form UNITE-HERE, but in 2010 UNITE seceded and merged with the Service Employees International Union.

[*See also* **American Federation of Labor; Congress of Industrial Organizations; Garment Industry; Hillman, Sidney; Immigration; Jewish American Labor Movement; Labor Movement, Decline of the; Labor Movements; Service Employees International Union; Textile Industry;** *and* **Uprising of 20,000.**]

BIBLIOGRAPHY

Fraser, Steven. *Labor Will Rule: Sidney Hillman and the Rise of American Labor*. New York: Free Press, 1991.

Katz, Daniel. *All Together Different: Yiddish Socialists, Garment Workers, and the Labor Roots of Multiculturalism*. New York: New York University Press, 2011.

Parmet, Robert D. *The Master of Seventh Avenue: David Dubinsky and the American Labor Movement*. New York: New York University Press, 2005.

Paul Adler

INTERNATIONAL MONETARY FUND

The International Monetary Fund (IMF) is an influential intergovernmental financial institution composed of 187 member states, headquartered in Washington, D.C. Its role in the international economic system has changed substantially since its creation at the end of World War II. At that time, Allied leaders feared that peace would lead to a return of the Great Depression. To forestall such a disaster, Allied representatives met at a conference in Bretton Woods, New Hampshire, in July 1944. Their goal was to fashion agreements that would facilitate a stable postwar financial system. The products of this planning were the IMF and the International Bank for Reconstruction and Development, better known as the World Bank.

When the IMF began operating in 1947, it developed two primary means of promoting postwar economic stabilization. First, it lent governments foreign currencies when they faced temporary cash shortages in paying for imports. Second, it maintained stable currency exchange rates. To achieve stability, member nations were expected to maintain the value of their currency as measured against the American dollar, though they could, in a crisis, devalue their currency if they obtained permission from the IMF. In the early 1970s the system of fixed exchange collapsed and was replaced by a "floating" system in which a currency's exchange rate fluctuated in relation to its current market value. Ever since, the IMF's focus has shifted increasingly toward promoting development in the global south and post-Communist countries. To achieve its new goals the IMF has integrated lending and economic-analysis functions more thoroughly into its everyday business.

The IMF is capitalized by contributions from its member states, with votes apportioned based on financial contribution: the more money a country invests, the more votes it gets. The United States controls nearly one fifth of the votes and exercises a de facto veto on major decisions. Policy is made by a board of governors that has representatives from every member nation. Daily operations are controlled by the twenty-four executive directors who make up the executive board. The executive board, in turn, appoints the organization's chief officer—called the "managing director"—who, by convention, is always a European.

Civil-society groups have criticized the IMF for decisions that favor developed nations at the expense of the developing world. Its decision-making process has also been criticized for lacking transparency. Critics further accuse the IMF of using a one-size-fits-all approach in its advice to governments, often exacerbating the economic problems that initially called for intervention. Critics argue that the conditions imposed on borrowing countries through IMF structural-adjustment loans—such as cutting government spending, liberalizing trade, and privatizing state enterprises—often result in lowering the living standards of the country's poor. Since the late 1990s the IMF has initiated a series of reforms that it claims address these issues, but many critics remain unconvinced.

[*See also* **Bretton Woods Conference; Foreign Trade; GATT and WTO; Globalization;** *and* **World Bank.**]

BIBLIOGRAPHY

Boughton, James M., and Domenico Lombardi, eds. *Finance, Development, and the IMF.* New York: Oxford University Press, 2009.

Schild, Georg. *Bretton Woods and Dumbarton Oaks: American Economic and Political Postwar Planning in the Summer of 1944.* New York: St. Martin's Press, 1995.

Vreeland, James Raymond. *The International Monetary Fund: Politics of Conditional Lending.* New York: Routledge, 2007.

Paul Gibson

INTERNATIONAL UNIONISM AND INTERNATIONAL SOLIDARITY

International unionism appears to follow Karl Marx and Frederick Engels's call, "Workers of all countries, unite!" Since the mid-nineteenth century, unionists have voiced moving rhetoric, created international institutions, and supported workers outside their own countries. Actual unity, however, has been limited as unions responded to national, regional, and local concerns. Political and ideological conflicts further divided international labor.

International Organizations. International unionism has two main global arenas, one for federations of unions and the other for individual trade unions. U.S. labor has intermittently participated in both arenas.

International organizations have included the International Workingmen's Association (1864–1876); the international trade secretariats (1889–2001), which have continued since 2001 under the name global union federations; the International Secretariat of the National Trade Union Federations (1901–1914), which, renamed in 1914 the International Federation of Trade Unions, disbanded during World War I but continued afterward (1919–1945); the International Federation of Christian Trade Unions (1920–1940 and 1945–1968), which was renamed the World Confederation of Labour (1968–2006); the Red International of Labor Unions, or Profintern (1921–1937); the World Federation of Trade Unions (since 1945); the trade union internationals (since 1949); the International Confederation of Free Trade Unions (1949–2006); and the International Trade Union Confederation (since 2006).

World federations. Founded in London in 1864, the first international labor organization, the International Workingmen's Association, embraced radical anticapitalist goals, while also seeking to prevent the recruitment and importation of foreign strikebreakers. In 1869 the American National Labor Union (NLU) resolved to "aid the one high purpose of all who work for our reform; that of the complete unity and enfranchisement of labor everywhere." The NLU collapsed before joining the International Workingmen's Association, but Socialists did create an American branch. The whole organization, damaged by factional disputes and political repression, dissolved in 1876.

Internationalism through the early twentieth century usually meant exchanges of letters between union leaders, connections derided by radicals as "letterbox internationalism." Still, such correspondence between the American Federation of Labor (AFL) and Europeans led to the first coordinated international demonstrations for the eight-hour day, held on 1 May 1890.

The Europeans formed the International Secretariat of the National Trade Union Federations in 1901. The AFL affiliated nine years later because its president, Samuel Gompers, hoped that internationalism would be effective in preventing the recruitment of strikebreakers, building international solidarity, and bringing "possibly the entire abolition of the fratricidal wars between nations of men."

Under American prodding, the International Secretariat became the International Federation of Trade Unions (IFTU) in 1914. After World War I the AFL rejected the socialism of the European unions and left the IFTU. It rejoined the IFTU in 1938, but only to prevent the affiliation of the Congress of Industrial Organizations (CIO). Other political divisions roiled the interwar years, with Christian and Communist unions forming their own internationals.

The World War II alliance of Great Britain, the United States, and the Soviet Union encouraged the CIO and British and Soviet unions to initiate the World Federation of Trade Unions (WFTU) in 1945. The WFTU brought together Communist, Socialist, and nonideological union federations for the first time. The AFL refused to participate alongside Communists. As the Cold War deepened in 1949, the CIO and other non-Communist unions abandoned the WFTU. Instead they joined with the AFL in the International Confederation of Free Trade Unions (ICFTU). The American Federation of Labor and Congress of Industrial Organizations (AFL-CIO) left the ICFTU in 1969 largely because President George Meany's rigid anti-Communism conflicted with the beliefs of most other affiliates. It rejoined in 1982 after Meany's influence had waned.

After 1949 the WFTU sat squarely in the Soviet camp. Splits in world Communism in the 1950s, the development of "Eurocommunism" after 1968, and the collapse of Communism in the 1980s and 1990s decimated the organization. In 2010 the WFTU claimed that it had 82 million members who support its "proletarian internationalism," but these numbers were likely exaggerated.

In contrast, during the 1980s and 1990s the ICFTU expanded by including independent eastern European, African, and South American unions. In 2006 the religious World Confederation of Labour and the secular ICFTU merged, naming the new organization the International Trade Union Confederation (ITUC). The ITUC in 2011 claimed 305 affiliates in 151 countries, representing 175 million members. It works in "defense of workers' rights and interests" largely by publicizing labor struggles and by advocating labor positions at global forums. Although the AFL-CIO is a member, it limits its involvement, and in 2012 no AFL-CIO officers served on the ITUC's executive board.

International trade secretariats. The most important international organizations for individual unions have been the international trade secretariats (ITSs), renamed the global union federations (GUFs) in 2001. Cigar makers formed a short-lived ITS in 1871, but most emerged at the end of the nineteenth century. By 1914 there were thirty-three ITSs, largely covering skilled craftsmen, but also with strong representation of industrial workers. After waves of consolidations beginning in the 1970s, ten GUFs remained by 2012.

Whereas the world federations have stressed political issues, the ITSs and GUFs have aided strikes, tried to coordinate standards, and provided other support for individual unions around the world. Beginning with shipyard strikes in the 1890s, the ITSs organized boycotts and raised funds for miners, maritime workers, and other strikers. The ITSs notably led a boycott of South African goods during the antiapartheid struggles. Since then, the GUFs have facilitated alliances of unions negotiating with multinational corporations and have supported global corporate campaigns that target antilabor employers. They have also negotiated so-called framework agreements with a variety of multinationals and industry groups that attempt to establish labor rights around the globe.

Labor and global institutions.
Labor has been a participant in the evolving system of global institutions. Gompers fathered the International Labour Organization (ILO) in 1919. It reflected his corporatist thinking by including representatives of business, government, and unions. The ILO seeks to regulate capitalism through a series of international agreements called "conventions." It remains an important source of information about labor, and its conventions establish fundamental labor rights. Yet U.S. isolationism kept it from joining the ILO until 1934. By 2012 the United States had ratified only 14 of 188 ILO conventions. Unions also have a formal voice in several bodies of the United Nations and at the Organization for Economic Co-operation and Development. The AFL-CIO's participation at the United Nations, as in other international venues, has been spotty.

International unions.
International unions, those with branches in more than one country, played a significant role in North American labor. International unions in imperial countries also represented workers in colonial possessions. Skilled craftsmen in the 1800s found union cards from their home country useful for entry into the brotherhood of their craft abroad. These interconnections happened most often where unionists shared a common language. As American unions grew in the second half of the nineteenth century, they accepted Canadian locals and then dubbed themselves "international unions." The typographers were the first to do so. The Knights of Labor in the 1880s and 1890s had many Canadian members, particularly in Ontario. The radical Industrial Workers of the World had followings in Canada, Australia, Britain, and New Zealand, and even among miners in northern Mexico.

In the twentieth century some international unions coordinated bargaining with transborder corporations. However, tensions within the internationals led to autonomy and, eventually, independence for many Canadian locals. In contrast to their work in Canada, the internationals have made limited efforts to coordinate Mexican–U.S. labor solidarity. Occasional attempts involved mining, agriculture, and the maquiladora sector of industrial production, but no long-lasting collaborations were created.

American Unions and U.S. World Power.
U.S., British, and, more recently, German unions built their own international structures that functioned in harmony with their governments' foreign policy. Funded secretly by the U.S. government, in the early twentieth century the AFL attempted to influence Latin American labor through the Pan-American Federation of Labor. By midcentury, cooperation between the AFL and the government had expanded to Europe, Africa, and Asia. The AFL

influenced elections in post–World War II France and Italy and underwrote breakaway anti-Communist unions. The AFL-CIO also actively combated radicals in Latin American unions and politics. The AFL and then the AFL-CIO acted through a series of regional institutes and committees. The U.S. government, particularly the State Department, the Labor Department, and the Central Intelligence Agency, funneled large amounts of money through union channels to aid anti-Communist unions and strengthen politically reliable leaders.

The Americans advocated an ideology of "free trade unionism," which meant unions independent of a political party or government. In practice, however, U.S. labor often supported foreign unions of questionable legitimacy or undemocratic politics. Foreign policy occasionally divided American labor, particularly in World War I, the early Cold War, and the Vietnam War. On the whole, however, unions rarely opposed U.S. foreign policy. In 1997 under President John Sweeney the AFL-CIO reformed its overseas operations by disbanding the regional institutes and replacing them with the new Solidarity Center. The Solidarity Center has been more judicious in its support of foreign unions. However, it usually supports U.S. foreign policy, receives most of its funding from the government's National Endowment for Democracy, and remains secretive about its activities.

[*See also* **Globalization; International Confederation of Free Trade Unions; Labor and Anti-Communism; Trade Union Educational League and Trade Union Unity League;** *and* **World Federation of Trade Unions.**]

BIBLIOGRAPHY

Alexander, Robert J., with Eldon M. Parker. *International Labor Organizations and Organized Labor in Latin America and the Caribbean: A History*. Santa Barbara, Calif.: Praeger/ABC-CLIO, 2009.

Carew, Anthony, ed. *The International Confederation of Free Trade Unions*. New York: Peter Lang, 2000.

Daele, Jasmien van, ed. *ILO Histories: Essays on the International Labour Organization and Its Impact on the World during the Twentieth Century*. New York: Peter Lang, 2010.

Gordon, Michael E., and Lowell Turner, eds. *Transnational Cooperation among Labor Unions*. Ithaca, N.Y.: ILR Press, 2000.

Windmuller, John P. *International Trade Secretariats: The Industrial Trade Union Internationals*. Washington, D.C.: U.S. Department of Labor, Bureau of International Labor Affairs, 1995.

Victor Silverman

INTERNET COMMERCE

Online commerce did not originate on the Internet. In the early 1970s, companies such as Lexis-Nexis and Dialog started selling information online in lucrative niches such as law and finance. Belief in a pending "revolution" caused by information technology soon spurred governments and businesses across the developed world to develop consumer networks. People were expected to order goods online, trade stocks, bank, book travel, and pay for access to information sources. These networks usually coupled a cheap terminal based on the Videotex standard with a standard television. Videotex was unsuccessful in the United States, but during the 1980s commerce was an increasingly important part of personal-computer-based online services such as CompuServe and America Online.

Origins of Internet Commerce. Only in 1994 was it possible to purchase anything at all using a web browser. The Internet was created in the early 1980s, but only from the mid-1990s was it used to support the exchange of goods and services for money. The Internet began as a collection of interconnected networks used primarily by universities, research laboratories, and the military. Until 1992 commercial activity was expressly forbidden. Its architecture and protocols lacked many of the features found in networks designed for consumer or business use. Data was transmitted without encryption, meaning that credit-card numbers and passwords were vulnerable to eavesdroppers. There was no centralized system of user accounts to validate identities or bill for services consumed.

Despite these technical handicaps, the Internet proved impossible for business to resist. Previous electronic commerce platforms had been centralized, requiring merchants to make deals with the network operators to have their services listed. Setting up a website was cheap and easy and gave unmediated access to customers. The Internet soon had more users than the proprietary online services had, as a wave of enthusiasm for everything Internet-related directed a flood of investment toward online retailers. This, in turn, pushed established businesses to announce their own web projects to counter the threat posed by start-ups. Talk of revolutions, paradigm shifts, and explosive change was rampant during the late 1990s.

Business Models. The conventional wisdom was that each area of online retail would support one or two big and highly profitable companies. "First-mover advantage" meant that the key to success was to spend massively on advertising, promotion, and expansion to achieve this dominant position. Hundreds of well-financed start-up companies applied this model to areas as diverse as pet supplies (Pets.com), office products, books (Amazon.com), recorded music (CDNow), furniture (Furniture.com), groceries (Webvan), garden equip-

ment (Garden.com), toys (eToys.com), cars (Autoweb.com), and drugs (Drugstore.com).

They competed with conventional retailers by offering a wider selection of goods and by lowering overhead costs by shipping directly from a warehouse. This was the same model used by catalog retailers such as L. L. Bean, Dell Computers, and Fingerhut, albeit with further cost savings from eliminating paper catalogs and compelling customers to enter their own data. User-contributed reviews, pioneered by Amazon.com, also harnessed customers to do work formerly carried out by sales staff. Firms such as Amazon.com and Buy.com offered a huge range of goods, echoing the breadth of the Sears & Roebuck catalog that a century earlier had featured items from toys to house-building kits and farming equipment.

The online store was not the only business model. eBay quickly won a dominant position in the online auction business. Its success was self-reinforcing: buyers are attracted by a wide selection of goods, and sellers are drawn by a large population of buyers. eBay transferred the expense and complexity of handling goods to the seller, and it took a commission on each sale.

Soon eBay moved beyond auctions, allowing sellers to list products for immediate purchase at fixed prices. This, and the equivalent Amazon Marketplace system, provided a giant online bazaar in which small businesses could hawk goods of all kinds.

Other new businesses helped customers compare prices across retailers (MySimon), read professional evaluations of Internet vendors (Gomez.com), or share their own reviews of companies and products (Epinions.com). These were usually supported by advertising. Internet users of the era were reluctant to pay for information services, with the notable exceptions of pornography (Whitehouse.com) and investment-oriented publications (the *Wall Street Journal*).

Business-to-Business. Internet commerce fell, and falls, into two areas: "business-to-business," or B2B, and "business-to-consumer," or B2C. Internet commerce between businesses has the lower public profile but accounts for a larger portion of the economy. Its roots are in what was known during the 1980s as electronic data interchange, usually between producers and suppliers. This was pioneered within the automobile industry to send engineering diagrams and parts orders and, in retail, by Wal-Mart to replenish stock from major suppliers such as Proctor & Gamble without human intervention. Electronic integration across organizational boundaries helped to tighten supply lines, lowering administrative and inventory costs and enabling just-in-time production. By the early 2000s this communication was increasingly shifting to the Internet, using the new XML, or extensible markup language.

The Internet boom also saw the creation of many industry-specific electronic marketplaces in which orders could be posted for suppliers to bid on by means of rules that had been programmed into the system. The idea was to extend the commodities-exchange model of spot prices from a small set of metal, energy, and agricultural commodities to a much broader range of products and services. This failed, but online exchanges did help organizations to shift their routine procurement activities online.

The Bubble Bursts. In 2000 the bubble in Internet stocks burst, and their prices crashed. With the prospect of a rapid public offering withdrawn, investors stopped funding new companies. The strategy of spending money freely to win customers and boost revenue growth was no longer viable. Profitability was suddenly more important than growth, and many of the highest-profile online retailers were bankrupt within months. In some niches, such

as furniture and pet supplies, all the major online retail start-ups failed.

Surviving online retailers tended either to be either tiny firms targeting small niches—such as water filters or *Star Trek* collectibles—or large, diversified companies whose progress was convincing enough to win continued investor support, such as Amazon.com. Amazon began in 1995 as an online book retailer, but within five years it had diversified into music, videos, electronics, home improvement, and toys. This required massive investment in warehousing and promotions, as well as the development of efficient logistics. Amazon finally began to produce profits at the end of 2002, and by 2011 it reported revenues of $48 billion—significantly higher than those of the combined Sears and K-Mart group. To give an idea of just how inflated the Internet commerce bubble was, Amazon's shares regained their peak 1999 value only in 2009, by which point it had increased revenues by a factor of fifteen and gone from increasing losses to substantial profits.

Infrastructure. The shift to Internet commerce reversed the long-term decline of home delivery. Retailers used to deliver all kinds of products to homes, but with the spread of cars, shopping malls, and big-box stores, Americans got used to driving their purchases home. Some Internet retailers set up their own local distribution networks, including Kozmo.com, which offered free one-hour delivery of consumer items, and Webvan, which offered free home delivery of groceries from highly automated warehouses. Most, however, relied on the delivery infrastructure provided by Federal Express and United Parcel Service to serve a national market with rapid and reliable delivery.

Internet retailers also relied on the existing banking infrastructure for electronic processing of credit and debit cards, supplemented for smaller businesses by nonbank payment systems. The most successful of these was PayPal, acquired by eBay in 2002.

Impacts. Bookshops and music retailers were hit hardest by online competition. Most national chains liquidated, including such once-common fixtures as Virgin, Tower, Borders, and Sam Goody. Electronics retailing has also appeared to be in terminal decline. Conversely, online retail brought many new choices to residents of rural areas and smaller cities.

According to Forrester Research, by 2010 Internet retail volume had reached $176 billion—8 percent of all retail sales in the United States. An unexpected outcome was the disappearance of the "mall rat." Socializing in shopping malls had been a major pastime for teenagers, but as their shopping and socializing patterns shifted online, now Americans between the ages of fourteen and seventeen were visiting malls less frequently than the population as a whole was (see Lambert and Connolly, 2011).

[*See also* **Advertising; Consumer Credit and Credit Cards; Consumer Culture; Department Stores; Mass Marketing;** *and* **Technology.**]

BIBLIOGRAPHY

Aspray, William, and Paul E. Ceruzzi, eds. *The Internet and American Business.* Cambridge, Mass.: MIT Press, 2008.

Cassidy, John. *Dot.Con: The Greatest Story Ever Sold.* New York: HarperCollins, 2002.

Evans, Philip, and Thomas S Wurster. *Blown to Bits: How the New Economics of Information Transforms Strategy.* Boston: Harvard Business School Press, 2000.

Lambert, Jean, and John Connolly. "After the Recession: Surprising New Patterns of U.S. Mall Shoppers." *Retail Property Insights* 18, no. 2 (2011): 27–32.

Schmidt, Susanne K., and Raymund Werle. "Interactive Videotex." In their *Coordinating Technology: Studies in the International Standardization of Telecommunications,* pp. 147–184. Cambridge, Mass.: MIT Press, 1998.

Thomas Haigh

INTERSTATE COMMERCE COMMISSION

See **Economic Deregulation and the Carter Administration;** *and* **Economic Regulation.**

IRON AND STEEL INDUSTRY

The history of iron making and steelmaking in the United States reflects the rise, fall, and partial recovery of the productive capacity of the nation's industrial sector, from its origins in the Colonial Era, through the enormous productivity of the 1880–1970 period, to the cutbacks and restructuring of the 1980s and 1990s. This history has been marked by dramatic events, triumphant technological innovations, and well-known entrepreneurs.

Through the early 1800s, the three essential stages in the production of finished metal, typically conducted in small, rural ironworks, consisted of smelting, which melted iron ore into a raw, intermediate material; refining, which imparted properties such as hardness or malleability; and shaping, which molded the metal into rails, beams, sheets, or tools and other objects. In the mid-nineteenth century, highly skilled workers refined and shaped the smelted metal. These workers, called "puddlers," produced high-quality wrought iron through a demanding and expensive process. Before the iron could be used, however, it had to be rolled through grooved cylinders. Skilled rollers then controlled the production of small amounts of finished iron.

When the Civil War began, U.S. mills output only a million tons per year through a slow and costly process that produced a wrought iron too weak to be made into rails, a much-demanded product. Fortunately for the ironmasters, a new technology, named for its English inventor, Henry Bessemer, became available in the postwar years. The Bessemer process bypassed puddlers by mechanizing the refining process. In a large, egg-shaped "converter," workers combined molten pig iron and a blast of air that produced an explosion so powerful that virtually all the impurities were removed. The result was a new, hard metal, Bessemer steel, ideal for making rails. The new process sparked mechanical improvements throughout the industry, prompting steelmasters to integrate all stages of the production process. These integrated mills employed thousands of workers, many of them recent immigrants, and made three thousand tons of steel per day. The Bessemer process and its successor, the open-hearth method, underlay the Second Industrial Revolution, which transformed the United States into the world's premier industrial and military power.

Andrew Carnegie was the first to see in the Bessemer process new possibilities for industrial organization. At his mammoth mills near Pittsburgh, Pennsylvania, he streamlined and automated production. Significantly, Carnegie's mills required less and cheaper labor than had been necessary in the days of puddling, and thousands of workers were displaced by the innovations that swept the metals industry in the late nineteenth century. Carnegie's initiatives essentially eliminated trade unionism in the steel industry until the 1930s, when the Steel Workers Organizing Committee succeeded in creating an industry-wide union open to workers of all skill levels. Throughout the twentieth century, industrial relations in steelmaking were marked often by acrimony and occasionally, as in the nineteenth century, by violence.

The United States retained its premier position in metal making until the 1970s, when international competition, higher production and labor costs, and questionable managerial decisions led to the collapse of the U.S. Steel Corporation, the direct heir of Carnegie's empire. In Pittsburgh and other locales in the Northeast, the effects were devastating. This region, which had profited so handsomely in the age of steel, was forced to look to service industries, education, and information technologies to rebuild its economic base. In other venues, however, the American steel industry staged a renaissance by the 1990s and succeeded in producing quality products in efficient and profitable mills, some large, others belonging to smaller competitors.

[*See also* **Amalgamated Association of Iron, Steel, and Tin Workers; Carnegie, Andrew; Congress of Industrial Organizations; Homestead Strike (1892); Industrialization and Deindustrialization; Little Steel Strike (1937); Rust Belt and Deindustrialization; Steel Strike of 1919; Technology and Labor;** *and* **United Steelworkers.**]

BIBLIOGRAPHY

Hoerr, John P. *And the Wolf Finally Came: The Decline of the American Steel Industry.* Pittsburgh, Pa.: University of Pittsburgh Press, 1988.

Hogan, William T. *Economic History of the Iron and Steel Industry in the United States.* 5 vols. Lexington, Mass.: Heath, 1971.

Paul Krause

J

JEWISH AMERICAN LABOR MOVEMENT

The Jewish labor movement in America was more than simply a gathering of unions from the garment trades. As an expression of the dynamic urban subculture of Jewish immigrants from the Russian Empire, it developed into a multifaceted movement, comparable to European models of social democratic organizations. The movement's main pillars were the International Ladies' Garment Workers' Union (ILGWU), representing workers in the women's apparel industry, and the Amalgamated Clothing Workers of America (ACWA), representing workers in the men's clothing industry. Surrounded by a number of smaller unions and seconded by the mutual help association the Workmen's Circle, these unions were the center of a densely organized network of economic, social, cultural, and political interests. Embodying a strong socialist current in American labor, the movement was supported by a prolific Yiddish-language press, among which Abraham Cahan's *Jewish Daily Forward* had the greatest circulation.

David Dubinsky, the ILGWU president from 1932 to 1966, and Sidney Hillman, the founding president of the ACWA from 1914 to 1946, were exiles from the 1905 Russian revolution. They brought to Progressive Era America the ideals of economic justice and democracy that they had fought for in tsarist Russia. Early adopting the inclusive principles of industrial unionism and institutionalized collective bargaining, they rationalized the Darwinian world of the garment industry, regularizing labor relations in this strike-prone and fragmented sector of small shops, subcontractors, and sweated workers. Beyond obtaining wage increases and shorter hours for garment workers, the ILGWU and ACWA developed social and educational services for their members: the ACWA began a workers' bank and housing projects, and both unions sponsored an array of evening classes to sustain the members' original cultures while facilitating their adaptation to American life. These services, however, as well as the unions' growth, were decimated by the Great Depression. But by the mid-1930s, with the effects of industrial recovery and revived union militancy, the combined membership of the garment-trades unions reached half a million. The predominant Jewish majority from eastern Europe had by then partly given way to a more varied labor force that included many Italians and more recent migrants from Puerto Rico and the American South. The unions retained a Jewish identity, however, so long as their original leaders imprinted their charismatic and strong governance on the unions during the New Deal and World War II.

Both Dubinsky and Hillman were at the forefront of the movement for industrial unionism that split the American Federation of Labor (AFL) and led to the creation of the Congress of Industrial Organizations (CIO) in 1938. The ACWA was one of the founding unions in the new federation, but the ILGWU returned to the AFL in 1940 because Dubinsky feared the strong impact of the CIO's Communist-led unions. Dubinsky's anti-Communism derived from an internecine battle within the garment trades, the so-called civil war in the unions, that had raged in the mid-1920s when Communist activists tried to take power in key ILGWU and ACWA locals. The conflict left a deep-seated hostility to Communism in the ILGWU ranks. Except for the furriers' union under Ben Gold's leadership, Communist influence weakened within the Jewish American labor movement.

Hillman, who won a reputation as labor statesman, played a central role in the enactment of New Deal labor legislation and industrial reforms. Strongly advocating state intervention in labor–management relations and economic regulation, he was closely associated with such New Deal labor legislation as the National Industrial Recovery Act, the National Labor Relations (Wagner) Act, and the Fair Labor Standards Act. During World War II, as a member of President Franklin D. Roosevelt's National Defense Advisory Committee, Hillman chaired the labor division of the War Production Board.

The New Deal's inclusion of such Jewish American labor leaders as Hillman and Dubinsky in its inner circles led the garment unions to break with their socialist loyalties. In 1936, Jewish labor leaders in New York created the American Labor Party as an alternative to the Tammany Hall–dominated New York City Democratic Party in order to secure the votes of Jewish workers for Roosevelt's second and third terms. Thereafter the Jewish American labor movement and its members solidified their loyalty to the Democratic Party.

[*See also* **Congress of Industrial Organizations; Hillman, Sidney; Immigration; International Ladies' Garment Workers' Union and Amalgamated Clothing Workers of America; Jewish Labor Committee; Labor and Anti-Communism;** *and* **Labor Movements.**]

BIBLIOGRAPHY

Dubinsky, David, and A. H. Raskin. *David Dubinsky: A Life with Labor*. New York: Simon and Schuster, 1977.

Fraser, Steven. *Labor Will Rule: Sidney Hillman and the Rise of American Labor*. New York: Free Press, 1991.

Green, Nancy L. *Ready-to-Wear and Ready-to-Work: A Century of Industry and Immigrants in Paris and*

New York. Durham, N.C.: Duke University Press, 1997.

Howe, Irving, with Kenneth Libo. *World of Our Fathers: The Journey of the East European Jews to America and the Life They Found and Made.* New York: Simon and Schuster, 1976.

Parmet, Robert D. *The Master of Seventh Avenue: David Dubinsky and the American Labor Movement.* New York: New York University Press, 2005.

Catherine Collomp

JEWISH LABOR COMMITTEE

The Jewish Labor Committee (JLC) was founded in New York City in February 1934 by the non-Communist elements within the Jewish labor movement. Its main pillars were the garment trades unions and the Workmen's Circle. The JLC proposed to help victims of Nazism and fascism abroad and to combat anti-Semitism in the United States. Before immigrating to the United States, the JLC's founder and first president, Baruch Charney Vladeck, and many of its leaders—most notably, David Dubinsky, Nathan Chanin, Jacob Pat, and Emanuel Tabachinsky—had been left-wing political activists as Bundists in the Russian Empire or in interwar Poland. They thought that Nazism must be resisted not only by Jewish organizations alone, but also by a broad coalition of progressive forces grounded in the international labor movement. During World War II the JLC rescued more than eight hundred European labor and socialist leaders from German-occupied France and simultaneously from Lithuania (annexed by the Soviet Union). It saved from extermination key European leaders of the Labour and Socialist International, as well as their counterparts in national political parties, trade unions, and cultural institutions. The JLC cooperated with the American Jewish Joint Distribution Committee in broad relief operations to support Jewish people in war-torn Poland, while also allocating funds to the underground labor movements in countries under Nazi occupation.

After the war the JLC participated in the reconstruction of Jewish lives. It assisted the re-settlement of displaced persons. In France and Poland it financed children's homes for Jewish orphans and organized a program to sponsor their education. In later years the JLC supported the American civil rights movement and shaped public opinion about anti-Semitism in the Soviet Union. In the twenty-first century the JLC remains active and describes itself as "a Jewish voice in the labor movement and the voice of labor in the Jewish community."

[*See also* **Jewish American Labor Movement.**]

BIBLIOGRAPHY

Collomp, Catherine. "The Jewish Labor Committee, American Labor, and the Rescue of European Socialists, 1934–1941." *International Labor and Working-Class History* 68 (Fall 2005): 112–133.

Jacobs, Jack. "A Friend in Need: The Jewish Labor Committee and Refugees from the German-Speaking Lands, 1933–1945." *Yivo Annual* 23 (1996): 391–417.

Malmgreen, Gail. "Comrades and Kinsmen: The Jewish Labor Committee and Anti-Nazi Activity, 1934–41." In *Jews, Labour, and the Left, 1918–48,* edited by Christine Collette and Stephen Bird, pp. 4–20. Aldershot, U.K.: Ashgate, 2000.

Malmgreen, Gail. "Labor and the Holocaust: The Jewish Labor Committee and the Anti-Nazi Struggle," *Labor's Heritage* 3, no. 4 (October 1991): 20–35.

Catherine Collomp

JOINT-STOCK COMPANIES

Designed for business purposes, joint-stock companies are institutions owned by shareholders in which each share represents a measure of the value of the capital stock of the company. The management of the company is divorced from the ownership, although share-owners—usually organized as a board of directors—can hire and fire the managers. Owners often possess unequal shares, all of which are transferable. Shareowners' liability for corporation losses is limited to the value of the shares that they own. Membership is limited to those who can afford to subscribe to the shares. Such companies have existed for hundreds of years and became particularly important in the development of trade and business in early modern Europe: evolving from guild and fraternal organizations into money-making organizations, often as arms of the state, often they were granted governing powers that today might be considered more appropriate for states.

No Renaissance and early modern state, with the exception of Spain, proved able to muster resources for successful overseas colonization without the leadership of interested private individuals, so the majority of early European efforts in the Atlantic and the East used some form of private associations, whether official or ad hoc, to pool capital. In the colonization of North America, joint-stock companies became a significant vehicle for combining wealth and limiting risk. Although a variety of forms of private associations participated in English expansion, two chartered types of joint-stock organizations propelled the expansion of the English overseas: the so-called semi-joint-stock company, which allowed investors to gain shares in particular voyages or specific trading missions, and the permanent joint-stock company, which created a permanent stock of shares in a company that could be purchased by interested investors. These companies possessed monopoly privileges granted by the sovereign. Shareowners remained separate from the management of the enterprises, but they received dividends from the companies' management

based on corporate profits. Voyages of discovery, exploration, and trade, conducted across great distances and exposing the adventurers to great risk, benefited from the ability of such companies to raise large sums of money from numerous people. The companies often were required to maintain diplomatic missions, outfit military expeditions, and govern territories and so benefited from the legal institution of the charter as well as the financial strength of the pool of investors.

The earliest important English joint-stock company was the Muscovy Company, chartered in 1555, which signaled English interest in developing trade relationships with newly discovered Russia. The company provided a model for private financing for trading companies and colonizing companies to settle new lands. The East India Company, chartered in 1600, and the Virginia Company, chartered in 1606 (expanded in 1609 and 1612, and also known as the Virginia Company of London), were joint-stock companies of great political significance in early English expansion. The Virginia Company of London possessed a monopoly on trade and the power to establish a government over new territories in much of what became southern North America. The company oversaw the establishment of the first permanent English-speaking settlement at Jamestown, developed a system of labor importation that greatly expanded the production of tobacco, fought numerous wars against the native peoples, and established the first representative political institutions in North America. The company ultimately lost its charter after the Indian uprising and massacre of 1622. After an investigation of the company, the crown revoked its charter and took over governance of the colony. Even so, joint-stock companies continued to be important in the first century of English expansion, and the initial governments of Rhode Island, Connecticut, and Massachusetts Bay were influenced by the corporate charter form—reflecting their origins as joint-stock companies. Joint-stock companies continued to be an essential form of corporate organization in the expansion of trade and commerce in the seventeenth and eighteenth centuries.

[*See also* **Capitalism;** *and* **Corporatism.**]

BIBLIOGRAPHY

Davis, Joseph Stancliffe. *Essays in the Earlier History of American Corporations.* 2 vols. Cambridge, Mass.: Harvard University Press, 1917.

Ekelund, Robert B., and Robert D. Tollison. "Mercantilist Origins of the Corporation." *Bell Journal of Economics* 11 (1980): 715–720.

Fisher, F. J. "Some Experiments in Company Organization in the Early Seventeenth Century." *Economic History Review* 4 (1933): 177–194.

McCusker, John J., and Russell R. Menard. *The Economy of British America, 1607–1789.* Chapel Hill: University of North Carolina Press for the Omohundro Institute of Early American History and Culture, Williamsburg, Va., 1985.

Scott, William Robert. *The Constitution and Finance of English, Scottish, and Irish Joint-Stock Companies to 1720.* 3 vols. Cambridge, U.K.: Cambridge University Press, 1910–1912.

Doug Bradburn

JONES, MARY "MOTHER"

(1837–1930), labor activist. Born in Ireland, Mary Harris immigrated to North America around 1851. She attended school in Toronto, Ontario, and later worked as a teacher and a dressmaker in Michigan, Chicago, and Memphis, Tennessee. In 1861 she married George Jones, an iron molder and union member. Six years later, she lost her spouse and their four children to an epidemic of yellow fever. This tragedy forced her back into life as a wage earner. In her often spurious and apocryphal autobiography, Jones claims to have joined the Knights of Labor in Chicago in 1871 and to have helped organize striking railroad workers in Pittsburgh, Pennsylvania, in 1877, yet the Knights became active in Chicago only in the 1880s, and Jones was nowhere near Pittsburgh during the year of the strike. What is clear is that by the 1880s, her resentment of social inequality had found an outlet in the labor movement, and her career as an agitator was well under way.

A tiny woman dressed in black, with striking blue eyes, Jones became known as "Mother Jones" and the "angel of the miners," a beloved figure in the mine fields of West Virginia, Pennsylvania, Illinois, Arizona, and Colorado. Her incendiary speeches made her a legend. She was arrested four times in the years before World War I, and in 1912, amid a bitter miners' strike, she was convicted in West Virginia of conspiracy to commit murder. Pardoned by the governor, Mother Jones continued her peripatetic activity among miners and other industrial workers.

Socialists embraced Mother Jones, but she remained politically unaffiliated. A founding member of the Industrial Workers of the World in 1905, she also worked for the American Federation of Labor, campaigned for the Democratic Party, and made her last public appearance in 1924 at the convention of the Farmer-Labor Party. Although she became a late twentieth-century feminist icon, Jones, like other radical labor activists of her day, viewed woman suffrage as trivial and the women's rights movement as bourgeois. She reserved her compassion, her boundless energy, and her always tart tongue for the workingman and his family. She died in Silver Spring, Maryland.

[*See also* **Labor Leaders; Labor Movements; Mining Industry; Radicalism and Workers;** *and* **Strikes.**]

BIBLIOGRAPHY

Fetherling, Dale. *Mother Jones, the Miners' Angel.* Carbondale: Southern Illinois University Press, 1974.

Foner, Philip S., ed. *Mother Jones Speaks: Collected Writings and Speeches.* New York: Monad Press, 1983.

Gorn, Elliott J. *Mother Jones: The Most Dangerous Woman in America.* New York: Hill and Wang, 2001.

Parton, Mary Field, ed. *The Autobiography of Mother Jones.* Chicago: C. H. Kerr, 1925.

Ann Schofield

JUNGLE, THE

Published in 1906, Upton Sinclair's *The Jungle* remains one of the most influential novels in American political and social history. Sinclair was a socialist writer who had just published a book on chattel slavery and an article on the meatpackers' failed 1904 strike for the socialist periodical *Appeal to Reason.* Invited by the journal's editor, Fred Warren, to do another exposé, this time of wage slavery, Sinclair in the autumn of 1904 lived for seven weeks in Chicago's meatpacking district, investigating both the plants and the adjoining workers' residences.

Based on this research, Sinclair wrote a graphic description of conditions encountered by a fictional family of Lithuanian immigrants. Jurgis Rudkus, the protagonist, is optimistic that he will succeed in America because of his physical strength and his work ethic. Instead, the industrial order grinds down not only Jurgis but every member of his family, several of whom die or suffer other terrible fates.

Though Sinclair's goal was to expose the evils of industrial capitalism and demonstrate the need for socialism, the public's reaction was very different. At a time when middle-class consumers were being taught to trust national name brands as symbols of purity and quality, Sinclair offered a very different message. *The Jungle* portrayed an industry in which monopolistic corporations sold diseased and damaged meat and invested in advertising rather than in pure and safe products. In the resulting uproar, Congress passed the Pure Food and Drug Act and the Meat Inspection Act in 1906. Commented a disappointed Sinclair: "I aimed at the public's heart and by accident I hit it in the stomach." Later critics attacked the pessimism of the book, especially Sinclair's failure to recognize the resourcefulness of immigrant workers.

[*See also* **Meatpacking and Meat-Processing Industry** *and* **Pure Food and Drug Act.**]

BIBLIOGRAPHY

Barrett, James. "Introduction." In *The Jungle,* by Upton Sinclair, pp. xi–xxxii. Urbana: University of Illinois Press, 1988.

Robert A. Slayton

K

KEATING–OWEN ACT

The anti-child-labor movement viewed President Woodrow Wilson's signing of the 1916 Keating–Owen Act as a triumph. Cosponsored by Representative Edward Keating, a Democrat from Colorado, and Senator Robert L. Owen, a Democrat from Oklahoma, the act passed by a vote of 337 to 46 in the House of Representatives and a vote of 50 to 12 in the Senate. The act's drafters turned to the Constitution's interstate commerce clause to weaken federal judicial resistance to the legislation as an unconstitutional extension of federal authority. The act levied fines on enterprises that shipped and sold the products of mines that employed children under the age of sixteen and factories that employed children under the age of fourteen.

President Wilson cited the legislation as evidence of his progressive credentials. Nonetheless, some parents, children, and religious leaders objected to child-labor regulations as unwelcome interference in family life. Many business owners also opposed efforts to end child labor.

The U.S. Children's Bureau was assigned responsibility for enforcing the new law—no mean task, considering that verifying the age of young workers would be complicated. Few adolescents at the time had birth certificates, and physical standards left little room for individual differences. Poverty encouraged many parents and their children to devise ways to circumvent child-labor laws. Yet the Children's Bureau hoped that the Keating–Owen Act would encourage states to tighten their laws beyond the federal minimums.

On 31 August 1917, however, one day before the Keating–Owen Act was to be implemented, a North Carolina judge ruled the law unconstitutional. Twenty days earlier, Roland H. Dagenhart had filed suit enjoining the Charlotte district attorney, William C. Hammer, from enforcing the law. Dagenhart argued that the act violated the constitutional rights of his two sons, fourteen-year-old Ruben and twelve-year-old John, and denied him as their father the right to their wages. The editor of the *Southern Textile Bulletin*, a supporter of child labor, urged Roland Dagenhart to bring the suit and probably paid the legal fees.

On 3 June 1918, in a 5-to-4 decision in the case, *Hammer v. Dagenhart*, the U.S. Supreme Court held the Keating–Owen Act unconstitutional. Although the Court ruled that Congress could not invoke the interstate commerce clause to prevent child labor, the majority opinion deemed child labor evil. Children's rights activists were disappointed in the decision, but they were also encouraged that the Court recognized a need to end exploitive child labor.

Congress passed another law, this one imposing taxes rather than fines on the employers of children, but it was also declared unconstitutional by the U.S. Supreme Court (*Bailey v. Drexel Furniture Co.*, 1922). That was followed by a constitutional amendment that passed Congress in 1923 but failed to obtain ratification by the necessary number of states. During the ensuing Great Depression, with its mass unemployment and the reform impulses behind the New Deal, Congress in the 1938 Fair Labor Standards Act outlawed child labor. The emergent New Deal Supreme Court upheld the law.

In an interview about the Keating–Owen Act published in 1924, twenty-year-old Ruben Dagenhart said that he lost by winning the case. In fact, he lamented, "Look at me! A hundred and five pounds, a grown man and no education. . . . From 12 years old on, I was working 12 hours a day—from 6 in the morning till 7 at night, with time out for meals. And sometimes I worked nights besides. . . . It would have been a good thing for all the kids in this state if that law they passed had been kept."

[*See also* **Child Labor; Factory and Hours Laws;** *and* **Fair Labor Standards Act.**]

BIBLIOGRAPHY

Hindman, Hugh D. *Child Labor: An American History.* Armonk, N.Y.: M. E. Sharpe, 2002.

Lindenmeyer, Kriste. *A Right to Childhood: The U.S. Children's Bureau and Child Welfare, 1912–46.* Urbana: University of Illinois Press, 1997.

Mellet, Lowell. "The Sequel to the Dagenhart Case." *American Child* 6, no. 1 (1924): 3. Reprinted in *Children and Youth in America: A Documentary History,* edited by Robert H. Bremner, vol. 2, *1866–1932,* pp. 716–717. Cambridge, Mass.: Harvard University Press, 1971.

Sallee, Shelley. *The Whiteness of Child Labor Reform in the New South.* Athens, Ga.: University of Georgia Press, 2004.

Trattner, Walter I. *Crusade for the Children: A History of the National Child Labor Committee and Child Labor Reform in America.* Chicago: Quadrangle, 1970.

Wood, Stephen B. *Constitutional Politics in the Progressive Era: Child Labor and the Law.* Chicago: University of Chicago Press, 1968.

Kriste Lindenmeyer

KELLEY, FLORENCE

(1859–1932), social reformer. Florence Kelley was born into a patrician Philadelphia Quaker and Unitarian family, the daughter of William Darrah Kelley, a leading Republican Party politician, and Caroline Bonsall Kelley. Graduating from Cornell University in 1882, Kelley then studied at the University of Zurich, where in 1884 she married Lazare Wischnewetzky, a Russian Jewish socialist medical student, and forged a lifelong identity as a socialist. Between 1885 and 1888 she gave birth to three children. Returning to New York City in 1886, she found it impossible to continue the political commitments begun in Zurich. In 1891, after Lazare began beating her, she fled with their children to Chicago, residing at Jane Addams's Hull House until 1899. In 1895 she completed a law degree at Northwestern University.

Kelley established her national reputation during a three-year tenure as Illinois's Chief Factory Inspector (1893–1896), enforcing the state's pathbreaking eight-hour law for working women and children. In 1899 she assumed the position that she occupied until her death, secretary-general of the newly formed National Consumers League (NCL). Returning to New York City, she lived at the Henry Street Settlement on Manhattan's Lower East Side.

Building sixty-four local leagues by 1906, Kelley, in cooperation with other women's organizations, worked to make American government more responsive to the needs of working people, especially wage-earning women and children. Using gender-specific legislation as a surrogate for class legislation, Kelley defended the constitutionality of legislation limiting the hours of working women, then successfully extended those protections to men. Similarly, the NCL pioneered the passage of state minimum-wage laws for women that in 1938 led to a federal minimum-wage law for women and men.

[*See also* **Child Labor; Consumer Movements; Eight-Hour Day; Labor Movements; Living-Wage Campaigns;** *and* **Women Workers.**]

BIBLIOGRAPHY

Sklar, Kathryn Kish. *Florence Kelley and the Nation's Work: The Rise of Women's Political Culture, 1830–1900.* New Haven, Conn.: Yale University Press, 1995.

Sklar, Kathryn Kish, ed. *Notes of Sixty Years: The Autobiography of Florence Kelley.* Chicago: C. H. Kerr for the Illinois Labor History Society, 1986.

Kathryn Kish Sklar

KEYNESIAN ECONOMICS

The term "Keynesian economics" refers in the first instance to the concepts set forth by the British economist John Maynard Keynes (1883–1946) in *The General Theory of Employment, Interest, and Money* (1936). The term also encompasses the many variations and permutations of Keynes's ideas that developed over time.

The Keynesian Era. Keynes crystallized his concepts during the Great Depression. He concluded that the length and severity of the Depression belied the classical theory that recovery from economic collapse occurred automatically through the market mechanism. Instead, Keynes posited, an economy could come to rest in a state of equilibrium that included idle resources and mass unemployment. The shock of collapse and perceptions of a paucity of investment opportunities caused businessmen to lack inducement to invest. In such conditions interest rates, however low, could not overcome the uncertainty undermining the will to invest. Hence, Keynes concluded, only a force external to the economic system per se could galvanize recovery. That external force would be government spending, or public investment, to compensate for the deficiency of private investment. With adequate investment assured by government, the economic system with its market mechanism would be spurred to operate more productively and to resume growth. Direct government intervention in the market would not be needed. Especially in the wake of the recession of 1937–1938, and as set forth by Keynes's leading American advocate of the time, Alvin H. Hansen, Keynesianism's initial thrust was secular rather than cyclical. What Hansen saw as an underlying tendency toward stagnation caused by a secular deficiency of private investment required massive and permanent public investment to keep the economy humming.

The third of a century after 1940 was dubbed the "Keynesian era," given the growing dominance of Keynesianism in the economics profession and the impact of Keynesianism on public policy—the latter reaching its apogee in the 1960s. But the Keynesian economics of the time differed in significant ways from its initial incarnation. Keynesianism during the so-called great boom was viewed primarily in cyclical rather than secular terms. It was often advanced in terms of demand management rather than in terms of public investment. And it was sometimes promoted in terms of tax reductions rather than in terms of government spending. Economists and policy makers geared fiscal policy to cyclical fluctuations: as the economy contracted, government could compensate by infusing money to increase demand. Tax cuts could also be designed to stimulate private investment. Rather than viewing public investment as a necessary engine of growth given businesspeople's lack of an inducement to invest, fiscal policy became a way to fine-tune a dynamic and expanding economy driven by consumer demand and private investment. Further, the assertion by Keynes that fiscal policy would provide a macro solution to economic problems—a solution not requiring public microeconomic intervention—in turn contributed to a theoretical alteration of great moment. Through a neoclassical synthesis, economists began to treat Keynes's general theory as a special case that did not displace orthodox theory as the ruling paradigm. This

had the consequence of converting Keynesian economics from a proclaimed general theory to a practical kit of short-run public-policy tools.

Decline and Revival. So long as the great boom lasted, the neoclassical version of Keynesian economics held sway. When the boom dissipated after 1973, the appeal of Keynesianism as practiced during the 1960s dissipated as well, leading to the end of the Keynesian era. The great problem from 1973 into the early 1980s was recession coupled with inflation, or what became known as "stagflation." As growth slowed and prices rose, the neoclassical Keynesian toolkit seemed not to work. To infuse money into the economy to combat recession or stagnation would intensify inflation. To withdraw money from the economy to combat inflation would intensify recession or stagnation. The original version of Keynesian economics had a long-term dimension, which had been lost after World War II as a cyclical version became dominant. Hence Keynesianism now appeared to lack explanatory power for the stagnation and declining economic growth. And lacking a concern for how the economy actually worked—a lack for which Keynes himself was partly responsible—Keynesianism appeared hapless in dealing with manifestations of inflation purported to arise from corporate power. In this climate, Keynesian economics, as it was understood during the boom, became widely and deeply discredited, and a new generation of economists and policy makers turned to concepts and policy instruments with pre-Keynesian and pre–Great Depression roots.

Nonetheless, a minority of economists labored to revise—or restore—Keynesianism to meet the exigencies of the time. Post-Keynesians, as they came to be known, undertook to provide what they felt Keynesian economics lacked from its inception: micro foundations to fit its macro theory. To them the great lacuna in Keynesianism was its failure from the beginning to address the impact of the modern corporation on the macroeconomy. Additionally, especially in the wake of the recession of the early 1990s that appeared, if only temporarily, to discredit the economic policies of the 1980s, many economists called for large-scale public investment to spur economic growth, an effort to refashion a secular version of Keynesianism.

A more drastic turn in the fortunes of Keynesianism, however, occurred with the economic collapse of 2008. That collapse, the worst since the Great Depression, led economists and policy makers to reconsider the ideas of the man, Keynes, who had wrestled most impressively with the disasters of the 1930s. Massive public spending was legislated in 2009 to stop the economic freefall, and concepts discarded decades earlier reappeared. Once again it was argued that the economic system could reach a condition in which it was unable to right itself; that low interest rates alone would not suffice to stimulate private investment and renewed economic growth; and that only external intervention in the form of a massive public fiscal package could avert a catastrophe on the magnitude of the 1930s. With the freefall and the sense of panic that accompanied it stopped, however, the question arose of whether the Keynesian revival would result in only a short-term policy prescription to avert immediate disaster and would lack a concomitant reorientation of economic theory to recognize the salience of long-term public investment.

[*See also* **Business Cycles; Depressions, Economic; Economic Theories and Thought; Inflation and Deflation; Long Swings and Cycles in Economic Growth; Monetary Policy, Federal; Neoclassical Economics; Neoliberalism as Public Economic Policy;** *and* **Stagflation.**]

BIBLIOGRAPHY

Clarke, Peter. *Keynes: The Rise, Fall, and Return of the 20th Century's Most Influential Economist.* New York: Bloomsbury Press, 2009.

Rosenof, Theodore. *Economics in the Long Run: New Deal Theorists and Their Legacies, 1933–1993.* Chapel Hill: University of North Carolina Press, 1997.

Skidelsky, Robert. *Keynes: The Return of the Master.* New York: Public Affairs, 2009.

Stein, Herbert. *The Fiscal Revolution in America: Policy in Pursuit of Reality.* 2d rev. ed. Washington, D.C.: AEI Press, 1996.

Theodore Rosenof

KNIGHTS OF LABOR

The Noble and Holy Order of the Knights of Labor (KOL) was the first significant labor federation in the United States and the first to establish an international presence among the world's working class.

Uriah Stephens and eight colleagues fashioned the KOL from a collapsed Philadelphia garment cutters' union in 1869. Because most trade unions barely survived the post–Civil War economic contraction, Stephens—who served as the KOL's first General Master Workman, or president—patterned the KOL after fraternal organizations. The Knights created a quasi-Masonic ritual and operated in secrecy until 1882. Fraternal ideals were embedded in the KOL's motto—"an injury to one is the concern of all"—and in the oath known as the SOMA, for secrecy, order, and mutual assistance, to which initiates swore fealty.

At its first convention in 1878, the KOL adopted a platform and statement of principles that defined the organization. Knights rejected as parochial and exclusionary the bread-and-butter principles of trade unions, and they bitterly denounced the hegemonic ideals of social

Darwinism. Knights noted that many rich men were neither self-made nor clever; rather they acquired wealth through inheritance, cutthroat business practices, protective tariffs, graft, and outright thievery. Knights insisted that the collective wealth of society was more important than individual wealth; that cooperative productive and distributive networks should replace acquisitive capitalism; that society should be based upon mutualism rather than individualism; and that producers, not investors, created wealth. The KOL's platform included calls for cooperatives, reserving public lands for settlers rather than speculators, laws requiring employers to pay their employees regularly, the creation of a bureau of labor statistics, an eight-hour workday, an end to child labor, equal pay for men and women, women's suffrage, banking reform, and (ultimately) an end to the wage system. Although it conducted strikes, the KOL opposed them in principle and usually launched primary or secondary boycotts before striking. Hundreds of disputes were resolved in this fashion, though Knights felt that the enactment of mandatory arbitration laws would better resolve disputes between capital and labor.

Growth. In 1878 the KOL had fewer than ten thousand members, but conditions favored its growth. The U.S. economy had entered the takeoff phase of its Industrial Revolution, but it underwent boom-and-bust cycles in which nineteen of the years between 1870 and 1900 were marred by recession. The Panic of 1873 and a crackdown against organized labor after the nationwide railroad strikes of 1877 sent trade unions into severe decline. Moreover, many states considered labor unions to be illegal conspiracies. The KOL's secrecy isolated it from the assault, just as it later insulated the KOL's predominantly Irish American membership base from being associated with the Molly Maguires, a Pennsylvania-based miners' group that was alleged to use terror.

In 1879, Stephens resigned and was replaced by Terence V. Powderly, a machinist and the mayor of Scranton, Pennsylvania. Powderly wanted the KOL to operate more openly, in part to attract more members, but also to overcome the Roman Catholic Church's condemnation of the KOL's secrecy oath. Powderly served until 1893 and oversaw both the Knights' rapid growth and its equally dramatic contraction. The KOL grew to 42,500 members in 1882, by which time it had expanded into most major cities. It welcomed as members all except liquor tradesmen, bankers, land speculators, gamblers, Chinese immigrants, and lawyers. By the mid-1880s it contained trade unionists, reformers, small-scale employers, Lassallean socialists, immigrants, agrarian radicals, Greenbackers, unskilled workers, temperance advocates, ministers, women, African Americans, and a smattering of Marxists and anarchists. These diverse groups made volatile comrades, and the KOL experienced numerous internal squabbles, fissures, and splits.

The Knights experienced explosive growth in the 1880s during the waves of activism between 1885 and 1889 that are collectively called the "Great Upheaval." Membership stood at 111,000 in 1885, the year in which the KOL won a strike against the Southwest railroad lines, owned by the hated Jay Gould. Strike success led to destabilizing growth. Paid membership soared to 729,000 by mid-1886, with legions more unofficially claiming affiliation with the Knights. Many new members viewed the KOL as labor's savior, but they were dimly aware that many of its principles called for government-instituted reform rather than action at the point of production. The KOL's complex structure made it difficult to enforce policy across its membership. In addition to a national executive board, power was also spread among national trade districts, state and district assemblies, various ad hoc committees, and thousands of local assemblies—some of which were so-called mixed bodies in which all Knights met, and some of which were segregated by trade, ethnicity, race, or gender.

The KOL reached its apex in 1886 when KOL third-party candidates contested power in 189 towns and won in 60 of them. The KOL established itself in every state and formed more than ten thousand local assemblies. At its height the KOL employed a congressional lobbyist, operated hundreds of cooperatives and public reading rooms, published dozens of newspapers, held massive rallies, and created its own sports teams, debate societies, bands, theaters, restaurants, and nurseries. It also established bodies outside of the United States and Canada, with assemblies forming in England, Germany, Ireland, France, Scotland, South Africa, and Australasia. The KOL did spectacularly well in New Zealand, where it elected members to Parliament that enacted the most advanced social legislation of any industrial democracy.

Decline and Significance. Clashes with trade unions and backlash against the Great Upheaval caused the KOL's contraction. The KOL shared blame for the 1886 Haymarket bombing in Chicago, though it declined to endorse the strike or protest that preceded it. More serious were lost railroad strikes and setbacks in the Chicago stockyards and New England textile mills. By 1890 the KOL had 100,000 members, roughly its pre-1885 total. It shed a quarter of that reduced number by 1893, when Iowa's James Sovereign replaced Powderly. Most historians consider the KOL defunct by then. Yet the KOL remained active, retreating to its rural base in the 1890s, where it fused with the rising Populist movement. The KOL closed its national office in 1917, though assemblies continued to operate as late as 1949.

The KOL demonstrated that a labor federation could serve as a countervailing force to organized capital. Its early successes inspired the 1886 creation of the American Federation of Labor (AFL), the body that supplanted it. Numerous KOL locals also experimented with industrial-union models that later reached full expression in the Congress of Industrial Organizations (CIO) in the 1930s. Both the AFL and the CIO had unfettered access to organizing Catholic workers, courtesy of KOL's role in convincing the Vatican to issue the 1891 papal encyclical *Rerum Novarum*, which removed church condemnation of labor unions. The KOL also anticipated the political potential of organized labor. Its decline was a setback for women, African Americans, recent immigrants, and unskilled workers, all of whom it had welcomed into its ranks but whom the AFL neglected.

[*See also* **American Federation of Labor; Haymarket Affair; Labor Movements; Powderly, Terence V.;** *and* **Strikes.**]

BIBLIOGRAPHY

Fink, Leon. *Workingmen's Democracy: The Knights of Labor and American Politics.* Urbana: University of Illinois Press, 1983.

Hild, Matthew. *Greenbackers, Knights of Labor, and Populists: Farmer-Labor Insurgency in the Late-Nineteenth-Century South.* Athens, Ga.: University of Georgia Press, 2007.

Weir, Robert E. *Beyond Labor's Veil: The Culture of the Knights of Labor.* University Park: Pennsylvania State University Press, 1996.

Weir, Robert E. *Knights Down Under: The Knights of Labour in New Zealand.* Newcastle, U.K.: Cambridge Scholars, 2009.

Robert E. Weir

KUHN, LOEB & CO.

Kuhn, Loeb & Co. was the leading German American investment banking firm in the

United States—and second overall only to J. P. Morgan and Company—in the late nineteenth and early twentieth centuries. Founded in 1867 in New York City by Abraham Kuhn and Solomon Loeb, two German Jewish immigrants who had been dry-goods merchants in Cincinnati, Ohio, until the 1920s the firm remained largely a family partnership. In 1875, Kuhn recruited the able young German Jewish banker Jakob Heinrich (anglicized to Jacob Henry) Schiff, who married Loeb's daughter. Until his death in 1920, Schiff dominated Kuhn, Loeb. His close connections with a network of European Jewish-led banks, headed by the Rothschild firms, facilitated Kuhn, Loeb's access to overseas capital, winning it a leading position in financing American railroad construction. Kuhn, Loeb had close ties with Edward H. Harriman's Union Pacific railroad interests, while the Morgan firm worked with James J. Hill's Great Northern Railway. During the 1905–1906 Russo-Japanese War, Schiff's fierce opposition to tsarist Russia's anti-Jewish policies impelled him to organize major American loans for Japan. In World War I, however, the German-born Schiff's refusal to participate in

American financing for the Allies—he feared that doing so might assist Russia—left Kuhn, Loeb somewhat marginalized within New York's financial community. After Schiff's death, Kuhn, Loeb remained a small partnership with a limited capital base, underwriting bonds, advising corporate clients, and specializing in mergers and acquisitions, but it steadily lost ground to the much larger commercial banks. In 1977, Lehman Brothers bought Kuhn, Loeb, ending its independent existence.

[*See also* **Harriman, E. H.; Hill, James J.; Lehman Brothers; Morgan, J. P.;** *and* **Railroads.**]

BIBLIOGRAPHY

Carosso, Vincent P. *Investment Banking in America: A History.* Cambridge, Mass.: Harvard University Press, 1970.

Chernow, Ron. *The Warburgs: The Twentieth-Century Odyssey of a Remarkable Jewish Family.* New York: Random House, 1993.

Ferguson, Niall. *High Financier: The Lives and Time of Siegmund Warburg.* New York: Penguin, 2010.

Priscilla Roberts

L

LABOR AND ANTI-COMMUNISM

From the Bolshevik revolution to the fall of the Berlin Wall, anti-Communism bedeviled the American labor movement. Antiunion forces indiscriminately charged strikers and radicals with being Communists to discredit labor action, while union leaders and activists developed an independent labor critique of Soviet Russia and the international Communist movement. In the 1920s and 1930s, long before the rise of McCarthyism, many unions enacted their own anti-Communist rules to contain Communist influence in the labor movement. After the Cold War began, government anti-Communist initiatives coincided more closely with union priorities, and labor anti-Communists collaborated with domestic and foreign-

policy efforts to stamp out Communism. This combination of internal and external pressure destroyed Communist cadres in unions and helped legitimize anti-Communism and McCarthyism.

Before 1945. The history of labor and anti-Communism can be broken into two periods, before 1945 and after 1945. Antiradicals and employers sometimes cast unionists as "Communistic" before Russia's 1917 Bolshevik revolution, but these attacks escalated with the creation of a durable Communist state and Soviet efforts to cultivate Communist unions abroad. During World War I and the 1919 Red Scare, American Federation of Labor (AFL) strikers and members of the Industrial Workers of the World (IWW, or Wobblies) alike were denounced as "Bolshevistic," although Wobblies and radicals endured far more repression. But the statutory apparatus of anti-Communism did not outlive the Red Scare; the Espionage and Sedition Acts expired, and by 1924 the Federal Bureau of Investigation (FBI) lost its mandate to police radicals and Communists inside or outside unions. Through the late 1930s, labor Communists organized with little fear of federal repression, although several cities fielded so-called Red squads.

In the early years, labor unions generated their own anti-Communist apparatus. Labor anti-Communism grew organically from the antistatist, antiradical politics of many AFL unions, and even in unions with strong socialist and Communist blocs, clumsy Communist organizing efforts alienated many members—including the syndicalist Wobblies, who disliked the Soviets' state-centered autocracy. The AFL immediately opposed the Bolshevik revolution, and AFL leaders continually whipped up anti-Communist animus among union members through indictments both of labor conditions in the Soviet Union and of the motives of Communist efforts like William Z. Foster's Trade Union Educational League, which sought to radicalize and unify discontented AFL union members. In the 1920s, most AFL unions, including John L. Lewis's United Mine Workers of America (UMWA), banned Communists from union leadership, and many union officers surreptitiously collaborated with federal repression of Communists, although unionists rejected extensions of federal antisedition laws for fear of becoming their targets. Labor anti-Communism extended also overseas; the AFL lobbied against American diplomatic recognition of the Soviet Union and campaigned in Europe against Communist unions during and after World War I. As a result, by the late 1920s American Communists had little presence in the labor movement.

In the mid-1930s, just as the National Labor Relations (Wagner) Act forced a split over in-

dustrial unionism in the AFL, Communist unionists embracing Popular Front liberalism remade themselves into outstanding organizers of the mass-production industries. Lewis's Congress of Industrial Organizations (CIO) enrolled Communist organizers and enraged AFL leaders already disaffected with the statist New Deal. In August 1938, AFL leaders helped launch the House Un-American Activities investigation led by Representative Martin Dies Jr. by supplying evidence of collaboration between the CIO and Communists, and AFL leaders Red-baited CIO-friendly members of the National Labor Relations Board (NLRB). The 1939 Nazi–Soviet pact unleashed a little Red Scare in the United States and emboldened AFL anti-Communists to support new statutory limits on Communist activity, including the Hatch Act and the Smith Act. Meanwhile the pact turned many liberal and radical labor allies against Communism, and many CIO unions banned Communists from leadership. By the end of 1941, anti-Communist union practice and government policy converged. Soviet enlistment in the Allies froze this anti-Communist consensus in place.

After 1945. After World War II, union leaders and state policy purged labor of Communism. Congressional conservatives and employers charged strikers as subversives and Communists, and the 1947 Taft–Hartley Act withheld NLRB protection from Communist-led unions. Taft–Hartley gave CIO union leaders a new tool, speeding the anti-Communist push that was already underway. By 1949 the CIO had expelled the Communist-led United Electrical Workers and charged ten other unions with being Communist-dominated. Meanwhile AFL unions advertised their anti-Communism to employers and workers, snatching up members from the left-led unions. Many historians and observers believe that anti-Communist purges robbed unions of their most militant leaders and drained labor's vitality. To longtime labor anti-Communists, though, the purges removed distracting conflicts and restored unions to their proper leaders.

Government repression also squeezed labor Communists. Mounting concern about Soviet espionage gave justification to the House Un-American Activities Committee and the Senate Internal Security Subcommittee for investigating Communist subversion in defense-industry strikes. AFL leaders generally endorsed these domestic anti-Communist efforts but disliked Senator Joseph McCarthy's slapdash approach, whereas CIO leaders more often denounced both McCarthyism and anti-Communism. (By the twenty-first century no evidence had been found to suggest that labor Communists used unions for espionage, except for unionized nuclear engineers like Julius Rosenberg.) Sustained scrutiny by the FBI, the Internal Revenue Service, and the Immigration and Naturalization Service harmed labor Communists as much as congressional tribunals did. By the early 1950s, Communists had again been driven from the mainstream American labor movement.

International anti-Communist campaigns became a far more important focus for labor anti-Communists after the war. Labor anti-Communists backed the Korean War, the Vietnam War, and U.S. interventions in Central America in the 1980s. As the Cold War polarized labor movements around the world, American unions also lent important intelligence and operational support to anti-Communist unionists around the world. First in Europe, later in Asia and Africa, AFL operatives like Jay Lovestone and Irving Brown helped organize non-Communist and anti-Communist unions and insurgencies, often in collaboration with the Central Intelligence Committee and the State Department. These efforts continued through the 1980s, with the Solidarity movement of Polish workers in 1981

trumpeted by the AFL-CIO as a crowning victory. These international campaigns, undertaken in countries where Communism attracted mass followings of workers, had far deeper implications than labor anti-Communism in the United States, where Communism won comparatively few adherents.

With the fall of the Soviet Union in 1989, the rationale for domestic and international anti-Communism also fell, freeing American unions of an old bugbear and leaving unionists and historians to grapple with the legacy of anti-Communism orchestrated by and against labor.

[*See also* American Federation of Labor; Congress of Industrial Organizations; Industrial Workers of the World; International Unionism and International Solidarity; Labor Movements; Labor Spies and Pinkertons; Radicalism and Workers; *and* Taft–Hartley Act.]

BIBLIOGRAPHY

Cherny, Robert W., William Issel, and Kieran Walsh Taylor, eds. *American Labor and the Cold War: Grassroots Politics and Postwar Political Culture.* New Brunswick, N.J.: Rutgers University Press, 2004.

Levenstein, Harvey A. *Communism, Anti-Communism, and the CIO.* Westport, Conn.: Greenwood Press, 1981.

Radosh, Ronald. *American Labor and United States Foreign Policy.* New York: Random House, 1969.

Schrecker, Ellen. *Many Are the Crimes: McCarthyism in America.* Boston: Little, Brown, 1998.

Jennifer Luff

LABOR CONSPIRACY LAW

Labor law in the United States originated with English common law that interpreted and implemented several medieval statutes that governed the wages and conditions of laborers. Because the Black Death decimated the working population in the late 1300s, both farm laborers and craftsmen were in great demand, enabling them to seek greater compensation and to search aggressively for more attractive places of employment. Medieval employers, landowners, and master craftsmen responded by enacting statutes that set maximum wages and criminalized the behavior of workers who abandoned jobs to seek better-compensated employment. As the English common law evolved, the magistrates who enforced it made it a criminal offense for an employer to offer higher wages to a worker employed elsewhere or for a worker to accept such enticement. This common-law tradition that regulated wages and employment relations traveled across the Atlantic to the British colonies in the New World.

So, too, did the subsequent eighteenth-century English common law that treated so-called combinations (unions) among craft workers to improve their wages and conditions as criminal conspiracies, especially when such combinations engaged in strikes or boycotts against unfair employers. First English jurists and then American colonial and early-national jurists criminalized collective action by workers. In England, parliamentary statutes criminalized collective organization by workers, but in the United States it was left for judges to rule that although there was nothing unlawful about workers combining for a common purpose or about individuals refusing to work or demanding better working conditions, for workers to unite to accomplish such ends constituted a criminal conspiracy.

Most judges concluded that collective labor activity was dangerous because it hurt the economy, interfered with the "natural" workings of the market, and invaded the rights of employers. They rejected workers' arguments that greater worker purchasing power helped the economy, that workers were "natural" parts of the market, too, and that the labor conspiracy doctrine invaded workers' rights because they owned their own labor. Judges perceived strikes and boycotts as selfish actions by workers to increase their compensation at the expense of employers and the greater community.

Under the common-law doctrine that allowed courts to determine what constitutes criminal activity, a Pennsylvania court in 1806 in *Commonwealth v. Pullis* adopted the labor conspiracy doctrine, declaring unions to be intrinsically criminal. The court summarily rejected the arguments by workers that, as free people in a newly free republic, they could combine to price their own labor. In 1821 in *Commonwealth v. Carlisle* when a union ingeniously tried to claim that employer combinations were equally criminal, another Pennsylvania court rejected the argument, stating that "the combination of capital for purposes of commerce" was benevolent, not harmful. Two decades later, in a famous Massachusetts case, *Commonwealth v. Hunt* (1842), the court rejected the notion that unions were by definition criminal conspiracies. The ruling legalized unions in the state of Massachusetts but left it to the judiciary to determine whether specific union actions were criminal; the ruling suggested that many strikes or boycotts might well be criminal conspiracies. The labor conspiracy doctrine persisted in the United States into the 1890s: then labor conspiracy law was replaced by the labor injunction as a judicial method of regulating strikes and boycotts.

Scholars differ about the impact of the law and judicial rulings on workers and their unions. Victoria Hattam (1992) argues that conspiracy law shaped the formation of the American working class only after about 1865. Before that time, according to Hattam, judges adopted long-standing eighteenth-century conceptions of political and economic relations—that is, the English common law and free-market economics—not the views of employers. She fails to explain how the two were different.

Peter Karsten (1990) rejects the notion of judicial bias, as do many scholars, finding that labor law followed its own internal legal dynamic. He claims that judges were professionals who understood that entrepreneurialism unfettered by worker combinations efficiently allocated resources, did not benefit their own socioeconomic class, and served the common welfare. He also fails to explain why judicial rulings did favor employers at the expense of their employees.

[*See also* **Antitrust Legislation; Class Consciousness; Master and Servant Law;** *and* **Repression of Unions.**]

BIBLIOGRAPHY

Hattam, Victoria C. "Courts and the Question of Class: Judicial Regulation of Labor under the Common Law Doctrine of Criminal Conspiracy." In *Labor Law in America*, edited by Christopher L. Tomlins and Andrew J. King, pp. 44–70. Baltimore: Johns Hopkins University Press, 1992.

Holt, Wythe. "Labor Conspiracy Cases in the United States, 1805–1842: Bias and Legitimation in Common Law Adjudication." *Osgoode Hall Law Journal* 22 (1984): 591–663.

Karsten, Peter. "'Bottomed on Justice': A Reappraisal of Critical Legal Studies Scholarship concerning Breaches of Labor Contracts by Quitting or Firing in Britain and the U.S., 1630–1880." *American Journal of Legal History* 34 (1990): 213–261.

Steinfeld, Robert J. "The Philadelphia Cordwainers' Case of 1806: The Struggle over Alternative Legal Constructions of a Free Market in Labor." In *Labor Law in America*, edited by Christopher L. Tomlins and Andrew J. King, pp. 20–43. Baltimore: Johns Hopkins University Press, 1992.

Tomlins, Christopher L. *Law, Labor, and Ideology in the Early American Republic.* Cambridge, U.K., and New York: Cambridge University Press, 1993.

Wythe Holt

LABOR JOURNALISM

In her memoir, *Footnote to Folly* (1935), the veteran reporter Mary Heaton Vorse argues that a strong labor movement requires a good network of communication and the support of a free press, for two reasons: first, because mainstream coverage of labor and workers shapes public opinion, and second, because labor unions need sources of information that are independent from corporate-owned media. Throughout American labor history, labor advocates have taken on the role of reporting, editing, and commenting on the news, especially if they first worked in the printing trade. Beginning in the early nineteenth century, labor leaders accorded fair labor reporting and independent labor journalism the respect—if not always the resources—needed for the job of informing working people. Labor newspapers, however, have run into significant obstacles in their efforts to report the news. Facing even more limited revenue and higher costs than commercial newspapers, and intermittently faced with government censorship and political opposition, labor publications have struggled and often folded. Conflict between labor and capital in the post–World War II era led to a decline in the quantity and quality of labor reporting, along with increasingly negative coverage not only of the labor movement but also of American workers.

An Alternative Press. Labor journalism began with the emergence of the penny press in the early nineteenth century. City sheets, filled with ship arrivals and commercial advertising, had little interest in or need to cover working-class experience and politics. Indeed, because early newspapers were little more than partisan publications, working-class and labor organizations were either invisible or greeted with hostility and derision. But as general news coverage came to dominate city newspapers, and newspapers as businesses became more dependent on working-class readers, reporters and editors directed more attention to working-class subjects. These papers had little interest in workers' organizations, and newspaper editors often saw labor conflict, especially strikes and boycotts, as illegitimate. In response, workingmen's parties and organizations established their own news publications. The *Mechanics' Free Press* in Philadelphia, the *Working Man's Advocate* in New York City, and the *Voice of Industry* in Lowell, Massachusetts, were among the first labor newspapers. Like many other small newspapers of the day, labor newspapers folded as working-class subscriptions declined and the costs of business overwhelmed their meager resources.

Labor journalism rebounded after the Civil War. In particular, the growth of local, regional, and national organizations affiliated with the Knights of Labor, the railroad brotherhoods, and the American Federation of Labor led to the creation of hundreds of new labor newspapers for both English-speaking and foreign-language readers. The *Journal of United Labor* (1880–1889), later known as the *Journal of the Knights of Labor* (1889–1917), provided the Knights with a national platform for labor and political advocacy. The *American Federationist* (since 1894) served to give the trades unions both a national presence and a political voice. The *Federationist* marked the coming of age for the labor press: unlike earlier publications, it began to rely on advertising revenue and published not only local organizing reports and financial statements but also investigations and political editorials. Though Samuel Gompers claimed the title of editor, this monthly news journal was shaped by the associate editor and publicist Eva McDonald Valesh, who previously published in and edited labor-reform publications and worked as a reporter for William Randolph Hearst. Radical newspapers and

journals such as the *Appeal to Reason* and the *International Socialist Review* gave extensive coverage to labor politics and covered major strikes and boycotts.

The Industrial Workers of the World, founded in 1905, published a newspaper that reflected a shift in labor coverage. Rank-and-file workers made regular contributions to the *Industrial Worker*, and other local and regional labor newspapers reflected the growing militancy of the new unionism. More than a thousand labor and radical newspapers, many of them foreign-language papers, existed before World War I. The war increased the cost of newspapers doing business: newspapers faced higher prices for and shortage of paper, new war taxes, and new restrictions on newspaper publication and government censorship. Increased hostility toward unions, immigrants, and radical organizations eroded labor's public support. Further, the publication of false reports during wartime and postwar strikes directly contributed to the failure of unions in mass-production industries.

By 1920, labor advocates recognized the weakness of the alternative press and, more specifically, its lack of information networks, even to the failure of news gathering abroad and in national and regional markets. The argument for independent sources of information led to the creation of the Federated Press. Under the leadership of Carl Haessler and with such editors as Harvey O'Connor and such reporters as Lawrence Todd, Art Shields, and Jessie Lloyd O'Connor, the Federated Press provided a news service to labor and progressive publications from its inception until it closed in 1956. The Federated Press news service also published its own syndicated labor news bulletin in the 1920s. City labor newspapers such as the *New Majority* (Chicago), the *Seattle Union Record*, and the *Minneapolis Labor Review* were instrumental in providing revenues to the labor news service and printing its extensive news reports.

After more than a decade of rebuilding the labor movement, culminating in the labor uprising of the 1930s, hundreds of new newspapers, such as the *CIO News*, the *United Auto Worker*, and the *UE News*, were quickly established, with the number of labor newspapers keeping pace with union membership.

Mainstream Media. Coverage of labor by the mainstream press, or the labor beat, was intermittent throughout the twentieth century. Louis Stark, the labor reporter at the *New York Times*, was the dean of a new generation of labor reporters and helped to shape labor coverage. At times, national news media, such as the Hearst newspapers, presented themselves as defenders of labor; small-city newspapers and chains such as Scripps courted working-class subscribers and readers. In so doing, the national and local press gave more balanced coverage of labor conflicts. With the rise of the powerful Congress of Industrial Organizations, the labor beat grew in strength and numbers, and expanded beyond the local press to take in large city and national newspapers, magazines, and national news media. Mass-market newsmagazines such *Time, Newsweek, Business Week*, and *U.S. News and World Report* and major newspapers such as the *New York Times* and the *Washington Post* had regular labor features. Professional journalism, however, championed narrow objectivity in reporting, a professional code that criticized political advocacy and limited reporting of social movements.

By the 1960s, as media corporations increasingly dominated print and broadcast news, labor reporting became narrower, more limited, and overtly critical. The journalist and critic Westbrook Pegler, for example, writing from the late 1930s to the 1960s, targeted labor unions as the source of graft and political influence that undermined American prosperity. Presenting themselves as reformers, conservative journalists painted the labor movement as big, subversive, and corrupt. By the 1970s, even as the labor movement entered a period of decline, it was common to read negative commentary on American workers in general and on strikes in both the private and the public sectors. Framing the debate was the assumption that labor conflict pitted the interests of the public—of taxpayers, consumers, stockholders, and employers—against the interests of the few workers who had access to union wages and benefits.

[*See also* **Labor Movements;** *Little Red Songbook;* *and* **Printing and Publishing.**]

BIBLIOGRAPHY

Conlin, Joseph, ed. *The American Radical Press, 1880–1960*. 2 vols. Westport, Conn.: Greenwood Press, 1974.

Faue, Elizabeth. *Writing the Wrongs: Eva Valesh and the Rise of Labor Journalism*. Ithaca, N.Y.: Cornell University Press, 2002.

Garrison, Dee. *Mary Heaton Vorse: The Life of an American Insurgent*. Philadelphia: Temple University Press, 1989.

O'Connor, Jessie Lloyd, Harvey O'Connor, and Susan M. Bowler. *Harvey and Jessie: A Couple of Radicals*. Philadelphia: Temple University Press, 1988.

Rondinone, Troy. *The Great Industrial War: Framing Class Conflict in the Media, 1865–1950*. New Brunswick, N.J.: Rutgers University Press, 2010.

Witwer, David. *Shadow of the Racketeer: Scandal in Organized Labor*. Urbana: University of Illinois Press, 2009.

Elizabeth Faue

LABOR LEADERS

The fundamental dynamic shaping both the character and the content of working-class leadership involves the interaction of workers' demands and the changing social, economic, and political landscape in which those demands are made. Labor leaders imperfectly represent the interests of their constituents to the outside world, while frequently also trying to mold their constituents' demands in response to perceived external limitations. In important ways, then, the nature of labor leadership at any given historical moment is shaped by the interaction of working-class demands and external opportunities.

Education and Reform. Labor leadership is not necessarily the same as union leadership, and through much of the nineteenth century, extra-union organization was the primary forum for the emergence of labor leaders. The first American trade unions emerged in the late eighteenth century as a historically specific response to changes in the production and marketing of finished goods, which for the first time sundered the connection between master craftsmen and journeymen artisans. Though the initial responses to changes in production tended to come through localized job actions, by the 1820s these trade organizations began to cohere into broader, citywide movements. These organizations, which were mostly confined to the most industrialized urban centers, produced some of the first visible labor leaders in the United States. William Heighton was the intellectual and organizational force behind Philadelphia's Mechanics' Union of Trade Associations, the first attempt at a formal alliance of organized trade in a major city.

But for the most part, working-class leadership in the antebellum era was marked by educational rather than organizational purposes. Heighton organized a library company and a debating program, and he edited and published a weekly newspaper for the Mechanics. In New York City, Langston Byllesby and Thomas Skidmore pursued similar blends of intellectual and organizational activism, blending contemporary republicanism with various strands of European radicalism to produce a language that challenged both the emerging economic order and the American political system and targeted everything from the length of the workday to slavery.

This reform orientation persisted into the second half of the nineteenth century, even as the first truly national labor unions began to emerge in railroad, printing, and some metal trades. Founded in 1866, the National Labor Union (NLU), the first sustained effort at a national labor movement, launched an ambitious campaign for the eight-hour day before it fell victim to the Panic of 1873. The main successor to the NLU, the much larger Knights of Labor (KOL), similarly mixed economic and political objectives. The KOL provided the United States its first national labor leader, Grand Master Workman Terence V. Powderly, but his leadership of the organization was largely symbolic, with little meaningful control over local assemblies. A series of failed job actions, most notably the disastrous railroad strike in the Southwest in 1886, reinforced Powderly's fears about economic action and redirected the KOL's energies toward political action and social reform, where it was modestly successful on the local level. The most famous example of the reformist strand in American labor leadership was Eugene V. Debs, who headed the American Railway Union before its destruction propelled him on a political career that saw him run for president five times as the candidate of the Socialist Party.

Business and Politics. The emergence of national craft and industrial unions during the last quarter of the nineteenth century fundamentally altered the responsibilities of working-class leadership. Beginning with the Federation of Organized Trades and Labor Unions in 1881 and continuing after 1886 in the

American Federation of Labor (AFL), the mainstream of the organized labor movement was marked not by a commitment to political reform, but by a pragmatic brand of "business unionism." Samuel Gompers, who headed the AFL for all but one year between 1886 and 1924, was an articulate advocate for a variant of unionism that combined generous benefits, high dues, and centralized control over strikes to curtail and direct the explosive growth of shop-floor militancy. This vision of the labor movement generally accepted the broad outlines of the status quo, despite occasional outbursts of rhetorical radicalism, eschewing the transformative agenda of the earlier movement in favor of efforts to enhance the material well-being of American workers within the existing economic system.

The consolidation of industrial capitalism thrust a new set of responsibilities upon labor leaders at the turn of the twentieth century. Though Gompers continued to serve as the symbolic spokesman for the American working class—despite the racial and gendered limits in the ranks of union membership—he increasingly occupied a more practical role as well, sitting with political and business leaders as the representative of all or some organized workers. Gompers served as the vice president of the National Civic Federation, founded in 1900, which aimed to resolve industrial disputes through informal mediation. Beginning with President Theodore Roosevelt's intervention in the anthracite coal strike of 1902, union leaders like John Mitchell of the United Mine Workers also found it necessary to mediate among their own union membership, elected officials, and the public, increasingly through the press.

This new range of responsibilities was only amplified by the changes brought by World War I, which further centralized the labor movement and linked its fate more tightly to the state. By allowing union leaders to participate in the government boards coordinating the mo-bilization effort, Woodrow Wilson also made union leaders more responsible for controlling an increasingly restive workforce. Enforcing contracts was added to negotiation as a key responsibility, and both responsibilities were undertaken by an increasingly professional class of union leaders.

This trend exploded after the start of the Great Depression, when unions gained unprecedented access to the levers of state power. As the working class moved more fully into the Democratic Party's political coalition, Sidney Hillman and John L. Lewis emerged as essential insiders, responsible for bartering as much with New Deal agencies and Democratic leaders as with representatives of major textile and mining firms. To be sure, Lewis in particular retained an older element of rabble-rousing oration and independence from the Democrats, but displays of workplace militancy were increasingly geared toward putting pressure not on employers, but rather on the agencies of the state.

In the postwar era, the consolidation of major industries and the proliferation of national pattern-bargaining added another dimension to union leadership. When Walter Reuther negotiated the famous Treaty of Detroit with Ford, General Motors, and Chrysler in 1950, he established a pattern of collective bargaining that conceded managerial prerogatives over the production and distribution of goods in return for the long-term material security of unionized workers.

The decline of private-sector union membership during the second half of the twentieth century also keyed changes in union leadership. The concession bargaining typical of many key American industries since the 1980s has forced union leaders into a more defensive posture with their own memberships. The weakened state of the institutional labor movement has, in some sense, fostered a return to an older brand of reformism, wherein union leaders claim the symbolic role of spokesmen for the American working class in an effort to secure social reforms through political channels rather than through collective-bargaining agreements. The growth of public-sector unions, which bargain directly with the state, has only reinforced the centrality of political activity to labor leadership.

[*See also* Collective Bargaining; Debs, Eugene V.; Gompers, Samuel; Hillman, Sidney; Labor Movements; Labor Organizations, Pre–Civil War; Labor's Role in Politics; Lewis, John L.; Powderly, Terence V.; Reuther, Walter; Strikes; *and* Treaty of Detroit and Postwar Labor Accord.]

BIBLIOGRAPHY

Brody, David. "Career Leadership and American Trade Unionism." In *The Age of Industrialism in America: Essays in Social Structure and Cultural Values*, edited by Frederic Cople Jaher, pp. 288–303. New York: Free Press, 1968.

Dubofsky, Melvyn, and Warren Van Tine, eds. *Labor Leaders in America*. Urbana: University of Illinois Press, 1987.

Mills, C. Wright. *The New Men of Power: America's Labor Leaders*. New York: Harcourt, Brace, 1948.

Van Tine, Warren. *The Making of the Labor Bureaucrat: Union Leadership in the United States, 1870–1920*. Amherst: University of Massachusetts Press, 1973.

Joseph E. Hower

LABOR MARKETS

The term "labor market" does not refer to a particular location or set of institutions. Instead it describes the processes of labor allocation in an economy, that is, the methods by which employers fill vacancies and workers find jobs, as well as the internal allocation of labor within businesses, households, and other economic organizations. The interaction of supply and demand in the market determines wages and employment.

The historical study of labor markets has two major objectives. The first is to describe how labor is allocated over time and how markets have evolved. The second is to document the consequences for wages, employment, the distribution of income and jobs, and the overall efficiency of the market. Although American labor markets have rarely, if ever, achieved perfect efficiency, the American economy's sustained growth and American workers' high standard of living could not have been achieved without the development of effective labor-market institutions.

The Colonial Period. From the beginning of European settlement in North America, American labor markets have been characterized by the scarcity of labor compared to the abundance of land and natural resources. Natural abundance raised the productivity of labor, enabling ordinary Americans to enjoy a higher standard of living than comparable Europeans could. Realizing these economic opportunities required labor-market mechanisms capable of overcoming the obstacles of high passage costs from Europe and imperfect communication.

In the colonial period, labor moved in three ways: free migration, indentured servitude, and the forced migration of African slaves. Because of the high cost of transatlantic passage, only a small fraction of potential migrants could afford transport to the Americas. The cost barrier was especially problematic for the young, landless laborers who stood to gain the most from such migration.

Under the indenture system, migrants signed contracts with merchants in Europe that committed the migrants to work for a specified number of years in exchange for passage to the

New World. Once in America, the merchants sold these contracts to planters needing labor. Because land abundance made it hard for planters to hire free labor, the use of unfree workers—either indentured servants or slaves—was the only way they could expand cultivation beyond the limits set by their family's labor. Demand for servants varied geographically, depending on crops and climates. Consistent with the existence of a well-functioning market, terms of service appear to have varied with individual productivity and employment conditions in the specific locality.

In the mainland British colonies, African slaves began to replace indentured servants as the principal source of unfree labor in the late seventeenth century. In the Chesapeake region the proportion of the population that was black grew from 13 percent in 1700 to around 40 percent in 1770. In South Carolina and Georgia, the black proportion of the population climbed from 18 percent to about 45 percent in the same period. The transition from indentured European to enslaved African labor reflected the effects of shifting supply-and-demand conditions. Improved economic conditions in Europe after 1650 reduced the supply of servants and raised their cost. Meanwhile, increasing competition in the slave trade caused slave prices to fall.

Because export opportunities were more limited in northern colonies, these colonies imported few slaves. Yet abundant land created opportunities for small-scale agriculture in Pennsylvania, New York, and New Jersey that enabled employers to attract indentured servants throughout the eighteenth century. In New England, where farming was less profitable and little demand existed for hired labor, immigrants, either free or slave, were infrequent.

By 1776, market forces had created a sharp regional division in labor-market regimes. Across the South, large-scale plantation agriculture utilizing slave labor was well established.

In the North, family farms predominated. Hired labor might be used on occasion, but limited markets meant that expansion was not justified. What had emerged by accident was soon codified into law. After the Revolution, all the northern states adopted some form of gradual emancipation, and in 1787 the Northwest Ordinance prohibited the introduction of slavery into territories north of the Ohio River.

Independence to World War I. Three related developments dominated the history of labor markets between the Revolutionary War and World War I: westward expansion, the growth of manufacturing, and mass immigration. From 1800 to 1910 the labor force grew from 2.3 million to 37.5 million. In these same years, the agricultural labor force's share of total employment dropped from 74 percent to 31 percent. Manufacturing, which had employed 3 percent of the labor force in 1800, employed 22 percent of all workers in 1910.

American independence eliminated British restrictions on expansion and initiated a century-long process of western settlement. Fertile land and abundant natural resources drew people toward less densely settled regions in the West. This movement was accelerated by improvements in transportation, which lowered shipping costs while increasing the speed, comfort, and reliability of travel.

Northern and southern responses to frontier expansion differed, with profound effects on settlement patterns and regional development. The large size of southern slave plantations made it relatively easy for planters to recover the fixed costs of obtaining information and relocating production onto new lands. Plantations were also largely self-sufficient, requiring little urban or commercial infrastructure to make them economically viable. Well-established slave markets facilitated migration by enabling western planters to acquire additional labor in the East. In the North, the small scale of family farms made it more difficult to recover the costs of migration. Consequently, the task of mobilizing labor fell on promoters who bought up large tracts of land at low prices and then subdivided them. Promoters offered generous loans, invested heavily in recruiting settlers, and actively encouraged the development of such urban services as blacksmith shops, grain merchants, wagon builders, and general stores. Population density, urbanization, and industrialization thus were all much higher in the North than in the South in 1860.

As improved transportation lowered the cost of midwestern agricultural products, the value of agricultural land and labor declined in New England. The result was a pool of underemployed agricultural labor—especially young women—who were available to work in the manufacturing establishments that developed in the Northeast during the War of 1812 and after the imposition of protective tariffs in 1816.

Throughout the nineteenth century, migration costs remained a significant though declining obstacle to transatlantic labor movements. Immigration accelerated in the late 1840s following the Irish potato famine of 1845–1847 and the failed German revolution of 1848. Whereas northeastern industries drew arrivals who had few resources (mostly Irish), agriculture and commerce in the Midwest attracted wealthier immigrants (mostly German). Few immigrants, however, settled in the South.

More than 25 million immigrants arrived in the United States between 1870 and 1915. By 1900, about 20 percent of the population was foreign-born, but because working-age males immigrated in disproportionate numbers, they constituted about 25 percent of the labor force. Immigrants were especially concentrated in manufacturing, where they often constituted a majority of the labor force. In 1907–1908, for example, foreign-born workers represented 72 percent of the factory labor force in textiles, 58 percent in iron and steel, 61 percent in slaughtering and meatpacking, and 34 percent in boots and shoes.

The close correlation between immigration levels and the American business cycle on the one hand, and the narrowing of transatlantic wage differentials on the other, indicates a growing integration of American and European labor markets. The links between European villages and American factories relied on informal networks of friends and family, as well as the recruitment efforts of steamship agents, employment agencies, and employers. The increased supply of labor that resulted appears to have depressed wages among less-skilled workers, who competed directly with the new arrivals. Workers with more skills, however, may actually have benefited from the influx of unskilled labor. Rising immigration and its adverse effects on less-skilled workers produced increasing anti-immigrant sentiments. But efforts to limit immigration proved unsuccessful, except on the West Coast, where the Chinese Exclusion Act (1882) effectively constrained labor supplies.

Mass immigration and the post–Civil War expansion of manufacturing brought substantial changes in the nature of employment relationships. In the antebellum era, most people worked on family farms or in small artisanal workshops. After the Civil War, however, urbanization, improved transportation and communication, and the introduction of high-volume, capital-intensive production processes created enormous factories. Workers became more isolated from managers and more dependent on wage labor.

One symptom of these changes was growing public concern about industrial unemployment and other labor issues. The late nineteenth century also saw a considerable increase in labor conflict. Early labor organizations had functioned primarily as benevolent associations—providing mutual insurance for illness, death, or unemployment. But after the Civil War, effective labor unions began to emerge for the first time.

During the 1880s the Knights of Labor enjoyed a brief surge of popularity, but membership collapsed after a series of failures in 1886. In the 1890s the American Federation of Labor (AFL) consolidated the union movement, with membership reaching 2 million, or 5.9 percent of the labor force, by 1910.

The First World War to the Early Twenty-First Century.

Declining rates of natural increase and immigration restrictions imposed in the 1920s slowed the growth of population and the labor force in the twentieth century. Nonetheless, by 2011 the labor force had increased to around 153 million. Agricultural employment continued to decline, now falling in both absolute and relative terms. By 2008, just 2.01 million workers, or 1.4 percent of the labor force, were employed in agriculture. Meanwhile, manufacturing's share of the labor force had dropped to only 14.2 percent. The service-producing and government sectors grew most rapidly, employing close to three quarters of all workers by 2008. Accompanying these sectoral shifts were pronounced changes in the composition of the labor force, as more women entered the workplace and children and older men exited. By 2009, 47 percent of the labor force was female, up from about 18 percent in 1900. Westward expansion had ceased, but shifting regional fortunes continued to produce substantial population redistribution. Finally, the twentieth century was characterized by the growth of long-term employment relationships and increasing government regulation of labor markets.

World War I ended mass immigration, and following the war Congress imposed a stringent quota system. Immigration rates remained low until 1965 when Congress liberalized immigration policies. The number of arrivals increased from 3.3 million in the 1960s to 4.5 million in the 1970s, and the number continued to grow into the first decade of the twenty-first century, raising concern about the impacts of uncontrolled immigration on the labor market.

The interruption of immigration caused by World War I initiated new patterns of internal population movements. Although the South's defeat in the Civil War ended slavery, postbellum southern labor markets had remained largely isolated from the rest of the country. The shock of the war, emancipation, and the slow growth of demand for the region's principal crop—cotton—caused southern wages to fall well below northern levels by the 1880s. Yet migration of southerners to the North was limited. Northern employers could meet their labor needs with immigrant labor, and potential southern migrants lacked contacts to help them find work in northern cities. Only during World War I did northern employers begin actively to recruit southern workers. Northward migration, once begun, continued into the 1970s, interrupted only by the Great Depression.

The effects of this population redistribution on regional wages became apparent in the 1960s: there was a significant narrowing of interregional differences in wages and earnings. By 1980, per capita incomes in much of the South had reached approximately 90 percent of the national average, up from about 60 percent in 1940.

In the 1970s and 1980s the industrial heartland of the Northeast and Midwest experienced a series of shocks caused by rising energy prices and increasing international competition. Declining manufacturing employment, coupled with the shift of service-sector jobs to the South and West, initiated a new pattern of population movements in the 1980s.

World War I also contributed to changes in employment relationships. Prompted partly by the high costs of labor turnover, employers had adopted policies to encourage longer-term employment relationships. Tight wartime labor markets accelerated this process and led companies to establish centralized personnel departments that shifted responsibility for hiring, promotion, wage setting, and discipline away from shop foremen. These developments heralded the emergence of modern "internal" labor markets.

The twentieth century also brought expanded government intervention in labor markets. Protective legislation limiting hours and regulating working conditions initially affected mainly women and children. The turning point came in the 1930s with New Deal legislation, which regulated industrial relations and other aspects of the labor market. In 1938 the Fair Labor Standards Act for the first time established national minimum-wage and maximum-hours standards.

New Deal laws contributed to a rapid expansion of union membership. Between 1934 and 1938, membership nearly doubled, reaching close to 30 percent of nonagricultural workers. It continued to climb in the 1940s, reaching an all-time high of close to 40 percent of nonagricultural workers in 1953. Despite a rise in public-sector unions after the 1960s, unionization rates declined consistently after the early 1950s, dropping to just 11.9 percent by 2010.

The introduction of federal unemployment insurance and the passage of the Employment Act of 1946, which committed the government to pursue macroeconomic policies intended to ensure full employment, represent other important instances of government intervention in the labor market. Though scholars disagree over the effect of macroeconomic policies on employment, workers in the early twenty-first century were much less likely than workers in 1900 were to become unemployed, although those who did were likely to spend considerably more time between jobs.

Women and African Americans.

The pattern of women's participation in the labor force has changed markedly. In 1900, less than 6 percent of married women worked outside the home; by 2010, more than 50 percent held paying jobs. This dramatic shift is attributable to changes in both supply—falling fertility rates, increased education, and the women's movement—and demand—the rise of white-collar and clerical jobs, evolving social attitudes, and technological changes that reduced the physical demands of most kinds of work. With rising female participation came an increase in relative wages. Median female earnings for full-time workers were about 82 percent of median male earnings in 2010, up from around 55 percent in 1900. Women continued to be disproportionately concentrated in some occupations and substantially underrepresented in others, however.

As women entered the labor force, other groups of workers left. Rising education and legal prohibitions substantially reduced child labor. Participation among elderly people declined with a shift toward earlier retirement. More years of education and earlier retirement contributed to a reduction in total work over the average worker's lifetime, as did the decline in the length of the average workweek from sixty hours at the turn of the century to around forty hours by 1940.

The economic progress of African Americans was painfully slow from emancipation until the mid-twentieth century, but between 1940 and 1980 black male wages rose from 43 percent of white male wages to just over 84 percent. Though considerable evidence indicated that increases in the quality and quantity of education and training were important in improving economic conditions among blacks, equally compelling evidence suggested that federal antidiscrimination programs adopted in the 1960s were also instrumental in promoting progress.

Assessment.

Labor markets have played a prominent role in shaping the development of the United States. The early settlement of the colonies, slavery, westward migration, industrialization, immigration, the changing status of blacks and women, the rise of high school and college education, and the growth of retirement are among the many phenomena that cannot be understood without examining the influence of labor markets. Despite the impressive efficiency with which changing labor-market institutions have mobilized human resources in response to economic incentives, imperfections in market allocation have been at least as important in shaping the country's history.

[*See also* **Agricultural Workers; Artisanal Labor; Child Labor; Clerical Workers; Factory and Hours Laws; Factory System; Immigration; Indentured Labor; Industrialization and Deindustrialization; Internal Labor Markets; Labor Movements; Migratory Labor and Migrant Workers; Segmented Labor Markets, Primary and Secondary; Slavery; Transportation Revolution; Undocumented Workers; Unemployment; Vagrancy and Workers;** *and* **Women Workers.**]

BIBLIOGRAPHY

Bodnar, John. *The Transplanted: A History of Immigrants in Urban America.* Bloomington: Indiana University Press, 1985.

Fogel, Robert W. *Without Consent or Contract: The Rise and Fall of American Slavery.* New York: W. W. Norton and Company, 1989.

Galenson, David W. "The Settlement and Growth of the Colonies: Population, Labor, and Economic Development." In *The Cambridge Economic History of the United States*, edited by Stanley L. Engerman and Robert E. Gallman, vol. 1, pp. 135–208. Cambridge, U.K.: Cambridge University Press, 1996.

Goldin, Claudia. *Understanding the Gender Gap: An Economic History of American Women.* New York: Oxford University Press, 1990.

Jacoby, Sanford M. *Employing Bureaucracy: Managers, Unions, and the Transformation of Work in American Industry, 1900–1945.* New York: Columbia University Press, 1985.

Keyssar, Alexander. *Out of Work: The First Century of Unemployment in Massachusetts.* Cambridge, U.K.: Cambridge University Press, 1986.

Laurie, Bruce. *Artisans into Workers: Labor in Nineteenth-Century America.* New York: Hill and Wang, 1989.

Lebergott, Stanley. *Manpower in Economic Growth: The American Record since 1800.* New York: McGraw–Hill, 1964.

Margo, Robert A. *Race and Schooling in the South, 1880–1950: An Economic History.* Chicago: University of Chicago Press, 1990.

Nelson, Daniel. *Managers and Workers: Origins of the New Factory System in the United States, 1880–1920.* Madison: University of Wisconsin Press, 1975.

Rosenbloom, Joshua L. *Looking for Work, Searching for Workers: American Labor Markets during Industrialization.* Cambridge, U.K.: Cambridge University Press, 2002.

Rosenbloom, Joshua L., and William A. Sundstrom. "Labor-Market Regimes in U.S. Economic History." In *Economic Evolution and Revolution in Historical Time*, edited by Paul W. Rhode, Joshua L. Rosenbloom, and David F. Weiman. Stanford, Calif.: Stanford Economics and Finance, 2011.

Wright, Gavin. *Old South, New South: Revolutions in the Southern Economy since the Civil War.* New York: Basic Books, 1986.

Joshua L. Rosenbloom

LABOR MOVEMENT, DECLINE OF THE

From its emergence in the late nineteenth century until the mid-1950s, the modern American labor movement waxed and waned cyclically. It grew rapidly from 1897 to 1903, stagnated the ensuing decade, expanded during the World War I years, nearly collapsed between 1922 and 1933, and then rebuilt itself during the Great Depression and World War II. Peak union density occurred at the end of the war and again in the midst of the Korean War, 1951–1953. By 1953 unions represented nearly one third of the nonagricultural labor force, including a majority of mass-production workers, workers in the transport industry, and craftsmen and laborers in the building and construction trades.

After the mid-1950s the labor movement's pattern of cyclical variation ended. Unions initially tended to increase membership when the economy expanded and the labor market tightened and to lose members when the economy contracted and the labor market loosened. For a time, growth in the absolute number of union members and substantial increases in public-employee unionism cloaked a steady, secular decline in union density, with union membership increasing more slowly than the growth of the labor force. Beginning in the 1970s and then accelerating, the number of union members began to decline absolutely, and union density plunged. By 2011, although union membership rose slightly that year, only 6.9 percent of private-sector employees belonged to a union, and 37 percent of public-sector workers did so; overall, less than 12 percent of all workers belonged to unions.

Factors Causing Union Decline.

Numerous factors explain the decline of the labor movement. Though many employers may have come to terms with unions by the 1950s, few truly accepted them. Most recognized and bargained with unions only from necessity and jealously regarded nonunion enterprises such as IBM, Eastman Kodak, Sears, Roebuck & Co., DuPont, and, later, Intel. Most employers preferred to operate union-free and seized any opportunity to do so.

The labor force declined in regions of union strength, while it expanded in southern and southwestern states where unions remained weak. Population shifts coincided with political changes that strengthened the influence of anti-union officeholders in both the Republican and the Democratic Parties. After the 1947 Taft–Hartley Act enabled states to enact so-called right-to-work laws, unions were weakened in some of the fastest-growing states, including Texas and Florida, where populations swelled when enterprises relocated there to avoid unions. In federal and state courts, unions found their rights increasingly restricted, most especially the right to strike.

Technological innovation played an equally large part in setting the labor movement back. Automation dramatically reduced employment in some industries in which unions had made their greatest gains, including automobiles, steel, electrical goods, meatpacking, rubber, and longshoring. Unions maintained their contracts with automobile and steel companies, General Electric and Westinghouse, and Armour and Swift, but they represented substantially fewer workers. Before long, moreover, many of those companies lost market share to new and emerging nonunion competitors, further reducing the number of workers covered by union contract.

Perhaps the most important factor that underlay the decline of the American labor movement was the emergence of global competitors. For nearly two decades after the end of World War II, the United States enjoyed global economic supremacy. Oligopolistic corporations that dominated domestic markets and faced little competition from foreign competitors could afford to treat their workers relatively generously and to recognize unions. By the late 1950s, however, the war-ravaged nations overseas had rebuilt their economies, experienced what the Germans called the *Wirtschaftswunder* (economic miracle), and challenged American enterprises for a share of domestic and foreign markets. By the late 1970s the Japanese invasion of American markets in automobiles and electronics was all the rage, and soon the so-called Asian Tigers, most notably South Korea and Taiwan, posed an additional challenge to U.S. corporations, including such unionized companies as General Motors and Ford.

To compete with technologically sophisticated foreign competitors, American employers demanded that unions offer concessions, or they even eliminated unions altogether. Foreign competitors also began to build their own manufacturing facilities in the United States in order to manage changes in currency exchange rates and barriers against imports. They usually located their American plants in states and localities antipathetic to unions. German and Japanese enterprises that dealt with unions at home operated union-free in the United States and took increasing market share from American competitors.

Deregulation and Globalization.

In the mid-1970s a newly discovered economic disease, "stagflation," afflicted the United States. As prices and the cost of living rose, the economy contracted, and unemployment grew, many blamed unions for the economic malaise. Governments found it difficult to pay their bills or balance their budgets, implementing tax increases that ignited taxpayer rebellions. Public-employee unions bore the brunt of the discontent, and local officials found it popular to attack unionized public employees, limiting the growth of public-employee unionism. A common plaint heard at all levels of government alleged that union monopolies extorted extravagant contracts, which generated excessive inflation. Deregulation became a preferred means to combat union monopolies, especially in transportation, where federal rule setting had stifled competition, enhanced union power, and generated high prices. The administration of Jimmy Carter deregulated commercial airline passenger and freight operations, as well as interstate trucking, causing union membership

losses for airline unions and the Teamsters. Policies of deregulation and the privatization of many municipal, county, and state services further weakened unions and reduced their membership.

The attack on unions reached its apex in 1981 when the administration of Ronald Reagan broke a strike initiated by the Professional Air Traffic Controllers Organization (PATCO) through the use of replacement workers. Private employers also began aggressively to hire replacements during strikes, to refuse to reemploy strikers, and, often, to end their relationship with the union. Frequently employers precipitated strikes as a means to eliminate unions. It was as though the age of Homestead and Pullman had returned.

As the twentieth century ended, hyperglobalization had become the rule. Capital scoured the globe for the lowest-cost labor, and container ships carried cargoes at relatively low cost around the world. Thanks to a bountiful labor supply, modern technology, and low wages, the People's Republic of China became the world's dominant exporter and attracted many U.S. corporations that chose to invest in China and other low-wage foreign nations rather than at home. By the end of the first decade of the twenty-first century, many U.S. corporations earned greater profits abroad than at home.

Meanwhile, the American labor movement found itself unable to adjust successfully to changing circumstances. At first, the core of the movement, the American Federation of Labor and Congress of Industrial Organizations (AFL-CIO), rejected any suggestion that unions needed to change. Proud of its accomplishments—including making union members contented homeowners and consumers and promoting political reforms, such as Medicare and what labor leaders deemed a successful Cold War against international Communism—organized labor ignored critics inside and outside. When labor leaders finally realized that their movement was in peril, the combined impact of stagflation, the PATCO strike, corporate strikebreaking, and globalization left them at a loss. An internal palace revolution in 1995 in which an insurgent leadership replaced the AFL-CIO's longtime power brokers brought little relief. A second internal schism less than a decade later, in which unions that represented nearly a third of the federation's total membership formed a new confederation, Change to Win, proved equally fruitless.

By the second decade of the twenty-first century, the labor movement appeared caught in a paradox. As unions lost density and weakened, their opponents' attack on union power intensified. Organized labor had become either the victim of a vicious circle or an example of the cost of path dependency.

[*See also* **Antilabor Mobilization after 1945; Economic Deregulation and the Carter Administration; Globalization; Repression of Unions; Right-to-Work Committees and Organizations, State Laws Related to; Stagflation; Taft–Hartley Act;** *and* **Unionization Rates.**]

BIBLIOGRAPHY

Davis, Mike. *Prisoners of the American Dream: Politics and Economy in the History of the U.S. Working Class.* New York: Verso, 1986.

Goldfield, Michael. *The Decline of Organized Labor in the United States.* Chicago: University of Chicago Press, 1987.

Greenhouse, Steven. *The Big Squeeze: Tough Times for the American Worker.* New York: Alfred A. Knopf, 2008.

Lichtenstein, Nelson. *State of the Union: A Century of American Labor.* Princeton, N.J.: Princeton University Press, 2002.

Moody, Kim. *An Injury to All: The Decline of American Unionism.* New York: Verso, 1988.

Melvyn Dubofsky

LABOR MOVEMENTS

Protective organizations appeared among working people as early as the 1750s, well before the Industrial Revolution in the United States. Craft guilds provided artisans some insulation against the vagaries of an emerging market system through regulation of apprenticeship and admission to the trade. Artisans also at times used the benevolent functions of their friendly societies as a facade for adopting the regulatory practices of a trade society. In the era of the American Revolution, rising debt levels, deteriorating trade conditions, and competition from moonlighting British troops pushed many artisans toward collective action to protect wages and uphold prices for the goods that they produced. Their nascent trade societies became vehicles for political activism and crucibles for the formation of a distinctive "artisan republican" ideology, forcefully articulated by Tom Paine.

By the first years of the nineteenth century, journeymen artisans organized independently of their masters in more formal trade societies to protect the prices for their work and their terms of employment and apprenticeship. So-called labor unrest concentrated primarily in a handful of trades—shoemaking, carpentry, tailoring, construction, and printing—in which the erosion of craft traditions was most pronounced. In other traditional trades—baking, butchering, blacksmithing, gold- and silversmithing, and cartering—the artisanal workshop and its norms remained relatively intact. Prior to 1830, prosecutions brought by employers against journeymen's trade societies for conspiracy to uphold wages and enforce trade rules resulted in numerous convictions but with relatively mild punishment. After 1830, reflecting the deepening polarization between masters and journeymen, many craftsmen were found guilty and imprisoned. As the traditional master–journeymen relationship evolved into a more market-oriented relationship, journeymen ignited a period of intense labor organization and conflict.

The Antebellum and Civil War Eras.

Most early trade unionists were skilled artisans, but others moved toward new forms of collective organization and concerted action as well. Female textile operatives in Lowell, Massachusetts, and other factory towns, women shoe binders throughout Massachusetts and northern New England, and less-skilled common laborers caught the infectious spirit of revolt. In Lowell, young women led strikes of operatives in 1834 and 1836 against the mammoth mills over wages and the cost of living in company-owned boardinghouses. The seaport cities bred a new kind of movement that combined trade grievances with a search for political remedies. Between 1828 and 1832 workingmen's parties probed the limits of Jacksonian politics but ultimately were reabsorbed into the dominant partisan alignment of Democrats and Whigs. During the prosperous years of the mid-1830s, journeymen's societies formed citywide general trades unions (GTU) to agitate around common economic grievances. A handful of loose-knit national trade associations (NTA) formed but proved premature given the infant state of national markets. The demand for shorter hours created a common bond that transcended craft, and the movement for a ten-hour day gathered support in 1834–1835 in Boston, Philadelphia, and other cities. Those efforts peaked in 1835 with a general strike in Philadelphia led by the city's GTU that won broad support from the city's skilled artisans and unskilled laborers and for a brief time saw the wide adoption of a ten-hour standard for the working day. However, a depression between 1837 and 1843 led to the collapse of this first general trade union movement. Economic hardship and rising levels of immigration pro-

duced deep ethno-cultural divisions that crippled the effectiveness of trade societies.

Following the return of prosperity in the mid-1840s, the ten-hour movement regained some of its predepression vitality, most notably in New England, where working-class activists such as Sarah Bagley were joined by reformers whose broad agenda included land reform, women's rights, and the abolition of slavery. The labor movement took on new life during the 1850s. Trade unions of skilled iron molders, iron puddlers, and textile workers joined struggling societies of artisan craftsmen—printers, shoemakers, and tailors—in a new surge of organizational activity. New industrial craftsmen carried their trades into emerging areas of industrial expansion in urban areas of the Great Lakes region of the Old Northwest and along the Ohio and Mississippi river valleys. The massive immigration of Irish and German workers between 1845 and 1855 provided cheap labor for railroad and canal construction, as well as craftsmen to compete in urban labor market. German refugees from the failed 1848 revolutions and Irish nationalists infused the labor movement of the 1850s with new currents of radicalism. A great shoemakers' strike in 1860 reflected a last, massive stand by craft workers in the trade—but not the new factory operatives, who would come to dominate the industry.

The Civil War profoundly changed the American labor movement. By the war's end, the trade union movement included new and old trades such as the Brotherhood of the Footboard (locomotive engineers) and a revived iron molders' union. Declining real wages and stagnant manufacturing and railroad construction during wartime fueled new organization. In 1866 the first truly national organization, the National Labor Union (NLU), led by the iron molders' leader William Sylvis, appeared. The NLU—like the new unions of wage earners in shoemaking, the Knights and the Daughters of

St. Crispin—demanded the eight-hour day and the right to organize. It also challenged the basis of the wage system by calling for land reform and cooperative production. For trade unionists like Sylvis and the printer Ira Steward, the eight-hour day was essential for workers to exercise their rights as citizens in an industrial order in which they would labor as wage earners for life.

Led by the ship caulker Isaac Myers, freedmen organized under the auspices of the Colored National Labor Union in such cities as Baltimore, Maryland, and Richmond, Virginia, giving added salience to labor's demand that wage slavery, like chattel slavery, must be ended. The war had been a watershed for women and African Americans. Through war work, more women than ever entered the wage labor force, most notably in the garment trades, and in the South emancipated slaves joined numbers of urban freedmen in the building trades, tobacco factories, railroad construction, and domestic service. Freedmen's status in the labor market proved precarious as southern states returned to white conservative rule in the 1870s and African Americans faced new barriers to the exercise of their political and economic rights.

The Gilded Age and the Progressive Era.

The NLU collapsed during the early 1870s, soon to be replaced by a new fledgling national organization, the Noble and Holy Order of the Knights of Labor (KOL). Founded in 1869 by Philadelphia garment cutters as a secret, local fraternal society, the KOL grew rapidly, spreading into the coal fields of Pennsylvania and westward along rail lines after the 1877 railroad strikes. The railroad strikes represented an unprecedented eruption of labor conflict that enlisted the solidarity of workers in related industries and the urban poor of the large railroad centers in the East and Midwest and in smaller railroad division towns. The strikes also witnessed significant destruction of railroad property and the loss of more than a hundred lives at the hands of state militia and U.S. troops in Baltimore, Pittsburgh, Chicago, and other railroad transportation hubs.

Under Terence V. Powderly the KOL became the dynamic center of labor organizing after 1878. The Knights organized all sectors of workers, regardless of skill, and also attracted women and African Americans in unprecedented numbers. At its 1886 general assembly, the KOL took a principled public stand for interracial unionism, even as it warily maintained separate local assemblies for white and black workers. But white hostility to black workers remained—especially in the South, where black workers were concentrated. The leadership's refusal to protect interracial organizers—for instance, among Louisiana sugarcane workers in 1887—doomed the KOL's attempt to practice biracial unionism.

The labor movement reached its nineteenth-century peak in 1886 with more than 700,000 workers in the Knights and another 250,000 in trade unions, a level of union density not reached again until the World War I era. After an impressive beginning to the 1 May 1886 general strike for the eight-hour day in Chicago and other cities, the explosion of a homemade bomb among the ranks of Chicago police squads as they sought to break up an anarchist-led protest meeting in Haymarket Square shattered the movement. The incident brought the virtual collapse of the strike and severe repression against labor radicals, who had provided significant leadership to the city's labor movement. The subsequent trial of eight anarchists, none of whom was directly linked to the bombing, and the execution of Albert Parsons and three of his comrades accentuated already deep divisions within the KOL. The Great Upheaval of 1886, as it came to be called, provided fuel for a surge in independent labor politics, most notable in several hundred smaller industrial cities where workers elected their own to local government office under the banner of the Union Labor Party. The Knights' growth quickly eroded, however, as employers resisted union growth and broke strikes. Internal divisions in the KOL over defense of the Haymarket martyrs, the interests of skilled workers, and support for independent politics contributed to the decline. By 1890, KOL membership had dwindled to 200,000, and it declined even more rapidly thereafter. Rising levels of strike activity, especially in the railroad industry, and the advent of sympathy strikes produced an imminent sense of social crisis fueled by class polarization between a rising class of robber barons and workers faced with unemployment and deepening poverty in a chronically depressed economy.

The 1890s represented a turning point for the labor movement. The American Federation of Labor (AFL), led by the former socialist cigar maker Samuel Gompers, preached a philosophy of "pure and simple" trade unionism and opposed independent working-class politics. Gompers urged skilled workers to "look to your union" and to distance themselves from what the AFL argued were utopian campaigns inspired by the KOL and socialist trade unionists to overthrow capitalism. While Gompers and his ideological compatriots, Adolph Strasser and P. J. McGuire, stressed caution, some workers and AFL-affiliated unions during the 1890s proved more inclined to maintain broader industrial forms of organization, particularly the United Mine Workers of America (UMWA), the Brewery Workers, the Western Federation of Miners, and the Boot and Shoe Workers, organizations that included among their membership former Knights, Populists, and socialists.

The American Railway Union (ARU), led by the former railroad fireman Eugene V. Debs, embraced all categories of railroad workers and organized widely from Chicago into much of the West. A sympathy boycott called by the ARU in support of car-shop workers at the Pullman works near Chicago grew into a massive strike that tied up much of the nation's rail traffic and economic activity through late June and early July 1894. But the strike precipitated intervention by the federal government and the dispatch of U.S. troops on orders from the Democratic president Grover Cleveland. With the strike crushed and leaders of the ARU arrested and under indictment, the most serious labor crisis of the nineteenth century passed.

Unions affiliated with the AFL benefited from the economic growth that followed the depression of 1893–1897. Trade unions expanded rapidly between 1897 and 1904. In relative terms, this was perhaps the period of most rapid union growth in American history: the number of union members rose from 450,000 to more than 2 million in only seven years. The UMWA secured a national agreement in 1898 for most bituminous-coal production, and the International Association of Machinists in 1901 won a national contract covering major firms in the metal trades. In response to these and other labor gains, many employers mounted an open-shop (antiunion) drive that stymied labor's growth in most economic sectors. Still, the UMWA, which had only 14,000 members in 1897, claimed as many as 300,000 by 1914. Between 1910 and 1914, newer unions in the garment trades—led by recent immigrants who excelled at organizing their immigrant brethren, male and female—added nearly 400,000 members to the ranks of labor. Buoyed by rising union membership yet threatened by employers' counterattacks, the AFL turned first to more intensive legislative lobbying for the eight-hour day, the restriction of antilabor injunctions, and immigration restriction and then, in the congressional campaigns of 1906 and beyond, to partisan politics. With few exceptions the AFL supported the Democratic candidates in the hopes of winning more union-friendly government policies.

Socialists and syndicalists contested Gompers's power before World War I. In 1902 and 1912, socialists challenged his presidency. The syndicalist Industrial Workers of the World (IWW), formed in 1905, confronted the AFL from another direction. First in the West, the IWW and its largest affiliate, the Western Federation of Miners (WFM)—which gave to the organization two of its most famous leaders, Vincent St. John and William D. "Big Bill" Haywood—challenged employers and their political allies in strikes and in free-speech fights. In 1909 and the years immediately following, IWW organizing shifted eastward. Revolts by less-skilled immigrant workers in McKees Rocks, Pennsylvania; Lawrence, Massachusetts; Paterson, New Jersey; and other eastern manufacturing centers foreshadowed a new phase of labor mobilization inspired by the IWW, as had the IWW's initial organizing success among western miners, timber workers, and migratory agricultural workers. These strikes set the stage for the bitter class war between miners and John D. Rockefeller Jr.'s Colorado Fuel and Iron Company that resulted in the massacre of nineteen strikers and family members in the tent colony at Ludlow, Colorado, on the morning after Easter 1914 and the subsequent guerrilla warfare between strikers and company guards and state militia in the weeks immediately following. Eugene Debs's Socialist Party of America, with strong support from segments of the labor movement, elected hundreds of members to local political office and in 1910 won control of the municipal government in Milwaukee, Wisconsin, and a number of other cities.

World War I. The outbreak of World War I created both opportunities and perils for the labor movement. As war orders drove unemployment levels to near zero and American workers struck widely to win improvements in wages, hours, and work rules, the administration of Woodrow Wilson designed new federal machinery to maintain labor peace. This included initially a labor advisory committee to the Council of National Defense, with Samuel Gompers a leading member, and the Adamson Act of 1916 that established the eight-hour day for the critical railroad industry. Following America's entry into the war in April 1917, Wilson appointed the President's Mediation Commission to investigate labor disputes, especially those that affected industries essential to the war effort, such as copper mining and smelting, and the War Labor Policies Board (WLPB) to originate plans for more durable industrial peace. Eventually Wilson created the War Labor Board (WLB), which mediated disputes in war-related industries and endorsed wage increases, the eight-hour day, collective bargaining for union members, and representation of nonunion workers through shop committees.

By the war's end, 4.2 million American workers belonged to unions. The AFL now included quasi-industrial unions in steel and meatpacking. Following the unprecedented so-called Great Migration of African Americans from the Deep South during the war years, large numbers of black workers for the first time entered the mass-production industries of northern cities, where they maintained, at best, an uneasy relationship with white-dominated unions. Racial tensions erupted into riots that saw significant casualties in the black communities of East Saint Louis, Illinois; Washington, D.C.; Tulsa, Oklahoma; and Chicago during and immediately following the war. Steelworkers in unprecedented numbers struck in late 1919 to protect wartime gains and their right to organize, but efficient and aggressive antistrike actions by companies, including in some instances large-scale recruitment of African American replacement workers, crushed the strike, leaving the vast majority of steelworkers unrepresented until 1937. The defeat of the strike showed that without support from the federal government, which terminated with the end of the war in November 1918, workers in the mass-production industries could not prevail against employer opposition. Defeat for the steelworkers also presaged the fate of many unions during the 1920s.

The 1920s. The immediate postwar years weakened the labor movement. Unemployment rose and employers, freed from the oversight of the WLB, fought to roll back wartime union gains. The major strike wave in 1919 resulted in labor defeats. Weakened and marginalized by wartime persecution, left-wingers split into rival Socialist and Communist factions following the Bolshevik revolution in Russia, and a wave of antiradical hysteria, the Red Scare, fostered by a federal government roundup and threatened deportation of immigrant radicals, shattered leftist influence within the labor movement. Employers promoted a revitalized open-shop movement through the so-called American Plan, which stressed the right of workers to obtain employment without union membership. Employers also fought unions with company welfare programs, improved forms of scientific management, professionalized personnel departments, and tacit support for new immigration-restriction measures. Major strike defeats in meatpacking, coal mining, and among railroad shopmen in 1922 further weakened key sectors of the labor movement. As a result, the proportion of organized workers fell by half.

Key industrial unions—precursors to the Congress of Industrial Organizations (CIO)—were decimated. The United Mine Workers of America, under the leadership of John L. Lewis, lost its national contract in the bituminous branch of the industry and by the early Depression years had a dues-paying membership of under 100,000, a catastrophic decline

from its wartime high of nearly 600,000. The International Ladies' Garment Workers' Union (ILG), one of the great union success stories of the immediate pre–World War I years for its organization of new immigrant and young women workers, was nearly bankrupt by 1932. Sidney Hillman's Amalgamated Clothing Workers (ACW), like the ILG a notable success in unionizing newer immigrants and women workers in the garment industry, saw its growth diminish and its ability to win improved conditions for members weaken—though thanks to Hillman's astute leadership, it suffered fewer debilitating losses than the UMWA or the ILG did. The International Association of Machinists lost all the gains that it had won during the war in the railroad industry's repair shops and elsewhere in the metal trades, while Prohibition practically put the United Brewery Workers out of business.

Only the Teamsters and the unions in the building trades and the printing industry, all concentrated in local markets in which they bargained primarily with smaller employers who lacked inordinate power, made substantial gains and increased their memberships during the 1920s. By decade's end, they dominated the AFL and its executive council, giving the federation a distinctively conservative character that opposed such progressive public policies as minimum wages, maximum hours, and unemployment insurance. These so-called barons of labor condemned Communists and Socialists, turned a cold shoulder to less-skilled workers, demanded the restriction of immigration from eastern and southern Europe, and often supported the Republican Party, endorsing the elections of presidents Calvin Coolidge and Herbert Hoover. A union federation led by such men (no women sat on the AFL's executive council) was ill prepared to deal with the gale of destruction that the Great Depression inflicted on working people.

The Great Depression and the New Deal. The Wall Street panic in late 1929 and the Great Depression of the 1930s brought massive unemployment and economic hardship to broad segments of the working class, but it also reenergized labor organizing across industrial America. The groundwork for that organizing came initially through efforts of unemployed workers to demand relief and resist evictions and home foreclosures. Unemployed Councils, often organized by Communists and Socialists at the local level, sparked mass mobilization and direct action that proved to be an important catalyst and preparation for renewed union organizing. Left-wing organizers in African American communities in the North and parts of the South laid the basis for broader union organizing on an interracial basis that would be one of the hallmarks of the CIO.

The inauguration of Franklin Delano Roosevelt as president in 1933 brightened the prospects for the labor movement's renewal: labor's political influence within the New Deal coalition stimulated expectations of a more sympathetic government climate. Passage of the National Industrial Recovery Act (NIRA) and its Section 7(a), which promised the right to union representation, ignited a wave of labor organizing in the mass-production industries. In the coal fields, miners responded to John L. Lewis's hyperbolic assertion that failed to distinguish between the two presidents Lewis and Roosevelt: "The president wants you to join a union." By the end of 1933, miners had largely reestablished the UMWA in the soft-coal fields. Similar early success brought rising membership and collective-bargaining victories for the ILG and the ACW.

The gains achieved by coal miners and garment workers resonated among workers in automobile plants, in textile and steel mills, and on the docks who walked off the job but failed to achieve victories. In 1934 major and at times violent strikes swept the nation, most notably in textile towns across the South—where workers participated in a massive nationwide walkout that spread from Maine to the hills of Alabama—among auto-parts workers in Toledo, Ohio, among teamsters in Minneapolis, and among dockworkers in San Francisco. The southern textile workers and the Ohio auto-parts workers suffered bitter defeats as local and state public officials helped employers break the strikes. The Minneapolis teamsters and the San Francisco waterfront workers emerged from their battles—which generated brief but effective citywide general strikes—victorious partly as a result of intervention by state (Minnesota) and federal (San Francisco) officials. Elsewhere, however, as had been the case with southern textile workers and Toledo strikers, efforts at organizing unions faltered in the face of corporate intransigence and government ambivalence.

Congressional friends of labor led by Senator Robert F. Wagner of New York drafted legislation designed to promote union recognition. The National Labor Relations (Wagner) Act that Roosevelt signed in 1935 firmly established the right to collective bargaining and created orderly procedures for workers to choose union representation. Union support for Roosevelt's reelection and Democratic legislative victories in 1936 hastened the process of union organizing.

Emboldened by rising worker militancy and the Wagner Act, leaders of a number of AFL unions joined Lewis, the president of the UMWA, in November 1935 to form the Committee for Industrial Organization (CIO). Charged by AFL leaders with splitting the labor movement, Lewis and his allies persisted in organizing mass-production workers. The division in the labor movement became formal with the suspension of the UMWA and its seven allied unions at the fall 1936 meeting of the AFL executive council. While Lewis and his allies, most notably Sidney Hillman and David

Dubinsky, clashed with their opponents who dominated the AFL executive council, they also encouraged and helped finance new organizing among steelworkers, automobile workers, rubber workers, and other employees in mass-production industries. Left-wing organizers, often associated with the Communist Party, played critical roles in organizing workers in the electrical, farm equipment, meatpacking, and other mass-production industries.

Not long after the AFL suspended the unions associated with CIO, the insurgent organization achieved a dramatic victory, helped in no small part by the recently elected New Deal Democratic governor of Michigan, Frank Murphy, and the triumphantly reelected Roosevelt. On 30 December 1936 a militant minority of union members organized a sit-down strike at a key General Motors (GM) plant in Flint, Michigan. The sit-down strikers fought off efforts by company guards and city police to dislodge them from the occupied plant. Governor Murphy ordered the National Guard to preserve the peace in Flint by separating the strikers inside from the company-influenced city police who had tried to dislodge them. Unable to dislodge the sit-downers from the initial plant that they had occupied and a second one in which they also had begun a sit-down, GM on 11 February 1937 agreed to recognize the fledgling United Auto Workers (UAW)—the first crack in the united anti-union, open-shop fortress of mass-production industry. Three weeks later, in March 1937, John L. Lewis secretly negotiated a contract with U.S. Steel that brought significant gains to the company's workers but fell short of the contract signed by GM. These victories catapulted the CIO into national prominence and made it a real rival to the AFL—and, according to one wag, made sit-downs as American a pastime as baseball.

By midsummer, however, the CIO's organizing drive stalled, first in a defeat suffered during a strike against the so-called Little Steel companies, during which the president and governors in states affected by the strike turned cold shoulders to union pleas for support against corporate use of heavily armed private guards, city police, and state troops to protect strike-breakers. Even following the so-called Memorial Day massacre at Republic Steel in Chicago—eleven workers were shot and killed by Chicago police—Roosevelt declared a pox on both houses, labor and management. The CIO also suffered severely as a result of the so-called Roosevelt depression that began in the late summer of 1937 and that was precipitated by the president's decision to balance the federal budget by reducing federal spending. As a result of this decision, employment fell in the mass-production sector, where CIO gains had been concentrated.

In October 1938 when the CIO held its first constitutional convention and emerged as the fully independent Congress of Industrial Organizations, it had lost much of its vigor and faced serious financial difficulties and splits within some of its newer affiliates, most especially the UAW. Meantime, the AFL's leaders learned lessons from the CIO's success. Realizing that less-skilled workers could be organized, that the AFL's affiliated unions had a presence in more areas of the nation than the CIO's did, and that generally employers who had no choice other than to recognize unions preferred the AFL to the more militant and radical CIO, the AFL began its own aggressive organizing among heretofore unorganized and less-skilled workers in mass-production and other industries. By the fall of 1938 the AFL had millions more dues-paying members than the CIO.

World War II. When European war erupted with full force in 1939 and with rising levels of employment, the CIO again began to grow, as did its larger rival, the AFL. By the time the United States entered World War II in

December 1941, virtually all American mass-production industries had signed union contracts. The war brought direct labor participation in wartime economic planning but also new restraints on worker and union actions. In early 1942, Roosevelt created the National War Labor Board (NWLB): the board soon established both the so-called Little Steel formula, which essentially limited wage increases in order to restrain inflation (exceptions to the formula were made for the lowest-paid workers), and also a maintenance-of-membership principle that guaranteed unions the right to retain their members then in the union for the duration of the war. In return, labor agreed to enforce for the duration of the conflict a no-strike pledge that its leaders had signed after Pearl Harbor. The NWLB pressured employers to bargain with unions in return for labor peace and in light of wartime "cost-plus" contracts from which they profited handsomely.

Wartime labor scarcity also brought large numbers of women and African Americans into the mass-production industries and their unions. Some CIO unions, such as the United Packinghouse Workers of America, took aggressive action to attack racial intolerance among their rank and file and actively promoted civil rights. In June 1941, before U.S. entry into the war, President Roosevelt, under pressure from A. Philip Randolph and other African American activists who threatened a massive march on Washington, signed an executive order that prohibited employment discrimination based on race and established the Fair Employment Practices Committee to enforce the order. Nonetheless, spasms of racial conflict punctuated the war effort. The most serious conflicts were precipitated by white autoworkers who walked off the job to protest the transfer of African American workers into jobs formerly held by whites. UAW leaders, in support of local civil rights leaders, acted quickly to end such wildcat hate strikes. Never before had

unions, especially those in the CIO, had so many African American and women members. Their wartime gains provided a new threshold for postwar organizing among women and minority workers.

As the war neared its end, fears based on memories of the massive joblessness associated with the Depression of the 1930s caused many labor leaders and public officials to expect a substantial rise in unemployment as the economy adjusted from defense production to a peacetime economy. Many women war workers, symbolized by "Rosie the Riveter," faced significant pressure to leave the workforce or to return to so-called women's jobs at lower pay in order to make room for the returning war veterans who had been assured that they would have their old jobs restored when peace came. Women's employment levels would, however, never return to prewar levels. By war's end, the labor movement had made unprecedented gains, having unionized nearly 35 percent of the nonagricultural labor force.

The Post–World War II Years. A postwar strike wave—the largest in American history—swept through the nation's mass-production industries in 1945–1946. The most significant, pattern-setting strike pitted the UAW against GM. The union linked its claim for a substantial wage increase to a demand for no increase in prices. When GM refused to consider such a demand, the strike leader, Walter Reuther, then a UAW vice president, challenged the company to "open its books," which the company also refused to do. The strike settlement produced a more modest wage increase, based on one that the federal government had already devised to settle a national steel strike, with no guarantees of price restraint. Large strikes had also erupted in the electrical, meatpacking, coal, and steel industries: the strikers had comparable demands, and the strikes were settled on similar terms.

With the wartime Office of Price Administration about to be eliminated, labor feared a postwar inflation that would further undermine wages. Unlike during the 1919 strikes, however, this time employers did not seek to break the unions. Instead they established a pattern of postwar collective bargaining in which workers conceded management's "right to manage" in return for higher wages and improved fringe benefits. A 1950 agreement between General Motors and the UAW, the so-called Treaty of Detroit, exemplified the postwar union–management bargain. In return for health insurance, vacation pay, cost-of-living adjustments, and pensions, the UAW agreed to a five-year contract and a promise of labor peace. The postwar bargain between management and labor created a sort of domestic cold war in which management contained its union enemies' most ambitious goals and worker discontent rarely erupted into heated conflict.

Politically, the labor movement suffered a number of defeats in the immediate postwar years. Republicans regained control of Congress in 1946 and the following year passed the antiunion Taft–Hartley Act. The new law revised key provisions of the Wagner Act by mandating "management rights" to balance those granted labor in 1935. Management gained the right to speak to its employees aggressively about the liabilities of union membership through company publications, inserts in pay envelopes, mandatory in-plant meetings, and supervisors' conversations with employees. These new management rights made union organizing more difficult. Union officers were required to sign so-called non-Communist affidavits in order for their unions to qualify for the services of the National Labor Relations Board and the rights guaranteed under the Wagner Act as amended by Taft–Hartley. And the law empowered states to pass so-called right-to-work laws that prohibited labor–management contracts that made union membership a condition of employment.

Taft–Hartley, combined with rising anti-Communist and anti-Soviet hysteria, caused a split in the CIO. In 1949–1950 the CIO expelled eleven left-led unions, either because their leaders refused to sign non-Communist affidavits or because the leaders had opposed the government's Cold War foreign policy. CIO leaders were most angry with the leaders of the expelled unions because they had supported Henry Wallace and the Progressive Party in the election of 1948, a policy that risked returning the Republicans to the White House and to a majority in Congress. The passage of Taft–Hartley, rising domestic anti-Communism, and the expulsion of its left-wing unions all played a part in the collapse of the CIO's Operation Dixie, an effort to build on the organization's wartime gains in the South, bring unionism to the region's largest industry, textiles, and transform the Democratic Party in the South into one more like its northern wing.

Despite the booming postwar economy, the labor movement, especially the CIO, reached its peak power and density during the Korean War and its immediate aftermath, 1950–1955. In the ensuing years, automation swept across unionized mass-production industries, simultaneously increasing productivity and reducing the demand for workers in automobiles, steel, rubber, meatpacking, and associated industries. War-ravaged economies abroad began to recover and compete for markets, capturing market share from U.S. competitors. Domestically, employment began to shift from the manufacturing sector to the service sector, where unions historically had less of a presence. Despite the merger of the AFL and the CIO in 1955, the labor movement entered a period of gradually declining membership that was followed by one of steep decline. With the Landrum–Griffin Act of 1959, the federal government intruded more directly into the oversight of internal union financial affairs and democratic governance. A number of unions, notably the United Packinghouse Workers and the UAW, provided financial support and organizing assistance to the growing civil rights movement in the South. But union organizing in the South was hampered by state right-to-work laws and the obstacles erected as whites mobilized against the civil rights demands of African Americans.

The factors that curtailed postwar organizing and union power intensified after 1960. Unions found themselves restrained by new government regulations and rising corporate resistance. The Vietnam War produced inflation and stagnating wages and put pressure on manufacturing workers to increase productivity. A younger, post–World War II generation of workers rebelled in a series of strikes that prefigured a deepening economic crisis. The strike of rank-and-file autoworkers at the GM plant in Lordstown, Ohio, in 1972 reflected these new tensions. Farmworkers in California organized the United Farm Workers of America (UFW) under the leadership of Cesar Chavez and Dolores Huerta. With broad support through consumer boycotts of grapes and lettuce, striking farmworkers won union recognition from California grape growers that improved their wages and benefits. Success, however, prompted a strong counterattack by growers and ranchers, as well as raids by the Teamsters, which sought to use to its own advantage the UFW's gains. Thus the success achieved by the UFW in the late 1960s and 1970s proved challenging to sustain and build on.

Wherever one looked in the late 1960s and early 1970s, one saw tensions in the labor movement. In Detroit, black autoworkers formed firm-specific "revolutionary union" units—DRUM, the Dodge Revolutionary Union Movement, and FRUM for Ford—as well as the League of Revolutionary Black Workers, to challenge the UAW leadership on issues of race.

Women used the new Civil Rights Act of 1964 to demand equal rights at work and in their unions. The war in Southeast Asia also deeply divided the labor movement: Walter Reuther of the UAW led a revolt against AFL-CIO support for the war. Insurgencies challenged many union leaders who had lost touch with younger rank-and-file workers. One of the more prominent opposition movements, Miners for Democracy, an effort to end half a century and more of autocratic leadership in the UMWA, witnessed the 1969 assassination of its popular leader, Jock Yablonski, by hirelings of the UMWA president Tony Boyle. In steel, rank-and-file insurgencies challenged leaders who had negotiated labor–management cooperation through a series of "productivity" bargaining agreements.

The Late Twentieth Century. Economic contraction, deindustrialization, and runaway plants in the 1970s and early 1980s accelerated the decline in union membership. Unions perceived the wage-price controls that the administration of Richard M. Nixon imposed to dampen inflation as unfairly restricting their ability to bargain. Although Nixon did sign legislation creating the Occupational Safety and Health Administration (OSHA), his economic policies generally contributed to declining rates of unionization in basic industry. Nevertheless, many states in the North and Midwest passed legislation establishing public workers' right to bargain collectively, and these workers' unions saw the beginnings of significant growth that lasted for several decades.

Conservative Republican Party hegemony in national politics by the 1980s weakened labor and limited the effectiveness of the National Labor Relations Board in protecting workers' right to unionize. Although the labor movement continued to serve as the backbone for the Democratic Party and as the most important defender of key social legislation such as Social Security, Medicare and Medicaid, and civil rights measures that guaranteed voting rights and equal-employment protection, the Democrats suffered critical losses in Congress in 1994 and a declining capacity to protect and defend such programs. Important strike losses by the Professional Air Traffic Controllers Organization in 1981, by Hormel packinghouse workers in Austin, Minnesota, in 1985–1986, and by corn-processing workers both in Clinton, Iowa, in 1980 and in Decatur, Illinois, in 1994 further depleted union ranks and morale. Isolated victories, such as the Pittston coal strike of 1989 and the United Parcel Service strike of 1997, failed to stem the tide of declining union membership. By the mid-1990s, union membership had reached its lowest point since the early 1930s: less than 15 percent of the nonagricultural labor force and less than 10 percent in the private sector. Work stoppages declined precipitously from their peak in the early 1970s. And foreign competitors, most notably the Asian nations—first Japan, then South Korea, and then Taiwan and the People's Republic of China—took market share from American enterprises, further diluting demand for American workers and eliminating jobs. In the early 2000s the so-called BRIC nations (Brazil, Russia, India, and China) enjoyed positive economic growth and displaced American competitors in numerous markets.

Two signs of revival appeared in the late 1990s. First, service-sector workers won significant gains, largely as a result of the growth of public-sector unions and the entry of women, minority, and immigrant workers into unions, led by a new cadre of organizers dedicated to building a more diverse and militant labor movement. Symptomatic of those changes, by the century's end the nation's most unionized city was not Detroit, Chicago, or Pittsburgh, but Las Vegas. Second, the AFL-CIO chose a new leadership in 1995, with John Sweeney of the Service Employees International Union as president. Sweeney promised to revitalize organizing campaigns, encouraged city and state federations to act politically, and sought to rebuild labor's alliances with other social movements. The U.S. labor movement, moreover, evinced new interest in building international alliances with workers overseas, while simultaneously fighting international trade agreements, such as the North American Free Trade Agreement (NAFTA), that freed capital from national regulation.

The Twenty-First Century. The promises of the 1990s gave way to continuing crises for the labor movement in the new century. The Republican administration of George W. Bush hampered the effectiveness of the NLRB by making antilabor appointments that resulted in an enormous backlog of cases. The administration reduced funding and curtailed the regulatory capacity of key agencies that protected labor—the Department of Labor, the Mine Safety Administration, and OSHA. In 2005 a group of unions, including the Service Employees International Union, UNITE HERE (garment unions and hotel and restaurant employees), and the Teamsters, left the AFL-CIO to form Change to Win, a coalition dedicated to rebuilding the labor movement through more aggressive and better-funded organizing campaigns. After some initial success, Change to Win was beset by internal conflicts over jurisdictions and strategy, and a number of affiliates rejoined the AFL-CIO. The election of the United Mine Workers president Richard Trumka to the presidency of the AFL-CIO in 2009 prepared the way for a reunification of the labor movement.

The labor movement participated enthusiastically in the campaign of the Democrat Barack Obama for the presidency in 2008. It was hoped that through new appointments to the National Labor Relations Board he would restore some of the federal government's capacity to protect the right of collective bargaining and that through new appointments to the Labor Department and the Occupational Safety and Health Administration he would achieve more robust and effective regulation of worker rights and safety. Yet by the end of 2011, according to data from the Bureau of Labor Statistics, union density had nevertheless fallen overall to 11.8 percent. Public-sector workers had a rate of 37 percent, and workers in local government had the highest rate, 43.2 percent. By contrast, workers in the private sector had a union density of 6.9 percent. Black workers were unionized at a rate of 13.5 percent, compared to whites at 11.6 percent, Asians at 10.1 percent, and Hispanics at 9.7 percent.

The severe economic crisis that hit the U.S. and world economies in 2008 and that intensified in the following year saw unemployment rise sharply. The pump-priming efforts of the Obama administration were hampered by congressional conservatives who limited stimulus spending. Obsessed by a rising deficit, Republicans resisted tax increases on the wealthy, the continuation of extended unemployment benefits, and better efforts to regulate a financial industry that had precipitated the crisis. Ideological polarization and right-wing mobilization against virtually every measure that the Obama administration undertook set the stage for midterm elections that gave the Tea Party Republicans a working majority in the House of Representatives and a minority in the Senate that was large enough to enable them to block almost all initiatives by the Democratic Party to restart the economy and reduce unemployment. For the labor movement this meant a setback in its efforts to win legislation that might enable unions to organize more effectively. Most dramatically, Republican governors in a number of states—Wisconsin, Ohio, Indiana, New Jersey, and others—tried to strip public workers of their collective-bargaining rights and to pass a new wave of right-to-work legisla-

tion. In the face of falling revenues, states everywhere reduced public employment and sought to curtail the salaries and benefits earned by public employees in order to balance their budgets as required by law. In response, with broad public support, unions in both the public and the private sector mobilized to reverse these initiatives through direct action, such as occupying state capitol buildings, and by conducting aggressive recall and referendum drives. These efforts contributed to changing the public discourse and energizing a broad "Occupy" movement that focused public attention on income inequality and the new class war of corporate elites on labor and the public interest.

[*See also* **African American Labor Organizations; American Federation of Labor; American Federation of Labor and Congress of Industrial Organizations; Artisanal Labor; Closed Shop; Collective Bargaining; Congress of Industrial Organizations; Dockworkers' Unions, Multiracial; Eight-Hour Day; Industrialization and Deindustrialization; Industrial Relations; Industrial Workers of the World; Jewish American Labor Movement; Knights of Labor; Labor Leaders; Labor Movement, Decline of the; Labor Organizations, Pre–Civil War; Labor's Role in Politics; National Labor Union; Radicalism and Workers; Railroad Brotherhoods; Resistance to Management; Strikes; Technology and Labor; Treaty of Detroit and Postwar Labor Accord; Union Corruption; Unionization Rates; Union Reform Movements; Union Shop; Utopian and Communitarian Movements; Women Workers; Work;** *and* **Worker Training.**]

BIBLIOGRAPHY

Barrett, James R. *William Z. Foster and the Tragedy of American Radicalism*. Urbana: University of Illinois Press, 1999.

Barrett, James R. *Work and Community in the Jungle: Chicago's Packinghouse Workers, 1894–1922*. Urbana: University of Illinois Press, 1987.

Brody, David. *Steelworkers in America: The Nonunion Era*. Cambridge, Mass.: Harvard University Press, 1960.

Cobble, Dorothy Sue. *The Other Women's Movement: Workplace Justice and Social Rights in Modern America*. Princeton, N.J.: Princeton University Press, 2004.

Cohen, Lizabeth. *Making a New Deal: Industrial Workers in Chicago, 1919–1939*. New York: Cambridge University Press, 1990.

Cowie, Jefferson. *Stayin' Alive: The 1970s and the Last Days of the Working Class*. New York: New Press, 2010.

Deslippe, Dennis A. *Rights, Not Roses: Unions and the Rise of Working-Class Feminism, 1945–80*. Urbana: University of Illinois Press, 2000.

Dubofsky, Melvyn. *We Shall Be All: A History of the Industrial Workers of the World*. Chicago: Quadrangle Books, 1969.

Dubofsky, Melvyn, and Warren Van Tine. *John L. Lewis: A Biography*. New York: Quadrangle, 1997.

Fink, Leon. *Workingmen's Democracy: The Knights of Labor and American Politics*. Urbana: University of Illinois Press, 1983.

Fink, Leon, ed. *Workers across the Americas: The Transnational Turn in Labor History*. New York: Oxford University Press, 2011.

Foner, Eric. *Tom Paine and Revolutionary America*. New York: Oxford University Press, 1976.

Fraser, Steven. *Labor Will Rule: Sidney Hillman and the Rise of American Labor*. New York: Free Press, 1991.

Gabaccia, Donna R., and Fraser M. Ottanelli, eds. *Italian Workers of the World: Labor Migration and the Formation of Multiethnic States*. Urbana: University of Illinois Press, 2001.

Green, James. *Death in the Haymarket: A Story of Chicago, the First Labor Movement, and the Bombing That Divided Gilded-Age America*. New York: Pantheon Books, 2006.

Greene, Julie. *The Canal Builders: Making America's Empire at the Panama Canal*. New York: Penguin Books, 2009.

Greene, Julie. *Pure and Simple Politics: The American Federation of Labor and Political Activism, 1881–1917*. Cambridge, U.K.: Cambridge University Press, 1998.

Gutman, Herbert G. *Work, Culture, and Society in Industrializing America: Essays in American Working-Class and Social History*. New York: Alfred A. Knopf, 1976.

Haverty-Stacke, Donna T., and Daniel J. Walkowitz, eds. *Rethinking U.S. Labor History: Essays on the Working-Class Experience, 1756–2009*. New York: Continuum, 2010.

Hunter, Tera W. *To 'Joy My Freedom: Southern Black Women's Lives and Labors after the Civil War*. Cambridge, Mass.: Harvard University Press, 1997.

Jones, Jacqueline. *Labor of Love, Labor of Sorrow: Black Women, Work, and the Family from Slavery to the Present*. Rev. ed. New York: Basic Books, 2010.

Kersten, Andrew. *Race, Jobs and the War: The FEPC in the Midwest, 1941–46*. 2000.

Kessler-Harris, Alice. *Out to Work: A History of Wage-Earning Women in the United States*. New York: Oxford University Press, 1982.

Laurie, Bruce. *Artisans into Workers: Labor in Nineteenth-Century America*. New York: Hill and Wang, 1989.

Lewis-Colman, David M. *Race against Liberalism: Black Workers and the UAW in Detroit*. Urbana: University of Illinois Press, 2008.

Lichtenstein, Nelson. *The Most Dangerous Man in Detroit: Walter Reuther and the Fate of American Labor*. New York: Basic Books, 1995.

Lichtenstein, Nelson. *State of the Union: A Century of American Labor*. Princeton, N.J.: Princeton University Press, 2002.

McCartin, Joseph A. *Collision Course: Ronald Reagan, the Air Traffic Controllers, and the Strike That Changed America*. New York: Oxford University Press, 2011.

McCartin, Joseph A. *Labor's Great War: The Struggle for Industrial Democracy and the Origins of Modern American Labor Relations, 1912–1921*. Chapel Hill: University of North Carolina Press, 1997.

Montgomery, David. *Beyond Equality: Labor and the Radical Republicans, 1862–1872*. New York: Alfred A. Knopf, 1967.

Montgomery, David. *The Fall of the House of Labor: The Workplace, the State, and American Labor*

Activism, 1865–1925. Cambridge, U.K.: Cambridge University Press, 1987.

Moody, Kim. *An Injury to All: The Decline of American Unionism.* London and New York: Verso, 1988.

Morris, Richard B. *Government and Labor in Early America.* New York: Columbia University Press, 1946.

Rachleff, Peter J. *Black Labor in the South: Richmond, Virginia, 1865–1890.* Philadelphia: Temple University Press, 1984.

Rock, Howard B. *Artisans of the New Republic: The Tradesmen of New York City in the Age of Jefferson.* New York: New York University Press, 1979.

Roediger, David R. *The Wages of Whiteness: Race and the Making of the American Working Class.* London and New York: Verso, 1991.

Rosswurm, Steve, ed. *The CIO's Left-Led Unions.* New Brunswick, N.J.: Rutgers University Press, 1992.

Stromquist, Shelton. *A Generation of Boomers: The Pattern of Railroad Labor Conflict in Nineteenth-Century America.* Urbana: University of Illinois Press, 1987.

Stromquist, Shelton, ed. *Labor's Cold War: Local Politics in a Global Context.* Urbana: University of Illinois Press, 2008.

Vargas, Zaragosa. *Labor Rights Are Civil Rights: Mexican American Workers in Twentieth-Century America.* Princeton, N.J.: Princeton University Press, 2005.

Wilentz, Sean. *Chants Democratic: New York City and the Rise of Working-Class America, 1788–1850.* New York: Oxford University Press, 1984.

Zieger, Robert H., and Gilbert J. Gall. *American Workers, American Unions: The Twentieth Century.* 3d ed. Baltimore: Johns Hopkins University Press, 2002.

Shelton Stromquist

LABOR ORGANIZATIONS, PRE–CIVIL WAR

Labor organizations emerged in an American workforce fragmented by a broad spectrum of practices, including the actual ownership of workers. The numbers of skilled white workingmen who had sufficient freedom to organize their own societies grew disproportionately after the Revolution. Nonagricultural wage labor reached about 200,000 in the 1820s and nearly 1.5 million on the eve of the Civil War. In the 1830s an estimated 30,000 to 35,000 workers participated in local "trades' unions," and those of the early 1850s involved as many as 120,000. A significant proportion of workers who had sufficient freedom to organize themselves did so.

Workers' associations in the crafts reflected broadly shared concerns. Although rapid labor turnover generated by economic growth ordinarily diminished worker discontent, general trends in wages relative to the cost of housing and food created labor grievances. Population growth in emerging industrial cities that had insufficient rental housing caused workers to dwell in cramped quarters at high cost, while new technology that subdivided labor devalued older skills and often made them obsolescent.

Craft organizations that united workers who had the same skills established short-lived citywide bodies in Philadelphia in 1796 and again in 1827. The latter year marked the first in a wave of citywide trades' unions that sustained the National Trades' Union for a part of the mid-1830s. The Panic of 1837, however, eroded the power of most unions, and the national movement imploded until its reemergence after 1849; a second peak occurred in the 1850s. The Panic of 1857 caused another collapse, but it was less complete, and labor organizations recovered more quickly from it. The late antebellum years also saw the emergence of new kinds of national unions within the crafts and industries, though local unions without national affiliations functioned all over the nation.

The character of the labor movement reflected the ethnically stratified nature of the American workforce. The core of the Anglo-American skilled workforce included some Irish, German, and other immigrant workers, but new crafts tended to draw disproportionately from immigrant sources. The labor movement increasingly reflected this tendency, as well the growing role of women and mechanized factory work in the economy.

Workers drew leadership from those among them dedicated to an ethos of self-improvement. The Pennsylvanian William H. Sylvis, the president of first the iron molders' union and then the National Labor Union, had been a temperance advocate and Sunday-school teacher. Alonzo Granville Draper shared a similar background before leading the largest strike to date in U.S. history, the 1860 walkout in Massachusetts by some seventeen thousand shoemakers, including two thousand women.

The broad enfranchisement of propertyless white men made electoral politics a perennial issue. Workers couched their grievances in the republican legitimacy of a social contract grounded in the consent of the governed. As early as 1809, New York City carpenters explicitly described the workplace as a "social compact" that mandated workers' inalienable natural rights both to wages sufficient to raise a family and sustain themselves in old age and also to a voice in such issues as the length of the workday. By the 1840s, workers spearheaded national petition campaigns for radical land reform and a restriction on landownership by the rich.

Such views contributed to a deepening sectional conflict over the nature of labor in America. When Abraham Lincoln visited New England in 1860, a newspaperman asked him about the ongoing strike, the largest yet experienced in the United States. Pleading ignorance of the shoe industry, Lincoln noted: "I know one thing, *there is a strike!* And I am glad to know that there is a system of labor where the laborer can strike if he wants to! I would to God that such a system prevailed all over the world."

[*See also* **Artisanal Labor; Deskilling; Industrialization and Deindustrialization; Labor Movements;** *and* **Strikes.**]

BIBLIOGRAPHY

Burke, Martin J. *The Conundrum of Class: Public Discourse on the Social Order in America.* Chicago: University of Chicago Press, 1995.

Laurie, Bruce. *Artisans into Workers: Labor in Nineteenth-century America.* New York: Hill and Wang, 1989.

Roediger, David R. *The Wages of Whiteness: Race and the Making of the American Working Class.* London: Verso, 1991.

Wilentz, Sean. *Chants Democratic: New York City and the Rise of the American Working Class, 1788–1850.* New York: Oxford University Press, 1984.

Mark Lause

LABOR PRODUCTIVITY GROWTH

In 1956 the MIT economist Robert Solow published "A Contribution to the Theory of Economic Growth" (*Quarterly Journal of Economics* 70 [1956]: 65–94), laying out a theoretical framework for modeling long-run growth in the neoclassical tradition. A year later he published "Technical Change and the Aggregate Production Function" (*Review of Economics and Statistics* 39 [1957]: 312–320), an empirical application of the model developed in "Contribution." In the second article Solow introduced a method for separating the measurement of the growth of technical progress from the growth of labor and capital inputs. Solow's formalization of growth accounting became the standard method for studying trends in the growth of labor productivity.

Growth Accounting. Growth accounting drew on standard production-function analysis of the quantity and quality of labor and capital stocks, as well as on something that came to be known as the "Solow residual." The residual—which, as Moses Abramovitz famously remarked in a 1956 article, is a measure of our ignorance of the processes behind economic growth—was intended to capture the effects of advances in technological and organizational change on labor productivity. Because it refers to growth in labor productivity under the assumption of full utilization of both labor and capital, the formal name for the residual is "total factor productivity" (hereafter "TFP"), but its function as a catchall term has remained.

Most of the research produced in the neoclassical tradition of growth accounting has focused first on technological, organizational, and other supply-side factors. A relatively understudied aspect of labor productivity growth is the centrality of demand-side forces. In fact, Adam Smith recognized the importance of demand in his *Wealth of Nations* (1776). Smith qualified his praise of the division of labor by observing that "the extent of the market … limits the division of labor." In other words, market demand has a significant effect on the productive capacity of the economy. Demand for goods generates pressure to specialize, leading to advances in worker learning, technology, and organization of production. The Dutch economist Petrus Verdoorn advanced an idea, now known as Verdoorn's law, that is widely seen as an alternative theory to mainstream supply-side explanations of TFP growth that assume constant demand. Verdoorn's law represents a significant contribution to understanding TFP growth: for example, the period of rapid productivity growth in the post–World War II era can be at least partially explained by reference to a strong and vital middle class during the golden age of American capitalism.

The growth-accounting method dominated much of the empirical research on labor productivity growth for several decades after the initial publication of Solow's article. Angus Maddison, an eminent British scholar of economic growth and economic history, used growth-accounting techniques for his well-known *Economic Growth in the West: Comparative Experience in Europe and North America.* Edward F. Denison, an economist at the Brookings Institution, was one of the leading experts on the history of economic growth in the United States. His studies include the books *Accounting for United States Economic Growth, 1929–1969* (1974) and *Accounting for Slower Economic Growth: The United States in the 1970s* (1979). Denison's work combined meticulous data collection with careful analysis of the particular causes of labor productivity growth, including worker education and changes in total hours worked. For example, Denison asserted that a main reason for high productivity growth from the late 1940s to the late 1960s can be found in the dramatic increase in the number of hours worked per worker over the course of this period. Later research confirmed the importance of total hours per worker and extended the phase to 1973, when labor productivity growth—and economic growth more generally—began to decline.

From 1973 until 1995, labor productivity growth suffered a slump even as computers began to revolutionize tasks in almost every sector of the economy (Solow quipped in 1987 that "you can see the computer age everywhere but in the productivity statistics"). Productivity revived from 1995 to 2001, and the resurgence accelerated from 2001 to 2004 during the boom in information technology and communications (in 2000, Solow redacted his earlier quip, noting that "you can now see computers in the productivity statistics"). A well-known study of this resurgence in productivity growth in relation to the information-technology revolution is Erik Brynjolfsson and Lorin Hitt's "Computing Productivity: Firm-Level Evidence" (*Review of Economics and Statistics* 85 [2003]: 793–808). Data has shown another upward trend in productivity growth after the 2008–2009 recession.

Impact of Technological and Organizational Change.

Aside from studying the effects of labor quality and capital deepening, scholars have also focused on technological and organizational change represented in TFP growth. Research in this area can focus on demand-led forces such as those discussed above, but more often they focus on supply-side changes. For example, Paul A. David (1975) has identified workers' learning by doing as a key factor behind labor productivity growth in early American industrialization. In David's study, he describes learning on the job as a type of technological growth, since it refers to workers' improving their method of production based on increased knowledge of the production process. Stephen Marglin (1974) has highlighted the particular organizational characteristics of the capitalist firm—particularly its ability to order production in a time-efficient manner. Marglin emphasizes the importance of the manager's overseeing production processes, inculcating the discipline and obedience necessary for economic growth. More recently, Alexander Field (2011) has argued that the Great Depression was marked by a period of substantial labor productivity growth driven primarily by technological and organizational change in the firm. Field notes that throughout the Great Depression, advertisements for scientists, engineers, and academics were common, as were rising wages. Field asserts that these phenomena are explained by the fact that firms were forced to cut back on laborers and adopted new, more efficient technologies and organizational methods.

Research on labor productivity growth has thus mostly focused on management-led changes in the method and organization of production. Nevertheless, since 2008 renewed interest in the causes and consequences of inequality, coupled with continued economic malaise marked by slow growth and high unemployment, might bring researchers interested in the topic to examine more closely the role that demand plays in labor productivity growth. The redistribution of wealth to the top income earners may have dramatically tempered productivity growth by weakening the middle class and thereby limiting the extent of the market.

[*See also* **Business Growth and Decline; Capitalism; Economic Development; Economic Theories and Thought; Education and Human Capital;** *and* **Productivity.**]

BIBLIOGRAPHY

Abramovitz, Moses. "Resource and Output Trends in the United States since 1870." *American Economic Review* 46 (1956): 5–23.

Abramovitz, Moses, and Paul A. David. "Reinterpreting Economic Growth: Parables and Realities." *American Economic Review* 63 (1973): 428–439.

David, Paul A. *Technical Choice, Innovation, and Economic Growth: Essays on American and British Experience in the Nineteenth Century.* London: Cambridge University Press, 1975.

Denison, Edward F. *Accounting for Slower Economic Growth: The United States in the 1970s.* Washington, D.C.: Brookings Institution, 1979.

Denison, Edward F. *The Sources of Economic Growth in the United States and the Alternatives before Us.* New York: Committee for Economic Development, 1962.

Field, Alexander J. *A Great Leap Forward: 1930s Depression and U.S. Economic Growth.* New Haven, Conn.: Yale University Press, 2011.

Gordon, Robert J. "Interpreting the 'One Big Wave' in U.S. Long-Term Productivity Growth." In *Productivity, Technology, and Economic Growth*, edited by Bart van Ark, Simon Kuipers, and Gerard Kuper, pp. 19–65. Boston: Kluwer, 2000.

Maddison, Angus. *Economic Growth in the West: Comparative Experience in Europe and North*

America. New York: Twentieth Century Fund, 1964.

Marglin, Stephen. "What Do Bosses Do? The Origins and Functions of Hierarchy in Capitalist Production." *Review of Radical Political Economics* 6, no. 2 (Summer 1974): 60–112.

Daniel MacDonald

LABOR SPIES AND PINKERTONS

Among the many tools at employers' disposal to monitor their workers is the labor spy. Because of the secretive nature of industrial espionage, the degree to which labor spies have been used by companies, as well as their effectiveness, is open to question. Still, few subjects have drawn more intense scorn from organized labor and its sympathizers than the labor spy.

The origins of industrial spying in the United States have often been traced to the Pinkerton National Detective Agency, a name synonymous with labor spying in the Gilded Age. Established in 1850 in Chicago by the Scottish immigrant Allan J. Pinkerton (1819–1884), the private company developed a strong reputation as an investigative agency and private police force at a time when local, state, and federal policing remained weak or nonexistent. The firm initially gained fame as it pursued counterfeiting rings and outlaws like Jesse James, the Younger brothers, and the Dalton gang. Pinkerton's agency won further publicity when it provided espionage services for the Union during the Civil War. After the war the agency built relationships with large corporations for "industrial work" as it was retained to curb the rise of armed train robberies and employee theft on the nation's expanding railroads. As more disgruntled workers turned to organized labor for help in the late nineteenth century, employers turned to the Pinkerton agency and similar private detective firms to help them anticipate labor troubles and combat unionization.

One of the earliest and most significant examples of Pinkerton's services in labor struggles involved the notorious Molly Maguire episodes in northeastern Pennsylvania. It remains unresolved whether such an Irish American secret society ever existed under the rubric "Molly Maguires." A wave of violence, including the murder of mine officials, did grip the anthracite coal region beginning in the early 1860s, but some scholars suggest that the mine and railroad operators used the incidences of violence to create the mythology of the Molly Maguires as part of an effort to demonize such emerging trade unions among anthracite miners as the Workingmen's Benevolent Association (WBA). Franklin B. Gowen, the ambitious president of the Philadelphia and Reading Railroad (which dominated the area's mines), met with Pinkerton in 1873 to discuss criminal activity in the region. Afterward the Pinkerton detective James McParlan infiltrated the Mollies for approximately two years. McParlan claimed to have found evidence of a terrorist organization operating under the guise of the Ancient Order of Hibernians (AOH), an Irish American fraternal organization. McParlan, using the alias James McKenna, observed and participated in planning Molly Maguire killings. After fleeing the region in March 1876, he acted as the lead witness during the Molly Maguire trials. Some scholars view McParlan's testimony with skepticism, believing him to have acted as an agent provocateur. Significantly, during McParlan's undercover activities, suspected members of the Molly Maguires and their families suffered vigilante attacks. Following their conviction at trial, twenty Irishmen alleged to be Molly Maguires were hanged.

Allan Pinkerton furthered the public perception of the Molly Maguires as a band of ruthless, alcoholic cutthroats with the publication of his ghostwritten 1877 dime novel, *The Molly Maguires and the Detectives.* The novel enhanced McParlan's national reputation as an investigator, and he rose in the ranks of the Pinkerton National Detective Agency, eventually becoming superintendent of the firm's office in Denver, Colorado, in 1885. Two decades later, he again gained national prominence as the detective who had uncovered the conspiracy by William D. "Big Bill" Haywood and other officials of the Western Federation of Miners to assassinate the former governor of Idaho, Frank Steunenberg. This time, however, during a trial for murder in which the union officials were defended by Clarence Darrow, a jury found them not guilty.

The Spread of Labor Spying.

By the early twentieth century, industrialists confronted with labor troubles could choose from among several hundred agencies besides the Pinkerton National Detective Agency. Other major players in the booming labor-spy business included the William J. Burns International Detective Agency, the Thiel Detective Service Company, and the Railway Audit and Inspection Company. Such agencies, which openly advertised their union-busting services, established offices in major cities throughout the nation. In some instances, employers retained informants to learn more about the behavior of individual workers. For example, when professional baseball was in its infancy, some team owners, concerned about the drinking habits of certain players and their impact on the players' performance on the field, retained Pinkerton detectives to tail players to saloons. More complex cases involved investigations of labor unions. Detective agencies planted spies within unions to gather intelligence about activists and tactics. The labor spy's techniques included employee monitoring, provocation, intimidation, and "missionary work," or spreading unfounded rumors about union members. Often, the agencies managed to place their operatives into official union positions where they gathered critical information and spread dissension. As early as 1880, the use of labor spies had grown so widespread that unions sought to identify and ostracize them.

When strikes and lockouts occurred, labor-spy agencies further served their clients. They guarded industrial facilities and protected strikebreakers. Some recruited strikebreakers for employers. The Pinkerton agency developed its own small private army to defend company property. It has been estimated that the Pinkerton agency protected property in more than seventy strikes throughout the country between 1866 and 1892. The agency was linked to many key moments in labor history: the Great Railroad Strike of 1877, the Haymarket affair of 1886, and the Pullman strike and boycott of 1894. The use of armed Pinkerton guards during labor struggles came into question as labor conflicts brought rising numbers of deaths and injuries. In the strike at the coal wharves in Jersey City, New Jersey, in 1887, a fourteen-year-boy—an innocent bystander—was shot and killed by a Pinkerton guard. A turning point in the use of armed industrial armies occurred in 1892 at Andrew Carnegie's plant in Homestead, Pennsylvania, when the use of three hundred Pinkerton guards led to the deaths of ten strikers and three guards. The public outcry over the use of Pinkerton's troops at Homestead prompted the passage of legislation that made the use of private security agents by the government illegal. The Pinkerton agency gradually curtailed its use of armed labor policing, but its reputation as an enemy of working people lingered.

Labor Spies and Their Critics.

As trade unionism continued to be advanced in the twentieth century, the use of labor spies came under greater scrutiny. For example, the United States Commission on Industrial Relations (CIR), established in 1912 to investigate the roots of the nation's labor struggles, condemned the industrial espionage industry. Similarly, the final report of the La Follette Civil Liberties

Committee (1936–1941), formed to investigate violations of workers' civil liberties during the industrial conflicts sparked by the Great Depression, detailed the extensive use of labor spies by companies seeking to destroy unions and break strikes. Several pro-labor publications also called attention to the abuses of the labor-spy industry, such as Morris Friedman's *The Pinkerton Labor Spy* (1907), Edward Levinson's *I Break Strikes: The Technique of Pearl L. Bergoff* (1935), and Leo Huberman's *The Labor Spy Racket* (1937).

The major shift in the capital–labor relationship wrought by the National Labor Relations (Wagner) Act of 1935 prompted companies to use subtler methods of industrial espionage and union busting. Private detective agencies, whose importance had been diminished by improvements in public policing, gradually withdrew from involvement in labor conflict and provided more traditional security services for institutions like banks. In the twenty-first century, employers seeking to maintain nonunion status, decertify existing unions, or skirt labor laws turn to such labor-consulting agencies as Modern Management Methods, Inc., or West Coast Industrial Relations Associates. Echoing the era of Pinkertonism, twenty-first-century companies can still obtain replacement workers during strikes by using temporary employment agencies. Though some agencies, such as Manpower, Inc., have avoided involvement in labor disputes, others maintain databanks of potential strikebreakers. Other firms, similar to those that developed during the Gilded Age, specialize in security matters during labor struggles. One example occurred during the Detroit newspaper strike of 1995 when the newspaper's management contracted with Alternative Work Force (AWF) to provide hundreds of replacement workers. To protect the replacement workers, Huffmaster Strike Services hired security guards. Vance International's Asset Protection Team (APT)—an agency more militant than Huffmaster, which it replaced during the Detroit strike—used guards dressed in black riot gear, helmets, and combat boots to intimidate pickets.

A new chapter in employee surveillance has opened as employers turn to modern, digital technology to monitor employees through keystroke logging, email filters, and video cameras. There is also evidence that employers can use the latest technology as a tool to fight unionization. The retail giant Wal-Mart allegedly maintains an extensive surveillance system that gathers information to retard union organizing among employees by monitoring their phone calls and emails.

[*See also* **Computer Monitoring of Office Workers; Molly Maguires; Repression of Unions;** *and* **Strikes.**]

BIBLIOGRAPHY

Jeffreys-Jones, Rhodri. "Profit Over Class: A Study in American Espionage." *Journal of American Studies* 6 (1972): 233–248.

Morn, Frank. *"The Eye That Never Sleeps": A History of the Pinkerton National Detective Agency.* Bloomington: Indiana University Press, 1982.

Norwood, Stephen H. *Strikebreaking and Intimidation: Mercenaries and Masculinity in Twentieth-Century America.* Chapel Hill: University of North Carolina Press, 2002.

Smith, Robert Michael. *From Blackjacks to Briefcases: A History of Commercialized Strikebreaking and Unionbusting in the United States.* Athens, Ohio: Ohio University Press, 2003.

Mark Noon

LABOR'S ROLE IN POLITICS

Organized labor has pressured government for favorable laws and supported sympathetic candidates for public office since American workers first organized to advance their interests. After the Civil War, as trade unions grew, many participated in coalitions that won federal and state laws declaring the legal workday to be eight hours. Some unions worked for the Greenback and Populist Parties—the Greenbacks had a plank in support of the eight-hour day in their 1878 national platform, as did the Populists in 1892—and for select Democratic and Republican candidates. From the late 1860s through the 1880s, the National Labor Union, the Knights of Labor, and the American Federation of Labor (AFL) all fought to establish federal and state labor agencies. These efforts culminated in 1913 with the creation of the separate U.S. Department of Labor, expected to be organized labor's "voice" in the Cabinet.

Gravitation toward the Democrats.

Labor leaders disputed political strategy as unionization further strengthened in the early twentieth century. Many miners, machinists, brewery workers, and garment workers urged the need for a broader political agenda and supported an independent labor or socialist party. But other leaders, mainly those concentrated in the crafts and building trades, rejected broad political involvement in favor of lobbying for specific laws that directly benefited unions. Locally, however, many of these unions allied with the political parties that dominated municipal and county politics and thus controlled the award of contracts for public construction and printing. The longtime AFL president Samuel Gompers placed top priority on unions' economic power, based on a theory of "voluntarism." Gompers rejected an independent labor party in favor of opportunistically rewarding labor's friends and punishing its enemies regardless of a candidate's party affiliation. In 1902, AFL leaders narrowly defeated a proposal to commit the AFL to socialism. Gompers and his allies feared that endorsement of a single party would create schisms in a labor move-

ment in which many members already held firm traditional attachments to the Democratic, Republican, or Socialist Parties. Thereafter, the growing muscle of the craft unions fortified Gompers's anti-labor-party position. The Industrial Workers of the World, a militant union organization, eschewed political engagement in favor of syndicalism, although many of its members sympathized with and voted for Socialists. The United States became the only advanced industrial nation without a major labor or socialist party. Yet the AFL lobbied forcefully for legislation that strengthened unions' bargaining position, that established public offices to advance labor's agenda, and that regulated the employment of women and children.

In the early 1900s, hostile Republican legislators, along with adverse court rulings, prompted Gompers and other AFL leaders to gravitate toward an informal alliance with the national Democratic Party. Gompers personally campaigned against the reelection of the House speaker Joseph Cannon, a Republican from Illinois, whom Gompers viewed as "the strategic center to the opposition to labor." The Democratic Party was more welcoming to the AFL because its candidates needed votes from union members to contest Republican power in northern industrial states. Federation leaders built an informal alliance with the Democrats in the Progressive Era that grew stronger and more formal during the New Deal and after. But the AFL maintained an official position of nonpartisanship because it needed the votes of such Progressive Republicans as the U.S. senators Robert M. La Follette of Wisconsin and George Norris of Nebraska.

Organized labor's political role surged along with union membership during the New Deal. The administration of Franklin D. Roosevelt actively promoted unions and built an especially strong alliance with the industrial unions that formed the Congress of Industrial Organizations (CIO), an AFL rival. Although the CIO president John L. Lewis grew unhappy with the New Deal, toyed with independent labor politics, and endorsed the Republican presidential candidate Wendell Willkie in 1940, most unions and their members, including those who belonged to Lewis's own union, the United Mine Workers, remained loyal to Roosevelt and the Democratic Party. Since 1936, organized labor has reliably provided armies of campaign workers and sizable campaign contributions for Democratic candidates.

Peak and Decline in Strength. Union economic and political strength peaked in the 1950s and 1960s. The AFL and the CIO merged in 1955, and they amalgamated their political action committees into COPE (the Committee on Political Education), a pathbreaking political action committee. Organized labor formed a close and effective partnership with the Democratic presidential administrations and congressional majorities in the late 1940s, 1950s, and 1960s. George Meany, the president of the AFL-CIO from 1955 to 1979, and Walter Reuther, the president of the United Auto Workers from 1946 to 1970, were major forces in bringing about the reforms of the Great Society.

By the 1970s, technological innovations and competitive global trade patterns decimated unionized manufacturing jobs, eroding union membership and organized labor's political strength. The rapid unionization of service workers and public employees in such unions as the Service Employees International Union and the American Federation of State, County, and Municipal Employees enhanced labor's political strength but did not stem the overall decline in unionization, which fell to about one in eight American workers in 2010. National election exit polls have shown that voters who live in union households have continued to cast about 60 percent of their ballots for Democratic presidential candidates, but the percentage of voters who live in such households declined from nearly 30 percent in 1976 to about 20 percent in 2008. By the late 1970s, the AFL-CIO found it more difficult—indeed, almost impossible—to advance its top legislative priorities, whether Democrats or Republicans held power. Organized labor built a poor relationship with Jimmy Carter (1977–1981) and an adversarial one with Ronald Reagan (1981–1989). During the administration of Bill Clinton (1993–2001), labor failed to win reform of labor law and suffered a bitter defeat with the passage of the North American Free Trade Agreement (NAFTA). The administration of George W. Bush (2001–2009) wasted little time in showing its disdain for organized labor. Even the administration of Barack Obama (from 2009) disappointed union leaders by declining to fight for legislation to make it easier to organize workers.

[*See also* **Greenback Labor Party; Secretaries of Department of Labor;** *and* **Voluntarism.**]

BIBLIOGRAPHY

Dark, Taylor E., III. *The Unions and the Democrats: An Enduring Alliance.* Ithaca, N.Y.: ILR Press, 1999.

Greene, Julie. *Pure and Simple Politics: The American Federation of Labor and Political Activism, 1881–1917.* Cambridge, U.K.: Cambridge University Press, 1998.

Robertson, David Brian. *Capital, Labor, and State: The Battle for American Labor Markets from the Civil War to the New Deal.* Lanham, Md.: Rowman & Littlefield, 2000.

David Brian Robertson

LABOR UNIONS

See **Labor Movements.**

LA FOLLETTE'S SEAMEN'S ACT

Although the Civil War brought an end to slavery in the United States, merchant sailors continued to be bound to the masters of the ships they served. Sailors who tried to terminate their yearly contracts, even when their ships were in port, could be deprived of payment and imprisoned. Although no other laborers were subject to such extreme controls, the Supreme Court upheld the conditions of this servitude in 1897, exempting merchant sailors from the Thirteenth Amendment by confirming that the contracts of seamen involved to some extent the surrender of personal liberty. In 1910, at the urging of the president of the International Seamen's Union, Andrew Furuseth, Senator Robert M. La Follette, a Republican from Wisconsin, introduced corrective legislation. Signed into law by President Woodrow Wilson in 1915, the Seamen's Act enabled merchant sailors to quit at their own discretion once their ships were docked and unloaded.

The act offered protection not only to sailors but also to passengers. The sinking of the *Titanic* in 1912 created outrage over the disproportionate loss of life among third-class passengers. That scandalous tragedy fueled support for the portions of the act that required that every ship leaving an American port be equipped with sufficient lifeboats and rafts for all passengers and crew. Another element of the act required that commercial vessels carry enough experienced seamen for two to be assigned to each lifeboat.

La Follette's Seaman's Act was an important Progressive achievement in safety and fair-employment practices. In regulating the powerful shipping industry, it advanced the Progressive goal of equal protection for all Americans.

[*See also* **Freedom of Contract** *and* **Maritime Transport.**]

BIBLIOGRAPHY

Berwick, Arnold. *The Abraham Lincoln of the Sea: The Life of Andrew Furuseth.* Santa Cruz, Calif.: Odin Press, 1993.
Fink, Leon. *Sweatshops at Sea: Merchant Seamen in the World's First Globalized Industry, from 1812 to the Present.* Chapel Hill: University of North Carolina Press, 2011.

Nancy C. Unger

LAISSEZ-FAIRE AND CLASSICAL ECONOMICS

That government should not be involved in economic activity is a relatively recent concept in Western society. Into the nineteenth century, governments regulated banks and the currency, controlled international trade, regulated land use and migration, granted businesses monopoly privileges to encourage particular activities, and carefully regulated relations between employers and their wageworkers or slaves. The campaign against regulation pitted progressive farmers, aggressive merchants, rising capitalists, and frustrated wageworkers against established interests sheltered by government-granted monopoly. Opponents of monopoly privilege used laissez-faire economics to promote populist and democratic politics.

Beyond the self-interest of the excluded, a larger vision of laissez-faire rooted itself in the ideas of deist philosophers such as Gottfried Leibniz and Adam Smith. From the premise that God is both all-powerful and all-good, optimistic philosophers argued that God created a beneficent natural order that, if left alone, would lead to a just and productive economy. The self-serving actions of bad governments were what caused misery and suffering by undermining the working of natural benevolence.

Smith. Laissez-faire ideas of natural order are most commonly associated with the work of the great eighteenth-century Scottish moral philosopher Adam Smith. Though credited with, or blamed for, being the first economist, Smith was a professor of moral philosophy, not economics, and though he was an advocate of natural benevolence, his economic arguments for laissez-faire are much more limited than has been recognized by many of those who proclaim themselves to be his followers.

Smith called for an active government to provide social and physical infrastructure to support economic development and also to restrain private selfishness. He criticized policies that established monopolies, such as restriction on entry into medieval guilds, and he certainly believed that a benevolent nature had created a form of self-interest that benefited society: "It is not from the benevolence of the butcher, the brewer, or the baker, that we expect our dinner, but from their regard to their own interest." Otherwise, the *Wealth of Nations* (1776) is filled with exceptions to laissez-faire, not support of it. For example, as a way of limiting financial speculation, Smith favored usury laws that limited interest rates. Though such regulations violated "natural liberty," he favored them because "exertions of the natural liberty of a few individuals, which might endanger the security of the whole society, are, and ought to be, restrained by the laws of all governments." He also believed in government management of infrastructure, because the selfish behavior of the owners of turnpikes and other public conveyances inflated the cost of transportation and trade. He favored public action to protect market competition, to restrain monopolies, to prevent conspiracies of employers, and to require payment of wages in legal tender in a timely fashion.

Some of Smith's ardent followers agreed that public intervention was needed to provide education and public goods and to restrain monopoly. In their enthusiasm for the moral imperative to respect benevolent nature, however, others forgot Smith's economic nuance. This certainly was the case, for example, with the French economist Frédéric Bastiat or the American Francis Wayland. "The principles of Political Economy," Wayland proclaimed, "are so closely analogous to those of Moral Philosophy" that "God intended" governments to confine

> themselves to their own appropriate duties, and leaving every-thing else alone. The interference of society with the concerns of the individual, even when arising from the most innocent motives, will always tend to crush the spirit of enterprise, and cripple the productive energies of a country.

Neoclassicists. These views were given a more sophisticated exposition in the work of a new generation of laissez-faire economists, including the early neoclassicists John Bates Clark and Léon Walras. Walras in particular developed an economic model proving that competitive markets might develop a set of prices under which individual demand for goods would equal the supply of goods. Walras's model was extraordinarily limited. It holds only under extreme assumptions about the nature of individual preferences and the production technology, it ignores public goods, and it never implies that market prices would be in any way optimal or lead to a desirable distribution of income. Nonetheless, proof of the possibility of competitive general equilibrium meant for advocates of laissez-faire proof that the economy could operate without government regulation.

The same response greeted the work of the neo-Walrasian Nobel Prize winners Kenneth Arrow and Gérard Debreu in the 1950s. This was far from Arrow and Debreu's intention, which was to demonstrate the need for nonmarket regulation because of the difficulty of achieving a competitive general equilibrium.

Nonetheless, neoclassical economists still believed that it was possible for competitive markets to find an equilibrium set of prices and that such prices might be stable. They ignored Arrow and Debreu's findings that such a set of prices was not necessarily optimal, was rarely stable, and would be reached only under extraordinarily unrealistic assumptions.

Much of the work in economic theory since Arrow and Debreu has confirmed their judgment that competitive markets will produce a set of stable prices only under assumptions that fail to guarantee optimality. The Nobel laureates Joseph Stiglitz, Michael Spence, and George Akerlof, for example, have demonstrated how information asymmetries produce inefficient markets or prevent mutually beneficial market exchanges. The Nobel laureates Robert Solow, Paul Krugman, and others have demonstrated how technological progress can be a public good and that research and learning and economies to scale in production can lead to situations in which society would be better off restricting trade to encourage technological progress.

Though sophisticated economic theory has rejected Walrasian equilibrium and moved beyond the economic harmonies of Bastiat and Wayland, it has failed to influence advocates of laissez-faire. This may be because the exponents of laissez-faire never expounded solely about economics but instead were actuated by the moral certainty that a benevolent deity had created a good world and that changing it in any way through social action would make things worse.

[*See also* **Capitalism; Economic Theories and Thought; Neoclassical Economics; Neoliberalism; Neoliberalism as Public Economic Policy;** *and* **Rational Choice Theory.**]

BIBLIOGRAPHY

Akerlof, George A., and Robert J. Shiller. *Animal Spirits: How Human Psychology Drives the Economy, and Why It Matters for Global Capitalism.* Princeton, N.J.: Princeton University Press, 2009.

Ely, Richard T. *The Past and the Present of Political Economy.* Baltimore: N. Murray for Johns Hopkins University, 1884.

Mill, John Stuart. *Principles of Political Economy, with Some of Their Applications to Social Philosophy.* Edited by Sir William James Ashley. London: Longmans, Green, 1909.

Schlefer, Jonathan. *The Assumptions Economists Make.* Cambridge, Mass.: Belknap Press of Harvard University Press, 2012.

Smith, Adam. *An Inquiry into the Nature and Causes of the Wealth of Nations* (1776). 2d ed. Great Books of the Western World 36. Chicago: Encyclopaedia Britannica, 1990.

Wayland, Francis. *The Elements of Political Economy.* Abridged. Boston: Gould, Kendall & Lincoln, 1837.

Gerald Friedman

LANDRUM–GRIFFIN ACT

Officially titled the Labor-Management Reporting and Disclosure Act, the Landrum–Griffin Act was passed in 1959. Its passage followed extensive congressional hearings on union corruption that were held from 1957 to 1959 by the McClellan Committee. The hearings had revealed abuses in union governance, violent organizing activities, and the influence of organized crime in some sectors of the labor movement, especially the Teamsters union. Public outrage ensured passage of a law that was designed to impose new restrictions on unions and that sought to promote internal union democracy. In this way the hearings proved fortunate for a range of groups within the business community and on the political right who were disturbed by the growing power of the labor movement.

The law addressed the right's concerns by imposing new legal barriers on activities related to union organizing. It limited the ability of unions to use pickets in their organizing drives, and it eliminated a loophole in the Taft–Hartley Act that had allowed some labor organizations to continue to engage in secondary boycotts. In a swipe at the allegations surrounding James R. Hoffa, the president of the Teamsters, the law banned individuals convicted of particular crimes from holding union office for thirteen years. And in the continued context of the Cold War, it also imposed a similar ban on current or former Communist Party members. Other provisions of the law sought to make union finances more transparent and to foster union democracy by providing a bill of rights for union members. The law hampered unions' organizing efforts, but the impact of its provisions for union democracy proved limited.

[*See also* **Hoffa, James R.; International Brotherhood of Teamsters; Taft–Hartley Act; Union Corruption;** *and* **Union Reform Movements.**]

BIBLIOGRAPHY

Bellace, Janice R., and Alan D. Berkowitz. *The Landrum–Griffin Act: Twenty Years of Federal Protection of Union Members' Rights.* Philadelphia: Industrial Research Unit, Wharton School, University of Pennsylvania, 1979.

Leiter, Robert. *The Teamsters Union: A Study of Its Economic Impact.* New York: Bookman Associates, 1957.

Witwer, David. *Corruption and Reform in the Teamsters Union.* Urbana: University of Illinois Press, 2003.

David Witwer

LASCH, CHRISTOPHER

(1932–1994), a leading and often controversial historian and social critic of the mid- and late twentieth century. Born in Omaha, Nebraska, Lasch graduated from Harvard University in 1954. In 1961 he completed a dissertation in history at Columbia University on the response of American liberals to the Russian revolution. The *New Radicalism in America, 1889–1963: The Intellectual as a Social Type* (1965), a withering examination of the rise of American intellectuals as a flawed social class overeager to serve power, won its young author great praise for the style and force of his social criticism. Thereafter Lasch regularly contributed trenchant pieces to journals such as the *New York Review of Books.* Never comfortable with student protests or the New Left, and after briefly experimenting with organized socialism, in the 1970s he entered what he characterized as a period of "retrenchment," during which he read deeply into European social thought. These labors bore fruit in a trio of books, *Haven in a Heartless World: The Family Besieged* (1977), *The Culture of Narcissism: American Life in an Age of Diminishing Expectations* (1979), and *The Minimal Self: Psychic Survival in Troubled Times* (1984), that both identified an assault on older sources of selfhood inherent in advanced bourgeois society and traced the emergence of a new social type in American life: the self-serving, parasitic narcissist. In *The True and Only Heaven: Progress and Its Critics* (1991), Lasch questioned the notion of progress as the dominant trope underlying American life and espoused a new populist vision. At its heart lay a counter-strand of history, running from Jonathan Edwards to Martin Luther King Jr., whom he brought together to offer an alternative historical tradition, one founded on skepticism about the assumptions of progress, especially the belief in limitless growth and expansion as hallmarks of improvement. In that vein, Lasch urged his country to embrace a localized, small-is-beautiful "culture of limits" in place of the untenable assumptions behind global consumerism.

After teaching stints at the University of Iowa and Northwestern University, Lasch spent most of his career, from 1970 until his death from cancer, at the University of Rochester.

[*See also* **Consumer Culture.**]

BIBLIOGRAPHY

Brown, David S. *Beyond the Frontier: The Midwestern Voice in American Historical Writing.* Chicago: University of Chicago Press, 2009.

Miller, Eric. *Hope in a Scattering Time: A Life of Christopher Lasch.* Grand Rapids, Mich.: Eerdmans, 2010.

Jeffrey Ludwig

LAWRENCE "BREAD AND ROSES" STRIKE (1912)

The Lawrence, Massachusetts, textile strike of January–March 1912 was notable for several reasons. It later became memorialized in poetry and song as a demand for roses (beauty) as well as bread (sustenance), and that is how it remains embedded in historical memory. It also marked a dramatic moment in the history of the Industrial Workers of the World (IWW): the Lawrence strike was the IWW's first significant strike victory among an ethnically mixed and heavily female labor force in the Northeast. Newspapers and magazines filed stories and articles heralding a rising tide of socialism or syndicalism. Lawrence also introduced a new tactic to industrial conflict in the United States: socialists from New York City and Philadelphia, adopting a tactic used in Europe, transported the children of Lawrence strikers to families elsewhere who cared for the strike's "orphans." The strike, moreover, led to congressional investigations of its causes.

The strike was both a spontaneous reaction to the impact of a new state maximum-hours law on workers' earnings and the result of pre-existing organization by Italian immigrant workers who belonged to the IWW. When the Massachusetts maximum-hours law reduced the workday, employers cut wages proportionately—as workers discovered when they received their first pay envelope in January. Upon discovering the wage reduction, Polish women workers in one mill called upon their sister and brother workers to quit in protest. From that mill the protest spread over the following days to all the textile mills in Lawrence. The strikers represented a remarkable diversity of people, including immigrants from Poland, Lithuania, and Italy, eastern European Jews, and Middle Eastern Christians. Italians formed the largest and most committed of the strikers, and the IWW members among them invited their organization's two most famous Italian leaders, Joseph Ettor and Arturo Giovannitti, to Lawrence. Ettor and Giovanitti transformed strikers who spoke different languages, practiced divergent religions, and socialized in competing clubs into a cohesive force. Despite a frigid New England winter, Lawrence's occupation by heavily armed state militia, opposition by city and state officials, and incidents of violence that led to the arrest, indictment, and trial of Ettor and Giovannitti for murder, the strikers held firm. Two of the IWW's most famous leaders, William D. "Big Bill" Haywood and the "rebel girl," Elizabeth Gurley Flynn, came to Lawrence to bolster the strikers' spirits. Worker solidarity won an increase in wages, a promise of improved working conditions, and the belief that through organization workers could bargain more equally with their employers.

Unfortunately for Lawrence's textile workers, their triumph proved short-lived. Within a year, the IWW had nearly disappeared, and the strikers, lacking effective organization, were at their employers' mercy. When Selig Perlman visited Lawrence in 1913 as a federal investigator, he concluded that the IWW had failed because of the millowners' power and because certain ethnic groups chose to identify more strongly with employers than with fellow workers.

[*See also* **Flynn, E. G.; Haywood, William D.; Industrial Workers of the World; Strikes;** *and* **Textile Industry.**]

BIBLIOGRAPHY

Cameron, Ardis. *Radicals of the Worst Sort: Laboring Women in Lawrence, Massachusetts, 1860–1912.* Urbana: University of Illinois Press, 1993.

Watson, Bruce. *Bread and Roses: Mills, Migrants, and the Struggle for the American Dream.* New York: Viking, 2005.

Melvyn Dubofsky

LEHMAN BROTHERS

The investment banking house Lehman Brothers was founded in 1850 by Henry Lehman, a dry-goods merchandiser, in Montgomery, Alabama. In 1868 its activities—mainly the trading of commodities, particularly cotton—were moved to New York City, and until the 1890s the firm's focus continued to be commodities trading. It became a member of many of the futures exchanges in New York, and from 1887 it was also a member of the New York Stock Exchange.

After the turn of the twentieth century, the firm slowly entered into investment banking. It underwrote stocks of newly emerging companies in growing industries, notably retailing. Before World War I, it joined with Goldman Sachs in underwriting many new issues, the best known of which was for Sears, Roebuck in 1906. Lehman also underwrote new stock issues for companies such as the Underwood Corporation, the Studebaker Corporation, and the F. W. Woolworth Company. After the Glass–Steagall Act was passed in 1933, Lehman Brothers became purely an investment banking firm,

and it remained a partnership in the post–World War II years.

In 1977 the firm acquired Kuhn, Loeb & Co., and in 1984 it held merger talks with Shearson/American Express. Shearson acquired Lehman; the company changed its name to Shearson Lehman/American Express and became the second-largest securities house on Wall Street. In the mid-1990s, American Express began to restructure itself, and Lehman Brothers was spun off as a public company, reassuming its original name. After the deregulatory legislation of 1999, Lehman expanded its activities and became a more full-service institutional firm, heavily reliant on funding in the money market and on the market for securities related to residential mortgages. The firm ran into financial difficulties during the credit-market crisis in 2008 and declared bankruptcy on 15 September 2008. It was the largest bankruptcy filing in American history.

[*See also* **Deregulation, Financial; Financial Crises, 1980s–2010; Glass–Steagall, Repeal of; Goldman Sachs; Kuhn Loeb & Co.;** *and* **Shadow Banking System.**]

BIBLIOGRAPHY

Chapman, Peter. *The Last of the Imperious Rich: Lehman Brothers, 1844–2008.* New York: Portfolio, 2010.

McDonald, Lawrence G., with Patrick Robinson. *A Colossal Failure of Common Sense: The Inside Story of the Collapse of Lehman Brothers.* New York: Crown Business, 2009.

Charles Geisst

LEWIS, JOHN L.

(1880–1969), labor leader. Born in Lucas, Iowa, to Welsh immigrant parents, John Llewellyn Lewis as a young man wandered the West and attempted to establish several businesses. He became a coal miner and in 1908 moved to Panama, Illinois. A year later, Lewis became president of the United Mine Workers (UMW) local. Thereafter he rose rapidly in the labor movement, becoming in 1917 a UMW vice president. Lewis's political ability and his adroit handling of the 1919 coal strike won him the union's presidency in 1920.

The union over which Lewis assumed command soon entered an era of decline. Ironically, as the power of the UMW eroded in the 1920s, Lewis's personal power in the union grew. With Franklin Delano Roosevelt's election in 1932, Lewis rebuilt the UMW. In 1933 he launched a spectacular organizing drive that brought more than 90 percent of the nation's coal miners into the union. With the passage in 1935 of the pro-labor National Labor Relations (Wagner) Act, he created the Committee for Industrial Organization (CIO) within the American Federation of Labor (AFL) to unionize workers in the mass-production industries. As president of the CIO—which was expelled from the AFL in 1938 and changed its name to the Congress of Industrial Organizations—Lewis helped unionize the automotive industry, the iron and steel industry, and others.

At first allied with Roosevelt and the New Deal, Lewis broke with the president during the 1940 election. Roosevelt's reelection caused Lewis to resign as president of the CIO and in 1942 to withdraw the UMW from the CIO.

During World War II, Lewis played the militant loner. In 1943 he led a series of unpopular strikes. After the war, Lewis led more massive coal strikes that spurred the passage of the 1947 Taft–Hartley Act. In the 1950s he shifted from militancy to accommodation with mine owners. He transformed himself into an industrial statesman, urging trade policies that would increase coal exports, building a string of union hospitals, and seeking the passage of the first federal mine-safety law. When he retired from his union presidency in 1960, Lewis left an ailing industry and a debilitated, corrupt union.

[*See also* **Congress of Industrial Organizations; Labor Leaders; Labor Movements; Labor's Role in Politics; Mining Industry; Steel Strike of 1919; Strikes; Union Reform Movements;** *and* **United Mine Workers.**]

BIBLIOGRAPHY

Dubofsky, Melvyn, and Warren Van Tine. *John L. Lewis: A Biography*. New York: Quadrangle, 1977.

Warren Van Tine

LITTLE, FRANK

(1879–1917), labor leader and martyr. The Industrial Workers of the World (IWW, or Wobblies) and subsequent historians of the organization have lionized the martyred part-Indian agitator Frank Little, who served the IWW as the quintessential hobo agitator. He was born in 1879 to Dr. Walter Little and Almira Hays Little; Almira claimed some Indian heritage, most probably Cherokee. In the 1880s the family moved to Oklahoma Territory in order to homestead. Frank Little left the territory in 1899 shortly after his father's death and headed west, working as a miner and as an organizer for the Western Federation of Miners (WFM). Eventually he joined the Industrial Workers of the World in 1906 in Arizona. Little threw himself into organizing for the IWW, distinguishing himself as a committed radical in strikes and protests across the western half of the United States. By the time the United States entered World War I in April 1917, Little had become a committed revolutionary and an outspoken critic of the war.

In July 1917 a battered Little arrived in Butte, Montana—he had broken his leg in a car accident in Arizona—to help organize miners in their struggles against the Anaconda Copper Mining Company. Early on the morning of 1 August, six masked men burst into his room and dragged him outside to a waiting car. Little's kidnappers tied him to the bumper and dragged him to a railroad trestle at the edge of town, severely beat him, and tossed him over the side of the bridge with a rope around his neck; pinned to Little was a note bearing the words, "Others take notice, first and last warning, 3-7-77," and the initials "L-D-C-S-S-W-T"—likely references to the dimensions of a grave and the initials of future victims of vigilantism.

[*See also* **Industrial Workers of the World; Labor Leaders; Labor Spies and Pinkertons;** *and* **Radicalism and Workers.**]

BIBLIOGRAPHY

Chaplin, Ralph. *Wobbly: The Rough-and-Tumble Story of an American Radical.* Chicago: University of Chicago Press, 1948.

Flynn, Elizabeth Gurley. *The Rebel Girl, an Autobiography: My First Life (1906–1926).* Rev. ed. New York: International Publishers, 1973.

Gerald Ronning

LITTLE RED SONGBOOK

Originally titled *Songs of the Workers, on the Road, in the Jungles, and in the Shops: Songs to Fan the Flames of Discontent*, the songbook of the Industrial Workers of the World (IWW, or Wobblies) was first published in 1909 by the IWW section in Spokane, Washington, as a red-jacketed booklet with twenty-four songs. In 2010 the union distributed the thirty-eighth edition of what had become known as the *Little Red Songbook*. Its objectives were to educate workers and to transmit the principles of the so-called One Big Union (revolutionary syndicalism), using the songs as entertainment and propaganda; songs could be more easily understood than pamphlets or manifestos. Lyrics and poems, reinforced by cartoons, translated Wobbly ideology into a simple language that workers could understand: the goal was "to fan the flames of discontent," as one of the alternative titles put it. Singing also served to overcome national, ethnic, linguistic, and gender barriers among workers whom the Wobblies wanted to organize. Many songs employed a humorous and satirical tone about class war and capitalist exploitation, adapting lyrics from well-known popular musical or religious melodies such as gospel hymns and vaudeville tunes. Ordinary workers and IWW members wrote songs relating their hard working and living conditions, including their experiences as migrant (hobo) workers.

Wobblies have repeatedly been associated with their boisterous singing at rallies, during strikes both successful and unsuccessful, during free-speech fights, and while imprisoned. Songs served to create group cohesion, emotional participation, and cooperation among segmented workers, as well as to build a revolutionary spirit among workers. The most famous IWW songwriters—Joe Hill, Ralph Chaplin, Richard Brazier, and T-Bone Slim—penned lyrics that have become immortal and continue to be sung by various social movements: songs such as "Solidarity Forever," "There Is Power in a Union," "The Preacher and the Slave," and "Hallelujah I'm a Bum."

[*See also* **Hill, Joe; Industrial Workers of the World;** *and* **Labor Journalism.**]

BIBLIOGRAPHY

Green, Archie, David Roediger, Franklin Rosemont, and Salvatore Salerno, eds. *The Big Red Songbook:*

250-plus IWW Songs! Chicago: Charles H. Kerr, 2007.

Kornbluh, Joyce L. *Rebel Voices: An IWW Anthology.* New ed. Chicago: Charles H. Kerr, 1998.

Arturo Lahera-Sánchez

LITTLE STEEL STRIKE (1937)

The so-called Little Steel strike, which began on 26 May 1937, pitted the Steel Workers Organizing Committee (SWOC) of the Committee for Industrial Organization (CIO), led by Philip Murray, against six smaller steel companies. The companies were small only in comparison to the industry giant, U.S. Steel, which was led by the chief executive of Republic Steel, Tom Girdler, a strident antiunion opponent. The strike began two months after U.S. Steel signed a contract recognizing the SWOC as the bargaining agent for its members, a victory that workers had won without a strike. U.S. Steel's smaller competitors—Republic, Bethlehem, Jones and Laughlin, Inland, Youngstown Steel and Tube, and Wheeling—refused to recognize or bargain with the SWOC. Instead, led by Girdler, they prepared to fight the union, hiring private detectives to infiltrate local unions and protect company property, stocking arms and ammunition, wooing loyal employees, and seeking strikebreakers, or replacement workers. Buoyed by the CIO's February victory over General Motors and U.S. Steel's concessions to the SWOC, the SWOC's leaders prepared to challenge Girdler and his corporate allies. For Murray, his lieutenants, and union troops, the moment seemed ripe for action. Labor was on the march, New Deal Democratic governors held power in the states of Pennsylvania, Ohio, Indiana, and Illinois where the battle would be fought, and a friend occupied the White House.

Within a week of its eruption, the Little Steel strike became a bitter and violent struggle. Battles raged between company guards and strikers in Pennsylvania, Ohio, and Indiana. In all three states, the Democratic governors dispatched state police and National Guard units to protect company property and replacement workers, in effect acting as strikebreakers. Their properties protected by state power, the steel companies organized back-to-work marches in which loyal employees paraded to work behind large American flags. The strike's single most violent moment occurred on the south side of Chicago on Memorial Day during a demonstration that included nearly two thousand Republic steelworkers, their wives and children, and numerous sympathizers who were there to protest police interference with legal picketing. As the peaceable demonstrators neared the mill gates, an altercation with the city police erupted. Police opened fire with their weapons—guns and tear-gas canisters—at the marchers, who turned tail and fled. When the shooting stopped, ten marchers lay dead, victims of police bullets; thirty more were wounded by gunshots; and an equal number suffered other injuries. A U.S. Senate investigating committee later reported that "wounded prisoners of war might have expected and received greater solicitude" than did the victims of the so-called Memorial Day massacre. When John L. Lewis appealed to President Franklin Delano Roosevelt for support, Roosevelt replied, "the majority of the people are saying just one thing, a plague on both your houses."

The president's reply presaged the SWOC's defeat. It demonstrated the limits of CIO power and political influence, as well as how far public opinion had turned against labor and its forward march. The SWOC's defeat marked the beginning of an internal crisis and decline for the CIO, a process not to be reversed until war erupted in Europe in the summer of 1939.

[*See also* **Congress of Industrial Organizations; Iron and Steel Industry; Murray, Philip;** *and* **Strikes.**]

BIBLIOGRAPHY

Baughman, James L. "Classes and Company Towns: Legends of the 1937 Little Steel Strike." *Ohio History* 87 (Spring 1978): 175–192.

Sofchalk, Donald. "The Chicago Memorial Day Incident: An Episode of Mass Action." *Labor History* 6 (Winter 1965): 3–43.

Zieger, Robert H. *The CIO, 1935–1955.* Chapel Hill: University of North Carolina Press, 1995.

Melvyn Dubofsky

LIVESTOCK INDUSTRY

Various means of marketing livestock developed in colonial America. Boston became a market town in the seventeenth century, as did nearby Brighton a century later; holding pens surrounded slaughterhouses where citizens purchased fresh meat. Similar arrangements existed at Lancaster, Pennsylvania, and on Manhattan Island in the middle colonies, and farther south they existed in Carolina "cowpens." As settlers migrated westward to Kentucky and Ohio, Louisville and Cincinnati emerged as leaders in the livestock industry. Processing techniques introduced by German hog butchers influenced the mid-nineteenth-century meat industries, and turnpikes and canals facilitated marketing.

The industry boomed after the Civil War thanks to three new developments: cattle raised on the west Texas frontier were driven northward to reach more lucrative markets, the transcontinental railroad expanded westward through Kansas, and insulated (later, refrigerated) railroad cars were built to carry processed meat to burgeoning eastern cities. Businessmen like Gustavus Swift and Philip Armour of Chicago, investing in modern meat-slaughtering facilities near railroad terminals and becoming part-owners of large stockyards adjacent to the meatpacking plants, made the livestock industry the nation's largest business in the 1880s and 1890s.

Early market centers included Chicago in 1865 and Milwaukee, Wisconsin, in 1869—the dates given are the incorporation dates of the cities' stockyards. Kansas City, Saint Louis, and Saint Joseph, Missouri; Peoria, Illinois; and Indianapolis, Indiana, followed in the 1870s. The 1880s brought very rapid growth, with stockyards incorporated in Omaha, Nebraska; Sioux City, Iowa; Denver, Colorado; Saint Paul, Minnesota; Fort Worth and San Antonio, Texas; and Wichita, Kansas. Between 1889 and 1916 a new group of livestock centers combining stockyards with packing plants emerged, including Sioux Falls, South Dakota; San Francisco; Portland, Oregon; Oklahoma City; and Ogden, Utah. Facilitated by this network of large market centers, packing facilities, stockyards, and booming railroads, the nation's livestock moved rapidly, expanded to a world market, and supplied the nation's allies during World War I. Fears of excessive profits and monopoly brought calls for regulation, resulting in the creation of the federal Packers and Stockyards Administration in 1921. This agency in the U.S. Department of Agriculture began court proceedings and forced meatpackers to divest themselves of stockyards, railroads, cattle-loan companies, and similar businesses. The agency remains a watchdog for the industry.

Following World War II, the livestock industry accelerated an earlier decentralization into country auctions or direct sales to packers that avoided federal regulation. In addition, railroads declined in importance as large trucks increasingly carried animals to market. As consumers demanded grain-fed beef, feedlots developed near grain-producing areas, and modern meatpacking facilities relocated near the feedlots. The large stockyards' century of dominance faded as more and more of them closed.

By the end of the twentieth century a new group of packers with a new process called "boxed beef" marketed a large percentage of the nation's meat supply. The twenty-first-century livestock industry involves computer technology in management and marketing, stricter environmental and pollution laws, and increased trading opportunities in animal futures. Country auctions for small operators, video sales, new breeds, specialty breed shows, and the use of private airplanes to locate animals all have had a place in this enduring and ever-evolving industry.

[*See also* **Agriculture; Commodity Futures Markets;** *Jungle, The*; **Meatpacking and Meat-Processing Industry; Swift, Gustavus;** *and* **Transportation Revolution.**]

BIBLIOGRAPHY

Ball, Charles E. *The Finishing Touch: A History of the Texas Cattle Feeders Association and Cattle Feeding in the Southwest*. Amarillo, Tex.: The Association, 1992.

Pate, J'Nell L. *America's Historic Stockyards: Livestock Hotels*. Fort Worth, Tex.: TCU Press, 2005.

Pate, J'Nell L. *Livestock Legacy: The Fort Worth Stockyards 1887–1987*. College Station: Texas A&M University Press, 1988.

J'Nell L. Pate

LIVING-WAGE CAMPAIGNS

The living wage, defined as earnings computed on the official poverty threshold for a four-person family, is based on the idea that people who labor full-time, as well as their families, should not have to live in poverty. The first victory of the late twentieth-century living-wage movement occurred with the passage of a living-wage statute in Baltimore in 1994 with the active participation of the Industrial Areas Foundation (IAF) and the American Federation of State, County, and Municipal Employ-

ees (AFSCME). The launching of subsequent living-wage campaigns in many municipalities during the 1990s involved not only the IAF and the AFSCME but also other religious and community organizations and labor unions, including the Religious Society of Friends (Quakers), the Association of Community Organizations for Reform Now (ACORN), the Service Employees International Union, and the Hotel and Restaurant Employees Union. Ten years after that implemented in Baltimore, 130 living-wage statutes had been implemented throughout the nation, including in Denver, Colorado, and in Minneapolis and Saint Paul, Minnesota.

In spite of the widespread implementation of living-wage statutes, by the early twenty-first century only an estimated 100,000 to 250,000 workers had received the mandated pay raises. This is because the statutes apply only to (1) businesses that possess contracts with the city or county, (2) employees of companies benefiting from economic-development grants, (3) subcontractors of the first two groups, (4) employees of businesses with city leases, and (5) direct government employees working for the city or county.

Moreover, because they include card-check or neutrality clauses that weaken employer resistance, many living-wage statutes have made it somewhat easier for unions to organize low-wage workers. Because the Taft–Hartley Act (1947) forbids cities or states from compelling private companies to concede card-check union recognition or to act neutrally during organizing campaigns, private companies can be included in living-wage statutes only if it can be shown that in the statutes' absence, strikes or industrial disputes would threaten a city's financial solvency.

Two examples of victorious union-organizing drives linked to living-wage campaigns by the early 2000s include the unionizing of fifteen hundred city workers by the Communication Workers of America Local 7026 in Tucson,

Arizona, and the acquisition of union recognition and a collective-bargaining agreement for 150 van and bus drivers by the United Transportation Union Local 23 in Santa Cruz, California. Moreover, living-wage campaigns have aided in successful unionization drives in Berkeley and San Jose, California, in Miami-Dade County, Florida, and in Chicago during the same time period. Finally, the struggle to obtain living wages has contributed to the creation of labor–community coalitions, which advance broad progressive political programs, including labor rights, throughout the country.

Thus living-wage campaigns have increased awareness, initiated discussions, and educated the public about how increasing wage inequality and the persistence of low wages has had a detrimental impact on the nation. Because economic studies have indicated that the increased costs to companies and municipal governments from implementing living-wage policies are small and that redistributing income to low-wage workers benefits the community, it seems likely that living-wage campaigns will continue to flourish.

[*See also* **Poverty** *and* **Wages, Real and Nominal.**]

BIBLIOGRAPHY

Luce, Stephanie. *Fighting for a Living Wage*. Ithaca, N.Y.: Cornell University Press, 2004.
Pollin, Robert, and Stephanie Luce. *The Living Wage: Building a Fair Economy*. New York: New Press, 1998.

Victor G. Devinatz

LOCHNER v. NEW YORK

In 1895, New York State passed a law limiting the hours of work for employees in bakeries to ten hours per day and sixty hours per week. Spearheaded by the bakers' union and tenement-house reformers, this statute reflected the labor movement's long struggle to achieve shorter work hours. In 1902 the Utica bakeshop owner Joseph Lochner was fined for violating the new law. Appealing to the U.S. Supreme Court, Lochner claimed that the statute violated the Fourteenth Amendment guarantee that no person shall be denied life, liberty, or property without due process of law. Voting 5 to 4, the Court in 1905 voided Lochner's conviction and ruled the bakeshop law unconstitutional. Justice Rufus Peckham's majority opinion reasoned that among the liberties protected by the Fourteenth Amendment was "liberty of contract," including the right of the employee and employer voluntarily to contract about the hours of work. A state might interfere with that liberty, Peckham admitted, but only if its regulation fell under the legitimate police powers of the states. Peckham defined the police power narrowly, saying that the bakeshop law was not a reasonable use of the state's power to protect the bakers' health.

Justice Oliver Wendell Holmes Jr. dissented vigorously. Attacking the majority's underlying premise, he argued that the majority had based its decision on laissez-faire economic theory rather than on the Constitution, substituting its own judgment for that of the state legislature.

Lochner became the symbol of laissez-faire constitutionalism and judicial activism. For more than thirty years, critics complained that the Court had erected an insurmountable barrier to economic reform. The so-called *Lochner* era came to an end in 1937 when *West Coast Hotel v. Parrish* rejected the liberty-of-contract doctrine.

[*See also* **Adkins v. Children's Hospital**; **Employment-at-Will**; **Factory and Hours Laws**; **Freedom of Contract**; *and* **West Coast Hotel v. Parrish.**]

BIBLIOGRAPHY

Gillman, Howard. *The Constitution Besieged: The Rise and Demise of Lochner Era Police Powers Jurisprudence.* Durham, N.C.: Duke University Press, 1993.

Kens, Paul. *Judicial Power and Reform Politics: The Anatomy of "Lochner v. New York."* Lawrence: University Press of Kansas, 1990.

Paul Kens

LONDON ECONOMIC CONFERENCE (1933)

The World Monetary and Economic Conference, commonly called the London Economic Conference, took place during the depths of the Great Depression, with fascism and Communism on the rise and the capitalist system in crisis. Most countries had abandoned the gold standard as their currencies faced collapse, tariff wars raged, World War I debts were in default, and Germany refused to pay its reparations. Hoping to cure these ills by stabilizing currencies, settling debt issues, and reducing trade barriers, the League of Nations called an economic conference to convene in London. The conference opened in June 1933 with sixty-six nations represented. The U.S. delegate was Secretary of State Cordell Hull. Despite initial optimism, squabbling soon erupted among three divergent groups: a bloc of European nations that favored returning to the gold standard as a way of stabilizing world currencies; a sterling bloc made up of nations of the British Commonwealth and Scandinavia that backed a silver standard; and an independent bloc made up of nations, including the United States and those in South America, determined to follow their own monetary policies.

Domestic political considerations dictated the U.S. position. The administration of Franklin Delano Roosevelt was in the process of abandoning the gold standard at the very time that the London conference was taking place, and President Roosevelt was unwilling to support any international currency-stabilization measures that would tie his hands in dealing with the domestic currency crisis. Moreover, Roosevelt did not want national attention diverted from what he saw as the more fundamental problem: U.S. economic recovery. The administration did support tariff reduction, but the gold-bloc nations saw this as secondary to currency stabilization.

The conference ended in late July with no significant accomplishments. Many blamed the United States for its failure—and even, in retrospect, for hastening the onset of World War II. In reality, the war's fundamental causes were already in place, and adjusting world currencies and tariffs would probably have done little to change the course of events.

[*See also* **Gold Standard; Tariffs;** *and* **Trade Policy, Federal.**]

BIBLIOGRAPHY

Gardner, Lloyd C. *Economic Aspects of New Deal Diplomacy.* Madison: University of Wisconsin Press, 1964.

Moley, Raymond. *After Seven Years.* New York: Harper & Brothers, 1939.

David E. Conrad

LONGSHOREMEN AND LONGSHOREMEN'S UNIONS

Historically, longshore work was defined by its backbreaking manual gang labor, dangerous conditions, oppressive hiring system, and casual nature. Because many dockside jobs required minimal skill and employers took advantage of port cities' large and diverse populations, unions were slow to develop. Despite these challenges, longshoremen (until recently, this work was done only by men) repeatedly attempted to organize. The workers' militancy and drive for unions can be explained by, among other factors, the dangerous nature of their work and that they toiled in gangs.

Founded in 1892, the International Longshoremen's Association (ILA) remains the dominant union on the Atlantic and Gulf coasts. The ILA organized marine transport workers into locals based upon a specific skill or cargo, such as lumber handler or checker, as well as by race. ILA craft unionism fit perfectly within the emerging "business union" model of the American Federation of Labor (AFL), which the ILA joined in 1895. The ILA spread rapidly and in 1914 absorbed an independent union in New York City, by far the nation's largest port.

In the 120 years between its founding in 1892 and 2012, only six men had served as ILA president, the most notorious being the so-called lifetime president Joseph P. Ryan from 1927 to 1963. The union's self-proclaimed conservatism has been a hallmark of the ILA—particularly its New York City leadership—since its inception. The ILA frequently has clashed with leftist dock unions and internal challengers.

Despite its smaller size, the International Longshore and Warehouse Union (ILWU) has played a major role in U.S. labor history. In 1934, ILA renegades in San Francisco, then the West's leading port, struck after employers refused union demands, beginning a historic coast-wide strike dubbed the "big strike." The longshoremen ultimately were led by the Australian-born Harry Bridges, a radical who was a member of the Communist Party. In July, after two strikers were killed in San Francisco on a day known as Bloody Thursday, 100,000 area workers joined a short, citywide general strike. The longshoremen won a union-controlled hiring hall—which decasualized work and eliminated abusive hiring practices—and a coast-wide contract. Subse-

quently, the ILWU organized warehouse workers both dockside and beyond the waterfront. Headquartered in San Francisco and with a leftist leadership and base, the union has commanded great loyalty from its members and been among the unions most committed to racial inclusivity. Significantly, West Coast longshoremen split from the ILA and joined the nation's other labor federation, the Congress of Industrial Organizations (CIO). In 1950, owing to the anti-Communism of the Cold War, the CIO expelled the ILWU. It joined the merged AFL-CIO in 1988.

An enormous change faced by all longshore workers concerned containerization. Starting in the 1950s, containerization transformed waterfront labor, facilitating the movement of goods, in large metal containers, from ship to rail to truck. Containerization rendered work less physically demanding, but it also reduced substantially the need for workers. Seeing no alternative, in 1960 the ILWU signed the historic Mechanization and Modernization Agreement with employers; later that decade, the ILA signed a similar, if inferior, deal. Accepting the inevitability of change, unions bargained to protect current workers, essentially trading future workforce reductions for higher compensation and greater job security for longshoremen with work seniority. Nevertheless, unlike in many other industries, both unions have maintained a surprising amount of power, even into the twenty-first century.

[*See also* **Bridges, Harry; Dockworkers' Unions, Multiracial; Labor and Anti-Communism;** *and* **San Francisco General Strike (1934).**]

BIBLIOGRAPHY

Kimeldorf, Howard. *Reds or Rackets? The Making of Radical and Conservative Unions on the Waterfront.* Berkeley: University of California Press, 1988.

Nelson, Bruce. *Workers on the Waterfront: Seamen, Longshoremen, and Unionism in the 1930s.* Urbana: University of Illinois Press, 1988.

Schwartz, Harvey. *Solidarity Stories: An Oral History of the ILWU.* Seattle: University of Washington Press, 2009.

Winslow, Calvin, ed. *Waterfront Workers: New Perspectives on Race and Class.* Urbana: University of Illinois Press, 1998.

Peter Cole

LONG SWINGS AND CYCLES IN ECONOMIC GROWTH

There have been two types of long-term movements or long swings that have been important for economic and historical studies. The approximate fifty-year long-term movements first statistically analyzed by the Russian economist Nicolai Kondratiev in 1924, and the fifteen to twenty-five year cycles described by Simon Kuznets in 1930, and then the focus of study by Kuznets, Moses Abramowitz, and Richard Easterlin in the 1950s and 1960s. The Kondratiev cycles are generally regarded to be changes in prices, not output. For some unclear reason they have come to play a more political role in evaluating the economy's prospects, and have been given attention by Marxist-influenced economists when the economy is in recession and used to argue for a permanent decline. Why the Kondratiev is used as the basis for this contention does not seem to be an inevitable interpretation. The long swing of fifteen to twenty-five years has been used mainly as a tool of economic forecasting and understanding. Its major impact has been to link demographic and economic change to describe the factors leading to change in the present day as well as the past. Given that these are two quite different sources of economic variability, attention has been given to different sets of causes and behavior in each case.

To understand the nature and role of long swings (or long cycles) in economic development, it will be useful to describe two different means of time-series decomposition for economic and demographic data. One distinguishes among trends, cycles, seasonal variation, and irregular movements. Trends are the basic long-term movements of anywhere from fifty to one hundred years that reflect the basic, persistent underlying movements. Cycles are fluctuations, of varying length, around the trend; they are much shorter time movements and are basically symmetrical and reversible. Seasonal variations are the intra-year movements, caused by weather or holidays, that are basically expected and predictable. "Irregular" is a catch-all term to reflect the differences between the actual value of the variable and that predicted from the outcome of trend, cycle, and seasonal variation, presumably caused by unusual and unexpected occurrences. A description of the different types of cyclical movements, of varying length, was presented by the eminent economist Joseph Schumpeter in his major two-volume 1930s work entitled *Business Cycles.* The Kitchin cycle was of forty months' duration, its movement attributed to changes in inventories. The Juglar, of seven to ten years, was based upon movements in fixed investment, primarily of plant and equipment for business purposes. The Kondratiev was a fifty-year cycle (forty to sixty years), generally of prices but not necessarily in production.

More recently, based on the pioneering work of Simon Kuznets, there has been attention to what have been called variously "long cycles," or, to avoid a sense that these were symmetrical movements over time, "long swings," or, after their earliest advocate, "Kuznets cycles." The initial claim was that there were movements of some fifteen to twenty years, most typically about seventeen years, that were based upon movements in housing and other forms of building construction and long-term fixed investments such as railroads and public utilities. These swings, unlike the other cycles described, combine demographic and economic movement and deal with immigration and other rates of population increase, fertility, and the mortality of the mature population, as well as with the effects of these on household formation. One scholar dates long swing peaks in the growth of output and economic activity as 1814, 1834, 1846, 1864, 1881, 1889, 1899, 1914, 1922, and 1939 and dates troughs at 1819, 1840, 1858, 1874, 1892, 1911, 1920, and 1930. As will be discussed below, the dates of long-swing troughs are often particularly severe business-cycle downturns. The characteristics and duration of these cycles differ, just as did their triggering mechanisms. This is meant to suggest, however, that such economic movements are often not smooth or symmetrical and that growth cannot be described as a continuous process. Rather, such fluctuations are characteristic of a growing economy.

Long Swings.   As with other types of cyclical movements, there is debate about whether these are true economic occurrences or merely artifacts of a statistical collection of random, unrelated factors. And there is some question of whether they reflect a series of isolated events that play out over time, such as war, natural disasters, or other isolated, important political events. Since economic cycles are not smooth and periodic, uniformity over time is not to be expected. Yet the frequent recurrence of particular relationships among economic variables, which can be described through theoretical connections, suggests that these are true economic episodes and not statistical artifacts.

There is some question of whether changes in the belief in and willingness to undertake economic policy may have dramatically changed the nature and magnitude of these long swings. Prior to the Keynesian revolution of the 1930s, there was only a limited belief in the desirability or efficacy of policies to affect or prevent cyclical movements that might otherwise have occurred. Fiscal and monetary stabilization policies, including measures to smooth changes in housing and other forms of construction, may remove these cycles or else change this timing in unexpected ways.

Befitting the early work on these long swings, their analysis has most frequently been applied to the study of the United States in the nineteenth and twentieth centuries. Though it is argued that most countries have experienced long swings at roughly the same time, such swings in other countries have not attracted the attention that those in the United States have. The leading economist to notice and write about the U.S. movements was Simon Kuznets in his study of U.S. economic growth in the period after 1869, based on his pioneering estimates of national income. Other scholars who wrote extensively on long swings were Moses Abramovitz and Richard Easterlin, both associated with Kuznets at the National Bureau of Economic Research. Earlier and relevant discussions include writings by Arthur Burns, Clarence Long, and Walter Isard in the United States. The writings on long swings have become less common since the later twentieth century, perhaps reflecting the claim in the title of a 1968 article by Abramovitz, "The Passing of the Kuznets Cycle," and the greater interest of economic historians in describing long-term trends.

The literature has pointed to long swings in output, prices, population growth, immigration, household formation, housing construction, and other related economic variables. The key to understanding long swings is that there is not just a simultaneous movement in these variables: they interact with each other in determining their movements.

Population and Long Swings.   The key addition to the usual cyclical movements in examining long swings is the importance of population movements and changes in the labor force in initiating or responding to output movements, whether because of immigration or natural population increase or because of external migration or internal migration. The population movement emphasized in the nineteenth through the first half of the twentieth century was immigration from abroad, which responded to the wages that were rising because of the economic expansion in the United States and attracted European adult men ready to work in the labor force. Such adjustment took place until the magnitude of immigration was sharply reduced in the 1920s. This did have some perverse effects on the pattern of internal migration. The population of blacks residing in the South did not respond to the initial wage increases in the northern states. Subsequently, the ending of the immigration constraint opened economic circumstances for blacks, and after 1910 a northward movement of blacks began.

The clearest movement of long swings can be seen in the antebellum years in the United States. There were two cycles in this period, from 1820 to 1837 and from 1838 to 1857, with large upward movements in output ending in severe economic decline. These were the years of major cotton booms that led to considerable westward movement, with some shift from rural to urban areas. This period also saw the onset of extensive immigration from Europe, with some short lag after the increase of output and wages. The increased demand for output caused labor incomes to rise and led to internal and external migration. The destruction and destabilization caused by the Civil War would seem to have affected the nature and timing of long swings, but the next major downturn was in 1873 (sixteen years after its predecessor) and again in 1893, in years when immigration remained high and was related to the U.S. business cycle. In the early twentieth century, World War I reduced immigration, though it increased domestic migration, and after the war Congress legislated restrictions in the quantity and composition of immigration, resulting in changes in population growth and in the composition of the labor force. More attention was now given to the effect of wages on labor-force participation rates and household formation. As Moses Abramovitz and others have argued, with these demographic changes and with government economic policy affecting housing construction, the Kuznets cycle had "passed on," and economic changes would no longer take on the character of long swings.

After the immigration restrictions of the 1920s, population movements relied more on fertility changes. Fertility, it was argued, responds to economic circumstances, leading to growth in population and eventually growth in the labor force. Leading to the growth in fertility were changes in rates of marriage and in rates of household formation. Resulting changes in the age structure and labor-force participation rates of the population determined the size of the labor force and production growth. These changes are, of course, not instantaneous, but come with lags of varying lengths, so that no two long swings are identical. In presenting the timing of cycles, the story begins with an increase in expenditures, generally by consumers, leading to increased wages. Then the increased demand for labor makes for a movement in the long-cycle components. Immigration from Europe becomes more desirable or, if immigration is not feasible, both domestic labor-force participation rates and also the marriage and fertility rates of native-born populations rise.

Yet another term for "long swing" has been "growth cycles," in part because these tend to be movements in the rate of growth output rather than on the level of income, as were the moves during the traditional business cycles. A notable characteristic of the relation between long swings and traditional business cycles concerns the events when both are in a stage of decline. The major downturns and panics of the nineteenth century occurred when the business-cycle decline coincided with the long-swing decline—thus generating key years of economic disturbance. Yet there always followed a cyclical upturn that brought the economy to higher levels of output.

[*See also* **Business Cycles; Capitalism; Depressions, Economic; Economic Development; Economic Growth and Income Patterns;** *and* **Economic Theories and Thought.**]

BIBLIOGRAPHY

Abramovitz, Moses. "The Nature and Significance of Kuznets Cycles." *Economic Development and Cultural Change* 9 (1961): 225–248.

Abramovitz, Moses. "The Passing of the Kuznets Cycle." *Economica* 35 (1968): 349–367.

Easterlin, Richard A. *Population, Labor Force, and Long Swings in Economic Growth: The American Experience.* New York: Columbia University Press, 1968.

Kuznets, Simon. *Secular Movements in Production and Prices: Their Nature and Their Bearing upon Cyclical Fluctuations.* Boston: Houghton Mifflin, 1930.

Kuznets, Simon. "Long Swings in the Growth of Population and in Related Economic Variables." *Proceedings of the American Philosophical Society* 102 (1958): 25–52.

Schumpeter, Joseph. *Business Cycles: A Theoretical, Historical, and Statistical Analysis of the Capitalist Process.* 2 vols. New York: McGraw–Hill, 1939.

Stanley Engerman

LOWELL SYSTEM

The cotton-textile mills of Lowell, Massachusetts, were the most famous factories in the United States in the first half of the nineteenth century. From them emanated innovations in technology, the organization of work, and business practices that made signal contributions to industrial capitalism in the United States.

In the early 1820s, Boston capitalists, organized as the Boston Manufacturing Company of Waltham, sought a site for expansion. They purchased land, a transportation canal, and waterpower rights at the Pawtucket Falls of the Merrimack River in East Chelmsford. There they began manufacturing printed cotton cloth in 1823.

Implementing their grand vision, the mill owners incorporated the town of Lowell in 1826, naming it for the late Francis Cabot Lowell, a founder of the Waltham venture. High profits led to rapid expansion, and by 1850 the Lowell mills, employing more than ten thousand workers, were the nation's leading textile-manufacturing center. With a population of thirty-three thousand Lowell was the second-largest city in Massachusetts.

Mill towns patterned after Lowell arose across New England and collectively came to constitute the Waltham–Lowell system. Large, redbrick, water-powered mills housed all the machinery needed to manufacture cotton cloth from raw cotton. Employing a workforce consisting of native-born single daughters of Yankee farmers, the mills erected boardinghouses for their workers. Combining corporate paternalism with monthly cash wages, the owners of the Lowell mills sought to industrialize without replicating the social ills associated with contemporaneous English factory towns. Later, immigrant workers replaced native-born young women.

The Lowell mills offered the first major source of wage work for women in the nation. After the Civil War, Lowell occupied a less important place in the textile industry and the industrial economy. Employment and production in Lowell grew until World War I but declined thereafter, as textile production shifted to the South. By 1980 only scattered, minor textile production continued in Lowell, the dominant center of the early American Industrial Revolution. In 1978, Congress created the Lowell National Historical Park on the site of a restored mill and associated buildings.

[*See also* **Factory System; Industrialization and Deindustrialization; Textile Industry; Welfare Capitalism; Women Workers;** *and* **Work.**]

BIBLIOGRAPHY

Dalzell, Robert F., Jr. *Enterprising Elite: The Boston Associates and the World They Made.* Cambridge, Mass.: Harvard University Press, 1987.

Dublin, Thomas. *Women at Work: The Transformation of Work and Community in Lowell, Massachusetts, 1826–1860.* 2d ed. New York: Columbia University Press, 1993.

Thomas Dublin

LUDLOW MASSACRE

The Ludlow massacre began on the morning of 20 April 1914 when a gun battle erupted between the Colorado National Guard and striking coal miners at their tent colony outside Ludlow, Colorado. Nobody knows who fired the first shot, but this incident entered historical memory as a massacre because the miners and their families bore the brunt of the casualties. At least nineteen people died that day: one guardsman, five miners, and thirteen women and children who suffocated in the pit where they sought safety from the gunfire. More died in violence throughout southern Colorado over the next few days. No matter how the casualties are counted, the total makes the Ludlow massacre one of the bloodiest events in American labor history.

Events.   The massacre was the culminating event of the 1913–1914 Colorado coal miners' strike. Miners waged the strike with two main goals in mind: requiring coal operators to follow the state of Colorado's mining law and gaining representation by the United Mine Workers of America (UMWA) for the state's miners. The dispute proved bloody from the outset, with deaths on both sides. The state's largest private employer, the Colorado Fuel and Iron Company (CF&I), employed most of the striking miners. Since it had more resources than the miners had, its efforts to intimidate union members into ending the dispute made the deepest impression on the public. For example, on 17 October 1913 an armor-plated car—quickly dubbed the "Death Special"—attacked the miners' tent colony at Forbes, Colorado, killing one and scaring many. In response to such company tactics, miners heavily armed their tent colonies. In turn, the governor of Colorado deployed the National Guard to control the miners. The guard members were dispatched to maintain the peace, but because the mine owners financed the cost of their deployment, the troops only caused more trouble. In addition, many of the guardsmen, veterans of the Spanish–American War and the Philippine insurrection, treated the Mexican and southern and eastern European miners as racially inferior.

No matter which side fired first on 20 April, it is fair to conclude that the battle began as a result of mutual distrust and fear. Granted the strike's already violent history, any minor incident was likely to lead to a major conflict. Once that conflict started, most of the residents of the miners' tent colony evacuated. Thinking that it had been abandoned, guardsmen burned the tents to the ground. Nobody knew about the thirteen women and children hiding in the pit until their bodies were found the next morning, suffocated by the fumes from the fire—not, as the miners alleged, executed in cold blood. A more accurate indicator of the guard's unbridled hostility toward the miners was its cold-blooded execution of three leaders under a flag of truce. Guardsmen shot Louis Tikas, a Greek American leader of the striking miners, three times in the back.

Ramifications. Ramifications from the massacre began instantly. When other miners heard of the events at Ludlow, they began a killing spree across the region, shooting mine supervisors and guards. Mine property was destroyed. Innocent victims fell on both sides. It is impossible to determine how many people died in the days after the massacre, although it was certainly a greater number than those who died during the initial tragedy. Rumors of a slaughter by the National Guard ran rampant, fueled by the inability of outsiders to confirm exactly what had happened at Ludlow or in its aftermath. On 28 April 1914, President Woodrow Wilson dispatched the U.S. Army to Colorado, thereby ending the violence and restoring order to the region.

The 1913–1914 Colorado coal strike ended in December 1914 with union failure. Nevertheless, the deaths of the women and children in the "death pit" captured the public imagination. In an era that remained Victorian, or patriarchal, in outlook, killing unarmed women and children, even if by accident, was completely unacceptable to the American public. Therefore, despite the hostile press that portrayed striking miners before the massacre, media outlets attacked the mine owners with gusto afterward. Indeed, it was not the miners, but rather a Denver newspaper, the *Rocky Mountain News*, that coined the term "Ludlow massacre." A clever media campaign by the UMWA, which included sending female survivors of the massacre on a nationwide speaking tour, won the union further support. An investigation of the strike and

"massacre" by the U.S. Commission on Industrial Relations under Chairman Frank Walsh kept the tragedy in the news for years afterward.

John D. Rockefeller Jr., the oil baron's son and the primary stockholder in the CF&I, became the primary object of union and public hostility after the Ludlow massacre. The writer Upton Sinclair and others protested outside his New York City office. Sinclair also participated in a mock trial of Rockefeller for murder near the upstate New York town where the industrialist lived. As a result, Rockefeller hired a former labor minister of Canada (and future prime minister), W. L. Mackenzie King, to design the so-called Rockefeller Plan, an employee representation plan—or "company union," to critics—that was designed to offer miners just enough concessions to assuage their grievances. To commemorate the massacre, in 1918 the United Mine Workers erected a statue on the site of the tent colony. The union continues to commemorate the event annually. In 2009 the U.S. Department of the Interior declared the site a National Historic Landmark, one of only two such sites in the United States related to labor history.

[*See also* **Company Unions; Employee Representation Plans; Mining Industry;** *and* **Strikes.**]

BIBLIOGRAPHY

Andrews, Thomas G. *Killing for Coal: America's Deadliest Labor War.* Cambridge, Mass.: Harvard University Press, 2008.
Martelle, Scott. *Blood Passion: The Ludlow Massacre and Class War in the American West.* New Brunswick, N.J.: Rutgers University Press, 2007.
McGovern, George S., and Leonard F. Guttridge. *The Great Coalfield War.* Boston: Houghton Mifflin, 1972.

Jonathan Rees

LUMBERING

From the early Colonial Era, European settlers tapped North America's forests. Initially, lumbering was more an adjunct of farming than an industrial activity. In the early eighteenth century, however, a primitive lumber industry arose on land in northern New England. By 1830, Bangor, Maine, was the world's largest lumber-producing center, supplying markets along the Atlantic seaboard and in Europe.

In the mid-nineteenth century, lumbering flourished in Pennsylvania and New York. Williamsport, Pennsylvania, became the new leader in production. There in 1872 the industry's first great strike occurred, its failure hastening the collapse of the National Labor Union. The Erie Canal opened new opportunities. Vast quantities of lumber went eastward over it, especially from Saginaw and Bay City, Michigan, which by the 1880s had come to primacy as producers. Albany, New York, the canal's eastern terminus, became the nation's major wholesale lumber mart.

As settlement pushed westward, the industry followed. Chicago became a distribution center, production expanded into Wisconsin, and large mills arose that served markets down the Mississippi River and on the Great Plains. In the upper Midwest, Frederick Weyerhaeuser and his associates created the industry's largest enterprise. Customarily, however, timber companies evinced little concern for the environment or conservation, generally clear-cutting timber lands as they moved west from northern New England across New York and Pennsylvania and on into Michigan, Wisconsin, and Minnesota. And, everywhere, they left behind what became known as infertile, cutover land.

Owing to natural barriers, lumbering lagged in the well-forested antebellum South. However, a few centers emerged that catered to markets in New Orleans and in the Caribbean sugar islands. With extensive railroad construction following the Civil War, the southern pine industry burgeoned in Louisiana and eastern Texas. Much of its expansion derived from northern capital and leadership. At Bogalusa, Louisiana, for example, Pennsylvania's Goodyear brothers in 1904 built the world's largest sawmill.

In the early twentieth century, many companies transferred to the Far West—primarily Idaho, Washington, and Oregon—competing with older mills that had arisen following California's gold rush, while continuing to serve midwestern markets by rail.

In the late nineteenth century, operators in the South and Far West had turned increasingly to timberland acquisition to ensure stable supplies of logs and to justify investments in logging railroads, which were ever more necessary as stands near floatable streams disappeared. Earlier lumbermen had put nearly all their investment capital into production facilities—and, in the West, into ships to carry their output—but this no longer sufficed. The need to acquire timberland, combined with expensive technological advances, fostered bigger enterprises, yet the industry remained highly fragmented. Bulky, abundant raw material, still relatively simple technology, and ease of entry discouraged centralization. Repeated efforts at cooperation or consolidation failed.

By the end of World War II, private timber holdings in the West had been heavily cut. A few of the larger, more heavily capitalized firms such as Weyerhaeuser tried to practice environmentally sustainable forestry, replanting forests that they cut, but their smaller competitors continued to cut at will. With no new forested frontiers available, lumbermen turned to the national forests for logs. This led to changes in the U.S. Forest Service, previously largely a custodial agency, and to clashes with environmentalists, who extolled the noncommodity values of forests. Partly in response, some producers shifted back to the South, where new forests had grown and most timber was on private land more insulated from environmentalist pressure.

Declining per capita lumber consumption and rising demand for more sophisticated wood products accompanied these shifts and encouraged consolidation anew, but as the twentieth century ended the industry remained decentralized and fragmented. Early in the twenty-first century, lumbering continued to flourish in the South, where the costs of labor and land remained relatively low, but in the Far West's Inland Empire, business failure and unemployment plagued traditional forest operations and sawmills in Idaho, Oregon, Washington, and California. By then, much of the forest land east of the Mississippi and north of the Ohio Rivers had regenerated and remained safe from aggressive lumbering in a region no longer home to the timber industry.

[*See also* **Environmental Regulations; Forests and Forestry;** *and* **Renewable Energy and Climate Change.**]

BIBLIOGRAPHY

Cox, Thomas R., et al. *This Well-Wooded Land: Americans and Their Forests from Colonial Times to the Present.* Lincoln: University of Nebraska Press, 1985.

Williams, Michael. *Americans and Their Forests: A Historical Geography.* Cambridge, U.K.: Cambridge University Press, 1989.

Thomas R. Cox

M

MADAR, OLGA

(1915–1996), top-ranking officer and leader in the United Auto Workers (UAW). The daughter of Czech immigrants who worked her way through Eastern Michigan University, from which she earned a BS in 1938, Madar briefly taught physical education before taking better-paid defense work. She was hired by UAW Local 50 to administer its recreation programs, and from that position Madar quickly rose to office in the international union in 1947. Thereafter she headed many UAW departments, combining a passion for social unionism with work toward gender equality, civil rights, and an improved quality of life for workers.

In 1966, Madar became the first woman elected to the UAW's International Executive Board, and in 1972 she became a vice president of the UAW. A pioneering activist, she helped found the Women's Equity Action League in 1968 and the National Women's Political Caucus in 1971, and she was instrumental in persuading the UAW and later the American Federation of Labor and Congress of Industrial Organizations to support the Equal Rights Amendment. In 1974 she was elected the first president of the Coalition of Labor Union Women (CLUW), which she also helped found.

Madar—whom Doug Fraser, the UAW's president from 1977 to 1983, called "a trailblazer in the struggle for equal rights"—extended her activism to other departmental work even after her 1974 retirement. She led the UAW's Recreation Department, where she was an effective advocate for racial integration.

As the first director of the Consumer Affairs Department, she lobbied for consumer protection. As the first director of Conservation and Resource Development, she helped organize around emerging environmental issues. In 1989, Madar was inducted into the Michigan Women's Hall of Fame.

[*See also* Labor's Role in Politics; United Auto Workers; *and* Women Workers.]

BIBLIOGRAPHY

Balser, Diane. *Sisterhood and Solidarity: Feminism and Labor in Modern Times.* Boston: South End Press, 1987.

Cobble, Dorothy Sue. *The Other Women's Movement: Workplace Justice and Social Rights in Modern America.* Princeton, N.J.: Princeton University Press, 2004.

Deslippe, Dennis A. *Rights, Not Roses: Unions and the Rise of Working-Class Feminism, 1945–80.* Urbana: University of Illinois Press, 2000.

Fones-Wolf, Elizabeth. "Contested Play: Company, Union, and Industrial Recreation, 1945–1960." *Labor's Heritage* 6, no. 1 (1994): 4–22.

Gabin, Nancy F. *Feminism in the Labor Movexment: Women and the United Auto Workers, 1935–1975.* Ithaca, N.Y.: Cornell University Press, 1990.

Jacquelyn Southern

MAIL-ORDER HOUSES

In the latter half of the nineteenth century, populations in the United States increasingly spread more widely across the nation's broad geographic expanse as a result of improvements in electrical distribution and mass transportation. The streetcar systems that private investors financed spread population beyond urban cores, and new towns in the West located close to railroad tracks. In the late nineteenth century, Congress passed legislation authorizing the U.S. Post Office to provide rural free delivery (RFD) to the nation's widely spread population. In response, innovative entrepreneurs created retail businesses to provide eager rural consumers with goods previously available only in distant city markets or country general stores. Sears, Roebuck and Montgomery Ward most notably mailed lavishly illustrated catalogs to potential consumers, who could then order by mail the goods that they desired and, courtesy of RFD, receive the goods the same way. Sears and Montgomery Ward grew into the nation's dominant mass-distribution retailers.

Such companies also decided to participate in the vast expansion of single-family housing that flourished between the late nineteenth century and the 1920s. Although most housing continued to be built on-site by hand, the availability of lumber and the ability to transport it by rail offered builders additional options. Companies began to sell construction plans and building materials to order. Soon such companies began to offer precut materials that would not have to be altered on-site. Between 1908 and 1940, Sears played its part in promoting the new method of building private homes by offering 450 different plans for mail-order homes.

Such homes varied in size from modest bungalows to large colonials. Sears seamlessly added the mail-order homes to its basic consumer catalog. In 1908 it reorganized the department that sold building materials and created a catalog with house plans and building materials specifically for the construction of private homes. Other companies also established mail-order-home businesses to meet the rising demand for new housing that developed at the end of the nineteenth century. The Hodgson Company, Montgomery Ward, and Aladdin Homes all attempted to satisfy such demand for inexpensive housing.

The precut homes proved to be particularly profitable for Sears. Its precut construction materials made the homes attractive in less-populated areas that might lack adequate skilled labor or the tools needed to build a home from a plan and raw materials. Sears led in the marketing of such homes, selling thirty thousand homes by 1925 and fifty thousand by 1930.

Much of the success of the mail-order homes can be attributed to the companies' aggressive marketing strategies. But even with their marketing campaigns, the top two mail-order-house companies, Sears and Aladdin, managed to sell only 73,200 homes during the housing boom of the 1920s, while traditional building techniques produced most of the 6 million homes then constructed across the United States. Aladdin Homes sold mail-order houses until 1982, but its sales declined after the 1920s. During the 1970s, however, a new generation of homeowners rediscovered the virtue of mail-order homes as an interest in historic preservation developed, and many individuals sought to renovate the homes ordered by previous generations of home builders.

[*See also* Consumer Culture; Mass Marketing; *and* Postal Services.]

BIBLIOGRAPHY

Paradis, Thomas W., ed. *The Greenwood Encyclopedia of Homes through American History*. 4 vols. Westport, Conn.: Greenwood Press, 2008.
Stevenson, Katherine Cole, and H. Ward Jandl. *Houses by Mail: A Guide to Houses from Sears, Roebuck and Company*. New York: Wiley, 1986.
Thornton, Rosemary. *The Houses That Sears Built: Everything You Ever Wanted to Know about Sears Catalog Homes*. Alton, Ill.: Gentle Beam, 2002.
William Jordan Patty

MARITIME TRANSPORT

Waterborne transportation has been central to the American economy since Europeans first crossed the Atlantic. Oceans, bays, and rivers offer surfaces across which heavy vessels can be moved with comparatively little effort, and the earliest European settlers knew how to build boats and use the wind to propel them. Maritime transport remained the only practical way to move freight long distances until canals and railroads began to be built in the 1820s and 1830s. In the nineteenth and twentieth centuries, new modes of transportation created new markets and greatly diversified the ways people and goods travel.

Three basic distinctions help explain the rise and decline of maritime transport in the United States. First, commercial ships normally operate in two quite distinct geopolitical settings. Coastal voyages between U.S. seaports and inland navigation along the country's rivers and canals are governed by state and federal laws. Foreign trade, on the other hand, is governed by agreements among the nations involved. From its beginnings, the United States, like the nations of Europe, restricted its coastal and internal trade to vessels built, owned, and crewed by its citizens. In international trade, however, the lowest-cost carrier who provides acceptable service normally prevails.

A second broad distinction concerns what is being carried. Ships, trains, automobiles, and airplanes can all move people, but in maritime transport the movement of commodities and goods is of greater significance. The development of railroads, automobiles, and airplanes reduced the importance of passengers in maritime transport, yet ships are still needed to carry commodities such as petroleum and the huge volume of manufactured goods and agricultural commodities that moves among continents.

A third distinction focuses on the evolving technologies employed in maritime transport. The nineteenth-century displacement of wooden-hulled, wind-driven ships by steam-driven iron- and then steel-hulled ships was profoundly important. Many other new technologies have been introduced during the long history of maritime transport, yet none has been nearly as consequential as the shift from wood and wind to metal and steam power.

These distinctions help illuminate the history of maritime transport in the United States. The period from the Revolutionary War to the Civil War was a flourishing age of sail. In this early industrial phase, Americans drew upon the shipbuilding skills of their ancestors, the timber resources of the continent, and their own talents as seafarers and merchants to create a vibrant commercial society centered on such seaport cities as Boston, Philadelphia, and Savannah, Georgia. Americans applied the lessons that they had learned as colonists operating within the British Empire to the global opportunities available to them after they had been excluded from imperial trade. In this phase, American ships ranked as the best and the least expensive in international trade, and U.S. ships consistently carried a high percentage of the nation's foreign trade. The development of steam propulsion on inland waterways, especially on the Ohio and Mississippi river systems, enabled the United States to expand rapidly into its trans-Appalachian hinterland.

A second phase in U.S. maritime transport began in the second half of the nineteenth century as British-built iron steamships increasingly dominated the international carrying trade, gradually squeezing out the United States. The loss was hardly noticed, however, as the nation turned westward and focused on the continental drama of railroad building. Although the coastal and inland trades remained protected from foreign competition, the railroads soon captured most of their markets. By 1900, U.S. ships were carrying only a small percentage of the nation's trade.

A third phase encompassed the world wars of the twentieth century, including the Cold War. Even before the United States entered

World War I, President Woodrow Wilson and Congress had committed the nation to building and operating a world-class merchant marine, a service capable of providing auxiliary support for the armed forces fighting abroad and ensuring that the nation's international trade would not again be disrupted by the withdrawal of foreign carriers. The massive shipbuilding programs of World War I and World War II provided the hulls, while government operating programs, subsidies, and cargo-protection laws sustained the maritime industry through the Cold War. The rapid expansion of global markets that followed the end of the Cold War, together with increasing deregulation of U.S. industry, created conditions that worked against the survival of the U.S. merchant marine. By the early twenty-first century the U.S. merchant marine was limited basically to coastal and interior-lake shipping services.

Meanwhile a series of innovations in maritime transport has been essential to the increase in world trade and globalization. Supertankers, among the largest ships ever built, have made possible a global carrying trade in oil shipments at lower cost. Even more important by the early twenty-first century has been the triumph of containerization for the shipping of general cargo. Containerization has made possible the shipping of larger cargoes at lower cost, has reduced substantially transaction costs owing to breakage and theft, and has reduced the labor, time, and effort needed to load and unload cargo.

In the twenty-first century, global shipping on the oceans has become dominated by ships that sail under flags of convenience and are registered in such nations as Panama and Liberia. Moreover, nearly all merchant seamen originate among poorer nations in the Southern and Eastern Hemispheres. The increasing globalization of markets, services, and manufacture may render this transformation a matter of limited significance. Although maritime transport services have come to be dominated by non-U.S. companies, maritime transport continues to play a vital role in America's participation in the global economy.

[*See also* **Canals and Waterways; Foreign Trade; Globalization; Shipbuilding; Steam Power;** *and* **Transportation Revolution.**]

BIBLIOGRAPHY

Bauer, K. Jack. *A Maritime History of the United States: The Role of America's Seas and Waterways.* Columbia: University of South Carolina Press, 1988.

Hutchins, John G. B. *The American Maritime Industries and Public Policy, 1789–1914: An Economic History.* Cambridge, Mass.: Harvard University Press, 1941.

Fink, Leon. *Sweatshops at Sea: Merchant Seamen in the World's First Globalized Industry from 1812 to the Present.* Chapel Hill: University of North Carolina Press, 2011.

Gibson, Andrew, and Arthur Donovan. *The Abandoned Ocean: A History of United States Maritime Policy.* Columbia: University of South Carolina Press, 2000.

Labaree, Benjamin W., et al. *America and the Sea: A Maritime History.* Mystic, Conn.: Mystic Seaport, 1998.

Arthur Donovan

MARKETING COOPERATIVES

American promoters of farm cooperatives at the turn of the twentieth century sought to help small farmers pool their resources to meet the economic challenges posed by such large-scale corporations as railroads and chain stores. The first farm cooperative developed primarily for marketing purposes was the Southern California Fruit Exchange, established in 1893 and later renamed the California Fruit Growers'

Exchange (CFGE). Led by G. Harold Powell, the CFGE developed innovative advertising campaigns using the brand name "Sunkist" to boost consumption of citrus products. A host of similarly influential marketing cooperatives, including the California Almond Growers' Exchange (Blue Diamond brand, established in 1910), the California Associated Raisin Company (Sun-Maid, 1912), and the Minnesota Cooperative Creamery Association (Land O'Lakes, 1921), followed the CFGE's creation. By 1921 there were 6,476 marketing cooperatives in the United States. All of these organizations worked to coordinate the packing, pricing, grading, and shipping of produce to national markets. Promoters of cooperation insisted that adopting the organizational forms and trade methods of industrial businesses would allow independent farm producers to maintain farm incomes against corporate competition.

The most important federal statute regulating farm cooperatives is the 1922 Capper–Volstead Act. It provides cooperatives with immunity from most antitrust actions, allowing them to exert significant control over farm prices and to capture extraordinary market share without legal reprisal. A decade after the act's passage, the number of farm marketing cooperatives ballooned to 10,255, with $1.7 billion in gross sales. By 2009 there were 1,169 farm marketing cooperatives, with gross sales of more than $102 billion.

[*See also* **Advertising; Agriculture,** *subentries on* **The Golden Age (1890 to 1920)** *and* **Since 1920; Antitrust Legislation; Cooperatives; Corporate Agriculture;** *and* **Mass Marketing.**]

BIBLIOGRAPHY

Postel, Charles. *The Populist Vision.* Oxford: Oxford University Press, 2007.

Stoll, Steven. *The Fruits of Natural Advantage: Making the Industrial Countryside in California.* Berkeley: University of California Press, 1998.

Woeste, Victoria Saker. *The Farmer's Benevolent Trust: Law and Agricultural Cooperation in Industrial America, 1865–1945.* Chapel Hill: University of North Carolina Press, 1998.

Shane Hamilton

MARXIAN ECONOMICS

Karl Marx (1818–1883) was a German philosopher whose interest in philosophic materialism led him to study economic theory and whose political radicalism led him to develop a theory of the transformation of modern capitalism into a socialist system. A revolutionary scholar seeking not only to understand the world but to change it, his ideas have inspired political radicals, and his theories have remained the subject of continuing controversy.

Marx's Theories. Trained as a philosopher, Marx was a follower of Georg Hegel, the German idealist philosopher who saw society developing through dialectical conflict between ideas. Each new idea would provoke an alternative idea, an antithesis, and conflict between the two ideas would lead to the development of a new synthesis, which itself would lead to a new antithesis and further conflict. An idealist, Hegel built his system around ideas in conflict, but many of his followers sought to ground his dialectics on material conflicts. While questioning Hegel's idealism, Marx and his friend and coauthor, Friedrich Engels, also challenged the simple structure of the materialist arguments of the so-called young Hegelians. In their *Theses on Feuerbach,* they criticized previous materialism for treating human activity as nothing but a response to material circumstances, leaving the active side of human life to be developed abstractly by idealist philosophy. Instead, Marx and Engels would treat "human activity itself as objective activity" and explain the coincidence of changing circumstances and changing people, "or self-changing," as "revolutionary practice."

On this philosophic basis, Marx developed a theory of social change that posits that material conflicts create class conflict that in turn leads, through revolution, to a new society. This led him to the study of political economy. He developed his economic ideas from studying the English classicists, including Adam Smith and David Ricardo, and their labor theory of value, in which commodity prices are associated with the labor used to produce them. This study led Marx to the fundamental dilemma of classical economics: how to explain, based on the labor theory of value, capitalist profits. Whereas others had used ad hoc arguments to associate profits with the nefarious maneuvers of privileged monopolists, Marx explained that capitalists could profit from the normal functioning of a competitive market in which all commodities trade at their value, which represents the labor needed for their reproduction. Capitalists, Marx argued, purchase a special commodity—namely, labor power or the potential to labor—that they then use to produce commodities embodying more labor than is needed to reproduce the labor power that they purchase.

Because capitalists profit by selling commodities embodying more labor than they pay in wages, capitalists always face a realization problem. Because the wages that they pay are never enough for their workers to buy the commodities that they produce, capitalists, as a class, need to find someone else to buy their commodities, either other capitalists or people outside the capitalist system. This gives capitalism its expansive nature, with capitalists always looking for new markets.

From his value theory and his explanation of capitalist profit, Marx identified two additional contradictions in which the search for profit by individual capitalists undermines the conditions for profit making for the capitalist class as a whole. A continuing drive for expansion by reinvesting profits in hiring more labor power leads capitalists to produce ever more commodities, magnifying the realization problem. Worse still, capitalist expansion undermines profitability when competition for labor power leads capitalists to bid up wages above the cost of reproducing labor power. Once the so-called reserve army of the unemployed is drained, capitalists must find additional workers either on an extensive dimension, expanding to new countries or colonies, or else on the intensive dimension, in which homeworkers and others outside the capitalist system are pulled into capitalist production. Otherwise, without additional workers, capitalist expansion will be halted when rising wages eliminate profits.

In his analysis of these contradictions, Marx applied dialectical thinking to economic dynamics. He anticipated that eventually, when the measures that capitalists took to maintain profitability heightened the system's internal contradictions, capitalism would collapse. Expanding production and sales enlarged the size of the proletariat, the wage-earning class that Marx expected to replace capitalism with socialism. When capitalists try to restore profits by replacing workers with machines, they reduce the portion of their investment on which they earn profits—namely, the labor power—leading in the long run to a declining rate of profit. Once profits decrease sufficiently, workers will overthrow capitalism.

The Soviet Experience. Inspired by Marx's theory that capitalism would collapse from its own contradictions, some revolutionaries assumed that they need only wait for changing material conditions to end capitalism: revolutionary organization and agitation would not be needed. The Russian revolutionary

Vladimir Lenin argued, however, that capitalists would find ways to prolong their rule and that capitalism would collapse only when toppled by a revolutionary party of the working class, a party led by educated, professional agitators. The collapse of the Russian Empire during World War I gave Lenin the opportunity to put his theories into action, and in 1917 his faction of the Russian Social Democratic Party seized power in Russia, inaugurating more than seventy years of Communist rule in the Soviet Union.

Disenchantment with the Soviet experience led many, especially in the English-speaking countries, to return to Marx's philosophic roots in Hegelian dialectics. The English historian E. P. Thompson, for example, differed with Lenin by arguing that true revolutionary practice and a true socialist revolution will come only when a working class has been "made" through a democratic revolutionary movement.

Yet as theorists and as revolutionaries, Marxists continue to wrestle with a dilemma that Marx posed in the *Eighteenth Brumaire of Louis Bonaparte*: "Men make their own history, but they do not make it as they please; they do not make it under self-selected circumstances, but under circumstances existing already, given and transmitted from the past." Then, perhaps in a moment of sad frustration, he added: "The tradition of all dead generations weighs like a nightmare on the brains of the living."

[*See also* **Capitalism; Class Consciousness; Economic Theories and Thought; Profits, Changes in Rates of; Proletarianization; Reserve Army of Labor;** *and* **Simple Commodity Production.**]

BIBLIOGRAPHY

Lenin, V. I. *State and Revolution: Marxist Teaching about the Theory of the State and the Tasks of the Proletariat in the Revolution.* New York: International Publishers, 1932.

Lenin, V. I. *What Is to Be Done? Burning Questions of Our Movement.* New York: International Publishers, 1929.

Marx, Karl. *Capital: A Critique of Political Economy.* 3 vols. Chicago: C. H. Kerr, 1906–1909.

Marx, Karl. *The Eighteenth Brumaire of Louis Bonaparte.* Translated by Daniel De Leon. New York: International Publishers, 1898.

Marx, Karl. *The German Ideology: Including "Theses on Feuerbach" and Introduction to "The Critique of Political Economy."* Great Books in Philosophy. Amherst, N.Y.: Prometheus Books, 1998.

Marx, Karl. *Wage-Labor and Capital.* Translated by J. L. Joynes. Chicago: C. H. Kerr, 1899.

Thompson, E. P. *The Making of the English Working Class.* London: V. Gollancz, 1963.

Thompson, E. P. *The Poverty of Theory and Other Essays.* New York: Monthly Review Press, 1978.

Gerald Friedman

MASS MARKETING

Mass marketing involves targeting a large percentage of the relevant population as purchasers of a particular product or service. The size of the market depends on the nature of the product sold and the goals of the company. Typically, mass marketers want to sell in a range between half the relevant population and everyone.

The history of photography offers a good example of the mass-marketing process. In 1877 when George Eastman purchased his first picture-taking equipment at a cost of some $55, photography was a mysterious art that demanded chemical knowledge, mechanical ability, and a considerable sum of money. Photographers were either professional portraitists or serious amateurs. Few Americans had ever taken a picture or mastered the technical processes of developing and printing. Eastman set out to eliminate these financial and technical hurdles by devising photographic methods that were simple and cheap. As he did so, however, he discovered that barriers related to consumer behavior remained. Finding a less-than-enthusiastic response to his innovations, he concluded that "in order to make a large business we would have to reach the general public and create a new class of patrons." Eastman consciously "created" a mass market for his camera and film. He intensively distributed his product, simplified it so that a child could use it, advertised it widely, and—most important—slashed the price. The Kodak Brownie camera sold in 1900 for $1, and film sold for 15 cents. By the time of Eastman's death in 1932, cameras and photography had become ubiquitous features of American mass culture.

Eastman's story contains within it many of the elements that defined mass marketing from the late nineteenth century through the 1960s. These elements include the vision of the mass market; the willingness to sacrifice profit margin for volume; and the preconditions, in terms of income, logistics, and psychology, for the creation of a receptive market.

Vision. Without the belief that a product will have a broad appeal, there would be no mass marketing. When mass marketing began in earnest in the United States, that belief did not grow from systematic market research. Instead it came from entrepreneurs' sense of what people wanted. Thus Eastman intuitively grasped that people would like to take pictures. When they did not respond at first, he coaxed them with persuasive advertising. Such visionary mass marketers have played a vital role in American business history. Henry J. Heinz knew that people really wanted his pickles, relishes, and beans in cans or jars. He went bankrupt in the 1870s seeking to mass-market his products but tried again in the 1880s and had happier results. Henry Ford felt the same way about the automobile. The American people wanted and deserved the benefits of automotive transport, he was convinced. Therefore the fact that the first two companies with which he was associated failed was merely a historical accident. Only after such failures and at a relatively advanced age did Ford produce his first Model T in 1908. Through this product, Ford became the most important mass marketer in the twentieth century. He put a high-quality automobile within the reach of a market of unprecedented size.

Visionary mass marketers enabled millions of Americans to purchase products and services undreamed of when mass marketing began in the 1880s. These include all the apparatuses of kitchen and bathroom, of home entertainment, and of personal computers. They also include air travel, telephones, and financial investment services.

Margin and Volume. The decision to be willing and, indeed, determined to sell many units of a product and make money on volume, rather than to sell fewer units and make money on the margin between cost and selling price, is an exceptionally difficult decision to make and sustain. Mass marketers sometimes have made decisions that seem contrary to the logic of the profit system. Henry Ford, for example, continuously cut the price of the Model T. When he did, demand skyrocketed. Even when demand exceeded supply, Ford permitted shortages to occur rather than raise prices. This seemed economically irrational but illustrates the commitment to low prices that is a crucial element in mass marketing.

Preconditions. America would have had no mass marketing without mass consumption. Mass consumption required a population with enough wealth to purchase the products being marketed, the means to deliver these products to their purchasers, and the desire to buy. All these existed in the United States by the 1880s. After the devastating Civil War and a deep de-

pression in the 1870s, America's economic and political life by the 1880s had achieved a level of stability that allowed for increased consumption. The producers of expensive consumer durables developed time-payment programs, placing their products within reach of ever-widening circles of consumers. But economic well-being was not constant. The overall trend toward greater mass purchasing power was punctuated by periodic collapses. When those occurred, as in the 1930s, the mass market, especially for expensive consumer durables, quickly shrank in size.

A second essential precondition is logistics. The United States is a continental nation of more than 3 million square miles. For a mass market to arise, goods had to be transported and business information transmitted at affordable prices. The railroads and the telegraph initially made this possible.

A third precondition for the mass-marketing revolution was that Americans had to harbor wants that exceeded their needs for survival such as food, clothing, and shelter. People had to feel that they deserved consumer products, that they would be happier owning them, and that they could afford them. A socialist once deplored "the damned wantlessness of the poor." Thanks to a deep-rooted national ideology of personal fulfillment that is summed up in the resonant phrase "the pursuit of happiness" and that has been powerfully reinforced by advertising, "wantlessness" has not been a problem in the United States.

Marketing Segmentation. Perhaps the most important trend in marketing in the later twentieth century was the rise of market segmentation and the relative decline of mass marketing. Market segmentation sought to divide a market in a multitude of ways—the most common being demographic (age, income, and education) and psychographic (lifestyle). Market segmentation permitted price customization. For example, an airline that charged the same fare for every seat of a jumbo jet might be thought of as following a mass-market approach to travel. The same airplane with three classes—first class, business, and tourist—has segmented its service in accord with customers' willingness to pay and has thus made possible higher revenues.

With the spread of personal computers, the Internet, smartphones, and other new information technologies at the end of the twentieth century and beginning of the twenty-first, many observers envisioned a data-rich environment in which products could be customized to individual taste, giving currency to the phrase "mass customization." At the same time, however, such giant firms as Wal-Mart used information technology to build a mass market through low prices. Mass marketing remains a vital part of the American economy in the twenty-first century, but the new technologies and forms of retailing make it possible to create highly specialized and segmented markets for more-affluent consumers.

[*See also* Advertising; Consumer Culture; Ford, Henry, and Fordism; *and* Mass Production.]

BIBLIOGRAPHY

Chandler, Alfred D., Jr. *The Visible Hand: The Managerial Revolution in American Business*. Cambridge, Mass.: Belknap Press of Harvard University Press, 1977.

Chandler, Alfred D., Jr., Thomas K. McCraw, and Richard S. Tedlow. *Management, Past and Present: A Casebook on the History of American Business*. Cincinnati, Ohio: South-Western College, 1996.

Dolan, Robert J., and Hermann Simon. *Power Pricing: How Managing Price Transforms the Bottom Line*. New York: Free Press, 1996.

Hounshell, David A. *From the American System to Mass Production, 1800–1932: The Development of Manufacturing Technology in the United States*. Baltimore: Johns Hopkins University Press, 1984.

Tedlow, Richard S. *New and Improved: The Story of Mass Marketing*. Boston: Harvard Business School Press, 1996.

Richard Tedlow

MASS PRODUCTION

At the beginning of the twentieth century, mass production transformed the way Americans lived and worked. Understandable only as part of the larger socioeconomic system in which it operates, mass production encompasses far more than a set of manufacturing principles and technologies. Thanks to its role in creating mass consumer culture, it constitutes a vital part of modern life. It was responsible for the dehumanizing assembly-line work of the twentieth century, as well as for the physical comfort enjoyed by most people in industrialized countries. The 1926 edition of the *Encyclopaedia Britannica* formally introduced the term in an article titled "Mass production." Ghostwritten by the Ford Motor Company's publicity secretary, the article appeared over Henry Ford's name. The actual authorship matters little, for Henry Ford is indeed recognized as the man who popularized the term and, more important, made mass production work.

Mass production is characterized by the high-volume manufacture of standardized goods that results in lower prices. Dependent on economies of scale and efficiency in production, it relies heavily on a mechanized workplace, the division of labor, and a far larger proportion of machine operators than of skilled workers. It also requires absolute uniformity in production: each piece or component must be made exactly the same each time. This feature of mass production—the manufacture of interchangeable parts—proved so

MASS PRODUCTION · 497

difficult and expensive that it took almost a century to achieve.

The idea that work could be made routine and more productive through mechanization, standardization, and the division of labor long antedated Henry Ford; it can be found in eighteenth-century England, France, and America. In *From the American System to Mass Production* (1984), David Hounshell traces the technical development of mass production in the United States, beginning with the arms industry and proceeding through the sewing machine and woodworking industries; agricultural equipment and bicycles; and, finally, the automotive industry. Like that of any invention, mass production's history is one of genius and frustration. With the support of the U.S. government, early nineteenth-century armories successfully experimented with the mechanized production of guns with interchangeable parts, the essential components of mass production. One after another, American industries mechanized production, but the manufacture of interchangeable parts proved too expensive for many, and without perfect interchangeability, true mass production remains impossible. Lacking this, some manufacturers, such as the Singer Sewing Machine Company, settled for the older system of "fitting" the parts together machine by machine. This resulted not in mass-produced machines whose parts could be assembled randomly, but in unique machines whose components had to be filed by trained machinists to make the parts fit properly.

The response to mass production is as interesting as the story of its invention. Perfected and most widespread in the United States, mass production and its products have been introduced around the world, rejected nowhere. The inspiration for art, architecture, poetry, and music, mass production was also criticized as the root cause of the modern ecological crisis and twentieth-century alienation. Mass production was one of the icons, both beloved and reviled, of the so-called American century—the twentieth—when the United States became the world's premier military and industrial power.

As the new system of manufacturing developed, workers complained about the growing restrictions in the workplace. Some expressed their discontent by quitting, others by joining unions. No factory had more trouble keeping workers than did the Ford Motor Company's Highland Park plant near Detroit, Michigan, where the assembly line in its fully realized form was introduced in 1914. Workers quit in such large numbers that in 1913, even before the assembly line became fully operational, turnover was 380 percent. Henry Ford addressed the turnover and made himself famous with a single act: to keep his employees on the job in the face of work that many deemed unacceptable, Ford offered them an unheard-of wage rate of $5 per day.

The European response to Ford's style of mass production, known as "Fordism," is surprising compared to the labor response in the United States. During the interwar years, Fordism, along with Frederick W. Taylor's scientific management, was praised, especially in Germany and the Soviet Union, by both conservative engineers and socialist reformers as the way to economic security. Fordism and Taylorism were seen as the keys to the success of modern America and the obvious path for any country that sought modernity.

A widespread and diverse artistic response to mass production can be found in film, painting, photography, literature, and music. The central inspiration for this response, sometimes called "machine-age modernism," was the mass-production factory. Film provides the clearest and most unambiguous initial reaction to mass production. Movies such as Charlie Chaplin's *Modern Times* (1936), which used Ford's factory as a model; René Clair's *A nous la liberté* (1931); and Fritz Lang's *Metropolis* (1926) unabashedly criticized mass production and the socioeconomic system that supported it. Other artists, however, found the modern factory a positive inspiration. The painters Charles Sheeler and Diego Rivera both portrayed Ford's Detroit factories and praised them (in very different ways) in their art. Modern architecture, beginning with the Bauhaus designs of Walter Gropius, derived much of its inspiration from American factories. As practitioners of a wide range of art forms embraced the symbols of mass production and the machine age in general, these technological developments became increasingly accepted as part of modernist culture, no longer questioned but taken for granted as integral components of the social and economic landscape.

[*See also* **American System of Manufacturing and Interchangeable Parts; Consumer Culture; Deskilling; Factory System; Five-Dollar Day; Ford, Henry, and Fordism; Industrialization and Deindustrialization; Labor Productivity Growth; Mass Marketing; Productivity; Proletarianization; Scientific Management; Technology and Labor; Vertical Integration, Economies of Scale, and Firm Size;** *and* **Work.**]

BIBLIOGRAPHY

Biggs, Lindy. *The Rational Factory: Architecture, Technology, and Work in America's Age of Mass Production.* Baltimore: Johns Hopkins University Press, 1996.

Chandler, Alfred D., Jr. *The Visible Hand: The Managerial Revolution in American Business.* Cambridge, Mass.: Belknap Press of Harvard University Press, 1977.

Hughes, Thomas P. *American Genesis: A Century of Invention and Technological Enthusiasm, 1870–1970.* New York: Viking, 1989.

Kanigel, Robert. *The One Best Way: Frederick Winslow Taylor and the Enigma of Efficiency.* New York: Viking, 1997.

Meyer, Stephen, III. *The Five Dollar Day: Labor Management and Social Control in the Ford Motor Company, 1908–1921.* Albany: State University of New York Press, 1981.

Tichi, Cecilia. *Shifting Gears: Technology, Literature, Culture in Modernist America.* Chapel Hill: University of North Carolina Press, 1987.

Lindy Biggs

MASTER AND SERVANT LAW

The key question in the labor market is, Who is in control, the employer or the employee? Can the employer mandate everything a worker does? Can the worker quit, in order to accept a better opportunity elsewhere? The law of employment relations in English feudal times was called "master–servant law." The legal relation between masters and servants—mostly youths in agricultural and domestic work—was unequal. Masters ordered servants, servants obeyed; and servants could not terminate the relationship without the master's consent. Servants' labor was the property of masters, who controlled all aspects of work. Criminal penalties—the state—enforced masters' authority.

The great lesson of the American Revolution was personal sovereignty—"freedom." Workers in the new republic refused to accept the status of servants; they demanded to be treated as free men. However, employers' greater economic and political power and the preference of most American judges to respect English common-law traditions ensured that master–servant law continued to apply in the workplace. The work of "free" wage laborers came to be governed by master–servant law during the late eighteenth and early nineteenth centuries. The contradiction between control by the boss and worker sovereignty remains a matter of intense struggle in the twenty-first century.

There have been worker victories. The criminal law has not been used in America since at least 1700 to enforce the authority of employers, masters no longer may use physical force to chastise servants, and an employer cannot get an injunction forcing a contracted employee back to work. In 1821 a previously enslaved black woman, Mary Clark, was moved to a free state, Indiana, and a state court ruled that "employment must be at the will of the employee." Between 1800 and 1850, as nonagricultural wage laborers grew from under 3 million to over 8 million, factory workers claimed and won the right to change jobs, quitting freely so that they could switch to employment that seemed more attractive.

Employers responded by having workers sign contracts of employment for a year and by holding back some or all of the wages until the terms of the contract were completed. When workers quit before their term was up, courts overwhelmingly disallowed their claims for unpaid wages they had earned. Corporate employers were allowed to claim masters' legal powers. Courts refused to void employment contracts because of unequal bargaining power or workers' ignorance; they ruled that posted regulations were part of the employee's contract whether bargained for or not.

The concentrated power of workers and other reformers has since the Civil War produced state and federal statutes requiring regular wage payment in real money; setting maximum hours, minimum wages, and restrictions on children's and women's labor; prohibiting discrimination based upon race, religion, gender, national origin, or sexual preference; protecting civil servants; and asserting workers' rights to bargain through unions and to have access to formal grievance processes.

Although collective bargaining has gained better wages and conditions for the minority of workers who are unionized, many protective labor laws and those that enhance worker power have been struck down or restricted by courts,

and enforcement of the laws that remain in effect weakens as the power of organized labor weakens. Employers have outsourced to low-wage nonunion locations many of the jobs that they still "own." And by and large they still "own" workers' labor during work time. Employers remain masters.

[*See also* **Apprenticed Labor; Contract, Sanctity of; Employment-at-Will; Freedom of Contract; Labor Conspiracy Law;** *and* **Labor Markets.**]

BIBLIOGRAPHY

Hay, Douglas, and Paul Craven, eds. *Masters, Servants, and Magistrates in Britain and the Empire, 1562–1955.* Chapel Hill: University of North Carolina Press, 2004. See in particular pp. 1–58.

Holt, Wythe. "Recovery by the Worker Who Quits: A Comparison of the Mainstream, Legal Realist, and Critical Legal Studies Approaches to a Problem of Nineteenth Century Contract Law." *Wisconsin Law Review* (1986): 677–732.

Karsten, Peter. "'Bottomed on Justice': A Reappraisal of Critical Legal Studies Scholarship concerning Breaches of Labor Contracts by Quitting or Firing in Britain and the U.S., 1630–1880." *American Journal of Legal History* 34 (1990): 213–261.

Orren, Karen. *Belated Feudalism: Labor, the Law, and Liberal Development in the United States.* Cambridge, U.K.: Cambridge University Press, 1991.

Steinfeld, Robert J. *Coercion, Contract, and Free Labor in the Nineteenth Century.* Cambridge, U.K., and New York: Cambridge University Press, 2001. See in particular pp. 1–38 and 253–314.

Steinfeld, Robert J. *The Invention of Free Labor: The Employment Relation in English and American Law and Culture, 1350–1870.* Chapel Hill: University of North Carolina Press, 1991.

Tomlins, Christopher L. *Law, Labor, and Ideology in the Early American Republic.* Cambridge, U.K., and New York: Cambridge University Press, 1993.

Wythe Holt Jr.

MAYO, ELTON, AND WORK CULTURE

Elton Mayo (1880–1949) pioneered in industrial psychology. Born in Adelaide, Australia, George Elton Mayo was one of five children of George and Henrietta Mayo. A graduate of the University of Adelaide, Mayo treated veterans of World War I for shell shock, and in doing so he established his reputation in the relatively new field of applied psychology. In 1922 he left for the United States, where he delivered a series of speeches about individuals and their relationship to industrial society that caught the attention of both social scientists and business owners. The two groups were convinced by Mayo that experts in the human behavioral sciences held the key to avoiding labor unrest.

Through the efforts of Vernon Kellogg of the National Research Council, Mayo received an appointment as a professor of industrial research at the Harvard Business School. Shortly after arriving at Harvard, Mayo developed an ambitious project experimenting with workers at the Hawthorne Works, near Chicago, of the Western Electric Company. Between 1927 and 1932, Mayo examined a team of six female employees under a variety of different working conditions. However much the women's pay and working conditions varied, their productivity remained high. Mayo concluded that group psychology acted as the primary factor in accounting for both worker satisfaction and productivity. Business leaders embraced Mayo's conclusions in part because they could now argue that pay and working conditions were not the primary causes of labor discontent. In 1933, Mayo published *The Human Problems of an Industrial Civilization*, a book that summarized his theories about the psychology of work groups and that received lavish praise from reviewers. Mayo had established himself as the leading figure in the emerging science of human relations.

[*See also* Industrial Relations; *and* Productivity.]

BIBLIOGRAPHY

Gillespie, Richard. *Manufacturing Knowledge: A History of the Hawthorne Experiments.* Cambridge, U.K.: Cambridge University Press, 1991.

Hawthorne Works Museum. http://www.morton.edu/museum/index.html.

Trahair, Richard C. S. *The Humanist Temper: The Life and Work of Elton Mayo.* New Brunswick, N.J.: Transaction, 1984.

David Cullen

MAZZOCCHI, ANTHONY "TONY"

(1926–2002), labor leader. Born in Brooklyn, New York, on 13 June 1926, Anthony "Tony" Mazzocchi was a skilled organizer and high-ranking union officer who worked with environmentalists, feminists, antiwar and antinuclear activists, scientists, and—last but not least—rank-and-file workers. At his death on 5 October 2002, he was considered "one of the greatest innovators and mavericks in the labor movement" (Greenhouse).

Mazzocchi is best remembered for his pioneering environmental activism, which began in the 1950s with opposition to nuclear testing and with alliances forged with dissident scientists. By the 1960s, as legislative director of the Oil, Chemical, and Atomic Workers (OCAW), he was a leader among a handful of union officers seeking answers about how radiation, toxic chemicals, and other hazards might affect workers. He famously publicized the plight of Navajo uranium miners, and he acted as a major force behind congressional passage of the Occupational Safety and Health Act of 1970. In 1973, he masterminded a historic strike against Shell Oil in which toxics and employee health were central issues; he also elicited support for it from major environmental organizations, building an alliance that proved a watershed in the environmental movement. He backed OCAW member Karen Silkwood in exposing nuclear mismanagement at the Kerr–McGee nuclear facility in Oklahoma, then demanded a union investigation into her mysterious death in 1974.

Mazzocchi also served as the OCAW's health and safety director, vice president, and finally secretary-treasurer, but he narrowly lost election to the union presidency in 1979 and 1981. Nevertheless, he continued his labor and environmental activism in the 1980s and 1990s, including pursuing right-to-know legislation, working with a broad coalition on the 1984 environmental disaster in Bhopal, India, starting *New Solutions: A Journal of Environmental and Occupational Health Policy*, and founding the independent Labor Party in 1996.

[*See also* **Environmental Regulations; Labor Leaders; Labor's Role in Politics;** *and* **Occupational Safety and Health Administration.**]

BIBLIOGRAPHY

Gordon, Robert. "'Shell No!' OCAW and the Labor–Environmental Alliance." *Environmental History* 3, no. 4 (October 1998): 460–487.

Greenhouse, Steven. "Anthony Mazzocchi, 76, Dies; Union Officer and Party Father." *New York Times*, 9 October 2002, p. A25.

Leopold, Les. *The Man Who Hated Work and Loved Labor: The Life and Times of Tony Mazzocchi.* White River Junction, Vt.: Chelsea Green, 2007.

Mazzocchi, Tony. "Crossing Paths: Science and the Working Class." In *Barry Commoner's Contribution to the Environmental Movement: Science and Social Action*, edited by David Kriebel, pp. 25–30. Amityville, N.Y.: Baywood, 2002.

Jacquelyn Southern

McCARTHYISM AND ANTILABOR ACTION

See **Labor and Anti-Communism.**

McCORMICK, CYRUS

(1809–1884), inventor and manufacturer. Cyrus Hall McCormick was born on a farm in Rockbridge County, Virginia. In 1831 he took up the project that his father had pursued unsuccessfully for twenty years: building a reaper to speed the harvesting of small grains. In July 1831 he gave a public demonstration of his new design, which embodied key innovations common to every subsequent reaper. McCormick started a business to manufacture his reaper, locating in Chicago in 1847 so as to be closer to the agricultural heartland. His company quickly became the industry leader, maintaining that position until the Civil War.

During the war, while McCormick lived in London, his company lost its position as the leading manufacturer of farm machinery, though it remained important. After the war, he left the management of the company to his brother Leander. When the devastating Chicago fire destroyed his factory in 1871, Cyrus McCormick considered abandoning the business, but his wife, Nettie Fowler, whom he had married in 1858, intervened, urging reconstruction of the factory. Thereafter she played a central role in the management of the McCormick Harvesting Machine Company and its successor, the International Harvester Corporation.

From 1857 until his death, McCormick was deeply involved in Democratic Party politics.

He was also a committed Presbyterian layman. In 1859 he endowed four professorships at the Presbyterian Theological Seminary of the Northwest, Chicago, which in 1886 was renamed McCormick Theological Seminary. McCormick's inventive genius transformed grain harvesting and agricultural practices, yet the success of his company—and, perhaps, his reputation—resulted primarily from the business acumen of his wife and, subsequently, of his eldest son, Cyrus Jr.

[*See also* Agriculture; Farm Machinery; Grain Processing; Technology; *and* Technology and Labor.]

BIBLIOGRAPHY

Hurt, R. Douglas. *American Farm Tools: From Hand-Power to Steam-Power.* Manhattan, Kan.: Sunflower University Press, 1982.

Hutchinson, William T. *Cyrus Hall McCormick.* 2 vols. New York: Century, 1930–1935.

Rikoon, J. Sanford. *Threshing in the Middle West, 1820–1940: A Study of Traditional Culture and Technological Change.* Bloomington: Indiana University Press, 1988.

Fred V. Carstensen

McDONALD'S

The brothers Richard and Maurice McDonald introduced assembly-line techniques at the hamburger drive-in that they opened in San Bernardino, California, in the 1940s. Their "Speedy Service System," combined with economies of scale made possible by serving many customers quickly, proved far more profitable than the traditional labor-intensive approach was. Their success attracted potential franchisees, including Ray Kroc, who supplied the Multimixers used to prepare McDonald's milk shakes. Overcoming the McDonalds' reluctance to invest time or money in franchising, Kroc offered to take all responsibility as the sole franchise agent. The brothers accepted Kroc's offer, and in 1955 McDonald's restaurants began to appear nationwide. Kroc bought out his contract with the McDonald brothers in 1962. Kroc's vision of clean, quick-service family restaurants with an instantly recognizable logo—the golden arches—fit beautifully with postwar trends of suburbanization, highway expansion, working mothers, and consumer preference for standardized, mass-marketed products.

Fast-food franchising had a mixed record before Kroc. Earlier franchisers had tended either to sell off large territories to raise capital quickly or—as the Howard Johnson's restaurants did in the 1930s—to operate as the supplier for the franchisees, creating potential conflicts of interest and temptations to overcharge franchisees. Kroc emphasized efficient restaurant operations and guaranteed franchisees' profits before the McDonald's Corporation took its cut. A key to the success of McDonald's was its chief financial officer Harry Sonneborn, who structured franchise deals that ensured profitability not by food sales alone, but also through the real estate that the restaurants occupied.

In the twenty-first century, McDonald's remains one of the world's largest private real estate enterprises, as well as one of the largest food-service providers, serving nearly 40 million meals daily in more than one hundred countries, with annual sales in excess of $30 billion. A host of competitors such as Kentucky Fried Chicken, Taco Bell, Wendy's, and Burger King testified to the success of the McDonald's formula, but none has matched its success.

[*See also* Advertising; Consumer Culture; Food and Diet; *and* Mass Marketing.]

BIBLIOGRAPHY

Kroc, Ray, with Robert Anderson. *Grinding It Out: The Making of McDonald's*. Chicago: H. Regnery, 1977.

Love, John F. *McDonald's: Behind the Arches*. Toronto: Bantam, 1986.

Christopher Berkeley

McGUIRE, P. J.

(1852–1906), labor leader. The founding president of the United Brotherhood of Carpenters and Joiners (UBCJA), P. J. McGuire was an early leader of the American Federation of Labor (AFL). Under McGuire the UBCJA fought a long and successful series of strikes against employers, consolidated power through a sequence of jurisdictional disputes with rival organizations, and successfully maintained the wages and influence of carpenters in a period of rapid and disruptive technological change. McGuire was also central to the rise and success of the AFL in the first twenty years after its founding in 1886 and is often cited as the first person to propose Labor Day as a national holiday. Throughout his career, McGuire held fast to a blend of trade union socialism; he was an advocate of practical, craft-centered organization and direct labor action, as well as of national and international working-class political action.

Born in New York City in 1852, Peter J. McGuire attended parochial schools and worked at a number of stores and odd jobs before his apprenticeship in a piano shop. While working as a carpenter in New York City, he took evening classes at the Cooper Institute, where he first met Samuel Gompers. McGuire emerged publicly in early 1873 as a passionate spokesman for the Committee of Public Safety, advocating government assistance for the unemployed. His political beliefs were closer to those of Adolph Strasser than to those of Gompers, and he worked with Strasser to found the Social Democratic Workingmen's Party of North America. As editor of the journal *The Toiler* in the 1870s, McGuire supported the Greenback Labor Party's campaign for the eight-hour workday, and as a carpenter and a member of the Knights of Labor, he also led the carpenters in a successful strike for the eight-hour workday in Saint Louis, Missouri.

In 1881, McGuire organized the convention of carpenters' unions that formed the United Brotherhood of Carpenters and Joiners of America. The UBCJA set out to protect the craft and craftsmen from new technologies, in particular the installation of machine-made wooden trim by less-skilled workers. He also fought to prevent the subcontracting of woodwork and the imposition of piece rates, as well as continuing to lead the campaign for the eight-hour workday. McGuire believed that his campaigns required a unified national organization, and he led the UBCJA through twenty years of conflict and, ultimately, unification with rival organizations. Also in 1881, McGuire again worked with Gompers, this time at early meetings that led to the founding of the Federation of Organized Trades and Labor Unions. McGuire served as a vice president both of the new federation and of its successor, the American Federation of Labor, for the next two decades. By the turn of the twentieth century, the UBCJA had emerged both as the dominant labor organization among carpenters and woodworkers and, together with the AFL, as a powerful force in the nation's economy and politics.

McGuire's career ended in 1901 when he was arrested for embezzlement. The membership of the UBCJA voted him out of office in 1902. Peter McGuire died in Camden, New Jersey, in 1906.

[*See also* **American Federation of Labor; Eight-Hour Day; Federation of Organized Trades and Labor Unions; Gompers, Samuel;**

Greenback Labor Party; Labor Leaders; Union Corruption; *and* United Brotherhood of Carpenters and Joiners.]

BIBLIOGRAPHY

Christie, Robert A. *Empire in Wood: A History of the Carpenters' Union.* Ithaca, N.Y.: Cornell University Press, 1956.

Cummins, E. E. "Jurisdictional Disputes of the Carpenters' Union." *Quarterly Journal of Economics* 40, no. 3 (May 1926): 463–494.

Galenson, Walter. *The United Brotherhood of Carpenters: The First Hundred Years.* Cambridge, Mass.: Harvard University Press, 1983.

Timothy J. Houlihan

MCNARY–HAUGEN BILL

In the years following World War I, farmers received prices for their products that represented a purchasing power far below prewar levels. This resulted in an effort by the farm bloc in Congress to secure a larger share for these producers, in part by making the protective tariff as effective for agricultural products as it was for manufactured goods. In 1924, Senator Charles McNary of Oregon and Representative Gilbert Haugen of Iowa introduced a bill designed to assist farmers by requiring the federal government to sell surplus crops abroad at whatever price the commodities could command, thereby allowing domestic prices to rise. The cost of the program would be met by an equalization fee levied on farmers. Congress passed two versions of McNary–Haugen, but President Calvin Coolidge vetoed both: in his view, the bills fixed prices and abused the power to tax. Although unable to override the president's vetoes, congressional supporters did succeed in bringing the plight of agriculture to national attention. Both political parties included planks in their 1928 platforms calling for legislation to give equality to agriculture.

The goal of the McNary–Haugen bills was to achieve parity, a fair exchange value between agricultural prices and the general price index. Considering the huge agricultural surpluses of the 1920s that kept prices low, it is doubtful that the law could have succeeded. During the Coolidge presidency, moreover, the government lacked the administrative ability and facilities to manage complex agricultural production and storage programs. But the campaign for the McNary–Haugen bills laid the foundation for some of the agricultural reforms of the New Deal era and for the federal agricultural programs that were in place from the 1940s into the 1990s.

[*See also* Agriculture, *subentry on* Since 1920; Farm Bureau Federation; Subsidies, Agricultural; Tariffs; *and* Trade Policy, Federal.]

BIBLIOGRAPHY

Fite, Gilbert. *George N. Peek and the Fight for Farm Parity.* Norman: University of Oklahoma Press, 1954.

Hamilton, David E. *From New Day to New Deal: American Farm Policy from Hoover to Roosevelt, 1928–1933.* Chapel Hill: University of North Carolina Press, 1991.

Kelley, Darwin N. "The McNary–Haugen Bills, 1924–1928: An Attempt to Make the Tariff Effective for Farm Products." *Agricultural History* 14, no. 4 (1940): 170–180.

Williams, C. Fred. "William M. Jardine and the Foundations for Republican Farm Policy, 1925–1929." *Agricultural History* 70, no. 2 (1996): 216–232.

Richard Lowitt

MEANY, GEORGE

(1894–1980), labor leader. Born in New York City, George Meany in 1915 joined the United

Association of Plumbers and Steam Fitters, his father's union. In 1922 he attained his first union office, winning election as business agent of New York City Local 463. He served as president of the New York State Federation of Labor from 1934 to 1939 and in 1939 was elected secretary-treasurer of the American Federation of Labor (AFL). Upon the death of William Green in 1952, the executive council elected Meany president of the AFL. In 1955, successful in his efforts to effect a merger with the once-rival Congress of Industrial Organizations (CIO), Meany was elected president of the AFL-CIO, a post that he held for twenty-four years.

Meany acted forcefully as an advocate of labor's views from within the political system. He supported civil rights legislation but rarely challenged the racially discriminatory practices of craft unions. Meany was an ardent cold warrior who fought pro-Communist unionism at home and abroad, as well as supported the Vietnam War. During his AFL presidency, union membership declined as a proportion of the non-agricultural labor force, a circumstance that Meany viewed with equanimity so long as the AFL-CIO remained influential in government and Democratic Party circles. Meany clashed frequently with the United Auto Workers president Walter Reuther, who urged revitalization of labor's activist traditions and a less strident approach to foreign-policy questions.

As a labor leader, Meany championed workers' economic interests and allied with the mainstream civil rights movement. He did little, however, to accommodate the concerns of women, minority or marginal workers, or more-militant trade unionists.

[*See also* **American Federation of Labor; American Federation of Labor and Congress of Industrial Organizations; Labor Leaders; Labor Movements; Labor's Role in Politics;** *and* **Reuther, Walter.**]

BIBLIOGRAPHY

Goulden, Joseph C. *Meany*. New York: Atheneum, 1972.

Zieger, Robert H. "George Meany: Labor's Organization Man." In *Labor Leaders in America*, edited by Melvyn Dubofsky and Warren Van Tine, pp. 324–349. Urbana: University of Illinois Press, 1987.

Robert H. Zieger

MEATPACKING AND MEAT-PROCESSING INDUSTRY

Commercial meatpacking in North America dates from 1660 when the entrepreneur William Pynchon began selling preserved pork from an abandoned warehouse in Springfield, Massachusetts. In the antebellum era, meatpacking and meat processing concentrated in Cincinnati, Ohio, where the Ohio River provided low-cost transport of pork to distant markets. By the late 1840s, Cincinnati boasted more than forty pork-packing plants using an advanced division of labor that integrated packing with slaughtering and dressing. By the end of the Civil War, however, Cincinnati had been displaced as the meatpacking capital by Chicago, strategically located along rail lines that linked western livestock supplies to eastern, urban markets.

Between 1865 and World War I, meatpacking changed from a mostly local, seasonal, and small-scale business into a giant, nationally integrated, and year-round industry dominated by five massive corporations, the largest of which were Swift and Armour. At the heart of this transformation lay Chicago-based firms' use of refrigerated railroad cars to ship dressed beef from Chicago and other western packing centers to eastern, urban markets. These firms also developed networks of refrigerated branch distribution outlets, deployed armies of salespeople, developed and marketed broad ranges of animal by-products, and subdivided a mostly unskilled labor force in massive, multi-species packing establishments. Collectively keeping labor costs low and pricing their goods on the basis of average costs rather than supply and demand, they dominated the industry through the 1940s.

After World War II, the advantage shifted to three upstart firms—ConAgra, Excel, and especially Iowa Beef Processors—that challenged the older rail- and river-connected packing centers and by 1989 slaughtered 70 percent of the nation's cattle. These companies deployed new technologies to eliminate skilled labor, advance the industry's legendary specialization of tasks, and increase productivity. They built single-species plants closer to livestock supplies and revolutionized the meat trade by trimming red meats to retail specifications within their slaughterhouses and selling the resulting "boxed beef" directly to grocery stores and supermarkets. They undertook an effective campaign against established wage standards, reduced plant safety, sped up production, and recruited nonunion workers from rural areas in the United States, Latin America, and Asia.

By the beginning of the twenty-first century, the meatpacking and meat-processing industry remained one of the nation's leading employers, important to the economies of midwestern and mid-Atlantic states, as well as of Texas and California. In many ways it also continued to resemble the industry as described by Upton Sinclair's *The Jungle* (1906), an exposé of labor exploitation and unsanitary conditions in the meatpacking industry that led to stricter federal regulation. Despite such regulation, the industry has continued to be plagued by charges of labor exploitation, noxious conditions, workplace danger, nutritional risk, and environmental damage.

[*See also* **Corporate Agriculture; Factory Farming; Hormel P-9 Strike (1985);** *Jungle,* **The; Livestock Industry; Pure Food and Drug Act; Swift, Gustavus; Transportation Revolution;** *and* **Vertical Integration, Economies of Scale, and Firm Size.**]

BIBLIOGRAPHY

Horowitz, Roger. *"Negro and White, Unite and Fight!": A Social History of Industrial Unionism in Meatpacking, 1930–90.* Urbana: University of Illinois Press, 1997.

Skaggs, Jimmy M. *Prime Cut: Livestock Raising and Meatpacking in the United States, 1607–1983.* College Station: Texas A&M University Press, 1986.

Paul Street

MECHANIZATION OF AGRICULTURE

See **Farm Machinery.**

MELLON BANKS

The Mellon banks were a group of financial institutions instrumental in the industrial development of the greater Pittsburgh area in Pennsylvania, as well as, to a lesser degree, of other regions of the United States. Mellon funding played important roles in the development of coal, fabricated (but not primary) steel, aluminum (in particular Pittsburgh Reduction, which became Alcoa), and oil (in particular Gulf). Other notable companies benefiting from Mellon funding and oversight were Carborundum, a maker of grinding materials, and Koppers, a maker of advanced coking ovens that captured rather than simply vented valuable by-product gases such as toluene and benzene. Mellon banks at various times also provided financial resources for real estate development, lumber, mining, traction, railroad-car construction, and electricity-generating enterprises, both in the Pittsburgh area and elsewhere.

The first Mellon financial intermediaries, ventures of Thomas Mellon, were the East Liberty Savings and Deposit Bank, a joint-stock institution founded in 1867, and T. Mellon and Sons, a private bank founded in 1869. Thomas Mellon's son, Andrew Mellon, cofounded with Henry Frick the Fidelity Title and Trust Company in 1886 and, with others, the Union Transfer and Trust Company in 1889 (eventually Union Trust Company). In 1902, Mellon converted T. Mellon and Sons along with a number of other banks into the federally chartered Mellon National Bank, with Andrew and Richard Mellon—another son—as principal shareholders. In 1946 the Mellon National Bank and the Union Trust Company, along with the Mellbank Corporation, which held various smaller, regional banks, combined to form the Mellon National Bank and Trust Company. Through a succession of subsequent acquisitions and mergers, this institution survives in the twenty-first century as Bank of New York Mellon (BNY Mellon).

Through these banks, investments on their own account, and interlocking directorates, the Mellon family and in particular Andrew Mellon became some of the wealthiest and most influential capitalists in the region and eventually the country. Shrewd businessmen, the Mellons were at the right place at the right time, able to take advantage of new technologies and new materials during the most dynamic period of Pittsburgh's economic development, from the end of the Civil War through World War I. They often took an active role in the management of companies in which they had a controlling interest, although standard operating procedure was to install capable management and then take a relatively hands-off approach unless and until a business ran into difficulty.

Andrew Mellon went on to serve as treasury secretary under presidents Warren G. Harding, Calvin Coolidge, and Herbert Hoover and subsequently as U.S. ambassador to the United Kingdom. He survived an indictment for income-tax evasion, and before he died he donated his art collection and provided the funding for the National Gallery of Art in Washington, D.C.

BIBLIOGRAPHY

Cannadine, David. *Mellon: An American Life*. New York: Alfred A. Knopf, 2006. The best single resource on the evolution of Mellon banks and their contributions to U.S. economic growth and development.

Alexander J. Field

MEMPHIS SANITATION STRIKE (1968)

On 1 February 1968 a faulty packing ram on a "wiener barrel" sanitation truck in Memphis, Tennessee, crushed to death Echol Cole and Robert Walker. These two African American men had been riding in the truck's garbage bin to stay out of the rain. The city of Memphis under Mayor Henry Loeb, as a fiscal austerity measure, had continued to use such outmoded equipment in the Public Works Department. The city paid most of its thirteen hundred sanitation workers a minimum wage of $1.60 per hour. They worked until their routes were done, often putting in sixty hours a week at forty hours of pay; some 40 percent of them drew welfare while working full-time jobs. The city hired and fired unskilled black workers at will and provided them with no showers or other sanitary facilities, no access to supervisory jobs, no rights and no respect, and minimal health and accident insurance. Cole and Walker, both in their thirties, left behind wives and children with no source of income. T. O. Jones had tried to organize the sanitation workers into a union to change these conditions, but Loeb refused to recognize or bargain with them or to deduct union dues. Sanitation workers were part of the African American community's vast working poor, doing full-time work at part-time wages.

A few days after the deaths of Cole and Walker, Public Works supervisors sent the sewer and drain workers home with no wages during a rainstorm, while white supervisors stayed at work and drew their pay with little to do. After a Sunday night meeting to air their grievances, the sanitation workers went on strike on Monday, 12 February, Abraham Lincoln's birthday. Jones, leader of Local 1733 of the American Federation of State, County, and Municipal Employees (AFSCME), did not ask for approval from his national office—he knew that it would not approve—and had no strike fund. City police escorted garbage trucks and scabs to break the strike, and during the next six weeks they attacked workers and their supporters with clubs and mace. Workers put up picket signs declaring "I Am a Man," and the strike evolved into a huge battle over dignity and respect for the city's black citizens. The city's African American community, representing some 40 percent of the city's population of half a million, though reluctant at first, largely rallied to the side of the workers. The civil rights veteran Reverend James Lawson and other black ministers opened their churches to nightly rallies, while the AFSCME organized mass picket lines, women led a boycott of downtown merchants, and the Memphis AFL-CIO Labor Council passed a resolution and held a demonstration of support. Led by its president Jerry Wurf and various staff members, the AFSCME international office put everything on the line to support the strike.

The civil rights leaders Roy Wilkins and Bayard Rustin came to speak, but the strike re-ceived little national attention until 18 March when the Reverend Martin Luther King Jr. gave an impassioned speech at Charles Mason Temple to a packed mass meeting. King declared that "all labor has dignity" and made Memphis part of his Poor People's Campaign to take impoverished people to the nation's capital to demand that Congress shift its war spending to address health care, jobs, housing, education, and other human needs. King pledged to return to lead a general strike of black workers and students against the city, but when he did so, on 28 March, Memphis police attacked, leading to chaos and the death of a teenager, Larry Payne. King returned again, intending to lead a peaceful mass march, but an assassin murdered him with a single bullet on 4 April. While evidence points to James Earl Ray, he was never convicted in a jury trial. Many saw white America as complicit in King's death, and mass insurrections took place in more than a hundred cities. Mayor Loeb still refused to sign a union contract or accept deduction of union dues from workers' paychecks, but under pressure from President Lyndon B. Johnson, Governor of Tennessee Buford Ellington, and the U.S. Labor Department, the city council signed an agreement on 16 April.

The assassination of King undermined his Poor People's Campaign and, along with the assassination of the presidential candidate Robert F. Kennedy six weeks later, provided a crushing blow to the social-change movements of the 1960s. However, the example of the strike's success inspired municipal, hospital, and service workers in the South, and the AFSCME, viewing the strike as a seminal moment, evolved into one of the largest unions in the United States. Although historians once viewed the Memphis story largely as the backdrop for King's assassination, recent historical treatments have seen this civil rights strike as the spark for a remarkable community and labor movement and as part of the black freedom struggle's turn toward economic justice and union rights for racial minorities and the working poor. This historical treatment of the strike as an epochal event also represents a turn toward seeing Dr. King not only as a civil rights leader, but also as a union and human rights advocate, one whose message continues to resound in the struggles of the working poor in the globalized economy and antiunion political climate of the twenty-first century.

[*See also* **American Federation of State, County, and Municipal Employees; Labor Movements; Poor People's Movement; Poverty; Racism;** *and* **Strikes.**]

BIBLIOGRAPHY

Beifuss, Joan Turner. *At the River I Stand: Memphis, the 1968 Strike, and Martin Luther King.* Memphis, Tenn.: B&W Books, 1985.

Honey, Michael K. *Black Workers Remember: An Oral History of Segregation, Unionism, and the Freedom Struggle.* Berkeley: University of California Press, 1999.

Honey, Michael K. *Going Down Jericho Road: The Memphis Strike, Martin Luther King's Last Campaign.* New York: W. W. Norton and Company, 2007.

Honey, Michael K. *Southern Labor and Black Civil Rights: Organizing Memphis Workers.* Urbana: University of Illinois Press, 1993.

King, Martin Luther, Jr. *All Labor Has Dignity.* Michael K. Honey, ed. Boston: Beacon Press, 2011.

Michael K. Honey

MERCANTILISM

Mercantilism is a body of political thought that encourages a state to maximize its own wealth in a competitive world of states and nations, often at the expense of other states, by dominating trade and manufacturing. Developed during periods of warfare and coinciding with the rapid rise in the cost of fighting wars, mercantilist policy attempted to enhance the ability of states to mobilize money for military combat. Only wealthy states could survive and dominate in a competitive world, so mercantilists were primarily concerned with how states became wealthy at the expense of their rivals. One state's gain would be another's loss. A great concern of political economy during the so-called age of mercantilism, roughly 1650–1830, was the balance of payments. Because the wealth of a nation was measured in bullion, the goal of mercantilism was to channel gold and silver into the country through a favorable balance of trade. Theoretically, states needed to export more than they imported. Because goods and services were purchased in specie, mercantilist policies attempted to encourage national self-sufficiency by ensuring that specie was always flowing into or remaining within the boundaries of the state. Internally, mercantilists believed that the pursuit of private wealth should be regulated to ensure that private competition did not harm the public good and the balance of payments. An ideal mercantilist policy would protect home manufactures with high tariffs on imports, would guard trade secrets to ensure that manufacturing advantages remained proprietary, and would exploit foreign and colonial raw materials to increase the self-sufficiency of the nation and encourage the dependence of rival powers.

Although numerous nations and empires in the early modern world practiced such a political economy, the English and British were particularly important in the articulation and later critique of mercantilist thought. Indeed, their own rise from a weak and marginal kingdom with one notable export in the late sixteenth century—unfinished wool—to a worldwide imperial power and dominant manufacturer by the mid-eighteenth century coincided with the development of mercantilist policy and thought. Although they amassed colonies from private initiatives as part of a rivalry with Spain in the early seventeenth century, by the middle of the century the English began to develop a policy that would eventually reflect the ideal of mercantilist economic development, in which the colonies both produced raw materials and exotic goods that would be in demand in Europe and also consumed manufactured items from the mother country. With the navigation acts in the 1660s, the English forced foreigners out of their colonial trade, shaped that trade to reach Europe solely through the control of the mother country, and pushed their colonies to maximize their extractive and staple capacities even as manufacturing at home was encouraged and protected.

By the mid-eighteenth century it was commonplace within ministerial circles in England that mercantilism explained the great rise of British power in the world and should be pursued forever. In *The Wealth of Nations* (1776), however, Adam Smith famously criticized mercantilist thought and policy by asserting that protectionism and heavy regulation of trade, as well as the high barriers to competition that the nation imposed to check the pursuit of private wealth, actually created inefficiencies that weakened the nation and served the interests of specific merchants and manufacturers. Nevertheless, mercantilist thought remained powerful into the nineteenth century. Alexander Hamilton, for instance, believed that the United States could become strong and economically independent after the American Revolution by emulating mercantilist policies. Although classical liberal economists follow Smith's critique of the danger of too much government involvement in economic development, many twentieth-century economists looked to the mercantilists as an example of the important place of state planning in a nation's economic strength, particularly the need to check the unregulated pursuit of private gain and to ensure and protect the maintenance of public goods and resources.

[*See also* **Capitalism; Foreign Trade; Hamilton, Alexander, and Economic Development; Tariffs;** *and* **Trade Policy, Federal.**]

BIBLIOGRAPHY

Heckscher, Eli F. *Mercantilism.* Translated by Mendel Shapiro. 2 vols. London: Allen and Unwin, 1935.

Magnusson, Lars. *Mercantilism: The Shaping of an Economic Language.* London: Routledge, 1994.

McCusker, John J., and Russell R. Menard. *The Economy of British America, 1607–1789.* Chapel Hill: University of North Carolina Press for the Omohundro Institute of Early American History and Culture, Williamsburg, Va., 1985.

Smith, Adam. *An Inquiry into the Nature and Causes of the Wealth of Nations* (1776, 1789). Edited by Edwin Cannan (1904). 2 vols. Chicago: the University of Chicago Press, 1976.

Doug Bradburn

MERGER MOVEMENT

The merger movement of 1898 to 1904 transformed the U.S. economy from one of predominantly small-scale firms to one of large corporations. Though many railroads and some extractive and manufacturing companies had developed into expansive corporations before 1898, some as early as the 1870s, mergers were rare outside of transportation before the turn of the century, and market shares in manufacturing and extractive industries were dispersed among many producers. This began to change—and to change rapidly—with the beginning of the merger movement. In 1898, 303 firms, representing 4 percent of the value of the gross domestic product (GDP) in that year, disappeared as a result of mergers—a more than fivefold increase in the average per year disappearance of firms from mergers between 1895 and 1897. In 1899, 1,208 firms, representing 12.9 percent of the value of the GDP in that year, disappeared as a result of mergers. And in 1901, 423 firms, representing 9.8 percent of the value of the GDP in that year, disappeared as a result of mergers. This merger frenzy trailed off with 379, 142, and 79 firms disappearing in 1902, 1903, and 1904, respectively (Nelson, 1959, p. 37).

Though happening within a short time span, these mergers left the U.S. economy fundamentally changed. Market concentration increased significantly in many manufacturing industries. Twenty-one companies resulting from mergers of 3 to 74 firms achieved control of 42.5 to 62.5 percent of their industry's market. Twenty-five companies resulting from mergers of 4 to 171 firms achieved control of 62.5 to 82.5 percent of their industry's market. And 16 companies resulting from mergers of 2 to 163 firms achieved control of 82.5 percent or more of their industry's market. Such giants as U.S. Steel, which achieved control of 65 percent of the steel market after combining 171 steel firms in 1901, and General Electric and Westinghouse, which achieved control of 90 percent of its market after combining 9 firms in 1901 and 1902, were created by 1904.

Historians have offered several explanations for the merger movement. Alfred D. Chandler argued that it represented an effort by business to increase efficiency through economies of speed and scale. In order to capture such efficiencies, business needed to revolutionize management and organization. Although many of the mergers at the turn of the twentieth century were horizontal—that is, the combination of competitors—successful combinations resulted from effective managerial organization that enabled companies to capture the increased efficiency of economies of speed through vertical integration—that is, the combination of companies that provided intermediate and raw

materials, companies that produced final goods, and marketing. Indeed, those at the top, such as Andrew Carnegie of U.S. Steel, understood the gross inequality that went hand in hand with consolidation. Carnegie was familiar with the ideas of the British philosopher Herbert Spencer, which are similar to those of Chandler. "The businessmen had accumulated their fortunes ... not because they were more righteous, more pious, more industrious, or more diligent than their employees, but because they possessed what Carnegie called the special 'talent for organization and management' required in the new industrial age" (Nasaw, 2005, pp. 127–128)—that is, an age in which vertical integration was of utmost importance.

Ralph L. Nelson has argued that the development of financial markets and of institutions that allowed nonfinancial companies to exploit these markets were the most important factors in the merger movement. Certainly, huge sums were involved in these combinations. Combining 163 competitors between 1895 and 1904, the American Tobacco Company represented assets worth $502 million—representing 14 percent of gross capital formation in 1904. Many contemporaries also argued that finance played a major role in the merger process. For example, John Moody, a Wall Street conservative, praised the role of finance in *The Truth about the Trusts* (1904), whereas Louis Brandeis, a Progressive activist, advocated trust-busting in *Other People's Money and How the Bankers Use It* (1914).

Yet subsequent scholars have argued that the merger movement represented the search by firms for market control so that they could raise prices and profits. Indeed, the majority of mergers between 1898 and 1904 involved the combination of competing firms—and thus concentrated market share. A large market share gives a firm more power to control prices, thus increasing the firm's revenue at the expense of the consumer. This was the complaint of southern and western farmers in the 1870s, 1880s, and

1890s about railroads. These grievances burst into politics through the Granger movement, the antimonopoly movement, the Greenback and Populist Parties, and even the Democratic Party, in its 1896 presidential platform.

Naomi Lamoreaux has explained that the economic distress of the Panic of 1893, combined with large fixed costs and growth during the boom years before the panic, pushed many firms into ruinous price wars. Earlier attempts at price-fixing between competing firms through association almost never lasted; the price-fixing did not stymie the competition between firms or prevent legal action. Thus firms merged in order to provide more direct control over production and prices. Indeed, in testimony before the Industrial Commission—appointed by President William McKinley and in existence from 1898 to 1902—many firms that had merged explained that they did so because of the "ruinous" price competition that took place in the mid-1890s. The choice was either bankruptcy or merger (Lamoreaux, 1985, pp. 109–110).

Richard Edwards (1979) has emphasized that market control went hand in hand with increased political power, a factor that motivated firms' decisions to merge. The large size of the new companies certainly placed many more workers and much more capital under an executive's control and may, therefore, have given the executives more political influence. Speaking of the 1880s, one historian suggested that Standard Oil's interests were looked after by Senator Henry Payne of Ohio, the father of the Standard Oil treasurer, and that the Union Pacific's interests were protected by Senator Leland Stanford of California, himself a director of the company. This easily could have factored into the cost–benefit analysis of executives in the merger wave of 1898 to 1904.

[*See also* **Antitrust Legislation; Northern Securities Case;** *and* **Vertical Integration, Economies of Scale, and Firm Size.**]

BIBLIOGRAPHY

Chandler, Alfred D., Jr. *The Visible Hand: The Managerial Revolution in American Business.* Cambridge, Mass.: Belknap Press of Harvard University Press, 1977.

Edwards, Richard. *Contested Terrain: The Transformation of the Workplace in the Twentieth Century.* New York: Basic Books, 1979.

Lamoreaux, Naomi R. *The Great Merger Movement in American Business, 1895–1904.* Cambridge, U.K.: Cambridge University Press, 1985.

Nasaw, David. "Gilded Age Gospels." In *Ruling America: A History of Wealth and Power in a Democracy*, edited by Steve Fraser and Gary Gerstle, pp. 123–148. Cambridge, Mass.: Harvard University Press, 2005.

Nelson, Ralph L. *Merger Movements in American Industry, 1895–1956.* Princeton, N.J.: Princeton University Press, 1959.

Sundquist, James L. *Dynamics of the Party System: Alignment and Realignment of Political Parties in the United States.* Washington, D.C.: Brookings Institution, 1973.

Mark Stelzner

MESABI RANGE AND MICHIGAN HARD-ROCK MINERS' STRIKES (1907–1916)

Strikes in 1907, 1913–1914, and 1916 by mine workers in the Lake Superior basin pitted the budding power of organized labor in these mining frontiers against the entrenched power of concentrated capital. Already by 1903, union organizers from the Western Federation of Miners (WFM) had made inroads on the Minnesota iron ranges and in Michigan's Copper Country. As early as 1904 in Minnesota and by 1906 in Michigan, mine workers began organized strikes against mining companies. By 1905 the WFM, then perceived by mine owners as a militant industrial union and beginning its two-year association with the Industrial Workers of the World (IWW), hurried to organize miners for collective labor action.

By 1907, the WFM had signed up more than twenty-five hundred mine workers on the Mesabi iron range. The WFM sent one of its most capable organizers, the Italian American Teofilo Petriella, to work on the Mesabi iron range. With the help of Finnish Socialist Federation locals, which were scattered throughout the region, the WFM succeeded in building enough strength to call a strike in July 1907. Finnish immigrant strikers especially gained notoriety for their actions during the strike, but the strike failed, and the union's critics condemned it for neglecting immigrant workers.

Though the 1907 strike failed, the WFM had planted the seeds of revolt among Lake Superior mine workers, and the result was a bitter, massive, and sometimes violet strike six years later. The 1913–1914 strike among copper miners in Michigan's Upper Peninsula proved especially bitter and lasted nine months. The strike garnered national attention and even saw Mary "Mother" Jones deliver fiery speeches on behalf of Copper Country mine workers. This strike represented both the peak and the end of major organizing by the WFM in the Midwest.

The causes of the 1913 Michigan copper strike included the hard-rock miners' standard grievances, as well as one unique to the Upper Peninsula: the workers demanded abolition of the so-called one-man drill. Its inclusion among strike grievances brought skilled labor into the WFM for the first time in the Copper Country. Skilled Cornish, German, and American miners joined Finns, Italians, Slovenians, and Croatians, among other recently arrived immigrant groups, in the union ranks.

No incident during the nine-month strike was more tragic than events on 24 December 1913 at a multiethnic Christmas party for strikers and their families at the Italian Hall in Calumet. In the waning hours of the afternoon, a stampede of men, women, and children streamed down the stairs of the hall's second floor. Bodies of fallen people piled up on one another as panic gripped the fleeing partygoers.

Mystery has forever shrouded the events of 24 December, but some maintain that a cry of "fire" initiated the fateful rush, and some union advocates suggest that a man wearing a pro-mining-company Citizens' Alliance button falsely shouted "fire." Even the precise toll of the dead, the majority of them children, remains in question. The best modern estimates place the number of victims at between seventy and seventy-four. Whatever the precise count, the Italian Hall tragedy signaled the strike's ultimate defeat. In early April 1914 the WFM ended the strike.

The WFM's defeats in 1907 and 1913–1914 led Lake Superior miners to seek the more militant unionism associated with the Industrial Workers of the World (IWW). By 1916, helped by radical Finnish immigrants, the IWW had built a strong following among Minnesota mine workers. In June 1916, Mesabi iron miners walked off the job from Aurora to Virginia, Minnesota, followed by workers from other mines on the range, ultimately shutting down the Vermilion and Cuyuna iron ranges, as well as the Mesabi. By mid-June the IWW had enlisted fifteen thousand iron miners in its strike.

Such famous IWW organizers and agitators as Carlo Tresca, Sam Scarlett, Frank Little, and Elizabeth Gurley Flynn came to the range. Violence on the part of the mining companies and the strikers ensued, with the public authorities and their courts exacting severe justice on strikers and their leaders. With strike leaders imprisoned or facing trial, in September the IWW called off the strike. Congressional investigations later concluded that many of the strikers' grievances were legitimate.

[*See also* Industrial Workers of the World; Mining Industry; Strikes; *and* Western Federation of Miners.]

BIBLIOGRAPHY

Dubofsky, Melvyn. *We Shall Be All: A History of the Industrial Workers of the World*. 2d ed. Urbana: University of Illinois Press, 1988.

Karni, Michael G. "The Founding of the Finnish Socialist Federation and the Minnesota Strike of 1907." In *For the Common Good: Finnish Immigrants and the Radical Response to Industrial America*. Superior, Wis.: Työmies Society, 1977.

Kaunonen, Gary. *Challenge Accepted: A Finnish Immigrant Response to Industrial America in Michigan's Copper Country*. East Lansing: Michigan State University Press, 2010.

Lamppa, Marvin. *Minnesota's Iron Country: Rich Ore, Rich Lives*. Duluth, Minn.: Lake Superior Port Cities, 2004.

Lankton, Larry. *Cradle to Grave: Life, Work, and Death at Lake Superior Copper Mines*. New York: Oxford University Press, 1991.

Ollila, Douglas J., Jr. "From Socialism to Industrial Unionism (IWW): Social Factors in the Emergence of Left-Labor Radicalism among Finnish Workers on the Mesabi, 1911–19." In *The Finnish Experience in the Western Great Lakes Region: New Perspectives*, edited by Michael G. Karni, Matti E. Kaups, and Douglas J. Ollila Jr. Turku, Finland: Institute for Migration, 1975.

Gary Kaunonen

METAL SMELTING AND REFINING

See Mining Industry.

METAL TRADES

See Iron and Steel Industry.

MIGRATORY LABOR AND MIGRANT WORKERS

Migratory laborers are workers who cross geographic boundaries and stay away from home in order to work for wages. Migrant workers also migrate within countries, usually their own, mainly in pursuit of seasonal work. They live in temporary accommodations for extended periods of time, ranging from a few days to many years. Migrant laborers can be single men without families or married men who leave their families in order to support them. Some migrants work in family units and accept migratory labor as a last resort to survive. Twenty-first-century migrant workers often lack proper immigration documents and are thus called "undocumented" or "illegal," that is, illegally residing in the United States. Employers, labor contractors, and foremen often overcharge them for jobs, transportation, food, and housing. In the United States, migrant workers were best memorialized in John Steinbeck's 1939 novel *The Grapes of Wrath*, which illustrated how the Great Depression forced so many Americans to migrate in search of work, and in Edward R. Murrow's 1960 CBS television documentary *Harvest of Shame*, which focused largely on migrant farmworkers in the states of the Eastern Seaboard.

Characteristics. Definitions of migrant workers vary and are ripe with stereotypes. Under most definitions, workers or their families moving north from Texas to pick cucumbers for three months in Ohio are considered migrants, but a teenager who moves to Kansas for a few months to drive his uncle's tractor is not considered a migrant, and neither are college students who leave their campuses to work in Yosemite Valley for the summer. An undocumented Mexican worker who picks strawberries is usually considered a migrant worker, although Mexican strawberry pickers usually settle in a community and commute daily to farm jobs—much like office workers traveling from the suburbs to the city. Migrant farmworkers can also be skilled and well-paid white men who operate combines on a string of midwestern grain farms. Many workers who satisfy the migrant stereotype are not migrants.

Migrant workers are not a new phenomenon. Wandering workers such as troubadours, tramp craftsmen, gypsies, vagabonds, and "masterless men" traveled throughout Europe. In the United States, mobile workmen were a common sight in the eighteenth century. Because there were no railroads, most traveled near their home. Some were artisans and craftsmen. People wandered because the country was not yet industrially developed and because farmers needed help during the planting and harvesting seasons. Skilled craftsmen with their tools were needed to fix plows, patch harnesses, construct beds, and otherwise accept odd jobs. Migratory labor increased after the Civil War when hundreds of thousands of men were suddenly released from military duty. Many had no homes or family ties. The rapidly expanding railroad transportation system provided a means to cross vast distances easily and quickly at a time when numerous seasonal industries were developing. Migrants used the new rail system to work as loggers, railroad workers, beggars, miners, cannery workers, sheep shearers, cigar makers, and ice cutters. Mobile and highly adaptable, they were known variously as "floating laborers," "hoboes," "tramps," "transients," and "bindlemen" (men who traveled with their belongings wrapped inside a tight bundle, or "bindle"). Another wandering worker of this era was the cowboy, whose seasonal employment bringing cattle to market, roping, and branding or driving herds to better pasture closely resembled the work of the transient laborers traveling between jobs.

During the late nineteenth and early twentieth centuries, periodic economic depressions, such as those of 1873–1878 and 1893–1897, cast millions of people out of work. Gilded Age newspapers labeled this the "tramp crisis," although it was actually a migrant-labor crisis.

The composition of the migrant labor force was both multiracial and multinational, varying according to industry, region, and time period. By the end of the nineteenth century, about a million men were on the road looking for work. Many headed for the wheat fields of the Great Plains. Because large population centers were few and far between, and most farming was restricted to family-size units, a huge amount of labor was required to harvest and thresh the ripening tide of grain. Beginning in early June and continuing into October, more than 100,000 men worked for a week or two, sometimes for five months or more. City laborers, craftsmen, and factory employees temporarily out of work, as well as small-scale farmers from the hills of Missouri and Arkansas, all came together to thresh and harvest. Roughly two thirds were American-born; the other third were recent immigrants from Europe. Climbing on board boxcars, they stole rides and followed the grain crop, some moving from Oklahoma as far north as Ontario and Alberta in Canada. In the 1920s, combines drastically diminished their numbers, and the introduction of the automobile ended the era of stealing rides on trains.

Around the United States. After the Florida Everglades were developed as citrus groves and winter vegetable districts, a heterogeneous stream of African American and white migratory laborers began moving along the Eastern Seaboard states harvesting crops as far north as Maine. At the same time, employment agents, known as *enganchadores*, recruited Mexicans in Texas, mainly for the sugar-beet fields of Michigan, Ohio, Wyoming, Wisconsin,

Minnesota, Colorado, the Dakotas, and Nebraska. Despite reports that millions of poor Hispanic immigrants follow the migrant agricultural circuit, in the twenty-first century the stereotypical migrant family that packs up its belongings to follow the ripening crops from south to north is less and less common. Temporary family housing is less available for them, and employers prefer single men. The largest group of domestic migrant workers consists of unskilled field hands who follow the ripening crops in California, Texas, and Florida. In California, where fruit and vegetable farms specializing in only one crop spread across entire valleys, large crews ranging from dozens to several thousand people are required.

Since the gold rush, California farmers have profited from successive waves of immigrant workers. The Chinese of the 1870s and 1880s, the Japanese of between 1890 and 1920, the Filipinos and Mexicans of the 1920s and 1930s, and the braceros—Mexican nationals brought north under a government program between 1942 and 1964—all served as migrant farmworkers. Others included displaced American and European immigrants and the 350,000 so-called Okies who migrated to California from the southern Great Plains states between 1935 and 1939. Because most migrants or their children escape from seasonal employment, in the twenty-first century, waves of newly arrived undocumented Mexican immigrants have come to constitute the bulk of the migrant labor force.

Around the World. Outside the United States, migrant labor is on the rise. In the early twenty-first century, about 120 million migrant workers circulate throughout China. Workers from China's impoverished interior stream into the more prosperous coastal regions. Most are farmers and farmworkers who have been displaced by modern farming practices. As new opportunities opened up in the interior, migra-

tion patterns have begun to reverse. Opportunities in the European Union draw large numbers of migrants from Turkey and North Africa. Most migrant workers in northwest Europe originate in former colonial territories—West Indians and Pakistanis working in Britain, Algerians working in France. Three quarters of all migrant workers travel to France and Germany. Local tradition sets migration patterns—Turks to Germany, Portuguese to France, Greeks to Sweden. Migrant workers in Germany are called *Gastarbeiter* and constitute about one in seven manual laborers and 12 percent of the total labor force. They have historically concentrated in the hardest, most disagreeable jobs in the plastics, rubber, and asbestos-processing industries. In France, Switzerland, and Belgium, about one in four industrial workers is a foreign migrant. In the late 1970s, migrants constituted 40 percent of the labor force at the Ford factory in Cologne, Germany; 40 percent of the labor force at Renault shops in France; and 45 percent of the labor force at the Volvo factory in Göteborg, Sweden. Exact numbers are impossible to tabulate. Many of the twenty-first-century European migrant workers lack proper documentation and live illegally. In less than a generation, Italy, once a net exporter of labor, shifted to being a net recipient. Italian farmers, especially those in the north, as well as fruit growers around Calabria, rely entirely on migrant workers, mostly from North Africa.

Migratory workers transfer valuable economic resources of labor from poor to rich countries. Economists sometimes refer to migratory labor as a "capital export," similar to the export of goods, and as a "labor subsidy." German policy makers agree that migrant workers hold down labor costs and increase the country's competitiveness, in both export and domestic markets. Sending countries confirm that migration abroad relieves pressure at home and that explosive conditions might develop without the "safety valve" provided by out-migration. Since the formation of the European Union, economic activity has relied increasingly on migrant labor. Cheap migrant labor generated higher profits for employers and increased consumption of goods and services by consumers. As the twenty-first century progresses, demographic pressures, especially an aging population, are likely to increase the demand for migrants, even as economic slumps tug at the shifting relationship between the continuing requirement for migrant workers and increasing anger at their presence.

[*See also* **Agricultural Workers; Agriculture; Braceros; Dust Bowl Era and Farm Crisis; Foreign Trade; Globalization; Immigration; Labor Markets; Transportation Revolution; Undocumented Workers;** *and* **Vagrancy and Workers.**]

BIBLIOGRAPHY

Berger, John, and Jean Mohr. *A Seventh Man: Migrant Workers in Europe.* New York: Viking, 1975.

Hahamovitch, Cindy. *The Fruits of Their Labor: Atlantic Coast Farmworkers and the Making of Migrant Poverty, 1870–1945.* Chapel Hill: University of North Carolina Press, 1997.

Higbie, Frank Tobias. *Indispensable Outcasts: Hobo Workers and Community in the American Midwest, 1880–1930.* Urbana and Chicago: University of Illinois Press, 2003.

Martin, Philip L. *Harvest of Confusion: Migrant Workers in U.S. Agriculture.* Boulder, Colo.: Westview Press, 1988.

McWilliams, Carey. *Ill Fares the Land: Migrants and Migratory Labor in the United States.* Boston: Little, Brown, 1942.

Monkkonen, Eric H., ed. *Walking to Work: Tramps in America, 1790–1935.* Lincoln: University of Nebraska Press, 1984.

Peck, Gunther. *Reinventing Free Labor: Padrones and Immigrant Workers in the North American West, 1880–1930.* New York: Cambridge University Press, 2000.

Street, Richard Steven. *Beasts of the Field: A Narrative History of California Farmworkers, 1769–1913.* Stanford, Calif.: Stanford University Press, 2004.

Wormser, Richard. *Hoboes: Wandering in America, 1870–1940.* New York: Walker and Company, 1994.

Richard S. Street

MILITARY–INDUSTRIAL COMPLEX

In January 1961, President Dwight D. Eisenhower's farewell address introduced the term "military–industrial complex," which some have claimed that he originally intended to call a "military–industrial–congressional complex." The term resonates on three different levels: political, economic, and technical.

Politically, the Democrats criticized the Eisenhower administration on the basis of an imaginary so-called missile gap in which the Soviet Union held a dominant lead. The Democratic establishment had absorbed enough of John Maynard Keynes's *General Theory of Employment, Interest, and Money* (1936) to understand that a stimulative fiscal policy was a useful instrument for increasing employment. Although many Republicans lambasted both Keynes and his leading American protagonists as socialists, profligate spending on the military remained immune from charges of anti-American socialism.

This narrow vision of fiscal policy became known as military Keynesianism. Congress played a large role in appropriating money and the Democrats had the majority in Congress at the time. Eisenhower's warning about the military–industrial complex was a subtle, seemingly nonpartisan way of criticizing the Democrats for their promotion of spending on the military.

The military–industrial complex also reflected changing technical conditions. Historically, the military had produced most of its own weaponry. U.S. Army arsenals had been pioneers in the development of methods of mass production, such as the use of interchangeable parts. Eventually, the facilities that produced military armaments lacked the resources to match the demand for increasingly capital-intensive weapons.

The Civil War created an initial surge in demand for capital-intensive industries, such as railroads, to support the military effort. Given the increasing scale of demand for modern armaments, business learned to harness capital-intensive production methods to full advantage. The military was slower to develop a comparable technological capacity.

During World War I, an awkward mix of military departments and civilian agencies dominated by businessmen shared responsibility for administering war production. Businessmen gained valuable insights into how to navigate the political and defense establishment. This early manifestation of a military–industrial complex created considerable public unease when in the 1920s the Special Committee on Investigation of the Munitions Industry, led by the North Dakota Republican senator Gerald P. Nye, revealed how weapons manufacturers and their military allies had influenced the United States' decision to enter World War I. Nevertheless, the power and influence of the complex only grew as industry and the military won plaudits for their part in winning victory for the Allies in World War II.

Eisenhower's subsequent warning, which was prompted by Cold War–inspired militarization between 1947 and 1960 and the ever-growing size of appropriations for the military, proved ineffectual. The official military budget for 2011 reached $548.9 billion, excluding the cost of ongoing wars in Iraq and Afghanistan, as well as the military expenditures outside the Department of Defense, including the Department of Energy's production of nuclear weapons and the Department of Agriculture's work on biological warfare. In 2012, U.S. expenditures on the military exceeded the total spent by the rest of the world's countries and was nearly six times greater than that of the country's closest competitor in military spending, the People's Republic of China.

Retired generals and admirals have often rotated from procurement positions in the military to corporate offices in private industry, where they use their contacts and influence in Congress and other government agencies to secure lucrative contracts for their new employers. Further, by 2012 private contractors had supplanted military support services in carrying out many of the necessary functions ancillary to combat operations. To an extent once inconceivable, parts of the military, like many other municipal, state, and federal government services, had been privatized.

[*See also* **American System of Manufacturing and Interchangeable Parts; Industrial Research Laboratories;** *and* **Technology.**]

BIBLIOGRAPHY

Perelman, Michael. *The Confiscation of American Prosperity: From Right-Wing Extremism and Economic Ideology to the Next Great Depression.* New York: Palgrave Macmillan, 2007.

Perelman, Michael. *The Invisible Handcuffs of Capitalism: How Market Tyranny Stifles the Economy by Stunting Workers.* New York: Monthly Review Press, 2011.

Perelman, Michael. *Manufacturing Discontent: The Trap of Individualism in a Corporate Society.* London: Pluto, 2005.

Perelman, Michael. *Railroading Economics: The Creation of the Free Market Mythology.* New York: Monthly Review Press, 2006.

Michael Perelman

MINING INDUSTRY

Mining has played a central role in American economic development. Coal, petroleum, natural gas, and uranium helped fuel industrialization. Iron, cement, copper, and other mine products were transformed into manufactured goods and buildings. Gold and silver have at times served as official bases for the money supply. Mining contributed to the accumulation of numerous family fortunes, including those of the Guggenheims, the Rockefellers, and the Mellons. Until the later twentieth century the growth of mining and the growth of the economy were strongly intertwined. Between 1880 and 1970, mining output was cyclical, and the trendrates of growth for mining and for real gross domestic product were similar. Since 1970, however, mining output has fluctuated around a flat trend.

Iron, copper, and coal were originally mined from outcroppings at or near the earth's surface, and gold was panned in streams. As the demand for mine products increased, miners searched farther afield, dug deeper, and drilled in the ocean. The increased difficulty of tapping the resources led to increased capital investment and dramatic changes in mine technologies. Through the early 1920s, many mines depended on workers using hand tools and rule-of-thumb techniques, and mules and steam-run hoists or pumps were used to move the materials to the surface. Increases in mine output required more mine workers, even though technological changes in blasting and machinery fueled by steam, compressed air, and then by electricity contributed to steady growth in output per miner. After the 1920s the pace of technological change increased dramatically. New machinery dug, drilled, pumped, and clawed underground, and many mines began using large-scale earthmovers to strip the hillsides above the mine seams. Consequently, mine output has risen nearly eightfold since the mid-1920s, despite a 40 percent reduction in the number of miners. The improvements in mining technology also cut accident rates in half.

Mining was often the leading edge of development in many isolated areas. Gold and silver rushes opened up California, Nevada, Arizona, and the Black Hills. When coal and copper mines opened, employers attracted workers from outside the region by establishing company towns where there had been little agricultural settlement or prior infrastructure. As the number of mines increased or other industries developed, company towns gave way to independent towns and cities. In some isolated regions, however, the population left when the resource was depleted, leaving ghost towns behind.

During the employment booms in the early 1900s, competition among mine owners for labor was fierce. Thus miners were often highly mobile, they earned high hourly earnings to compensate for the dangers of mining, and employers hired an ethnically diverse workforce. Competition among numerous mines, in combination with the miners' use of collective action, limited the employer's ability to exploit monopoly power in company towns. Miners went on strike more frequently than other workers did, and several famous violent episodes occurred in mining areas. Mine workers often were leaders in the major union movements: William D. "Big Bill" Haywood led the radical Industrial Workers of the World. The United Mine Workers of America, including its longtime president John L. Lewis, played leading roles in the American Federation of Labor, the Congress of Industrial Organizations, and the later merger of the two organizations.

[*See also* **Colorado Labor Wars** (1903–1905); **Gold Rushes; Industrial Workers of the World; Iron and Steel Industry; Mesabi Range and Michigan Hard-Rock Miners' Strikes** (1907–1916); **Petroleum Industry; United Mine Workers;** *and* **Western Federation of Miners.**]

BIBLIOGRAPHY

Freese, Barbara. *Coal: A Human History*. Cambridge, Mass.: Perseus, 2003.

Lynch, Martin. *Mining in World History*. London: Reaktion, 2002.

Price V. Fishback

MINNEAPOLIS TEAMSTERS AND GENERAL STRIKE (1934)

The strike of the Teamsters in Minneapolis, Minnesota, was one of four major strikes in 1934 that signaled the reemergence of the labor movement. Strikes of the longshoremen's union in San Francisco, the Auto-Lite workers in Toledo, Ohio, and textile workers nationally had as their context the new federal support for collective bargaining under the National Industrial Recovery Act and resurgent trade unionism. In Minneapolis the strike began when more than two thousand truck drivers and other workers from Local 574 of the Teamsters participated in a citywide organizing campaign that began in February with a coal drivers' strike. The conflict resurfaced with a general truckers' strike in May and concluded with a thirty-six-day strike in July and August 1934.

Pervasive violence occurred during the strike, including minor skirmishes and two major battles in the city's central market. Hundreds were injured, and four men were killed—two strike supporters and two from the business-oriented Citizens' Alliance. After weeks of conflict, employers sought to break the strike, and the Minnesota Farmer-Labor governor Floyd B. Olson brought in the National Guard to intervene in the face of recurrent violence. Though Olson, who supported the strike, hoped that his actions would be neutral, guard officers freely issued permits to trucking firms. Commercial truck traffic, which had ground to a halt, now resumed. Through back channels, the governor and federal officials brokered an end to the labor conflict, with few employer concessions but union recognition.

The success of the strike in Minneapolis was principally thanks to union leadership. Bill Brown, a Farmer-Labor trade unionist, and the Trotskyists Farrell Dobbs, Carl Skoglund, and the brothers Ray, Grant, and Miles Dunne were able to forge a powerful alliance between progressive forces and labor. In local memory, the 1934 strike took on epic dimensions, as Minneapolis, an open-shop city, became the staging ground for the rebirth of unionism regionally.

[*See also* **Labor Movements; National Industrial Recovery Act and National Recovery Administration; San Francisco General Strike (1934); Strikes; Textile Strike (1934);** *and* **Toledo Auto-Lite Strike.**]

BIBLIOGRAPHY

Faue, Elizabeth. *Community of Suffering and Struggle: Women, Men, and the Labor Movement in Minneapolis, 1915–1945*. Chapel Hill: University of North Carolina Press, 1991.

Walker, Charles Rumford. *American City: A Rank and File History of Minneapolis*. New York: Farrar and Rinehart, 1937.

Elizabeth Faue

MOLLY MAGUIRES

The Molly Maguires were allegedly a secret Irish society that terrorized the anthracite-coal-mining area of Pennsylvania in the 1860s and 1870s. Over the course of two decades, sixteen men, mostly midlevel mining officials, were assassinated by Irish or Irish American mine laborers. The conventional depiction of the Mollies as an organized conspiracy of murderous fanatics was largely built by their antagonists: local journalists, Pinkerton agents, and industry leaders looking to inhibit unionization in the area.

There were two distinct waves of violence that came to be known as "Molly Maguireism." The first occurred between 1862 and 1868. Six men were assassinated, five of whom were mine superintendents or foremen. Concurrently, workers engaged in a vigorous effort to establish a labor union in the area. Since mine operators and local officials viewed any disruption to coal production as a threat to the Union war effort, they labeled as treason attempts at labor organization. Anti-Irish nativism, combined with high Irish participation in efforts to organize a labor union in the area, meant that the term "Molly Maguireism" came to mean any violence or disorder caused by Irish mine workers.

By 1868, anthracite miners in northeastern Pennsylvania had established the Workingmen's Benevolent Association (WBA). Bringing together workers of different ethnicities and skill levels who had previously been at odds, the WBA was responsible for a period of relative calm, during which only two assassinations attributed to the Molly Maguires took place.

In 1874, however, Franklin B. Gowen, president of the Philadelphia and Reading Railroad, consolidated control of anthracite coal production. The WBA stood as a major obstacle to Gowen's economic interests, so he embarked upon a slander campaign, claiming that the WBA and the Molly Maguires were one and the same. During the Long Strike of 1875, some Irish members of the WBA broke ranks and once again began taking violent action against mine bosses, who were mostly of Welsh and English origins. Gowen successfully linked the new wave of violence, and therefore the WBA, to the Molly Maguires. By June 1875 he had broken the union, and in doing so he precipitated heightened ethnic tensions among workers of different skill levels and their supervisors. The result was a new wave of assaults and assassinations.

Between January 1876 and August 1878, more than fifty alleged Molly Maguires were tried on charges of murder and conspiracy. Though some of the men may have been guilty as charged, they experienced trials that were nothing short of travesties of justice. Twenty Irish or Irish Americans were condemned to execution by hanging for their supposed involvement with the Molly Maguires. Newspapers published detailed, profusely illustrated reports of the hangings, thus solidifying in the imaginations of Americans the Molly Maguires as a depraved group of lawless immigrants who had been brought to justice by the power of the state.

The violence of the Molly Maguire era demonstrates the bitterness engendered by conflict between labor and capital in the 1860s and 1870s in northeastern Pennsylvania. More important, it underscores the impact of ethnicity, religion, and migration on capital–labor relations in a developing industrial society.

[*See also* **Labor Movments; Labor Spies and Pinkertons; Mining Industry; Racism;** *and* **Repression of Unions.**]

BIBLIOGRAPHY

Coleman, James Walter. *The Molly Maguire Riots: Industrial Conflict in the Pennsylvania Coal Region.* Richmond, Va.: Garrett and Massie, 1936.

Kenny, Kevin. *Making Sense of the Molly Maguires.* New York: Oxford University Press, 1998.

Mimi Cowan

MONETARISM

The economic theory known as monetarism holds that the money stock exerts an important influence on economic activity and prices. Economists who embrace monetarism hold that changes in the quantity of money are crucial in increasing aggregate income and productivity in the short run, as well as in determining the inflation rate in the long run. The University of Chicago economist Milton Friedman was the most prominent twentieth-century proponent of monetarism, but the theory's intellectual origins extend back more than two centuries to the quantity theory of money of classical economics. According to such theories, changes in the money stock or the velocity of the circulation of money—that is, the ratio of total spending to the money stock—determine nominal spending. Because velocity changes less over the longer run than the total money stock does, the effects of the money stock dominate.

Friedman and Anna Schwartz offered important empirical support for monetarism in *A Monetary History of the United States, 1867–1960* (1963). They showed that since the Civil War, fluctuations in the rate of monetary growth led the peaks and troughs of all U.S. business cycles. Moreover, they associated especially severe economic downturns, such as that of 1929–1933, with large monetary contractions. Though money powerfully affected the economy in the short run, its long-term effect was less predictable. This fact underlies another precept of monetarism: rather than actively using monetary policy to smooth business cycles, as Keynesians advocate, the monetary authority—in the United States, the Federal Reserve System (the Fed)—should adhere to a fixed rule, such as maintaining a constant rate of growth of the money supply.

Although changes in the money supply may affect the physical volume of output in the short run, over the long run nonmonetary factors determine economic growth. Monetary changes primarily affect the price level. Hence, monetarists argue, inflation and deflation are directly related to the rate of growth of the money supply.

Implementation of monetarist monetary policy has had something of a rocky road. As a result of the influence of the monetarists—led by Milton Friedman, who advocated a steady growth rate of monetary aggregates—in the 1970s the Federal Reserve, under the chairmanship of Arthur Burns, began to shift away from its dual focus on both monetary and interest-rate targets toward a policy that concentrated more on the money supply and its determinants. In October 1979, shortly after Paul Volcker became chairman of the Fed's Board of Governors, the Fed announced that it would focus much more on monetary aggregates (nonborrowed reserves) and much less on interest rates. Ironically, however, at just about that time, inflation and banking deregulation—which allowed, or even promoted, the development of new financial assets—had made it easier for the public to move in and out of holding money balances, thereby undermining a stable demand-for-money function, a fundamental precept of monetarism. The Fed proved to be no more successful in hitting its monetary targets than it was before, and interest rates soared. To be sure, one interpretation of this period is that the focus on monetary aggregates was only a smokescreen that allowed interest rates to rise to promote disinflation. In any case, the concentration on monetary aggregates was short-lived. In 1982 the Fed deemphasized monetary targeting, and in 1993 the Fed's chairman Alan Greenspan announced that the Fed would no longer rely on monetary aggregates in the conduct of monetary policy.

[*See also* **Business Cycles; Economic Growth and Income Patterns; Economic Theories and Thought; Federal Reserve System; Free Silver and Bimetallism; Friedman, Milton, and the Chicago School of Economics; Gold Standard; Inflation and Deflation; Monetary Policy, Federal;** *and* **Volcker, Paul.**]

BIBLIOGRAPHY

Friedman, Milton. *A Program for Monetary Stability.* New York: Fordham University Press, 1959.

Friedman, Milton, and Anna Jacobson Schwartz. *A Monetary History of the United States, 1867–1960.* Princeton, N.J.: Princeton University Press, 1963.

Hirsch, Abraham, and Neil de Marchi. *Milton Friedman: Economics in Theory and Practice.* New York: Harvester Wheatsheaf, 1990.

John A. James

MONETARY POLICY, FEDERAL

Encompassing two major components, the coining of currency and the creation of a banking system, U.S. monetary policy is as old as the national government itself.

Currency. Following Alexander Hamilton's recommendations, the Coinage Act of 1792 established the dollar as the official unit of account and established a bimetallic standard that defined the dollar in relation to gold and silver. The silver dollar contained fifteen times as much silver as the gold dollar contained gold. Originally the 15-to-1 ratio was close to the prevailing market value, but as market values changed over time, one of the metals became overvalued at the mint price. In the early nineteenth century, silver became overvalued, and its possessors presented silver to the mint for coinage. Gold coins began to disappear from circulation. In 1834 the Treasury adjusted the mint ratio to around 16 to 1, now overvaluing gold. Hence, gold began to replace silver in circulation, causing the latter to be hoarded or exported.

This system whereby the value of the dollar and foreign currencies was defined by their specie (gold or silver) content in turn fixed the value of currencies relative to each other. In other words, a system of fixed exchange rates enabled specie, dollars, and foreign exchange all to be freely convertible. Civil War economic exigencies, however, led Congress to pass the Legal Tender Act of 1862, which provided for the issue of fiat money, commonly known as greenbacks, not convertible into specie at a fixed rate, and made them legal tender for settling all debts and in all transactions save the payment of customs duties. In a system of floating or flexible exchange rates, market forces determined the value of the greenback (paper) dollar relative to gold and foreign currencies. At one point, greenbacks in New York fell to a price as low as thirty-five cents on the (gold) dollar.

To restore the prewar parity between the U.S. dollar and the British pound sterling (the standard for global exchange rates), the post–Civil War American government adopted fiscal policies to deflate prices and bring greenbacks onto a par with gold. This active contractionary policy was short-lived—Congress stopped retirement of greenbacks in 1868—but prices fell nevertheless, primarily as a result of strong increases in real incomes. The continuing sharp deflation, which hurt debtors and aided creditors, caused fierce opposition. The Greenback Labor Party, founded in 1874, appealed to debtors and entrepreneurs who wanted to expand the issue of greenbacks, increase the money supply, and raise the price level. Later, the free-silver movement advocated the free and unlimited coinage of silver at the old ratio (16 to 1) to accomplish the same ends. Only after a decade of deflation did Congress pass the Resumption Act of 1875 and commit the Treasury to exchanging gold dollars and paper dollars at par. On 1 January 1879, greenbacks became freely convertible to gold, with fixed exchange rates restored at the prewar parity.

The victims of deflation, however, continued to condemn the gold standard as the congressional "Crime of '73": in 1873, ancillary to its deflationary policy, Congress had demonetized silver by ordering the U.S. Mint to stop making silver coins. The 1880s and early 1890s remained a period of intense controversy as to the appropriate monetary standard. The election of William McKinley over William Jennings Bryan in 1896 and, subsequently, rising prices stilled the protests of debtors and free-silver advocates. In 1900 the United States formally committed itself to the gold standard: the value of the dollar was formally and explicitly defined only in terms of gold. During the Great Depression, however, in 1933, though still remaining on gold, the dollar was devalued.

At the 1944 Bretton Woods Conference, after the financial crises and disruptions of the 1930s and World War II, the United States and its major allies agreed to restore fixed exchange rates. The dollar, set at a price of $35 per ounce of gold, replaced the pound sterling as the international currency of record. The Bretton Woods system lasted into the early 1970s when domestic inflation and balance-of-payments imbalances prompted President Richard M. Nixon to end fixed exchange rates. Afterward the dollar floated against other currencies, its value determined by the demand and supply of foreign exchange.

Banking. Congress chartered the First Bank of the United States in 1791 as proposed by Alexander Hamilton, who modeled it after the Bank of England. The bank was a combined public and private enterprise with branches in major cities, the authority to issue notes, and a role as both a commercial bank and the fiscal agent of the government. When the bank's charter came up for renewal in 1811, the recharter bill failed in the Senate after a hotly contested debate about its constitutionality.

Difficulties in financing the War of 1812 and the general suspension of payments (outside New England) in 1814—in which private commercial banks refused to convert into specie at face value, as required by law, the notes and deposits that they had issued—led the federal government to rethink central banking. Shortly thereafter, in 1816, Congress established the Second Bank of the United States, with charter provisions similar to those of the first. It, too, was an interstate branch bank with offices in major cities across the country and headquarters in Philadelphia. After a rather undistinguished early history, the Second Bank came into its own in 1823 with the appointment of Nicholas Biddle of Philadelphia as director. Biddle actively pursued a policy of pressing state banks to redeem their outstanding banknotes at promised par or face value in specie. Such a policy restrained the temptation of such banks to "overissue" notes, dampened inflation, and increased public confidence in circulating banknotes. During the 1820s Biddle's policy narrowed the range of discounts among state banknotes. This policy promoted soundness and confidence in the banking system but produced discontent in western regions and among individuals desirous of easier credit.

President Andrew Jackson, who vetoed a bank recharter bill in 1832, represented the enemies of Biddle. In his veto message, Jackson criticized the bank's monopoly status, its domination by financiers and foreigners, and its (sound) money policies that were said to have been restrictive and hampered economic growth in the West. He also questioned its constitutionality. Jackson resolved to cripple the bank's power by removing government deposits and redepositing them in selected state banks known as "pet banks." Jackson's war against the Second Bank was followed by a speculative boom—one that saw the highest peacetime inflation rate before the 1970s—and an ensuing financial panic and deep depression (1837–1843). After 1836 the federal government withdrew from the banking system altogether, later establishing an independent treasury to administer revenues and their disbursement.

This system lasted nearly three quarters of a century until the establishment in 1913 of the Federal Reserve System.

To replace the circulation of heterogeneous state banknotes with a uniform currency and simultaneously increase the demand for government bonds, the National Banking Acts of 1863–1864 established a national banking system. Banks with national charters were allowed to issue banknotes backed by U.S. government bonds. Initially relatively few state-chartered banks were interested in converting to national charters. Only the imposition in 1865 of a 10 percent tax on state banks' notes in circulation prompted a mass conversion to national banking. By the late 1860s more than 80 percent of chartered banks had federal charters. The dominance of national banks proved short-lived, however. Increasing use of checks and demand deposits made state-chartered banks' effective inability to issue notes less of a disadvantage, so that by the 1890s the number of nonnational banks had surpassed that of national banks. This system of small, independent local banks (as opposed to branch banks) proved particularly vulnerable to financial crises. In the late nineteenth century, financial panics and subsequent suspensions of cash payments by banks became virtually regular events. A panic in 1907 was the last straw, leading Congress to establish the congressional National Monetary Commission to consider banking reform. The result was the Federal Reserve Act of 1913.

The Federal Reserve System created a central bank to alleviate the problem of recurrent panics. The new institution was to furnish "an elastic currency," to provide smooth seasonal money-market stringencies, and to act as the lender of last resort during crises. The law established a decentralized structure that dispersed power and reflected popular and congressional suspicion of the concentration of economic power in Washington, D.C., or among Wall Street bankers. Twelve regional Federal Reserve Banks operated under a coordinating board in Washington. In its initial years the new system appeared successful in adjusting seasonal credit flows and smoothing seasonal interest rates. The Federal Reserve, however, failed to avert the Great Depression of the 1930s. Indeed, many economists cite its inaction as the principal factor underlying the severity of that depression. The failure of the Federal Reserve System between 1929 and 1933 led the administration of Franklin Delano Roosevelt to propose further reforms. The Banking Act of 1933, known as the Glass–Steagall Act, created the Federal Deposit Insurance Corporation (FDIC) to protect depositors' accounts. Glass–Steagall also divorced investment and commercial banking operations. The Banking Act of 1935 further centralized and extended the power of the Federal Reserve Board, now called the Board of Governors. Thereafter, the Federal Reserve Board had greater power to regulate the money supply and set interest rates.

The high inflation and interest rates of the 1970s created great problems for regulated banks, which were limited as to the loans that they could make and the rate of interest that they could pay. Depositors thus withdrew funds from banks and redeposited them in unregulated money-market mutual funds that offered higher interest rates. The Depository Institutions Deregulation and Monetary Control Act (DIDMCA) of 1980 partly deregulated commercial banks and savings and loan associations, allowing them to offer higher interest rates by making more diverse investments. The ensuing pattern of highly speculative investment led to the savings and loan scandal of the 1980s. The trend toward greater banking deregulation, however, was set. Among several other bills passed in this period, the Riegle–Neal Act of 1994, for example, established the basis for nationwide branch banking, allowing—notwithstanding state laws to the contrary—bank holding companies to acquire banks in other states. The Gramm–Leach–Bliley Financial Services Modernization Act of 1999 overturned the Glass–Steagall separation of commercial from investment banking. In addition, over this period, nonbank financial intermediaries, the so-called shadow banking sector, subject to much less stringent or minimal regulation, grew rapidly. Such structural changes, plus the development of new financial practices such as securitization, set the stage for the financial collapse of 2007–2008. Undoubtedly with the experience of the Great Depression in mind, the Federal Reserve responded aggressively to the financial crisis. Short-term interest rates (the federal funds rate) were reduced virtually to zero, and large amounts of liquidity were injected into the financial system by making it easier to borrow from the Fed, thereby damping the downturn, although not, of course, completely counteracting it.

Over the late twentieth century there were also marked changes in the conduct of monetary policy by the Federal Reserve. As a result of the influence of the monetarists—led by Milton Friedman, who advocated a steady growth rate of monetary aggregates—in the 1970s the Federal Reserve, under the chairmanship of Arthur Burns, began to shift away from its dual focus on both monetary and interest-rate targets. In October 1979, shortly after Paul Volcker became chairman of the Fed's Board of Governors, the Fed announced that it would focus much more on monetary aggregates (nonborrowed reserves) and much less on interest rates. Ironically, however, at just about that time, inflation and deregulation—which allowed, or even promoted, the development of new financial assets—had made it easier for the public to move in and out of holding money balances, thereby undermining a stable demand-for-money function, a fundamental precept of monetarism. The Fed proved to be no more successful in hitting its monetary targets than it was before, and interest rates soared. To be sure, one interpretation of this period is that the focus on monetary aggregates was only a smokescreen that allowed interest rates to rise to promote disinflation. In any case, the concentration on monetary aggregates was short-lived. In 1982 the Fed deemphasized monetary targeting, and in 1993 the Fed's chairman Alan Greenspan announced that the Fed would no longer rely on monetary aggregates in the conduct of monetary policy.

In view of the breakdown of the relationship between monetary aggregates and inflation, many central banks in the 1990s then turned to inflation targeting as their preferred strategy—following the example of New Zealand, which adopted such a policy in 1990. Ben Bernanke, the Fed's chairman since 2006, has been one of this strategy's strong proponents, and perhaps the Fed might move in that direction, even though by 2012 it had not ever used explicit inflation targets. An advantage of such a strategy, in addition to its clarity and transparency, is that it does not rely on stability of the relationship between money and inflation. Instead, the central bank might use whatever information and tools that might be necessary to meet its goal. Typically that is price stability—which is actually, in practice, low inflation; the European Central Bank, for example, aims at an inflation rate of 2 percent per year. The situation is, however, a bit more complicated for the Federal Reserve. In contrast to the European Central Bank, which has a single mandate, price stability, the Fed has a dual mandate, price stability and maximum employment.

[*See also* **Bank of the United States, First and Second; Bretton Woods Conference; Deregulation, Financial; Federal Deposit Insurance Corporation; Federal Reserve Act; Federal Reserve System; Financial and Banking**

Promotion and Regulation; Free Silver and Bimetallism; Glass–Steagall, Repeal of; Gold Standard; Greenback Labor Party; Greenbackism; Inflation and Deflation; Monetarism; National Banking System (1863); New Deal Banking Regulation; Shadow Banking System; Tariffs; *and* Trade Policy, Federal.]

BIBLIOGRAPHY

Friedman, Milton, and Anna Jacobson Schwartz. *A Monetary History of the United States, 1867–1960.* Princeton, N.J.: Princeton University Press, 1963.

Hammond, Bray. *Banks and Politics in America from the Revolution to the Civil War.* Princeton, N.J.: Princeton University Press, 1957.

Studenski, Paul, and Herman E. Krooss. *Financial History of the United States: Fiscal, Monetary, Banking, and Tariff, Including Financial Administration and State and Local Finance.* 2d ed. New York: McGraw–Hill, 1963.

Temin, Peter. *The Jacksonian Economy.* New York: W. W. Norton and Company, 1969.

Timberlake, Richard H., Jr. *The Origins of Central Banking in the United States.* Cambridge, Mass.: Harvard University Press, 1978.

White, Eugene Nelson. *The Regulation and Reform of the American Banking System, 1900–1929.* Princeton, N.J.: Princeton University Press, 1983.

John A. James

MORGAN, J. P.

(1837–1913), banker, financier, and art patron. The son of the international banker Junius Spencer Morgan and his wife Juliet Pierpont, John Pierpont Morgan became America's dominant financier of steel and railroad enterprises. Born in Hartford, Connecticut, and schooled in Boston, Switzerland, and Germany, he returned to New York in 1857, a year of economic panic. Joining a banking firm representing the London-based George Peabody and Company, he acted as his father's eyes and ears. In 1861 he married Amelia Sturges, of a Manhattan cotton-trading family. Soon after her death in 1862 he married Frances Louise Tracy; they had four children.

During the Civil War, Morgan arranged Union loans on the London market, but he also resold guns originally bought from the army, the often-defective Hall carbines, making a substantial and perhaps unethical profit. Avoiding military service by paying for a substitute (as did many other well-to-do young men), Morgan instead sold government bonds and supported charities for war widows and the wounded. He also became a partner in the new banking house of J. S. Morgan and Company, which became Drexel, Morgan in 1871 and J. P. Morgan and Company in 1895.

Coming of age in the era of ruthless capitalist entrepreneurs such as Cornelius Vanderbilt, Daniel Drew, Andrew Carnegie, and Jay Gould, Morgan invested heavily in and eventually gained control of Gould's Erie Railroad. He also combined the New York Central and Wabash railroads and acquired or reorganized the Lehigh Valley and Northern Pacific railroads. In 1895, at a considerable profit, he successfully halted a run on the gold reserves of the U.S. Treasury. Purchasing Carnegie Steel in 1901, he combined it with other holdings to form the United States Steel Corporation, which dominated the industry. During a financial panic in 1907, Morgan led a consortium of New York bankers who ended the crisis by guaranteeing the stability of weaker banks—a demonstration of his dominance over the economy that intensified pressures for reform of the nation's banking system. His vast economic power prompted congressional investigators to call him to testify in 1912 before the Pujo Committee, which investigated the small circle of New York financiers who controlled the nation's banks, corporations, railroads, and stock exchange. Morgan emerged with his prestige intact, his position unchallenged.

A collector even as a boy, Morgan during his many trips to Europe acquired a horde of valuable works. Among the first patrons of the Metropolitan Museum of Art, he also supported the American Museum of Natural History. His acquisitions included Chinese porcelains, medieval and Renaissance paintings, and rare books, especially on religion. His treasures became the nucleus of the Morgan Library, housed in his Madison Avenue mansion.

Some of Morgan's contemporaries saw him as ruthless, secretive, and acquisitive to an extreme, taking more from society than he gave. Others viewed him as a major contributor to corporate growth, philanthropy, and American culture. Larger than life, he was simply J. P. Morgan.

[*See also* **Federal Reserve Act; Iron and Steel Industry;** *and* **Railroads.**]

BIBLIOGRAPHY

Chernow, Ron. *The House of Morgan: An American Banking Dynasty and the Rise of Modern Finance.* New York: Atlantic Monthly Press, 1990.

Strouse, Jean. *Morgan: American Financier.* New York: Random House, 1999.

Leo Hershkowitz

MOTOR VEHICLES

See **Automotive Industry.**

MULLER v. OREGON

A 1908 U.S. Supreme Court decision that granted states the right to regulate the hours of women workers, *Muller v. Oregon* began when the laundry owner Curt Muller, convicted of violating Oregon's ten-hour law for women, carried his appeal to the Supreme Court, arguing that the law infringed his right to contract freely with his workers. At issue, then, was whether states had the power to intervene on behalf of employees in employment relationships. In *Lochner v. New York* (1905), the Supreme Court had overthrown a New York law that regulated the hours of bakers. The opportunity to prepare evidence in defense of the Oregon law fell to Florence Kelley and her research chief at the National Consumers League (NCL), Josephine Goldmark. The case exemplified Kelley's strategy of using gender-specific means to achieve class-wide goals. Goldmark collected extensive evidence to prove that long hours jeopardized women's health and morals, and her brother-in-law Louis Brandeis argued the case before the Court. His famous Brandeis Brief, a compilation of sociological and medical evidence, persuaded the high court to uphold Oregon's law. Writing for the majority, Justice David Brewer accepted the argument that overwork was injurious to women and that the state bore a responsibility for protecting women "to preserve the strength of the race."

The ruling led many more states to regulate working conditions. It also popularized the practice of introducing sociological and medical data to establish legal claims. This approach, central to the concept that came to be known as "legal realism," helped lay the groundwork for such later landmark decisions as *Brown v. Board of Education* (1954). Although women's organizations supported the *Muller* decision at the time, changes in working conditions and in ideology brought about a reversal of attitude, and in the 1960s and 1970s the National Organization for Women and other feminist organizations successfully campaigned for the removal of gender-specific laws.

[*See also* Contract, Sanctity of; Eight-Hour Day; Factory and Hours Laws; Freedom of Contract; Kelley, Florence; *Lochner v. New York*; State Regulatory Laws; *West Coast Hotel v. Parrish*; *and* Women Workers.]

BIBLIOGRAPHY

Goldmark, Josephine. *Impatient Crusader: Florence Kelley's Life Story*. Urbana: University of Illinois Press, 1953.
Woloch, Nancy. *Muller v. Oregon: A Brief History with Documents*. Boston: Bedford Books of St. Martin's Press, 1996.

Kathryn Kish Sklar

MURRAY, PHILIP

(1886–1952), labor leader. A self-taught immigrant coal miner, Philip Murray became vice president of the United Mine Workers (UMW), president of the United Steelworkers of America (USWA), and president of the Congress of Industrial Organizations (CIO).

Murray's rise as a labor leader started in western Pennsylvania, where the UMW was weak and riven by factions. Intelligent, articulate, and willing both to fight and also to be conciliatory, he attracted the attention of union leaders. Elected UMW vice president in 1919, he worked closely with the union's president, John L. Lewis, until they broke in 1941 over Murray's support of President Franklin Delano Roosevelt's foreign policy.

Earlier than other labor leaders, Murray became convinced that unions needed the backing of the federal government to succeed in confrontations with corporations. In return he was willing to compel workers who struck in violation of contracts to return to work, to suppress Communist union dissidents, and to back mobilization against Nazi Germany and the Soviet Union.

When Lewis and Murray split, Lewis accused his former loyal associate of betraying the United Mine Workers, though Murray had fought fiercely for the union. And unlike Lewis and other union leaders who dominated their members, Murray mixed easily with workingmen and workingwomen. Unpretentious, affable, deeply patriotic, and religiously devout, he became extremely popular, especially with steelworkers, whose union he led from its founding until his death. In a long series of battles with coal and steel magnates from the 1910s through the Korean War, Murray achieved major improvements in compensation, working conditions, and pensions for his coal-miner and steelworker members. He also successfully defended most of the CIO unions when national politics shifted to the right during the 1950s.

[*See also* Congress of Industrial Organizations; Industrial Democracy; Labor Leaders; Lewis, John L.; Little Steel Strike (1937); United Mine Workers; *and* United Steelworkers.]

BIBLIOGRAPHY

Schatz, Ronald. "Philip Murray and the Subordination of the Industrial Unions to the United States Government." In *Labor Leaders in America*, edited by Melvyn Dubofsky and Warren Van Tine, pp. 234–257. Urbana: University of Illinois Press, 1987.

Ronald W. Schatz

MUSTE, A. J.

(1885–1967), minister, pacifist, and political and labor activist. Abraham Johannes "A. J." Muste was born in Zeeland, a province in the Netherlands. When he was six years old, his family immigrated to the United States and settled in Grand Rapids, Michigan, where his father worked as an unskilled laborer in a furniture factory. Muste graduated from Hope College in Holland, Michigan, in 1905 and a year later enrolled in the New Brunswick Theological Seminary in New Jersey. In 1909 he was ordained in the Dutch Reformed Church and assumed his first pastorate at Fort Washington Church in Washington Heights, New York City. He resigned in 1914 because he no longer ascribed to Calvinist doctrine. Soon thereafter, he became minister of the Central Congregational Church in Newton, Massachusetts, where he remained until 1917 when he was forced to resign because of his opposition to World War I. As a radical Christian pacifist, Muste worked briefly for the National Civil Liberties Bureau (a forerunner of the American Civil Liberties Union), but then he became deeply involved in the labor movement. In 1919 he led some thirty thousand textile workers in Lawrence, Massachusetts, in a strike that lasted three months and culminated in victory for the workers. He served as the general secretary of the subsequently formed Amalgamated Textile Workers of America until 1921, when the union was decimated during the postwar Red scare. From 1921 until 1933 he was a faculty member and dean of the Brookwood Labor College in Katonah, New York. He also served as a vice president of the American Federation of Teachers and as an editor of the progressive labor monthly *Labor Age*.

In 1928, Muste became the target of Red-baiting by the American Federation of Labor, which denounced Brookwood as a "Communistic" institution and called on its internationals to disaffiliate from the college. Muste responded by forming the Conference for Progressive Labor Action (CPLA) in May 1929 to coordinate progressive activities in the labor movement. The CPLA became the seedbed for the so-called Musteite movement, which stood for the organization of industrial workers, an independent labor party, and a pragmatic, independent Marxism. The CPLA was deeply involved both in a textile revolt that swept the southern Piedmont, particularly the strike in Marion, North Carolina, in 1929, and also in the Reorganized United Mine Workers of America, which challenged John L. Lewis's leadership of the mine workers. The CLPA's greatest success, however, was in organizing hundreds of thousands of unemployed workers into its Unemployed Citizens Leagues. In 1933 the CPLA reorganized as the American Workers Party (AWP), which is best known for leading the Toledo Auto-Lite strike of 1934. In December 1934 the AWP fused with the Trotskyist Communist League of America to become the Workers Party of the United States, with Muste as general secretary. Muste left the party in 1936 to return to Christian pacifism. From 1941 until his death, he was the unofficial head of the American peace movement, leading the Fellowship of Reconciliation, the Committee on Nonviolent Action, and the Spring Mobilization against the War in Vietnam, among other organizations. He continued to champion workers' rights and to oppose capitalism, yet he no longer viewed labor as the vehicle for radical social change.

[*See also* **Brookwood Labor College; Labor Leaders; Labor Movements;** *and* **Toledo Auto-Lite Strike.**]

BIBLIOGRAPHY

Hentoff, Nat, ed. *The Essays of A. J. Muste*. Indianapolis, Ind.: Bobbs–Merrill, 1967.

Robinson, Jo Ann Ooiman. *Abraham Went Out: A Biography of A. J. Muste*. Philadelphia: Temple University Press, 1981.

Leilah Danielson

MUTUAL FUNDS AND RETIREMENT ACCOUNTS

Retirement accounts allow individuals to save for retirement on a tax-favorable basis. Prior to the 1980s, retirement accounts were insignificant to the mutual fund industry; defined-benefit plans, managed primarily by banks and insurance companies, held most of Americans' retirement assets. By the twenty-first century, however, retirement accounts had come to play a major role in the fund industry's business, accounting for 40 percent of its $11.8 trillion assets at the end of the year 2010.

This shift occurred in the 1980s and 1990s after federal legislation created individual retirement accounts (IRAs) and defined-contribution 401(k) plans. Congress passed the Employee Retirement Income Security Act in 1974 to help Americans who lacked access to retirement accounts. Section 408 authorized IRAs. In 1978, mutual funds managed just 2.5 percent of all IRA assets, but because of its major marketing campaigns and strong fund performance, by 2001 the industry controlled 45 percent of the $2.6 trillion IRA marketplace.

The Revenue Act of 1978 added Sections 401(k) and 402(a)(8) to the Internal Revenue Code. Clarification of these sections in 1981 allowed employees to divert some of their pay, before taxes, into a new type of defined-contribution plan, the 401(k) plan. In the 1980s the fund industry successfully lobbied Congress for reforms and regulations pertaining to 401(k) plans that made funding the plans with mutual funds more favorable than using other financial products. By 1990, Fidelity Management and Research Company and the Vanguard Group dominated the 401(k) marketplace. By the end of 2010, the fund industry managed $1.8 trillion, or 58 percent, of all 401(k) assets.

[*See also* **Financial and Banking Promotion and Regulation; Insurance; Shadow Banking System; Taxation;** *and* **Taxes, Federal Income.**]

BIBLIOGRAPHY

Fink, Matthew P. *The Rise of Mutual Funds: An Insider's View*. New York: Oxford University Press, 2008.

Investment Company Institute. "2011 Investment Company Fact Book." 2011. http://www.ici.org/pdf/2011_factbook.pdf.

Emily Louise Martz